2/5/01

Sciences of the Earth

Garland Encyclopedias in the History of Science (Vol. 3)
Garland Reference Library of Social Science (Vol. 745)

Advisory Board

Sciences of the Earth

An Encyclopedia of Events, People, and Phenomena

Volume 1
A–G

Edited by
Gregory A. Good

GARLAND PUBLISHING, INC.
A member of the Taylor & Francis Group
New York & London
1998

Library of Congress Cataloging-in-Publication Data

Sciences of the earth: an encyclopedia of events, people, and phenomena / edited by
    Gregory A. Good.
            p.   cm. — (Garland encyclopedias in the history of science ;
    vol. 3) (Garland reference library of social science ; vol. 745)
        Includes bibliographical references and index.
        ISBN 0-8153-0062-X (set : alk. paper)
        1. Earth sciences—History—Encyclopedias.   I. Good, Gregory.
    II. Series.   III. Series: Garland reference library of social science ; v. 745.
    QE11.S38   1998
    550'.9—dc21   97-25163
                                                                        CIP

Cover photograph: Zabriskie Point, Death Valley, California. Earth Scenes © Esther Kivat.

Cover design: Robert Vankeirsbilck.

In memory of Kenneth O. May, who understood the importance
of reference works for establishing new scholarly fields and who taught me
that a passion for the world and the living augments scholarship.

Contents

Preface

The scope of this volume is wide, its coverage and approaches diverse. It addresses both the questions of tradition and of change in knowledge of the Earth. It is a basic reference in the history of sciences of the Earth, an introduction for newcomers to this field: students, scientists, scholars from specialties beyond the history of science, and the general public. The volume reflects "the state of the art." Although it is not and could not be complete, this volume provides an overview of the status of our knowledge of the history of the geosciences.

These essays introduce not only the ways human understanding of the Earth has differed from time to time and place to place, but also the historiography of studying the history of geoscience. For readers who aren't historians by training, one might say simply that historiography is anything that historians fight about: what methods are valid in their research, which interpretations of events are valid, which events are important, what the goals of historical writing are, and so on. These are the issues that enliven history. Historians want to know more than what happened and who did it, and historians base their writing on assumptions, sometimes examined and sometimes not, just as any other researcher must. Historiographical issues in the history of the geosciences may be as simple as the decision to include geologists but not geographers in a story. Historians of geoscience may disagree about the relative importance of political and social issues in the stories of their sciences, or about the degree of autonomy of science. Many entries in the volume are devoted to such major historical issues, approaches, and disputes: for example, the articles on Colonialism and Imperialism; Humboldtian Science; and Presentism. Other entries consider changes in the way historians have viewed historical figures and events, mixed in with a more expected summary of those events.

Some entries provide the first and only known historical discussion on their given topic. The articles on Dew; Geysers; and Sea Level are such instances. These articles discuss the scientists and their investigations directly, sometimes offering historical interpretation. Some topics, readers should note, are omitted because no historical literature has yet been developed, or because no historian is currently working on them. These lacunae represent some of the best opportunities for future contributions to the history of geoscience.

The reader should note that this is not an encyclopedia of the geosciences themselves. The titles of many articles in the volume sound as though they belong in such an encyclopedia: Airglow, Geosyncline, Greenhouse Effect, Ice Ages, Stratigraphy. Nevertheless, the task of this volume is not to explain currently accepted facts and theories, nor is it to justify the geosciences of today. Certainly, others may choose to apply history in that way. Nor is the purpose of this volume only to chronicle how we have come to our current knowledge of terrestrial phenomena, though it does that, too. Instead, its goal is to provide coherent and understandable accounts of what has been accepted as knowledge of earthly occurrences, even if those earlier ideas appear strange or fabulous to today's science. The goal is always to embed earlier ideas in the contexts of their times and to ask how it was that intelligent thinkers considered them reasonable and acceptable. Hence, the reader should automatically insert the phrase "history of" in most article titles.

The history of science transcends the investigation of former explanations for phenomena, and that fact is reflected in this volume. Although the history of ideas about the Earth and the history of researches about terrestrial phenomena figure prominently here, these are not the only approaches to the history of these sciences. Articles of two other major types are also represented. The first type relates to institutions that have supported and shaped science. The second type probes the relationships between science and practical activity, or between science and social or political developments.

Particular institutions of geoscience are explored in such articles as Bergen School of Meteorology; Deutsche Seewarte (German Naval Observatory); Geological Surveys, U.S. State; Intergovernmental Oceanographic Commission (IOC); International Council for the Exploration of the Sea, and Woods Hole Oceanographic Institution. Although institutions that have been important in some geosciences are not covered here, issues raised in these articles may help future historians to approach them.

Moreover, articles are included on some more general classes of institutions, which address developments in some of the geosciences not represented by specific articles. These include the roles of scientific societies in various geosciences, the activities of the Jesuits, the Masons, mining academies, international organizations, and Enlightenment encyclopedias. These articles usually focus on some specific geoscience and then consider exemplary individual institutions within that science.

Historians of science most fully become energized, it seems, in debating the very nature of science, a set of historiographic issues that mark this history off from, say, political or social history, or regionally defined history. Some of the most controversial articles in these pages review and perhaps advocate particular positions in that debate. These articles include Foucault's *Order of Things*; Hypotheses, Method of Multiple; Lakatos's Idea of Scientific Research Programs; Novel Facts; Popper's Ideas on Falsifiability; and Sociological/Constructivist Approaches. The central features of this class of historiographical debate revolve around the logical structure of science and the degree of its independence from other human activities.

Another set of important historiographical issues are those interpretive questions raised more directly by developments in the geosciences. A fresh look is taken at the question of the pace and regularity of geological change and agents of change in Actualism, Uniformitarianism, and Catastrophism. Issues of political context of geography are explored in Geography and Imperialism; and Geopolitics. Such issues that emerge from close examination of individual sciences are the meat of most entries.

Another sort of article focuses on the relation between practical knowledge and geoscience: Mining and Knowledge of the Earth; Weather Modification; and Earthquakes, Prediction, to name a few. As is emphasized in Historiography (Eighteenth-Century England), the neglect by historians of science of practitioners' knowledge is a widespread problem that requires remedy.

Although the entries in this volume concentrate mostly on mainstream geosciences, several articles examine topics that might initially seem strange. Occult Philosophy and the Earth in the Renaissance; Geography and Renaissance Magic; Shifting Crust Theory; Velikovsky's *Worlds in Collision*: a reader might wonder what these have to do with science. Also included are Popular Understanding of the Earth, since 1900 and several articles on folklore and mythology. The relations between geoscience and religion are spotlighted in Jesuits and the Earth; Masons and the Earth; and Sacred Theory of the Earth. Some ideas are explored, too, that were once explicitly accepted parts of science, but which have been rejected: Phlogistic Chemistry; the Deluge, and Expanding Earth Theories, for example. These are here because the volume addresses understanding of the Earth, broadly defined. That is necessary if we are to explore the boundaries and standards of geoscience. One last opportunity for investigating these standards is provided by specific controversies: Mass Extinction and the Impact-Volcanic Controversy; Taconic Controversy; and Plutonists, Neptunists, Vulcanists.

History rests predominantly on the written and printed text. There are, however, other types of evidence available. A small selection of articles examine the utility of images and artifacts and their histories. General questions of visual representation are treated in Geological Maps; Humboldtian Science; and Isolines. Among the scientific instruments discussed are the geomagnetic, meteorological, and seismic. The possibilities of new historical understanding arising from nonverbal evidence are rich, and much such history remains to be written.

Although the focus of this volume is strongly on Western science, the condition of knowledge of the Earth in a few other cultures receives some attention. Examples of this are Cosmology and the Earth, Pre-Modern Orient; Atmospheric Optics to 1600; and Meteorological Ideas in Pre-Modern Orient. It is hoped that this volume will stimulate similar research for African, American, and other cultures, and that scholars will make explicit connections to the history of science from any research on such topics that exists in other literatures.

A multidisciplinary volume like this one allows for inclusion of articles that cut across disciplinary lines. For example, articles often discuss approaches to the history of one science that are suggestive for the history of another. Articles about instruments or computers in a given science, for example, carry much broader implications. Articles about practitioners' knowledge or about theological views do, too. Articles about a tightly defined subdiscipline in one country or about one geoscientific institution may suggest how one context affects science differently than does another.

Another advantage of having, say, geography, geology, and geophysics considered in one volume is that it lets us examine how these sciences have related to each other over time. Moreover, having entries on Ecology; Evolution and the Geosciences; Environmental History; and Environmentalism in one volume makes it easier not only to see how these relate to each other, but especially to see their differences. A similar opportunity is provided by articles that appear to cross disciplinary boundaries: Agricultural Chemistry; Agricultural Geology; and Agricultural Meteorology; Geological Astronomy; Meteorology, Marine; and Meteorology, Medical are examples.

Readers will readily note that this volume contains no biographies. There simply would have been too many, given the number of sciences covered. The difficulty of defining workable selection criteria has led instead to integrating people into the thematic essays as appropriate. An advantage to this approach is that, as historical figures pop up in unexpected contexts, readers will begin to see new links possible between fields that otherwise seem disconnected. Checking the index for Charles Lyell, for example, reveals that his interests ranged much more widely than geology. The "Resources for Research" chapter at the beginning of the volume offers some suggestions for ways in which to track down more biographical information than is contained in this volume. Special effort has been exerted to include in the names index almost all individuals mentioned in the book, as is indicated by the unusual length of this index.

The 230-some articles in this volume only begin to scratch the surface of the history of the geosciences. This is one of the richest areas in the history of science, and it lies yet wide open for exploration. My greatest gratification would be if my efforts and those of the 120 authors who have worked with me led to greatly expanded historical investigation of these sciences. If these essays spur younger students to a deeper understanding of the planet and of our relationships to it, perhaps an even more critical purpose will be achieved.

Acknowledgments

A volume of this length and complexity requires the editor to call in favors hither and yon and to become indebted for the rest of his life. My utmost thanks go to my advisory board and the authors of the articles, who have been unstinting in their aid. Likewise, I thank the series editor, Marc Rothenberg, and my original editor at Garland, Kennie Lyman, for the appropriate mixture of patience and insistence. For help with the many problems of incompatible computer formats, my thanks go to Patrick Connell, Padma Madurie, and Carol Hando at West Virginia University. My current and former graduate students Yuegen Yu, Valerie Morphew, Matthew Rhodes, Blaine Jack, Mike Caplinger, and Jeff Drobney helped in compiling lists of many kinds and in tracking down biographical information. As usual, the university's interlibrary loan team of Judi McCracken and Todd Yeager made scholarship possible. I want, lastly, to thank the office staff of the History Department at West Virginia University: Nancy McGreevy, Sharonlee Huffmann, Diane Barnes, Jen Nestor, and Michelle Taft.

D.E. Cartwright, author of the article "Tides after Newton," wishes to express his thanks to the Leverhulme Foundation, which has supported his historical research.

Series Introduction

Since World War II, the historical study of science has grown enormously. Once the domain of a few scientists interested in their intellectual genealogy and a scattering of intellectual historians, philosophers of science, and sociologists of knowledge, it is now a mature and independent discipline. However, historians of science have not had a way until now to make the essentials of their subject accessible to high school and college students, scholars in other disciplines, and the general public. The encyclopedias in this series will furnish concise historical information and summarize the latest research in a form accessible to those without scientific or mathematical training.

Each volume in the series will be independent from the others. The focus of a particular volume may be a scientific discipline (such as astronomy), a topic that transcends disciplines (such as laboratories and instruments, or science in the United States), or a relationship between the science and another aspect of culture (such as science and religion). The same entry title may appear in a number of volumes, perhaps with a different author, as individual volume editors and co-editors approach the subject from different perspectives.

What is common to each of the volumes is a concern for the historiography of the history of science. By historiography, I mean the recognition that there is never an undisputed explanation of past events. Instead, historians struggle to come to a consensus about the facts and significant issues, and argue over the most valid historical explanations. The authors of the entries in this and the other volumes in the series have been asked to provide entries that are accurate and balanced, but also cognizant of how historical interpretations have changed over time. Where historiographic debate has occurred, authors have been asked to address that debate. They have also been given the freedom to express their own positions.

The extent to which historiographic issues are prominent in the entries varies from entry to entry, and from volume to volume, according to the richness of the historical literature and the depth of the debate. Even for a subject with a rich historiographic literature, such as science in the United States, there are topics for which there is little scholarship. The one or two scholars working on a particular topic may still be laboring to uncover the facts and get the chronology correct. For other fields, there may have been too few active scholars for the development of a complex debate on almost any topic. The introductions to each of the individual volumes clearly lay out the historiographic issues facing scholars in that particular area of the history of science.

To aid the interested reader, each entry provides a concise, selected bibliography on the topic. Further bibliographic information can be obtained from the volumes in the Garland series "Bibliographies on the History of Science and Technology," edited by Robert Multhauf and Ellen Wells.

Marc Rothenberg
Smithsonian Institution

Introduction

Some time after the Renaissance, sciences of the Earth began to emerge in Europe and the regions Europeans were beginning to dominate. There had been knowledge of the Earth and of earthly phenomena before and in other cultures, of course. But these were new kinds of knowing, with new motivations and new methods and new capabilities. The Earth and its knowing would never again be the same.

This volume is about the wide variety of ways in which the Earth has been known. It is especially concerned with forms of knowing the Earth in recent centuries, partly because those are the best documented and partly because it is mostly in that period that our current opportunities and dilemmas have been created. Those who are aware of the Earth, of our environment, as we approach the year 2000 are at least dimly aware that what we know of our home planet has changed dramatically. They are also aware that this knowledge has been used in ways that have maximized human ability to extract resources from the Earth and that simultaneously it has revealed to us the damage done to ecosystems on all scales by our increasing ability to get what we want from the planet. That is, sciences of the Earth, motivated often by a simple urge to understand, have also been tied to other human urges: to control, to profit, to increase material living standards, to revere, to repair, to heal, to cohabitate.

This history, like all histories, is no single, simple story. It is a flow of many rivulets, each with its own relations, its own movement and force. Ideally it includes the perceptions of all peoples of this world, of all times. Ideally it includes the mythology of ancient cultures, along with their practical knowledge of weather or ocean currents. The rivulets of understanding of the Earth among recent farmers, miners, or navigators should stand in this history alongside the research programs of meteorologists, geologists, and oceanographers. Otherwise, we embrace as complete a mere partial understanding of how the human race has come to its current relationships to the Earth. This history should consider not just what now seem to be reasonable ideas, but the full range of ideas about earthly events.

Earth as an Object of Knowledge, Control, and Awe
It is wisest to begin a search for knowledge with greatest humility. In this case, we should not presume that we know what the Earth is, let alone what a science of the Earth might be. Especially in earlier centuries or different cultures (but even in the twentieth century), the meaning of "earth" has varied widely. Did Anaximander, Xenophenes, and other early Greeks really refer to a large singular body when discussing the origin of "earth"? Indeed, one must seriously question translators' own knowledge in rendering the modern word "earth." What does it mean to say that Thales believed "the earth floated in water" (Bowler, *Norton History*, p. 39)? When various American Indian stories tell of Turtle Island, or of Mother Earth (see Sam D. Gill's excellent *Mother Earth: An American Story*), is it simplistic cultural misinterpretation by non-Indians (or perhaps metaphor) to see these as referring to the planet? Much that

is written about the place of "earth" in cosmologies is ill-defined or makes unwarranted parallels to twentieth-century Western ideas.

This is far more than a quibble. Before Copernicus argued in 1543 that the Earth is a planet traveling around the Sun, before globes became fairly common in the Renaissance, and before travelers circumnavigated the globe, what meaning did "earth" have? Clearly, an Earth at the center of the universe was not a planet; it had unique properties. Even after Copernicus and circumnavigation, local and more regional views of our home remained far more probable than any whole-Earth view.

Moreover, knowledge of "earth" has included much more than what is now recognized as science. Historian of science Peter Bowler is correct to point out that there is something different from previous understandings about the "rational" approach to nature, and that one important task of the history of science is to investigate the emergence of this approach in the last few centuries, especially as it regards the Earth (*Norton History,* pp. 4–5). However, we must also be open to mythic, poetic, metaphoric, organic, anthropomorphic, theological, and practical views of "earth."

Indeed, myths of both ancient peoples and contemporary cultures may well provide clues to extensive knowledge of geo-processes and events. One model of the careful reinterpretation of myth is provided by Mott Greene in his *Natural Knowledge in Preclassical Antiquity.* Greene argues that early Greek people had detailed knowledge of phenomena associated with prehistoric volcanic eruptions (chaps. 3, 4). Several entries in this encyclopedia call attention to other neglected areas of folklore and mythology relating to the weather, aurora, and other phenomena. The appreciation of natural knowledge expressed through myth, especially where it concerns the Earth and terrestrial processes, requires careful application of techniques and insights from the history of science, as well as from linguistics, anthropology, and other fields. To place this knowledge of the Earth in the contexts of both use and awe is critical in interpreting myth. Knowledge about the Earth among peoples of Africa, the Americas, and elsewhere certainly still needs to be incorporated into historical investigation. This volume takes some very tentative steps in that direction.

The word "earth" is one of the most problematic in the English language, and probably in other languages too. It can mean the surface we walk on or the soil of our gardens. It can mean Nature, the source of life and fecundity. It can mean one of the four elements—earth, water, air, and fire—that provide the basis of many cultures' conceptual frameworks. It can mean an alchemical principle. Or it can mean a planet. This latter is but one of the most recent meanings. Because this word can be used in so many ways, it must be treated carefully. Throughout this volume, every effort has been made to keep the meaning clear. When reference is to the planet, the word is capitalized as any other planet's name would be: Mercury, Venus, Earth, and so on. This is a standard followed by both astronomers and geophysicists, and seems appropriate for historians of those sciences, too. To say "the atmosphere of *earth*" but "the atmosphere of *Mars*" is at least inconsistent. However, if the reference is to any other use of the word "earth," it is not capitalized. This usage forces us to think more carefully. Situations in which it is difficult to decide this issue underscore that our concept of "earth" is problematic.

From the most pragmatic perspective, Earth is simply the place where we humans live. Much of the time humans don't think about the planet at all, nor do we always intentionally act on it or wonder at it. Rather we go about more immediate tasks. Then sometimes, some humans try to understand the processes that have produced or that maintain the Earth: the relation of environmental factors to human activity, the movement of tectonic plates, electrical discharge in the upper atmosphere, the flow of nutrients and energy in an ecosystem. We also sometimes act directly and willfully on the Earth in an effort to control riverine floods, to extract mineral resources, or to tap its living wealth. And in moments perhaps altogether too rare, we marvel at the spectacle of clouds, volcanoes, or rivers, or at a chemistry that supports so many life forms. But whether or not we realize that Earth is an object of our knowledge, control, or awe does not vitiate the actuality of our knowing, controlling, and wonderment.

This three-way relationship between humans and the Earth has certainly existed in every culture in all times, most likely predating history. And yet it is a relationship that only recently has become an object of self-conscious, critical examination. This awareness is now becoming essential. The sheer mass of humanity on the face of the planet now demands that we be aware of what we know about it, how we affect it, and how it affects us. Historical perspective is an important part of this awareness. An object of *Sciences of the Earth: An Encyclopedia of Events, People, and Phenomena* is to contribute substantially to this need.

Sciences of the Earth: A Special Consideration for the History of Science
Although there are many ways to look at the Earth, this encyclopedia concentrates on the history of the scientific investigation of the planet. The use of the word *sciences* in its title implies that focus. One of the most important figures in defining a science of the Earth, John Herschel (1792–1871), argued that science must exclude all facts and ideas that relate to "emotions of wonder or terror, to passion or interest." Although he certainly considered knowledge useful and nature full of wonder, science was about precision, abstraction, and measurement alone (Herschel, "Whewell on the Inductive Sciences," p. 244). Some readers may readily accept this portrayal of science: disinterested objectivity, a purposeful and regulated method. To some readers it may also imply a permanence of result and a superiority over other forms of knowing. Let us say merely (for now) that each of these presumed characteristics of science (hence of geoscience) is contested among historians of science and other scholars. To thoroughly evaluate the legitimacy of our various judgments about the characteristics of scientific knowledge of the Earth, we need to know much more about what has counted as such knowledge in different times and places.

Two different ways of looking at the Earth—both within the perspective of science—are represented by two excellent recent books. One emphasizes the Earth seen in the context of human society: David Livingstone's *The Geographical Tradition.* The second, Peter J. Bowler's *Norton History of the Environmental Sciences,* stresses the Earth as the habitation of living things. These are two very useful perspectives, and they set knowledge of the Earth in important contexts. Throughout history, the greatest interest in the Earth has indeed been stimulated by practical relationships to humanity. Strabo saw geography as primarily a knowledge in service of governments. To the fifteenth-century Portuguese navigators, who corrected extensive geographical errors of the ancients, empirical knowledge derived much of its value from the profits it promoted. Beyond that, geography has long had another human side in its connection to studies of peoples encountered.

Livingstone's book reflects the new levels to which scholars are elevating the history of geography. No longer is it restricted to the history of exploration or to lightly grounded theoretical warfare. He approaches geography as a science, and convincingly places its history in the context of the history of science. One of the strengths of his book is its combination of the history of geographical thought with the history of the social and institutional settings of geography's practitioners. He places geography in "situated messiness" and strives for a "reciprocity of text and context" (pp. 28–31). Geography as a word and as a science goes back to ancient Greece, but Livingstone argues that geography has transformed over time, not simply grown. (One could make a similar case for the other ancient geoscience, meteorology.) The episodes he highlights almost all concern relations between people and the Earth, from correspondences pointed out by John Dee (1527–1608) between the human microcosm and the cosmic macrocosm (pp. 75–80) to twentieth-century debates about whether or to what degree human societies are determined by their physical environments (for example, chap. 8). Livingstone is aware of the side of geography that has concerned the investigation of the physical Earth; it's simply not his focus.

Bowler's emphasis on the Earth as the abode of life is sustained throughout his analysis, although he does mention some physical geosciences. Given his many publications on the history of evolution, this emphasis is both well supported and not surprising. His discussion of Aristotle includes his *Meteorologica* but looks more closely at his *Historia Animalium* (pp. 46–54). He argues that eighteenth-century studies of the Earth included topics we would divide among geography, geology, meteorology, oceanography, and other disciplines, but which were then organized very differently (pp. 100–112). Bowler's discussions of research regarding the Earth are interspersed with others about the living world for every period examined. This is a valuable juxtaposition, but it necessarily (and legitimately) focuses attention on some episodes and sciences at the expense of others. Bowler's topic is the history of sciences of the environment, not generally of the Earth.

These human and biological perspectives on the Earth are important parts of the story of the geosciences, but one can also look at the Earth itself as an object of knowledge. Geosciences can take the form of the examination of Earth's physical properties, or of its chemical history, of its structure, or of the forces that drive events anywhere between Earth's center and the upper atmosphere. Life is not a factor in these extremes, and it is not always a factor even on the surface. Of course, when life is a factor and science has taken it into account, historians should, too. While geosciences can intersect with human and biological situations, they can also include phenomena and sciences in which such matters aren't germane. Hence, a history of geoscience intersects with the history of geography and with the history of the environmental sciences, but they are not the same. Much of the history of research about ocean currents, for example, can be written with more regard for changing understanding of physical principles than for how such knowledge improved shipping or connected to ocean life. The history of oceanic research also should include information on who these researchers were (whether biologists, physicists, engineers, or other scientists) and it should investigate the characteristics that differentiated their careers and institutions from those of other sciences whose histories are better known.

This volume emphasizes these physical geosciences without intending undue omission of questions of the relations of the Earth to humanity and living things. Indeed, it includes a number of essays directly related to both Livingstone's and Bowler's perspectives. All of these geosciences are subject to a broad range of analysis, from the story of the development of theory to that of how these sciences participate in and are shaped by social and political situations. No primacy inheres in the history of physics, or of evolutionary biology, geography, environmental science, or geoscience. The history of science is enriched by the multiplicity of ways in which past science can be examined.

Scale and Method in the Geosciences

Some characteristics of sciences of the Earth have made it difficult to consider them in historical terms. Two of the most important arise, first, in the scale of these sciences and second, in the methods employed in them. The question of scale is elusive. With regard to our knowledge of the Earth, it runs from processes as minute as the mingling of waters or the growth of fungi in the soil to others as great and distant as the auroral glow or the effects of the Sun's gravity on the oceans. Scientists have investigated crystalline structure, the generation of individual landslides, and the worldwide effects of geomagnetic storms. Moreover, the timescale of geo-processes runs from the flash of a lightning strike to the billions of years of geological time. For any individual to slide readily from the local to the global, from the immediate to the deep past, requires an uncommon mental agility.

The second problematic characteristic of the geosciences relates to their methods. There are two distinct methodological problems: one relates to the inherent requirement of geosciences for rafts of data, the other to their peculiar use of both universalist and historical methods. In more common terms, the geosciences draw on the methods used in physics and in geology, although these two sciences have no exclusive claim to either.

Historians and other commentators on the geosciences have often portrayed them as methodologically impoverished in contrast with the better-known sciences of physics and biology. These latter are often viewed as mature sciences, in which the phenomena have been brought within the scope of theory, often stated in mathematical terms, and in which deductions may be made and then tested in rigorous circumstances. Geosciences, such as geology or meteorology, are often portrayed as naively inductive, or as is often said, Baconian. This is a reference to Francis Bacon, who in the early seventeenth century established a method of science based on observation and classification. Although certainly there have been investigators of the Earth who have interminably collected observations with nary an idea of what the observations meant, they have been, I believe, no more common in these than in other sciences. Researchers have usually had theories in mind. Ancient ideas about the connection of climate to disease or of earthquakes to subterranean winds might not be acceptable today, but they were indeed theories in their times and they guided both scientific discourse and research efforts. Assertions by historians about rampant naive inductivism in the geosciences in earlier centuries are themselves too simplistic and uninformed to be taken seriously. One goal of the history of geoscience is to investigate how research in various sciences was actually done.

Another version of inductivism often pointed out is usually connected to the work and inspiration of Alexander von Humboldt (1769–1859), under the tag Humboldtianism. Humboldt advocated exhaustive observation of terrestrial phenomena. Qualitative description was acceptable in some instances, but he had precision measurement foremost in mind. Although often seen as a romantic, Humboldt gave the impression through much of his writing that the only science of any value rigorously excluded theory or heuristic speculation. He gave his work *Cosmos* the subtitle *A Sketch of a Physical Description of the Universe* and restricted himself to "positive knowledge of the phenomena" or "mere objective representation" (vol. 5, p. 153). Nevertheless, of all scientists of the Earth in the nineteenth century, Humboldt was among the most willing to let hypotheses guide his research. He demanded, however, rigorous quantitative agreement between deductions from them and observational results. Likewise with John Herschel, perhaps the English scientist most like Humboldt. Herschel readily entertained hypotheses as long as they could be stated in quantitative terms and tested rigorously against observational results. The supposed inductivists were in fact much more complex in the methods they used. Nor did such scientists employ a hypothetico-deductive approach exclusively. They used analogies, *vera causa,* and a variety of other methods. As diverse as the geosciences have been, this should not be surprising. A wealth of opportunity exists in the history of the geosciences for analysis of scientific methods.

Historical versus Universalist Approaches to the Earth
Perhaps the more problematic question of method in the geosciences relates to their use of both universalist and historical methods. This requires some explanation, since I don't believe that this particular historiographic problem has been addressed directly in this context. When most historians of science speak of scientific method, natural laws, or causality, they have in mind examples such as Galileo's search for a law of falling bodies or Isaac Newton's universal laws of motion. Physical science, even in its earlier guise of natural philosophy, is and was seen to seek after ultimate properties, ultimate constituents of matter, the universal natures of heat, light, electricity, and so on. If the positions of all particles and their motions were known, along with the laws governing those motions, the future of the universe was utterly predictable (at least in principle). Moreover, from Descartes's mechanical universe until the discovery of entropy in the mid-nineteenth century, there was a sense that these processes were reversible. Different scientists had different ideas about the human ability to reach such ultimate knowledge, but they nevertheless saw it as the goal of science. And although there was disagreement about the relative utility of induction, hypotheses, mathematics, and so on for learning about universal laws and ultimate reality, the hope and intent was still to obtain indubitable knowledge of Nature, applicable everywhere.

Meanwhile, however, not everyone saw all knowledge as timeless nor all phenomena as amenable to such universal, mechanical accounts. Some situations seemed to be contingent on specific previous events in ways that went deeper than the careful (and presumably repeatable) specifics of experimental design. Some events seemed simply not to be repeatable. Human history seemed capricious at worst, but some saw it as directional, with events unfolding toward the Millennium, or perhaps toward decay or progress. The eighteenth-century view that society and individuals might follow natural law was notable precisely because it was so unusual.

Likewise regarding the Earth. Since Aristotle, the Earth was taken to be the scene of generation and corruption, becoming and decay. The combination of this detailed metaphysics with the creation story of Genesis produced a sense that the story of the Earth was intimately linked to the story of humanity and God. There was a timeline, most famously embodied perhaps in the sacred history of the Earth of Thomas Burnet, although much more variable in its telling than is commonly acknowledged. Another famous history of the Earth was the Neptunist tale that the Earth began as a body covered by a world-ocean, the directionality of Earth's history produced by that ocean's gradual recession and the appearance of ever more dry land. This story was not reversible. A late-nineteenth-century tale tied the directionality instead to the heat-death of the Earth.

Historians often speak as if this historical approach in geoscience died with the success of uniformitarian and actualistic geology at the hands of James Hutton and others. Such writers saw geological processes as a perpetual balance of constructive and destructive forces; uplift and volcanoes balanced against erosion. The Earth was changing, but in no particular direction. Nevertheless, the methods of these geologists were fundamentally historical. William Whewell proclaimed that the object of geology and similar sciences was to "ascend from the present state of things to a more ancient condition from which the present is derived by intelligible causes" (quoted in Herschel, p. 183). The evidences of strata and fossils were, like historical documents, unique products of particular times and places. Their explanations read like historical narratives. Periodization and characterization were just as important as in the stories of civilizations. By far the strongest areas of history of the geosciences have concentrated on exactly this niche.

In one of the few points on which I differ from Peter Bowler's description of the environmental sciences, he aligns these sciences strictly with this historical method, saying that they "have methodological requirements of their own that should not be analysed in terms of categories devised for the study of the physical sciences" (Bowler, *Norton History*, pp. 6–7). He argues that to understand the Earth as an isolated system requires investigation of its structure and of the historical laws that have produced what we see around us. Not denying the importance of this historical method in the geosciences, I would stress that many geosciences have drawn heavily upon the universalist method, too.

The geosciences that have been explored the least in histories are those that leaned toward this universalist method, or that relied on it and a historical method both. On the one hand missed by historians of geology and geography, these more physical geosciences have also been relatively ignored by historians of physics, who have focused on the investigation of prominent issues in "pure" physics: the development of classical mechanics, electromagnetic field theory, or relativity. Nevertheless, terrestrial phenomena have figured in physical science since antiquity, and many of the "universal" aspects of Nature have been investigated specifically in a terrestrial context. The pace of work in this strain of geoscience began to quicken with the Scientific Revolution, and it became undeniably important at exactly the time that geology was emerging as a more-or-less independent discipline—that is, in the nineteenth century.

The Rise of Disciplines in the Geosciences: A Historical Phenomenon
The sciences have become an ingrained part of our view of the world and our place in it. Sciences and their divisions are often mistaken for the world and its parts. Disciplines are taken to represent that world. Geology is the science of the rocks near the Earth's surface, meteorology of its atmosphere, and oceanography of the open waters of the surface. But geology did not exist until the eighteenth century, meteorology had included earthquakes and comets for almost two thousand years, and oceanography has been born only in the last century. The current disciplinary landscape of the geosciences is often inappropriate to other periods and to non-Western cultures, and it can obscure the very different intellectual and institutional boundaries that have characterized geoscience.

Hence it might seem strange to emphasize disciplinary history, as this volume does. This may appear unabashedly presentist, requiring a historian to look backward with the current boundaries, methods, problems, theories, and so forth of some scientific discipline in mind. Disciplinary history can indeed include as a step in its pursuit—but not as its primary goal—

investigation of the origins of a discipline. These origins may be well known, as in the foundation of chemistry in the late eighteenth century, or they may be obscure or convoluted, as in the case of geophysics. Although some historians might maintain that an inherent quality of the universe dictates the shape of disciplines, historical investigation generally indicates that the boundaries between disciplines and the various standards within disciplines are subject to nearly continuous negotiation among scientists. That is, disciplines are constructed by their practitioners, based partly on the natures of phenomena, but also on personal or professional priorities, social or institutional realities.

Disciplinary history requires an openness to the unexpected. The historian must be willing to set aside the current context and ferret out the different contexts of other times and places. Hence a disciplinary history of geology requires one to consider how rocks, the genesis of ores, minerals, and fossils were thought of before the construction of geology in the eighteenth and nineteenth centuries. A disciplinary history of meteorology forces one to take seriously questions of method and substance that allowed Aristotle to discuss rain and comets in the same work.

All sciences are constructs in an important way, without their facts and theories being "unscientific." The environmental sciences are a construct and so are the geosciences. The genesis of so many disciplines in the last two hundred years is evidence of this. The establishment of geology, biology, geophysics, and so on required not only the "professional" accoutrements of journals, societies, professorships, and institutes, but also the declaration and defense of bounded intellectual zones, problem areas, and methodological restrictions.

Clearly it is illegitimate to seek geology or geophysics before these constructs existed. But is it also illegitimate to look for knowledge of the Earth, even scientific knowledge of the Earth, before these existed? Absolutely not. To do so requires a suspension of expectations—a peeling away—as one investigates what has counted as a legitimate topic of research about the Earth, a legitimate method, and so on, in earlier times. Paradoxically, the purposeful concentration on disciplinary histories allows scholars to reveal the boundaries—both temporal and conceptual—of current disciplines. It reveals the contingency of these boundaries and eliminates some of the more egregious errors of this most invisible of presentist assumptions. Disciplinary walls are high in the late twentieth century, and well defended, but they need not blind us to their historical character.

Words: Rhetoric, Multiple Designators, and Appropriation
Much could be made of the appearance of new words as indicators of the emergence of new sciences. This requires great care, since critical terms can become the focus of much contention; meaning is tied as much to connotation and association as to overt definition. Political debates about such words as communist and liberal indicate this well. Words become invested with emotion and innuendo. Take the well-known but jarring word *geognosy* (the German original being *Geognosie*), and the related word *geology*. Its early meanings around 1800 ranged from the stratigraphic and mineralogical structure of a region—for example, the Saxon *Erzgebirge*—to an intensely pejorative dismissal by British geologists of German approaches to their roughly common subject area: rocks, minerals, and stratigraphic structure. To some, geognosy and geology were synonymous. To others, geognosy implied wildly unfounded speculation about the origin of Earth or why mountain chains were oriented in particular directions. Ironically, the word *Geologie* often carried the same connotation to German-speaking researchers! Geology, like geography and cosmography, often implied the comprehensive study of the planet, including its waters and atmosphere. Historians could certainly still learn much from careful analysis of the rhetoric surrounding such words, but their meaning is not transparent (Dean, passim).

The invention of a term for the physical investigation of the Earth is instructive in other ways. Such study was becoming sufficiently common in the early nineteenth century that many investigators felt the need for a new word or phrase. François Arago (1786–1853) used *physique du globe,* C.F. Schönbein (1799–1868) and Julius Fröbel (1805–1893) used first *Physik der Erde,* then *theoretische Erdkunde* (theoretical Earth-knowledge), and finally *Geophysik.* John

Herschel called this study terrestrial physics or physical geography (Buntebarth, pp. 99–104; Kertz, passim; Herschel, *Preliminary Discourse*, p. 350). Through the mid and into the late nineteenth century, writers continued to use variants of all these terms, all the while debating the appropriate methods and goals of particular subsets of physical geoscience, from tectonics and the study of earthquakes to geodesy and terrestrial magnetism. The relations among these subsets and between them and better-known disciplines like geography and astronomy are just beginning to be investigated (see Good, passim). Although the term *geophysics* did not become well accepted until nearly 1900, the activity was being developed and debated throughout the century. The historical inquiry into the appearance and significance of new disciplines and research concentrations is much needed if we are to get beyond simplistic categories of the sciences and beyond the sense that there is something permanent and necessary about disciplines, something beyond human contingency.

Some last examples of the way meanings have shifted and confused some issues are evident in the words *environmental* and *environmentalism*. The most common meaning today connotes a political movement and a commitment to saving the planet from degradation: Green Peace, reversing the growth of the ozone hole, and so on. But other meanings are extant. The environmental sciences, as in the title of Bowler's book or in the names of university courses and professorships, are at least separable from this meaning and connote scientific research concerning the environment of living things: physical and chemical processes that affect life. A related meaning had a short life around 1970 in the U.S. federal bureaucracy, when the Environmental Sciences Service Administration encompassed the sciences of the ocean, the atmosphere, and some related to the solid Earth, along with elements of the life sciences. A very different meaning than any of these has long been used among geographers, not to mention among social scientists. When William Morris Davis (1850–1934) discussed environmentalism, he meant the determination of human society by the environment—that is, environmental determinism. The extent to which human beings and societies can overcome the determinants of their surroundings and impose their wills has long been a central issue among geographers (Livingstone, passim). A last use to mention is the term *environmental technology*, frequently appearing in the 1990s attached to activities such as waste management and acid-mine-drainage remediation. These shades of meaning in environmental and environmentalism caution us that words must be read carefully, and interpreted in context. Such focal words reflect a concentration of importance attributed to an area of activity during a given age, in a given culture. Such words can also transfer credibility or be appropriated to activities where their use is at variance with other meanings. All of this is subject to historical investigation and interpretation.

Conclusion: What We Stand to Gain
In 1994 the Geological Society of America convened a Penrose Conference called "From the Inside and Outside: Interdisciplinary Perspectives on the History of the Earth Sciences." Discussions centered on the different approaches and interests that geoscientists bring to the study of their fields and those brought by historians and other outsiders. Common ground was also considered. Each clearly brings strengths and weaknesses, characteristics that are undoubtedly reflected in many essays in this volume, since the contributors include about a fifty-fifty split. But neither has an exclusive claim to writing good, interesting, challenging, or credible history. Indeed, both have an obligation to do so.

Writers of history of the geosciences, like all writers of history, write with a reason or reasons, even if this is unacknowledged or denied. History can be written to address current needs of the subject of the history. Historians of geology, for example, could write in defense of geology. This is possible in any history and is not necessarily to be disparaged, although there are certainly dangers in doing so, such as glorifying earlier figures who apparently did things your way and vilifying those who did not. Charles Lyell's introductory chapter to his *Principles of Geology* (1830–1833) is a classic case of history in the service of a particular view of a science. It ridiculed catastrophic geology, buttressed the case for uniformitarian geology, and butchered the historical record. It long led the history of geology astray. It should be noted, however, that scientists do not always write such self-serving history, as many articles in this volume attest.

Writers of history may also, at the other extreme, set their own agendas and standards. Indeed, they do. The standards of history generally—and of history of science in particular—are exacting. Standards of argument and the use of sources are debated continuously in the journals. There is even *An Introduction to the Historiography of Science* written by Helge Kragh, which explores these questions with the thoroughness of a philosopher.

As to the agendas of history, these are constantly emerging and shifting. Sometimes the agenda is to buttress the credibility of science, sometimes to question it. More often, it is neither. Sometimes the agenda is simply to understand better how science works, or how research problems are resolved, or to bring into account an area of science that has been neglected in the history of science. At another level, the agenda can be to take on a particular historical interpretation and evaluate its strengths and weaknesses. Most history, like most science, is undertaken for a reason. To paraphrase historian E.H. Carr, if a piece of history has no agenda, its author is a dull dog.

Our understanding of the Earth and of the history of the geosciences stands only to be enriched by entertaining the widest variety of histories possible. This means entertaining histories even if we disagree vehemently with the reasons for which they were undertaken. Peter Bowler suggests that just as science has often been pursued in the service of industry, it can also be pursued in the service of environmentalism. Both groups of scientists, he writes, have political interests to defend (*Norton History*, p. 29). Likewise, historians can seek out different instances to investigate, depending on whether the writer thinks in terms of the control of nature or environmental coherence. Bowler believes that environmentalism provides a new and valid agenda to historians of science. It encourages the historical investigation of neglected sciences, "once dismissed as too technical to be of interest to non-specialists," and of earlier periods in which scientists pursued a less specialized, more unified science (p. 3). As Bowler writes elsewhere, an environmental focus might make possible "the integration of a whole range of important, yet hitherto ignored, topics into mainstream history of science" ("Science and the Environment," p. 9). In the end, histories from both agendas must measure up to the same standards of investigation and argument.

Geoscience has indeed been used often to benefit industry and individuals, nations and national ideologies. The application of geophysical techniques, for example, helped create a petroleum-based way of life. The ocean bottom was mapped in the 1950s in large part to aid in submarine navigation, a part of the Cold War. This history should be written, and it should be done coolly and analytically. The history of the geosciences, however, is more than just a story of science in the service of environmental exploitation, or even of increasing fragmentation of our understanding. The geosciences have also at times sought unities of understanding we have forgotten. They have at times been driven by an urge to wonder. They have sought to heal damage done to the Earth and to living things. Historians of the geosciences can legitimately tell all these stories.

It would be naive to think that the use of geoscience by private and limited interests will cease, but it is certainly to be hoped that the common good of the human race, of other living things, and of the planet as a whole will call forth a new application of geoscience, an application intended to repair ecosystems on all scales. Ultimately, is it too much to ask that our expanding understanding of the physical and biological processes of this planet will produce a new wonderment, a new awe that will temper our behavior? Let history be a repository for our memories of what we have tried, of what has been good and what has not. And let this history be based on an honest, hard-nosed evaluation of what we have known about the Earth.

Gregory A. Good

Bibliography
Bowler, Peter J. *The Norton History of the Environmental Sciences.* New York and London: W.W. Norton, 1993. First published in England as *The Fontana History of the Environmental Sciences,* 1992.
————. "Science and the Environment: New Agendas for the History of Science?" In *Science and Nature. Essays in the History of the Environmental Sciences,* edited by

Michael Shortland, pp. 1–21. (British Society for the History of Science, Monograph 8.) Oxford: Alden Press, 1993.

Buntebarth, Günter. "Zur Entwicklung des Begriffes Geophysik." *Abhandlungen der Braunschweigischen Wissenschaftlichen Gesellschaft* 32 (1981): pp. 95–109.

Carr, E.H. *What Is History?* New York: Vintage Books, 1961.

Dean, Dennis R. "The Word 'Geology.'" *Annals of Science* 36 (1979): pp. 35–43.

Gill, Sam D. *Mother Earth: An American Story.* Chicago and London: University of Chicago Press, 1987.

Good, Gregory A. "Geomagnetics and Scientific Institutions in 19th-Century America." *Eos: The Transactions of the American Geophysical Union* 66 (1985): pp. 521–526.

Greene, Mott T. *Natural Knowledge in Preclassical Antiquity.* Baltimore and London: Johns Hopkins University Press, 1992.

Herschel, John. *Preliminary Discourse on the Study of Natural Philosophy.* London: Longman, 1830.

———. "Whewell on the Inductive Sciences." *Quarterly Review* 68 (1841), pp. 177–238. Reprinted in *Essays from the Edinburgh and Quarterly Reviews.* London: Longman, Brown, Green, Longmans, and Roberts, 1857, pp. 142–256.

Humboldt, Alexander von. *Cosmos. A Sketch of a Physical Description of the Universe.* Translated by E.C. Otté. 5 vols. New York: Harper, 1867–1868.

Kertz, Walter. "Die Entwicklung der Geophysik zur eigenständigen Wissenschaft." *Mitteilungen der Gauss-Gesellschaft* 16 (1979): pp. 41–54.

Kragh, Helge. *An Introduction to the Historiography of Science.* Cambridge: Cambridge University Press, 1987.

Livingstone, David N. *The Geographical Tradition. Episodes in the History of a Contested Enterprise.* Oxford, U.K., and Cambridge, Mass.: Blackwell, 1992.

Categorical Listing of Entries

Air, Meteorology, and Climate

Agricultural Meteorology
Airglow
Atmosphere, Chemistry of
Atmosphere, Discovery and Exploration of
Atmosphere, Structure of
Atmospheric Optics to 1600
Auroras in Folklore and Mythology
Auroras, before the International Geophysical Year
Auroras, since the International Geophysical Year
Ballooning
Bergen School of Meteorology
Chemical Revolution
Climate, Ancient Ideas
Climate Change, before 1940
Climate Change, since 1940
Climates, Pleistocene and Recent
Computers and Meteorology
Cosmology and the Earth in Antiquity
Cosmology and the Earth in Medieval Europe
Cosmology and the Earth in Pre-modern Orient
Cosmology and the Earth in the Renaissance
Cosmology and the Earth in the Scientific Revolution
Dew
Greenhouse Effect
Ice Ages
Instruments, Meteorological
Instruments, Upper Atmospheric and Near Space
Isolines
Mathematics and Meteorology
Meteorological Ideas in Classical Greece and Rome
Meteorological Ideas in Europe, Fifteenth to Eighteenth Centuries
Meteorological Ideas in Folklore and Mythology
Meteorological Ideas in Pre-modern Orient
Meteorological Observing Systems
Meteorological Services
Meteorological Societies
Meteorology: Disciplinary History
Meteorology, Marine
Meteorology, Medical
Ocean Currents
Ocean Currents, Circulation Patterns
Ocean-Atmosphere Interactions
Ozone
Phlogistic Chemistry
Precipitation, Theories of
Radiosondes and Related Instruments
Scientific Rocketry to *Sputnik*
Sky Brightness during Solar Eclipses
Storms and Cyclones
Weather Modification

Earth's Interior

Artesian Water
Continental Drift and Plate Tectonics
Convection within the Earth
Cosmology and the Earth in Antiquity
Cosmology and the Earth in Medieval Europe
Cosmology and the Earth in Pre-modern Orient
Cosmology and the Earth in the Renaissance
Cosmology and the Earth in the Scientific Revolution
Deluge, The
Drilling
Drilling, Scientific
Earthquakes, Historic
Earthquakes, Prediction
Earthquakes, Theories from Antiquity to 1600

Resources for Research in the History of Geosciences

Perhaps after reading some of the articles in *Sciences of the Earth: An Encyclopedia of Events, People, and Phenomena,* you will want to learn more about the history of some special topic. How can you go further? The first place that an initiate into the history of science might turn for information on, say, the history of geology is likely to be a standard encyclopedia. The *Encyclopedia Britannica,* or any of a dozen others, does indeed provide the skeleton chronologies in articles such as "Earth," "Earth Sciences," and "Earth: Its Properties, Composition, and Structure."

These, however, must not be mistaken for historical analyses. Such articles are generally intended as introductions, not complete discussions. The emphasis of such sources on facts often does not allow for discussion of questions of historical interpretation. The contexts of events are seldom explored. Nor can such articles offer critical examination of sources or of what historians have made of them. For those, one must turn to articles and books written by historians and to the original scientific literature. Once these materials are found, the reading of both types to learn more about the history of a science requires judgment and critical analysis. History is an inquiry, not a mere reporting of facts. But how does one find this literature in the first place?

A distinction must be made at the start of this section. Historians and scientists use the phrases "primary literature" and "secondary literature" in very different ways. To a scientist, primary literature consists of publications that present the results of original research, mainly in journal articles. Secondary literature includes various materials that reflect on, critique, or summarize the results contained in primary literature: review and encyclopedia articles, textbooks, and the like.

Historians use these words quite differently. Primary literature to a historian is any source upon which historical research can be based. It includes both research results and virtually all other publications by scientists, including literature reviews and encyclopedia articles. Moreover, it may include their popular essays and lectures, their personal memoirs, or their publications on research methods, goals, or other concerns. Primary sources for historians go much further than the published literature. They can include unpublished correspondence, research notebooks, private diaries, internal agency reports, sketches or photographs, instruments, models, maps, and more. Primary sources to the historian are, simply put, the data from which history is written. Another way of saying this is that primary sources to the historian include all materials produced at the time of the events being studied.

Secondary sources are, equally simply, the results of historical research. Historical investigators, whether trained historians or scientists looking at former periods of scientific activity, contribute to the secondary literature. Anyone conducting historical research would be wise to know this literature, just as scientists who remain ignorant of the results of other scientists' research do so at their own peril. The least that might happen is that researchers might duplicate work already done. The worst is perhaps that their historical research would be un-informed of important interpretations or results. It is equally important that historical investigators exhaustively explore both the primary and secondary literature, in the historian's sense of these terms (see Kragh, chaps. 11, 12 [listed in section VIII below]).

For two reasons, a brief look at resources for investigators of the history of the geosciences is needed. First, the simple number of geosciences means that those familiar with one contemporary specialty, such as geology, might be unaware of the relevant sources in another, such as geography. This point is all the more obvious if one enumerates specialties in finer detail: solar-terrestrial relations, aeronomy, soil science, landscape ecology, and so on. Clearly, when one is investigating real historical problems, all relevant trails of evidence must be considered, even those beyond today's disciplinary boundaries. Second, finding historical investigations and older scientific materials presents unique challenges, especially to researchers accustomed to disregarding literature more than a few years old. In the history of science, older works are often the most important, whether they are secondary or primary works.

Many useful sources are listed in the bibliographies of the individual articles in this volume. Others of more general use are listed below. These are divided into sections: I. Technical Dictionaries and Encyclopedias; II. Historical and Humanistic Dictionaries and Encyclopedias; III. Sources of Biographies; IV. Bibliographies of Primary Sources; V. Bibliographies of Secondary Sources; VI. Periodical Indexes and Abstract Services; VII. On-line Data-Bases and CD-ROMs; and VIII. Journals and Newsletters.

I. Technical Dictionaries and Encyclopedias

Clark, Audrey N. *Longman Dictionary of Geography, Human and Physical.* Harlow, U.K.: Longman, 1985. Quite useful for terms in physical geography, geophysics, geology, and so forth.

Dunbar, Gary S. *Modern Geography: An Encyclopedic Survey.* New York: Garland, 1991.

Durrenberger, Robert W. *Dictionary of the Environmental Sciences.* Palo Alto: National Press Books, 1973.

Fairbridge, Rhodes Whitmore. *The Encyclopedia of Atmospheric Sciences and Astrogeology.* New York: Reinhold, 1967.

―――. *The Encyclopedia of Geochemistry and Environmental Sciences.* New York: Van Nostrand Reinhold, 1972.

―――. *The Encyclopedia of Geomorphology.* New York: Reinhold, 1968.

―――. *The Encyclopedia of Oceanography.* New York: Reinhold, 1966.

―――. *The Encyclopedia of Paleontology.* Stroudsburg, Pa.: Dowden, Hutchinson, and Ross, 1979.

―――. *The Encyclopedia of World Regional Geology.* Stroudsburg, Pa.: Dowden, Hutchinson, and Ross, 1975.

Fairbridge, Rhodes Whitmore, and Charles W. Finkl, Jr. *The Encyclopedia of Soil Science.* Stroudsburg, Pa.: Dowden, Hutchinson, and Ross, 1979.

Franck, Irene, and David Brownstone. *The Green Encyclopedia.* New York: Prentice Hall, 1992.

James, David E. *Encyclopedia of Solid Earth Geophysics.* New York: Van Nostrand Reinhold, 1989.

Magill, Frank N., ed. *Magill's Survey of Science: Earth Science Series.* 5 vols. Pasadena and Englewood Cliffs, N.J.: Salem Press, 1990. Index in vol. 5.

National Referral Center (U.S.). *A Directory of Information Resources in the United States: Geosciences and Oceanography.* Washington, D.C.: Government Printing Office, 1981.

Paehlke, Robert C. *Conservation and Environmentalism: An Encyclopedia.* New York: Garland, 1995.

Parker, Sybil P., and Robert A. Corbitt. *McGraw-Hill Encyclopedia of Environmental Science and Engineering.* 3d ed. New York: McGraw-Hill, 1993.

Runcorn, S.K., et al., eds. *International Dictionary of Geophysics. Seismology, Geomagnetism, Aeronomy, Oceanography, Geodesy, Gravity, Marine Geophysics, Meteorology, the Earth as a Planet and Its Evolution.* 3 vols. New York: Pergamon, 1967.

Small, John, and Michael Witherick. *A Modern Dictionary of Geography.* London: Edward

Arnold, 1986. Good on physical geography.

Stiegeler, Stella E. *A Dictionary of Earth Sciences*. New York: Pica Press, 1976.

Sullivan, Thomas P. *Directory of Environmental Information Sources*. 4th ed. Rockville, Md.: Government Institutes, 1992.

Wood, David N., Joan E. Hardy, and Anthony P. Harvey, eds. *Information Sources in the Earth Sciences*. 2d ed. London: Bowker-Saur, 1989. Includes excellent bibliographical essays for different branches of geoscience and one on the history of geology.

Wyatt, Antony. *Challinor's Dictionary of Geology*. 6th ed. Cardiff: University of Wales, 1986. Compiled on historical principles.

II. Historical and Humanistic Dictionaries and Encyclopedias

Bynum, William F., E. Janet Browne, and Roy Porter, eds. *Dictionary of the History of Science*. Princeton: Princeton University Press, 1981.

Gill, Sam D. *Dictionary of Native American Mythology*. Santa Barbara: ABC-CLIO, 1992.

Hammond, N.G.L., and H.H. Scullard. *The Oxford Classical Dictionary*. 2d ed. Oxford: Clarendon, 1970.

Hetherington, Norriss S. *Encyclopedia of Cosmology: Historical, Philosophical, and Scientific Foundations of Modern Cosmology*. New York: Garland, 1993.

Holland, Clive. *Arctic Exploration and Development, c. 500 B.C. to 1915: An Encyclopedia*. New York: Garland, 1993.

Lanjue, Frédérique, and Carmen Salazar-Soler. *Dictionnaire des termes miniers en usage en Amérique espagnole, XVIe–XIXe siècles. Diccionario de términos mineros para la América española, siglos XVI–XIX*. Paris: Editions Recherche sur les Civilisations, 1993.

Olby, R.C., G.N. Cantor, R. Christie, and M.J.S. Hodge, eds. *Companion to the History of Modern Science*. London: Routledge, 1990.

Weiner, Philip E., ed. *Dictionary of the History of Ideas: Studies of Selected Pivotal Ideas*. 5 vols. New York: Scribner, 1974.

III. Sources of Biographies

American Men and Women of Science. 13th ed. 6 vols. and index. New York: Bowker, 1976. (Formerly *American Men of Science*.) Older editions are useful for previous generations.

Arnim, Max. *Internationale Personalbibliographie, 1800–1943*. 2 vols., (A-K) and (L-Z). Zweite, verbesserte und stark vermehrte Auflage. Stuttgart: Anton Hiersemann, 1952. Vol. 3, Stuttgart: Anton Hiersemann, 1963.

Axelrod, Alan, and Charles Phillips. *The Environmentalists: A Biographical Dictionary from the 17th Century to the Present*. New York: Facts on File, 1993.

Daintith, John, Sara Mitchell, Elizabeth Tootill, and Derek Gjertsen, eds. *Biographical Encyclopedia of Scientists*. 2d ed. 2 vols. Bristol and Philadelphia: Institute of Physics Publishing, 1994.

Debus, Allen G. *World Who's Who in Science: A Biographical Dictionary of Notable Scientists from Antiquity to the Present*. Chicago: Marquis Who's Who, Inc., 1968.

Dictionary of American Biography, London: Milford, 1928–.

Dictionary of National Biography, British, London: Oxford University Press and others, 1882–, with supplements.

Elliott, Clarke. *Biographical Dictionary of American Science: Seventeenth through the Nineteenth Centuries*. Westport, Conn.: Greenwood Press, 1979.

Geological Society of America. *Memorials*. Boulder, Colo.: 1973+. From 1973 to 1996, 26 volumes appeared, with short biographical notes on over 1,000 geologists.

Gillispie, Charles Coulton, ed. *Dictionary of Scientific Biography*. 16 vols. with index, plus supplements. New York: Scribner, 1970–1976. This is the foremost basic source. The subject headings in the index are useful entries into the histories of specific sciences.

Larkin, Robert P., and Gary L. Peters. *Biographical Dictionary of Geography*. Westport, Conn., and London: Greenwood, 1993. Seventy-seven biographies, including several of physical geographers.

McGraw-Hill Modern Men of Science. 3 vols. New York: McGraw Hill, 1966–1980.

Muir, Hazel. *Larousse Dictionary of Scientists. From the Pioneers of Science to the Innovators of Modern Research*. Edinburgh: Larousse, 1994.

National Academy of Sciences. *Biographical Memoirs*. Washington, D.C.: National

Academy Press, 1958–. A cumulative index appears in vol. 57, 1987.

Poggendorff, J.C. *Biographisch-literarisches Handwörterbuch zur Geschichte der exacten Wissenschaften; enthaltend Nachweisungen über Lebensverhältnisse und Leistungen von Mathematikern, Astronomen, Physikern, Chemikern, Mineralogen, Geologen, u.s.w. aller Volker und Zeiten.* 7 vols. Amsterdam: B.M. Israel, 1970. Extremely valuable for the nineteenth and earlier centuries and international in scope. Each entry includes a bibliography of the scientist's main publications.

Porter, Roy. *The Hutchinson Dictionary of Scientific Biography.* Oxford: Helicon, 1994.

IV. Bibliographies of Primary Sources

Hazen, William B., and Adolphus W. Greely, eds. *The International Bibliography of Meteorology: From the Beginning of Printing to 1889.* 4 vols. in 1. Upland, Pa.: Diane Publishing, 1994. Originally issued in limited quantity in 1889–1891. With an index and historical introduction by James Rodger Fleming.

Knight, David. *Sources for the History of Science, 1660–1914.* Ithaca, N.Y.: Cornell University Press, 1975. (Sources of History: Studies in the Uses of Historical Evidence.) Discussions of the varieties of evidence available, with selective bibliographies.

Long, Harriet K. *A Bibliography of Earth Science Bibliographies of the United States of America.* Washington, D.C.: American Geological Institute, 1971.

Pearl, Richard M. *Guide to Geological Literature.* New York: McGraw-Hill, 1951.

Royal Society of London. *Catalogue of Scientific Papers, 1800–1900.* New York: Johnson Reprint Corp., 1965– (1867–1925). 19 vols. (plus 3 vols. subject index). Useful guide to nineteenth-century scientific works. For many scientists, this catalogue provides the most complete listing of their research publications available, although it often omits their more popular publications.

Sarjeant, William A.S. *Geologists and the History of Geology: An International Bibliography from the Origins to 1978.* 5 vols. plus supplements. New York: Arno Press, 1980. Includes both primary and secondary literature and more than geology. Indexes by country and by field make this extremely valuable.

Sen, S.N., and Santimay Chatterjee. "A Bibliography of Physics, Astronomy, Astrophysics, and Geophysics in India, 1800–1950." *Indian Journal of History of Science* 27 (1993): S1–S77; 28 (1993): S79–S219, S221–S501.

Sinkankas, John. *Gemology: An Annotated Bibliography.* 2 vols. Metuchin, N.J.: Scarecrow Press, 1993. Primary literature since the beginning of printing.

Ward, Dederick C., and Marjorie Wheeler. *Geological Reference Sources: A Subject and Regional Bibliography of Publications and Maps in the Geological Sciences.* Metuchin, N.J.: Scarecrow Press, 1972. 2d ed. with Robert A. Bier, Jr., 1981. The two editions complement one another, the first being better for historical sources. Includes geophysics and "extra-terrestrial" geology.

Wheaton, Bruce R. *Inventory of Sources for History of 20th Century Physics. Report and Microfiche Index to 700,000 Letters.* With the assistance of Robin E. Rider. Stuttgart: Verlag für Geschichte der Naturwissenschaften und der Technik, 1993. Although the title says physics, this includes references to many geoscientists.

V. Bibliographies of Secondary Sources

Bibliografia Italiana di Storia della Scienza. Florence: Olschki. Published annually by the Istituto e Museo di Storia della Scienza.

Bridson, Gavin. *The History of Natural History: An Annotated Bibliography.* New York: Garland, 1994.

Brush, Steven G., and Helmut E. Landsberg. *The History of Geophysics and Meteorology: An Annotated Bibliography.* New York: Garland, 1985. Extremely useful. Includes many primary sources, too.

Bulletin Signaletique 522: Histoire des sciences et techniques. Paris: Centre de Documentation du C.N.R.S. Published quarterly.

Current Bibliography of the History of Technology. Published annually in the journal *Technology and Culture.*

Deacon, M.B. *The History of Oceanography: An Annotated Bibliography.* New York: Garland, 1993.

Dunbar, Gary S. *The History of Modern Geography: An Annotated Bibliography.* New York: Garland, 1990.

Hurt, R. Douglas, and Mary Ellen Hurt. *The History of Agricultural Science and Technology: An International Annotated Bibliography.* New York: Garland, 1993.

ISIS Critical Bibliography appears annually in *ISIS,* the journal of the History of Science Society, vol. 1, no. 1, 1913–. Called *ISIS Current Bibliography* from 1989 on. The most valuable guide to current literature in the history of science. These are available on-line via RLIN from 1976 to the present. Use with the *ISIS Cumulative Bibliography,* below.

ISIS Cumulative Bibliography: A Bibliography of the History of Science Formed from ISIS Critical Bibliographies 1–90, 1913–1965. Edited by Magda Whitrow. London: Mansell, in conjunction with the History of Science Society, 1971–1982. 5 vols. A must, the first place to turn to.

Vol. 1: Personalities (A-J)
Vol. 2: Personalities (J-Z) and Institutions
Vol. 3: Subjects
Vol. 4: Prehistory to Middle Ages
Vol. 5: Fifteenth to Nineteenth Centuries

ISIS Cumulative Bibliography, 1966–1975. A Bibliography of the History of Science Formed from ISIS Critical Bibliographies 91–100, indexing literature published from 1965 through 1974. Edited by John Neu. Suppl. 1. London: Mansell in conjunction with the History of Science Society, 1980.

Vol. 1: Personalities and Institutions
Vol. 2: Subjects, Periods, and Civilizations

ISIS Cumulative Bibliography, 1976–1985. A Bibliography of the History of Science Formed from ISIS Critical Bibliographies 101–110, indexing literature published from 1975 through 1984. Edited by John Neu. Boston: G.K. Hall, in conjunction with the History of Science Society, 1989.

Vol. 1: Persons and Institutions
Vol. 2: Subjects, Periods, and Civilizations

Mills, Eric L. "A Handlist of Printed Sources on the History of Oceanography." *Earth Sciences History* 12 (1993): 2–4.

Molloy, Peter M. *The History of Metal Mining and Metallurgy: A Selected, Annotated Bibliography.* New York: Garland, 1986.

Ogilvie, Mary Bailey. *Women and Science: An Annotated Bibliography.* New York: Garland, 1995.

Porter, Roy. *The Earth Sciences: An Annotated Bibliography.* New York: Garland, 1983.

Rothenberg, Marc. *The History of Science and Technology in the United States: A Critical and Selective Bibliography.* 2 vols. New York: Garland, 1982, 1993.

Sarjeant, William A.S. *Geologists and the History of Geology: An International Bibliography from the Origins to 1978.* 5 vols. plus supplements. New York: Arno Press, 1980. Includes both primary and secondary literature and more than geology. Indexes by country and by field make this extremely valuable.

Selin, Helaine. *Science across Cultures: An Annotated Bibliography of Books on Non-Western Science, Technology, and Medicine.* New York: Garland, 1992.

Whitrow, Magda. "Bibliographical Developments in the History of Science." In *The Book Encompassed: Studies in 20th Century Bibliography,* edited by Peter Davidson, pp. 151–160. Cambridge: Cambridge University Press, 1992.

VI. Periodical Indexes and Abstract Services

Marconi, Joseph V. *Indexed Periodicals: A Guide to 170 Years of Coverage in 33 Indexing Services.* Ann Arbor, Mich.: Pierian Press, 1976. Useful for researchers unfamiliar with older indexes.

Commonly used current indexes include:

> *Bibliographical Index*
> *Biography Index*
> *British Humanities Index,* supersedes *Subject Index to Periodicals*
> *Ecological Abstracts*
> *Education Index*
> *Essay and General Literature Index*
> *Geographical Abstracts*
> *Geological Abstracts*
> *Geoscience Abstracts*
> *Historical Abstracts*
> *Humanities Index,* supersedes in part *Social Sciences and Humanities Index*
> *Internationale Bibliographie der ZeitschriftenLiteratur*
> *International Bibliography of Periodical Literature*
> *International Index to Periodicals in the Social Sciences*
> *Nineteenth Century Readers' Guide to Periodical Literature, 1890–1899*
> *Oceanographic Literature Review*
> *Pool's Index to Periodical Literature,* covers thirty-seven important periodicals for 1815–1899
> *Readers' Guide to Periodical Literature*—remains valuable, especially for the early twentieth century
> *Social Sciences and Humanities Index,* is superseded by *Humanities Index* and by *Social Sciences Index*
> *Social Sciences Index,* supersedes in part *Social Sciences and Humanities Index*
> *Subject Index to Periodicals,* is superseded by *British Humanities Index*

VII. On-line Data-Bases and CD-ROMs

Hundreds of on-line data-bases, most of them simply bibliographies (some evaluative, others not) and abstracting services are becoming available on computer networks and are accessible via personal computers. Many of these services are available at research libraries on CD-ROMs. Because these are becoming available over Internet and Worldwide Web, however, these are listed together here. There is also a new Web page for the history of the geosciences. This is being organized by "Friends of Geo-Clio," a loose network of scientists, historians, and other scholars who investigate the histories of geology, geophysics, oceanography, and related fields. GeoClio is located at http://geoclio.st.usm.edu. (See table on p. xxxiii for additional web sites.)

Recent scientific literature is the most thoroughly treated in computerized data-bases. Several history and social science data-bases are also available. A few cautionary notes are needed. First, this is a quickly changing source of information and any listing or advice goes out of date as soon as it appears. Second, there is a tendency to think that if one searches an on-line service or a CD-ROM that all possible information has been found. This is a false impression; human imagination is still required. Most computerized resources of any type reach back only a few years for sources. A user must always check to see what period is indexed, as well as what list of journals, what countries, what languages, and so on, are covered. Lastly, the printed sources listed above are still necessary tools. The information in some of them will probably never be entered into any computer resource.

> *Academic Index* includes citations to articles from general and social science periodicals for the current five years.
> *Agricola* lists agricultural publications.
> *Applied Science and Technology* includes citations for articles from 335 journals in applied science. Coverage extends from 1983 to the present.
> *ASFA* indexes journals in aquatic and marine sciences.

ADDITIONAL WEB SITES

URL	Description
http://weber.u.washington.edu/~hssexec/index.html	History of Science Society
http://www.aescon.com/geosociety/index.html	Geological Society of America
http://earth.agu.org	American Geophysical Union
http://www.geobyte.com	American Association of Petroleum Geologists
http://www.uwyo.edu/ahc/ahcinfo.htm	American Heritage Center, University of Wyoming
http://www.uwyo.edu/ahc/iaeg/iaeg.htm	International Archive of Economic Geology, University of Wyoming
http://www.uwyo.edu/ahc/mha/mha.htm	Mining History Association
http://www.uidaho.edu/special-collections/Other.Repositories.html	University of Idaho: Listing of over 650 web sites useful for researchers
http://www.asap.unimelb.edu.au/hstm/hstm_ove.htm	WWW Virtual Library for History of Science, Technology, and Medicine
http://www.aip.org/history/	American Institute of Physics, Center for History of Physics
http://feature.geography.wisc.edu/histcart/	History of Cartography Project
http://www.physics.mcgill.ca:8081/physics-services/physics_history.html	A listing of web sites in history of physics, including some geophysics
http://www.ciw.edu/DTM.html	Access to library of catalog of the Department of Terrestrial Magnetism, Carnegie Institution of Washington
http://www.ngdc.noaa.gov/seg/potfld/oldmag.html	Historical Geomagnetic Data, National Geophysical Data Center, Boulder, CO, USA
http://www.observe.ivv.nasa.gov/observe/exhibit/rem_sen/history/history_0.html	NASA, Remote Sensing in History

Please note that addresses on the World Wide Web often change.

GEOBASE has several versions and a user should carefully note the scope of the version used. Some reach back only to 1990, others to 1980. The strength of the series is in its topical breadth, not being limited to any one geoscience. Abstracts are included with citations. Published by Elsevier and SilverPlatter.

Geophysics and *The Leading Edge* are available on CD-ROM.

GeoRef is a data-base of publications on North American geology since 1785 and on other regions since 1933. Compiled by the American Geological Institute.

GPO-1976 to Present is a data-base for locating U.S. government publications from 1976 to present.

ISIS Current Bibliographies are available annually on disk, beginning in the early 1990s. These bibliographies are also available over RLIN for 1976 to the present, see above.

NTIS lists U.S. government–sponsored research.

RLIN is the Research Libraries Information Network. It is an immensely valuable for-fee service, available on-line at many research facilities.

WilsonDisc indexes 111 science journals.

VIII. Journals and Newsletters

Archiv für Geschichte der Mathematik, der Naturwissenschaften und der Technik

British Journal for the History of Science

Earth Sciences History, the journal of the History of the Earth Sciences Society.

Environmental History Review, the journal of the American Society for Environmental History. *Environmental History* since January 1996.

Imago Mundi: A Review of Early Cartography

INHIGEO *Newsletter,* published by the International Commission on the History of Geological Sciences (INHIGEO).

Mitteilungen, Arbeitskreis Geschichte der Geophysik, a journal of the German Geophysical Union.

EOS: Transactions of the American Geophysical Union, not indexed in the *ISIS Current Bibliographies.*

Historical Studies in the Physical and Biological Sciences

History of Science

History of Technology

NTM: Internationale Zeitschrift für Geschichte und Ethik der Naturwissenschaft, Technik und Medizin

Bibliography

Kragh, Helge. *An Introduction to the Historiography of Science.* Cambridge: Cambridge University Press, 1987.

Contributors

Filippo Affronti
Facoltá di Scienze
Universitá di Catania

Duncan Carr Agnew
Institute of Geophysics and Planetary Physics
University of California, San Diego

William Randall Albury
Science and Technology Studies
University of New South Wales

Alan O. Allwardt
Rogers E. Johnson and Associates
Santa Cruz, California

Sandra Barney
Social Studies Department
Lock Haven University

Maria Valeria Barone
Facoltá di Scienze
Universitá di Catania

David Barraclough
British Geological Survey

Marco Beretta
Istituto e Museo di Storia della Scienza

Lee Blackledge
Department of Geology
University of Kansas

William J. Boone
School of Education
Indiana University

Kennard B. Bork
Department of Geology and Geography
Denison University

David F. Branagan
Department of Geology and Geophysics
University of Sydney

Michael Bravo
*Department of the History and Philosophy
    of Science*
Cambridge University

Hendrik J. Bruins
Jacob Blaustein Institute for Desert Research
Ben-Gurion University of the Negev

Günter Buntebarth
Institut für Geophysik
Technische Universität Clausthal, Germany

John J. Butt
History Department
James Madison University

Gerhard C. Cadée
Netherlands Institute for Sea Research

David Edgar Cartwright
*Fellow of the Royal Society of London
    and of the American Geophysical Union*

Stefano Casati
Istituto e Museo di Storia della Scienza
Florence, Italy

Peggy Champlin
Independent Scholar

Henry Charnock
Department of Oceanography
University of Southampton

Marco Ciardi
Istituto e Museo di Storia della Scienza

E.W. Cliver
*Chair, History Committee, American
    Geophysical Union*
Geophysics Directorate, Phillips Laboratory
(USAF)

D. Philip Commander
Waters and Rivers Commission
W. Australia

M. Yavuz Corapcioglu
Department of Civil Engineering
Texas A&M University

Lesley Cormack
Department of History
University of Alberta

Arnold Court
Emeritus Professor of Climatology
California State University, Northridge

Scott W. Daley
History Department
West Virginia University

Margaret B. Deacon
Department of Oceanography
University of Southampton

Dennis R. Dean
Department of History and Geosciences
Oregon State University

David H. DeVorkin
Department of Space History
National Air and Space Museum,
Smithsonian Institution

Ronald E. Doel
Department of History and Geosciences
Oregon State University

H.A. Doyle
Department of Geology
University of Western Australia

Laurence Draper
Institute of Oceanographica Studies
Surrey, U.K.

Dean A. Dunn
Department of Geology
University of Southern Mississippi

Matthew H. Edney
Osher Map Library and Smith Center for

Cartographic Education
University of Southern Maine

Evelyn Edson
Professor of History
Piedmont Virginia Community College

Anne B.W. Effland
U.S. Department of Agriculture

William R. Effland
U.S. Environmental Protection Agency

Alv Egeland
Department of Physics
University of Oslo

George R. Ehrhardt
Independent Scholar

K.O. Emery
Senior Scientist Emeritus
Woods Hole Oceanographic Institution

Patricia Fara
Darwin College

Theodore S. Feldman
Department of History
University of Southern Mississippi

Graziano Ferrari
Storia Geofisica Ambiente
Bologna, Italy

Irene K. Fischer
*Formerly with National Oceanic
    and Atmospheric Administration*

William E. Fischer, Jr.
Formerly with History Department,
U.S. Air Force Academy

James Rodger Fleming
Science-Technology Studies Program
Colby College

Henry Frankel
Department of Philosophy
University of Missouri, Kansas City

Gerald M. Friedman
Department of Geology
Brooklyn College and Graduate School
City University of New York

Gregory A. Good
Department of History
West Virginia University

Judith R. Goodstein
Institute Archives
California Institute of Technology

Gérard Grau
Institut Océanographique

Emanuela Guidoboni
Storia Geofisica Ambiente

Ernst P. Hamm
University of British Columbia

Michael J. Heffernan
Department of Geography
Loughborough University of Technology,
U.K.

J. Douglas Helms
National Historian
Natural Resources Conservation Service
U.S. Department of Agriculture

Russell J. Hemley
*Geophysical Laboratory and Center for High
    Pressure Research*
Carnegie Institution of Washington

Norriss S. Hetherington
Institute for the History of Astronomy
University of California, Berkeley

Karl Hufbauer
Department of History
University of California, Irvine

Andrew Jackson
Department of Earth Sciences
Leeds University

Christopher Jackson
*Department of History and Philosophy
    of Science*
University of Melbourne

Ian S.F. Jones
Marine Studies Centre
University of Sydney

Joyce E. Jones
Marine Studies Centre
University of Sydney

Jo Ann Joselyn
Environmental Research Laboratories
National Oceanic and Atmospheric
Administration

M.A. Khan
*School of Ocean and Earth Science
    and Technology*
University of Hawaii

William Kimler
Department of History
North Carolina State University

Edgar S. Laird
Department of English
Southwest Texas State University

Léo F. Laporte
Earth Sciences
University of California, Santa Cruz

Homer Le Grand
*Department of History and Philosophy
    of Science*
University of Melbourne

Peter Lessing
West Virginia Geological Survey

David N. Livingstone
Professor of Geography, School of Geosciences
Queen's University of Belfast

Gretchen Luepke
U.S. Geological Survey

William J. McPeak
Institute for Historical Study
San Francisco

Benjamin Malphrus
Department of Physical Sciences
Morehead State University

Giovanni Martinelli
Storia Geofisica Ambiente
Bologna, Italy

Gerard V. Middleton
School of Geography and Geology
McMaster University

Anne Millbrooke
Department of History and Philosophy
Montana State University—Northern

Keith L. Miller
Independent Scholar

Eric L. Mills
Department of Oceanography
Dalhousie University

Nicoletta Morello
*Dipartimento di Storia Moderna
e Contemporanea*
Università di Genova

Valerie N. Morphew
Department of Education and Social Work
Longwood College

David T. Murphy
Department of History and Political Science
Anderson University

Shigeru Nakayama
STS Center
Kanagawa University

Sally Newcomb
Department of Physical Sciences
Prince George's Community College

Richard Nunan
Department of Philosophy
College of Charleston

Max Oelschlaeger
*Department of Philosophy and Religion
Studies*
University of North Texas

David Oldroyd
Science and Technology Studies
University of New South Wales, Australia

Naomi Oreskes
Gallatin School of Individualized Study
New York University

W. Dudley Parkinson
Geology Department
University of Tasmania

Richard E. Peterson
Department of Geosciences
Texas Tech University

Andy Pintus
Department of Philosophy
West Virginia University

Stephen Pumfrey
Department of History
Lancaster University, U.K.

Ronald Rainger
Department of History
Texas Tech University

Maria Basso Ricci
Istituto di Fisica Generale Applicata
Università di Milano

Richard E. Rice
General Education Program
James Madison University

G.S. Ritchie (Rear Admiral)
*Former President, International Hydrographic
Bureau*

Hans Ulrich Roll
*President (retired), DHI (German Hydro-
graphic Institute)*

James R. Rossiter
Knowledge Connection Corporation
Toronto, Canada

Stephen M. Rowland
Department of Geoscience
University of Nevada, Las Vegas

Paul Salstrom
Department of Social and Behavioral Sciences
Saint-Mary-of-the-Woods College

Howard Sankey
*Department of History and Philosophy
of Science*
University of Melbourne

Wilfried Schröder
Geophysical Station, Bremen-Roennebeck
Germany

Adrian P. Sharpe
*Department of History and Philosophy
of Science*
University of Melbourne

Sam Silverman
Physics Department, (retired)
Boston College

Jens Smed
*Formerly with International Council
for the Exploration of the Sea*
Denmark

A. Mark Smith
Department of History
University of Missouri

David I. Spanagel
Emerson College

William Stauder, S.J.
Department of Earth and Atmospheric Sciences
Saint Louis University

Don W. Steeples
Department of Geology
University of Kansas

Lester D. Stephens
Department of History
University of Georgia

Wesley M. Stevens
Department of History
University of Winnipeg

Richard E. Stoiber
Department of Earth Sciences
Dartmouth College

George Sweetnam (deceased)
Program in History of Science
Princeton University

John P. Tandarich
Hey and Associates

Joseph N. Tatarewicz
Department of History
University of Maryland—Baltimore Campus

Liba Taub, Curator
Whipple Museum of the History of Science
Department of History and Philosophy
   of Science
Cambridge University

Roger D. K. Thomas
Department of Geosciences
Franklin and Marshall College

Philip D. Thompson (deceased)
National Center for Atmospheric Research

David Thorndill
Essex Community College

Keith J. Tinkler
Department of Geography
Brock University

Pasquale Tucci
Istituto di Fisica Generale Applicata
Università di Milano

Anne-Marie Turnage
History Department
West Virginia University

Susan Turner
Queensland Museum

Agustín Udías, S.J.
Departamento de Geofísica y Meteorologia
Universidad Complutense

Ezio Vaccari
*Dipartimento di Storia Moderna
   e Contemporanea*
Università di Genova

David A. Valone
Department of History and Political Science
Quinnipiac College

William Wallace
Department of Natural Science
San Diego State University

Spencer R. Weart
American Institute of Physics

George E. Webb
Department of History
Tennessee Technological University

Thompson Webb III
Department of Geological Sciences
Brown University
Providence, Rhode Island 02912–1846

R. William Weisberger
History Department
Butler County Community College

Charles W.J. Withers
Department of Geography
University of Edinburgh

Hatten S. Yoder, Jr.
Geophysical Laboratory
Carnegie Institution of Washington

Charles A. Ziegler
Anthropology Department
Brandeis University

Sciences of the Earth

Volume 1
A–G

Actualism, Uniformitarianism, and Catastrophism

A set of ideologically and methodologically distinct positions on the character, rate, and intensity of geological forces, which stem from geological controversies set in the 1830s in Great Britain. The contrasts among these "isms" arose not from necessary philosophical consequences, but rather from the appropriation of these terms as labels to identify adversaries in the ongoing controversies of that specific historical setting.

Actualism is most commonly defined by the aphorism that geologists should try to explain the past by reference to causes now in operation. In most European languages other than English, cognates of the word *actual* carry the meaning "present," rather than "real" (Gould, p. 120). Hence, the rhetorically powerful term "actualism" was useful to English-speaking advocates of a historical geology dependent entirely on ordinary everyday processes, most notably Charles Lyell (1797–1875).

Uniformitarianism is the term that has come to be most closely identified with Lyell's methodology since he published his landmark three-volume text, *Principles of Geology* (1830–1833). The many specific senses of the root word *uniform* helped Lyell to sustain an ideologically potent claim in behalf of his own collection of assumptions about how geology ought properly to be done. Uniformitarianism embraces and sometimes confounds some or all of the following: uniformity of law (which is a prerequisite to scientific inquiry); uniformity of process (in other words, actualism); uniformity of rate (that is, a gradual-

ism which, for Lyell, also meant that the shaping of the Earth's features must have taken a very long time); uniformity of scale (so that, for example, the strictly local observable natural disasters like floods, earthquakes, and volcanic eruptions ought not be supposed to ever operate in a global manner); and uniformity of state (that is, the rejection of the popular contemporary idea that the Earth had undergone a purposeful progressive development to its present condition—one designed for human habitation) (Gould, pp. 99–126; Huggett, pp. 4–5). Taken all together or in convenient subsets, these various senses of *uniform* have enabled uniformitarianism to rule the practice of geology, at least in name, ever since 1832 when William Whewell (1794–1866) coined the term to denominate Lyell's doctrine.

Catastrophism was the name Whewell attached to the doctrine of Lyell's opponents. Both terms were coined in a review by Whewell of *Principles*, in order to set Lyell's program apart from its contemporary competitors. During the 1820s, England's leading geologist was the Reverend William Buckland (1784–1856). An extremely popular lecturer at Oxford, internationally respected for his interpretation of hyena bones found in caves, Buckland supported a diluvialist theory that attributed universal deposits of gravel and loam, as well as the excavation of some valleys, to the action of a sudden and transient deluge. Evidence of cataclysmic flooding abounded in a world not yet seen as molded by the ice ages. Gigantic boulders perched atop high hills, displaced from their native rock by hundreds of miles, were only the most obvious of a host of phenomena that seemed to testify to the inadequacy of "causes now in operation."

Drawing on the most sensational aspects of diluvialism, Whewell dubbed those who were opposed to Lyell's uniformitarianism "catastrophists." Interestingly enough, in subsequent reiterations of this distinction, Whewell consistently failed to cite Buckland as a representative of catastrophism, mentioning instead the French theorist of mountain-building Léonce Elie de Beaumont (1798–1894) and even Scottish-born Roderick Murchison (1792–1871), who harbored ideas about an ancient time of "paroxysmal turbulence" in the Earth's history (Rupke, p. 199).

Nineteenth-century intellectual historians saw catastrophism primarily in negative terms from the start. In the black-and-white heroic tradition of scientific biography, such as *Founders of Geology* (1897) by Archibald Geikie (1835–1924), any theory or explanatory mechanism that could be accused of not adhering to some sense of uniformity was potentially catastrophist. Thus, from a historical perspective, it becomes clear that the label "catastrophism" has served more an ideological than a logical categorical function.

As a case in point, uniformitarians branded all flood theorists as old catastrophists by lumping together any diluvialist with the so-called Scriptural geologists, who saw Moses' account of the Deluge as unimpeachable scientific evidence. In this way Buckland was accused of defending an outmoded cosmogony. For well over a century, this portrayal of Lyell's contemporaries as biblical literalists, uninformed by the real world of observable processes and phenomena, was faithfully reproduced by historians of geology.

The characterization is particularly unfair to Buckland, who had done such important work in establishing an actualist basis and evidence to corroborate fossil-based stratigraphic technique and who had consistently argued against a literal reading of the Genesis account (Rupke, pp. 33–41, pp. 60–61). The automatic identification of actualism with uniformitarianism (again, translation to non-English European languages often freely interchanges these two) bears the unfounded implication that catastrophists were not actualistic. Typically, as a matter of fact, catastrophists relied upon present-day processes to explain most of their observations, insisting only that some phenomena may fall outside the explanatory power of cumulative effects of gradual everyday processes.

In other words, catastrophists were good empiricists who preferred to keep an open mind about explanatory mechanisms when faced with extraordinary evidence. Ironically, given Lyell's success in portraying the catastrophists as unscientific fantasists, it was really the uniformitarians who were metaphysically attached to an a priori belief—that is, the sufficiency of causes now in operation, at presently observable rates, to explain all past changes in the Earth's surface (Hooykaas, "Catastrophism," pp. 336–338).

It is interesting to note how some now-standard elements of the uniformitarian understanding of the Earth's history had their roots in theories originally branded as catastrophist. For example, the promulgation by Alpine geologist Jean Louis Rodolphe Agassiz (1807–1873), in 1837, of sudden and universal glacial action (an ice age) to explain rock displacement and striation throughout Europe was initially ridiculed by English geologists as a catastrophist scenario. The plausibility of the agency of mile-thick ice was not widely accepted until after 1858, when expeditions reported a massive sheet of slowly moving ice in the interior of Greenland.

True to his uniformitarian creed, Lyell, though initially receptive to Buckland's 1840 presentation of Agassiz's ideas, quickly reverted to a theory that he and Murchison had developed to explain the rock striation by the motion of water-borne icebergs across formerly submerged land (Rupke, pp. 98–103). At that point, iceberg transportation of boulders was preferable (in an actualist sense) to universal glaciation, even though climate change was otherwise one of Lyell's favorite mechanisms to explain geographically surprising fossil discoveries.

Recent historians of geology have noted the misleading dichotomy of uniformitarianism and catastrophism, and have attempted to offer a conscientious analysis of the points of contrast between the two along the lines of the discussion above. First among these must be counted Reijer Hooykaas, whose work beginning in the 1950s has made possible a more contextually sensitive reading of Lyell's emergence as the "father of modern scientific geology" than the idea that all who preceded or opposed him were captives to speculation about supernatural causes and extraordinary events. In his writings about the principle of uniformity, Hooykaas delineates the philosophical typology of catastrophisms, actualisms, and uniformitarianisms to which all subsequent students of this subject have referred (Hooykaas, *Natural Law;* Hooykaas, *Principle of Uniformity*).

Beyond this important first task of setting straight these terms and their possible interactions, other historians have sought to disaggregate or substitute for one or the other elements of the problematic catastrophist-uniformitarian dichotomy. Needless to say, this effort entails the introduction of yet more "isms." For example, Martin Rudwick proposes to substitute the name "directionalism" for "catastrophism" as a better representative of the synthesis Lyell sought to displace (Rudwick, pp. 213–218).

Nicolaas Rupke, Buckland's biographer, offers a more direct challenge to Whewell's dichotomy, so well preserved by historians of English geology, when he charges that no catastrophist synthesis ever existed. Instead, according to Rupke, the school of geology to which Buckland belonged was that of historical geology, a school that produced progressivism as its synthesis. Progress in this case had much more to do with continuity and long periods of gradual change than with the catastrophic interruptions which, after all, are embedded in the very periodization of historical geology. The boundaries separating Primary, Secondary, Tertiary, and Quaternary epochs are universally abrupt and recognizable (Rupke, pp. 194–195).

In his most recent and succinct deliberations on catastrophism in geology, Hooykaas reiterates his typology of catastrophisms while providing representative proponents of the various combinations. Actualist catastrophists include the eighteenth-century French cosmologist G.L. LeClerc (Comte de) Buffon (1707–1788), the aforementioned Elie de Beaumont, and their late-nineteenth-century countryman Charles Saint-Claire Deville (1814–1881). Nonactualist catastrophists include the following: the Russian neptunist (that is, Wernerian) geologist Count Gregor Razumovsky (1759–1837); the French theorist impatient with gradualistic arguments about mountain-building Deodat de Dolomieu (1750–1801); and Lyell's self-designated nemesis, Baron George Cuvier (1769–1832), who, like Murchison, argued that long periods of tranquillity, such as the present, must in the past have been interrupted by brief periods of great convulsion in order to produce the dramatically overturned rock masses observable in the Alps (Hooykaas, "Catastrophism," pp. 316–331).

A brief reflection upon this list raises two significant historical questions. First, to what degree were catastrophist ideas characteristic of Continental European, as opposed to insular English, geology (and, if so, for what reasons)? And second, to what degree were mountain-building theories especially problematic for dogmatic uniformitarians? Historian Mott Greene suggests in his book on nineteenth-century geology that the story to be told revolves around these two questions rather than upon the ultimate "triumph" of Lyellian uniformitarianism (Greene, p. 76).

Noting that the study of global tectonics by Europeans has proceeded primarily in the hands of French- and German-speaking geologists—for example, Elie de Beaumont, Horace Benedict de Saussure (1740–1799), and Eduard Suess (1831–1914)—Greene tacitly illustrates the inability of British geology and of the Lyellian paradigm to answer questions about processes that were necessarily monumentally dynamic. England's strength lay, rather, in its rich record of secondary strata. These bore both the wondrous variety of fossilized life forms that sustained the reputation of British science, and the concomitant stores of iron ore, coal, and limestone that fueled the ascent of British industry. For these reasons, perhaps, the preeminence of Britain in discussions of the history of nineteenth-century geology can be understood. But that does not mean that terms and categories peculiar to the English geological context are universally applicable.

Greene's purpose in calling attention to Great Britain's post-Lyellian shortcomings is not to make a strictly linguistic or cultural discrimination. Indeed, he credits English-speaking North American geologists—such as James Hall (1811–1898), the Rogers brothers (Henry Darwin [1808–1866] and William Barton [1804–1882]), and James Dwight Dana (1813–1895)—with the original development of the geosynclinal view of orogenesis, an approach to the theory of mountain-building that was subsequently adopted by geologists worldwide (Greene, pp. 122–143). The key difference, therefore, had to do with access to salient phenomena. Geologists were more or less likely to accept the plausibility of catastrophic processes, depending on the suggestiveness presented by their native landscapes. Americans were confronted with the wavelike ripples of the Appalachian Mountains, and so were led to speculate about dynamic causes for such a structure.

On the other hand, Lyell's acquaintance and collaboration with Italian geologists was what ultimately set him apart from his English

(Buckland, et al.) contemporaries (Rupke, p. 181). In Italy, Lyell transcended the experience of his own quiescent landscape. There he learned about earthquakes and volcanoes, and gained the insight that gave uniformitarianism such an advantage over catastrophism. Lyell interpreted local cataclysms as cumulatively tremendous in their effects. Thus, actualism combined with an expanded timescale made extraordinary causes, forces, and scales less compelling. Paradoxically, natural disasters only added to the repertoire of gradualism. Evidence of a past gigantic, catastrophic event could even become fodder for uniformitarianism if some pattern, even an irregular one, of recurrence could be shown.

Lyell's escape from nationalistic limitations in nineteenth-century geological theory and speculation only reinforces the general validity of the rule. Further research might explore some other sources of ideological predisposition highlighted by this review of the controversy typically cast as one between catastrophists and uniformitarians. For example, vernacular language and its connotations did enter that century's controversies. It played a role that can be illustrated both by contrasting it to the preceding (Enlightenment) era, when Latin tended to be the universal language of science, and by attending to persistent efforts by scientists and mathematicians in the late nineteenth century to construct international standards of measurement, nomenclature, and even hybrid languages (for example, Esperanto).

Another valuable exercise would be to devote more attention to the periphery of the English-speaking geological community. So much is known and published about the English geologists themselves that the nonspecialist historian of science might conclude that geological controversies were confined to the British Isles. Clearly, however, these controversies had active partisans, as well as vociferous, historically interesting analogues, overseas, such as in North America and Australia. Correspondence among English-speaking geologists operating hemispheres apart has yet to receive central attention in the literature. The imperial model of knowledge acquisition has amplified the myopic concerns for local central concerns at the expense of global geological practices. In other words, the English-speaking scientific community comprised more than its London and Oxbridge circles.

Finally, taking the cues offered by Hooykaas, Rudwick, and Rupke, alternate formulations of what Lyell's geology tri-umphed over deserve the kind of critical and thoughtful elaboration that has been foisted upon the dead horse of catastrophism. What is interesting, after all, is that a creed named uniformitarianism established hegemony over 150 years of geological discourse. That catastrophism was the name chosen for the enemy goes far to explain some geologists' resistance to provocative ideas in that time span, but other questions remain unaddressed. What effect did uniformitarian suppression of directionalism have, especially with regard to Darwinian evolution? What impact can be traced to the demotion of historical geology's progressivism? Although historian-philosophers of science (such as Rachel Laudan and Stephen Pyne) have analyzed geology's practical dilemma between being a natural history and being a physics of earth processes, none have examined the role played in this struggle by Lyell's triumph.

Actualism, uniformitarianism, and catastrophism stand as significant reminders that history tends to be written, especially in the first instance, by the winners. The task for students of the history of earth science is to carefully examine the terms they use; to distinguish essential denotative meanings from the connotative burdens borne in a remote time and place.

David I. Spanagel

Bibliography

Gould, Stephen Jay. *Time's Arrow, Time's Cycle: Myth and Metaphor in the Discovery of Geological Time.* Cambridge: Harvard University Press, 1987.

Greene, Mott T. *Geology in the Nineteenth Century: Changing Views of a Changing World.* Ithaca, N.Y.: Cornell University Press, 1982.

Hooykaas, Reijer. "Catastrophism in Geology, Its Scientific Character in Relation to Actualism and Uniformitarianism." In *Philosophy of Geohistory,* edited by Claude C. Albritton, Jr., pp. 310–356. Stroudsburg, Pa.: Dowden, Hutchinson, and Ross, 1975.

———. *Natural Law and Divine Miracle. A Historical-Critical Study of the Principle of Uniformity in Geology, Biology and Theology.* Leiden: E.J. Brill, 1959 (revised and published under the title *The Principle of Uniformity in Geology, Biology and Theology,* 1963).

Huggett, Richard. *Cataclysms and Earth History: The Development of*

Diluvialism. Oxford: Clarendon Press, 1989.

Rudwick, Martin J.S. "Uniformity and Progression: Reflections on the Structure of Geological Theory in the Age of Lyell." In *Perspectives in the History of Science and Technology,* edited by Duane H.D. Roller, pp. 209–227. Norman: University of Oklahoma Press, 1971.

Rupke, Nicolaas A. *The Great Chain of History: William Buckland and the English School of Geology (1814–1849).* Oxford: Oxford University Press, 1983.

See also Climate, Ancient Ideas; Climate Change, before 1940; Climate Change, since 1940; Deluge; Diluvialism; Evolution and the Geosciences; Geosyncline; Ice Ages; Plutonists, Neptunists, Vulcanists; Polar Exploration; Presentism; Stratigraphy; Velikovsky's Worlds in Collision

Age of the Earth, before 1800

Period when Europeans considered several very different ideas of the Earth's age.

In Europe from ancient times through the eighteenth century there were several competing concepts about the age of the Earth. Aristotle considered the Earth to be ageless and eternal. Other Greek philosophers taught that the Earth was periodically destroyed and regenerated. Beginning in the second century C.E., Christian scholars used chronologies in the Bible and other ancient texts to determine the age of the Earth; the pinnacle of this scholarly tradition was the mid-seventeenth-century work of Archbishop James Ussher, who calculated that the Earth was formed in the year 4004 B.C.E. in the evening preceding October 23. Also in the mid-seventeenth century, with the writings of Rene Descartes, a new concept appeared: that the Earth is very old, but not eternal. Compte de Buffon, in 1788, was one of the first to try to determine the Earth's antiquity using empirical methods, comparing the cooling rates of various size spheres and extrapolating to the size of the Earth. In his published writings, Buffon concluded that the Earth was about seventy-five thousand years old, although privately he thought it was much older. At the end of the eighteenth century there was still no European consensus about the age of the Earth or the appropriate epistemological approach to this question, although the publications of James Hutton had set the stage for the development of modern concepts of geologic time in the nineteenth and twentieth centuries.

The way one addresses the question of the age of the Earth is closely linked to one's philosophical and religious world view. To Aristotle the Earth was eternal and ageless. Other classical Greek and Roman philosophers, however, were impressed by the erosive processes that were degrading the Earth's surface. The Roman poet and philosopher Lucretius (ca. 99–55 B.C.E.), disciple of the Epicurean school of Greece, vividly described the degradation of the Earth in his famous poem *De Rerum Natura* (The Way Things Are, p. 168):

You see that stones are worn away by time,
Rocks rot, and towers topple, even the shrines
And images of the gods grow very tired,
Develop cracks or wrinkles, their holy wills
Unable to extend their fated term,
To litigate against the Laws of Nature.
And don't we see the monuments of men
Collapse, as if to ask us, "Are not we
As frail as those whom we commemorate?"
Boulders come plunging down from mountain
   heights,
Poor weaklings, with no power to resist
The thrust that says to them, Your time has
   come!
But they would be rooted in steadfastness
Had they endured from time beyond all time,
As far back as infinity. Look about you!

How could such degradation be accommodated by an eternal Earth without its surface being eroded to a featureless plain? Aristotle and his followers (the Peripatetics) reasoned that, in order to maintain the Earth, erosion in one place must be compensated for by rejuvenation elsewhere. The Stoics, on the other hand, adopted a cyclic view of Earth's history in which the world is repeatedly destroyed in a universal conflagration and then regenerated. In this world view, erosion is seen as proof of the impending end of the present world. Each regenerated world was thought to be identical to the previous one, with an identical history consisting of the same people and events repeating over and over again (Gohau, chap. 1).

The Epicureans, a third school of philosophy in ancient Greece, held that the external world is a series of fortuitous combinations of particles called atoms. Like the Stoics, they believed in periodic destruction and regeneration of the Earth, but the fortuitous aspect of their world view gave each regenerated Earth a unique history and personality. In *De Rerum Natura,* the Epicurean Roman poet Lucretius described in considerable detail the most recent regeneration of the Earth. Lucretius' descriptions influenced seventeenth- and eighteenth-century natural philosophers who were also attempting to explain the formation of the Earth (Gohau, chap. 1).

The contrasting views of Earth's history among the ancient Greeks foreshadowed many of the controversies and conflicts that arose much later over the age of the Earth and the nature of the Earth's history. For example, the Aristotelians' constantly rejuvenated Earth reappeared in the eighteenth century in the views of James Hutton, who envisioned a very cyclic process of simultaneous erosion and mountain building on a very ancient Earth. Meanwhile the Stoics' decaying Earth can be recognized in the teachings of the eighteenth- and early-nineteenth-century Neptunists, who thought that the process of mountain building on Earth had stopped long ago and the mountains were inexorably eroding away (Gohau, chap. 1).

There is a long history of Christian scholars who used biblical chronologies and other ancient texts to determine the Earth's age. The first known scholar to perform such a calculation was the Syrian St. Theophilus of Antioch (ca. 115–180 C.E.), who, in the year 169 used scriptural chronologies to calculate that the world had been created 5,698 years earlier, in the year 5529 B.C.E. (Dalrymple, p. 19). As with the more famous calculation of Archbishop Ussher in the seventeenth century, Theophilus was inspired by the need to disprove the writings of pagan philosophers who claimed that the world was eternal.

Following Theophilus, many other biblical chronologists calculated the age of the Earth. Alphonse des Vignolles, writing in 1738, claimed to have collected more than two hundred calculations for the date of Creation; these ranged from 3483 B.C.E. to 6984 B.C.E. (Reese et al.). The most famous is that of James Ussher (1581–1656), Archbishop of Armagh, who calculated that the Earth was created in the year 4004 B.C.E. Ussher's work was published in 1650 in Latin. The following excerpt is from the English version, published in 1658 (quoted in Brice, p. 18):

In the beginning God created Heaven and Earth, Gen. I. v. I. Which beginning of time, according to our chronologie, fell upon the entrance of the night preceding the twenty third day of October in the year of the Julian calendar, 710 [4004 B.C.E.]. Upon the first day therefore of the world, or October 23, being our Sunday . . . On the second day (October 24 being Monday) the firmament being finished, which was called Heaven, a separation was made of the waters above, and the waters here beneath enclosing the Earth.

Ussher was actually not the first biblical chronologist to deduce 4004 B.C.E. as the year of Creation; St. Basil the Great had reached the same conclusion in the fourth century, thirteen hundred years earlier (Reese et al.).

In 1642, eight years before Ussher's work was published, a contemporary of Ussher's named John Lightfoot had written a small book entitled *Observations on Genesis* in which he calculated that Creation had been in the year 3928 B.C.E., quite close to Ussher's date. Lightfoot further stated that man was created in "about the third hour of the day, or nine of the clock in the morning." Lightfoot's time of nine o'clock in the morning for the creation of man is very often incorrectly attributed to Ussher and incorrectly said to be the time of Creation of the world (Brice, p. 19).

Ussher's date, which is often the target of misguided ridicule today, is more famous than any of the others primarily because, beginning in the early eighteenth century, it was printed in most editions of the King James translation of the Bible as a marginal annotation next to the first verse of Genesis. Thus in English Bibles it came to represent, in effect, the authorized date of the origin of the world.

The detailed calculation by Archbishop Ussher was presented in a two-thousand-page treatise titled *Annales veteris testamenti, a prima mundi origine deducti* (Annals of the Old Testament, deduced from the first origin of the world, 1650). Far more than a divinely inspired pronouncement or a simple-minded adding up of the ages of biblical figures, the *Annales* was a comprehensive chronological synthesis of all history down to the fall of Jerusalem in 70 C.E. (Barr, p. 581). It represents the highest level of scholarship of its day.

The methodology employed by Ussher and other seventeenth-century and earlier chronologists is analogous to the methodology used by modern stratigraphers in their attempt to determine a stratigraphic synthesis for the Earth: key stratigraphic sections with good biostratigraphic and age control are studied intensively; correlation between sections is more or less successful depending on the co-occurrence of time-specific data (fossils, marker beds, magnetic reversals, secular isotopic excursions, and so forth) in two or more sections. The difference is, of course, that for modern stratigraphers the source of data is the stratigraphic record; for Ussher and members of his chronological tradition the source of data was ancient written records.

Biblical chronologists faced a variety of difficulties (Barr, pp. 579–603; Gould, "House of Ussher," pp. 16–21). From Creation to the reign of King Solomon, the biblical chronology is relatively straightforward because the Bible records a continuous male lineage and lists the father's age at the birth of his first son. However various early translations of the Bible are not always consistent. For example, the Septuagint (Greek translation of the Old Testament), which is still in use by the Eastern churches, gives different ages for the early patriarchs at the birth of their first son than does the standard Hebrew Bible used in the Western churches. In the Septuagint Adam is two hundred and thirty years old when Seth was born, while in the Hebrew text he is only one hundred and thirty. Nor is the Samaritan Pentateuch Bible consistent with either the Hebrew bible or the Septuagint. Ussher and most Western scholars used the ages in the Hebrew Bible, but some used the Septuagint (Barr, pp. 582–584).

From Solomon to Zedekiah, the first of the kings of Judah, the Bible records the length of each king's rule but includes many ambiguities, such as unspecified intervals of co-regency of a king and his successor. Ussher and his colleagues agonized over and debated such minutiae just as modern stratigraphers debate the age and definition of the Cambro-Ordovician boundary.

The worst problem faced by the biblical chronologists was connecting the Old Testament with the New. The Bible does not indicate how much time passed between the end of the Old Testament and any New Testament event. Stratigraphers facing an analogous problem of linking two nonoverlapping sections seek out a third section that overlaps with the other two. Ussher took the same approach. He sought an extra-biblical source that overlaps with the Old and New Testaments; he found it in Chaldean and Persian records which themselves contain a continuous chronology. The death of the Chaldean king Nebuchadnezzar II was cited in both the Old Testament and the Chaldean chronologies, while the Persian records reached the

period of Roman rule, which could then be correlated with the New Testament. This work obviously required a knowledge of rather obscure nonbiblical sources in addition to scriptural detail. Only about one-sixth of the two thousand pages of the *Annales* is devoted to biblical material (Barr, p. 581).

Astronomical cycles also played a role in the calculations of the biblical chronologists. It was a common belief that God would certainly have arranged the universe so that the Sun was at one of the solstices or equinoxes at the precise moment of Creation, this in spite of the fact that the Sun wasn't created until four days later. Ussher's date of October 23 was chosen, in part, for its relationship to the autumnal equinox (in the Julian calendar) and the Jewish New Year. Other scholars, arguing that God would have placed the birth of the world in the spring, chose the vernal equinox (Reese et al., p. 404).

Astrological factors were also considered by some chronologists, not, however, including Ussher (Barr, p. 601). The German astronomer Johannes Kepler (1571–1630), the discoverer of the laws of planetary motion, assumed that Creation occurred at the summer solstice and at a time when the solar apogee was at the head of Aries. Knowing the rate at which the apogee moved, Kepler calculated that Creation had occurred in 3993 B.C.E. (Reese et al., p. 404). The closeness of the dates of Kepler, Ussher, Lightfoot, and other workers served to reinforce the confidence of this research community that their approach was correct and that if they were diligent and perceptive enough they would almost certainly be able to accurately reconstruct the chronology of history.

The labors of the biblical chronologists were partially stimulated by a desire to quash Aristotle's concept of an eternal Earth. After demonstrating that the Earth must have been formed in the year 4004 B.C.E., Ussher triumphantly wrote: "What say you then to Aristotle . . . who laboreth to prove that the world is eternal?" (quoted in Gould, "House of Ussher," p. 21).

The knowledge and philosophy of the ancient Greeks had been mostly lost and forgotten in Europe until they were rescued from obscurity by Islamic scholars. During the Middle Ages, while intellectual development in the Christian West languished, Islam was rapidly expanding and aggressively absorbing the science and technology of conquered peoples. Islamic scholars translated the texts of ancient Greece into Arabic and kept them in great libraries such as the one in Toledo, in Moorish Spain. When Christians finally reconquered Toledo in 1085 they were astonished to find a vast unknown literature. Bilingual Toledan Jews and Christians, together with visiting scholars, spent the next 150 years translating the Arabic texts into Spanish and Latin. It was by this circuitous route that the work of Aristotle and other ancient Greeks, along with the commentaries of Islamic scholars, began to appear in Christian Europe, beginning in the twelfth century. As the translations from Spain were carried over the Pyrenees into France, they stimulated tremendous intellectual ferment throughout Europe. The ideas of the ancient Greeks about the Earth's history, among many other subjects, greatly influenced European thought for several centuries (Lindberg, pp. 203–206).

Also coming to medieval Europe by way of Islamic translations was the geocentric astronomy of Ptolemy, with its wonderfully complex system of cycles and epicycles. Islamic scholars had elaborated on primitive Greek observational instruments and recorded precise star positions. New approaches to the question of the age of the Earth emerged from Ptolemaic astronomy and Arabic astronomical tables. Ancient Greek astronomers had observed the phenomenon called precession, which is explained today as the wobble or oscillation of the Earth's axis. It causes a slow circling movement of the stars, returning them to their original position every twenty-six thousand years. In the Middle Ages the precession cycle was thought to be thirty-six thousand years long. A fourteenth-century French scholar named Jean Buridan, rector of the University of Paris, studied shorter astronomical cycles such as those of the planets (Gohau, pp. 27–31). In keeping with the Ptolemaic paradigm of cycles within cycles, it was thought that all of the planets must periodically return to the same position. But Buridan discovered that these short cycles are not perfect submultiples of the thirty-six-thousand-year precession cycle. The return of all of the planets to the same position in the precession cycle, Buridan realized, would occur only once in hundreds of millions of years. This very long cyclicity supported an elaborate concept that Buridan developed concerning sea-level change. Since ancient times people had found sea shells far inland and had inferred that the land had once been covered by the sea. Buridan concluded that the land was very slowly flooded by the sea and then exposed again on a regular cycle. The cyclicity

must have a very long period, he reasoned, because records in Egypt showed that the seashore has been in the same place for four thousand years. In the face of such long time periods, the logical conclusion for Buridan was that "the world has existed forever as Aristotle seemed to believe even though it is false in the opinion of our faith" (quoted in Gohau, p. 31). It was very unusual in medieval Europe for a prominent scholar to so boldly contradict the Church.

In the mid-seventeenth century, while biblical chronologists continued to calculate the date that God created the universe *ex nihilo,* French philosopher Rene Descartes proposed an alternative model. In *Principia Philosophiae* (1644) Descartes discussed the creation of the Earth, Sun, and all of the planets by mechanical rather than divine forces. He attempted to minimize Church censure by claiming that he was not addressing "the things actually found in the real world," and that his "description of the birth of the world" actually agrees much better than Aristotle's "with the verities of faith" (quoted in Rossi, p. 45). But such disclaimers could not conceal the fact that Descartes, for the first time since Lucretius, seventeen centuries earlier, had dared to propose a rational or mechanical theory for the formation of the Earth and the universe.

Descartes was not interested in the age or history of the Earth, only in its formation. It was Nicolaus Steno, in his famous *Prodromus of a Dissertation on Solids Naturally Contained within Solids* (1669), who developed Cartesian rationalism into a methodology for deducing a sequence of events in the Earth's history that ultimately led to empirical methods of determining the Earth's age.

By the end of the seventeenth century, Descartes's rational philosophy had become respectable enough to be the guiding principle behind the Reverend Thomas Burnet's reconstruction of Earth's history. Burnet was a prominent Anglican clergyman and the private chaplain to King William III. In his *Telluris Theoria Sacra, or Sacred Theory of the Earth: Containing an Account of the Origin of the Earth, and of All the General Changes which It Hath Already Undergone, or Is to Undergo till the Consummation of All Things,* published in four volumes between 1680 and 1690, Burnet pointedly avoided divine intervention in his reconstruction of Earth's history, instead relying on rational explanations based on natural laws (Gould, *Time's Arrow,* pp. 29–30). He combined a linear narrative element with a cyclical aspect. Like many other religious scholars, Burnet aggressively rejected the Aristotelian notion of an eternal Earth, but he revived the alternative Greek view of a cyclic history of destruction and regeneration.

During the eighteenth century Cartesian rationalism can be seen to have had a profound influence on the world views of many European scholars regarding the age and history of the Earth. For example, in 1715 English astronomer Edmond Halley completely ignored the biblical chronology and proposed an empirical method for determining the age of the Earth, using the rate of accumulation of salt in the sea. He reasoned that a constant amount of dissolved salt is added to the ocean every year by rivers, and he lamented that ancient Greek and Latin scholars had not measured and recorded the saltiness of the sea in their day. If they had, then by comparisons with modern levels one could calculate the age of the sea and therefore the Earth. Halley recommended that the Royal Society of London undertake a research program to obtain salinity measurements so that eventually such a calculation could be made. Like the work of many of his predecessors, Halley's approach was "chiefly intended to refute the ancient Notion, some have of late entertained, of the Eternity of all Things; though perhaps by it the World may be found much older than many have hitherto imagined" (Halley, pp. 296–300). In 1899, Irish scholar John Joly used this approach to actually calculate the age of the sea, using estimates of the amount of salt added to the sea each year by rivers (Badash, p. 92).

A provocative and influential mid-eighteenth-century publication by French diplomat Benoît de Maillet (1656–1738) also related changes in the sea to the age of the Earth, but in this case it was a progressive drop in sea level, rather than a rise in salinity, that was used as a chronometer. In a book entitled *New System on the Diminution of the Waters of the Sea,* posthumously published in 1748, de Maillet presented his theory of the Earth in the form of a lengthy conversation between two imaginary characters: a French missionary and an Indian philosopher named Telliamed (de Maillet spelled backwards). Based partly on de Maillet's own field observations of such phenomena as sea shells on mountains and retreating shorelines, his character Telliamed was able to determine that the sea level is falling at a rate of 3 inches per century by evaporation into outer space, and that Earth is more than two billion years old (Albritton, pp. 68–77).

A third example of an eighteenth-century European scholar's rejection of the biblical chronology in favor of a much older Earth is seen in the writing of the Russian scholar Mikhail Lomonosov (1711–1765). In *O Sloyakh Zemnykh* (Concerning the strata of the Earth), published in 1763, Lomonosov politely dismissed the biblical chronologists. He wrote that although biblical scholars have very precisely calculated the moment of Creation, "I must truthfully confess that I can find no access to such precision. I can only say that the age of the world appears to be greater than any such difficult calculations indicate" (Lomonosov, para. 165).

A direct experimental approach to the question of the age of the Earth was finally undertaken by the Frenchman Georges-Louis Leclerc, Compte de Buffon (1707–1788). In his *Des Époques de la Nature* (The epochs of nature), published in 1778, Buffon proposed that the Earth was originally molten material that formed when a comet collided with the Sun (Albritton, pp. 80–86). In order to determine the time required for the molten Earth to cool down to its present temperature, Buffon carried out an extensive series of experiments with iron balls of various sizes. He heated the balls to near melting and measured the time it took for each to cool to a point that it could be touched without burning his fingers, and then to the temperature of a nearby cave. Buffon repeated the experiments with other balls that were mixtures of metallic and nonmetallic materials, trying to simulate the composition of the Earth. Extrapolating the different cooling rates of his graduated spheres to the size of the Earth, Buffon calculated that it took the Earth about seventy-five thousand years to reach its current temperature, and that in another forty-five thousand years it will be frozen and lifeless. In unpublished manuscripts Buffon is seen to favor an even older Earth, as old as about three million years. He evidently published the much younger date in order not to strain the credulity of his readers: ". . . although it is quite true that the more we stretch time, the closer we get to the truth and the reality of the use that nature has made of it, still, we must shorten it as much as possible in order to conform to the limited power of our intelligence" (quoted in Rossi, p. 108). Buffon did not minimize his calculations of the Earth's age in order to placate the Church; seventy-five thousand years was sufficiently heretical that it might as well have been three million. Buffon's empirical approach to reconstructing Earth's history represents a major epistemological transition, from the reliance on ancient texts to the reliance on observational data.

During the concluding decades of the eighteenth century there had not yet emerged a consensus among European natural philosophers about the age of the Earth. There were four competing concepts (Dean, p. 275): The first was an eternal Earth. This Aristotelian concept was still being promoted in some quarters, most notably by George Hoggart Toulmin in *The Eternity of the World* (1785). The second was a scripturally derived age of about six thousand years, based on the work of Ussher and other biblical chronologists. This was still very much the view of religious orthodoxy. It was aggressively defended by two prominent opponents of James Hutton, Jean André Deluc (for example, in a 1796 review of Hutton's *Theory of the Earth*) and Richard Kirwan (for example, in a series of essays written in 1796 and 1797). Kirwan argued that, contrary to Hutton's view, the succession of geological events recorded in the Earth was in complete agreement with the Mosaic account written in Genesis (Dean, pp. 79–82).

The third concept separated human history from that of the Earth. Proponents of this view advocated a scripturally derived age of about six thousand years for the origin of humankind, but also a preceding interval of much greater extent before man was created. This prehuman interval was commonly explained in terms of figurative "days" of Genesis. According to this concept of geologic time, the Earth was assumed to have been created by God, but different theorists estimated different ages. For example, in the 1790s the Neptunist A.G. Werner guessed that about a million years had passed since a universal ocean had covered the Earth (Dean, p. 96). The boldest and ultimately most influential proponent of this concept was James Hutton (1726–1797), who in his *Theory of the Earth* (1788), argued that the age of the Earth is beyond our ability to measure. Invoking Newtonian imagery of revolving planets, Hutton concluded with the following often-quoted passage:

For having, in the natural history of this Earth, seen a succession of worlds, we may from this conclude that there is a system in nature; in like manner as, from seeing revolutions of the planets, it is concluded, that there is a system by which they are intended to continue those revolutions. But if the succession of worlds is established in the

system of nature, it is in vain to look for any thing higher in the origin of the Earth. The result, therefore, of our present enquiry is, that we find no vestige of a beginning, no prospect of an end.

Hutton did not, however, specifically challenge the biblical chronology of human history on Earth.

Lastly, the fourth concept incorporated an extended history of humanity as well as of the Earth, not limited by the biblical narrative. This concept was cautiously advanced by Buffon in the first three volumes of his monumental forty-four-volume *Histoire naturelle*, published in 1746. In describing the Earth's history, Buffon ignored biblical chronology as much as he thought he could get away with. When his work was attacked by the Faculty of Theology at the University of Paris, he did not address the specific criticisms, but disingenuously responded that he "abandoned all which in [his] book concerns the formation of the Earth, and in general all that might be contrary to the story by Moses." Then, thirty years later, in his *Epochs of Nature* (1778), he wrote that the six days of Creation "are merely six spans of time whose duration cannot be determined by the historian of religion" (Gohau, pp. 93–94).

Historians pursuing the history of ideas about the age of the Earth in the eighteenth century and earlier have primarily concentrated on British and French participants (see Dean, Gohau). Paolo Rossi provides the perspective of an Italian scholar. Dean has thoroughly examined the controversies surrounding the work of James Hutton, but comparably rigorous surveys of geological thought in, for example, France, Italy, and Russia, and of the flow of ideas throughout Europe, have not yet been conducted.

Stephen M. Rowland

Bibliography
Albritton, Claude C., Jr. *The Abyss of Time.* San Francisco: Freeman, Cooper, and Co., 1980.
Badash, Lawrence. "The Age-of-the-Earth Debate." *Scientific American* 261 (August 1989): pp. 90–96.
Barr, James. "Why the World Was Created in 4004 B.C.: Archbishop Ussher and Biblical Chronology." *Bulletin of the John Rylands University Library* 67 (1985): pp. 575–608.
Brice, William R. "Bishop Ussher, John Lightfoot and the Age of Creation." *Journal of Geological Education* 30

(1982): pp. 18–24.

Dalrymple, G. Brent. *The Age of the Earth.* Stanford: Stanford University Press, 1991.

Dean, Dennis R. *James Hutton and the History of Geology.* Ithaca, N.Y.: Cornell University Press, 1992.

Gohau, Gabriel. *A History of Geology.* New Brunswick: Rutgers University Press, 1991.

Gould, Stephen J. "Fall in the House of Ussher." *Natural History* 100 (November 1991): pp. 12–21.

———. *Time's Arrow, Time's Cycle: Myth and Metaphor in the Discovery of Geologic Time.* Cambridge: Harvard University Press, 1987.

Halley, Edmond. "A Short Account of the Cause of Saltness of the Ocean, and of the Several Lakes that Emit No Rivers; with a Proposal, by Help Thereof, to Discover the Age of the World." *Philosophical Transactions* 29 (1715): pp. 296–300.

Lindberg, David C. *The Beginnings of Western Science: The European Scientific Tradition in Philosophical, Religious, and Institutional Context, 600 B.C. to A.D. 1450.* Chicago: University of Chicago Press, 1992.

Lomonosov, Mikhail V. "O Sloyakh Zemnykh." In *The Complete Collected Works of M.V. Lomonosov.* Moscow: Academy of Sciences of USSR, 1952.

Lucretius. *The Way Things Are.* Translated by R. Humphries. Bloomington: Indiana University Press, 1968.

Reese, Ronald L., Steven M. Everett, and Edwin D. Craun. "The Chronology of Archbishop Ussher." *Sky and Telescope* 62 (1981): pp. 404–405.

Rossi, Paolo. *The Dark Abyss of Time: The History of the Earth and the History of Nations from Hooke to Vico.* Translated by Lydia G. Cochrane. Chicago: University of Chicago Press, 1984.

See also Actualism, Uniformitarianism, and Catastrophism; Age of the Earth, since 1800; Dendrochronology; Diluvialism; Earth in Decay; Geological Periodization; Geological Time; Ocean Chemistry; Paleomagnetism; Plutonists, Neptunists, Vulcanists; Sacred Theory of the Earth

Age of the Earth, since 1800

Modern history of efforts to establish a quantitative age for the Earth and solar system.

In the years between 1790 and 1841, an increasingly detailed standard chronology of the Earth was established in Western Europe, based on the relative ages of rocks representing the Cambrian and later periods of geologic time. The number of cycles of mountain building and erosion and the cumulative thickness of sedimentary rocks showed beyond any doubt that the Earth is orders of magnitude older than most people had previously supposed. This accomplishment set the stage for varied attempts, beginning in the 1850s, to determine or set limits on the age of the Earth. These yielded inconsistent results, ranging from a few tens to many hundreds of millions of years. Vigorous controversy ensued between those whose calculations based on physical models suggested ages of less, even much less, than one hundred million years and geologists convinced that the events documented in the rock record demanded a much longer history. By the 1890s, uneasy compromise had given way to stalemate between diverging estimates and the hardening positions of their proponents. This lasted until the discovery of radioactivity and its associated emission of heat, which undercut the principal assumption on which the model calculations were based. In 1904, Ernest Rutherford (1871–1937) recognized that the decay of radioisotopes could be used to date rocks. Within a decade, it became apparent that the Earth was another order of magnitude older than had hitherto been appreciated. However, fifty years would pass before theoretical advances and improved analytical techniques made it possible for F.G. Houtermans and Clair Patterson to arrive independently at ages close to the current best estimate of 4.54 billion years.

The appearance of John Playfair's *Illustrations of the Huttonian Theory of the Earth* in 1802 called attention to the emergence in Britain of what we would call a dynamic steady-state model of the Earth's continental crust. In the 1780s, James Hutton (1726–1797) had developed a cyclical "theory of the Earth" in which mountain building, driven by the Earth's internal heat, alternated with erosion powered by running water. Field observations indicated that this "earth machine" had operated over many cycles, spanning countless ages, and that the rocks of the Earth's crust showed no evidence of a beginning. Playfair (1748–1819) stripped this theory of its more philosophical speculations and frequent references to the intentions of the Creator. In his short, clear account of

Hutton's ideas, Playfair reasserted that natural history provides no data bearing on the origin of this system, which must be extremely ancient (Laudan).

Critics asserted that Hutton and Playfair had revived the heresy that the Earth is eternal, although that was not their intention. The inference that the Earth must be very old had already been drawn by some authors in the previous century, including even Abraham Werner (1749–1817), on the basis of different sorts of arguments. However, Hutton's theory and observations implied a much greater antiquity than had generally been imagined. This generated a sharp debate between naturalists who adopted Hutton's views and others who maintained that all natural phenomena could be explained in terms of the Mosaic account of the Creation, recorded in the book of Genesis and its traditional exegesis. The debate continued into the mid-nineteenth century and beyond, but by then it was conducted between geologists and a decreasing minority of churchmen (Haber).

Hutton's cycles of mountain building and erosion were large-scale, long-term phenomena that could not be matched, in the absence of other kinds of data, from one region to another. By 1800, the principles of correlation, based on characteristic sequences of sedimentary rock types and fossils, had been established. William Smith (1769–1839) in England and Léopold Cuvier (1769–1832) and Alexandre Brongniart (1770–1847) in France recognized the regularity of local sequences. Soon, many others would take up this stratigraphic work, drawing on Werner's methods and adapting his nomenclature to establish, over a period of forty years, a consistent, international geologic time scale (Rupke). As the work progressed, it became ever more apparent from the long sequence of events that the Earth must be extremely ancient, especially if processes operated in the past at rates comparable to those observed today. This led John Phillips (1800–1874) to suggest, in 1837, that the total thickness of strata represented in the time scale might serve as a basis for calculation of the age of the Earth's crust (Burchfield, p. 59).

In fact, Charles Lyell (1797–1875) had already recognized that a convincing demonstration of the Earth's antiquity called for some calibration, however approximate, of the relative time scale. He had established subdivisions of the Tertiary strata based on quantitative data, using ratios of extinct to still-living species of molluscan shells that occur in each formation, but this "clock" yielded only relative ages. Lyell recognized that he could use Mount Etna to link his Tertiary chronology to rates of modern processes. The Mount Etna volcano is 90 miles in circumference, and a typical lava flow is about a mile wide, near its base. Fewer than 90 flows have been recorded in historical time, so the mountain has on average been raised by less than the thickness of one flow during this interval. Given its great height, the age of the mountain must be very many times that of human civilization. Yet, fossils show that this volcanic edifice is geologically young, being built entirely on top of "newer Pliocene" strata. Lyell had constructed a compelling argument for the immense age of geologic phenomena, relative to the span of human experience (Rudwick). He was content to rest his case here. Lyell did not extrapolate from these results to calculate an age for Etna or the newer Pliocene strata, presumably because he was well aware of the uncertainties involved.

Charles Darwin (1809–1882) was uncharacteristically less cautious. Evolution by natural selection required even more time to permit the gradual divergence of living and extinct organisms. Impressed by the apparent slowness of marine erosion on rocky shores, Darwin set out to calculate the time required for this process to excavate the Weald, a predominantly lowland region within an eroded anticline in southeast England. Making quite arbitrary assumptions, he arrived at a figure of 306,662,400 years for the operation of a process that could not have begun before the end of the Mesozoic!

This calculation appeared in the first edition of *On the Origin of Species* in 1859 (p. 287). It was promptly attacked as the weakest argument in the book (Burchfield; Hallam). The Wealden anticline is dissected by streams and rivers. The idea that its complex topography could have been produced by the retreat of a single line of sea cliffs 500 feet high was implausible, quite apart from the fact that the argument used to estimate the rate of their retreat was invalid. Darwin soon recognized his error, adding a note of reservation in the second edition and eliminating the topic altogether from the third edition of 1861 (Burchfield). Darwin needed time sufficient for the existence of an enormous number of intermediate lifeforms in the course of evolution. As a result, like Benoît de Maillet (1656–1738), he had calculated a geologic age that would later prove to be a substantial overestimate.

Among Darwin's critics, John Phillips was moved by this issue to undertake the calculation he had previously proposed. Dividing the cumulative thickness of Cambrian and younger strata by an estimated average rate of sedimentation, he determined that the stratified rocks of the Earth's crust had accumulated over a period of ninety-six million years. The publication of this estimate, in 1860, marks the beginning of an intense controversy over the age of the Earth that persisted into the first years of the twentieth century (Hallam, pp. 82–107).

Geologists influenced by Hutton and Lyell argued that the rock record yields no evidence of conditions or processes radically different from those of the present day. From this uniformitarian perspective, they suspected that the Earth must be hundreds of millions of years old. Other early-nineteenth-century geologists, impressed by the need to explain the Earth's interior heat, supposed like Descartes and Buffon that the Earth had originated in a molten state. On this premise, the Earth's history must involve directional change, with more violent processes acting in the past than at later times, cooling of the Earth's interior, and a progressive refrigeration of its climate. To this argument, the Second Law of Thermodynamics, formulated by Rudolph Clausius (1822–1888) and William Thomson (later Lord Kelvin, 1824–1907) in 1851, brought a theoretical basis in physics and the possibility of a direct calculation of the Earth's age.

Kelvin, like Phillips, was prompted by Darwin's calculation to apply principles he had developed several years before to estimate the age of the Earth. In 1854, drawing on ideas of Hermann von Helmholtz (1821–1894), he had calculated the gravitational energy that would be released as heat by the collision of sufficient meteorites to constitute the Sun's mass. At that time, he observed this number to be twenty million times the rate at which the Sun's energy is being dissipated today. In 1862, he expanded on this concept, taking various uncertainties into account. He concluded that the Sun has probably been in operation for ten to one hundred million years, certainly not for more than five hundred million years. Later, in 1889, he was led by the lack of geological evidence for progressive cooling of the Earth's climate to reassess this problem. If the Sun's output of energy was determined by ongoing contraction, as Helmholtz had suggested, it could fluctuate about a constant value over a long period of time. Nonetheless, the Sun's total potential energy remained the same, so Kelvin fell back on his original calculation, now suggesting that the Sun could probably not have been shining for any more than twenty million years (Burchfield; Smith and Wise, pp. 524–544).

Kelvin's second approach was to calculate the Earth's age directly from its own cooling history. He assumed that the Earth was initially molten and that it solidified from the center outwards at a uniform temperature. If this were so, the Earth's initial temperature and that of its still uncooled center would be close to the temperature at which rock materials fuse. The temperature gradient at the Earth's surface had recently been determined, and Kelvin had himself measured the heat conductivities of several rock types. In 1863 he published his result, using Fourier's equation of heat transfer to determine the time required for the Earth to cool to its present state (Burchfield; Smith and Wise, pp. 559–573). The age he arrived at was ninety-eight million years, in remarkable accord with that of Phillips, with whom he had corresponded. However, acknowledging the uncertainties associated with his assumptions, Kelvin concluded that the age of the Earth must lie between twenty and four hundred million years.

In 1868, Kelvin developed a third argument against uniformitarian geology, based on the loss of angular momentum and consequent slowing of the Earth's rotation resulting from tidal friction. He documented this effect in detail, showing that the day must gradually be getting longer, as Kant had long since recognized, and the Moon further from the Earth. Kelvin perceived a possible measure of the Earth's age, based on its change in rate of rotation. The degree of flattening of a spheroid depends on its rate of rotation. Kelvin thought that the Earth had acquired its shape when it was still just fluid, at the time of its origin. If this were so, the Earth's shape should correspond to its initial rate of rotation. The difference between this shape and that predicted from the Earth's current rate of rotation would be a measure of its age. In fact, there was no detectable difference. This is not surprising, as the solid Earth behaves on this scale as if it were a fluid body, but this was not recognized at that time. Rather, Kelvin inferred that insufficient time had elapsed for a detectable difference to accumulate. Here then was further evidence, he supposed, for a limited age of the Earth (Burchfield). Subsequently, Sir George Darwin (1845–1912) took up this problem, calculating that a minimum of fifty-six million years would be required for the Moon to reach its current orbit from an initial metastable state. This figure was commonly cited as an independent estimate of the age of the Earth-Moon system, but Darwin himself inferred that the time involved must have been much greater (Dalrymple).

In later years, Kelvin revised his estimates successively downwards, citing new evidence and reducing the allowance for uncertainty. By 1881, he was advocating limits of twenty to fifty million years. In 1893, the American geologist Clarence King (1842–1901) argued, on the basis of experimental data and graphical models of changes in temperature with depth, that the Earth would have required six hundred million years to solidify, given the initial temperature assumed by Kelvin. A much lower initial temperature and an age of twenty-four million years would just permit complete solidification. This age, he pointed out, was consistent with that which Kelvin had estimated for the Sun (Burchfield). Two years later, Kelvin acknowledged King's result as the best estimate of the age of the Earth (Holmes).

Responses to Kelvin's calculations were very varied, with geologists and physicists on both sides of the debate (Smith and Wise, pp. 579–580). Some, such as Thomas Huxley (1825–1895) and later the mathematician John Perry (1850–1920), attacked Kelvin's assumptions. Charles Darwin, lacking an adequate rejoinder to Kelvin's arguments, continued to insist that the Earth must be much older than his results implied. Many geologists, especially in the 1870s and 1880s, were willing to accept an age on the order of one hundred million years, but this compromise broke down as Kelvin's estimates grew shorter and his allowance for error more constricted. Others followed Kelvin's example, setting up geological models from which they could extrapolate to obtain their own estimates of the age of the Earth.

In 1867, Charles Lyell took up James Croll's idea that the glacial period coincided with an interval of unusually great eccentricity in the Earth's orbit. Adopting one of two possible dates proposed by Croll, Lyell noted that 95 percent of living mollusc species extend back to the last ice age, a million years ago. Hence, he inferred the complete replacement of a fauna in twenty million years and the turnover of twelve such faunas since Cambrian time, for a total age of 240 million years.

Lyell did not stand by this calculation for very long. It was replaced in the next edition of *The Principles of Geology* by a statement to the effect that determination of numerical ages was, at that time, hopeless (Burchfield, pp. 67–69).

There were many attempts, nonetheless. Most were based, like that of John Phillips, on the aggregate thickness of sedimentary rocks and inferred rates of accumulation. A tabulation of results of fifteen such studies, published between 1860 and 1909 (Holmes, p. 86), shows ages for the Earth's crust ranging from 17 to 1,584 million years. These differences arose principally from the difficulty of arriving at an appropriate rate of sedimentation. Some authors used historically determined rates, usually with some allowance for different geologic settings and types of sediments. Most considered rates of sedimentation determined from the supply of material by erosion to be more reliable, but these depended in turn on estimates of erosion rates, the area and relative relief of the continents, and the area over which sediments accumulated.

All these estimates were fallible. When it became apparent from results of the *Challenger* expedition that thick sequences of sediments are restricted to continental margins, previous ages were revised downward by almost an order of magnitude. As Burchfield (p. 98) points out, these results were determined largely by the predisposition of the investigator. Few determinations—and none of those of the more prominent geologists, such as Archibald Geike (1835–1924) and Charles Walcott (1850–1937)—exceeded one hundred million years. The influence of Kelvin's first estimate of the Earth's age and its consistency with that of Phillips is clear.

Another approach, originally conceived by Edmond Halley in 1715, was to determine the concentration in river and ocean water of substances that accumulate in the ocean without being recycled to the continents. This idea was revived by T. Mellard Reade (1832–1909), who determined that the sulfates would have taken twenty-five million years, and the chlorides two hundred million years, to reach their current levels. In 1899, John Joly (1857–1933) refined the method, arguing that only sodium consistently accumulates in ocean water. He introduced various corrections and determined an age of eighty-nine million years for the oceans. Similar calculations made during the next decade yielded results ranging up to 150 million years. All were based on the false premise that sodium is not recycled to any significant extent in sedimentary rocks (Dalrymple, pp. 52–58).

With the end of the century came increasing recognition that no method then employed to determine the Earth's age was well founded. In 1899, Thomas Chamberlain (1843–1928) challenged the widespread supposition that the Earth had been initially molten. He attacked Kelvin's assumptions, developing an alternative model involving cold accretion for the Earth's origin. He also suggested that enormous energies might reside within the atom. Radioactivity had already been discovered in 1896 by Henri Becquerel (1852–1908), but the associated release of heat was not reported until 1903. In 1906, R.J. Strutt showed that the distribution of radioactive material within the Earth must be inhomogeneous, as that observed in igneous rocks of the crust was sufficient to generate more than fifty times the average amount required to account for the loss of heat by the Earth as a whole (Burchfield, p. 170). The alternative source of energy, which Kelvin himself had parenthetically envisaged and dismissed, was at hand.

This denouement is often heralded by geologists as a triumph of geologic reason over the tyranny of mathematical models that proved to be misconceived. The geologists were right about the Earth's great age, although most of them sought to arrive at results not too far out of line with Kelvin's allowance. On the other hand, Kelvin was right to argue that the Earth must have changed over time, albeit on a time scale different from that which he imagined. Kelvin was unaware of radioactivity, and the geologists lacked evidence of the Earth's violent early history. The opponents in this debate held different pieces of the puzzle, so their arguments failed to meet on common ground until a new discovery established the common context of the problem.

Rutherford's recognition in 1904 (Badash, p. 94) of radioactivity's potential for dating minerals was quickly taken up by Bertram Boltwood in the United States and by Strutt in England. Boltwood had recognized lead as the ultimate, stable daughter product of the uranium decay series, although these were not yet well understood. By 1907, he had determined ages of minerals apparently ranging up to 2.2 billion years, based on lead/uranium ratios (Hallam, p. 102). Strutt focused on the accumulation of helium as a decay product. He soon came to recognize that ages based on helium/radium or helium/uranium ratios were

minimum estimates, due to the escape of more or less helium. By 1911, Arthur Holmes (1890–1965), then a student in Strutt's laboratory, was able to compile a table of lead/uranium dates broadly consistent with the relative ages of the rocks from which they had been obtained (Dalrymple, p. 74). Numerous difficulties attended these early attempts to derive ages from radioactive elements. The atomic structure had not yet been elucidated, and isotopes were not recognized as such until 1911. Consequently, ages were calculated from ratios of elements including more than one radioisotope and lead derived from thorium as well as uranium. For the same reasons, the decay constants were not properly defined and most of the early age determinations were overestimates.

Even as these problems were resolved, severe experimental difficulties had to be overcome. Elements were accessible to chemical analysis but isotopes were not, so age determinations were restricted to minerals bearing uranium and thorium, those being the only common elements composed largely of radioisotopes. This severely limited the availability of suitable samples for dating rocks (Faul), but the isotopes of these elements provide the most direct means for determining the age of the Earth. In 1921, the American astronomer Henry Russell recognized that the time required for lead in the Earth's crust to accumulate if it were all produced by radioactive decay sets a maximum value for its age. Subsequently, in 1927, Arthur Holmes refined Russell's calculations, concluding that the age of the Earth must be close to but not much greater than 3.0 billion years (Dalrymple, pp. 76–77).

Theoretical and experimental uncertainties continued to foster skepticism, vigorously articulated by John Joly even in the mid-1920s, about the reliability of radioactive elements as chronometers. In the United States, the organization and assessment of research in this field took on a new style (Faul). The National Research Council appointed two committees, in 1923 and 1926, to coordinate the growing body of analytical results and to assess the status of different approaches to the problem. The 1931 report of the Committee on the Age of the Earth, two-thirds of it authored by Arthur Holmes, established beyond doubt that ages based on the decay of radioactive elements rested on fewer unverifiable assumptions than those obtained by any other method (Badash, p. 96). Even so, the committee accepted only six of the numerous rock age determinations that had by then been made as meeting the most stringent criteria of reliability. The Earth was inferred to be at least 2.0 billion years old, but there was no substantial evidence of its actual age (Knopf).

By this time, early mass spectrometers were being developed. An American, Alfred Nier, incorporated a new and extremely sensitive vacuum tube into one of these instruments. This gave him the precision, in 1939, to determine ratios of the lead daughter products of radioisotopes to nonradiogenic lead. His results gave rise to a model, based on changes in the proportions of isotopes with different decay rates, from which the age of the Earth could be determined. Generally associated with Holmes and Houtermans, who published it independently in Britain and Germany in 1946, this model had been first conceived in 1942 by E.K. Gerling in the Soviet Union. Holmes and Houtermans obtained inconsistent results using this model because terrestrial samples did not conform to their assumptions. However, the American Clair Patterson realized in 1953 that the initial lead isotope ratio could be determined from iron meteorites. Within the same year, he and Houtermans arrived at a common age of 4.5 billion years for the solar system, based on data from the Earth and meteorites (Dalrymple, pp. 305–356). This result has since been confirmed by independent methods, employing less abundant radioisotopes that are accessible to analysis by modern mass spectrometers to date meteorites and the Moon's primeval crust, which formed very soon after its accretion.

This essay has focused on our changing knowledge of the time of the Earth's origin, measured in years before the present, as does the existing literature. The nineteenth century witnessed a significant transition, from a world view in which the Earth was assumed to exist in a given framework of universal time that might be finite or eternal, to one in which material products of processes acting on the Earth serve as measures of its own, local time. This development, culminating in the use of radioisotopes to determine the age of the solar system, parallels the shift from an earlier hegemony of Newtonian physics to twentieth-century conceptions of time and space that have emerged from relativity.

Historical work on this subject has been predominantly internal, apart from studies relating the expansion of geologic time to changing religious and philosophical perspectives.

Inadequate attention has been paid to developments outside Britain and America. Little systematic work has been done on the kinds of people who have taken different positions, the means by which ideas were disseminated, or the circumstances in which new developments were possible. Such studies of the history of radioisotope dating and of its progress in relation to improvements in instrumentation would be particularly interesting.

Roger D.K. Thomas

Bibliography

Badash, Lawrence. "The Age-of-the-Earth Debate." *Scientific American* 261 (August 2, 1989): pp. 90–96.

Burchfield, Joe D. *Lord Kelvin and the Age of the Earth.* New York: Science History Publications, 1975.

Dalrymple, G. Brent. *The Age of the Earth.* Stanford: Stanford University Press, 1991.

Faul, Henry. "A History of Geologic Time." *American Scientist* 66 (1978): pp. 159–165.

Haber, Francis C. *The Age of the World. Moses to Darwin.* Baltimore, Md.: Johns Hopkins University Press, 1959.

Hallam, Anthony. *Great Geological Controversies.* Oxford: Oxford University Press, 1983.

Holmes, Arthur. *The Age of the Earth.* London and New York: Harper and Brothers, 1913.

Knopf, Adolph. "The Age of the Earth: Summary of Principal Results." In *Physics of the Earth—IV: The Age of the Earth,* edited by Adolph Knopf et al., pp. 3–9. Washington, D.C.: National Research Council Bulletin 80, 1931.

Laudan, Rachel. *From Mineralogy to Geology: The Foundations of a Science, 1650–1830.* Chicago: University of Chicago Press, 1987.

Rudwick, Martin J.S. "Lyell on Etna, and the Antiquity of the Earth." In *Towards a History of Geology,* edited by Cecil J. Schneer, pp. 288–304. Cambridge, Mass., and London: M.I.T. Press, 1969.

Rupke, Nicholaas A. *The Great Chain of History: William Buckland and the English School of Geology (1814–1849).* Oxford: Oxford University Press, 1983.

Smith, Crosbie, and M. Norton Wise. *Energy and Empire: A Biographical Study of Lord Kelvin.* Cambridge: Cambridge University Press, 1989.

See also Actualism, Uniformitarianism, and Catastrophism; Age of the Earth, before 1800; Dendrochronology; Earth in Decay; Geological Periodization; Geological Time; Heat, Internal, Eighteenth and Nineteenth Centuries; Heat, Internal, Twentieth Century; Nebular Hypothesis; Ocean Chemistry; Paleomagnetism; Plutonists, Neptunists, Vulcanists; Radioactivity in the Earth; Sacred Theory of the Earth; Stratigraphy

Agricultural Chemistry: Disciplinary History

A multidisciplinary science of the soil. Among other things, agricultural chemistry was concerned with the analysis of soil and served as a precursor of soil science.

Soil science is fairly recent as a discipline, germinating in the nineteenth and flowering in the twentieth century. However, the precursor disciplines of soil science, such as agricultural chemistry and agricultural geology, can be traced back to ancient times. According to John P. Tandarich's, and Stephen W. Sprecher's article "The Intellectual Background for the Factors of Soil Formation," agricultural chemistry developed from the agricultural interests within the parent discipline of chemistry and evolved simultaneously with it. Both disciplines drew upon the early natural philosophers as well as pioneer scientists from the Middle Ages onward. By the nineteenth century, agricultural chemistry was broadly defined to include "whatever has a relationship to agriculture in other sciences, more especially in chemistry, physics, geology, botany and plant physiology" (Bernhard Tollens, quoted in Charles A. Browne, pp. viii–ix). Browne also included mineralogy within the purview of agricultural chemistry. Consideration of the soil became an important part of agricultural chemistry throughout its history.

In the Western world, the organized understanding of the world began with the Greek natural philosophers. Thales of Miletus (ca. 640–546 B.C.E.) reduced nature to one element, water; Anaximenes of Miletus (contemporary of Thales) claimed that the one element was air; Heraclitus of Ephesus (540–475 B.C.E.) proposed fire as the basic element, which, when combined with air and water, was changed to earth. It was Empedocles of Agrigentum (ca. 495–435 B.C.E.) who proposed four elements as the basis for all existence: earth, air, fire, and water. The four-element model of Empedocles was adopted, developed, and refined by Aristotle (384–322

B.C.E.) and became the accepted model of existence for almost two thousand years.

Among the Romans, Caius Plinius Secundus (23–79 C.E.), called Pliny "the Elder," recognized that, within the Roman Empire, there were differences among the soils due to color, texture, and vegetation type, and certain crops did better on particular soils than on others (Browne, pp. 10–11). Pliny traced the differences among soils to the variable balance within them of the four basic elements. Lucius Junius Moderatus Columella (first century C.E.) was the first Roman writer to recognize the difference between what are called today the surface soil and subsoil.

The four elements of Empedocles were the model for understanding the world from the eighth through the fourteenth centuries, when knowledge centers were within monastery walls and royal courts. The Renaissance (fifteenth and sixteenth centuries), the scholarly rediscovery of the ancient Greek and Roman philosophers in Western Europe, revitalized scientific inquisitiveness and made possible changes in knowledge.

Philippus Theophrastus Paracelsus, the Bombast of Hohenheim (1493–1541) was a Renaissance scholar who broke with the classical philosophy. He began experimenting with analytical procedures to determine the proportions of three fundamental components of matter, sulfur, mercury, and salt, which he believed comprised the four elements of Empedocles. Paracelsus recognized that the soil, which he believed to be uniform in nature, gave these three components or "principles" to plants in the following forms: organic constituents (sulfur), water (mercury), and mineral matter (salt).

The Englishman Francis Bacon (1561–1626) was, like Paracelsus, an advocate of experimental discovery of knowledge, but rejected the three fundamental components of matter. Bacon conducted experiments on soil modification in an attempt to improve crop productivity. He first examined and analyzed the soil to see what improvements needed to be made, but he appears not to have made systematic surveys of specific soil characteristics.

The founding of the Royal Society of London in 1660 by Robert Boyle (1627–1691) and others provided a forum for discussion of scientific discoveries. Several members of the society formed the Georgical Committee to study agriculture. Boyle, who was chairman of this committee and is best known as a pioneer chemist, recognized the different types of the "soyls of England" as: "Sandy, Gravelly, Stony, Clayie, Chalky, Light-Mould, Marish, Boggy, Fenny, or Cold-weeping Ground" in the first volume (1665) of the society's *Philosophical Transactions*. He developed this basic list as necessary background for a potential natural history survey of England, and a history of agriculture and gardening. Years later, other society members such as Martin Lister proposed that "soyls" be mapped ("An ingenious proposal for a new sort of maps of countrys, together with tables of sands and clays, such chiefly as are found in the north parts of England, drawn up about 10 years since, and delivered to the Royal Society Mar. 12, 1683") as discussed in the *Philosophical Transactions* in 1684.

In northern Europe, Johann Joachim Becher (1635–1682) and his student Georg Ernst Stahl (1660–1734) advocated that earth and water were the primary terrestrial elements. Matter was seen as composed of a combustible material, which they called phlogiston, which when mixed with elementary earth and water gave rise to plant and animal substances. Stahl attempted a classification of earths (soils) based on cohesiveness in his *Philosophical Principles of Universal Chemistry* (London, 1730). His categories were "hungry, fat, opake, transparent, shining, and dull" (quoted in Browne, p. 101).

The first actual reference to agricultural chemistry as a discipline was in the work of Johann Gottschalk Wallerius (1709–1785). Wallerius and his student Gyllenborg at the University of Uppsala, Sweden, recognized that soils of differing textures exist in nature. In his dissertation *Agriculturae Fundamenta Chemica* (Chemical fundamentals of agriculture, Uppsala, 1761), Gyllenborg recognized that there is a subsoil below the surface soil (summarized in Browne, p. 134). Wallerius and Gyllenborg appear to have been the first agricultural chemists to recognize soil as a three-dimensional entity.

Joseph Black (1728–1799) attempted a rudimentary classification of marls (calcareous manures) in his *Lectures on the Elements of Chemistry Delivered in the University of Edinburgh* (Edinburgh, 1803, vol. 2, pp. 26–29), based upon their physical and chemical properties: shell (fresh water and sea water), clay, and stone. Black was part of a particularly brilliant group of intellectuals in Edinburgh that included geologist James Hutton and philosophers David Hume and Adam Smith.

The eighteenth-century Enlightenment marked a revolution in learning, as had the Renaissance three centuries earlier. Established theories such as phlogiston were cast aside in the wake of new, more rigorous experimental techniques. In France, Antoine Laurent Lavoisier (1743–1794), a leader in this new chemistry, in addition to developing modern elemental chemistry, also conducted experiments on the soil of his property, published in "Results of some agricultural experiments and reflections upon their relation to political economy," a paper read before the Paris Agricultural Society in 1788 (Browne, pp. 176–177). A disciple of Lavoisier's, Jean Antoine Claude Chaptal (1756–1832), reasoned that knowledge of the soil depended upon analysis of its chemical properties. Chaptal's approach was embraced and developed by Theodore de Saussure (1767–1845), who advocated complete chemical analyses of the soil. Jean-Baptiste Boussingault (1802–1887) emphasized the physical analysis of soil in addition to the use of chemical analyses, the prevailing method, to gain a more complete understanding of the soil.

In England, Humphry Davy (1778–1829) likewise stressed the need for chemical analysis of the soil. In his *Elements of Agricultural Chemistry, in a Course of Lectures for the Board of Agriculture* (London, 1813), Davy also emphasized the study of the physical and, particularly, of the geological properties of the rocks from which the soils had formed.

In northern Europe, Albrecht Daniel Thaer (1752–1828) developed a knowledge of soils and their constituents through detailed analyses of soils from different locales. He argued in his *Principles of Agriculture* (Philadelphia, 1844) that a soil's productivity is related directly to an optimum balance of the physical and chemical properties.

Jons Jakob Berzelius (1779–1848), a Swedish chemist, was one of several scientists who laid the foundations of modern agricultural chemistry. His analyses showed that soil organic matter is composed of various component acids important in plant nutrition. Many teachers of agricultural chemistry in nineteenth-century Europe and America were trained by Berzelius and his students, including Heinrich Rose (1795–1864) and Eilhard Mitscherlich (1794–1863) at the University of Berlin and Gerardus Johannes Mulder (1802–1880) at the University of Utrecht.

Gustav S. Schubler (1787–1834), an instructor at the University of Tübingen, proposed that a knowledge of physical and chemical properties of soils was important for their potential classification and agronomic use. His soil classification reflected this broader thinking: 1. physical properties (mass), 2. geognostic (geologic-elemental), and 3. chemical (proportion of constituents). He published *Grundsätze der Agrikultur-Chemie in näherer Beziehung auf land- und forstwirthschaftliche Gewerbe* (Principles of agricultural chemistry in closer relation to Agricultural and forest commerce) in Leipzig in 1830.

Carl S. Sprengel (1787–1859), a student of Thaer's, was instructor of agricultural chemistry at Göttingen University. He recognized the difference between surface soils and subsoils resulting from physical, chemical, and climatic factors, as well as from the character of the native vegetation. In his *Die Bodenkunde oder die Lehre vom Boden nebst einer vollständigen Anleitung zur Chemischen Analyse der Ackererden* (The knowledge or science of the soil including a complete guide to the chemical analysis of arable earth, Leipzig, 1837), Sprengel grouped soils into classes based on physical and chemical properties: gravelly, sandy, loamy, clayey, calcareous, marly, humic, peaty, swampy, talcose, gypseous, and ferruginous. Sprengel's work influenced a pioneer of pedology, Friedrich Albert Fallou (1794–1877).

In the Netherlands, Mulder developed a school of agricultural chemistry at the University of Utrecht. As with most of the contemporary agricultural chemists, Mulder was concerned with the analysis of soil humus and the improvement of soil by chemical means. His work was overshadowed by his contemporary, Liebig.

Justus von Liebig (1803–1873) of Hesse-Darmstadt established a school of agricultural chemistry at the University of Giessen that was the prototype of the modern chemical laboratory. At Giessen, Liebig's educational philosophy was based on scientific principles, a clear research design, and development of testable hypotheses. Although not directly concerned with classifying soils, Liebig's laboratory was the model for instruction in agricultural chemistry in other German states and many countries. Margaret Rossiter has examined this important case in detail in *Emergence of Agricultural Science.*

Liebig's contemporaries and students, along with those of Berzelius, trained many agricultural scientists of Europe, Russia, and the United States. Rossiter has identified Liebig's European and Russian students (indicated below by an asterisk) and contempo-

raries: Karl Friedrich Rammelsberg (1813–1899) at the University of Berlin; Karl Remigius Fresenius (1818–1897) at Wiesbaden; Robert Wilhelm Bunsen (1811–1899) at Marburg and Heidelberg; Friederich August Kekule (1829–1896) at Ghent and Bonn; August Wilhelm Hofmann (1818–1892) at the Royal College of Chemistry, London, and the University of Berlin; Emil Erlenmeyer (1825–1909) at Heidelberg and Berlin; Rudolf Fittig (1835–1910) at Göttingen, Tübingen, and Strassburg; Nikolai Nikolaievich Zinin at Kazan University and the Imperial University of St. Petersburg; and Aleksandr A. Voskresenskii at the Imperial University of St. Petersburg.

Some of Liebig's students who became educational leaders of agricultural chemistry (and agricultural geology) in the United States were Eben Norton Horsford (1818–1893), Samuel W. Johnson (1830–1909), William H. Brewer (1828–1910), and Josiah D. Whitney (1819–1896). These people and their academic descendants trained most of the agricultural chemists of the late nineteenth and early twentieth centuries, many of whom were important in the development of soil science.

There was a prevailing view in nineteenth-century America that the best education in agricultural chemistry was in Europe, despite the existence of universities such as Yale, the first in America to teach agricultural chemistry. The lectures of Benjamin Silliman, Sr. and Jr., and John Pitkin Norton in the Sheffield Scientific School and the Yale Analytical Laboratory, both founded in 1847, introduced these first coordinated efforts.

Norton, who had studied with Mulder at Utrecht, was designated professor of agricultural chemistry and wrote *Elements of Scientific Agriculture* (Albany, 1850), which became the basis for agricultural chemistry study at the Sheffield School and elsewhere. Norton's students included William H. Brewer and Samuel W. Johnson, both of whom became prominent agricultural chemists. Brewer, who had studied with Bunsen at Heidelberg and Liebig at Giessen, served with Josiah D. Whitney on the California Geological Survey from 1860 to 1864 prior to an appointment at Yale from 1864 to 1903. In 1869, Whitney had Brewer train young William Morris Davis (1850–1932) in geological and topographical mapping methods. Johnson, also a student of Liebig's and professor in the Sheffield Scientific School, became known for his analytical studies of soils and crops, and facilitated the establishment of the Connecticut Agricultural Experiment Station in 1875 (see Rossiter).

Forces of reform were at work at Harvard in the mid-1840s. The desire to create a German-style university was strong, particularly in applied sciences such as agricultural chemistry. A postgraduate program was also being contemplated and a new school was seen as the vehicle to effect these ends: the Lawrence Scientific School. Eben Norton Horsford (1818–1893) was chosen as Rumsford Professor of the Application of Science to the Useful Arts at Harvard. Horsford wished to establish a chemical laboratory like Liebig's in Giessen, where he had studied from 1844–1846. College students until that time had learned by demonstration and not by actual laboratory experience, a fact that Horsford wished to alter. Lack of funding kept Horsford from developing the laboratory. Students who graduated from the Lawrence Scientific School, including George Chapman Caldwell (1832–1906), who graduated in 1855, still sought advanced training in Europe. The attempt to bring Liebig's laboratory to Harvard ultimately failed and Horsford left in 1863. At the same time, Yale's attempt was succeeding and, as stated by Rossiter (p. 109): "Yale was to become the center of agricultural chemistry and soil analysis in the United States."

The history of agricultural chemistry and the transition to soil science at Cornell University has been well documented by Marlin G. Cline in *Agronomy at Cornell: Soils, Field Crops and Atmospheric Science. 1868–1980*. Cornell University selected George Chapman Caldwell as its first professor of (agricultural) chemistry in 1867. Many Cornell students of agricultural chemistry, and particularly Caldwell's, became notable soil scientists and had a large role in shaping the discipline, subdisciplines, and emphases of soil science. They included Franklin Hiram King, B.S. 1874 (soil physics); James A. Bizzell, Ph.D. 1903; Cyril George Hopkins, M.S. 1894, Ph.D. 1898 (soil survey); Jacob G. Lipman, M.A. 1900, Ph.D. 1903 (soil microbiology); Thomas Lyttleton Lyon, Ph.D. 1904 (soil fertility and management); and Merritt Finley Miller, M.S. 1901 (soil erosion and conservation).

Hopkins returned to his home state of Illinois and strengthened the soils program in the newly established Department of Agronomy. Lipman went to Rutgers University and became known as the founder of the journal *Soil Science*. Miller became head of the Soils Department at the University of Missouri, Columbia, and was known as the first to do controlled soil erosion experiments.

Lyon became head of the Department of Soil Technology at Cornell after Caldwell's retirement in 1903. Some of Lyon's many students distinguished themselves as soil scientists, including: Charles F. Shaw, B.S.A. 1906; Harry O. Buckman, Ph.D. 1908; and George John Boyoucos, Ph.D. 1911. Lyon, his student and faculty colleague Buckman, and faculty colleague Elmer O. Fippin became well known for their textbooks on soil science. The earliest texts were by Lyon and Fippin, *The Principles of Soil Management* (New York, 1909) and by Lyon, Fippin, and Buckman, *Soils: Their Properties and Management* (New York, 1909). Lyon and Buckman produced *The Nature and Properties of Soil: A College Text of Edaphology* (New York, 1922), which has enjoyed a long life through ten editions as of 1990 (now under the authorship of Nyle C. Brady).

Lyon's colleague on the Cornell faculty, Bizzell, also produced many students. One of the most notable was Raymond Stratton "R.S." Smith. After receiving his Ph.D. in 1918, Smith returned to Illinois, his home state, and worked with Hopkins and J.G. Mosier in soil survey and strengthened the Soils Department at the University of Illinois at Urbana-Champaign. Some of Smith's students included Frank F. Riecken, Guy D. Smith, Russell T. Odell, and Eugene P. Whiteside.

By the early twentieth century, students of agricultural chemistry interested in soils were also studying with Professor Georg Wiegner (1883–1936) in Switzerland. Several of his students became well known in soil science, including Hans Jenny, C. Edmund Marshall, and William Bradfield. One of Jenny's landmark works was *Factors of Soil Formation* (New York, 1941). Marshall's best known work was in soil chemistry and soil clay mineralogy.

By the early twentieth century, agricultural chemistry's concerns with soils had transitioned into the discipline of soil science. Many practitioners who had specialized in soils within agricultural chemistry were responsible for developing the distinct and independent discipline of soil science with its own scientific organizations, journals, and books.

John P. Tandarich

Bibliography

Browne, Charles A. "A Source Book of Agricultural Chemistry." *Chronica Botanica* 8 (1944): pp. 1–289.

Cline, Marlin G. *Agronomy at Cornell: Soils, Field Crops and Atmospheric Science. 1868–1980.* Agronomy Mimeo No. 82–16. Ithaca, N.Y.: Department of Agronomy, Cornell University, 1982.

Rossiter, Margaret W. *The Emergence of Agricultural Science: Justus Liebig and the Americans, 1840–1880.* New Haven and London: Yale University Press, 1975.

Tandarich, John P., and Stephen W. Sprecher. "The Intellectual Background for the Factors of Soil Formation." In *Factors of Soil Formation: A Fiftieth Anniversary Retrospective,* edited by Ronald G. Amundson, Jennifer W. Harden, and Michael J. Singer, pp. 1–13. SSSA Special Publication No. 33. Madison, Wis.: Soil Science Society of America, 1994.

See also Agricultural Geology; Agricultural Meteorology; Agriculture in the Seventeenth and Eighteenth Centuries; Disciplinary History; Geochemistry: The Word and Disciplinary History; Atmosphere, Chemistry of; Chemical Revolution; Chemistry, Terrestrial and Cosmical; Mineral Waters; Mineralogy; Minerals and Crystals, Fifteenth to Eighteenth Centuries; Ocean Chemistry; Pedology; Phlogistic Chemistry; Soil Conservation; Soil Science; Stratigraphy

Agricultural Geology: Disciplinary History

The study of the origin, nature, composition, and distribution of the soil from a geological viewpoint.

According to John P. Tandarich and Stephen W. Sprecher in "The Intellectual Background for the Factors of Soil Formation," agricultural geology developed as an interest, and eventually, a subdiscipline of geology and was named in the nineteenth century. But its origins reach much further back. It developed from the agricultural interests of natural philosophers and classical mineralogists. In her *From Mineralogy to Geology,* Rachel Laudan has traced the intellectual evolution of classical mineralogy to geology. According to Laudan, the model of the mineralogical classification of the earths and their being equated with agricultural soils began with Georgius Agricola (1494–1555) in his *De Natura Fossilium* (Basel, 1546).

Inquiries into "agricultural" mineralogy, as with agricultural chemistry, were fostered by the Royal Society of London. Martin Lister (1639–1712), a society member, proposed that the soils of England could be mapped, in his "Ingenious Proposal for a New Sort of Map of Countrys" in the society's *Philosophical Transactions* in 1684. Included in his proposal was what may be the first soil classification scheme. However, no map appears to have been made at that time. Proposals similar to Lister's were made by fellow society members John Aubrey (1626–1697) in his *Memoires of Natural Remarques in the County of Wilts* (London, 1685) and William Stukeley (1687–1759) in his *Itinerarium Curiosum* (London, 1724). Their ideas were not followed up until the mid-eighteenth century, when Christopher Packe (1686–1749) published his *Ancographia; sive convallium descripto* (Canterbury, 1743), a "philosophico-chorographical chart" of the area around Canterbury, England. Shading was used to indicate the darkness of the surface soils. Packe's chart also showed the topography by means of shading in a manner similar to a shaded-relief map of today.

In 1793, the Board of Agriculture was created for surveying English agriculture and preparing a series of reports. Arthur Young (1741–1820), a well-known agriculturalist and naturalist, was made secretary of the board. Young had spent much of his life assessing the agriculture of England and Scotland, and had developed a network of "farming correspondents" in each county. However, there were no standards or guidelines for the correspondents to use in the preparation of reports, except the model report that Young had prepared in his *General View of the Agriculture of the County of Suffolk* (London, 1794). Each report contained a soil map of a general nature. Basic soil information for the maps was gathered by interviewing farmers in the counties. These maps stressed the relationship of the soil to the surface geology. The Board of Agriculture continued preparation of new reports and reprinting of existing ones until it was disbanded in 1822. This effort marks the first general agricultural survey of a country, and perhaps served as a model for others, such as Russia.

In northern Europe, the influence in the late eighteenth and early nineteenth centuries of Abraham Gottlob Werner (1749–1817) of the Bergakademie of Freiberg, Saxony, is well documented (see Alexander Ospovat and Laudan). In particular, Werner's concept of geognosy is pertinent here. Geognosy *(Geognosie)* was defined by Werner and translated by Werner's biographer, Alexander Ospovat, literally as "the abstract systematic knowledge of the solid earth" (Ospovat, p. 101). Werner's geognostic writings on agriculture, although unpublished, are the foundation of what came to be called *Agrikulturgeognosie* in northern Europe and Russia, *geologie agricole* in France, and agricultural geology in the United States in the nineteenth century.

One of Werner's outstanding students was Alexander von Humboldt (1769–1859). Humboldt became well known for his physical geographic work, particularly on plant-soil-landform relationships. Humboldt developed modern concepts of mapping which he spread throughout Europe and Russia through personal visits and expeditions. His visit to Russia in 1829 was a stimulus to scientific developments there. He had applied geognostic principles to the Russian landscape, and wrote of the distribution of the black earth (Russian *chernoziom*) in his work *Central-Asien* (Berlin, 1844). A colleague of Humboldt's, Carl Ritter (1779–1859), also a well-known physical geographer, spread the geognostic ideas, modern mapping, and landscape-analysis methods throughout Europe and Russia.

In France, Georges Cuvier (1769–1832) and Alexandre Brongniart (1770–1847) were disciples of Werner's geognosy. They wrote *Description Géologique des Environs de Paris* (Paris, 1822), in which they described in detail the landscape and soils of the region around Paris. This is one of the first contributions to the literature on agricultural geology.

In Russia, some institutions important for the development of agricultural geology were the Academy of Sciences of St. Petersburg, founded in 1724 by Czar Peter the Great; the Free Economic Society of St. Petersburg, founded in 1765 by Empress Catherine II; the Imperial University of St. Petersburg, founded in 1819; and the St. Petersburg Society of Naturalists, founded in 1868. The Academy of Sciences originally consisted of foreign (mostly German) members, since Russia had few scholars at the time of the founding; this established the pattern of German economic and scientific influence felt in Russia through the nineteenth century. According to the historian of Russian science Alexander Vucinich, it is important to realize

that the type of governmental-scientific relationship that Peter the Great established in the St. Petersburg Academy was based on the Berlin Academy, which, like the French *Academie des Sciences*, was "an agency allied with the government" to "provide answers to various questions as they were set forth by agencies of government" (Vucinich, p. 68).

A notable exception to the foreign membership of the Academy was Russian-born Nikolai Mikhail Lomonosov (1711–1765), who was a "Renaissance man" versed in many aspects of knowledge. His pioneering work in geography and mineralogy is claimed to have paved the way for the establishment of soil studies in Russia. His treatise *On the Layers of the Earth* (St. Petersburg, 1763), an appendix of a larger work, *Metalurgia,* was the first Russian work to draw attention to soil. His works stimulated geographic, mineralogic, and geologic thought in Russia and elsewhere. According to Cuvier, the work of one of Lomonosov's students, Pierre Simon Pallas (1741–1811), substantially influenced Werner.

The Free Economic Society had as its primary aim the improvement of agriculture in Russia. To this end, the society, which counted within its membership both economists and scientists, worked with the government and the Imperial University to provide useful information on agricultural subjects such as soils.

One of the society members, Heinrich Storch (1766–1835), was an economist whom Vasilli V. Dokuchaev cites in *Cartography of Russian Soils* (1879) as influencing early soils work in Russia. Storch's works on land valuation as a source of wealth to the government were an impetus to begin the mapping of soils. According to Vucinich (p. 305), the visit of von Humboldt in 1829 marked the introduction of Werner's geognosy and of agricultural geologic mapping concepts into Russia. According to Dokuchaev, the first soil map was made in 1838; other soil maps were produced in 1842, 1851, 1853, 1857, and 1869. The legend and soil classification for a general map were completed for the society in 1873 by economic-statistician Vasilli Nikolaievich Chaslavskii (1834–1878), but they were not published until after his death by Dokuchaev in his *Cartography of Russian Soils*. Between the completion of the map legend by Chaslavaskii and his death, the society, at the urging of the eminent chemist Dmitri Mendeleev (1834–1907), turned to the Imperial University of St. Petersburg for assistance in the study of the Russian *chernoziom,* or black earth, region. Vasilli Dokuchaev, an agricultural geologist and mineralogist at the university, was selected to be chairman of a commission established to study the *chernoziom.* The work done by Dokuchaev contributed to the development of the subdiscipline of soil science known as pedology.

Although he did not study directly with Werner, William Maclure (1763–1840) credits Werner for the geognostic framework of knowledge that he used in his study of the geology and soils of the eastern United States. Maclure published "Observations on the geology of the United States, Explanatory of a Geological Map" in the *American Philosophical Society Transactions* in 1809. A native Scotsman, he was directly influenced by a student of Werner's, Robert Jameson (1774–1854), at the University of Edinburgh, and by a French friend, Comte de Volney (1757–1820), who had published *A View of the Soil and Climate of the United States of America* (Philadelphia, 1804).

Subsequent efforts of American geologists in the study of soils relied on the foundations laid by Maclure. This included Benjamin Silliman, Sr. (1779–1864) at Yale and his students Amos Eaton and Edward Hitchcock. Even before Maclure's scientific efforts, American colleges were beginning to offer geology courses. The history of soil-geologic studies may be now traced through the development of particular schools and the connections among the professors and students. Although geology was occasionally taught elsewhere, Yale University developed the first systematic curriculum in this subject.

Consideration of soils and geology continued with Amos Eaton (1776–1842). Educated at Yale under Silliman in geology and mineralogy, he was retained by Stephen Van Rensselaer to do the geological and agricultural survey of the Van Rensselaer property—on which he published *A Geological and Agricultural Survey of Rensselaer County in the State of New York* (Albany, 1822)—and along the site of the proposed Erie Canal. On the latter, Eaton published *A Geological and Agricultural Survey of the District Adjoining the Erie Canal in the State of New York* (Albany, 1824). He assisted Van Rensselaer in establishing the Rensselaer Institute (now Rensselaer Polytechnic Institute) in 1824. Eaton taught practical and applied science, stressing field and laboratory work, which made Rensselaer different from the memori-

zation method ongoing at Harvard or Yale. At the latter institutions, students had no field or laboratory experience until the establishment of the Lawrence and Sheffield Scientific Schools at Harvard and Yale, respectively, in 1847. Eaton published an agricultural map of New York, an early attempt to depict soil distribution, in *A Geological Nomenclature for North America Founded upon Geological Surveys Taken under the Direction of the Hon. Stephen Van Rensselaer* (Albany, 1828). He saw the soils as the uppermost geologic layer or stratum that supports plant life.

Many of Eaton's students became notable agricultural geologists, such as George Hammel Cook, Edward Hitchcock, and Ebenezer Emmons. They were hired to work in newly established state geological surveys that became active before 1850. The geology of agriculture was considered part of the domain of study of the state surveys.

Eaton's student Edward Hitchcock (1793–1864) worked on the geological surveys of New York, Connecticut, Massachusetts, New Hampshire, and Vermont. His agricultural map of Massachusetts in the *Final Report on the Geology of Massachusetts* (Amherst and Northampton, Mass., 1841) was another early effort to depict soil distribution. His concept of soil was similar to that of Eaton.

Another Eaton student, Ebenezer Emmons (1799–1863), co-founded the *American Quarterly Journal of Agriculture and Science* in 1844. In it he published an 1845 article, written with William Prime, entitled "Agricultural Geology," which defined this subdiscipline of geology and its practice in the United States.

Students produced by Rensselaer and other institutions staffed the newly formed state geological surveys or were connected with universities. Some of these investigators were David Dale Owen (1807–1860), who worked on the state surveys of Kentucky, Iowa, Illinois, Wisconsin, and Arkansas; George Hammel Cook (1818–1889) of Rutgers College, Scientific School and Agricultural Experiment Station, and the New Jersey Geological Survey; Alexander Winchell (1824–1891) at the Alabama Geological Survey, University of Michigan, and Michigan Geological Survey; and Eugene Woldemar Hilgard (1833–1916) of the University of Mississippi, Mississippi Geological Survey, University of Michigan, and the University of California, Berkeley.

Swiss-born and educated Jean Louis

Rodolphe Agassiz (1807–1873) was recruited by Harvard University in 1847 to accept a professorship in zoology and geology at the Lawrence Scientific School. Agassiz had studied with and was strongly influenced by both Cuvier and Humboldt, and had become well known through his work *Études sur les Glaciers* (Solothurn, Switzerland, 1841), advancing his glacial ice age theory. Although an expert in many areas of natural history, Agassiz appears not to have made soils an interest. However, during his tenure at Harvard from 1847 to 1873 he attracted many students, some of whom either practiced or taught those who practiced agricultural geology, such as Joseph Moore (1832–1905), Nathaniel Southgate Shaler (1841–1906), and William Morris Davis (1850–1932).

Joseph Moore, an Indiana native, had attended the Friends Boarding School (later Earlham College) at Richmond, Indiana, from 1853 to 1859, and then studied at Harvard University under Agassiz in 1859 to 1861 earning his bachelor of science degree in 1861. Returning to Earlham in 1861 as a faculty member, Moore remained there for the rest of his life as teacher, college president, and founder and curator of the museum that now bears his name. Of his students, Alan David Hole (1866–1940) is significant in the history of agricultural geology.

Nathaniel Southgate Shaler came from Kentucky in 1858 to study at Harvard, where he received the bachelor's degree in 1862 under Agassiz. He was appointed to the Harvard faculty in 1865 and remained active until his death in 1906. Shaler's interest in soils developed while he was director of the Kentucky Geological Survey (1873–1880), in which position he was exposed to the agricultural geologic work of David Dale Owen. Shaler's interest in soils resulted in several works: he published one of the earliest articles describing the effect of organisms in pedogenesis (soil formation), "Animal Agency in Soil Making," in *Popular Science Monthly* in 1888. He delivered a lecture, "The Soils of Massachusetts," before the Massachusetts State Board of Agriculture in 1890. He also published "The Origin and Nature of Soils," which appeared in his text *Aspects of the Earth* (New York, 1890) and in the *Twelfth Annual Report of the U.S. Geological Survey to the Secretary of the Interior 1890–'91,* which marked Shaler's peak of interest. His detailed discussion of "The Economic Aspects of Soil Erosion" in *National Geographic Magazine* in 1896 was one of the first, although futile, attempts to draw public attention to the devastation of erosion.

In "The Origin and Nature of Soils," Shaler recognized that the underclays of coal are ancient soils, emphasized the importance of organisms (now called pedoturbators) and of the energy of the Sun in the soil forming process, and discussed the effect of humans on soils. Also in this work, Shaler described and illustrated his idea of what we now call a soil profile.

A student of both Agassiz's and Shaler's, William Morris Davis had come to Harvard from Philadelphia in 1866 and graduated in 1870. He was invited to the faculty in 1876, remaining there for the rest of his career. In 1884, Davis formulated his idea of the cycle of erosion and, soon afterwards, the deductive method of physiographic investigation. His interests included agricultural geology, and he discussed soils and soil erosion in his text *Physical Geography* (Boston, 1898). Like Agassiz and Shaler before him, Davis attracted many students, some of whom are important in the history of agricultural geology, particularly Curtis F. Marbut (1863–1935) and Frederick V. Emerson (1870–1920). Emerson published the last textbook in the United States entitled *Agricultural Geology* (New York, 1920).

Curtis F. Marbut is of special interest, for he is regarded as the "father" of pedology in the United States. A native Missourian, Marbut was educated at the University of Missouri in Columbia (B.S. 1889) and Harvard University (M.A. 1894). He completed requirements for the Ph.D. at Harvard under William Morris Davis, but the degree was not awarded. Marbut taught at the University of Missouri from 1895 to 1910. Marbut's interest had turned to agricultural geology as a result of the influence of Shaler, but it was during his time at Missouri that he became active. His associations with Merritt F. Miller, head of the Soils Department, and Henry J. Waters, dean of the College of Agriculture, led to their collaboration on a soil map of Missouri that won a gold medal at the Louisiana Purchase Exposition in St. Louis in 1904. Waters appointed Marbut director of the Missouri Soil Survey from 1905 to 1910.

During this time Marbut became known to Milton Whitney, director of the Bureau of Soils, U.S. Department of Agriculture. Whitney recruited Marbut for a position with the Bureau of Soils. Marbut accepted various positions with the federal bureau from 1909 until 1935, including Chief of the Division of Soil Survey in the Bureau of Soils (after 1927, the Bureau of Chemistry and Soils).

Agricultural geology became established at the University of California, Berkeley, upon the arrival of Eugene W. Hilgard in 1874 as professor. Originally from Bavaria, Hilgard had settled in Belleville, Illinois, with his family in 1836. He was educated at the University of Zurich and the Bergakademie in Freiberg (where he studied geognosy), and the University of Heidelberg 1849–1853 (Ph.D. 1853 in chemistry, probably under Bunsen). He worked for the Mississippi Geological Survey from 1855 to 1872, where his first work on agricultural geology was published in the *Report of the Geology and Agriculture of the State of Mississippi* (Jackson, Miss., 1860). Hilgard was also professor at the University of Mississippi, 1866–1872. He was briefly on the faculty at the University of Michigan, 1872–1874. In 1874, he accepted a position at the University of California that he held for the remainder of his life (Jenny, *E. W. Hilgard*).

Hilgard worked vigorously in agricultural geology and was appointed special agent in charge of the cotton production report of the Tenth Census, which was published as *Report on Cotton Production in the United States* (Washington, D.C., 1884). He produced several agricultural geologic (soil) maps as part of the Tenth Census, including a general map of the cotton-producing states, California, Louisiana, and Mississippi. His work on the Tenth Census and his special interest in the "alkali lands" made him internationally famous and brought him to the attention of John Wesley Powell, director of the U.S. Geological Survey, who had similar interests in alkali lands and their reclamation. Hilgard's reputation in geologic and agricultural circles reached its zenith in the mid-1880s. In 1885, Hilgard was nominated for the position of commissioner of agriculture; however, Norman J. Colman of Missouri was appointed. Hilgard and Powell attempted to establish a national agricultural survey within the Department of the Interior. This attempt failed in 1888 because of opposition from Commissioner of Agriculture Colman, who wished the survey to be in the Agriculture Department (see Jenny, *E. W. Hilgard*). Nevertheless, agricultural geologic work received a strong measure of support from Powell, as evidenced by the Geological Survey's *Annual Report for 1890–1891*. Hilgard's agricultural geologic knowledge put him in the forefront of the development of pedology in the United States beginning in the 1890s.

Initial agricultural geologic work on soils in Wisconsin was done by Thomas Chrowder Chamberlin (1843–1928). A native of Mattoon, Illinois, Chamberlin attended Beloit College, graduated in 1866, and continued to teach there from 1873 to 1882, while working for the Wisconsin Geological Survey. While at Beloit, he studied for a year (1869–1870) with Alexander Winchell at the University of Michigan. Winchell's pamphlet *The Soils and Subsoils of Michigan* (Lansing, Mich., 1865) no doubt influenced Chamberlin, for a while at the Wisconsin Survey, Chamberlin published several treatises on the agricultural geology of Wisconsin from 1874 to 1882 and produced two soil maps based on the physical properties of soils: one of eastern Wisconsin in 1876 and the other a map of the state of Wisconsin in 1882. All of these are in *Geology of Wisconsin: Survey of 1873–1877* (Madison, Wis., 1882). These maps are notable, and they were recognized early in the twentieth century as being "modern" in approach by George N. Coffey in his "Development of Soil Survey Work in the U.S." (1912): the map units are based on a soil physical property, "texture" (a term used more qualitatively than today's concept). Chamberlin's approach was a departure from the practice of considering soils merely as a geologic formation.

Chamberlin was also interested in the problem of soil erosion as early as 1876. He recognized that farmers in eastern Wisconsin were beginning to farm newly exposed subsoils, and therefore he produced a map of eastern Wisconsin in 1876 showing the textural groups of the subsoils, in *Geology of Wisconsin: Survey of 1873–1877* (Madison, Wis., 1877). Chamberlin delivered an address on soil erosion in 1909 on "Soil wastage." He also published "Soil Productivity" in *Science* in 1911. The public address caught the attention of soil scientist Hugh Hammond Bennett (1882–1961), who afterwards decided to make soil conservation his life's work.

Chamberlin worked for the U.S. Geological Survey from 1882 to 1887 as head of the Glacial Geology Division, and taught at the Columbian (now George Washington) University from 1885 to 1887. While employed at the Geological Survey, he influenced two scientists toward agricultural geologic work, W.J. McGee and Frank Leverett. Chamberlin was president of the University of Wisconsin, Madison, from 1887 to 1892.

University of Chicago President William Rainey Harper invited Chamberlin to chair the geology department at that newly organized university in 1892. According to Fisher *(First Seventy Years)*, the first faculty members of that department and their geologic areas of teaching and research interest were Rollin D. Salisbury (1858–1922), physiographic, historical, and geographic; Charles Richard Van Hise (1857–1918), structural; Chamberlin, glacial and theoretical; Joseph Paxson Iddings (1857–1920), petrology, crystallography, and mineralogy; and Richard Alexander Fullerton Penrose, Jr. (1863–1931), economic.

Like Chamberlin, Salisbury also had an interest in soils, as evidenced by his work in New Jersey, published in the *New Jersey Geological Survey Annual Report for 1898*. Chamberlin and Salisbury were a prominent team in geologic research and education and the cornerstones of the early department. They wrote basic geology texts used in colleges for many years: *Geology* (New York, 1904–1906) and *Introductory Geology* (New York, 1914). These included soils and influenced many students toward both agricultural and Quaternary geology. Some students who became involved in Quaternary geologic-soil studies were William C. Alden, George F. Kay, Morris M. Leighton, and Paul MacClintock. Some of the students who did agricultural geologic work were Frederick V. Emerson, Allen David Hole, Andrew Robeson Whitson (1870–1945), and Carl Ortwin Sauer (1889–1975). Whitson had been a student of Chamberlin's and Salisbury's at the University of Wisconsin, and he completed his B.S. under them at the University of Chicago in 1894; he continued in graduate study there, 1894–1895 and 1899–1900, specializing in soils and crop production. After returning to the University of Wisconsin, Madison, Whitson became the head in 1905 of the first department of soils established in the country.

According to Francis D. Hole, Allen D. Hole, a student of Joseph Moore's at Earlham College (B.S. 1897), spent summers studying at the University of Chicago, 1902–1908, under a cooperative agreement between the university and the U.S. Geological Survey by which students could participate in field camps and field trips to many areas of the country. Hole was appointed to the Earlham College faculty in 1900, and received a Ph.D. from the University of Chicago in 1910. In 1911, he began a program of course work and field study in soil survey in cooperation with the Indiana Geological Survey and the U.S. Bureau of Soils. Hole's soil surveys were pub-lished by the Indiana Geological Survey in its *Annual Reports* in 1912 and 1915.

A few of Hole's students who took advantage of this training and pursued careers in agricultural geology (graduation dates from Earlham College) were: Mark Baldwin, 1912; Earl D. Fowler, 1915; and James Thorp, 1921. Baldwin, Fowler, and Thorp served on the soil survey staff of the Bureau of Soils and the Bureau of Chemistry and Soils (after 1927) under Marbut and Charles Kellogg.

An international society of agricultural geology or agrogeology formed and held its first meeting in 1909 in Budapest. In 1924 it changed its name to the International Society of Soil Science. Prior to that action a comprehensive bibliography of agricultural geology containing 3,302 entries had been published in English by Adolf Wulff. By the time of the First Congress of Soil Science held in Washington, D.C., in 1927, the name agricultural geology was no longer used by the practitioners of soil science.

John P. Tandarich

Bibliography

Chamberlin, Thomas C. "Soil wastage." In *Proceedings of a Conference of Governors in the White House, Washington, D.C., May 13–15, 1908*, pp. 75–83. Washington, D.C.: U.S. Government Printing Office, 1909.

Coffey, George N. "The Development of Soil Survey Work in the United States with a Brief Reference to Foreign Countries." *Proceedings of the American Society of Agronomy* 3 (1912): pp. 115–129.

Dokuchaev, Vasilli V. *Cartography of Russian Soils* [In Russian]. St. Petersburg, 1879.

Fisher, D. Jerome. *The First Seventy Years of the Department of Geology, University of Chicago, 1892–1961*. Chicago: University of Chicago, 1963.

Hole, Francis D. *Allen David Hole and Mary Doan Hole: A Biography of Two Hoosier Quaker Educators, 1866–1940*. Madison, Wis.: The Friend's Press, 1991.

Jenny, Hans. *E. W. Hilgard and the Birth of Modern Soil Science*. Collana Della Rivista Agrochimica No. 3. Pisa, Italy: Collana della Rivista Agrochimica, 1961.

Laudan, Rachel. *From Mineralogy to Geology*. Chicago and London: University of Chicago Press, 1987.

Ospovat, Alexander M., trans. *Short Classification and Description of the Various Rocks by Abraham Gottlob Werner.* New York: Hafner Publishing Company, 1971.

Tandarich, John P., and Stephen W. Sprecher. "The Intellectual Background for the Factors of Soil Formation." In *Factors of Soil Formation: A Fiftieth Anniversary Retrospective,* edited by Ronald G. Amundson, Jennifer W. Harden, and Michael J. Singer, pp. 1–13. SSSA Special Publication No. 33. Madison, Wis.: Soil Science Society of America, 1994.

Vucinich, Alexander. *Science in Russian Culture. A History to 1860.* Stanford: Stanford University Press, 1963.

Wulff, Adolf. "Bibliographica Agrogeologica." *Mededeelingen van de Landbouwhoogeschool en van de Daaraan Verbonden Instituten* 20 (1921): pp. 11–285.

See also Agricultural Chemistry; Agricultural Meteorology; Agriculture in the Seventeenth and Eighteenth Centuries; Chemical Revolution; Cycle of Erosion; Disciplinary History; Geology; Pedology; Soil Conservation; Soil Science; Minerals and Crystals, Fifteenth to Eighteenth Centuries; Mineralogy

Agricultural Meteorology

The influence of the weather upon agriculture.

Agricultural meteorology as a coherent discipline and in recognizably modern form dates from the twentieth century, perhaps even from after World War II. Very little has been written on its history. This article suggests a periodization and sketch of the main lines of development.

The roots of agricultural meteorology lie in ancient and even prehistorical agricultural practice. The division of the year into seasons, the selection of times for sowing and reaping, and other ancient weather lore embodied a knowledge of agricultural meteorology handed down over many generations. Ancient calendars and collections of weather lore—including Hesiod's *Works and Days* (before 700 B.C.E.) the *Book of Signs* (278 B.C.E.) of Aratus of Solis (ca. 315–240 B.C.E.), *On the Signs of Rain, Winds, Storms, and Fair Weather* (ca. 300 B.C.E.) of Theophrastus (ca. 371–287 B.C.E), and the *Georgics* (ca. 35 B.C.E.) of Virgil (70–19 B.C.E.)—put this material into written form. According to William Napier Shaw (Shaw, p. 100), Theophrastus recorded nearly all the weather signs known to us, and authors from Aratus to Erasmus Darwin (1731–1802) depended heavily upon him. Scholars such as William Jackson Humphreys in his *Weather Proverbs and Paradoxes* (1923), writing prior to World War II, have investigated the reliability of this material and its basis, if any, in actual weather patterns and atmospheric physics. Some, such as John Grand Carteret, in *Les almanachs français,* have treated it as social and cultural history. Emile Dominique Nourry argues in *L'astrologie populaire* (pp. 38–39, 65) that it is pointless to search for an empirical basis of traditional weather lore, since in a prescientific age traditions were not based on observation but rather themselves shaped observation and experience.

Much of traditional weather lore involved astrology. Especially in the Mediterranean region, with its regular weather patterns, a natural association grew up between the periodic behavior of the heavenly bodies and the changes of the weather. These regularities were extended to anticipate the vicissitudes of the weather in other climes. Based on symbolic associations, for example of the moon with growth or fermentation, astrological weather lore persisted among both the educated population and common farm-folk well into the twentieth century. Typical of such lore is the belief that plants grow faster during the waxing moon and that the weather of the solstices decides the weather of the succeeding six months. The abundant literature on the history of astrology and on the almanac provides many colorful examples.

The scientific and agricultural revolutions transformed but did not discard this body of tradition. Natural philosophers of the seventeenth and especially the eighteenth centuries replaced the earlier magical sympathies governing the weather with effluvia or lunar atmospheric tides. Giuseppe Toaldo (1719–1798), the leading proponent of this approach, claimed in *La meteorologia applicata all'agricoltura* to demonstrate from observations a lunar influence on the weather and speculated on the influence of "feeble emanations and impulsions of the stars and planets on sublunar fluids and solids." He was able to exploit the growing mass of weather observations collected by individuals like himself and by scientific institutions like the Royal Society of London, the Société Royale de Médecine at Paris, the Societas Meteorologica Palatina at Mannheim, and the numerous agricultural societies founded in this age of agricultural improvement. These observations were also examined by meteorologists such as H.-L. Duhamel du Monceau (1700–1782) and Louis Cotte (1740–1815). Less ambitious (or extravagant) than Toaldo, they aimed to discover correlations between weather patterns and the success of crops and began to develop concepts such as degree sums and mean annual, seasonal, and other such temperatures. Many of their correlations preserved traditional weather lore, which was well regarded by meteorologists into the twentieth century (Feldman, "Late Enlightenment Meteorology").

The establishment of modern climatology and plant geography in the early nineteenth century by Alexander von Humboldt (1769–1859) and others shifted interest from the accumulation of observations and the ferreting out of correlations and weather proverbs, toward an understanding of regional climates and their influence on the distribution of plants and animals. Plant geography was greatly stimulated by European imperialism and the exploration that accompanied it, and much of the agricultural meteorology of the first half of the nineteenth century involved questions of plant distribution or acclimatization that were natural concomitants of imperial activity. Investigations focused primarily on the role of temperature, especially mean and extreme seasonal temperatures, on the growth of various crops. In Russia, Adolph Theodor Kupffer (1799–1865) advocated in the 1830s the determination of temperatures at the boundaries of grain-growing regions, in order to determine suitable ranges for the introduction of crops; in the United States, the patent office collected agricultural statistics, including temperature and precipitation, for the same purpose. Jean-Baptiste Boussingault (1802–1887), whose *Economie rurale* includes one of the few systematic treatments of agricultural meteorology in the nineteenth century, adopted a similar position, closely following Humboldt. The geographical distribution of plants, he argued, is a consequence of the distribution of heat, so that temperature becomes the key to plant growth, along with light, air, moisture, and other factors. Boussingault's proximity to Humboldt extends to his reliance on information from the equatorial mountains of South America, from which he determined a minimum mean annual temperature capable of supporting plant growth. He claimed to have established an inverse proportion between a crop's growing season and the temperature.

As Boussingault well realized, agricultural meteorology was in its infancy around 1850. In the succeeding quarter century, nonagricultural problems claimed meteorologists' attention. The famous storm of 1854 at Balaklava inaugurated a preoccupation with maritime meteorology. The first International Conference of Meteorologists at Brussels in 1853 had emphasized this branch of meteorology, and the national meteorological services of France, England, the United States, the Netherlands, and Norway focused on storms and on storm warnings for oceangoing vessels. The emergence of steam travel diminished the need for maritime storm warnings after about 1870. But storm warnings could be of use in agriculture as well, and in the last quarter century, national weather services began to issue storm, frost, and flood warnings to farmers. At this time local networks of observers and agricultural stations proliferated, leading toward the study of microclimates that is essential to modern agricultural meteorology. Khrgian (chaps. 8, 16), who emphasizes Russian contributions, points to the role of district-council (or *zemstvo*) meteorology and to the work of A.I. Voeikov (1842–1916) and P.I. Brounov (1852–1927) in furthering detailed local studies and introducing new concepts such as "critical periods," during which plants particularly need moisture. According to Khrgian, Western European nations adopted these advances only in the next century.

Aviation and World War I once again distracted meteorologists from agricultural problems. But the war created agricultural crises as well. Friedman (chaps. 5, 11) has shown how the food shortage in Norway in 1918 led Vilhelm Bjerknes (1862–1951) to adapt maritime forecasting institutions to short-range weather forecasting for farmers. The dense system of observing stations he established for the purpose, coupled with the pressure for short-range, local forecasts, generated important theoretical advances, including the polar front model of cyclones and air mass meteorology.

Whether World War I stimulated agricultural meteorology in other countries as well must be the subject for further research. Contemporary agricultural meteorologists like Jen-Hu Chang in *Climate and Agriculture* and James A. Taylor in *Weather and Agriculture* imply that neither the war nor the Great Depression significantly affected the field. Only since World War II have detailed climatological and microclimatological studies been applied to agriculture. Increasing international competition combined with government intervention and growing sophistication in marketing arrangements have fostered a new appreciation for agricultural improvement. Interdisciplinary work among meteorologists, agriculturalists, geographers, and ecologists has altered the field; and television has transformed the weather advisory service. Only since the 1960s have agricultural meteorologists begun to study in detail the meteorology of the plant and soil surface.

The history of agricultural meteorology, especially in the modern period, remains largely uncultivated. Wide fields for historical research are open in the influence of plant geography and Humboldtian climatology; the roles of national weather services and of local networks and stations in the late nineteenth and early twentieth centuries; the impact of the two world wars and the Depression; a possible revolution in the discipline after World War II; and the influence in the last several decades of university departments and government programs.

Theodore S. Feldman

Bibliography

Boussingault, Jean-Baptiste. *Rural Economy, in Its Relations with Chemistry, Physics, and Meteorology.* Translated by George Law. New York: D. Appleton & Co.; Philadelphia: Geo. S. Appleton, 1845.

Chang, Jen-Hu. *Climate and Agriculture. An Ecological Survey.* Chicago: Aldine Publishing Co., 1968.

Feldman, Theodore S. "Late Enlightenment Meteorology." In *The Quantifying Spirit in the Eighteenth Century,* edited by Tore Frängsmyr, J.L. Heilbron, and Robin Rider, pp. 143–178. Berkeley, Los Angeles and Oxford: University of California Press, 1990.

Friedman, Robert Marc. *Appropriating the Weather. Vilhelm Bjerknes and the Construction of a Modern Meteorology.* Ithaca and London: Cornell University Press, 1989.

Grand-Carteret, John. *Les almanachs français.* Paris: J. Alisi, 1896.

Humphreys, William Jackson. *Weather Proverbs and Paradoxes.* Baltimore: Williams and Wilkins, 1923.

Khrgian, A. Kh. *Meteorology. A Historical Survey.* 2d. ed., revised. Edited by Kh.P. Pogosyan. Jerusalem: Israel Program for Scientific Translations, 1970.

Nourry, Emile Dominique. *L'astrologie populaire étudiée éspecialement dans les doctrines et les traditions relatives à l'influence de la lune.* Paris: J. Thiebaud, 1937.

Shaw, William Napier. *Manual of Meteorology.* Vol. 1. *Meteorology in History.* Cambridge: Cambridge University Press, 1926.

Taylor, James A., ed. *Weather and Agriculture.* Oxford, London and New York: Pergamon Press, 1967.

Toaldo, Giuseppe. *La meteorologia applicata all'agricoltura.* Venezia: Storti, 1775.

See also Agricultural Chemistry; Agricultural Geology; Agriculture in the Seventeenth and Eighteenth Centuries; Climate Change, before 1940; Meteorological Ideas in Folklore and Mythology; Pedology: Disciplinary History; Soil Conservation; Soil Science

Agriculture in the Seventeenth and Eighteenth Centuries

A period of central importance for experimental and scientific agriculture, rich with potential for historical study.

The history of the science of agriculture is new and still of limited scope. Historians have examined agricultural science in the nineteenth and twentieth centuries on the premise that the science of agriculture developed only then, and they have studied the practice of agriculture of medieval and early modern Europe and thoroughly scrutinized the Agricultural Revolution in the seventeenth century. Yet other than Reginald Lennard's one article in 1932, sections of Joan Thirsk's monumental works on agrarian history (vol. 5, sec. 2, pp. 533–589; vol. 6, 275–383), and Charles Webster's book on science and Puritanism, none have recognized that agricultural science originated as an important science of the Earth in the seventeenth and eighteenth centuries.

The Dutch and the English began to study and write about agriculture in the sixteenth century, mostly as observations of the best methods and crops. With the advent of the call for a scientific method that was both empirical and experimental by Francis Bacon (1561–1626), a new quest for accumulation of data began. Agriculture was one of Bacon's interests and, contrary to some claims against him, he carried out or reported on experiments in agriculture ranging from tree grafting to soil preparation. Following Bacon there was a tremendous outburst of books on agriculture in seventeenth-century England, many of which were experimental or diagnostic.

These new books focused on soil types, fertilizers, marls, and their effects on soil, seed preparation, plant and animal selection, crop rotation, grafting and theories of sap movement, and equipment and technology. However, these agriculturalists lacked an agricultural paradigm, and they experimented randomly without an overriding hypothesis. For example, soil experiments were conducted without any chemical understanding of soil properties beyond labels of "fat" or "not fat," but mineralogists in the seventeenth century, who followed the work of J.J. Becher (see Laudan, p. 44), believed the Earth was composed of three principles (earth, water, and air), and they could not decide whether earths and stones were separate classes until the eighteenth century. The source and role of nitrogen, unknown until the late eighteenth century, remained a problem for German and American researchers until the 1850s. Experiments on grafting and sap were performed with, at best, the rudimentary understanding of capillarity demonstrated by Giovanni Borelli (1608–1679), and without the knowledge of transpiration developed by Stephen Hales (1677–1761), or of osmosis, researched by R.J.H. Dutrochet (1776–1847).

Nevertheless, agriculture was a science in the seventeenth and eighteenth centuries. Many seventeenth-century authors used the term "science" or "experiment" or the phrase "new philosophy," which meant experimental science, and many of them attempted to quantify their observations. Francis Bacon in *Novum Organum* (1620) suggested experiments of observing planted seeds daily. Ralph Austen (d.1676) set up measured experiments on seed germination with hotbeds. Paracelsus (Theophrastus Bombastus, ca. 1493–1541) wrote of the importance of salt in manure as a fertilizer, a theory both French and English agriculturalists in the seventeenth century followed. The significance of salts, however, would not be realized until the late nineteenth century. John Evelyn (1620–1706), who had studied under two of the most famous chemists in Europe, analyzed soil samples using a microscope to determine their fundamentals and composition; he, as well as several others, concluded that "nitre" in soil was essential for plant growth. Evelyn also developed a device to measure plant growth. Nehemiah Grew (1641–1712), in experiments performed in the 1670s that he said would advance agriculture, developed a partial understanding of the cause of sap movement in plants. Grew was also one of the first to use the microscope in a methodical way for the study of plant physiology. Robert Boyle (1627–1691) thought that chemistry, geology, botany, and breeding would transform agriculture. Experiments in selective breeding of animals and plants were performed, and hybridization of plants and animals was recognized. The Royal Society of London was extremely interested in agriculture. Even though R.K. Merton completely ignored agriculture in his categories of seventeenth-century science, the second largest committee of the Royal Society was the Georgical Committee, whose interest was the earth sciences, mainly agriculture. Transcripts of Georgical Committee meetings, a survey sent to prominent agriculturalists around England and Wales, transactions of Royal Society meetings, and the correspondence of Henry Oldenburg (1618–1677), the secretary of the Royal society, indicate that agriculture was one of the most active areas of science in the society. The Georgical Committee's survey in 1665 was one of the first attempts in any area of science to gather all of the knowledge and data available and to quantify it. It included data on soils and fertilizers and their success with different plants in an attempt to correlate soil nutrients and specific plant growth.

In the mid-seventeenth century, England came close to establishing a college of agriculture under the influence of Samuel Hartlib (d. 1662) and his circle. Gabriel Plattes (fl. 1638–1640), one of the pioneers in the scientific approach to agriculture, pushed for a state laboratory intended for improvements in medicine and agriculture (Webster, pp. 47, 332). By the late seventeenth century, John Houghton (d. 1705), who was one of the first to note the potato as an agricultural vegetable, published a journal of agricultural science. The experimental use of new plants, many of which had come from the New World, occupied many of the researchers. Experiments on machines for agriculture were also common. In 1670 Evelyn presented to the Royal Society a new machine for plowing, sowing, and harrowing. Jethro Tull (1674–1741) experimented with the seed drill and horse-drawn hoe. Experiments were performed with water-meadow technology, in which meadows were flooded with a thin sheet of water from a series of sluices and gutters to determine the optimum exposure to air and water.

The eighteenth century experienced some consolidation and dissemination of the gains made in the previous century, although by the late eighteenth century agricultural science was becoming more focused on theoretical problems that could be attacked by specific procedures. In eighteenth-century France, Jean Antoine Nollet (1700–1770) experimented with the influence of electrification on the growth of plants and animals. Stephen Hales in 1727 published the most important eighteenth-century contribution to plant physiology and demonstrated that plants exchange gases. H.B. de Saussure (1740–1799), working in the 1780s on the source of nitrogen in plants, discovered that plants did not assimilate atmospheric nitrogen. Also in the 1780s, Joseph Priestley (1733–1804) wrote to Arthur Young (1741–1820), the renowned agriculturalist, describing his discovery of "dephlogisticated air" (oxygen) and recommending its value to agriculture, for Priestly suggested that plants transformed stale air into "dephlogisticated" air. Young worked on developing new strains of plants such as potatoes, yet despite his reputation as a great agriculturalist, he really did little scientific work. His greatest accomplishment was dissemination of ideas developed in the seventeenth century. The eighteenth century saw a great interest in hybridization, including the work of Carl Linnaeus (1707–1778), and a series of prizes offered by many of Europe's scientific academies encouraged this pursuit. New varieties of wheat and corn were produced to increase yields and control disease.

New machinery was developed, such as the threshing machine, but often it was a matter of alterations to existing machines, such as converting wooden plows to iron for greater strength and lightness, or the mathematically determined alteration of the curve of a plow moldboard for use on hillsides made in America by Thomas Jefferson (1746–1827). Jefferson was also interested in the new machine for cleaning rice that was being used in Italy in the late eighteenth century. But this had little to do with science.

Although agricultural science made great strides in the seventeenth and eighteenth centuries, historians have not acknowledged it as a science because it was practical, lacked a paradigm, and failed to establish a continuum of experimentation to the present. The accusation that agricultural science was overly practical and without a clear hypothesis should not detract from recognizing it as a science by seventeenth- and eighteenth-century standards. Other acknowledged sciences of these centuries did not employ a clear hypothesis or even use experimentation.

For example, medicine is recognized as a science for its practical triumphs and a continuum of research, especially through academic institutions with the application of chemistry and instruments such as the microscope—yet it had no clear hypothesis. Furthermore, natural history was sometimes atheoretical and used almost no experimentation, but it established its success in collection, description, and classification, and maintained a continuum of study in taxonomy.

Agriculture as a science in this period has been overlooked for a variety of reasons. Agricultural science has failed to gain recognition partly because of the seventeenth and eighteenth centuries' limitations in chemical experimentation and in the use of the microscope for plant science; partly because of its pragmatic orientation, in which the practitioners were viewed as farmers, not scientific experimenters; and partly because of a lack of continuum in the field. In addition, as agricultural science became more specific, and required closer examination of soil or plant, specialization took place. Botany originates, to a great extent, from agricultural science, but historians have missed the general and practical origins in favor of more narrow and theoretical science. Tremendous gains were made in the seventeenth century in the production of food and in the introduction of new plants and strains of plants and new breeds of animals. The success of agriculture in Europe and its expansion to the New World blunted the demand for new agricultural developments and led to consolidation in the eighteenth century. Not until the growing population of the nineteenth century placed new demands on food production was there renewed interest in agricultural science. In her 1975 book *The Emergence of Agricultural Science* (pp. xi–xiv) Margaret Rossiter argues that modern agricultural science originated in the period between 1840 and 1880 with the application of new knowledge in chemistry, physics, and biology. Chemistry had developed to the level that it could be used systematically to help solve problems in agriculture. Academic institutions began to study agriculture as a science and special institutions for its study arose. This indicates that by some historians' standards, the existence of a science depends not so much on the success of the applied science but on the acceptance of methods used in the modern scientific world and on the existence of established and continuous centers of study in the field.

Seventeenth- and eighteenth-century agricultural science needs to be investigated as a science by the standards of the time, as has been done for other sciences. Books of the period and manuscripts on agriculture need to be scrutinized for scientific methodology. Many of the seventeenth-century practitioners believed they were being scientific, and used logical methodologies to analyze the soil, plant anatomy and physiology, even though their concepts and tools were usually inadequate to build a progressive discipline. Practical application of agriculture and unorthodox experiments should not detract from the scientific methodology of diagnosis, experimentation, and quantification that flourished in seventeenth- and eighteenth-century Europe, and a new interpretation of the origins of agriculture as a science must be considered, as well as its connections to the development of related sciences such as geology, botany, zoology, and chemistry. Charles Browne's "Source Book" provides a good starting point for those unfamiliar with the literature.

John J. Butt

Bibliography

Browne, Charles. "A Source Book of Agricultural Chemistry." *Chronica Botanica* 8, no. 1 (1944): pp. 1–290.

Hall, A.R., and M.B. Hall, eds. *The Correspondence of Henry Oldenburg.* 11 vols. Madison: University of Wisconsin Press, 1966–1973.

Kerridge, Eric. *The Agricultural Revolution.* London: George Allen and Unwin, 1967.

Laudan, Rachel. *From Mineralogy to Geology: The Foundations of a Science, 1650–1830.* Chicago: University of Chicago Press, 1987.

Lennard, Reginald. "English Agriculture under Charles II: The Evidence of the Royal Society's 'Enquiries.'" *Economic History Review* 4 (1932): pp. 23–45.

Merton, R.K. *Science, Technology and Society in Seventeenth-Century England.* Reprint. Osiris, 1938. New York: Fertig, 1970.

Rossiter, Margaret W. *The Emergence of Agricultural Science.* New Haven: Yale University Press, 1975.

Thirsk, Joan, ed. *The Agrarian History of England and Wales.* Cambridge: Cambridge University Press, 1985, 1989.

Webster, Charles. *The Great Instauration: Science, Medicine and Reform 1626–1660.* London: Duckworth, 1975.

See also Agricultural Chemistry; Agricultural Geology; Agricultural Meteorology; Climate Change, before 1940; Chemical Revolution; Cosmology and the Earth in the Scientific Revolution; Meteorological Ideas in Europe, Fifteenth to Eighteenth Centuries

Airglow

Light of the night sky, first noticed in antiquity or earlier.

The fact that the night is not completely dark, even in the absence of moonlight, was interpreted in antiquity in religious terms, in terms of creation by God or Gods. Of seventeen accounts of the creation of the world quoted by Mircea Eliade, only one, that of the Boshongo, a Central African Bantu tribe, includes an explanation for the fact that the night is not dark. We are told that Bumba, the creator, after having vomited up the Sun, thus bringing light to everything, "vomited up the moon and then the stars, and after that the night had its light also." Of probably considerably earlier antiquity is the account in Genesis (1:14–15), in the Hebrew Bible: "And God said: 'Let there be lights in the firmament of the heaven to divide the day from the night; and let them be for signs, and for seasons, and for days and years; and let them be for lights in the firmament of the heaven to give light upon the earth.' And it was so." In addition to providing measures of time intervals, the passage allows for an interpretation of the fact that the night is not completely dark, even on moonless nights, and that this light comes from the stars. Parallels exist between the account in Genesis and that in the "Enuma Elis," the Akkadian account of creation, but the mention of the night light is not found in the place in the sequence to be expected from the corresponding position in Genesis. We may presume that knowledge of the "Enuma Elis" was widespread, as it was recited in Babylon, an inheritor of Akkadian civilization, each year during the New Year's festival. Comparison of the similarities and differences between the two accounts raises some interesting questions. The pertinent portions of the "Enuma Elis" are found in the fifth tablet (Landsberger and Wilson). This contains a description of the year, month, and week using the stars and Moon as markers so that the focus here is on time reckoning, important for an agricultural people. The early Hebrews were nomads for whom the light in the night sky would be of more importance, and perhaps that explains the different focus.

The next mention of atmospheric luminosity that can be interpreted as airglow comes with the development of Greek rationality—that is, descriptions of and hypotheses about natural phenomena without recourse to religion. Aristotle and Pliny described the phenomena of *chasmata,* which can be identified in part as auroras, and in part as bright airglow nights (Silverman, "On the Chasms"). Aristotle explained these as being the result of a condensation of the upper air resulting from a combustion process. The term *chasmata* for aurora remained in use up to at least the time of Johannes Kepler, around 1600. These two sources of the light of the night sky—the stars and some form of photochemical process within the atmosphere itself—are still our basic sources, though both are now considered to be important contributors.

Auroral observations continued to be made over the next two millennia, but no attention appears to have been paid to the light of the night sky until the late nineteenth century. A number of observations were made of the variability of the earth-light or earth-shine (see J. Maurer and his references). Quantitative measurements were first carried out by Gavin J. Burns in 1899 and 1902 and by Simon Newcomb (1835–1909), the astronomer who long directed the American Nautical Almanac Office, in 1901. The measurement of the light of the night sky by Newcomb at the turn of the century was motivated by the question of the total amount of light of all the stars that were too faint to see. This question became important for cosmological theory as a result of Olbers's Paradox. Briefly stated, Olbers in 1826 showed that if the universe were uniform in its physical characteristics and laws, and static, then the light reaching the surface of the Earth from all the stars would be equal to fifty thousand times that of sunlight when the Sun is in the zenith, corresponding to a surface temperature of over 5,500°C (9,900°F). The total light of all the stars then became an important parameter in attempts to resolve the discrepancy with reality.

Gavin J. Burns in 1906 and 1910 and L. Yntema in 1909 were the first since Aristotle to point out that the observations required a luminous layer within the Earth's atmosphere. Some additional photometric measurements were carried out up to the 1920s when Lord Rayleigh carried out the series of systematic measurements in restricted spectral ranges that marked the beginning of modern airglow research. Rayleigh also looked for correlations with solar and magnetic data.

A prominent feature of both the aurora and the airglow in the visible region of the spectrum is the 557.7 nm forbidden transition of atomic oxygen. The line was first discovered in aurora by Anders Angström in 1867. Angström's discovery led to spectroscopic observations of the aurora by many others, and eventually to the recognition that the line is always present in the night sky—sometimes called a permanent aurora. For many years the origin of the line remained a mystery. In 1925 it was finally conclusively demonstrated to be a line of atomic oxygen by J.C. McLennan and G.M. Shrum. Attention was then focused on the mechanism of this emission, with a major contribution to this question by Sydney Chapman in 1931.

In the twentieth century our understanding of the airglow progressed with the theoretical underpinning of quantum theory of spectral emissions, and with the growth of instrumental advances. Knowledge of the airglow spectrum has expanded into the ultraviolet and infrared regions, with high-resolution spectra now available. Instrumental measurements have expanded to many regions of the globe, and rocket and satellite measurements have produced in situ results at upper levels of the atmosphere. Considerable effort has also been expended on studies of emission mechanisms. A careful historical investigation of the researches on airglow would provide opportunities for considering the interdisciplinary nature of many topics in the geosciences.

Sam Silverman

Bibliography

Eliade, Mircea. *From Primitives to Zen—A Thematic Sourcebook of the History of Religion.* New York: Harper & Row, 1967.

Landsberger, B., and J.V. Kinnear Wilson. "The Fifth Tablet of Enuma Elis." *Journal of Near Eastern Studies* (1961): pp. 154–179.

McLennan, J.C., and G.M. Shrum. "On the Origin of the Auroral Green Line 5577 Å and Other Spectra Associated with Aurora Borealis." *Proceedings of the Royal Society of London* A108 (1925): pp. 501–512.

Maurer, J. "Erscheinungen des Erdlichts

1895–1899." *Meteorologische Zeitung* 16 (1899): pp. 257–260.

Silverman, S.M. "Night Airglow Phenomenology." *Space Science Reviews* 11 (1970): pp. 341–379.

———. "On the Chasms of Aristotle and Pliny." *Journal of Atmospheric and Terrestrial Physics* 24 (1962): pp. 1108–1109.

See also Atmosphere, Structure of; Atmosphere, Chemistry of; Atmosphere, Discovery and Exploration of; Auroras in Folklore and Mythology; Meteorological Ideas in Folklore and Mythology; Sky brightness during Solar Eclipses

Archaeology and the Geosciences

A relationship that became firmly established when Charles Lyell (1797–1875) published his *Geological Evidences of the Antiquity of Man* in 1863. It continues today as an interdisciplinary science known as geoarchaeology, defined as "the application of all earth sciences to archaeological problems" (Thorson and Holliday, pp. 19–20).

In the early decades of the nineteenth century, geology and archaeology developed upon similar principles. Both are historical in approach; both geologists and archaeologists work with materials that have been deposited over time. Both are concerned with determining the age of deposits: geologists use fossils, while archaeologists use human artifacts as criteria for division into named periods or epochs. Evidence from both sciences has been used as a sign of evolution and progress.

Until about the end of the nineteenth century, geology played an important part in helping to establish prehistoric archaeology on a scientific basis, making possible the study of humankind in the ages before the development of writing and written records. Just as early geologists divided geological time into three parts—Primary, Secondary, and Tertiary—so archaeologist Christian J. Thomsen (1788–1865), curator of Denmark's National Museum of Antiquities, proposed in 1836 a three-age system—the Stone, Bronze, and Iron ages—for the classification of tools of stone and metal that were being found in great numbers in Danish peat bogs, on the site of Swiss lake dwellings, and in English and European caves and alluvial gravels (Boorstin, pp. 605–607). In 1847 appeared *Antiquités Celtique* by Jacques Boucher de Perthes (1788–1868), in which he described the discoveries of stone tools associated with the bones of extinct animals in gravel deposits of the Somme River near Abbeville, France. This work, containing sections by a geologist illustrating the position of flint implements in the gravel beds, particularly interested English geologists Lyell and Joseph Prestwich (1812–1896), who confirmed that the human remains were from the same period as the animal bones, thus placing man much further back in time than had previously been thought. Lyell's *Geological Evidences of the Antiquity of Man* summed up the research that had been done on prehistoric man in England, Europe, and America up to 1863, and in 1865 the English archeologist Sir John Lubbock (1834–1913) was able to declare that "a new Science . . . has been born among us. . . . Archaeology forms the link between geology and history (Daniel and Renfrew, p. 44).

In the United States, geologists interacted with archeologists and physical anthropologists in the late nineteenth century in an effort to determine when humans had arrived in North America. Controversy over the age of "glacial man" stimulated the study of glacial and interglacial deposits, as the question could not be settled until the relative sequence of glacial periods could be defined. Many geologists, including William J. McGee (1853–1912), Josiah Dwight Whitney (1819–1896), and Nathaniel Shaler (1841–1906), investigated reports of human remains, encouraged perhaps by the constructive relationship that existed between the United States Geological Survey and the Bureau of American Ethnology in the 1880s, when John Wesley Powell (1834–1902) headed both bureaus. However, according to John A. Gifford and George Rapp, Jr., personal, institutional, and even political factors in American science polarized geological and archaeological opinions in the United States, with the result that the two sides in the early man controversy were often talking past one another. The differences were magnified as archaeology and anthropology became professionalized, reducing the influence of the generalist in geology in this field of study (Gifford and Rapp, "Early Development," pp. 412–415).

The most important aspect of the collaboration between geology and archaeology in the early years of the development of both sciences was the analysis of sediments to aid in the dating of prehistoric cultures. As F.E. Zeuner wrote in 1952 (p. 2), "The past could teach us much in respect of the rate of the evolution of cultures . . . provided sufficiently reliable *time-scales* were available." Guided by the stratigraphic methods of geologists, archaeologists applied principles of superposition and used imbedded artifacts to determine the relative order of deposition and to date similar deposits in other places. They also learned to recognize the significance of interfaces, which, like unconformities in geology, indicate the occurrence of an event that caused a break in deposition over an unknown period of time. Geologists and archaeologists measured thicknesses of both natural and artificial deposits to calculate the rate of growth, hoping to achieve a relative or absolute chronology. In 1910, in his paper "A Geochronology of the Last 12,000 Years," Gerhard De Geer (1858–1943) described his study of the thin layers of silt that had been deposited yearly in glacial lakes, and he proposed the counting of these layers, which he called varves, as a way to date glacial periods as well as human remains from the Pleistocene and to determine when cultures flourished and declined. These methods, supplemented by the counting of tree rings, were the principle means of determining chronology in archeology until the discovery of radiocarbon dating by Willard F. Libby in the late 1940s (Daniel, pp. 251–255).

Although geology was in at the birth of archaeology, and while many individual instances of interdisciplinary cooperation occurred, Gifford and Rapp think that archaeology and the geosciences became distanced from each other as graduate schools were established and disciplinary boundaries were formed, starting in the 1890s. Prehistoric archaeology became part of anthropology, a social science, while the geosciences developed their own disciplines (Gifford and Rapp, "History," pp. 10–11). A notable exception to this division was the work of geologist Raphael Pumpelly (1837–1923) at Anau in Turkmenistan, central Asia, where in 1904 he conducted excavations at a site that had been occupied intermittently since Neolithic times (Champlin, chap. 7). Pumpelly's report, *Explorations in Turkestan,* published in 1908 by the Carnegie Institution of Washington, described his investigations of the natural sedimentary deposits of the site, which he carried out in parallel with the excavations of human remains done by his archaeologist, Hubert Schmidt. Pumpelly also drew on the expertise of geomorphologist William Morris Davis (1850–1934), geographer Ellsworth Huntington (1876–1947), and other specialists to analyze the environmental conditions that had affected the growth and decline of the different societies that had inhabited the site.

In 1936 the English archaeologist F.J. North (North, p. 74) recognized that archaeologists should have a knowledge of geology when he wrote that "many of the factors that determined the trends of history," such as coastal access, surface relief, climate, water supply, agricultural potential, development of a road system, and exploitation of mineral wealth, "are influenced either directly or indirectly by the nature and distribution of rocks, and of the soil which has resulted from the destruction of rocks." Individual investigations of this nature had been done for many years, such as studies of the floodplains and changes in the course of the Nile and other rivers, changes in sea level, provenance studies including identification of the sources of building stone (for example, for Stonehenge) and other materials, and microscopic petrography of marble for statuary. Yet archaeologists were not cooperating with other disciplines in an organized way. After World War II, however, they became increasingly aware that the techniques of the natural and physical sciences could be used to solve specific problems in archaeology. Archaeometry, for example, which Renfrew (p. 1) calls a new discipline, developed as a result of the application of the physical sciences to such problems as remote sensing of sites and the chemical analysis and dating of artifacts.

During the 1960s the contributions of earth scientists to archaeology became centered less on chronology and more on the development of an understanding of the total environment of a site (Renfrew, p. 3). Karl Butzer helped to introduce this new phase of environmental archaeology, which was shortly to be labeled "geoarchaeology" or "archaeological geology," with his 1964 book *Environment and Archeology* and its later editions, in which he emphasized the importance of systematic studies of the Pleistocene for interpretation of prehistoric sites, including the study of soils, pollen analysis, climate, sea level fluctuations, and the geomorphology of human settlements. Butzer called for more organized interdisciplinary work by natural scientists in collaboration with archaeologists in the field to achieve a better understanding of human social and economic life.

The greater emphasis in the twentieth century on the application to archaeology of techniques from all the sciences ushered in what came to be called the "new archaeology" during the 1960s, and with it the beginnings of greater cooperation between archaeology and the geosciences. The "new archaeology," as outlined by British archaeologist Colin Renfrew in chapter 9 of *The Idea of Prehistory* (written with Glyn Daniel), was a turning from the classification and organization of remains by cultural groups toward an analysis of behaviors and underlying processes of societies in order to better understand how cultural systems work and how they change. It meant tackling in a coherent way problems such as the origins of agriculture and the emergence of urban life, which required an understanding of the geomorphology of sites, composition of soils, sources of traded items, and other subjects to which geology could contribute (Daniel and Renfrew, pp. 157–169).

By 1977 geologists who were working in archaeology and who needed a way to share their findings organized the Archaeological Geology Division of the Geological Society of America. In 1986 the journal *Geoarchaeology* was founded. With these developments what some see as a new discipline was formally recognized, although there is still debate over what to call it. Geoarchaeology is "archaeology pursued with the help of geological methodology," according to one definition, while archaeological geology is "geology pursued with an archaeological bias or application" (Gifford and Rapp, "History," p. 15). A broader scope for geoarchaeology is set forth by the journal *Geoarchaeology* in an editorial by Jack Donahue in the first issue in 1986; it states that the journal's goal is to cover "all aspects of the interface between the Earth Sciences and Archaeology." This interface involves a "two-way interaction," in which research using archaeological data to expand geological understanding is just as important as the reverse. The great diversity of current work in geoarchaeology can be seen in the pages of the journal, which include papers on archaeomagnetic dating, prehistoric coastal ecologies in Greece, geomorphological change and the origins of agriculture in Turkey, trade of millstones in Cyprus, and the soils and stratigraphy of a site in the Big Horn Mountains of Wyoming. Whether geoarchaeology can be called a discipline is still debated by those who work on investigations such as these, but it is clear that the field has many practitioners devoted to an interdisciplinary endeavor that is both archaeology and geoscience. Moreover, historical research concerning earlier investigators such as Lyell and Boucher de Perthes must take this dual context into account.

Peggy Champlin

Bibliography

Boorstin, Daniel. *The Discoverers.* New York: Random House, 1983.

Champlin, Peggy. *Raphael Pumpelly: Gentleman Geologist of the Gilded Age.* Tuscaloosa: University of Alabama Press, 1994.

Daniel, Glyn. *A Hundred and Fifty Years of Archaeology.* 2d ed., London: Duckworth, 1975.

Daniel, Glyn, and Colin Renfrew. *Idea of Prehistory.* 2d ed. Edinburgh: Edinburgh University Press, 1988.

Gifford, John A., and George Rapp, Jr. "The Early Development of Archaeological Geology in North America." In *Geologists and Ideas: A History of North American Geology,* edited by Ellen T. Drake and William M. Jordan, pp. 409–421. Boulder, Colo.: Geological Society of America, 1985.

———. "History, Philosophy, and Perspectives." In *Archaeological Geology,* edited by George Rapp, Jr., and John A. Gifford, pp. 1–23. New Haven: Yale University Press, 1985.

North, F.J. "Geology for Archaeologists." *Archaeological Journal* 94 (1938): pp. 73–115.

Renfrew, Colin. "Archaeology and the Earth Sciences." In *Geoarchaeology: Earth Science and the Past,* edited by D.A. Davidson and M.L. Shackley, pp. 1–5. London: Duckworth, 1976.

Thorson, Robert M., and Vance T. Holliday. "Just What Is Geoarchaeology?" *Geotimes* 35 (July 1990): pp. 19–20.

Zeuner, Frederick E. *Dating the Past: An Introduction to Geochronology.* 3d ed. London: Methuen, 1952.

See also Age of the Earth, since 1800; Climate Change, before 1940; Climate Change, since 1940; Climates, Pleistocene and Recent; Contemporary Use of Historical Data; Dendrochronology; Environmentalism; Geological Periodization; Geological Time; Paleomagnetism; Radioactivity in the Earth; Seismology, Historical; Stratigraphy

Artesian Water

Groundwater that flows to the surface under pressure.

Free-flowing groundwater was encountered during progressive deepening of hand-dug wells sometime in the first millennium B.C.E. at Dakhla Oasis in the western desert of Egypt. The first to explain the correct nature of artesian wells were Mohammad Karaji (d. 1016) and al Biruni (973–1048), but in Europe the explanation had to await an understanding of the hydrological cycle.

The name artesian comes from the flowing wells constructed in the twelfth century at the Carthusian monastery near Lillers in the province of Artois, France. However, it was in Italy where an explanation of the phenomenon was provided. Bernardino Ramazzini (1633–1714) described in 1691 the artesian wells that were commonplace in the city of Modena. He drew a geological section, although it appears he envisaged underground rivers rather than porous strata as the water source. In 1715 Antonio Vallisnieri (1661–1730), president of the University of Padua, published *Lezione accemica intorno all'origine delle fontane* (Academic Lesson concerning the Origin of Springs). In it he reasoned that rainfall on the mountains was the source of the artesian water at Modena, and he illustrated his work with geological sketches of the Alps made by Johann Scheuchzer.

The word *artesian* seems to have come into general use in the early 1800s at the time that Chinese drilling technology was introduced to Europe by French engineers. The exploitation of artesian water on an extensive scale followed the success of the Grenelle artesian bore near Paris, in which water rose to a height of 33 meters (108 feet) and flowed at a rate of 4,000 cubic meters per day. In the absence of suitable pumps, the availability of free-flowing water was an important factor in opening up new lands in the Americas and in Australia, where the existence of the Australian Great Artesian Basin, postulated in 1881, was proved by drilling in 1887. Such was the impact of free-flowing water on the public that drilling for artesian water was often carried out in geologically unfavorable places, with a widely held perception that artesian water would be encountered, provided the boring was deep enough.

Geological textbooks of the mid- to late 1800s illustrated the structure of classical artesian basins such as the Paris and London Basins, although it was recognized by the end of the century that flowing wells could also occur under different conditions. A series of papers by U.S. Geological Survey authors provided detailed explanations of artesian water. Thomas Chamberlin's classic paper of 1885, which is recognized as the beginning of the science of hydrogeology in North America, systematically laid down the conditions under which artesian flows would be obtained, and Oscar Meinzer's paper on elasticity of artesian aquifers in 1928 drew together much of the work from the intervening period.

However, there were many who denied the conventional theory (held in the main by Geological Surveys) that the origin of the water was meteoric (that is, due to precipitation), and that the pressure was related to the water table in the outcrop areas of artesian aquifers. In Australia, distinguished academic geologists such as J.W. Gregory (1906) and Alexander du Toit (1917) invoked juvenile (that is, originating in molten rock) and connate (that is, trapped in sediments during deposition) water, rock pressure, and gas bubbling to explain the origin of the water and pressure. These ideas were also supported by American geologists with oil-field experience.

There is still debate surrounding the explanation for the origin of artesian pressure, stimulated by studies of nonclassical basins such as the Hungarian Basin, and this has led to a better understanding of basin hydrodynamics. Because of confusion, the word *artesian* applied to groundwater and aquifers has gradually been replaced by the term *confined*. A full historical investigation of this topic remains to be undertaken.

D. Philip Commander

Bibliography

Chamberlin, Thomas C. "The Requisite and Qualifying Conditions for Artesian Flow." In *U.S. Geological Survey Fifth Annual Report,* pp. 131–141. Washington, D.C.: Government Printing Office, 1885.

Meinzer, Oscar E. "Compressibility and Elasticity of Artesian Aquifers." *Economic Geology* 23, no. 13 (1928): pp. 263–291.

Vallisnieri, Antonio. *Lezione accademica intorno all'origine delle fontane.* Venice: Appresso Pietro Poletti, 1715.

See also Dowsing; Drilling Techniques; Drilling, Scientific; Geysers; Hydrologic Cycle; Mineral Waters; Ocean Chemistry; Precipitation, Theories of; Water Quality; Water Wells in Antiquity

Atmosphere, Chemistry of

An important part of the history of the sciences of the Earth, beginning with the Chemical Revolution.

The discovery that air is chemically active produced a series of new discoveries, inconsistent with existing theories, especially that of Ernst Stahl (1660–1734). Antoine-Laurent Lavoisier (1743–1794) did not discover many gases, but he was the first to offer an image of the atmosphere close to the actual one. He observed that in phosphorus and candle combustion, as well as in metal oxidation and animal respiration, only a small part of air is consumed (from one-fourth to one-sixth), the purest part. Atmospherical air appeared to be a mixture formed by almost one part oxygen and four parts nitrogen. The interpretation of Lavoisier in the history of scientific thought has been and is still at the center of many debates (Donovan, passim; Crosland, passim). The discovery of rare gases in the nineteenth century belongs to another crucial point in the history of chemistry, made possible by great technical and analytical advancements such as spectroscopy, essential to obtain exact information on chemical and atomic constitution of substances. This technique was developed by Joseph Fraunhofer (1787–1826), and perfected by Gustave Kirchoff (1824–1887) and Robert Bunsen (1811–1899). However, research into the definition of the periodic table of elements (Van Spronsen, passim) of Dmitrij Ivanovic Mendeleev (1834–1907) and the revival of the hypothesis of William Prout (1785–1850) were also crucial (Brock, *From Protyle,* passim).

The chemical nature of atmospheric air was not recognized until the early eighteenth century; until then, it had been considered just from a physical point of view. Air was considered by Aristotle (384–322 B.C.E.) as an element. This belief survived long after the fall of the scholastic image of the world.

The English naturalist Stephen Hales (1677–1761), in his *Vegetable Statics* (1727), an experimental inquiry into plant physiology, first showed that air could combine with solid bodies. Hales did not single out any particular air or gas, but he wrote of a "fixed air" in solid bodies. He described the results of his experiments in a chapter called "Analysis of Air." Hale's discovery was a starting point for subsequent research on atmospheric air, which led to revolutionary consequences in chemical theory. Stahl's theory did not consider that air could have chemical properties. Therefore explanations resorted to the concept of phlogiston, which Stahl had used to explain chemical processes of decomposition. According to Stahl, during decomposition phlogiston was emitted from bodies. On the contrary, chemical reduction was explained as

a combination phenomenon. The discovery of the chemical nature of air caused the rise of several theories based on phlogiston, although the word had very different meanings within each theory (Beretta, pp. 180–187).

The first chemist to determine the characteristics of a specific aeriform substance differing from common air was Joseph Black (1728–1799), a Scottish physician. In his memoir *Experiments upon Magnesia Alba, Quicklime and Some Other Alcaline Substances* (1755), read at the Philosophical Society of Edinburgh, Black proved that the existence of this specific aeriform substance explained the transformation of calcium carbonate ($CaCO_3$) into quicklime (CaO), although he did not recognize this gas as carbon dioxide (CO_2). After Black's discovery, many other specific aeriform substances were isolated. This determined the birth of the chemistry of gases, or pneumatic chemistry. Henry Cavendish (1731–1810) presented a memoir at the Royal Society of London entitled *Three Papers Containing Experiments on Factitious Air* (1766), in which he pointed out the discovery of the so-called inflammable air (hydrogen), which he had obtained through the reaction of acids on metals. In 1772 the Scot Daniel Rutherford (1749–1819), in his thesis "Dissertatio inauguralis de aere fixo dicto, aut mephitico" ("Opening Dissertation on the So-called Fixed Air, and the Mephitic One"), announced the discovery of a mephitic or phlogisticated air (nitrogen) (Abbri, *Le terre,* pp. 132–135).

In the same year, the English theologian and philosopher Joseph Priestley (1733–1804) read at the Royal Society some *Observations on Different Kinds of Air.* He described his inquiries about fixed air, inflammable air, and phlogisticated air, and announced the discovery of two new airs: acid air and nitrous air (nitrous oxide). He also described a method for measuring the salubrity (healthfulness) of a sample of common air. In the *Philosophical Transactions* of 1775 Priestley gave information about his most famous discovery: the gas oxygen, or, as he called it, dephlogisticated air (Beretta, pp. 172–178).

A remarkable debate concerned the nature of fixed air. In 1773 Torbern Olaf Bergman (1740–1824), in his memoir *Om luftsyra* (On aerial acid), maintained that fixed air is an acid present in the atmosphere. Such a hypothesis was controverted by Felice Fontana (1730–1805) in his *Ricerche fisiche sopra l'aria fissa* (Physical research on fixed air, 1775) and by Marsilio Landriani (1751–

1816), in his *Ricerche fisiche intorno alla salubrità dell'aria* (Physical research on the healthiness of the air, 1775). Landriani, among other things, described a new instrument, the eudiometer, whose aim was to measure the salubrity of a sample of air. Many scientists thought of fixed air as the result of dephlogistication. Priestley, on the contrary, believed that this process produced nitrogen; therefore the nitrogen was not a component of the atmosphere, but the product of a chemical operation (calcination, combustion, respiration), leading to a phlogistication of atmosphere. This idea was widely denied by many phlogistical chemists, like Fontana, in the *Recherches physiques sur la nature de l'air nitreux et de l'air déphlogistiqué* (Physical research on the nature of nitrous air and dephlogisticated Air, 1776). In 1777 Carl Wilhelm Scheele (1742–1786), who had already discovered oxygen (1770–1773), which he called *Vitriol-Luft,* published his *Chemische Abhandlung von der Luft und dem Feuer* (Chemical treatise of air and fire), in which he proposed a fully alternative theory, in respect to other European chemists, like Priestley. Every scientist had to confront it. Scheele intended to define exactly the nature of fire, heat, and phlogiston (Abbri, *Science,* pp. 53–64).

In the second half of the eighteenth century innumerable phlogiston theories had been formulated, showing how complex and variegated the world of chemical research was before definitive affirmation of new theories by Lavoisier. This was especially true of the study of gases and therefore of the chemistry of the atmosphere. The recognition of specific airs by British and Swedish researchers was interpreted by Lavoisier in a completely different way. The history of Lavoisier's research on gases is fundamental for the understanding of the birth and success of the Chemical Revolution. Between 1772 and 1774 Lavoisier specified that combustion, calcination, and respiration processes were not caused by the loss of phlogiston, but to the fixation of air, whose features however he could not define. The results of his research went into the *Opuscules physiques et chimiques* (Physical and chemical works), published in Paris in January 1774. Subsequently, between 1775 and 1777, Lavoisier stated that fixed air was a compound of pure air (oxygen) and carbon, and that calcination and combustion processes were the result of the combination of metals and inflammable bodies. In his *Mémoire sur la combustion des chandelles dans*

l'air atmosphérique et dans l'air éminemment respirable (Memoir on the combustion of candles in atmospheric air and highly breathable air, 1777) Lavoisier clearly pointed out that atmospheric air was a mixture of gases, mainly constituted by pure air and an atmospheric mofette (nitrogen) (Abbri, *Le terre,* pp. 255–256).

Lavoisier's new theory of the fundamental phenomena of chemistry did not earn immediate and universal praise, for it was only one alternative among many. No chemist was ready to abandon phlogiston. Jean Senebier (1742–1809), in his *Recherches sur l'influence de la lumière solaire pour métamorphoser l'air fixe en pur par la végétation* (Research on sunlight's influence for transforming fixed air into pure air by vegetation, 1783), proposed an alternative hypothesis about the composition of gases. According to Senebier, the different kinds of air were but acids in a vapor state. Acids were composed of phlogiston and fixed air, in different proportions. Things began to change only after experiments upon the combustion of hydrogen and oxygen, made in 1783 by Lavoisier and by Pierre-Simon de Laplace (1749–1827), and those of the decomposition of water achieved by Lavoisier and Jean-Baptiste-Marie-Charles Meusnier (1754–1793), the results of which were published in 1784 and 1786. A favorable milieu for the reception of new discoveries had been determined by the visit of Alessandro Volta (1745–1827) in Paris, in the winter of 1781–1782; Volta had collaborated with Lavoisier and Laplace in electrical research (Guerlac, pp. 234–240).

Lavoisier's theories were strongly criticized by many naturalists who did not accept the decomposition of water. They still used the word phlogiston, even if their hypotheses were quite different from Stahl's theory. In 1785 Jean-Claude Delamétherie (1743–1817), editor of the *Journal de Physique,* published an *Essai analytique sur l'air pur, et les différentes espèces d'air* (Analytical essays on pure air and on the different kinds of air), in which earth, water, air, and fire were still considered as elementary principles of matter. According to La Métherie, inflammable air corresponded to phlogiston, the principle of inflammability. Balthazar-Georges de Sage (1740–1824) was one of Lavoisier's strongest opponents. Still in 1810 he published an *Exposé des effets de la contagion nomenclative* (Exposé of the effects of the naming disease), against the radical changes that *nouvelle chimie* had caused in chemistry (Beretta, p. 287).

Joseph Black converted to Lavoisier's theory in 1790; Priestley, on the contrary, fought against it until his death.

Further studies upon the constitution of atmosphere were made by John Dalton (1766–1844). Between 1793 and 1802 he succeeded in establishing the causes of air's homogeneity, formulating the law of partial pressures. In the attempt to give solid experimental bases to his studies, Dalton laid the foundations of future atomic theory, beginning an experimental inquiry into the proportions of different gases in the atmosphere (Dalton, passim; Thackray, chap. 8; Middleton, chap. 7). Important studies on atmospheric composition in the early nineteenth century were led by Joseph-Louis Gay-Lussac (1778–1850) and Jean-Baptiste Biot (1774–1862), who published a *Mémoire sur la vrai constitution de l'Atmosphère* (Memoir on the true composition of the atmosphere, 1841). Jean-Baptiste-André Dumas (1800–1884) and Jean-Baptiste Boussingault (1802–1887), authors of an *Essai de statique chimique des être organisés* (Chemical statics of organized beings, 1841) determined a method of separating the exact quantities of nitrogen and oxygen contained in perfectly dried air, purified from carbon dioxide (Affronti, p. 213).

However, decisive developments occurred only at the end of the century. The discovery of new substances in the air happened within the context of the search for new chemical elements, in particular after Mendeleev formulated the periodic table. The idea that some elements were lacking from this table led to new discoveries. At the same time, the hypothesis formulated in 1815 by William Prout that different elementary atoms are formed by a whole number of hydrogen atoms found new favor. In order to verify Prout's hypothesis, John William Strutt, Lord Rayleigh (1842–1919), professor at the Royal Institution of Great Britain in London, started a series of inquiries into the density of gases. In 1783 Henry Cavendish had obtained a residuum (about 1/120th of the air used) of atmospheric air, differing from foul air as well as from dephlogisticated air, but he did not attach much importance to it (Brock, *The Fontana History,* p. 331). In 1892 Rayleigh, who knew of Cavendish's investigations in this field, discovered that the density of atmospheric nitrogen is greater than that of nitrogen obtained by chemical means. Separating nitrogen from air, Rayleigh obtained a residuum, showing an unknown spectrum. The notice given in the review *Nature,* "Density

of Nitrogen" (1892), drew the attention of William Ramsey (1852–1916). In 1894 Rayleigh and Ramsey, during the meeting of the British Association in Oxford, communicated the discovery of a new, elementary atmospheric gas. The almost chemically inert element constituted about 1 percent of the volume of the atmosphere, and its density was over twice that of nitrogen. They called it argon, from the Greek word meaning inert (Strutt, passim). Rayleigh also recognized the presence in the atmosphere of a very small percentage of hydrogen (Brock, *The Fontana History,* pp. 331–335).

In 1895 Ramsey obtained a new inert gas working on a variety of pitchblende. The spectroscopic analysis by William Crookes (1832–1919) showed that its spectral lines were identical to those observed in the photosphere of the Sun during the solar eclipse of 1868 by the astronomer Pierre Janssen (1824–1907). These lines had been ascribed to an element called helium, unknown on the Earth. That observation had been confirmed by Joseph Lockyer (1836–1920). In 1895, Ramsey announced the existence of earthly helium. The same conclusion was reached independently by P. Theodore Cleve (1840–1905), professor at the University of Uppsala, only two weeks after Ramsey had.

Later, in 1898, Ramsey and Morris Travers (1872–1961) discovered three more inert gases through the application of a physical phenomenon, the fractionated distillation of liquid air. They called these gases krypton ("hidden"), neon ("new"), and xenon ("stranger"). All of these monotomic gases were characterized only by their densities and spectra, for the absence of chemical properties did not allow them to combine. In this way Ramsay defined the column of rare gases on the periodic table, and contributed enormously to the knowledge of atmospheric composition. Thanks to these discoveries, Ramsey was awarded the Nobel Prize for chemistry in 1904; in the same year, Rayleigh received the Nobel Prize for physics, for his research on the density of gases and the discovery of argon (Brock, *The Fontana History,* pp. 336–337). In 1913 the French physicist Charles Fabry (1867–1945) discovered ozone's presence in the atmosphere. Ozone (from a greek root meaning "to smell, reek") had been discovered in 1840 by a German chemist, Christian Friedrich Schönbein (1799–1869), who had noticed a strange odor near the electrical apparatus in his laboratory. Afterwards, Thomas Andrews (1813–1885), Irish chemist and physicist, described ozone as a sort of oxygen (an allotropic form of oxygen, O_3). The first theory about ozone's distribution in the atmosphere was formulated by Sydney Chapman, who published the results of his researches in the *Quarterly Journal of the Royal Meteorological Society* in 1934.

The story told above of the discovery of the many atmospheric gases has generally not been seen in the context of the investigation of the Earth. This shift of perspective may suggest new historical investigations. For example, to what extent did these chemists and physicists interest themselves in atmospheric field work? Did they participate in or encourage sampling of air in different latitudes or altitudes? If so, how did this participation affect the research, or how did it affect the social and disciplinary relations of these scientists? Such questions have not yet been considered by historians.

Marco Ciardi

Bibliography

Abbri, Ferdinando. *Science de l'air. Studi su Felice Fontana.* Cosenza: Edizioni Brenner, 1991.

————. *Le terre, l'acqua, le arie. La rivoluzione chimica del Settercento.* Bologna: Il Mulino, 1984.

Affronti, Filippo. *Atmosfera e meteorologia.* Modena: STEM, 1977.

Beretta, Marco. *The Enlightenment of Matter. The Definition of Chemistry from Agricola to Lavoisier.* Canton, Mass.: Science History Publications, 1993.

Brock, W.H. *The Fontana History of Chemistry.* London: Fontana Press, 1992.

————. *From Protyle to Proton: William Prout and the Nature of Matter, 1785–1985.* Bristol: Hilger, 1985.

Crosland, Maurice P. "Chemistry and the Chemical Revolution." In *The Ferment of Knowledge: Studies in the Historiography of Eighteenth Century Science,* edited by G.S. Rousseau and R. Porter, pp. 389–416. Cambridge: Cambridge University Press, 1980.

Dalton, John. *Meteorological Observations and Essays.* London: Richardson, 1793.

Donovan, Arthur, ed. "The Chemical Revolution: Essays in Reinterpretation." *Osiris* Second Series 4 (1988).

Guerlac, H. "Chemistry as a Branch of Physics: Laplace's Collaboration with Lavoisier." *Historical Studies in the Physical Sciences* 7 (1976): pp. 193–276.

Middleton, W.E. Knowles. *A History of the Theories of Rain and Other Forms of Precipitation.* New York: Franklin Watts, 1966.

Strutt, John William (Ramsay, William). "Argon, a New Constituent of the Atmosphere." *Philosophical Transactions of the Royal Society* 186A (1895): pp. 187–241.

Thackray, Arnold. *Atoms and Powers: An Essay on Newtonian Matter Theory and the Development of Chemistry.* Cambridge: Harvard University Press, 1970.

Van Spronsen, J.W. *The Periodic System of Chemical Elements: A History of the First Hundred Years.* Amsterdam: Elsevier, 1969.

See also Atmosphere, Discovery and Exploration of; Atmosphere, Structure of; Atmospheric Optics to 1600; Auroras, before the International Geophysical Year; Auroras, since the International Geophysical Year; Bergen School of Meteorology; Chemical Revolution; Climate Change, before 1940; Climate Change, since 1940; Climates, Pleistocene and Recent; Greenhouse Effect; Meteorology; Ozone; Precipitation, Theories of; Sky Brightness during Solar Eclipses; Weather Modification

Atmosphere, Discovery and Exploration of

A process of vital importance since the appearance of human civilization.

Tales can be found in all ancient mythologies showing a deep interest in the atmosphere. The first systematical work about atmospherical phenomena is undoubtedly the *Meteorologica* of Aristotle (384–322 B.C.E.). In the Aristotelian cosmology, the Earth, imperfect, was placed at the center of the universe, and composed of four elements: earth, water, fire, and air. These elements were characterized by rectilineal and discontinuous motion. Meteorology concerned phenomena involving elements of air and fire, therefore not only atmospherical phenomena, but also geological and heavenly ones. However, meteorology differed from astronomy. The latter studied celestial bodies' motion (that of the Sun, the planets, and the stars, composed of aether or quintessence), which was continuous and circular. As in his *Physica,* Aristotle's *Meteorologica* represented an undisputed point of reference until the Renaissance, and it was often confused with the magical-astrological tradition. Even in 1682, Pierre Bayle (1647–1706) found it necessary to write an anonymous work about heavenly wonders and superstitions that was to become famous. The destruction of Aristotelian meteorology must be linked to the Scientific Revolution.

The adoption of the Copernican system, a heliocentric system, led Galileo Galilei (1564–1642) to a full revision of the atmosphere's role and behavior. In fact, the invention of the barometer by Evangelista Torricelli (1608–1647) and Vincenzo Viviani (1622–1703) was achieved within the sphere of the Galilean school. However, such an invention was not only due to the new theoretical and philosophical vision of the world. The new scientific knowledge was also founded upon experience and technique; the use of new instruments, together with mathematics, produced considerable results in the physical exploration and structural knowledge of the atmosphere. A more problematic approach concerns the prediction of atmospherical phenomena. The possibility of using new instruments made possible a transition from mere observation to recording and collection of experimental data about temperature, moisture, and the direction and intensity of the wind. But the impossibility of applying mathematical laws to atmospherical phenomena made meteorology a branch of the descriptive natural sciences.

The collection of data on meteorological phenomena was often a secondary aspect of exploration travels. An empirical knowledge of atmospherical movements had already been reached in ancient times. Great navigators had acquired a good knowledge about the general circulation of atmosphere: the compilation of navigation manuals testifies to these achievements. But the attempt to collect and order observations and experimental data in a systematic way and to formulate a general theory was first made by Edmond Halley (1656–1742). He wrote *An Historical Account of Trade-Winds and Monsoons Observable in the Seas between and near the Tropics with an Attempt to Assign the Physical Cause of the Said Winds* (1686), in which he tried to describe the general movement of air masses, drawing a world map of winds (Affronti, p. 172). Subsequently, George Hadley (1685–1768) perfected Halley's theory, making a fundamental contribution to the comprehension of the atmosphere's general circulation.

The first modern network for meteorological measurement was the so-called *rete medicea,* promoted by the Grand Duke of Tuscany, Ferdinando II de' Medici (1610–1670). Observations were made in the stations of Paris, Warsaw, Osnabruck, Innsbruck, Florence, and Vallombrosa between 1650 and 1667. Systematic observations from the ground, whose specific purpose was to investigate the lower part of the atmosphere, took place in Europe by the early eighteenth century. The project was to record temperature, direction and strength of wind, and quantity of rains. Meteorological predictions were of significant social utility, especially for agricultural production. In Germany, Johann Kanold (1679–1729) began to publish the *Breslauer Sammlung* (Breslau Collection), a quarterly weather report. James Jurin (1684–1750), secretary of the Royal Society, and Louis Cotte (1740–1815) organized efficient meteorological networks in England (1724–1735) and France (1776–1786). In Italy, Giuseppe Toaldo (1719–1797), professor of astronomy and meteorology at the University of Padua, published a systematical data collection in the *Giornale Astro-Meteorologico* (Astro-meteorological Journal) (1773–1798) (Casati, passim). The first international meteorological experiment was organized by the Mannheim Meteorologische Gesellschaft (Meteorological Society) in the 1780s; fifty-five meteorological stations were connected.

A direct exploration of the higher atmosphere was attempted with mountain climbing. The first experiments organized in high mountains were made in order to verify the existence of atmospheric pressure. In 1648 Florin Périer (1605–1672), commissioned by Blaise Pascal (1623–1662), climbed the Puy-de-Dôme, a mountain near to Clermont-Ferrand in France. Jean André De Luc (1727–1817) and Horace Benedicte de Saussure (1740–1799), Genevan naturalists, were the first who organized mountain expeditions with the specific purpose of exploring the higher atmosphere. De Luc, with instruments such as a portable barometer he had built himself, could collect a great amount of data; he studied steam in the atmosphere and the influence of temperature and pressure on astronomical refraction, and he perfected the pressure-height formula. Atmospheric measurements were made by Alexander von Humboldt (1769–1859), who also collected samples of air during his numerous travels. In 1805 he published, together with Gay-Lussac, an important essay, *Expériences sur les moyens eudiométriques et sur la proportion des principes constituants de l'atmosphère* (Experiments on the Eudiometric Method and on the proportion of the principal constituents of the atmosphere) (Crosland, pp. 264–268).

The development of atmospheric research obviously was linked to the improvement of technical means and a connection among international observatories. In fact, one of the most eminent historians of meteorology, W.E.K. Middleton, dedicated most of his work to the study of instruments and their use. There were occasional attempts during the eighteenth century to explore phenomena of the air by sending instruments directly into the atmosphere: Alexander Wilson (1714–1786), professor of astronomy at Glasgow, was the first to use kites carrying thermometers to obtain information about the temperature of the air at different heights. Most famous were the experiments made by Benjamin Franklin (1706–1790), who used kites to study atmospheric electricity (Middleton, *Invention,* pp. 291–292). An indirect knowledge of the atmosphere's composition was reached through the observation of electrical, as well as acoustic and optical, phenomena. The effects of temperature on wave propagation, and the study of light refraction in the air, led to the formulation of theories about the stratified structure of the atmosphere.

However, the real systematic exploration of the atmosphere did not begin until the invention of balloons by Jacques-Etienne (1745–1799) and Joseph-Michel (1740–1810) Montgolfier in June 1783. The Montgolfier brothers (Gillispie, passim) blew warm air into a linen bag 10 meters (33 feet) in diameter; it went up to 457 meters (1,500 feet) and ran along two kilometers (1.2 miles) from the starting point.

Later that year a commission formed by Antoine Laurent Lavoisier (1743–1794), Gaspard Monge (1746–1818), and other scientists was charged to examine the Montgolfiers' aerostatic machine. That August, the physicist Jacques Alexandre César Charles (1746–1823), helped by the Robert brothers, built another balloon, using hydrogen instead of warm air. Afterwards, the French Académie des Sciences constituted a committee for developing balloons, built according to the methods of Charles and the Robert brothers; Lavoisier and J.B.M.C. Meusnier (1754–1793) were members of the committee. The importance of the Montgolfiers' invention was immediately recognized as fundamental to the improvement of atmospheric knowledge. In a letter to Joseph Banks (1743–1820), dated December 14, 1783, Joseph Priestley (1733–1804) wrote: "I thank you also for your account of the air balloons which though at present they only amuse the idle, may in time answer some important purposes in philosophy, enabling us to explore the upper regions of the atmosphere" (Middleton, *Invention,* p. 288).

The Montgolfiers organized another flight in Paris in September 1783: the aerostat ran along 10 kilometers, carrying not people but animals, and a great crowd attended the event, including Benjamin Franklin. Jean-François Pilâtre de Rozier (1756–1785) and François Laurent d'Arlandes (1742–1809) were the first men who made a balloon ascent, in November 1783. De Rozier died two years later, together with Pierre Romain, in an attempt to cross the English Channel (Affronti, p. 279). The idea of carrying scientific instruments on balloons was first realized by Charles, who took a barometer and a thermometer during an ascent of 3,467 meters (11,372 feet) on December 1, 1783.

But the first real exploration, organized for a specific scientific aim, was that of Joseph-Louis Gay-Lussac (1778–1850) and Jean-Baptiste Biot (1774–1862) in August 1804. The two young scientists were members of the Society of Arcueil, supported by Napoleon, whose eminent directors were Pierre-Simon de Laplace (1749–1827) and Claude-Louis Berthollet (1748–1822). The main purpose of the experiment was to observe the magnetic field of the Earth. An earlier attempt in that direction had been made by Etienne Gaspard Robertson (1763–1837), who had noted a decreasing intensity of the magnetic field at high altitude. On the contrary, Biot and Gay-Lussac did not notice variations until 4,000 meters. The mapping of magnetism was not the only aim of their expedition; they also measured temperature, air pressure, and moisture. In September 1804 Gay-Lussac made a further ascent, alone; he reached 7,016 meters (23,000 feet), a record that was not equaled for almost fifty years. He took samples of air, stating that the oxygen proportion was the same at high altitude as at sea-level; his recordings of temperature variations were particularly accurate (Crosland, pp. 262–264).

Further exploration of the atmosphere could be possible only when technological means were perfected. The improvement of the quality of balloons concerned the production of gas, the impermeability of materials, and the possibility of controlling the course. Among the most important ascents made in the second half of the nineteenth century is that of Barral and Bixio in 1850, supervised by the famous physicist and chemist Henri Victor Regnault (1810–1878), who specially ordered the construction of thermometers and other instruments (Middleton, *Invention,* p. 288).

Between 1862 and 1866, James Glaisher (1809–1903) carried out twenty-eight ascents in several places in England, under the auspices of the British Association for the Advancement of Science. The aim of the experiments was to make hygrometer and barometer recordings, meteorological observations, and inquiries into electrical, magnetic, acoustic, and chemical properties. During one of these ascents, they reached the height of 8,838 meters (28,990 feet).

In 1875 Gaston Tissandier (1843–1899), Teodoro Sivel (1834–1875), and Giuseppe Croce-Spinelli (1845–1875), with the balloon *Zenith,* went up to 8,600 meters (26,260 feet), but the rarefaction of air and low temperatures caused the death of Sivel and Croce-Spinelli (Tissandier, chap. 3). By the end of the century, thanks to the scientific supervision of Richard Assmann (1845–1918) and the support of the emperor, forty-seven ascents had been made in Germany; a new kind of thermometer, the Assmann's aspirated thermometer, was used. However, as Middleton points out, "the manned balloon was too expensive and sporadic a means of collecting data from the upper air, and various events contributed to the demise of this kind of scientific ballooning. In the 1890s there was a rapid development of the use of kites and captive balloons. The sounding balloon was invented in the same decade, and finally the mastery of heavier-than-air flight after 1903 shifted interest quite away from the manned balloon as anything but a piece of sporting equipment." (Middleton, *Invention,* pp. 290–291). The antecedent of the sounding balloon was the so called pilot-balloon, used throughout the nineteenth century, in order to determine speed and direction of wind. A pilot-balloon was usually sent up just before the ascent of a manned balloon. Little balloons, filled with hydrogen, had been used for observation of air currents since 1809. But this method was systematically adopted only in the 1870s by Urbain Le Verrier (1811–1877).

The idea of furnishing balloons with instruments for scientific observations was pro-posed by Gustave Hermite. A necessary step for the development of this technique was indeed the transformation of meteorological instruments from simple measurers to recorders. By 1892, Hermite and George Besançon began to send up sounding balloons with recording instruments. Three years later, the International Meteorological Organization instituted a Commission for Scientific Aeronautics, whose president, Hugo Hergesell (1859–1938), organized the first international experiment of launches (Affronti, p. 281). Sounding balloons were fundamental for the comprehension of the vertical structure of the atmosphere: famous experiments were made by Léon Teisserenc de Bort (1855–1913) and Richard Assmann. Further improvements were introduced by William Henry Dines (1855–1927), whose light meteorograph, provided with a complex recording system, earned great praise (Middleton, *Invention,* p. 311).

In the meantime, the invention of the electric telegraph, thanks to Sir Charles Wheatstone (1802–1875) and Samuel Morse (1791–1872), had opened the way to meteorological forecasting. The idea of using the telegraph for meteorological observation was driven by the necessity to obtain all the data simultaneously, in order to compare them and draw synoptic maps giving a complete picture of the weather situation. This helped global connection, the creation of an international organization, and led meteorology to assume an institutional role. A first telemeteorograph had been described in 1843 by Wheatstone. Telemeteorographs for surface observations had been subsequently employed in the late nineteenth century. Several attempts were made to furnish sounding balloons with such instruments. In 1917 an early method for transmitting information to the ground through the wire of kites and balloons was found. During the 1920s, the transmission of radio signals from balloons was tested, but the first successful results were reached only between 1927 and 1932 (Middleton, *Invention,* chap. 10).

Improved techniques permitted the exploration and knowledge of the upper atmosphere. Radio waves were also an indirect means of sounding the atmosphere beyond the stratosphere: studying interference of radio signals, the ionized layer was discovered; and the so-called Appleton layer was found thanks to the observation of shortwave reflection. Moreover, the idea of using manned balloons was not completely neglected. In order to avoid the lethal effects of rarefied air, the Swiss physicist Auguste Piccard (1884–1962) had designed a sealed aluminum aerostat; in May 1931 he succeeded in reaching the height of 15,781 meters (51,762 feet), and in August 1932 he went up to 16,201 meters (53,139 feet, or 10 miles).

There was a sudden progression in the development of exploration techniques with the advent of rocket-propulsion mechanisms and aviation, making possible the compilation of sophisticated synoptic maps of the upper atmosphere.

Exploration of the atmosphere is an important and not very well-known chapter of the history of the geosciences. For a reliable interpretation of this interesting subject, historians of science should pay more attention to primary sources, and analyze social, cultural, and institutional contexts.

Marco Ciardi

Bibliography

Affronti, Filippo. *Atmosfera e meteorologia.* Modena: STEM, 1977.

Casati, Stefano. "Giuseppe Toaldo: la Luna, il Saros e le Meteore." *Nuncius. Annali di storia della scienza* 5, no. 2 (1990): pp. 17–42.

Crosland, Maurice P. *The Society of Arcueil.* London: Heinemann, 1967.

De Luc, Jean-André. *Idées sur la météorologie.* 3 vols. Paris, 1787, and London: T. Spilsbury, 1786–1787.

Fierro, Alfred. *Histoire de la Météorologie.* Paris: Denoël, 1991.

Frisinger, H. Howard. *A History of Meteorology to 1800.* New York: Science History Publications, 1977.

Gillispie, Charles Coulston. *The Montgolfier Brothers and the Invention of Aviation.* Princeton: Princeton University Press, 1983.

Middleton, W.E.K. *A History of the Thermometer and Its Use in Meteorology.* Baltimore, Md.: Johns Hopkins University Press, 1966.

———. *Invention of Meteorological Instruments.* Baltimore, Md.: Johns Hopkins University Press, 1969.

Rossi, Paolo. *I filosofi e le macchine, 1400–1700.* Milan: Feltrinelli, 1962, 1971. Translated as *Philosophy, Technology, and the Arts in the Early Modern Era.* New York: Harper and Row, 1970.

Saussure, Horace-Benedict de. *Essais sur l'Hygrométrie.* Neuchatel: S. Fauche, 1783.

Tissandier, Gaston. *Les martyrs de la science.* Paris: Dreyfous, 1872.

See also Atmosphere, Chemistry of; Atmosphere, Structure of; Atmospheric Optics to 1600; Auroras before the International Geophysical Year; Auroras since the International Geophysical Year; Ballooning; Bergen School of Meteorology; Computers and Meteorology; Cosmology and the Earth; Exploration, Age of; Humboldtian Science; Instruments, Meteorological, before 1800; Instruments, Meteorological, since 1800; Instruments, Upper Atmosphere and Near Space; Mathematics and Meteorology; Meteorological Ideas in Europe, Fifteenth to Eighteenth Centuries; Meteorological Observing Systems, Early History; Meteorology, Marine; Ozone; Planetary Science; Radiosondes and Related Instruments

Atmosphere, Structure of

Primarily a topic of research in the twentieth century, although with roots in earlier periods.

The study of the atmosphere until the end of the nineteenth century was limited to the analysis of what is now commonly called the "troposphere"—that is, the principal seat of meteorological phenomena. After the discovery of atmospheric pressure, scientists were involved mainly in the determination of the atmosphere's height. For a history of this problem, a fundamental contribution has been given by H. Howard Frisinger's article "Mathematicians in the History of Meteorology." The discovery of vertical structure and the study of upper layers were possible only with the invention of instruments such as sounding balloons and meteorographs, and with the research on electromagnetism of Henrich Hertz (1857–1894). A direct exploration of the upper atmosphere was made after the advent of aviation; but new layers were discovered through the study of reflection and interference of radio waves.

The corporeality of air had been demonstrated since the fifth century B.C.E. by Empedocles (ca. 492–432 B.C.E.). Empedocles' theory of four elements was accepted by Aristotle (384–322 B.C.E.), who attributed weight and corporeality to air. Most of Aristotle's analysis of the physical properties of air is set out in his work *Meteorologica.* Meteorology was the study of *ta metéora*—that is, things in the regions of air and fire; it included not only atmospheric phenomena but also geological and astronomical ones. Aristotle asserted the stratified structure of air, and studied its features. Aristotle's physics was characterized by the *horror vacui* principle; the historical development of meteorology was influenced by the denial of the possibility of a vacuum. This affected not only ancient science, but also medieval thought, up to the Renaissance.

The fundamental turning point in the study of atmospheric air came with the Scientific Revolution, in particular with the research of the Galilean school (Segre, passim). The studies on the properties of air and on light refraction and movement by Galileo Galilei (1564–1642) were developed by the members of the Accademia del Cimento (Academy of Experiment), which was active in Florence from the mid-seventeenth century up to 1667. Scientists became aware of the possibility of the existence of the vacuum by observing pumping operations in mines: a column of water couldn't be pumped beyond a depth of 10 meters (32 feet). This caused the crisis of the scholastic *horror vacui* principle.

Evangelista Torricelli (1608–1647) made the famous experiment of the barometer with the help of Vincenzo Viviani (1622–1703) in 1644 (Segre, chap. 5). The identity of aerostatic and hydrostatic phenomena induced different interpretations, among which were those of René Descartes (1596–1650) and Gilles Personne de Roberval (1602–1675). Blaise Pascal (1623–1662) again proposed Torricelli's experiment, reporting his results in the *Experiences nouvelles touchant le vide* (New experiments on the vacuum, 1647); yet the fall of the *horror vacui* principle was not complete. The idea of nature's aversion to a vacuum was definitively refuted when Florin Périer (1605–1672), Pascal's brother-in-law, repeated the experiment at the top of the Puy-de-Dôme in September 1648. A description of the experience was given in a letter addressed to Pascal, who later included it in the *Récit de la grande experience de l'equilibre des liqueurs* (Account of the great experiment on the equilibrium of liquids, 1648). Pascal pointed out that there was a relationship between atmospheric pressure or weight, and altitude. Since increasing height corresponded to decreasing pressure, according to Pascal it should have been possible to measure the exact altitude with the aid of a barometer (Cajori, pp. 499–500).

One of the first attempts in this direction was carried out by Robert Hooke (1635–1703) in his *Micrographia* (1665). Using the volume-pressure law formulated by Robert Boyle (1627–1691) in the *New Experiments Physico-Mechanical Touching the Spring of the Air and Its Effects* (1660), Hooke argued that it would be impossible to establish the height of the atmosphere, because the pressure of its upper layer was so low that it should have a boundless volume. Hooke's and Boyle's new findings were spread on the continent by Edme Mariotte (1620–1684), who perfected Boyle's law in the *Discours de la nature de l'air* (1679). Stating that height increases in geometric ratio, while pressure decreases in arithmetic proportion, Mariotte could establish that the atmosphere's altitude should be nearly 35 miles. Mariotte's approach was followed by Edmond Halley (1656–1742), who represented the relation between height of mercury and expansion of air graphically as a hyperbola. Halley's formula allowed him to calculate the altitude of the atmosphere at 45 miles, but he realized that temperature variations could affect the density of air. In 1714 Halley conceived a model of the vertical structure of the atmosphere, based on theoretical calculus and experimental data obtained during mountain climbing. Halley described the atmosphere as formed by three layers: the first was characterized by a constant decrease of temperature, from sea level to 14 kilometers (8.7 miles); the second one, from 14 to 29 kilometers (18 miles), had a low and constant temperature; the third layer, from 29 to 72 kilometers (45 miles), showed a further decrease of temperature (Affronti, p. 171). Halley's formula, involving logarithms, received little attention for many years. During the eighteenth century, different rules were proposed by Jacques Cassini (1677–1756), Daniel Bernoulli (1700–1782), Pierre Bouguer (1698–1758), and Johann Heinrich Lambert (1728–1777). As H.H. Frisinger has pointed out, "By the second half of the eighteenth century the pressure-height problem was in a chaotic state. The many formulas advocated for the altitude as a function of the barometer reading gave different results" (Frisinger, p. 273).

A further step in the development of a general rule was made by Jean-André De Luc (1727–1817). First of all, he improved the quality of instruments used in meteorological observation. Basing his work on thorough data collections, he corrected Mariotte's and Halley's formula, with regard to temperature variations and capillarity. However, the great mathematician and physicist Pierre-Simon de Laplace (1749–1827) was the first to propose a complete formula, taking account of every variable, such as temperature, latitude, moisture, and gravity. The attention devoted to the latter is not fortuitous; in fact, Laplace was trying to extend the physics and mathematics of the *Philosophiae Naturalis Principia Mathematica* (Mathematical principles of natural philosophy, 1687) of Isaac Newton (1642–1727) to every aspect of natural phenomena (Frisinger, pp. 281–284).

One of the first scientists who used pilot and sounding balloons in the study of the upper air was Léon Philippe Teisserenc de Bort (1855–1913), founder and director of the Observatoire de Météorologie Dynamique of Trappes (Middleton, *Invention,* p. 301). In 1898 he discovered that the atmosphere's temperature decreases roughly up to 11 kilometers (6.8 miles), while at higher altitudes it remains constant. He repeated balloon launchings many times, in order to verify this surprising discovery. In 1902 Teisserenc de Bort could announce officially at the Academy of Sciences, Paris, the existence of what he called upper inversion. At the same time, Richard Assmann (1845–1918), director of the Meteorological Observatory near Berlin, verified the existence of the upper inversion during his frequent ascents in a new kind of rubber balloon (Middleton, *Invention,* p. 303). In 1908 Teisserenc de Bort defined the two layers as the troposphere, from the Greek root *tropos* (movement), for it is the region of meteorological phenomena; and the stratosphere, which means "even space," in which gases are disposed in undisturbed strata.

In December 1901, for the first time in the history of physics, Guglielmo Marconi (1874–1937) succeeded in linking Europe and America through radio waves, from Poldhu in Cornwall to St. John's in Newfoundland. Considering that radiowaves are propagated in a straight line and that the Earth is curved, it was difficult to explain how the broadcast could be possible. As an explanation, Oliver Heaviside (1850–1925) suggested that the upper atmosphere is formed by an ionized electrical layer that reflects radiowaves. In the meantime, Arthur Edwin Kennelly (1861–1939) had independently formulated the same hypothesis. The stratum was therefore called the Heaviside-Kennelly layer (Affronti, p. 293).

In 1913 the French physicist Charles Fabry (1867–1945), using a spectroscopic method, proved there are great amounts of ozone in the upper atmosphere, between 10 and 50 kilometers (6.2 and 31 miles). This region, later called the ozonesphere, showed a strong rise in temperature under spectro-scopic analysis. The existence of a warmer layer in the upper part of the stratosphere was not at first believed. But it was later confirmed by F.A. Lindemann and G.M.B. Dobson: to explain the phenomenon of falling stars, they proved the necessity of a higher-temperature layer in the upper atmosphere.

Edward Victor Appleton (1892–1965), studying the problem of the fading of radiowave signals at night, demonstrated it was due to an interference between reflected and straight-traveling radiowaves. With the aid of the British Broadcasting Corporation, he cast radio signals bouncing off the Heaviside-Kennelly layer, giving hence the first experimental proof of its existence. He thus determined that the stratum was at a distance of 90 kilometers (56 miles). In 1925 Gregory Breit and Merle Antony Tuve conceived a radioelectrical method for measuring the height of this strata (Gillmor, passim). Two years later Appleton discovered a further layer (called the Appleton layer), at 230 kilometers (143 miles) from the ground, reflecting shortwave radio signals. He also discovered that sunlight is responsible for modifications in upper atmospheric layers. Appleton was awarded the Nobel Prize for physics in 1947 for his research on the physical properties of the atmosphere. Robert Watt (1892–1973) named the whole of the ionized strata the ionosphere. Nowadays, the Heaviside-Kennelly layer is called the E-layer; the Appleton layer is known as the F-layer.

Thanks to satellites, it has been possible to explore extremely rarefied layers in the higher regions of the atmosphere; in 1961, the calculation of aerodynamical resistance in the orbit of the satellite *Echo I* led to the discovery of the heliosphere at 300 to 900 kilometers (186 to 559 miles). A remote region, composed essentially of hydrogen and spread over 65,000 kilometers (90,000 miles), was later identified.

Historical investigation of the designation of the various zones of the atmosphere is barely begun. One interesting question is the means by which the boundaries of this structure were agreed to. Another is the role of new technologies in this process. The development of knowledge of the structure of the atmosphere must overall be placed in cultural and political context.

Marco Ciardi

Bibliography
Affronti, Filippo. *Atmosfera e meteorologia.* Modena: STEM, 1977.

Cajori, Florian. "History of Determinations of the Heights of Mountains." *ISIS* 12 (1929): pp. 482–514.

De Luc, Jean André. *Recherche sur les modifications de l'atmosphère.* 2 vols. Geneva, 1772.

Frisinger, H. Howard. "Mathematicians in the History of Meteorology: The Pressure-Height Problem from Pascal to Laplace." *Historia Mathematica* 1 (1974): pp. 263–286.

Gillmor, C. Stewart. "The Big Story: Tuve, Breit, and Ionospheric Sounding, 1923–1928." In *The Earth, the Heavens and the Carnegie Institution of Washington,* edited by Gregory A. Good, pp. 133–141. Vol. 5 in the series "History of Geophysics." Washington D.C.: American Geophysical Union, 1994.

Middleton, W.E. Knowles. *The History of the Barometer.* Baltimore, Md.: Johns Hopkins University Press, 1964.

———. *Invention of the Meteorological Instruments.* Baltimore, Md.: Johns Hopkins University Press, 1969.

Segre, Michael. *In the Wake of Galileo.* New Brunswick, N.J.: Rutgers University Press, 1991.

See also Atmosphere, Chemistry of; Atmosphere, Discovery and Exploration of; Atmospheric Optics to 1600; Auroras before the International Geophysical Year; Auroras since the International Geophysical Year; Ballooning; Bergen School of Meteorology; Instruments, Upper Atmosphere and Near Space; Gravity, Newton, and the Eighteenth Century; Mathematics and Meteorology; Meteorological Ideas in Europe, Fifteenth to Eighteenth Centuries; Meteorology; Ozone; Ocean-Atmosphere Interactions; Radiosondes and Related Instruments

Atmospheric Optics to 1600

Various phenomena produced by light passing through the Earth's atmosphere.

From the early Hellenistic era to the seventeenth century, the Earth's atmosphere and its composition were generally understood on the basis of book I of Aristotle's *Meteorology.* According to the account given there, the terrestrial sphere consists of a solid core of earth more or less encased in a sheath of water. The resulting earth-water orb is in turn enveloped by a sphere of air reaching to the lunar region, where the celestial realm begins. This aerial envelope is differentiated into two main strata, the higher of which is formed by fire continually fed by hot, dry vapors rising from the Earth. The lower stratum is further subdivided into a relatively thick layer of pure air resting upon a far thinner blanket of air laden with moisture that ascends from the terrestrial surface and reaches to the highest mountaintops (that is, several miles). It is primarily to this lower blanket of moist air that we will refer when using the term "atmosphere" in the following discussion. Four specific issues thought to be connected with atmospheric optics were of particular concern during the period under scrutiny: the so-called Moon-illusion, the effect of atmospheric refraction on astronomical observation, the height of the optically effective atmosphere, and the formation of the rainbow.

The Moon-illusion involves the apparent enlargement of celestial bodies, particularly the Sun and Moon, as they approach the horizon. The earliest explanations for this phenomenon appealed to refractive distortion, the bodies in question supposedly being magnified by the thick, vaporous lower atmosphere, much like objects submerged in water. Since more of the vaporous air must be visually penetrated along the horizon than at zenith, size-distortion will be greater at the former than at the latter. Such, in essence, seems to have been the reasoning not only of Strabo (early first century C.E.) and Cleomedes (early second century C.E.?), but also of Ptolemy in book I of the *Almagest* (ca. 150 C.E.) (see Rashed).

Later, however, in the *Optics* (ca. 160 C.E.), Ptolemy shifted the grounds of explanation from physics to psychology, having realized that the Moon-illusion is just that: an optical illusion. Indeed, given his general analysis of refraction in the fifth book of the *Optics,* it is clear that, if refractive distortion were operative, celestial objects would appear diminished at the horizon, since, in passing from the humid atmosphere into pure air (and thence into ether), the line-of-sight, or "visual ray," enters an optically rarer medium. Ptolemy therefore reasoned that celestial bodies appear smaller overhead than they should because they are perceived under anomalous conditions:

Generally speaking, when visual radiation falls upon visible objects in a way other than is inherent to it by nature and custom, it perceives less clearly all [their] characteristics. . . . So too, its perception of [distance] will be diminished. This [is] why, among celestial objects that subtend equal visual angles, those . . . near the ze-

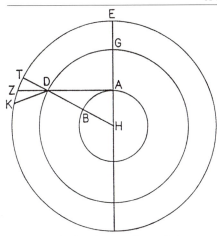

Figure 1. Ptolemy's explanation of atmospheric refraction.

nith appear smaller, whereas those . . . near the horizon are seen in another way that accords with custom. And [so], things that are high up seem smaller than usual and are seen with difficulty. (Optics, p. 151)

Precisely what Ptolemy meant by "nature and custom" in this passage is debatable, but he may well have had in mind the problem of correctly judging distance, and thus size, without relational data. Such data being absent at zenith, relative distance and size will therefore be misperceived when we look directly overhead.

Despite Ptolemy's ultimate repudiation of it, the refraction-based account of the Moon-illusion survived into the Middle Ages, in great part, no doubt, because it was primarily through the *Almagest,* not the *Optics,* that Ptolemy was known to subsequent generations. Among those imputing the phenomenon to refraction were Theon of Alexandria (mid-fourth century), Olympiodorus (early sixth century), and Aḥmad ibn 'Īsā (late ninth century), all of whom were either ignorant of, or chose to disregard, Ptolemy's appeal to psychology. In sharp contrast to these thinkers, the Arab polymath Ibn al-Haytham (or "Alhazen," fl. ca. 1000) was not only thoroughly acquainted with, but also profoundly influenced by, Ptolemy's *Optics* in the framing of his own optical masterpiece, the *Kitāb al-manāẓir (Book of Optics).* Accordingly, he looked to psychological rather than physical causes for the Moon-illusion, his account in book VII of the *Kitāb al-manāẓir* being grounded in the so-called size-distance constancy principle. Briefly, he argued that at zenith celestial bodies appear closer than at the horizon because we lack the requisite topo-

graphical clues by which to gauge their relative distance. Also, we tend to judge the arc of the sky above us as flat rather than concave. Lacking the appropriate clues for distance-judgment and perceptually flattening the celestial vault, we underestimate distances at zenith. Judging them to be nearer, then, we perceive the same celestial objects as smaller at zenith than at the horizon, even though they subtend the same visual angle throughout (see Sabra).

With the dissemination of the *Tanqīḥ al-manāẓir,* Kamāl al-Dīn's fourteenth-century recension of the *Kitāb al-manāẓir,* Ibn al-Haytham's account of the Moon-illusion soon gained currency in the Islamic East. In the Christian West that same account won adherents as the Latin version of the *Kitāb al-manāẓir* (translated in the late twelfth century?) was assimilated by the so-called Perspectivists, among whom Roger Bacon (fl. ca. 1260), Witelo (fl. ca. 1275), and John Pecham (fl. ca. 1280) figured prominently. On that basis, Ibn al-Haytham's explanation of the Moon-illusion eventually became so well-entrenched that, by 1600, no one of even moderate learning in Europe could seriously question it, at least not on principle.

That atmospheric refraction skews celestial observations, especially near the horizon, had been recognized by at least the time of Cleomedes, but the earliest known technical analysis of this effect was undertaken by Ptolemy in book V of the *Optics.* There he set out to demonstrate not only that atmospheric refraction causes a northward shift in apparent position along the meridian, but also that the closer to the horizon the apparent position, the greater the shift. Ptolemy's argument is simple. Suppose that circle AB in figure 1 represents the Earth and that line ADZ is a horizontal line of sight. Let GD represent the interface between air and ether, HDT the normal to that interface through D, and K a star. Then, since line-of-sight AD passes obliquely from a denser to a rarer medium (that is, from air to ether) through D, it will be deflected away from normal HDT along DK. But K will appear along continuation DZ of line-of-sight AD, so its apparent position at Z will lie above its true position at K. On the other hand, because line-of-sight AGE along the zenith strikes the air-ether interface orthogonally, no refraction occurs. The northward shift of apparent position is thus greatest at the horizon and least at zenith. The precise measure of this shift Ptolemy left moot, however, concluding that, until the height of the

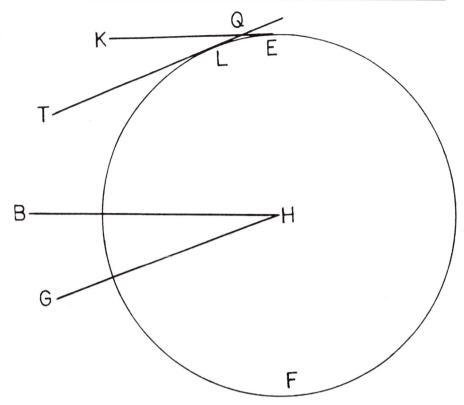

refractive atmosphere is definitively established, "it is impossible to provide a method for determining the size of the angles of deviation" (*Optics,* p. 242).

As in the case of the Moon-illusion, so in this case, it was through Ibn al-Haytham that Ptolemy's reasoning reached Medieval and Renaissance thinkers, the Perspectivists in particular. Yet these thinkers seemed content to rehearse the Ptolemaic account without any effort at finding the method whose possibility Ptolemy had so summarily dismissed. With the resurgence of interest in mathematical astronomy during the sixteenth and seventeenth centuries, though, came an increasing realization that, if the observational basis of astronomy were to be perfected, atmospheric refraction had to be taken into account. Addressing this issue in his *Progymnasmata* (Preliminary exercises) of 1602, Tycho Brahe (1546–1601) provided values for refractive deviation on a more-or-less empirical basis. Although reasonably accurate, Tycho's figures are nonetheless inconsistent, those for the Sun (ranging from 34' at horizon to 5" at 45°) being somewhat different from those for the Moon (ranging from 33' at horizon to 5" at 44°), and the figures for both being different from those for the stars (ranging from 30' at

horizon to 1' at 19°). Faced with these unsystematic tabulations, Tycho's protégé, Johannes Kepler (1571–1630), attacked the problem anew in chapter IV of the *Ad Vitellionem paralipomena* (Additions to Witelo, 1604), in which he undertook a rigorous theoretical analysis of refraction. Although the correct law of refraction eluded him, Kepler did manage to derive values for atmospheric refraction that were more consistent and somewhat more accurate than Tycho's. With the advent of telescopy and the development of a better understanding of refraction during the seventeenth century, Kepler's rough tabulations were eventually honed to effective accuracy by the eighteenth century.

In order to account fully for the observational displacement resulting from atmospheric refraction, one needs to know not only the refractive index of the medium, but also how deep it is. As noted earlier, Aristotle posited an atmosphere consisting of a relatively thin blanket of moist air surmounted by a far thicker layer of essentially unadulterated air. Nowhere did he offer an exact determination of either stratum's altitude, and several centuries later even Ptolemy despaired of such a determination. There matters apparently stood until the eleventh century, when the

Spanish Arab Ibn Mu'ādh al-Jayyānī (d. 1093?) proposed a method for computing the height of the optically effective atmosphere in his brief treatise "On Twilight and the Rising of Clouds."

Ibn Mu'ādh began by supposing that at the very first light of dawn the Sun lies 19° below the horizon. Accordingly, let circle ELF in figure 2 represent the Earth, EQK a horizontal line of sight from point E, and BH a line parallel to EQK through centerpoint H of the Earth. Hence, if GH represents the straight line connecting the Sun's center to centerpoint H of the Earth, angle BHG will be 19° at the crack of dawn. Now, let TLQ represent a solar ray tangent to the Earth at L. TLQ thus represents the leading edge of the cone of shadow cast by the Earth beyond point of tangency L at dawn's first light, and Q represents the point where this leading edge intersects line-of-sight EQK.

So much for geometry. As far as optics are concerned, Ibn Mu'ādh assumed that pure air and ether are perfectly diaphanous. Consequently, even when open to sunlight, they are not illuminated, because, instead of absorbing the light, they allow it to pass through unaffected. Air lying near the Earth's surface, however, is illuminated when open to sunlight, because the vapors permeating such air impede and absorb the incident radiation. What we see at the very break of day, therefore, is the tingeing of the topmost reaches of such vapor-laden air by the Sun's rays. In figure 2 this point is represented by Q, where horizontal line-of-sight EQK meets leading ray TLQ. Hence, to determine the height of the atmosphere we need only compute the altitude of Q above the Earth's surface. The resulting calculation depends upon knowing the length of the Earth's radius HE (just over

6,147 kilometers, or 3,818 miles by Ibn Mu'ādh's reckoning), the ratio of the solar to the terrestrial diameter (5.5:1), and the mean Earth-to-Sun distance (1,110 terrestrial radii). Using these parameters, Ibn Mu'ādh arrived at a figure of just under 84 kilometers (52 miles).

That Ibn Mu'ādh's analysis exerted some influence within the Islamic East is witnessed by at least two instances from the thirteenth century (see Saliba). But it was within the Christian West that "On Twilight" made its most significant inroads, at least if we are to judge by the relative wealth of Latin manuscript evidence currently available. Indeed, the value of 84 kilometers or 52 miles seems to have remained canonical in Europe until renewed interest in atmospheric refraction during the later sixteenth century forced a more critical evaluation of Ibn Mu'ādh's analysis, which ignored the atmosphere's refractive effect altogether. Realizing the fundamental deficiency of that analysis, therefore, Kepler saw fit in the *Ad Vitellionem paraliponena* to reduce drastically the figure for the height of the atmosphere from 84 to 3.2 kilometers (52 to 2 miles) (see Goldstein; Smith).

Among the optical phenomena attributed to atmospheric conditions in the third book of Aristotle's *Meteorology* (for example, haloes, mock suns, the aurora borealis, and comets), the rainbow was perhaps the most intriguing as far as theoretical implications are concerned. According to Aristotle, rainbows appear when visual rays reflect to the Sun from water-droplets within dark storm clouds. In elaboration, he offers the following mathematical analysis. Suppose that semicircle HML in figure 3 represents a section of a hemisphere whose base lies on the plane of the horizon. Let centerpoint K of

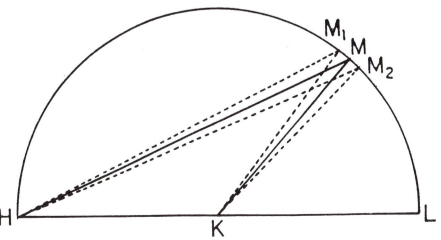

Figure 3. Aristotle's analysis of the rainbow.

that section represent the viewpoint, H the Sun at the horizon, and arc M_1MM_2 a portion of the storm cloud facing K. Accordingly, visual ray KM emanating from the eye reflects to H from some point M on the storm cloud. But such reflection is not governed by the equal-angles law, for in this case (Aristotle insisted) the reflecting surfaces, being tiny droplets, render confused impressions of color rather than coherent images. Mathematically speaking, then, the form and position of Aristotle's rainbow were functions not of an angular relationship but of a specific ratio between incident and reflected rays KM and HM. This ratio depends upon the position of point M, which is determined by the intersection of arc HML and the so-called Apollonian semicircle. The arc of the rainbow is thus described by point M as triangle HMK is rotated about axial line HKL, and the size of the arc depends upon how high above the horizon the Sun lies.

The rainbow itself, Aristotle contended, comprises a band centered on this mathematically generated arc. That band is subdivided into three distinct orders by color, the uppermost being red, the middle green, and the

bottom violet. These three primary colors are ranged according to relative weakness, with red the liveliest and violet the dullest; and each hue is ultimately determined by strength of illumination, which varies inversely with distance. Hence, the liveliest hue, red, occupies the region just above point M, at point M_1, because the relative distance between M_1 and H is shorter than that between M and H, which is in turn shorter than that between H and M_2, where the dullest (that is, violet) band lies. The intermediate colors, such as yellow, which appears between the primary red and green bands, are explained in perceptual terms, the lower part of the red appearing "whitened" by contrast to the neighboring green, and so forth.

While by no means wholly implausible, this model presented serious difficulties, especially when applied to the secondary rainbow (Aristotle denied the possibility of additional rainbows beyond the secondary one). Nevertheless, Aristotle's reflection-based explanation remained virtually unchallenged until the thirteenth century, when several significant theoretical changes were proposed. For instance, in his *De iride* (On the rainbow,

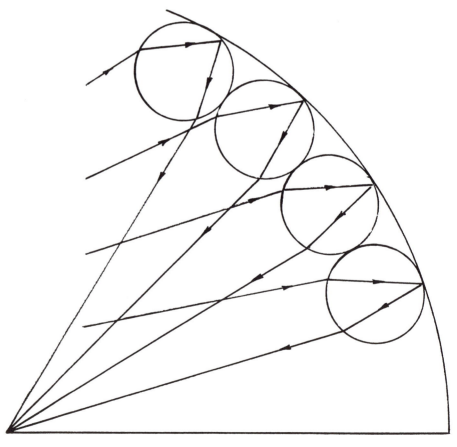

Figure 4. Theodoric's explanation of the rainbow

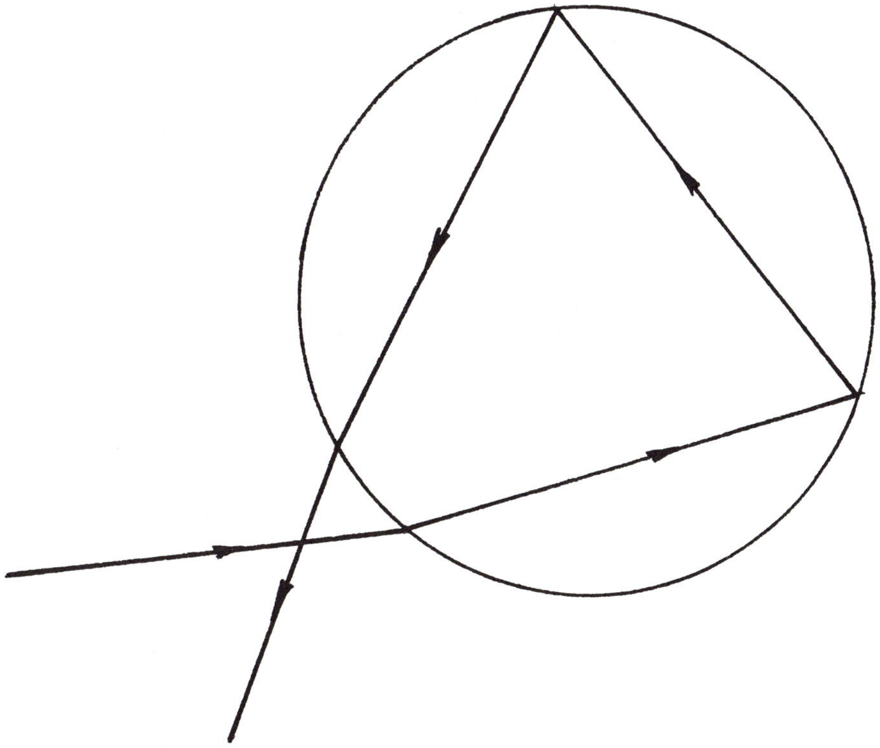

Figure 5. Explanation of the secondary rainbow.

ca. 1235), Robert Grosseteste suggested that, besides reflection, refraction is entailed in the rainbow's formation. Somewhat later, in the *Opus majus* (ca. 1265), Roger Bacon correctly determined the maximum height of the primary arc to be 42°. And in his *Perspectiva* of ca. 1275, Witelo observed that the coloring in the rainbow could be likened, at least to some extent, to the prismatic effect created by light shining through water-filled glass globes (see Boyer).

Yet despite such analytic insights, none of these authorities were able to apply them to a satisfactory account of the rainbow. The critical breakthrough, which came around the turn of the fourteenth century, was made independently by the Arab Kamāl al-Dīn (d. ca. 1320), author of the *Tanqīḥ al-manāẓir*, and the Latin Theodoric of Freiberg (d. ca. 1310), author of the *De iride et radialibus impressionibus* (On the rainbow and impressions due to radiation). For both writers the key to understanding the rainbow lay in using spherical flasks of water as an analytic basis and examining carefully the paths followed by beams of light passed at various angles into and through such flasks. As a result, both realized that the incident light was subject to a combination of refractions and internal reflections within the water-filled globes. Taking

the rainbow-producing cloud as a composite of myriad such globes, each representing a water-droplet, they concluded that the rainbow as a whole was the result of such refraction-reflection combinations and their angular variations.

The resulting model, as described by Theodoric, is illustrated in figure 4. The primary bow is formed when sunbeams penetrate the anterior surface of the droplets and suffer a refraction toward the normal upon passing through. Striking the posterior surface, they undergo a single reflection that reroutes them back through the droplets to the anterior surface, where they are refracted away from the normal at such an angle as eventually to reach the eye. The color that ensues is a function of the relative position of the droplets within the primary bow, those droplets higher within the bow reflecting and refracting at different angles than those lower within the bow. These angles therefore determine the colors—four according to both Theodoric and Kamāl al-Dīn—that will reach the eye. The highest droplets yield red, the next-highest yellow, the ones below that green, and the lowest blue. The secondary bow, for its part, results from a double rather than a single internal reflection within the droplets (cf. figure 5). Thus, the reversed order of colors in the secondary bow, a phenomenon that had so far resisted systematic explanation, follows automatically from the extra diversion of the beam's path inside the droplets (see Wallace).

Although essentially correct in their analysis, Kamāl al-Dīn and Theodoric lacked the necessary theoretical framework within which to perfect their model quantitatively. In particular, they needed an accurate measure of refraction and a satisfactory understanding of the prismatic dispersion of white light. It was only with the fulfillment of these needs during the seventeenth century that a truly scientific account of the rainbow could be developed by the likes of Descartes and Newton on the basis of the model proposed by Kamāl al-Dīn and Theodoric.

A. Mark Smith

Bibliography
Aristotle. *Meteorologica.* Translated by H.D.P. Lee. Cambridge: Loeb, 1952.
Boyer, Carl B. *The Rainbow: From Myth to Mathematics.* New York: Yoseloff, 1959.
Goldstein, Bernard R. "Ibn Mu'ādh's Treatise on Twilight and the Height of the Atmosphere." *Archive for History of Exact Sciences* 17 (1977): pp. 97–118.
Kepler, Johannes. *Ad Vitellionem paralipomena quibus astronomiae pars opticae traditur.* Translated by Catherine Chevalley, *Johan Kepler, and Paralipomènes à Vitellion.* Paris: Vrin, 1980.
Ptolemy. *Optics.* Translated by A. Mark Smith. "Ptolemy's Theory of Visual Perception: An English Translation of the Optics with Introduction and Commentary." *Transactions of the American Philosophical Society,* 86.2. Philadelphia: American Philosophical Society, 1996.
Rashed, Roshdi. "Fūthītos (?) et al-Kindī sur 'l'illusion lunaire.'" In *ΣΟΦΙΗΣ ΜΑΙΗΤΟΡΕΣ "Chercheurs de sagesse": Hommage à Jean Pépin,* pp. 533–559. Paris: Institut d'Études Augustiniennes, 1992.
Sabra, A.I. "Psychology versus Mathematics: Ptolemy and Alhazen on the Moon Illusion." In *Mathematics and Its Applications to Natural Philosophy in the Middle Ages,* edited by Edward Grant and John E. Murdoch, pp. 217–247. Cambridge: Cambridge University Press, 1987.
Saliba, George. "The Height of the Atmosphere According to Mu'ayyad al-Dīn al 'Urḍī, Quṭb al-Dīn Al-Shīrāzī and Ibn Mu'ādh." In *From Deferent to Equant,* edited by David A. King and George Saliba, pp. 445–465. New York: New York Academy of Sciences, 1987.
Smith, A. Mark. "The Medieval Latin Version of Ibn Mu'ādh's 'On Twilight and the Rising of Clouds.'" *Arabic Sciences and Philosophy* 2 (1992): pp. 83–132.
Wallace, William A. *The Scientific Methodology of Theodoric of Freiberg.* Fribourg: Fribourg University Press, 1959.

See also Airglow; Atmosphere, Discovery and Exploration of; Atmosphere, Structure of; Cosmology and the Earth; Earth, Size of; Meteorological Ideas in Classical Greece and Rome; Meteorological Ideas in Medieval Islam and Christian Europe; Sky Brightness during Solar Eclipses

Auroras in Folklore and Mythology

Aurora, with its variety of colors and forms, dynamics, and rapid movements, interpreted by nonliterate peoples. The aurora has served almost as a Rorschach test, reflecting the culture of the group observing it. This article summarizes the diverse ways in which many cultures have responded to the aurora.

Auroras have been interpreted by many peoples as related to gods or other heavenly beings. The Ottawa Indians of Canada believed that the world and its people were created by the demigod Nanahboozko. Subsequently he moved to his permanent home in the north, but promised always to keep a watchful eye on his people. As a sign of his continuing care he occasionally lights fires, and the reflections of the flames are the northern lights. In the Nordic countries the aurora was considered to be an active volcano in the north, placed there by the Creator to provide light and warmth in those cold and murky regions. For the Ostyaks of Siberia the northern lights were a flame kept burning by the fish god to help those out fishing after dark. For Indians in northern Canada a heavenly being, Ithenhiela, was a symbol of good, and they believed that when the northern lights flickered this god of happiness was sending them a greeting. By contrast, an old tradition in Sweden was that God was angry when the northern lights were active. The Cuvash of Siberia had a god named Suratan-Tura, roughly translated as "The sky gives

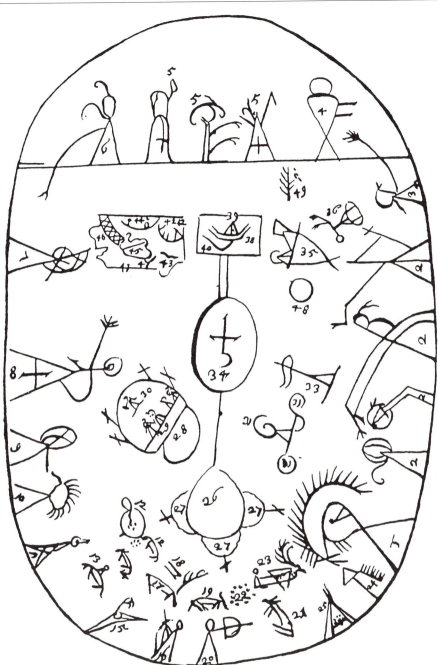

Symbols 38, 39, and 40 on a magic drum produced in the Sami culture of northern Finland probably represent auroras. From Brekke and Egeland, p. 12.

births." The aurora was given the same name, and they believed that when the aurora appeared Suratan-Tura would bear a son. Women who gave birth beneath the northern lights were thought to have an easier labor.

Other heavenly beings were also involved. In Finland it was believed that the archangel Michael lit up the northern lights in his battle with the devil, Beelzebub. They were thus a reminder that each individual had to do battle with his own sins. Finland also is the source of the belief that the aurora is caused by angels fighting each other with burning splinters of pitch-pine. Among the southern Sami/Lapps in Scandinavia it was believed that the northern lights originated in a battle between the god Thor and the mountain king. If the northern lights were seen to the south, it was the breath of Thor and his goats as they swept across the heavens, but if it came from the north, it was the mountain king breathing down their necks. The Estonians viewed the northern lights as a battle between heavenly beings.

Jean-Baptiste Dortous de Mairan (1678–1771) suggested that the Greek placement of the abode of the gods on Mount Olympus, the highest peak in Greece, derived from the aurora. He pointed out that its direction was also the most frequent direction of the aurora for those latitudes. The phenomenon, being rare, was also a marvelous one. Since the aurora generally was not too high above the horizon, it appeared as adjacent to these mountains and as touching the summits. This then was an unequivocal sign of the presence of gods. The dark segment below the bright aurora (often commented on prior to the present century) was taken as a cloud hiding the immortals from profane eyes. The fire-colored rays could be seen as the lightning bolts from the hand of Jupiter.

Many different ideas have been considered in folklore about the source of the aurora. In the Northern Hemisphere many peoples saw the aurora as the reflection of fires far to the north. Many North American Indian tribes believed that the northern lights were gatherings of medicine men and warriors feasting in the far north. Other Indians thought that on the ice farthest to the north there existed a tribe of very strong tiny Indians, and that the aurora was the reflection of the fires they used to cook whales. Similarly, the Maoris of New Zealand believed that some of their ancestors had settled farther south, and that in the aurora they were seeing an atmospheric reflection of the huge fires their distant relatives were lighting as a signal to them that they wished to be saved from their cold surroundings. In Scandinavia some believed that the source was the Sami searching for their reindeer with flaming torches. As late as the nineteenth century many in Scandinavia felt that the northern lights were reflections from the shields of the Valkyries (who were dead virgins). When the northern lights were seen in northern Scandinavia it was said that "the old maids are making a fire."

Natural phenomena were also seen as a source. In Norway and Sweden there was a belief that the aurora was a reflection from huge shoals of herring or other fish swimming at the surface and reflecting light toward the clouds. "Herring light" was a term used for the northern lights up to the twentieth century. In southeast Finland it was believed that there was a species of whale that created waves in the Arctic Ocean that were reflected in the sky. Danish folklore provided the romantic picture of attributing the aurora to swans that had flown too far north and become frozen in the ice. Reflections from the wings flapping as they tried to free themselves produced the northern lights. Similarly, in Swedish folklore the northern lights were said to be greylag geese beating their wings. In Finland the aurora was believed to be caused by a fox with a sparkling pelt running about the mountains, a spark of cold fire emanating from it each time it touched a blade of grass or other object. A common story in early-twentieth-century America was that reflection from icebergs causes aurora.

Astronomical phenomena have also occasionally been invoked as a source of the aurora. Among the Sami/Lapps of Finnmark, nothern Norway, the light was said to have come from Orion's belt. In the most northern part of Norway a linkage of the aurora with the Moon also seemed probable.

In lower latitudes the aurora typically has a reddish hue, and is thus easily mistaken for a fire in the distance. In 37 C.E., at the time of a probable aurora, the Roman emperor Tiberius, thinking that the town of Ostia was in flames, sent an army unit to help put out the fire. We have several examples of "auroral fires" right up to our own times. The aurora of September 15, 1839, for example, appearing in London as a reddish glow on the northern horizon, led to horses' being harnessed to almost all of London's fire engines. An aurora during the Franco-Prussian war of 1870 was believed by many in England to be the reflection of the fighting on the continent. The aurora of January 25, 1938, led to several such reports (Bernhard, p. 10). In England the Windsor Fire Department responded to a report that the Royal Castle there was on fire. In Bermuda the red tints led to a rumor that a ship at sea was on fire. In Gibraltar the aurora was seen as a sign that the end of the world was at hand.

The aurora has often represented activities of the dead. For the Eskimos the northern lights represented the home of their ancestors. Greenlanders felt that the flickering of the lights was the dead attempting to make contact with their living relatives. In some northern cultures the dead could be contacted by whistling. For the Chukchi of northern Siberia different aspects of the aurora reflected different fates of the dead: the whitish flecks showed those who had died of infectious diseases, the red flecks those who had been stabbed to death, and the dark flecks those who had died of nervous illness. In many parts of Scandinavia the aurora was

A Chinese sketch of auroras and other celestial phenomena, from a manuscript of 1652. Reprinted from Brekke and Egeland, p. 46.

considered to be the abode of virgins, generally elderly unmarried women. In the Nordic countries the northern lights were regarded as being especially dangerous for women.

The rapid movements of the aurora lend themselves readily to the concept of dancing. In Scotland and the islands to the north the aurora is known as "The Merry Dancers." This designation was imported to the Hudson Bay region of Canada by Scottish islanders who formed much of the personnel of the Hudson Bay Company. In Scotland these merry dancers are supernatural beings warring in the heavens for the favor of a beautiful woman. "The Merry Dancers" was also a common designation among the Indians of North America, where they were seen as gods dancing above the sky. The Scandinavians also associated the northern lights with dance, and an old Swedish name for it was *Polka*. In western Norway elderly unmarried women were thought to go to the northern lights after

death, and to be dancing and waving white mittens. "She is so old she'll soon be off to the northern lights," was a well-known expression.

The rapid movements of the aurora also lend themselves to the idea of the play of spirits. West Greenlanders felt that the aurora showed the dead spirits playing, using walrus tusks for balls. East Greenlanders also felt that the spirits were playing football, but here the balls were the afterbirth of still-born babies and those who had been born in secret. The Chukchi of northern Siberia believed that the flickering rays of the aurora were dead spirits playing ball with a walrus head. The Eskimos of Baffin Island believed that the aurora was the spirits of those who had committed suicide, playing with a living walrus head.

Violence has often been associated with the aurora. Some Scots saw the aurora as an unending battle between warriors. The Estonians also saw the northern lights as a battle between heavenly beings. The Tlingit Indians of Alaska believed that the souls of those who died in battle went up to the sky, and when they fought, the northern lights were formed, prophesying disaster and bloodshed on Earth. Similarly, the Chuchus assigned the northern lights as the home of those who had died a violent death. The Sami/Lapps also felt that the aurora represented the blood shed in fights between souls of the murdered and those who had fallen in battle.

In most folklore the aurora has been regarded with fear. Alaskan Eskimos would take their children inside when the aurora appeared, to prevent their heads' being taken to be used as balls. Similarly, in many districts of Norway it was believed that the northern lights would chop off the heads of those who stood watching them for too long. The Sami of Finnmark feared that the aurora could take, or even kill, their children. In Finnmark it was believed that the northern lights would oscillate rapidly if a child began to mock them, and would finally come down and take the child's life. Sami children feared that the lights might come down and tear their eyes out. A less drastic result was feared in the Faroe Islands: if children went outside bareheaded, the aurora would strike and singe their hair off. Among the Sami, women with their heads uncovered were faced with having their hair torn out during an aurora. In Sweden people were admonished not to cut their hair beneath the flames of the northern lights. Pregnant women in Iceland believed that gazing at the aurora would cause the child they were carrying to become cross-eyed.

Mocking the aurora was fraught with danger. In large areas of Norway there was a common belief that the aurora would kill those who mocked them. In northern Norway the inhabitants believed that waving at the northern lights would make them descend to Earth and wreak havoc and destruction. Around Tromsö it was believed that if anyone began to laugh at the aurora he would become paralyzed, "for in doing so one had scoffed at the power of the Almighty." Similarly, in other places in northern Scandinavia, the belief was that whistling at the northern lights would cause paralysis.

Despite the fact that aurora occur at altitudes of 80 kilometers (50 miles) and above, many cultures believe that the movement of the aurora can be influenced by actions of people on the ground. The Eskimos believed that by whistling the auroral movements could be increased, and if one could hear the rustling noise, sometimes reported as connected with the aurora, then contact had been made. The common Lappish/Samisk name for the northern lights, *Guovsahas*, actually means "the audible light." The northern lights were even a symbol on their magic drums. In many places in Scandinavia it was felt that the northern lights would crackle and sparkle even more brightly if one waved a large, white piece of clothing, or a sheet. Even in the 1990s most people in the Nordic countries have childhood memories of waving pieces of white clothing at the play of lights, and remember thinking that its movement increased vigorously as they waved. The Sami felt that chanting could result in auroral sound. The Fox Indians believed that by whistling they could summon the spirits, who would then light up the ground. Alaskan Eskimos believed that the harmful aurora could be staved off by waving a sharp knife or singing. Similarly, the Sami mitigated the dangers of the northern lights by pointing an iron implement at them. A more recent, and contrasting belief, was that of the well-known ice pilot Elling Carlsen (1819–1900), who would remove every piece of metal on him in order not to bring down the wrath of the northern lights upon him.

The aurora, occurring in the heavens, and often with red coloration, could easily be seen as an omen or portent of war and conflagration, or some other disaster. In China observations of heavenly phenomena, including auroras, were carried out by royal decree in order to aid in foretelling future events. As far back as 502 B.C.E. "burning spears" were seen in the sky above Rome, and interpreted as an omen of a subsequent enemy attack in which the Roman consul Posthumius lost a great battle. In 507 C.E. "incandescent armies" and "blood" were seen in the skies above Rome, accompanied by the sound of trumpets, about the time of the Lombard attack (Eather, chap. 2). Auroral displays in 1582 and 1702 seen in Bergen, Norway, were taken as omens portending subsequent major fires. In southern Norway there was a belief that the northern lights prophesied war if they extended south of the maximum solar height. A proverb from the same area states: "Northern lights red, war ahead." The memorable aurora of February 23, 1716, happened to take place on the day of Lord Derwentwater's execution, and were thereafter known for some time in the north of England as "Lord Derwentwater's Lights" (R.G.).

Where the individual or society was

The oldest known realistic representation from Scandinavia of an aurora, originally printed in K. Lem, Beskrivelse over Finnmarkens Lapper (A Description of Finnmark's Lapps, *1767). Reprinted from Brekke and Egeland, p. 13.*

deeply religious, the occurrence of an aurora reflected this. Thus when Martin Luther (1483–1546) witnessed the aurora in 1525 he was said to have quoted St. Paul: "Put on the whole armour of God, that ye may be able to stand against the wiles of the devil. For we wrestle not against flesh and blood, but against principalities, against powers, against the rulers of the darkness of this world, against spiritual wickedness in high places" (Ephesians 6: 11–12). In 1570, in Bohemia, an aurora was seen as having pillars with flames running down them like drops of blood. "Everybody was appalled at the sight and said they had never seen or heard about such a terrible sight in their living memory." The contemporary text of this description concludes: "Therefore, good Christian people, take this gruesome omen to heart and pray to God that he may lessen our punishment" (Brekke and Egeland, plate III). In New England the reappearance of the aurora in 1719, after a long absence, filled the country with alarm, and people believed that it was a sign of the second coming, and that the last judgment was about to begin. There was little sleep in New England that night (Lovering, p. 102).

It is not surprising that such a dramatic phenomenon as a large auroral display in the polar night against a background of a star-spangled firmament should occupy a central place in the mythology of people living in close contact with nature. Much of this article has been drawn from Brekke and Egeland (pp. 10–23), which should be referred to unless otherwise noted in the text. Analyses of these views of aurora by anthropologists, psychologists, and others would be most useful, especially in comparison with myth about other natural phenomena such as weather, floods, and volcanoes.

Sam Silverman
Alv Egeland

Bibliography
Bernhard, Hubert J. "Northern Lights Come South." *Sky* 2 (March 1938): p. 10.
Brekke, Asgeir, and Alv Egeland. *The Northern Lights: Their Heritage and Science.* Oslo: Grondahl Dreyer, 1994.
de Mairan, Jean Jacques Dortous. "Conjectures sur l'origine de la Fable de l'Olympe." *Memoires de l'Academie Royale des Inscriptions and Belles-Lettres* 25 (1754): pp. 183–215.
Eather, Robert H. *Majestic Lights.* Washington, D.C.: American Geophysical Union, 1980.
Lovering, Joseph. "On the Secular Periodicity of the Aurora Borealis." *Memoirs of the American Academy of Arts and Sciences* 9 (1867): pp. 101–111.
R.G. "The Earliest Mention of the Aurora Borealis." *Nature* 3 (1870): p. 46.

See also Atmosphere, Chemistry of; Atmosphere, Discovery and Exploration of; Atmosphere, Structure of; Auroras before the International Geophysical Year; Auroras since the International Geophysical Year; Cosmology and the Earth in the Pre-Modern Orient; Meteorological Ideas in Folklore and Mythology; Meteorological Ideas in the Pre-Modern Orient; Skybrightness during Solar Eclipses

Auroras, before the International Geophysical Year

Also known as northern lights, polar lights, and by other names; a rapidly changing display of color and motion in the night sky consisting of luminous emissions from particle excited atoms or molecules at heights typically above 80 kilometers (50 miles).

The aurora, like other heavenly phenomena, has stirred the human imagination and curiosity since earliest times. Certain passages in the Hebrew Bible can be interpreted as reflecting auroral phenomena. Thus the wheel that turned but did not move in the first chapter of Ezekiel can be interpreted as an aurora (Link, p. 301). Similarly, Frantisek Link lists biblical passages from Jeremiah (1:13) and Zechariah (1:7–8) as well as Ezekiel (1:1) as the first auroral notations in his catalogue (1962). Annals from the centuries before the Common Era in China, where heavenly phenomena were observed as omens and portents, also provide descriptions that are clearly auroral. Typically these notations are of fire in the sky, or similar descriptions, that can easily be identified as the diffuse red glow usually observed in low-latitude auroras.

In the classical Greek and Roman period such celestial observations were viewed as natural phenomena. In Aristotle, Pliny, and Seneca, descriptions of what are clearly auroras are denoted as *chasmata,* a term that continued to be used until at least the time of Tycho Brahe (1546–1601) and Johannes Kepler (1571–1630). Occasionally these were also seen as portents of coming events, typically wars, disasters, and plagues.

In the Medieval period auroras in Europe were usually again interpreted as omens and portents, and as such were included in the catalogue (1552) of Julius Obsequens. Auroral notations can be found in the annals of monasteries and cities during this period. A more naturalistic approach is found in the Norse literature in "The King's Mirror," dating from about 1250. In this book the aurora was described in detail, including the notation that when "these rays are at their highest and brightest, they give forth so much light that people can easily find their way and can even go hunting." The origin of the aurora was given as absorption of light from the midnight Sun during the summer and reradiation of this light in winter time; but reflections or sunlight were also listed as possibilities (Brekke and Egeland, p. 31).

In the sixteenth century, with the development of printing in Europe, notices or reports of noteworthy events appeared. These ephemera often contained illustrations of the aurora, seen as such things as armies fighting in the air, or as candles. Such an interpretation of the aurora can be found as late as 1870,

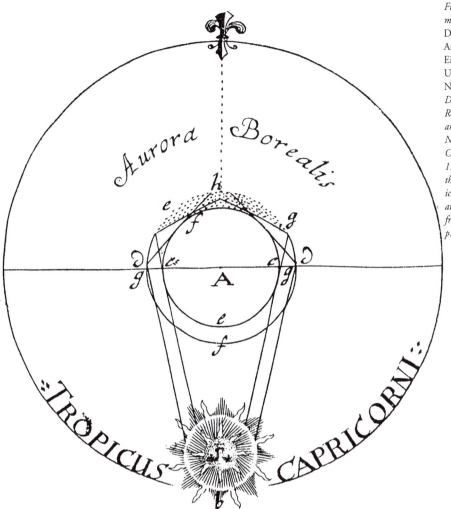

Figure 1. In his 1724 monograph Historische Demonstration und Anmerkung über die Eigenschaften und Ursachen der sogenannten Nord-Lichts *(Historical Demonstration and Remark on the Properties and Causes of the So-called Northern Lights), Jens Christian Spidberg (1684–1762) explained auroras as the Sun's rays reflected from ice crystals in the upper atmosphere. Reproduced from Brekke and Egeland, p. 59.*

when some people in England interpreted the great aurora of that year as being the light from battles of the Franco-Prussian war, which was then raging (*Nature* 2 [1870]: p. 520).

From the Renaissance to the present the aurora has been interpreted and discussed in naturalistic terms. Observations of the aurora from 1582 to 1598, in connection with his astronomical observations, were included in the register of Tycho Brahe. The internationally accepted term "aurora borealis" was first used in a publication by Pierre Gassendi (1592–1655) in 1649 in connection with the aurora of September 13, 1621. It is likely that the term actually originated with Galileo (Siscoe). The Norwegian priest Peder Clausson Friis (1545–1614), about the year 1600, by comparing old Norse records with his own observations, noted that the geographical position of the aurora had moved significantly equatorwards over the preceding four hundred years.

The eighteenth century saw major advances in auroral research (figure 1), perhaps stimulated by the increased activity that followed the prolonged solar activity minimum (roughly 1650–1715) now designated as the Maunder Minimum, named after Edward Walter Maunder (1851–1928), who wrote about it in detail in the 1890s (Eddy). The existence of the activity minimum in sunspots had been noted earlier by Derham in 1711, Lalande in 1792, William Herschel in 1801, and Sporer in 1887 and 1889. Jean-Jacques Dortous de Mairan (1678–1771) noted the minimum in auroral activity during this in-

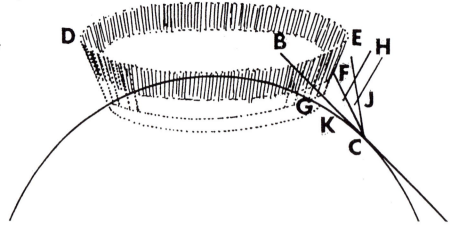

Figure 2. Christopher Hansteen (1784–1873) contributed most significantly to geomagnetic research. He also proposed the existence of the auroral oval in 1827. Reproduced from Brekke and Egeland, p. 80.

terval in 1733, and Agnes Clerke, in 1894, following the publication of Maunder's paper, noted the relative absence of auroras in England during that period.

Edmond Halley (1656–1742), after viewing the aurora of 1716, the first widely observed in England in more than a hundred years, postulated a connection between the aurora and the Earth's magnetism, and sought an explanation of the phenomenon as the result of the evaporation of gases into the atmosphere. Halley also realized that the auroral rays lie along the magnetic field lines, an observation later stated more explicitly by the Swedish scientist Johann Carl Wilcke (1732–1796) in 1770. Celsius (1701–1744) pro-

Figure 3. Fritjof Nansen (1861–1930), best known for his Arctic exploration, also studied auroras and made this striking print of a solitary individual walking beneath its sweeping form. He published this in Nord i Tåkeheimen *(In Northern Mists, 1911). Reproduced from Brekke and Egeland, p. 37.*

posed simultaneous observations from different sites. Correspondence between Celsius and Hiorter in Uppsala and Graham in London established simultaneity of auroral occurrence in England and Sweden. Celsius's brother-in-law, Hiorter (1696–1750) discovered that the aurora is correlated with variations in the magnetic compass needle (Brekke and Egeland, pp. 61–62).

The greatest stimulus to auroral studies in the eighteenth century was the publication of *Traité Physique et Historique de l'Aurore Boréale* by Mairan in 1733 (second edition, with numerous additions in 1754). This contained a wide-ranging and thorough discussion of all phases of auroral phenomenology and theory, and included a catalogue of auroras. Mairan dismissed many of the existing theories, and expressed the view that auroras are caused when gas of solar origin penetrates the Earth's atmosphere. Accordingly he proposed that auroras should also occur in the Southern Hemisphere, as was later observed by Captain James Cook in 1773.

That the aurora is an electrical phenomenon was proposed by Erich Pontoppidan (1698–1764) in 1752. Benjamin Franklin (1706–1790) saw the aurora as constituting the northern part of an electrical circulation system from the equator to the Arctic regions (Silverman). In the eighteenth and early nineteenth centuries auroral observations expanded in temperate latitudes and such observations in Arctic areas were extended as routine parts of scientific work carried out by survey and exploring ships (figures 2 and 3). Determinations of auroral heights and attempts to relate auroral occurrences to other solar and geophysical phenomena also began in this period. G.W. Muncke, in 1833, proposed the existence of zones of maximum

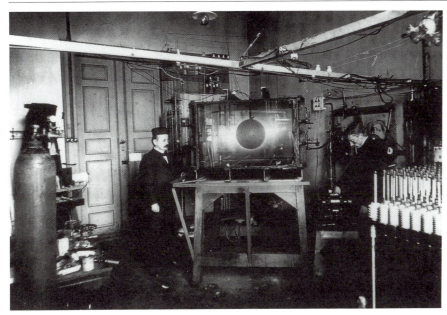

Figure 4. A critical development was the experimental study of auroras in laboratory simulations by Kristian Olaf Bernhard Birkeland (1867–1917). The work of Birkeland, here shown with assistant Karl Devik on the right, played a prominent role in the history of auroral research. Reproduced from Brekke and Egeland, p. 91.

auroral occurrence based on records of Arctic travels. The mid-nineteenth century was a period of production of auroral catalogues, the best known being those of Joseph Lovering (1813–1892) and Hermann Fritz (1830–1893). Studies of auroral periodicities, stimulated by the discovery of the sunspot cycle, were carried out, by, among others, Denison Olmsted (1791–1859), Lovering, and Fritz. The first auroral zone map was made in 1860 by Elias Loomis. The map of isochasms prepared by Fritz in 1874 remained standard until the late twentieth century. Anders Angström (1814–1874), in 1867, initiated spectroscopic work on the aurora with the discovery of the green line of atomic oxygen. The identification of this line as a forbidden transition of atomic oxygen was definitively made in 1924 by J.C. McLennan and G.M. Shrum. Angström's discovery was quickly followed by a host of spectroscopic observations by many observers. From then to the present time spectroscopic measurements have remained an important part of auroral research. Lars Vegard (1880–1963) carried out systematic spectrographic observations and, in 1912, was able to attribute part of the spectrum to molecular nitrogen. In 1939 Vegard detected auroral hydrogen lines and interpreted them as the result of showers of protons being neutralized in the Earth's atmosphere.

The 1890s brought the discovery of electrons. This knowledge was almost immediately put to use by Kristian Birkeland (1867–1917), who suggested that auroras occur as a result of solar electrons being bent toward the polar regions by the Earth's magnetic field. He performed laboratory experiments on a terrella to demonstrate the motion of electrons in the neighborhood of a magnetized sphere. As the electrons hit the fluorescent surface of the sphere the "auroral zones" were observed (figure 4). Intrigued by these experiments, Carl Störmer (1874–1957), in 1904, began mathematical studies of the motion of single charged particles in a magnetic dipole field. By tedious computations he was able to verify Birkeland's interpretation of the experiments. Störmer also started systematic photographic observations of auroras around 1900, and by triangulation of more than forty thousand auroral pictures was able to accurately determine its height. He found that the majority of auroras occur between 95 and 200 kilometers (59 and 124 miles).

Störmer's and Birkeland's view that the aurora is caused by streams of solar electrons was criticized, and in 1919 F.A. Lindemann suggested that neutral streams of ionized solar gas (that is, plasma) were the main sources. The first attempt to evaluate the complicated magnetohydrodynamic interactions between a stream of solar plasma and the Earth's magnetic field was made by Sidney Chapman and V.C.A. Ferraro in the 1930s. In the years around 1940 Alfven advanced a number of ideas and theories of lasting importance in the fields related to auroral physics. He suggested theories for auroras and magnetic storms which, although controversial, stressed the existence of electric fields in the space surrounding Earth. In order to compute the motion of charged particles in electromagnetic fields, he developed a perturbation technique, and introduced the guiding center concept together with the first adiabatic invariant, the magnetic moment of charged particles.

Auroral as well as other geophysical studies were much stimulated by the international cooperation developed during the International Polar Years of 1882–1883 and 1932–1933, and by the International Geophysical Year of 1957 (IGY) and the International Year of the Quiet Sun in 1964. The growth of complexity of instrumentation and in theoretical interpretations during and after the IGY represents a good stopping point for the present survey. For general background, readers are advised to consult Chamberlain, and Brekke and Egeland.

Sam Silverman
Alv Egeland

Bibliography

Brekke, Asgeir, and Alv Egeland. *The Northern Lights: Their Heritage and Science.* Oslo: Grøndahl Dreyer, 1994.

Chamberlain, Joseph W. *Physics of the Aurora and Airglow.* New York and London: Academic Press, 1961.

Eather, Robert H. *Majestic Lights.* Washington, D.C.: American Geophysical Union, 1980.

Eddy, J. "The Maunder Minimum." *Science* 192 (1976): pp. 1189–1202.

Link, Frantisek. "Observations et catalogue des aurores boréales apparues en occident de -626 à 1600." *Geofysikalni Sbornik* 10 (1962): pp. 297–392.

Silverman, S.M. "Franklin's Theory of the Aurora." *Journal of the Franklin Institute* 290 (1970): pp. 177–178.

Siscoe, George. "An Historical Footnote on the Origin of 'Aurora Borealis.'" *EOS* 59 (1978): pp. 994–997.

See also Atmosphere, Chemistry of; Atmosphere, Discovery and Exploration of; Atmosphere, Structure of; Auroras in Folklore and Mythology; Auroras since the International Geophysical Year; Cosmology and the Earth in the Pre-Modern Orient; Geomagnetism, Theories between 1800 and 1900; Geomagnetism, Theories since 1900; International Polar Years; International Geophysical Year; Meteorological Ideas in the Pre-Modern Orient; Meteorological Ideas in Folklore and Mythology; Skybrightness during Solar Eclipses; Solar Wind; Solar-Terrestrial Relations

Auroras, since the International Geophysical Year

A new era in international cooperation in auroral research.

With the International Geophysical Year (IGY) of 1957 and 1958, several important changes occurred that strongly affected the investigation of auroras. New instrumentation platforms such as rockets and satellites became widely used. Advanced optical instruments were also developed both for ground and space application. Moreover, auroral research was no longer limited to countries within or near the auroral zone; almost any country with a space program could become involved.

This article reviews some of the whys and hows of the significant progress in auroral research after the IGY. It also describes the most significant results of this research, including theories, and lastly it lists some unsolved problems related to auroral phenomena.

Auroras (the northern and southern lights) can be seen and admired without the aid of instruments. The earliest use of instrumentation involved the spectroscope, initiated by Anders Ångström in 1867, and cameras and spectrographs were used in the pre-IGY period (see, for example, Störmer, pp. 33–89).

In the post-IGY period several sophisticated optical instruments have been developed. In the 1950s an automatic auroral camera with 180° field of view was designed for auroral research. The early versions involved a configuration of mirrors, followed by fish-eye lenses for use in all-sky cameras. In the days of low-sensitivity film (that is, through the 1960s) the all-sky camera exposure time was typically 10 seconds. During the 1960s and 1970s more than one hundred all-sky cameras were in use, particularly within the northern auroral zone. It was not possible to record the weak, diffuse auroras with this camera. However, both the auroral oval and the auroral substorm concepts were first identified from the all-sky photographs (Feldstein and Starkov; Akasofu, *Polar and Magnetospheric Substorms*).

Auroral spectrometers use modern electronic and data handling instead of photographic film. Prisms were replaced by extremely finely ruled gratings, which give very good wavelength resolution.

The meridian scanning photometer was also introduced in the mid-1950s to measure selected emissions, determined by filters. Typical scan times were of the order of 20 seconds for a full scan of 180°. The sensitivity—less than one hundred Rayleighs, where the Rayleigh is defined as an apparent emission rate of 1 megaphoton/cm²(column) second (Chamberlain, pp. 569 ff.)—was at least a factor of ten better than that of a standard all-sky camera (roughly 1 kR). Thus, photometers were used as sensitive lightmeters. Auroral locations, dimensions, and movements were detected. Photometers were also ideal for recording auroral pulsations. From spectral ratios and absolute intensity measurements it has been possible to obtain information about fluxes and energies of electrons and protons, the source for these auroral emissions (Feldstein).

A significant improvement for studies of auroral structures and rapid temporal variations was the development of low-level television monitors—the so-called auroral TV-camera—in the 1960s. These instruments were further developed up to the 1990s. There has been a vast improvement from the time when images had a temporal resolution of about 10 seconds in the early 1960s to the present-day timing accuracy, on the order of 50 milliseconds. This temporal resolution is important for detailed studies of auroras and their correlations with space plasma instabilities. Thus, in recent years, it has been possible to study auroras with low intensities and rapid variations.

Even though the majority of auroral observations are still based on continuous ground observations, more and more satellites are now equipped with optical imagers. Even during daylight the optical aurora can be observed from space by recording within the ultraviolet band. Since the beginning of the 1960s auroral photometers and cameras have been flown on balloons and, particularly, on rockets and satellites. This three-front auroral attack—from a network of auroral ground stations and balloon observations from below, from rocket measurements inside the auroral forms, and from satellite recordings above the aurora—has provided a lot of new information about the auroral phenomenon. We have seen an explosion in published auroral literature.

Not until the early 1960s—when automatic all-sky cameras were operated over the whole polar area—was it shown that the instantaneous aurora appears along an oval-shaped zone. During the night the oval is—from quiet to disturbed conditions—located between 20° and 30° from the magnetic poles, and its halfwidth is typically 500 kilometers (310 miles). Auroras were also observed during daytime, located approximately 10° to 20° from the geomagnetic poles and with halfwidths of about 250 kilometers (155 miles). The oval-shaped zone varies considerably in both form and position and is closely correlated with geomagnetic activity.

The oval is not centered on the geomagnetic pole, but is fixed in relation to the Sun. Therefore, the oval maps onto different places of the Earth's surface at different universal times. The oval is permanently illuminated. Its form is closely associated with the large-scale magnetospheric structures. Because disturbances reach their maximum intensity in the auroral oval, considerable interest has been connected with this region. It should be noticed that the oval concept has developed from all-sky camera data. Important auroral parameters such as different auroral forms, auroral pulsations, and typical dayside auroral characteristics were not included when its shape was determined.

Systematic investigation of the dayside aurora did not start until around 1980. The main reason for that was probably the difficulty in finding conveniently located observation sites—about 10° to 15° from the geomagnetic pole with the Sun well below the horizon during daytime. In the Northern Hemisphere only sites in the islands north of Scandinavia satisfy those requirements. The spectra (dominated by the auroral red line at 630 nm), the height distribution (well above 250 kilometers [155 miles]), the intensity (typically less than 1 kR), and the character (mainly diffuse glowtype aurora during quiet conditions) of dayside aurora are all significantly different from the typical nightside auroras (Sandholt and Egeland).

Auroras also occur inside the ovals—the so-called polar cap aurora—as well as on the equatorward side of the ovals, normally called low-latitude auroras. However, the occurrence frequency, the intensity, and the dynamics are significantly lower than within the auroral oval—that is, within the zones between 10° and 30° from the magnetic poles. As a result of improved instruments, in the 1980s the auroral data-base increased enormously, and the space-time distribution of auroral luminosity was recognized as more complicated than had earlier been believed. In the 1990s the oval has been a useful concept for references and interpretation of space-time auroral variations at high latitudes. The application of a geomagnetic coordinate- and time-system has put the space-time distribution of auroral events in order.

An enormous amount of auroral data has become available from the new, sophisticated instruments with higher resolution in both space and time, as well as from additional auroral stations, both in the Northern, but particularly in the Southern, Hemisphere, well coordinated with both rocket and satellite measurements. Optical measurements by rockets have given for the first time accurate height profiles for different types of aurora. While the intensity at the lower border decreased rapidly, the situation at the upper border was quite different. Weak auroras can extend over a large height interval, up to several hundred kilometers.

New, small-scale structures were detected in the optical emissions, and for the first time subvisual aurora—from the ultraviolet to the infrared—were recorded and mapped in relation to the more intense, discrete auroral forms studied in the pre-IGY period. In particular, the auroral TV-data clearly illustrated the occurrence of auroral dimensions of much less than 1 kilometer (0.6 mile). But more important was the variation and dynamics within the large-scale auroral forms. New, important topics of auroral physics were auroral pulsations and the electrodynamics of both small- and large-scale auroral structures.

Auroral pulsations are per definition fairly rapid, often rhythmical or quasi-periodic fluctuations of brightness. The period ranges from a fraction of a second to a few minutes. Pulsating aurora even include flaming, flickering, and streaming forms. Only the more low-frequency (approximately 10 seconds) pulsations occurring in the morning auroras can be observed without sophisticated instruments.

An active auroral display may look rather chaotic. However, from a detailed study of IGY camera data, Syun-Ichi Akasofu in the 1960s found a sequence of systematic characteristics in all such displays that he called an "auroral substorm." The auroral features during a substorm, he said, consist of three main phases. To begin with, we observe—from a location within or close to the auroral zone—a system of quiet, normally weak (a few kR) arcs or bands. The activity starts with a brightening of one or more of the arcs and an equatorward motion. Then very abruptly, almost as an explosion, a significant increase

in intensity is observed. New auroral forms, with rayed structures, are observed all over the sky, and very rapid motions in different directions are noticed. Substorm auroras cover vast areas of the polar regions, as has been well documented by satellite images. The movements are generally away from the disturbance center. The auroras are very bright, but rapid intensity variations occur. This active phase often lasts less than 10 minutes. Then more diffuse forms occur, and the aurora gradually weakens. This recovery phase may last for typically 30 to 60 minutes. The magnitude and intensity of substorms vary greatly. During disturbed conditions we may observe several substorms in one night.

Today we know that the cause of auroras is more complicated than indicated by Kristian Birkeland's original 1896 theory of direct entry of solar particles into the Earth's polar regions, where they excite upper atmosphere atoms and molecules along ring-shaped belts. It should be noticed that the aurora is associated with several other ionospheric parameters, including an electrical current of more than 10^6 amperes along the nightside oval.

The cornerstones in the auroral theory in the 1990s are the following parameters: (1) the solar wind, (2) the solar wind-magnetospheric generator, (3) the Earth's magnetic field, (4) auroral particle precipitation, and (5) the atmospheric characteristics and dynamics above 90 kilometers (54 miles).

To explain the aurora, one must understand solar wind–magnetosphere-ionosphere coupling. Some problems related to the causes of the auroral emissions and why the auroral luminosity distribution is so closely related to the distributions of auroral particles in the near-Earth space will be briefly mentioned. When the continuous, supersonic solar wind interacts with the Earth's outer magnetosphere, it is equivalent to an enormous generator: more than 10^{12} watts are produced. As the Earth's magnetic field plays an important role in relation to both the location and the shape of the auroral oval and the auroral activity, its interactions with the solar wind are very important.

As a result of this generator process, accumulated magnetic energy is converted into kinetic energy, and auroral particles stream with high velocity along the magnetic field lines toward the Earth's polar regions. The interactions between the solar wind and the Earth's magnetic field create particle motion as the Earth rotates. The resulting electric currents also float along the magnetic field lines between the polar equatorial plane. These currents—called Birkeland currents—are closed in the auroral ionosphere at about 120 kilometers (75 miles) (Potemra). Thus, the auroral oval is coupled to the solar wind via electric and magnetic fields. During active periods on the Sun, the solar wind can be greatly enhanced. The result is more intense auroras farther equatorward than during quiet conditions. Even though several hypotheses for acceleration of the auroral particles to the required energy (that is, up to 20 keV) have been proposed, the mechanism is not understood. But this energy gain occurs well inside the magnetosphere. The connection between auroral motions and the magnetospheric plasma suggest that the plasma sheet/neutral layer is an important source region.

There is no doubt in the 1990s that the aurora is created by the precipitating particles penetrating the polar regions of the Earth along the geomagnetic field lines, but only 1 to 2 percent of the particle energy ends up as optical emissions. The dayside aurora, on the other hand, is closely linked with the solar wind entry via the cusp regions on the dayside.

The understanding of the origins and mechanisms of the aurora remains far from complete. Current thinking ascribes magnetic storms (with which the aurora is closely related) to different solar origins, depending on the phase of the solar cycle and the magnitude of the disturbance. The largest magnetic storms are related to coronal mass ejections, usually producing shocks when they overtake the solar wind, coupled with a southward-directed interplanetary magnetic field. Other storms may be related to solar flares. In and near the solar cycle minimum coronal holes appear to be responsible for the high-speed solar wind that produces disturbances. The understanding of these relationships, however, is in a state of flux at this time, though much recent progress has been made in our understanding of auroral phenomena.

A number of important questions remain for future investigations. What, for example, are the accelerations of the auroral particles, both on the night- and day-sides? The coupling and transport of ionization between the auroral ovals and the regions further poleward and equatorward are not well mapped or explained. In particular, vertical transport, the so-called polar wind, from high latitudes needs further experimental and theoretical attention. Exploration of the polar ionosphere and the complexities of the intri-cate couplings between regions also need further attention.

The number of scientists working in this area in the post-IGY period has been so great that referencing individual contributions becomes unmanageable. The bibliography includes references that should be helpful to the reader.

Sam Silverman
Alv Egeland

Bibliography

Akasofu, Syun-Ichi. *Polar and Magnetospheric Substorms.* New York: Springer Verlag, 1968.

———. "What Causes the Aurora." *EOS* (1992): pp. 209–214.

Chamberlain, Joseph W. *Physics of the Aurora and Airglow.* New York and London: Academic Press, 1961.

Feldstein, Y.I. "A Quarter of a Century with the Auroral Oval." *EOS* (1986): pp. 761–765.

Feldstein, Y.I., and G.V. Starkov. "Dynamics of Auroral Belt and Polar Geomagnetic Disturbances." *Planetary and Space Sciences* 15 (1967): pp. 209–229.

Kelley, Michael C. *The Earth's Ionosphere: Plasmasphere Physics and Electrodynamics.* San Diego: Academic Press, 1989.

Meng, Ching-I, Michael J. Rycroft, and Louis A. Frank, eds. *Auroral Physics.* Cambridge: Cambridge University Press, 1991.

Potemra, Thomas A. "Magnetospheric Currents." In *Encyclopedia of Earth System Science,* vol. 3, pp. 75–84. New York and London: Academic Press, 1992.

Rees, M.H. *Physics and Chemistry of the Upper Atmosphere.* Cambridge, Cambridge University Press, 1989.

Sandholt, P.E., and A. Egeland, eds. *Electromagnetic Coupling in the Polar Clefts and Caps.* Boston: Kluwer Academic Publishers, 1989.

Störmer, Carl. *The Polar Aurora.* Oxford: Clarendon Press, 1955.

See also Atmosphere, Chemistry of; Atmosphere, Discovery and Exploration of; Atmosphere, Structure of; Auroras in Folklore and Mythology; Auroras, before the International Geophysical Year; Cosmology and Geomagnetism, Theories between 1800 and 1900; Geomagnetism, Theories since

1900; International Geophysical Year; International Polar Years; Magnetic Storms or Disturbances; Radiosondes and Related Instruments; Scientific Rocketry to Sputnik; Skybrightness during Solar Eclipses; Solar Wind; Solar-Terrestrial Relations; Space Science

Ballooning

The exploration of the atmosphere with lighter-than-air craft.

No aeronautical component has had such enduring appeal as ballooning. From theoretical foundations in classical antiquity, practical lighter-than-air flight required the discoveries resulting from Europe's Scientific Revolution, specifically those of Henry Cavendish (1731–1810) and Joseph Priestley (1733–1804). Most notable among the early aeronauts were paper-makers Joseph (1740–1810) and Etienne (1745–1799) Montgolfier. Their first public demonstration, using a cloth and paper "aerostat," was held on June 4, 1783, in Annonay, near Lyon, France, and resulted in widespread popular and scientific interest in ballooning.

Competition soon developed between the Montgolfiers' hot-air balloons and the hydrogen gas-inflated rubber-coated cloth balloons of physicist J.A.C. Charles (1746–1823) and the Robert brothers, Jean (1758–1820) and Noel (1761–1828). Hazardous hydrogen-filled aerostats were replaced with helium balloons during the twentieth century. Both French factions succeeded in sending people aloft in free-floating (commonly referred to as "free") balloons before the end of 1783, with Charles developing the valve and ballast system for altitude control.

Instruments were quickly incorporated into the milieu of early aeronauts as scientists and scientific academies exploited the new medium by sponsoring ascensions in the pursuit of atmospheric inquiry. Physician John Jeffries (1744/45–1819) used a thermometer, barometer, and hydrometer, among other devices, to make observations during an ascent from London with Jean Blanchard (1753–1809) in November 1784. Jeffries also took air samples with vials provided by Cavendish. Blanchard's and Jeffries's triumphant crossing of the English Channel two months later further fueled a growing popular fascination that led to a golden age of ballooning throughout much of the nineteenth century (see Crouch, pp. 71–96).

Whether in free or captive (tethered) balloons, airborne experimentation was performed to answer a seemingly endless array of questions on such subjects as the evaporation rates of liquids, magnetism, solar rays, electrical matter, cloud formation, the flight of birds, and the human physiological effects associated with increasing altitude. Enlarging the data-base of temperature, humidity, and pressure observations remained a constant for scientific balloon ascensions. Furthermore, the apparent military value of aerial reconnaissance led Revolutionary France to establish the world's first, albeit temporary, balloon corps in 1794. Notable among the airborne scientists as aerostation entered a new century were Etienne Robertson (1763–1837), who ascended from St. Petersburg in 1804 at the request of the Russian Academy of Science, and physicists Jean-Baptiste Biot (1774–1862) and Joseph Gay-Lussac (1778–1850), who examined magnetic intensity during a flight in August 1804. The following month, Gay-Lussac reached a height of 7,010 meters.

During the nineteenth century many professional aeronauts, including Charles Green (1785–1870), Thaddeus Lowe (1832–1913), and John Wise (1808–1879), increasingly turned to the adventure of long-distance flight. Interestingly, the Union Army employed both Lowe and Wise for aerial reconnaissance during the American Civil War. Others sought to overcome nature through powered flight, with Henri Giffard (1825–1882) making the first successful airship voyage in September 1852. Additionally, aeronautical showmen, such as Eugène Godard (1827–1890), used the balloon to perform daring feats of skill or provided ascensions to a paying public at well-attended county fairs and urban celebrations—such aeronauts set the stage for twentieth-century barnstormers (Crouch, pp. 171–529). Yet the scientific community persistently saw the balloon as a tool for the exploration of the atmosphere.

In the late 1850s the British Association for the Advancement of Science resolved to sponsor a series of diurnal and nocturnal balloon ascensions by aeronaut Henry Coxwell (1819–1900) and meteorologist James Glaisher (1809–1903). The most memorable flight occurred in 1862 when the duo, in an open gondola, reached an estimated 9,144 meters (Glaisher contended it was 11,278 meters). Glaisher went unconscious because of the effects of hypoxia, with tragedy averted only through the dire exertions of Coxwell to vent gas and descend; others were not so fortunate (see Glaisher, pp. 50–58).

In 1894, Swedish engineer Salomon August Andrée (1854–1897) envisioned the conquest of the North Pole by means of balloon. Andrée and two companions ascended from Spitsbergen Island in July 1897 only to be forced down some five hundred miles short of the pole. Their dream now an impossibility and facing extreme cold and the reality of starvation, the trio marched for two and a half months before establishing a camp on barren White Island, where they perished. Almost thirty years later, Roald Amundsen (1872–1928) and associates succeeded in crossing the North Pole by dirigible just two days after Richard Byrd (1888–1957) and his pilot had done so by airplane, on May 9, 1926.

By the time Arthur Berson (1859–1942) and Reinhard Süring (1866– ?) reached the record height of 10,797 meters for human flight in 1901, a safer method of obtaining high-altitude meteorological data had been introduced, with the self-recording instrumented "registering balloons" (later known as balloonsondes) first deployed by Georges Besançon (1866–1934) in France in 1893. Richard Assmann (1845–1918) refined the process by developing small rubber balloons designed to burst at altitude and parachute the instruments safely back to earth. However, it was Teisserenc de Bort (1855–1913) who first noted an apparent temperature discontinuity in the atmosphere above 14,000 meters during an extensive series of balloon "soundings" between 1898 and 1903. Assmann's upper-air soundings, among others, confirmed the existence of the tropopause and stratosphere, a region that would witness the first Soviet-American "space race."

Just as Western armies had begun to seriously consider the value of aeronautics and to form balloon corps in the late nineteenth century, the successes of Thomas Baldwin (1854–1923), Charles Renard (1847–1905), and Alberto Santos-Dumont (1873–1932) helped shift military focus to soft and semirigid dirigible balloons. In contrast, Germany, under the leadership of Ferdinand von Zeppelin (1838–1917), concentrated on refining rigid airship technology. Yet captive balloons regained military importance during World War I for observation across a stagnated front and protection of vital centers from night airplane attack.

While the marvel of powered flight was capturing popular appeal at the turn of the century, a small minority of airminded individuals, among them Henri de la Vaulx (1870–1930), fostered a piloted ballooning renaissance. Soon aero clubs and, in 1905, the Fédération Aéronautique Internationale were formed, in part to provide organization and guidelines for sport ballooning. Local and national "races," actually distance events, were capped, beginning in 1906, by the James Gordon Bennett international balloon competition. Interrupted by World War I, the races for the Gordon Bennett Cup continued until 1939, when a second European war put an end to the annual event. The competition has only recently been resurrected (Crouch, pp. 531–589).

During the interwar period of the 1920s and 1930s the stratosphere took on a mystique reminiscent of earlier continental explorations, in which intrepidity and national honor were prizes more coveted than scientific findings. Hawthorne Gray (1889–1927), an American Air Corps balloonist, gained tragic hero status with three ascensions in 1927. His final flight, which peaked at 12,945 meters, cost Gray his life when the oxygen supply was expended at altitude. Human physiological limitations chronically hampered the conquest of the upper atmosphere.

A sealed, pressurized gondola offered one solution but also opened a host of engineering problems (Crouch, pp. 591–603).

Physicist Auguste Piccard (1884–1962) pioneered the development of such a platform to further his research of cosmic rays which, incidentally, were first detected by Victor Hess (1883–1964) during a balloon ascension in 1912. Though unanticipated problems prevented the gathering of scientific information from inside the *FNRS* (so named for the sponsorship provided by the *Fonds National de Recherches Scientifique*), Piccard and an assistant succeeded in setting an altitude record of 15,781 meters during their ascent from Augsburg, Germany, in May 1931; the following year he broke 16,200 meters (DeVorkin, pp. 9–38). The flights validated the use of the pressurized gondola and set the stage for conquest of the stratosphere, an exploit that increasingly became an ideological struggle between East and West once the Soviet Union joined the competition.

In September 1932, almost two months after the abortive flight of the *Century of Progress,* launched with much fanfare from the Chicago exposition of the same name (DeVorkin, pp. 56–82), a Soviet balloon successfully carried three "stratonauts" to a new height of 18,500 meters. American airmen quickly recaptured the record before the Soviets returned to the stratosphere in late January 1934. The *Osoaviakhim-1* rose from Moscow to a height of 22,000 meters but met with tragedy on descent when the balloon tore and the gondola broke free. Scientific initiative took on renewed emphasis when the National Geographic Society enthusiastically sponsored stratospheric exploration in cooperation with the United States Army Air Corps.

The *Explorer I* lifted off from the "Stratobowl," a natural depression near Rapid City, South Dakota, in July 1934 with a crew of three and a host of scientific instruments. While the balloon and gondola met a fate similar to that of the Soviet effort six months earlier, this time the aeronauts parachuted to safety, and much scientific information gathered during the flight was salvaged (DeVorkin, pp. 131–181). Other 1934 piloted upper-air ascensions were carried out by Max Cosyns (19?–?) and an assistant, and by Jean (1884–1963) and Jennette (1895–1981) Piccard, the first women to enter the stratosphere. An improved *Explorer II* reached 22,066 meters in November 1935 to end the era. During the flight, Orvil Anderson (1895–1965) and Albert Stevens (1886–1949) per-formed a host of experiments and studies on cosmic rays, ozone, atmospheric electricity, radio propagation, and aerial photography (DeVorkin, pp. 183–231). However, the high cost of such voyages, especially during a period of worldwide depression, resulted in a return to the use of balloonsondes, with the Soviets initially leading the way. Researchers Erich Regener (1881–1955) and William Coblentz (1873–1962) were but two among many scientists committed to refining balloonsonde instrumentation (DeVorkin, pp. 247–260).

High-altitude piloted ballooning made a resurgence during the Cold War as Soviets and Americans tested and refined technology in preparation for launching humans into space and ensuring their safe recovery. Both *Project Manhigh,* which resulted in high-altitude parachute jumps by Joseph Kittinger (b. 1928), the most daring from over 31,333 meters (102,800 feet), and *Project Stratolab,* in which ascensions culminated in May 1961 with the setting of the piloted balloon altitude record of 34,668 meters (113,740 feet) by Malcolm Ross (b. 1919) and Victor Prather (1926–1961), were developed to address such issues (see DeVorkin, pp. 295–317).

Yet, for all such spectacles, pilotless scientific missions were emphasized following World War II with newly developed polyethylene plastic balloons for atmospheric, meteorologic, and cosmic ray research. The medium soon became the focus of an alliance between American public and private sectors, including both the Office of Naval Research and General Mills, as military necessity in the fields of aerial reconnaissance, nuclear test detection, and high-altitude supersonic flight experimentation called for expanded scientific review (DeVorkin, pp. 261–294). The initial *Project Helios* became *Skyhook* and resulted in a wide variety of scientific pursuits, including the use of balloons to lift small solid-fuel rockets that were then launched into the ionosphere. Another outgrowth was the *Moby Dick* enterprise, which attempted photo reconnaissance of the Soviet Union during the 1950s. Beginning in 1960, the National Aeronautics and Space Administration (NASA) launched Echo-series aluminum coated balloons into orbit. Shining brighter than the North Star, these passive communication satellites caught the attention and imagination of people the world over (Crouch, pp. 644–651). NASA has continued to incorporate balloon technology for planetary research in the decades since Echo.

Scientific use of balloons led to a similar resurgence in sport ballooning during the 1960s, a trend that continues. The lure of transoceanic flight led many balloonists to attempt such ascents, yet the Atlantic was not crossed until the crew of the *Double Eagle II* landed in France in August 1978. Ben Abruzzo (1930–1985) and Larry Newman (b. 1947) followed their success by crossing the Pacific as part of the crew of the *Double Eagle V* in November 1981. Thousands of less venturous modern-day balloonists simply enjoy slipping the bonds of Earth, at least temporarily, to sail with the wind (Crouch, pp. 656–667).

For more than two hundred years balloons have served both popular and scientific inquiry in the exploration of the earth's atmosphere and beyond. As such, the history of scientific ballooning is only beginning to be written and deserves greater scholarly attention.

William E. Fischer, Jr.

Bibliography

Crouch, Tom D. *The Eagle Aloft: Two Centuries of the Balloon in America.* Washington, D.C.: Smithsonian Institution Press, 1983.

DeVorkin, David H. *Race to the Stratosphere: Manned Scientific Ballooning in America.* New York: Springer-Verlag, 1989.

Glaisher, James, et al. *Travels in the Air.* London: Bentley, 1871.

Jackson, Donald D. *The Aeronauts.* Alexandria, Va.: Time-Life Books, 1980.

National Geographic Society. "Explorer II." In *The National Geographic Society—United States Army Air Corps Stratosphere Flight of 1935 in the Balloon.* Washington, D.C.: National Geographic Society, 1936.

Rolt, L.T.C. *The Aeronauts: A History of Ballooning, 1783–1903.* New York: Walker, 1966.

See also Atmosphere, Discovery and Exploration of; Cosmic Rays, Early History; Exploration, Age of; Humboldtian Science; Instruments, Meteorological, before 1800; Instruments, Meteorological, since 1800; Instruments, Upper Atmosphere and Near Space; Meteorology; Oceanographic Expeditions up to H.M.S. *Challenger*; Polar Exploration; Popular Understanding of the Earth, since 1900; Radiosondes and Related Instruments; Scientific Rocketry to Sputnik; Underwater Research, Early History

Bergen School of Meteorology

A group of meteorological theorists in Norway noted for their research in atmospheric dynamics.

The rapid evolution of aviation during and immediately following World War I provided the needed impetus for expanded efforts to understand the weather. While researchers had long sought to explain weather phenomena, meteorology remained little more than a pseudo-science at the close of the nineteenth century and lacked credibility among scholars of the physical sciences. However, the emerging demands of flight, both commercial and military, for accurate weather forecasting provided an unparalleled opportunity for quantitative research in the field.

In 1897 Vilhelm Bjerknes, a physicist, became a leader in establishing a modern meteorology following his formulation of circulation theorems that were applicable to oceanic and atmospheric motions (Jewell, passim). His efforts to develop means of reliable weather forecasting resulted in his selection as a research associate of the Carnegie Institution of Washington in 1905. These grants continued until 1941. Bjerknes believed that only through the close interaction of theoretical (dynamic) and practical (forecasting) research could meteorology effectively serve not only the emerging needs of aviation but also of fisheries and agriculture in his native Norway. Hence his desire to develop a mechanical physics of the atmosphere became closely tied to improvements in weather observation methods.

After serving as director of the Leipzig Geophysical Institute (Good, pp. 304, 315), the first institution established for training aerologists, Bjerknes returned to neutral Norway in 1917 to organize the Bergen Geophysical Institute (Friedman, pp. 97–103). Collaborative efforts between theoretical atmospheric research at the institute and practical prognostication at the newly established West Norway Weather Bureau (WNWB) led to advances in both areas and resulted in what became known as the "Bergen School of Meteorology." Fundamental to the process were aerological, or upper-air, observations that were used to infer the three-dimensional structure of the lower atmosphere. When such means were unavailable the Bergen meteorologists used indirect aerology—observable weather phenomena, especially cloud type and associated precipitation. By melding synoptic observations and analysis of the sky, Bergen meteorologists became ever more successful in localized weather prediction (Friedman, chap. 8).

Jacob Bjerknes, son and research assistant of the elder Bjerknes and superintendent of the WNWB, developed the concept of frontal analysis when he derived a new cyclone (low-pressure) model while interpreting weather data from a dense network of observation stations along the Norwegian coast. His identification and explanation of steering and squall surfaces (warm and cold fronts, respectively) provided the Bergen meteorologists with identifiable weather phenomena for prognostication (Friedman, chap. 6).

As weather observation networks and international cooperation expanded after 1918, Bergen meteorologists Tor Bergeron, Ernst Calwagen, and Halvor Solberg, among others, refined air-mass analysis by postulating the concepts of the occlusion process, occluded fronts, and the polar front. As an example, the polar front was discerned on synoptic charts as a single line of discontinuity that covered the Northern Hemisphere. It provided a conceptual model for understanding general atmospheric circulation and the formation of cyclones and anticyclones (high-pressure systems) (Friedman, chaps. 9–11).

Weather services soon began implementing and modifying Bergen-school air-mass analysis. United States Weather Bureau adoption came in the mid-1930s. With international recognition achieved, researchers began to leave isolated Bergen to continue their work. Vilhelm Bjerknes accepted a professorship at Oslo in 1926. Jacob Bjerknes supervised the WNWB until 1931, then served as professor at the Bergen Geophysical Institute until 1940, when he became the first professor of meteorology at the University of California at Los Angeles. Tor Bergeron taught at Stockholm and Uppsala, where he became a leader in the field of cloud physics. During the interwar period meteorologists at the Bergen Geophysical Institute and the WNWB provided the foundations for the scientific rationalization of meteorology.

Some historical research on the Bergen School has already been undertaken, the most prominent example being Robert Marc Friedman's *Appropriating the Weather* of 1989. In addition to publications on Bjerknes listed in the bibliography, those by other Bergen meteorologists may be found in the *Monthly Weather Review,* the *Quarterly Journal of the Royal Meteorological Society,* and *Meteorologische Zeitschrift.*

William E. Fischer, Jr.

Bibliography

Friedman, Robert Marc. *Appropriating the Weather: Vilhelm Bjerknes and the Construction of a Modern Meteorology.* Ithaca, N.Y.: Cornell University Press, 1989.

Good, Gregory A. "The Rockefeller Foundation, the Leipzig Geophysical Institute, and National Socialism in the 1930s." *Historical Studies in the Physical and Biological Sciences* 21 (1991): pp. 299–316.

Jewell, Ralph. "Vilhelm Bjerknes's Duty to Produce Something Clear and Real in Meteorological Science." In *The Earth, the Heavens and the Carnegie Institution of Washington,* edited by Gregory A. Good, pp. 37–46. Vol. 5 in the History of Geophysics Series. Washington, D.C.: American Geophysical Union, 1994.

See also Atmosphere, Structure of; Ballooning; Geophysics; Instruments, Upper Atmosphere and Near Space; Mathematics and Meteorology; Meteorology; Meteorology, Marine; Ocean Currents; Ocean-Atmosphere Interactions; Oceanography, Physical; Precipitation, Theories of; Radiosondes and Related Instruments; Storms and Cyclones

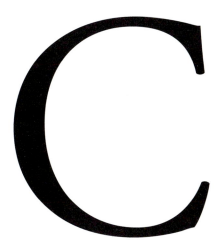

Carbonates

A sediment, mineral, or rock used for millennia and studied since the eighteenth century.

The term "carbonates" applies to one kind of sediment (carbonate sediment) and two kinds of rock: (1) limestone ($CaCO_3$), composed of the mineral calcite, its diagenetic precursors aragonite, or high-magnesian calcite; and (2) dolostone, composed of the mineral dolomite, $CaMg(CO_3)_2$.

Carbonates have attracted the attention of both geologists and nongeologists because of their use as building stones (the pyramids of Egypt, the Hebrew Temple of Solomon in Jerusalem, the Roman Wall in England, and the Tower and Tower Bridge of London), their use as ornamental stone (European and Canadian government buildings, the National Cathedral in Washington, the Empire State Building in New York), and because of the abundant fossils present in them.

The building and ornamental stones and those carbonates full of fossils are almost all limestones. Deodat Gratet de Dolomieu (1750–1801) noted the presence of magnesium in carbonates in what are now known as the Dolomite Mountains of northern Italy. Horace Bénédict de Saussure (1740–1799) named the magnesium-rich carbonate "dolomite" (1792). The English term dolomite, introduced in *Elements of Mineralogy* (second edition) in 1794 by Richard Kirwan (1733–1812), was meant for a mineral, not a rock. Independently in the United States, Amos Eaton (1776–1842) discovered the rock dolostone during his survey of the Erie Canal in the Geodiferous Limestone (1824), now the Silurian Lockport Formation, not knowing it had recently been named outside North America.

The first detailed studies of carbonates were those of Sir Charles Lyell (1797–1875) in his classic *Principles of Geology* (1830–1833), in which he compared modern and ancient reef deposits and discussed Italian travertine. The term "travertine" is derived from the Italian *travertino,* a former name of the locality now called Tivoli. Travertine is a calcareous spring deposit in which precipitation of $CaCO_3$ relates chiefly to biologic processes, especially microbial activity (Sanders and Friedman, p. 171).

The book by Charles Darwin (1809–1882) on H.M.S. *Beagle,* and other writings on coral atolls in the 1840s, emphasized the problems connected with the origin of modern carbonates. Many studies resulted from Darwin's stimulus; their culmination was in the drilling of many test borings by the U.S. Geological Survey in the decade after World War II as discussed by Ladd, Tracey, Wells, and Emery in 1953 (Sanders and Friedman, p. 171).

The presidential address by Henry Clifton Sorby (1826–1908) to the Geological Society of London (1879) is one of the most penetrating studies of carbonates ever made; he applied advanced methods to a study of the mineralogy and texture of limestones and modern carbonate sediments with great success. He concluded that limestones are derived mainly from cementation of broken up and decayed shells and corals; hence he indicated that a knowledge of the mineralogy and structure of shells is fundamental to understanding limestones. Sorby compared modern carbonate sediments with ancient limestones. The full significance of this study was unrealized until 1954, when Vincent Charles Illing (1890–1969) published his work on the carbonate deposits of the Bahamas (Sanders and Friedman, pp. 171–172).

However, Sorby's main contribution was his laboratory study of carbonates by means of thin-sections and the petrographic microscope that he reported on in his 1879 presidential address. To develop a body of information on the petrography and petrology of carbonates, Lucien Cayeux's 1935 book on the sedimentary rocks of France and a long article by Bruno Sander (1936) of Austria complemented and supplemented Sorby's research (Sanders and Friedman, p. 172).

Johannes Walther (1860–1937), one of the giants of geology at the turn of the century, wrote a three-volume textbook (1893–1894) that devoted considerable space to modern carbonates. An outstanding synthesizer and shrewd observer, Walther had traveled extensively on four continents (Europe, Asia, Africa, and North America) to make geological observations. His study of the Holocene and Pleistocene carbonates of the Red Sea is a classic and was many decades ahead of its time. Walther was an early advocate of the experimental approach to problems of carbonate diagenesis. However, Walther's publications, in German, were lost to the post–World War II English-speaking geological community that advanced the fields he specialized in. In the 1960s, even in his own country, he was barely known. Although there were several routes by which his memory and contributions were rekindled, it was the American petroleum industry in the 1960s that resurrected his contributions and brought him new recognition.

Around 1900 Andrew W. Grabau (1870–1946), the father of modern sedimentology, recognized most of the varieties of carbonates known today, yet few geologists bothered to penetrate his elaborate genetic terminology. One major change from Grabau's views on limestones, occasioned by subsequent research, is recognition of the importance of wave-working of deposits of calcareous material in the sea. Although Grabau's petrographic studies were terse, his treatment of the other aspects of carbonates was thorough. Although his bibliographies were cosmopolitan, he omitted Sorby's work on limestones, possibly because it is petrographic. Much of the new research on carbonates that occurred in the United States after

1950 would have been accomplished far earlier had these studies commenced with a combination of the material available in the published works of both Sorby and Grabau (Sanders and Friedman, p. 173).

Hans Klähn (1884–1933) was an active worker in the field of carbonate sedimentation and petrology in Germany in the 1920s and early 1930s, yet modern workers have largely ignored his extensive studies. Another prodigious student of carbonate sedimentation and petrology was Julius von Pia (1887–1943), who published a book *Die Rezenten Kalksteine* (*Recent carbonate sediments,* 1933) in which he summed up the entire field as then known. Although still one of the most comprehensive studies on this subject, it is now obsolete in many areas. The classic literature on limestones has been reviewed by Sanders and Friedman.

The early pioneers in the study of carbonates made little impact on the present generation of geologists. A breakthrough in this field has come during the last forty years. The sources of inspiration, energy, and progress were the major oil companies of the United States. The enormous petroleum reservoirs discovered in carbonates of the Middle East, in the Devonian of western Canada, and in the Permian of west Texas and New Mexico prompted the oil companies to increase their efforts in carbonate research. In 1959, a Carbonate Rock Subcommittee was established as a division of the American Association of Petroleum Geologists (AAPG). W.E. Ham edited an AAPG memoir in 1962 on the classification of carbonate rocks, which is a major milestone and turning point in the history of the study of carbonates.

Although geologists have studied carbonate rocks from various points of view for the past 150 years, surprisingly, the first widely adopted classifications did not appear in the geological literature until this 1962 AAPG Memoir. The interest of many geologists in limestones centered on faunal remains. Those who studied only the fossils did not bother about the other elements of limestones. In particular, they did not do much about classifying and naming these rocks. In fact, in the mid-1950s, when petroleum companies discovered major reservoirs of petroleum in carbonate rocks, the geological profession—specifically, geologists in oil companies—realized their widespread lack of basic understanding of limestones. The inadequate description of carbonate rocks prevailing at the time and the general lack of detailed petrological information are illustrated by descriptions of rocks on sample logs from well bores. A sample was commonly described simply as "limestone"; additional information sometimes added was: "limestone, tan, fossiliferous" and perhaps a "detailed" description cited "limestone, tan, fossiliferous, partially dolomitized." For a petroleum geologist, the purpose of data on a log is to help in interpreting the rock's origin. Such an interpretation must be based on good descriptive data, which includes carefully classifying and naming the rock.

To most geologists, limestones were "chemical" rocks that fizzed when hydrochloric acid is applied. Only a few others followed in the Sorby-Grabau tradition and considered limestones as the rock products of calcium-carbonate sediments that were sorted and transported as if the particles were silicate minerals. Finally, a few investigators studied the textural relationships of carbonate rocks. Despite the fact that the few followers of Sorby and Grabau were on the right track, their impact on the profession at large was not significant. The oil companies' need to develop their own programs indicates how widely the "chemical" view of limestones was accepted as opposed to the "mechanical-organic" ideas of Sorby and Grabau. Most older systems of carbonate rock classification proved inadequate because they were based more on philosophical concepts about limestones than on intimate knowledge of these rocks themselves (Friedman and Sanders, *Principles*).

The economic incentive spurred various crash programs among oil companies to develop usable classifications. Throughout much of the 1950s, geologists from several major oil companies worked simultaneously on the problem of classifying and naming limestones. For reasons of competition, these companies did not communicate. Coincident with and partly encouraged by the new economic interest was a stimulation of similar research in colleges, universities, and various geological surveys. It is surprising then that when the different classifications finally appeared in print in 1962, their differences were only slight. Still, some differences did exist, which reflected in part the area of study in which the geologists did their work or the particular philosophy the geologists adopted in classifying.

All classifications developed in the 1962 AAPG Memoir are based on the facies concept: distinction is made between (1) limestones that formed under high-energy conditions (waves, currents, storms, surge) in which particles, such as skeletal fragments or ooids, are separated from one another by pore space, or by cement that occupies this space; and (2) limestones that formed under low-energy conditions in which lime mud occluded potential pore space. This distinction between high- and low-energy accumulation is the key to all the limestone classifications. Of the several classifications in the 1962 AAPG Memoir, the most widely and currently used classification is that of Shell, for which R.J. Dunham acted as spokesman (in Ham, pp. 108–121).

The literature on dolomite and dolostones is enormous. Many papers have attempted to solve the dolomite problem or question, as it is widely known. The literature may be subdivided into papers written before and after the x-ray diffraction "revolution." Most of the modern breakthroughs in the dolomite question have resulted directly from studies that have used the x-ray diffraction technique (Friedman and Sanders, *Principles*).

Any review of the literature of dolomite and dolostone rightfully begins with the monograph (1916) of Francis M. Van Tuyl (1887–1975). In this classic paper Van Tuyl assembled all the available literature and examined all possible aspects of the subject. Steidtmann (1926) made an important early petrographic study that emphasized the replacement origin of most dolostones. Shorter summaries of the status of the dolomite question appeared in the *Treatise on Sedimentation*. Detailed summaries of the dolomite problem were presented by Rhodes Fairbridge in "The Dolomite Question" in 1957 (Friedman and Sanders, *Principles*, pp. 270–276).

G.I. Teodorovich summarized the extensive Russian literature on sedimentary dolostone in 1959 and attempted to relate dolostone occurrences to changing conditions in the Earth's atmosphere with geologic time. He showed that dolomite may form under a variety of conditions, but that the dominant process is replacement (Friedman and Sanders, *Principles*, p. 274).

Rapid progress in environmental interpretation of dolomite was closely linked with the x-ray revolution, which made dolomite identification simple, fast, and efficient. Yet the processes leading to dolomitization are still disputed.

In 1967 dolostones were first classified genetically into three major groups: (1) syngenetic, (2) diagenetic, and (3) epigenetic.

Syngenetic dolostone is dolostone that was formed penecontemporaneously in its environment of deposition. This kind of dolostone contrasts with diagenetic dolostone, which was formed by the replacement of calcium-carbonate sediments or of limestones during or following consolidation, such as within beds of carbonate sediments or limestones. The distinction between syngenetic and diagenetic may become difficult or impossible to make. Epigenetic dolostone is defined as dolostone formed by localized replacement of limestone along postdepositional structural elements, such as faults and fractures, or by deep burial (Friedman and Sanders, *Principles;* "Origin").

Three models for syngenetic-diagenetic dolomite have been debated since the 1960s. The seepage reflux model of J.E. Adams and M.L. Rhodes proposed in 1960 a downward flow of dense brine (Braithwaite, "Dolomites"). If the molar ratio of magnesium to calcium in the brine has been raised much higher than the normal value in seawater (5/1), owing to evaporation and precipitation of calcium sulfate, then the high-magnesium brine may cause dolomite to form. The capillary-concentration mechanism of G.M. Friedman and J.E. Sanders posited in 1967 that the capillary upward movement of seawater, initially of normal or near-normal salinity, flows through sediments on marginal supra-tidal flats and becomes concentrated by evapo-transpiration at the sediment-air interface. The mixed-zone dolomitization model of B.B. Hanshaw, W. Back, and R.G. Deike posited in 1971 that mixing marine and meteoric waters produces a solution that is at once undersaturated with respect to calcite and oversaturated with respect to dolomite, even at dilutions of 10:1 (Braithwaite). Such waters have been held to react with existing carbonates to form dolomite (Braithwaite). Hardie criticized this model in 1987, and it is now less widely accepted.

Epigenetic dolostone may form where limestone is contiguous to fault zones that transmitted the dolomitizing fluids (Friedman and Sanders, "Origin," pp. 330–334) or under conditions of deep burial in which a hydraulic pump can deliver sufficient volumes of fluids over long periods (Land; Sternbach and Friedman).

Recent reviews of the dolomite problem are those of Land, Hardie, and Braithwaite. These reviews demonstrate that the "dolomite problem" or "dolomite question" is still debated. As an example, in the Levant (Sinai subplate and along Dead Sea transform) modern dolomite has formed (1) by capillary concentration-evaporitic mechanism, (2) by detrital recycling, (3) through the methane pathway, and (4) by fluids from the mantle (Friedman). No wonder within this diversity the answer to the "dolomite question" is still elusive. Yet a recent reappraisal by S.Q. Sun of dolomite abundance and occurrence concludes: "Review leads me to concur with Friedman and Sanders . . . that most dolomite in the rock record formed under conditions of hypersalinity."

Gerald M. Friedman

Bibliography

Braithwaite, C.J.R. "Dolomites, a Review of Origins, Geometry and Textures." *Transactions of the Royal Society of Edinburgh: Earth Sciences* 82 (1991): pp. 99–112.

Eaton, A. *A Geological and Agricultural Survey of the District Adjoining the Erie Canal, in the State of New York.* Albany, N.Y.: Packard and Van Benthuysen, 1824.

Friedman, G.M. "Diverse Origin of Quaternary Dolomite in the Levant." *Geological Society of America, Abstracts with Programs* 25 (1993): p. A-397.

Friedman, G.M., and J.E. Sanders. "Origin and Occurrence of Limestones." In *Carbonate Rocks,* edited by G.V. Chillingar, H.J. Bissell, and R.W. Fairbridge, pp. 267–348. Amsterdam: Elsevier, 1967.

———. *Principles of Sedimentology.* New York: John Wiley, 1978.

Ham, W.E. "Classification of Carbonate Rocks. A Symposium." *Memoir of the American Association of Petroleum Geologists* 1 (1962): 279 pages.

Hardie, L.A. "Perspectives. Dolomitization: A Critical View of Some Current Views." *Journal of Sedimentary Petrology* 57 (1987): pp. 16–183.

Kirwan, R. *Elements of Mineralogy* 2d ed. London: J. Nichols, 1794.

Land, L.S. "The Origin of Massive Dolomite." *Journal of Geological Education* 33 (1985): pp. 112–125.

Sanders, J.E., and G.M. Friedman. "Origin and Occurrence of Limestones." In *Carbonate Rocks,* edited by G.V. Chillingar, H.J. Bissell, and R.W. Fairbridge, pp. 169–265. Amsterdam: Elsevier, 1967.

Saussure, T. de. "Analyse de la dolomie, 1792." *Journal de Physique* 40 (1792): pp. 161–173.

Sternbach, C.A., and G.M. Friedman. "Dolomites Formed under Conditions of Deep Burial: Hunton Group Carbonate Rocks (Upper Ordovician to Lower Devonian) in the Anadarko Basin of Oklahoma and Texas." *Carbonates and Evaporites* 1 (1986): pp. 61–73.

Sun, S.Q. "A Reappraisal of Dolomite Abundance and Occurrence in the Phanerozoic." *Journal of Sedimentary Research* A64 (1994): pp. 396–404.

Walther, J. *Einleitung in die Geologie als Historische Wissenschaft. 3. Lithogenesis der Gegenwart.* Jena: Fischer, 1893–1894.

See also Facies, Sedimentary; Geology; Hydrologic Cycle; Mineral Waters; Ocean Currents; Ocean Chemistry; Ore Formation, Theories since 1800; Petroleum Geology to 1920; Petrology; Sedimentary Geology; Sedimentology; Stratigraphy

Cartography: Disciplinary History

The development of mapmaking as a science with supporting insitutional structures, its own distinctive methods, and topics of investigation.

All humans acquire spatial knowledge through personal experience and by verbal communication with others. The inscription of the resultant "mental maps" into artifacts—maps per se—has occurred in all human societies that have required spatial knowledge to be stored and reproduced beyond the otherwise limited scope of individual memory. In this respect, maps predate writing as the oldest of humanity's inscriptive artifacts. Formal structures of mapmaking developed in conjunction with the intensification of commodity exchange and associated changes in social form. The traditional societies of Europe and Asia supported much cartographic activity, but as Harley and Woodward (vol. 2.1, p. 510) argue, the many "centers of map production were [otherwise] like islands in a sea of cartographic silence." It has only been in the modern world, with the development of the modern militarist and industrial state, that map use has permeated all levels of society and that mapmaking might be regarded as an organized discipline rather than a personal, unorganized, and intellectual practice.

Matthew Edney has classified the broad historical range of mapping practices into three interrelated "modes": maritime charting; small-scale mapping of the world and its regions ("chorography"), being part and parcel of general geographical description; and large-scale surveying of the land. Each mode entails a different conception of the world, employs different intellectual and instrumental techniques, and is organized for different social purposes. In early modern Europe, the overall level of mapping activity was sufficiently low that there were few specialized mapmakers, and distinctions between the three basic modes of cartographic practice and other artistic and scientific practices were weak. By the early nineteenth century, however, mapmaking had become sufficiently specialized that when, in 1839, the viscount of Santarém (1791–1856) coined the term "cartography" as the study of old maps, it was very quickly appropriated for all aspects of mapmaking (Harley and Woodward, vol. 1, p. 12).

The navigational tradition of early modern Europe derived from the *portolani* of the Mediterranean sailing tradition. The economic importance of navigational information in the fifteenth and sixteenth centuries led to conflicts between the pilots and chartmakers, who wished to profit from the sale of manuscript charts, and the maritime powers, who wished to control such information, and so established the earliest state regulation of cartographic practices. Spain established a hydrographic office in 1508 to maintain a master chart, the *Padron Real,* and to regulate chartmaking. England and France were less rigid and patronized the chartmakers of Dieppe in the mid-1500s. Manuscript chart production was challenged in the mid-sixteenth century by the free Dutch presses, although manuscript charts were not entirely replaced for another century (Brown, pp. 141–149).

The Renaissance introduction of classical models of geographical description, particularly the *Geography* of Claudius Ptolemy (ca. 90–168) further stimulated by the "great discoveries," led to the commercial publication of geographical texts and world and regional maps. Initially, these were published on both sides of the Alps, but the wealthy mercantilist economy of northern Italy created enough intellectual consumers to support dedicated commercial cartographers early in the sixteenth century. The subsequent rise of Dutch urban mercantilism and its bourgeois rejection of Hapsburg absolutism produced numerous free presses on which hitherto restricted materials, such as sea charts, were published for the rest of Europe. Dutch materialism drove a commercial trade in maps and geographic texts that soon predominated in northern and western Europe. The famous Gerard Mercator (1512–1594) was one of the few geographical scholars who were also map publishers in their own right. The rest had their maps and texts published for them by commercial publishers like Abraham Ortelius (1527–1598), who made a successful living as a book dealer specializing in geographical works. In 1570 Ortelius published his innovative *Theatrum orbis terrarum,* the first atlas to represent all the world in a systematic and ordered manner (Karrow, pp. 1–31, 376–406).

Commercial map publishing spread to France and the rest of Europe in the seventeenth century, becoming highly institutionalized. The larger Dutch, and subsequently French, publishing houses accumulated enough printing plates to issue huge, multivolume atlases, affordable only by the very wealthy. All geographical publishers plagiarized existing works and reused older plates—adding only their own name—in order to feed the much larger market for smaller atlases and single-sheet maps (Brown, pp. 168–174). This cartographic inertia was supported by the occasional addition of original information derived from several sources, whose wide variety is made evident by Robert Karrow's exhaustive biographies of sixteenth-century cartographers. For areas beyond Europe, they depended on travel narratives and on an active, if illegal, trade in maritime information. Within Europe they drew upon the mapping activities of the early states. Several of the essays edited by David Buisseret suggest that each new generation of bureaucrats was more cartographically literate than the previous one; by the 1580s, several states had underwritten the acquisition of basic geographic information for their territories in regional surveys like those by Pedro de Esquivel (d. 1575) of Spain in the 1560s and Christopher Saxton (1542/1544–ca. 1620) of England, completed in 1579.

The principal reasons for the steady increase in cartographic literacy in early modern Europe were perhaps the increased availability of maps through printing, humanist education, and the allure of foreign lands. A more practical factor was the commodification of land, which supplanted older feudal land tenures with cash rents and the active exchange of real property (especially of confiscated Church lands). Even as both innovations stimulated new forms of legal wrangling over property rights (the usual motive for the large-scale mapping in traditional societies), they also required the assessment of the quantity as well as the quality of land. Add to this the early modern agricultural improvements—of draining and reclaiming land in the Veneto and the Netherlands, for example—and the result was a dramatic increase in the localized measurement of land at very large scales. The seventeenth-century colonization of the Americas (and of Ireland by the English) usually required the formal subdivision of property by survey. Only a very few of the surveyed maps were sufficiently important to warrant publication. From the early seventeenth century on, this mode of cartography nonetheless supported a large number of texts on the techniques of large-scale mapping and the calculation of land areas from maps. The texts themselves were addressed to various audiences, from the aristocratic property owner to the lowly tenant. Similarly, there evolved a new profession of land surveyors, many self-educated, who ranged in the social scale from common "geometers" to the stewards of huge landed estates.

By the second half of the seventeenth century, there were thus four interrelated groups of cartographic practitioners who straddled the three modes of mapmaking: mariners, intellectual geographers, commercial publishers, and land measurers. After 1660, the increased intervention of each European state in the large-scale surveying of their territories led to a fifth grouping of "professional geographers," specifically the military and state surveyors, whose work melded the three modes into one, unified "mathematical cosmography."

The initial stimulus for increased state intervention was the reform and augmentation of revenues from property taxes. Sweden's Baltic provinces and the Netherlands were, early in the seventeenth century, the first states to initiate official cadastral surveys of all properties in each district in order to assess land taxes according to the quantity as well as the productivity of landed property. The financial dislocation of the Thirty Years War (1618–1648) accelerated the adoption of official cadastres, particularly in the sorely afflicted German states. The adoption by each central government of a statewide cadastre was usually accompanied by extensive negotiations between the central, provincial, and urban powers. In the worst case, the war left the Austrian Hapsburgs' fiscal structure in complete disarray, but political opposition prevented any cadastral survey until that of Lombardy (1718–1731; 1749–1759). Austria-Hungary proper was still reassessed without the benefit of surveys, but the Lombardy survey inspired similar surveys in Spain and the kingdom of Sardinia that encompassed all land and not just productive fields (Kain and Baigent, pp. 181–191).

Somewhat after the first general cadastres were begun, several European states began to map their own territories for general administrative and military purposes (Brown, pp. 241–279; Kretschmer et al.). The leader in this respect was the highly centralized French state. Between the geodesists and astronomers of the Académie royale des sciences (founded 1660), who provided a mathematical framework for France (in the first "Cassini survey" of 1680–1744), the engineers of the corps of the Ponts et Chaussées (Bridges and Roads, founded 1719), and the surveyors employed by César-François Cassini de Thury (1714–1784) on the second, topographical Cassini survey (1747–1789), France was thoroughly mapped. The Cassini surveys spawned similar surveys in Denmark (1757–1805) and Württemberg (1793–1828). The surveys of Italian and German states begun under French occupation during the Revolutionary and Napoleonic Wars (1794–1815) were subsequently continued after 1814. Military mapping by other European states was not so mathematically rigorous as the French surveys: the English mapped Scotland after the 1745 uprising, as well as their overseas colonies (such as Bengal, 1765–1771); military engineers mapped the Hapsburg domains (1763–1787), Prussia (1767–1787), and Saxony (1780–1825). The commonality of military surveys in the eighteenth century indicates a general increase in cartographic literacy among the European armies, although military maps generally remained in manuscript in order to reduce circulation and maintain confidentiality.

Neither the district cadastres nor the provincial military surveys entailed the creation of formal government agencies but were prosecuted on an ad hoc basis by military personnel or civilian surveyors under contract to the state. Note that provincial surveys occupied an ambiguous position: they applied the techniques of land surveying to large regions more commonly represented at much smaller scales. The surveyed maps were vast—the second Cassini survey took 180 sheets to cover France at 1:86,400—and their commercially published derivatives at smaller ("medium") scales were still huge. These maps were the cartographic equivalents of the monstrous, multivolume geographic texts that presented the world in all its particulars. They brought all geographic information into one encyclopedic enumeration of location and place. They helped destroy the apparent differences between the established cartographic modes; all geographic data could be fitted to an abstract and scaleless Foucauldian *table* of latitude and longitude, regardless of its quality or the nature of its source (marine explorations, regional surveys, or travel narratives). Indeed, the fundamental rationale of the British and French governments' support of cartographic science in the 1700s was the perfection of this geographic framework. Both states offered large prizes for an easy and accurate means of determining longitude; the Académie royale des sciences organized expeditions to Sweden and Ecuador to measure the size and shape of the Earth (1734–1744); finally, in 1784–1790, the two states measured the longitudinal difference between their principal observatories at Greenwich and Paris. The result was the consolidation of cartography into the single mode of "mathematical cosmography," which combined astronomy, geodesy, and mapmaking with the bourgeois worldview. It is this singular conception of an amalgamated and unified mapmaking that quickly adopted the name "cartography" after 1839 and that has been naturalized as the empiricist foundation of "geography" (Edney).

The logical next step in state mapping was to incorporate property information into the survey of entire countries, and so replace the numerous district cadastres with one all-purpose "national survey." Institutional difficulties prevented the archly rationalist *philosophes* of revolutionary France from completing such a survey, and it divided after 1814 into a separate cadastre and a military topographic survey. The British Ordnance Survey of Ireland (1824–1846) was however successful in conducting a very large scale cadastral survey, at 1:10,560, from which topographic maps could be derived, at 1:63,360, for military purposes. Political opposition initially prevented the resumption of the Ordnance Survey in Britain along similar lines (it had begun in 1791 as a strictly topographical survey). The "battle of the scales" was resolved only when it became clear that highly detailed maps at very large scales were utterly essential for resource inventory (including geological and land-use mapping), the planning and construction of the physical infrastructure necessary for an industrial economy (from railroads to sewers), the maintenance of an efficient cadastre, effective military strategies and tactics, and the myriad planning tasks required by an increasingly urban and regulated society (Kain and Baigent, pp. 225–235, 260–264).

The industrialized countries of Europe and their colonies followed the British experience after 1850: increasingly permanent and steadily larger military survey institutions mapped each state at ever larger scales. The poorer European states were not, however, so well mapped: despite their pretensions to the contrary, they simply could not afford state-of-the-art cartography. The national map of Spain at 1:50,000, for example, was begun in 1875 but took ninety years to complete. The cartographic surveys were usually undertaken in conjunction with population censuses. The collection of geographically defined statistics in the later eighteenth century had produced a new representational form, specifically "thematic cartography," in which statistical distributions are mapped across physical space (Robinson). By the later nineteenth century, thematic mapping was as essential an element for government and academic planners as the topographic mapping itself.

The state of formal mapping has been equally varied beyond Europe in the nineteenth and twentieth centuries. The United States largely recapitulated the European experience, although the geodetic and hydrographic work of the Coast Survey (first organized in 1807) and the topographical mapping by the Geological Survey (founded 1879) were complicated by constitutional relations between the federal and state governments; also, both surveys were begun primarily for commercial and economic reasons and are civilian institutions. British India and the colonies of white settlement (such as South Africa and Australia) have generally been well mapped by large military survey departments; the lesser, poorer colonies were mapped in a more ad hoc manner. At the height of European imperialism, 1870–1914, plans were initiated to construct an International Map of the World, but at the relatively small scale of 1:1,000,000 (Brown, pp. 299–307). The independent Asian countries eventually adopted European cartographic institutions. The Ottoman Turks, for example, adopted European techniques in the late 1700s and made cadastral surveys after 1858. But other than Thongchai's study of

Thailand (including the formation in 1885 of a modern state survey organization employing European staff), the cultural imperialism implicit in the spread of the national survey to Asia remains largely unexamined.

Increasing literacy through public education programs in the industrialized countries after 1800 meant a continued expansion of commercial cartography, an expansion facilitated by the introduction of lithography after 1800 as a cheap and easy printing technology. A few very large firms came to dominate the intellectual geographic market—Bartholemew (Edinburgh), Michelin (Paris), Justus Perthes (Gotha), and so on—and their principals mingled with the military and imperial surveyors, navy hydrographers, state-supported explorers, geodesists, and academic geographers in the metropolitan geographical societies: these were the cartographic elites. Then there were numerous commercial firms, both for surveying and publishing, who worked locally or in more specialized niches, such as the publication of school atlases.

Training and education in the mapping sciences was usually conducted within each specific cartographic institution, using the descendants of the survey texts first published in the 1600s. Academic and technical specialization has however split the discipline since the late 1800s into surveying, which has generally been taught in engineering colleges, and cartography, which was central to the development of academic geography after 1870. The first text to deal with the character of maps and mapmaking was *Die Kartenwissenschaft* (1921–1925) of Max Eckert (1868–1938). Since World War II, academic cartographers have sought to distance themselves from geography. They have founded their own academic societies and journals, for example the Deutsche Gesellschaft für Kartographie (founded 1950) and the American Cartographic Association (1961), and they have followed Arthur H. Robinson (b. 1915) at the University of Wisconsin in establishing separate degree programs, some even with the Ph.D. (Wolter, pp. 208–215, 252–280). The purpose of these programs has been to provide sufficient expertise for the remapping of the industrialized states at still larger scales (for example, the United States embarked on a national mapping program at 1:24,000 after 1945) and for the large-scale mapping of the world made necessary by global warfare. That need is evidenced in the thirty-five million copies of maps by the U.S. Defense Mapping Agency shipped to thirty thousand U.S. troops during the Gulf War in 1990–1991. As each European state completes its remapping, the mapping agencies have been turned over entirely to civilians. Similarly, as Europe has withdrawn from its empires, the colonial mapping agencies have been progressively transferred to local staff. Europe nonetheless maintains its cartographic supremacy through institutions such as the British Directorate for Overseas Surveys, which undertakes mapping in Africa through aid programs, and the International Training Center (at Enschede, in the Netherlands), which trains students from around the world in surveying, geodesy, and cartography.

The industrial states and the militaries on either side of the Cold War have prompted the development of new cartographic technologies to improve both surveying and map production. Remote sensing techniques have been perfected to allow examination of enemy territory from afar: first aerial photography in the 1930s and 1940s and subsequently satellite imagery. The world geographic data-base is steadily being converted into digital form for use with automated mapping programs. These developments, made in part by academic and commercial researchers funded by state grants, promise to perpetuate well into the next millennium the modern state's role in defining the disciplinary character of maps and mapmaking.

Matthew H. Edney

Bibliography

Brown, Lloyd A. *The Story of Maps.* New York: Little, Brown, and Co., 1949. Reprint. New York: Dover, 1979.

Buisseret, David, ed. *Monarchs, Ministers, and Maps: The Emergence of Cartography as a Tool of Government in Early Modern Europe.* Chicago: University of Chicago Press, 1992.

Edney, Matthew H. "Cartography without 'Progress': Reinterpreting the Nature and Historical Development of Mapmaking." *Cartographica* 30, nos. 2, 3 (1993): pp. 54–68.

Harley, J.B., and David Woodward, eds. *The History of Cartography.* 6 vols. in 8 books. Chicago: University of Chicago Press, 1987–. Vols. to date are: 1, *Cartography in Prehistoric, Ancient, and Medieval Europe and the Mediterranean* (1987); 2.1, *Cartography in the Traditional Islamic and South Asian Societies* (1992); 2.2, *Cartography in the Traditional East and Southeast Asian Societies* (1994).

Kain, Roger J.P., and Elizabeth Baigent. *The Cadastral Map in the Service of the State: A History of Property Mapping.* Chicago: University of Chicago Press, 1992.

Karrow, Robert W. *Mapmakers of the Sixteenth Century and Their Maps: Bio-Bibliographies of the Cartographers of Abraham Ortelius, 1570.* Chicago: Speculum Orbis Press for the Newberry Library, 1993.

Kretschmer, Ingrid, Johannes Dörflinger, and Franz Wawrik, eds. *Lexikon zur Geschichte der Kartographie von den Anfängen bis zum ersten Weltkrieg.* 2 vols. Vienna: Franz Deuticke, 1986.

Robinson, Arthur H. *Early Thematic Mapping in the History of Cartography.* Chicago: University of Chicago Press, 1982.

Thongchai, Winichakul. *Siam Mapped: A History of the Geo-Body of a Nation.* Honolulu: University of Hawaii Press, 1994.

Wolter, John A. "The Emerging Discipline of Cartography." Ph.D. Diss., University of Minnesota, 1975.

See also Disciplinary History; Colonialism and Imperialism; Earth, Models of before 1600; Exploration, Age of; Foucault's Order of Things; Geodesy; Geographical Societies; Geography and Imperialism; Geography; Geological Maps; Geological Surveys; Humboldtian Science; Isolines; Mappaemundi

Chemical Revolution

A period during the eighteenth century of extraordinary change in chemistry, both at the theoretical and institutional levels. One reason for this rapid progress was allied systematic researches in metallurgy and mining. In Sweden and Germany, for instance, most chemists were trained in the metallurgical tradition until the second half of the eighteenth century. This practical background had important effects in developing the art of assaying minerals and analyzing metals. The connections between early chemistry and the geosciences were thus very close. However, the radical change that occurred in chemistry during the 1770s found its primary cause in another research field.

In 1890 the French chemist Marcellin Berthelot (1827–1907) published an important study with the title *La révolution chimique:*

Lavoisier. In this work Berthelot tried to demonstrate the genesis and structure of the chemical breakthrough by Antoine-Laurent Lavoisier (1743–1794) and to emphasize the discontinuity between the achievement of the French chemist and those of his predecessors. Berthelot's claim that Lavoisier's work engendered a chemical revolution has been enforced by the historical investigations published by Hélène Metzger, Andrew Meldrum, Maurice Daumas, and Henry Guerlac, all of whom emphasized the original and innovative aspects of Lavoisier's chemical thought. In addition to this, the success of the historical use of the notion of chemical revolution was justified by the fact that Lavoisier himself regarded his own contribution as a "revolution in physics and chemistry."

In more recent times, J.B. Gough, Carleton E. Perrin, Frederic L. Holmes, and other historians of eighteenth-century science have reassessed the historical role of Lavoisier in the foundation of modern chemistry, and they have emphasized that his theory was in continuity with the chemical and experimental contributions of his contemporaries and predecessors. By doing so these historians aimed at diminishing the rupture that occurred in chemistry by the end of the eighteenth century, and they have claimed that chemistry was a specialized and autonomous science long before Lavoisier appeared on the scene. According to this interpretation, chemistry was an established discipline with deep concern for the makeup of the Earth, its waters, and its atmosphere by the beginning of the eighteenth century.

Both these interpretations were dominated by the general image of science that alternatively supported a revolutionary or a cumulative evolution of its historical development. Accordingly the notion of chemical revolution has been used to discredit or support a general conception of science rather than being the object of a genuinely historical reconstruction.

The notion of chemical revolution is, in fact, not a category created by historians to serve their aim; on the contrary, it is an historical entity that appeared during the second half of the eighteenth century. Lavoisier and many of his contemporaries used the notion of "revolution in chemistry" in order to denote the extraordinary progress enjoyed by chemistry during the period between 1770 and 1789. The experimental background for this revolution was founded on the extraordinary investigations on the nature of air performed by Joseph Black (1728–1799), Joseph Priestley (1733–1804), Carl Wilhelm Scheele (1742–1786), and several other chemists in the second half of the century. In 1755 Black recognized that air is not a simple element but that it is composed of different kinds of airs, and that some of them are capable of entering in combination with other bodies, thus modifying their chemical nature. Black was able to isolate one of these gases, which he called "fixed air," later denoted carbon dioxide. For centuries naturalists had regarded air as a simple and chemically passive element. We can understand the great excitement that Black's discovery provoked in the chemical community. A new investigative field was created, and during the last four decades of the century chemists focused their attention on the nature of gases.

In November 1772 Lavoisier observed that sulfur gains weight after its combustion, instead of losing it as Stahl believed. The phenomenon itself was not new to eighteenth-century chemists, but Lavoisier regarded it from a completely new perspective and assumed that the cause of the gain of weight of sulfur was the fixation of the air during the combustion. Although he was not yet able to isolate the gas, Lavoisier significantly regarded this discovery of crucial importance. Indeed, the chemical role of phlogiston, which was supposed to be the main cause of the combustion, was suddenly called into doubt by an unknown gas. However, Lavoisier's intuition was not supported by many chemists, who did not see any threat to phlogiston in Lavoisier's experiment.

In 1774 Scheele and Priestley simultaneously discovered a new kind of air, which was respectively named *Feuerluft* (air of fire) and "dephlogisticated air" (later denoted oxygen). Lavoisier immediately understood that the gas isolated by Scheele and Priestley was the active agent of calcination and combustion and that its isolation cast stronger doubts on the existence of phlogiston. On these early observations Lavoisier built a theory that was centered on the role of the newly discovered gas, which he called "eminently respirable air," and a new conception of the gaseous state. In 1779 Lavoisier gave his theory a more precise definition. In a historic memoir, *Considérations générales sur la nature des acides,* he claimed that the "eminently respirable air" was combined with all acids and that it could be regarded as the universal principle of acidity. In order to understand the boldness of this claim it is worth remembering that by 1779 chemists had determined the composition of fewer than five acids. Convinced of the validity of his supposition, Lavoisier named the new gas the "oxygen principle," which was derived from the Greek "begetter of the acids."

Simultaneous to the generalization of the theory of acidity, other crucial experiments threatened the traditional philosophy of matter. Between 1777 and 1783, Jean-Baptiste-Marie Bucquet (1746–1780), Charles Blagden (1748–1820), Henry Cavendish (1731–1810), and Lavoisier studied the effects of the combustion of "inflammable air" (hydrogen). Consistent with his theory, Lavoisier expected to see the formation of a new acid as a result of the combination of hydrogen and oxygen, but to his great surprise no visible product could be detected. In 1782 and 1783 Lavoisier repeated the experiment by using a more accurate apparatus, and, on June 24, 1783, by burning a large quantity of hydrogen, he was finally able to obtain water.

The implications of Lavoisier's extraordinary experiment were enormous, and another tenet of the Aristotelian theory of the four elements was destroyed. Water, which had been considered a simple liquid element, was in fact a combination of two gases. But, because of the strength of the traditional philosophy of matter, the consequences of Lavoisier's experiment were difficult to accept. How could a liquid substance, which had been regarded as simple for thousands of years, be the result of the combination of the airs? In Lavoisier's system this critical question found a logical and conclusive answer. The French chemist recognized the inner complexity of matter and rejected any reified principles or elements. Within this conception, the experiments on the composition and decomposition of water were not at all disconcerting, but rather a confirmation of Lavoisier's belief in the composite structure of matter.

But it was at the methodological level that Lavoisier's approach to chemistry was particularly innovative. Lavoisier shifted the focus from the traditional hierarchy of qualitative elements to a system of chemical reactions in which the reagents were detectable quantitatively. The emphasis on quantification of chemical analysis was undoubtedly one of the major contributions to a new vision of chemistry, and the experiments on water were possibly the most impressive applications of it. Many contemporaries of

Lavoisier could not accept the experimental results because they considered quantitative data as inconclusive evidence. The water that resulted after the combustion of hydrogen was claimed to have been already in the apparatus or to be the consequence of the atmospheric humidity absorbed during the experiment. To sum up, both Lavoisier's vision of matter and his interpretation of his experimental results found a wide opposition among European chemists.

By 1785 Lavoisier felt that most of this opposition rested primarily on the prejudices of tradition, rather than on the lack of evidence of its experiments, and he decided to launch a frontal attack against the phlogiston theory. In his *Réflexions sur le phlogistique,* the French chemist outlined all the weaknesses and contradictions entailed in the traditional philosophy of matter in a persuasive and elegant style. One of Lavoisier's major arguments was that after Stahl's creation of the notion of phlogiston, his successors used this idea in a completely different manner and in contradictory terms. It became "the *Deus ex machina* of metaphysicians: an entity which explains everything and which explains nothing, to which one ascribes in turn opposite qualities."

Lavoisier transformed his destructive attack into a constructive system in 1787 when he, together with Louis Bernard Guyton de Morveau (1737–1816), Claude Louis Berthollet (1748–1822), and Antoine François de Fourcroy (1755–1809), published the *Méthode de nomenclature chimique,* which was his first systematic work. The nomenclature of chemistry before Lavoisier was an extremely complicated terminology that was often rooted in the ambiguous language of alchemy and some mystical doctrines. As a consequence of this confusion one name could denote several different substances and, conversely, the same substance could be named in many different ways. The term "oxygen" is a good example of this confusion. Despite its late discovery in 1774, already in 1777 at least six different names circulated. Priestley called it "dephlogisticated air," Scheele *Feuerluft,* Lavoisier "pure air," "eminently respirable air," and "oxygen," and Condorcet "vital air." The case of oxygen is interesting also from another important aspect: each of the names given to it implied particular alternative visions of matter and of the gaseous state. The example of the denomination of oxygen could be extended to most of the chemical terms used before 1787.

Because of this confusion, most eighteenth-century chemists yearned for a reform of the chemical nomenclature. Between 1766 and 1784, Pierre-Joseph Macquer (1718–1784), Torbern Bergman (1735–1784), and Guyton de Morveau attempted to systematize the traditional nomenclature into an ordered and expressive chemical lexicon. The introduction of the binomial nomenclature for the classification of acids and salts was very successful, but most names were still rooted in the phlogistic and alchemical languages.

By publishing a book entirely devoted to the reform of nomenclature, Lavoisier was thus responding to a widespread need. However, the idea behind the book was not the result merely of this circumstance; Lavoisier attributed in fact great importance to scientific language, and since the very beginning of his chemical career he had been extremely reluctant to use the phlogistic nomenclature. Convinced that languages are analytical methods rather than subordinate instruments of human understanding, Lavoisier distinguished three fundamental elements in the scientific endeavor: (1) the facts that distinguish each science, (2) the ideas that recall those selfsame facts, and (3) the words that express them. Following the philosophy of language outlined by Étienne Bonnot de Condillac (1714–1780), Lavoisier claimed that the formulation of any scientific idea is simultaneous to the creation of the linguistic frame appropriate to it. False and ambiguous ideas correspond to false and ambiguous words. Accordingly, in the eyes of Lavoisier the phlogistic nomenclature was not simply an ineffective and complicated terminology that needed reform, but rather a false language to be rejected.

Lavoisier proposed to substitute for the old nomenclature a method of naming that indicated how to denominate. The publication of the *Méthode de nomenclature chimique* was indeed a methodological breakthrough that laid the foundation of the syntax of modern chemistry. The only new terms introduced were caloric, oxygen, hydrogen, and azote (nitrogen), but the entire chemical language was deeply affected by Lavoisier's definition of these four simple substances. All the acids were now considered as the combination of oxygen with a specific base; the metallic calces (oxides) were named after oxygen, and most chemical reactions orbited around the definition of caloric, oxygen, and hydrogen. The map of the new system was effectively illustrated in the "Table of chemical nomenclature," in which the fifty-five simple substances were represented in relation to their combination with oxygen and caloric. The table also represented the new quantitative approach in the introduction of the suffixes: *-ique, -eux, -ate, -ite,* and *-ure.* Lavoisier used the example of sulfur to distinguish five different denominations corresponding to five different states of saturation with oxygen:

Lavoisier (1787)	Modern Nomenclature
acide sulfurique (or sulfur saturated with oxygen)	sulfuric acid
acide sulfureux (or sulfur combined with a lower quantity of oxygen)	sulfurous acid
sulfate (generic name for all the salts formed from the sulfuric acid)	sulfate
sulfite (generic name for all the salts formed from the sulfurous acid)	sulfite
sulfure (generic name for a sulfuric compound not saturated with oxygen)	sulfide

The systematic introduction of suffixes represented a revolutionary innovation in the grammar of eighteenth-century chemistry. The idea behind the system was not only to provide different substances derived from the same base with the same denominative root, but also to give a quantitative indication of different degrees of saturations. A variation of the suffix corresponded to a variation of quantity of matter. Lavoisier's dream of expressing chemical reactions with the rigor of mathematics found an effective means of application in the use of suffixes.

The nomenclature presented in 1787 was a total break with the previous chemical language; the alchemical terminology, the synonymous, and the phlogistic names were all expunged. The practical advantages of the new language were clear to all chemists, but it was also obvious to them that by adopting it they had to abandon the principles of phlogiston theory and embrace Lavoisier's oxygen theory. Because of this tension, the European chemical community initially reacted against the new language and claimed that its break with tradition was too deep to be accepted. And indeed, the *Méthode de nomenclature chimique* introduced a dramatic shift from the past. In this respect it is noteworthy that Lavoisier's nomenclature listed 1,055 new names for which only 361 old synonyms existed; two-thirds of the new names referred to substances unknown before 1787.

On the eve of the French Revolution, in March 1789, Lavoisier published his masterpiece, the *Traité élémentaire de chimie*. In the first part of the *Traité* Lavoisier formulated for the first time the law of conservation of matter and stated that: (1) an equal quantity of matter exists both before and after a chemical reaction, (2) the quality and quantity of the reagents always remain the same, and (3) nothing exists in chemistry beyond changes and modifications in the combination of the reagents. In the second part of the *Traité* Lavoisier presented the famous table of thirty-three simple substances in which he established the frame of the complex mosaic of chemical matter. In the third part, the French chemist finally exhibited the pneumatic instruments he had used to illustrate his chemical analysis and experiments. With the publication of this milestone of scientific literature, chemistry became a science that aimed at a quantitative detection of chemical reactions. That idea, expressed in the concise and methodical nomenclature proposed in 1787, presented the contemporaries of Lavoisier with a tremendous challenge and led rapidly to the overthrow of phlogiston. It is in fact useful to remember that before 1785 Lavoisier was the only chemist in Europe to use the term "oxygen," whereas after 1800 only Priestley persisted in naming the same substance "dephlogisticated air." The chemical revolution was thus accomplished and a language that had survived for centuries was successfully eliminated in less than twenty years.

Marco Beretta

Bibliography

Abbri, Ferdinando. *Le terre, l'acqua, le arie. La rivoluzione chimica del Settecento.* Bologna: Il Mulino, 1984.

Beretta, Marco. *The Enlightenment of Matter. The Definition of Chemistry from Agricola to Lavoisier.* Canton, Mass.: Science History Publications, 1993.

Berthelot, Marcellin. *La révolution chimique: Lavoisier.* Paris: F. Alcan, 1890.

Donovan, Arthur. "Lavoisier and the Origins of Modern Chemistry." *Osiris* 4 (1988): pp. 214–231.

Gough, J.B. "Lavoisier and the Fulfillment of the Stahlian Revolution." *Osiris* 4 (1988): pp. 15–33.

Grimaux, Edouard. *Lavoisier 1743–1794, d'après sa correspondance, ses manuscrits, ses papiers de famille et d'autres documents inédits.* Paris: Félix Alcan, 1888.

Holmes, Frederick L. "Lavoisier's Conceptual Passage." *Osiris* 4 (1988): pp. 82–92.

Laudan, Rachel. *From Mineralogy to Geology. The Foundations of a Science, 1650–1830.* Chicago and London: University of Chicago Press, 1987.

Meldrum, A.N. *The Eighteenth Century Revolution in Science—The First Phase.* Calcutta, London and New York: Longmans, Green, and Co., 1930.

Perrin, C.E. "Research Traditions, Lavoisier, and the Chemical Revolution." *Osiris* 4 (1988): pp. 53–81.

See also Agricultural Chemistry; Atmosphere, Chemistry of; Chemistry, Terrestrial and Cosmical; Ecology; Geochemistry: The Word and Disciplinary History; Geology in the Laboratory circa 1800; Greenhouse Effect; Heavy Minerals; Mineral Waters; Mineralogy; Minerals and Crystals, Fifteenth to Eighteenth Centuries; Mining Academies; Mining and Knowledge of the Earth; Ocean Chemistry; Ozone; Petrology; Phlogistic Chemistry; Plutonists, Neptunists, Vulcanists; Water Quality

Chemistry, Cosmical and Terrestrial

The study of the elements making up celestial bodies, in comparison with the same elements on Earth, especially through spectroscopic analysis of the light they emit or absorb.

The spectroscope, which disperses light into a spectrum, provides a very sensitive means of detecting even trace quantities of elements and compounds in laboratory samples. Similarly, in conjunction with a telescope, it provides a means of identifying substances in stars, planets, and space. Historically, the two applications of the spectroscope were not disjoint; they developed alongside each other.

The guiding principle, that light emission or absorption at specific wavelengths signifies the presence of specific elements, pertained simultaneously to the Earth and the heavens. This principle overturned a more ancient conviction that the materials constituting the Earth and the heavens must be fundamentally dissimilar. In the older view, the Earth was the scene of change and corruption, while the heavens were perfect and immutable; the constituent materials differed accordingly (Pannekoek, p. 115). As late as the nineteenth century, the French philosopher Auguste Comte (1798–1857) stated that the composition of the stars is, for man, forever unknowable (quoted in Pannekoek, p. 407).

The first conceptual unification of terrestrial and heavenly matter came with the theory of gravity advanced by Isaac Newton (1642–1727) in the seventeenth century. In Newton's scheme, both terrestrial and celestial matter were ruled by the same gravitational force. However, a distinction between the two realms remained, in that heavenly bodies were not expected to deviate from their perfect orbits, while Earthly material eventually came to rest. This led some eighteenth-century scientists who considered themselves followers of Newton to doubt that meteorites, known since remote antiquity, actually originated in the sky. Instead, volcanic or atmospheric origins were envisioned. With others, Antoine-Laurent Lavoisier (1743–1794), after carrying out a chemical analysis of reputed sky-stones, ruled out the possibility of an extraterrestrial origin (Burke, pp. 10–11, 14, 27–28).

Leading academicians in Paris accepted the possibility of sky-fall only after the French Revolution, and upon the testimony of numerous common people who had witnessed an especially dramatic meteor in the countryside. Still, while sky-fall was accepted, the idea that meteorites actually came from beyond the Earth-Moon system gained acceptance only gradually, during the first half of the nineteenth century (Burke, chap. 2). When the idea took hold, knowledge that meteorites contain elements found on Earth meant that the ancient dichotomy between the terrestrial and the celestial was no longer absolute. Before space flight, of course, meteorites were the only samples of cosmic matter accessible for close scrutiny.

Prior to 1820, the German optician Joseph von Fraunhofer (1787–1826) began to map out the spectrum of the Sun. Fraunhofer found many dark lines crossing the solar spectrum, drew them, and designated the most distinct lines with letters for ease of identification. These lines were useful to Fraunhofer because he needed to understand the actions of optical glasses on light of various colors, and the fixed dark lines could mark distinct portions of the spectrum (Pannekoek, pp. 329–330). Fraunhofer designated one especially prominent pair of lines with the letter *D,* and noted that, in the laboratory, a flame might produce a pair of bright spectral lines at the same position.

Solids heated to incandescence give off continuous spectra, but gases emit light only at specific, discrete wavelengths, giving rise to spectra containing only sharp, bright lines, with dark spaces between. In the 1830s, the idea existed that the composition of materials might be discerned from their spectra.

In the 1850s, two pioneers began to pursue spectroscopy methodically in Heidelberg. Physicist Gustav Kirchhoff (1824–1887), in collaboration with chemist Robert Bunsen (1811–1899), assembled an apparatus consisting of a lens (to collimate light from a laboratory sample), a prism (to spread light into a spectrum), and a telescope (to view the result). Suitably arranged, these components enabled Bunsen and Kirchhoff to see laboratory spectra directly. The device as a whole is called a spectroscope (Weeks, p. 180). The spectrograph, which came later, made photography of the spectrum possible. (Bunsen is most widely known for a laboratory burner that provides a colorless flame.)

By 1859, Kirchhoff and Bunsen were certain that each element, in gaseous form, emits distinctive spectral lines. Two further insights followed. First, if illuminated brightly, an element might absorb the same wavelengths of light it previously emitted. (Others may have understood this, as well.) Second, Kirchhoff asserted that the dark *D* lines in the solar spectrum corresponded to bright lines emitted by the well-known element sodium in a laboratory flame. Therefore, the solar D lines resulted from light absorption by sodium in the sun. Kirchhoff quickly generalized this insight to other Fraunhofer lines, and concluded that a number of elements known on Earth were also present in the Sun. These included iron, calcium, and magnesium (Pannekoek, pp. 406–407).

Essentially, Kirchhoff had discovered the physical meaning of the Fraunhofer lines: gases in the solar atmosphere absorb light leaving the sun. If Kirchhoff's understanding was valid, then these hot gases also emitted light, but weakly. In the absence of light from below, they would furnish emission lines, rather than absorption lines. Among others, the American astronomer Charles Young (1834–1908) observed this reversal in the outer Sun during an eclipse in 1870 (Lockyer, p. 117).

The tools of Kirchhoff and Bunsen furnished insight equally into solar and terrestrial matter. They achieved an earthly success when they discovered two new terrestrial elements spectroscopically, in the laboratory:

cesium, named for the blue light it produces, in 1861, and rubidium, named for its distinctive red light, in 1862. (During the period 1859–1860, Bunsen also briefly collaborated at Heidelberg with Dmitri Mendeleev [1834–1907], although not necessarily on spectroscopy.) With the aid of the spectroscope, other investigators soon discovered a number of other, sometimes obscure, elements. William Crookes (1832–1919) detected a green line in 1861 that he attributed to a new element dubbed thallium, from a Latin term for green. Two Germans analyzing zinc ore in 1863 detected a bright, new indigo line from a heated sample, and named the new elemental source indium (Weeks, pp. 185–198, 211).

As for the solar spectrum, other investigators, including Anders Angström (1814–1874) in Sweden, took up Kirchhoff's and Bunsen's research agenda, making more detailed maps of the solar spectrum and assigning more lines to terrestrial elements (Lockyer, pp. 85–89). Angström's name is today used for units of wavelength. This work might variously fall under chemistry of the Sun, solar physics, or, in modern terms, astrophysics. As investigators extended their understanding of terrestrial elements to the Sun, they needed to distinguish between true solar absorption lines and telluric lines, originating from absorption of sunlight as it passed through the terrestrial atmosphere. In one instance, a French physicist observed a large bonfire from a distance of 21 kilometers (13 miles) across a lake, and detected many absorption lines that did not occur close to the fire (Lockyer, p. 66).

Some lines remained puzzling. In England, J. Norman Lockyer (1836–1920) concluded in 1868 that an absorption line near the Fraunhofer D line corresponded to no known element, and so suggested the existence of a new element, which he named helium, for the Sun. William Ramsay (1852–1916) eventually detected this element spectroscopically on Earth in 1895, deriving it from the mineral cleveite (Hearnshaw, pp. 84–85). More controversially, Lockyer formulated a "dissociation hypothesis," maintaining that complex elements would dissociate at the high temperatures in the Sun into simpler elements, of lower atomic weight. Lockyer also argued, as others did later, that light might arise from parts of atoms, not whole atoms (Brock, pp. 84–85). However, this argument antedated both the modern electron and the Bohr atom. Lockyer also made a common analogy, between particles emitting light and acoustic resonators emitting sound, that persisted in physics into the twentieth century. Lockyer wrote, "The law which connects radiation with absorption and at once enables us to read the riddle set by the sun and stars, is then simply the law of sympathetic vibration" (Lockyer, p. 63).

In the 1860s, astronomers extended terrestrial chemistry beyond the solar system, to the stars. The Sun was by far the most accessible celestial light source, and spectra from the stars were much fainter. As with the Sun, initial observations of stellar spectra were visual; then photography was introduced. English amateur William Huggins (1824–1910) pioneered stellar spectroscopy, and from spectral lines inferred the presence in stars of many terrestrial elements, including hydrogen, sodium, calcium, and iron. Wrote Huggins, "A common chemistry, it was shown, exists throughout the universe" (quoted in Hearnshaw, p. 70). Other leaders in the study of stellar chemistry were Angelo Secchi (1818–1878) in Italy and Hermann Carl Vogel (1841–1907) in Germany.

Huggins also studied astronomical nebulae, which he believed to be clouds of vapors or gas. Like Lockyer in the case of the Sun, Huggins found in the spectra of nebulae two green emission lines that corresponded to no known terrestrial element. He consequently named the emitting substance "nebulium." The question of the nature of nebulium was not settled until 1927, when the American physicist/astronomer Ira Bowen (1898–1973) found that the green lines arose from highly ionized oxygen, and not from a new element unique to the nebulae (Hearnshaw, pp. 71, 261–263).

Because of the faintness of stars and nebulae, spectroscopes could not disperse their light to a large scale; initial photographs of stellar spectra were less than 1 inch in length, limiting the amount of detail perceptible in spectral lines. The Sun, however, remained bright and accessible, allowing for much more detailed study. Among the physicists and astronomers who took up Kirchhoff's and Bunsen's program of interrelating solar and laboratory light, one of the most important was American physicist Henry Rowland (1848–1901). As in Heidelberg, the development of appropriate instruments was fundamental to Rowland's work. But unlike Kirchhoff and Bunsen, who used prisms to create a spectrum, Rowland, like Angström, used diffraction gratings, which produced a spectrum more easily measured.

Drawing by hand, Angström had recorded some one thousand absorption lines in the solar spectrum. Rowland, using photography and an improved grating of his own invention, recorded and measured more than ten times as many lines, and published extensive wavelength tables in the 1880s and 1890s.

Rowland hoped to bring the Heidelberg program to completion, identifying all solar lines with elements found on Earth, but the task was too immense for his laboratory at Johns Hopkins University. Even as late as 1965, the collective efforts of the spectroscopic community had identified only 73 percent of the lines (Hearnshaw, pp. 421–422). But Rowland's tables long remained a benchmark. By 1891, Rowland had identified some thirty-six elements in the Sun. Those producing the greatest numbers of lines were, respectively, iron, nickel, titanium, and manganese. The elements producing the most intense lines were calcium, iron, hydrogen, and sodium (Rowland, pp. 522–523).

From the belief that the composition of the heavens is ineffable, opinion had reversed to the effect that celestial matter was mundane. Not only were terrestrial elements present in the Sun and stars, but they were assumed to be present in similar proportions. In 1908, George Ellery Hale (1868–1938), the leading promoter of astrophysics in the United States, accepted Rowland's view that, if the whole Earth were heated to the temperature of the Sun, its spectrum would greatly resemble that of the Sun. Hale believed that, where the Earth possessed clouds of water vapor, the Sun possessed clouds of metallic vapor. The stars, he opined, were "enormous crucibles" (Hale, pp. 62, 191, 196). At the turn of the century, gradual shrinkage of the Sun was considered a possible source of the solar heat. Another hypothesis suggested a vast in-fall of meteorites as the source of heat.

The presence in the solar spectrum of strong lines from hydrogen, which is present only in scant quantities in the Earth's atmosphere, long remained problematic. Helium in the Sun, too, produced strong lines. Yet sophisticated analyses into the 1920s still concluded that the abundances of elements in the Sun and stars were comparable to abundances in the Earth's crust (DeVorkin and Kenat, pp. 181–183, 186). Strong hydrogen and helium lines were considered anomalous, but could not be explained away.

In the 1920s, physicists developed techniques by which to estimate the numbers of atoms required to produce spectral lines of a given strength, and these techniques led to a drastic revision of the accepted picture. Indian astronomer Meghnad Saha (1894–1956) derived a useful equation which could express the degree of ionization that atoms would undergo at stellar temperatures and pressures. American astronomer Henry Norris Russell (1877–1957), working with theories of the time and data obtained at Mount Wilson Observatory in California, was most important to the establishment of a new consensus, which finally conceded an overwhelming abundance of hydrogen. In 1929, Russell concluded that the solar atmosphere is mostly hydrogen (DeVorkin and Kenat, pp. 126, 197, 208–210, 216–217). That was hardly comparable to the composition of the Earth's crust. And although the stars might vary in exact makeup, all are more similar to the Sun than to the Earth. Russell, and contemporaries including Cecilia Payne (1900–1979) who furnished him with relevant knowledge, had effected a revolution.

Initial analyses of planetary light in the nineteenth century showed, unsurprisingly, that the planets shine by reflected sunlight; planetary spectra contain absorption lines familiar from the solar spectrum. Lockyer observed comets, and found that their spectra change on approach to the Sun. At a great distance, a comet typically shows only one bright emission line. As it begins to near the Sun, and presumably to gain heat, carbon appears. With decreasing distance from the Sun and increasing temperature, lines of manganese and lead emerge. At the highest temperatures, evidence of sodium and iron appear, as well (Fowler, p. 20). But planetary spectra did not show these striking changes.

Astronomers accepted the existence of an atmosphere on Venus in the late eighteenth century, from close observations of the planet when it appeared as a crescent. George Johnstone Stoney (1826–1911) had published a theory of planetary atmospheres in 1898. Based on considerations of temperature and gravity, he concluded that Mars must lack water vapor but possess frozen carbon dioxide. Stoney also concluded that Jupiter, because of its great mass, must retain helium and hydrogen, which escape the lesser gravity of Earth (Stoney, pp. 26, 46–47).

Spectroscopic understanding of the planets began to emerge before 1910. Vesto Slipher (1875–1969) found that the atmospheres of the major planets (Jupiter, Saturn, Uranus, Neptune) show strong absorption lines not originating in sunlight. By the 1930s, theory and observation by various astronomers led to the conclusions that Venus possesses carbon dioxide, but scant oxygen; Mars, too, possesses carbon dioxide and scant oxygen; Jupiter possesses ammonia and methane; and Saturn possesses methane and ammonia (Pannekoek, pp. 391–392). It later became clear that the atmospheres of the major planets contain much molecular hydrogen and helium. Not even the planets, it appeared, were necessarily like Earth. As is accepted today, "The chemical composition of the Earth is far from representative of the universe as a whole" (Ponman, p. 623). Hydrogen and helium are the most abundant elements, not only in the Sun, but throughout space.

The space age, of course, has made possible the study of cosmic chemistry by direct sampling, most extensively thus far on the Moon, rather than solely by remote spectroscopic observation. After the *Apollo* missions, it was certain that the lunar "seas" or maria are composed of basalts, resembling basalts on Earth.

Spectroscopy was, through the 1920s, a dominant specialty of physicists in the United States, until the emergence of atomic models that could explain the complexity of spectral lines from the elements, and the rise of nuclear physics. Now extended to electromagnetic radiations beyond the visible spectrum, spectroscopy remains an extremely sensitive—and routine—tool in chemical analysis, and is still virtually the only observational tool for determining the chemical composition of most of the known universe. Further historical research should better define the place of spectroscopy as a basis for physical knowledge.

George Sweetnam

Bibliography
Brock, W.H. "Lockyer and the Chemists: The First Dissociation Hypothesis." *Ambix* 16 (1969): pp. 81–99.
Burke, John G. *Cosmic Debris: Meteorites in History*. Berkeley: University of California Press, 1986.
DeVorkin, David H., and Ralph Kenat. "Quantum Physics and the Stars (II): Henry Norris Russell and the Abundances of the Elements in the Atmospheres of the Sun and Stars." *Journal for History of Astronomy* 14 (1983): pp. 180–221.
Fowler, A. "Objects for the Spectroscope." *Nature* 42 (1890): p. 20.
Hale, George Ellery. *The Study of Stellar Evolution: An Account of Some Recent Methods of Astrophysical Research*. Chicago: University of Chicago Press, 1908.
Hearnshaw, J.B. *The Analysis of Starlight: One Hundred and Fifty Years of Astronomical Spectroscopy*. Cambridge: Cambridge University Press, 1990.
Lockyer, J. Norman. *The Chemistry of the Sun*. London: Macmillan and Co., 1887.
McGucken, William. *Nineteenth-Century Spectroscopy: Development of the Understanding of Spectra, 1802–1897*. Baltimore, Md.: Johns Hopkins University Press, 1969.
Pannekoek, A. *A History of Astronomy*. New York: Interscience Publishers, 1961.
Ponman, Trevor. "Cosmic Chemistry." *Chemistry in Britain* 28 (1992): p. 623.
Rowland, Henry A. *The Physical Papers of Henry Augustus Rowland*. Baltimore, Md.: Johns Hopkins University Press, 1902.
Stoney, G. Johnstone. "Of Atmosphere upon Satellites and Planets." *Astrophysical Journal* 7 (1898): pp. 25–55.
Weeks, Mary Elvira. *The Discovery of the Elements*. Easton, Pa.: Mack Printing Co., 1933.

See also Age of the Earth, since 1800; Geochemistry; Nebular Hypothesis; Planetary Science; Solar-Terrestrial Relations; Space Science

Climate, Ancient Ideas

May have been derived from local experience of seasonal phenomena such as changing temperatures, wind directions, humidity, and heat from the Sun. Useful generalizations about these phenomena may be made in comparison with reports from those who have traveled in other lands. On a wider and more systematic scale however, ancient ideas about climate were derived from astronomy.

Early concepts of *klima* were expressed in terms of regions or zones. Eudoxos of Cnidos (d. 355 B.C.E.) used the term *klima* to designate an area on his drawings in *Circuit of the Earth* (cited by Strabo, *Geographia* IX:1:2). Such *klimata* were not like modern lines of latitude, but were wide bands of space extending around the sphere of Earth, perpendicular to the Earth's axis.

Greek and Roman astronomers used the terms *longitudo* (length) and *latitudo* (breadth) only with respect to the ecliptic, the central line of the zodiac. But the zodiac shifts across the sky with the seasons, so that a reference to parts of its length or of its breadth could not be directly transferred to the Earth's surface in order to locate a place or a zonal band.

One may notice however the relation of one *klima* to another in terms of daylight hours during the longest and the shortest days at one place corresponding with those at another. Having traveled the North Atlantic, Pytheas of Massalia (Marseilles), a contemporary of Alexander the Great (d. 323 B.C.E.), was the earliest to have expressed this method, in his work *On the Ocean.*

Later, the astronomer Hipparchos of Nicaea (190–120 B.C.E.) wrote *Against Eratosthenes* to ask "whether Alexandria in Egypt is North or South of Babylon and how far North or South it is," affirming that this may be learned only "by means of *klimata.*" Concerning the *klima* of a region he knew as Celtica at the mouth of the river Borysthenes, he reported that the Sun rose only nine cubits at summer solstice (that is, 18° in our terms). Other comments by Hipparchos allowed G. Aujac to form a table of correspondences by this method:

16 hours	9 cubits	[18 degrees]
17	6	[12]
18	4	[8]
19	3	[6]

The method is twofold: either count equinoctial hours during the Sun's course from horizon to horizon on the day of its longest visibility, which is the summer solstice (conversely, its shortest period at winter solstice); or, at noon on the day of a solstice, take the ratio of a length of shadow cast by a gnomon relative to its height (cotangent). The same number of equinoctial hours or the same *gnomon ratio* for several locations would place them within the same band of *klima.*

Any staff may serve as a gnomon without regard to its height; a building or a high bluff that casts a shadow will do just as well if the ratio of shadow length to gnomon height is determined. Often, however, Roman surveyors recorded only shadow lengths, a method that assumes that for the sake of comparison the gnomon will be like the hiking staff of an average man's height: six Roman feet, or 5 feet 9 $^9/_{16}$ inches English measure (Dilke, p. 89; Stevens, "Bede's Scientific Achievement," pp. 9–10, and notes 25, 26).

Special uses of a gnomon may be with a ball or disk at the top whose center is the top; the center of the oval shadow is then easier to determine than the indefinite end of a shadow caste by a straight stick. Another improvement was use of a very small opening in the disk: an aperture-gnomon gave greater precision to observations. (Lindberg; Bruin, pp. 21–25) An important special use is with a sundial whose gnomon castes its shadow on hour lines for either twelve variable seasonal hours of daylight or for twelve equal hours determined as twelve parts of daylight at the equinoxes (Turner). During the medieval centuries of Western Europe, all monastic schools taught and used equinoctial hours as necessary for the *computus* and applied them to hours of prayer, day and night (Stevens, "Bede's Scientific Achievement," pp. 8–10, notes 23–30).

Around such a band of *klima* it was possible to determine distances in terms of days and hours of travel, but the reports were quite diverse for travel even between the same places. Hipparchos thought that "we cannot accurately fix points at varying distances from us, whether to the East or the West, except by a comparison of eclipses of the Sun and the Moon"—that is, the difference of times at which an eclipse was observed on the arcs of lunar and solar paths would reveal the hours of *longitudo* along the ecliptic of the zodiac. A model globe or an armillary sphere would assist in the practice of those observations (Aujac).

Plinius Secundus (23–79 C.E.) said, "There are a number of segments of the Earth which we Romans have called circles, while the Greeks have called them parallels" (*Historia naturalis* VI, p. 39). Apparently, the term *klima* was not transliterated into Latin from Greek. But when he listed principal cities, regions, and people across his world from south to north, Pliny located them by the methods of *klimata:* lengths of shadows with their gnomon ratios, and hours during longest days.

When Ptolemy of Alexandria (100–170 C.E.) wanted to describe "our part of the inhabited world," he said that the surface "is approximately bounded by one of the two northern quarters" of the *orbis quadrata* (*Megale Syntaxis* II, p. 1, commonly called *Almagest*). Beneath the celestial parallels he had reckoned from his sources, Ptolemy enumerated eleven *klimata* at half-hour intervals for the longest day from the equator with 12 hours to Tanais with 17 (chap. 8). Again (chap. 12) he listed seven *klimata* on this basis from Meröe or Aswan with 13 hours to Borysthenes with 16 hours. The mouths of rivers Tanais (Don) and Borysthenes (Dnieper) are on the Black Sea. To these reports from his sources, he added calculations for one, one-half, or one-quarter hour between 33 *klimata* for his *oikumene* (chap. 1). Those were not his own observations.

Both in his *Syntaxis* and *Geographia* (if chap. 8 is actually his), Ptolemy expressed distances east or west within a *klima* by reference to the meridian of Alexandria. In *Geographia*, chaps. 2–7, however, his distances were stated relative to the Fortunate Islands of the Atlantic Ocean, a theoretical point outside of Europa and Africa, calculated in terms of hours of the Sun's course along the ecliptic, not degrees of the equator or degrees of the meridian.

On the *zonal rota* (see figure), the continents of Asia, Africa, and Europa were found within the northern temperate zone between the tropic of Cancer and the Arctic Circle, and the southern zone was also assumed to be habitable between the tropic of Capricorn and the Antarctic Circle. Between the tropics was the torrid climate of uninhabitable wasteland, with whose inhabitants (Ethiopians) nevertheless there was active trade. East/west lines could be multiplied on this model for identification of narrower bands of space in the known world from India to Spain and from Gothia to the northern seas and islands (Pliny, *Historia naturalis,* II). The lines on this zonal diagram are easily susceptible to modern terminology by attribution of degrees of north latitude, but that would be inappropriate. Both its lines and its spaces were thought of broadly as bands of land that enjoyed or suffered the same *klima, klimata.*

The method of *klima* and the recording of bands of *klimata* with lists of prominent cities and regions within them were used by all Roman and medieval scholars, notably by Isidore of Seville, Bede of Jarrow, Hraban of Fulda, Heiric of Auxerre, Abbo of Fleury, Johannes of Sacrobosco, and the many latter encyclopedists (Stevens, "Bede's Scientific Achievement," p. 5–10). Numerous *mappaemundi* of the *zonal rota* type attempted to display numerous bands of *klimata* for the Northern Hemisphere. But it was perhaps the *astrolabium planispherium,* an astronomical instrument invented perhaps in Alexandria (John Philoponos, sixth century C.E.) and found often in Persian and Arab courts, east and west (eighth century and later); the earliest Latin astrolabe dates from the late tenth

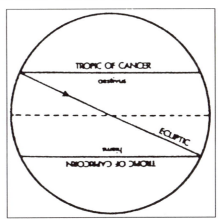

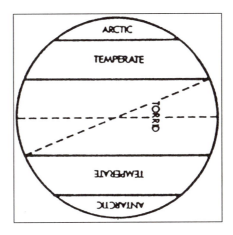

Eudoxian schemata for Heaven and Earth, known as zonal rota.

century, perhaps from Catalonia (Stevens, "Bede's Scientific Achievement," p. 9, note 25). That astronomical instrument was based upon the *zonal rota* but it described the heavens in a way that suggested a new means for describing the Earth.

The heaven of bright but fixed stars could be imagined on the early medieval astrolabe or quadrant in terms of circles of constant altitude, parallel to the horizon *(almucantars)* and equal arcs from zenith to horizon (azimuth): a grid of parallel curved lines. By analogy, the bands of *klimata* could be replaced by projection of parallel lines in a new grid for the whole Earth. Locations on the Earth's surface could be conceived in terms of 360° of longitude and 360° of latitude. This was probably accomplished only after the invention of graphs with *latitudo* and *longitudo* as coordinates by Nicole Oresme (1320–1382).

The temptation to express statements about *klimata* in terms of a scale of degrees has misled modern historians of geography and cartography. Thus, it has often been said that Ptolemy's method was to locate cities and regions "by a pair of coordinates." In fact Ptolemy used the methods of *klimata* and spoke of bands of *klimata* within his part of the *orbis quadrata.* Resolving his usages into modern terms of latitude and longitude is an entirely modern exercise that awaited four-teenth-century graphing and seventeenth century analytic geometry.

Wesley M. Stevens

Bibliography

Aujac, G. *Strabon et la science de son temps.* Paris: Les Belles Lettres, 1966.

Bruin, F., and M. Bruin. "The Limits of Accuracy of Aperture-gnomons." In *PRISMATA. Naturwissenschaftsge-schichtliche Studien. Festschrift für Willy Hartner,* edited by Y. Maeyama and W.G. Saltzer, pp. 21–42 (Wiesbaden: Franz Steiner Verlag, 1977).

Dilke, O.A.W. *Greek and Roman Maps.* London: Thames and Hudson, 1985.

Lindberg, D.C. "The Theory of Pinhole Images from Antiquity to the Thir-teenth Century." *Archive for the History of the Exact Sciences* 5 (1968): pp. 154–176.

Stevens, W.M. "Bede's Scientific Achieve-ment." The Jarrow Lecture for 1985. Jarrow-upon-Tyne: Parish of St. Paul's Church, 1986. Reprinted in *The Jarrow Lectures, 1935–1995.* Aldershot: Ashgate Publishing, 1994.

———. "The Figure of the Earth in Isidore's *De natura rerum.*" *ISIS* 71 (June 1980): pp. 268–277.

Turner, A.J. "Gnomon." *Enzyklopedie des Mittelalters* 2 (1988): p. 1525.

See also Atmosphere, Chemistry of; Cartog-raphy; Cosmology and the Earth; Earth, Models of before 1600; Earthquakes, Theo-ries from Antiquity to 1800; Flat Earth Mod-els; Gravity before Newton; Latitude; Mappaemundi; Meteorological Ideas in Clas-sical Greece and Rome; Meteorological Ideas in Medieval Islam and Christian Europe; Meteorology

Climate Change, before 1940

A topic of current scientific debate, with a history beginning in antiquity.

Any survey of ideas of climate change must take into account the masterly *Traces on the Rhodian Shore* by Clarence J. Glacken (1967), a study from antiquity to 1800 of three major themes in environmental history: the designed Earth, the influence of the en-vironment on humanity, and the role of hu-mans in modifying the environment. This last theme, along with ideas about natural causes of climatic change, has witnessed many changes and forms of expression.

The classical heritage related the climate of an area uniquely to its latitude. Climate—from *klima,* meaning "inclination"—was originally thought to depend only on the height of the Sun above the horizon, modi-fied in part by special local characteristics. In *Tetrabiblos,* Ptolemy divides peoples into southerly, northerly, and intermediate types based on their *klimata,* and assigns special traits to each. Theophrastus wrote of local changes of climate resulting from human agency. Draining wetlands removed the mod-erating effects of water and led to greater ex-tremes of cold; clearing woodlands for agriculture exposed the land to the Sun and resulted in a warmer climate. According to Glacken, accounts of climate change in Pliny's *Natural History* are derived from Theo-phrastus. In the thirteenth century, Albert the Great wrote in *De natura locorum* of humans modifying their environment by cutting down particular trees that either poison or stifle the air.

After a long period of relative inattention to this topic, European thought linking cli-mate change and culture began anew with Jean-Baptiste Abbé Du Bos (1670–1742). Du Bos argued in *Réflexions critiques sur la poësie et sur la peinture* in 1719 that artistic genius flourishes only in countries with suitable cli-mates (always between 25° and 52° north), and that changes in climate must have oc-curred to account for the rise and decline of the creative spirit in particular nations. Du Bos's idea that climate affects culture, derived in part from the writings of Jean Bodin, John Barclay, Fontinelle, and John Chardin. He in turn influenced other famous authors includ-ing Edward Gibbon, Johann Gottfried Herder, Montesquieu, and David Hume.

In his essay "Of the Populousness of Ancient Nations," Hume cited ancient au-thorities—Aristotle, Diodorus Siculus, and Strabo—as a basis for believing that the cli-mate of Europe and the Mediterranean area had been colder in ancient times. Hume be-lieved the moderation of the climate had been caused by the gradual advance of cultivation in the nations of Europe. Hume also thought that similar but much more rapid changes were occurring in the Americas. as the woods were felled. By the end of the eighteenth cen-tury, Enlightenment thinkers had come to the following conclusions regarding climate change, culture, and cultivation:

1. Cultures are determined or at least strongly shaped by climate.
2. The climate of Europe had moderated since ancient times.
3. This was caused by a gradual clearing of the forests and by cultivation.
4. The American climate was undergoing rapid and dramatic changes caused by settlement.
5. The amelioration of the American climate would make it more fit for European-type civilization and less suitable for the primitive native cultures.
6. Measurements of the American climate should begin immediately, before the climate changed too drastically.

Early settlers in the Americas, who found the climate harsher and the storms more violent than in the Old World, thought that clearing the forests, draining the swamps, and cultivating the land would change the temperature and rainfall patterns (Fleming, *Meteorology in America,* pp. 2–3). There was no general agreement, however, about the direction or magnitude of the change. Cotton Mather, Benjamin Franklin, Thomas Jefferson, and Hugh Williamson all believed it was getting warmer. According to Franklin, "cleared land absorbs more heat and melts snow quicker." In his *Notes on Virginia,* Jefferson summarized the positions of those who believed that the climate was milder than before. William Dunbar, however, saw the reverse trend and published his findings in the *Transactions of the American Philosophical Society.* Others speculated on the changes in rainfall that could result from cultivation.

Jefferson also thought that the progress of settlement inland from the seacoast would allow the sea breezes to penetrate farther inland than ever before. His concerns over rapid climate change induced him to begin a system of meteorological correspondence centered on the American Philosophical Society. Within two decades other groups, including the U.S. Army Medical Department, had begun widespread meteorological measurements across the country, in part to document potential changes in the climate.

The notion that human activity was causing climate change came under serious attack from several quarters. Noah Webster, in his essays of 1799 and 1806 together entitled "On the Supposed Change in the Temperature of Winter," criticized the poor logic and the misuse of ancient texts by those who thought the climate was changing. Climatologists subjected the growing amounts of thermometric data to statistical analysis and found no changes in the climate in recent times. For example, in 1844 Samuel Forry analyzed data gathered from over sixty Army medical officers and concluded that (a) climates are stable and no accurate thermometrical observations warrant the conclusion of climatic change; (b) climates are susceptible of amelioration by the changes wrought by the labors of man; but (c) these effects are extremely subordinate to physical geography: oceans, lakes, mountains, dimensions of continents over latitude, and so forth (Forry, p. 239). This tradition of citing stability in the historical temperature records was continued by Lorin Blodget in *Climatology of the United States* (1857), Elias Loomis in *Transactions of the Connecticut Academy of Arts and Sciences* (1866), and Charles A. Schott in *Smithsonian Contributions to Knowledge* (1876).

Cleveland Abbe, the chief scientist with the national weather service, agreed that the old debates about climate change had finally been settled. In an article entitled "Is Our Climate Changing?" Abbe defined the climate as "the average about which the temporary conditions permanently oscillate; it assumes and implies permanence" (p. 679).

As the debate over climate change caused by human activities was winding down in the mid-nineteenth century, the discovery that the Earth had experienced ice ages produced a plethora of complex but highly speculative theories of climatic change involving astronomical, physical, geological, and paleontological factors. Joseph Adhèmar offered one explanation in *Révolutions de la mer, deluges periodiques* in 1842. Later, James Croll, Svante Arrhenius, T.C. Chamberlin, and many others attempted explanations based on the behavior of the oceans, the Earth's orbital elements, and the global carbon budget (see Imbrie and Imbrie).

In the mid- to late-nineteenth century, infrared radiation was being measured at increasingly long wavelengths, first by Macedonio Melloni, with his "thermal telescope" in the very near infrared (see Barr). Samuel P. Langley published an account of his "bolometer" measurements at wavelengths of about 5 microns in the *Philosophical Magazine* in 1886. In the same journal in 1861, John Tyndall had related his pioneering work on the absorption and emission properties of atmospheric constituents, particularly aqueous vapor and carbonic acid (H_2O and CO_2). Increasingly in these decades national weather services and international exchanges of data were providing more global perspectives on the climate and its changes.

Also of note was the return, in the 1890s, of the concept of an anthropogenic role in climate change. In the 1896 *Philosophical Magazine,* Arrhenius specifically addressed the notion that burning fossil fuels may help ameliorate a deteriorating (cooling) climate and either prevent a rapid return to the conditions of an ice age, or inaugurate a new carboniferous age of enormous plant growth. Arrhenius, often cited as an intellectual ancestor of the greenhouse effect, had this to say on the topic:

We often hear lamentations that the coal stored up in the earth is wasted by the present generation without any thought of the future, and we are terrified by the awful destruction of life and property which has followed the volcanic eruptions of our days. We may find a kind of consolation in the consideration that here, as in every other case, there is good mixed with evil. By the influence of the increasing percentage of carbonic acid in the atmosphere, we may hope to enjoy ages with more equable and better climates, especially as regards the colder regions of the earth, ages when the earth will bring forth much more abundant crops than at present, for the benefit of rapidly propagating mankind (Arrhenius, p. 63)

This is quite different from both the pastoral view of the Enlightenment that clearing and cultivation would lead to beneficial changes in the climate, and the current view of a harmful, pollution-induced "super greenhouse effect" caused by industrial emissions and massive deforestation. For Arrhenius, as for most people throughout history, the dominant sentiment was that "warmer is better."

By 1900 most of the chief theories of climate change had been proposed, if not yet fully explored: changes in solar output, changes in the Earth's orbital geometry, changes in terrestrial geography, including the form and height of continents and the circulation of the oceans, and changes in atmospheric transparency and composition, in part the result of human activities. Based on studies of the intensity of solar radiation performed at the Smithsonian Institution, Langley and Charles G. Abbot concluded that the luminosity of the Sun varies by up to 10 percent, causing large effects on the climate. In the 1930s the Serbian astronomer Milutin Milankovitch outlined a comprehensive "astronomical theory of the ice ages," caused by periodic changes in the Earth's orbital elements, a topic that was debated until the 1980s. The continental drift ideas of Alfred Wegener also influenced the debate over paleoclimatic changes. Atmospheric heat budgets were first constructed early in the twentieth century by William Henry Dines and George Clark Simpson, among others. Both Dines and Simpson published in journals of the Royal Meteorological Society in Britain (see Hunt et al.). Measurements of infrared radiation at longer wavelengths—including the 8–12 micron atmospheric "window"—and at finer band resolutions were completed in the 1930s. Two examples are Paul Edmund Martin's "Infrared Absorption Spectrum of Carbon Dioxide," published in 1932, and L. Goldberg's 1954 "Absorption Spectrum of the Atmosphere." And in 1938 G.S. Callendar read a paper to the Royal Meteorological Society on the artificial production of carbon dioxide and its influence on climate. All these issues, especially whether the Earth would experience a new ice age or warm suddenly because of greenhouse gas emissions, continued to be debated after 1940.

James Rodger Fleming

Bibliography

Abbe, Cleveland. "Is Our Climate Changing?" *Forum* (New York) 6 (Feb. 1889): pp. 678–688.

Arrhenius, Svante. *Worlds in the Making: The Evolution of the Universe.* Translated by H. Borns. New York: Harper, 1908.

Barr, E.S. "The Infrared Pioneers II: Macedonio Melloni." *Infrared Physics* 2 (1962): pp. 67–73.

Fleming, James Rodger. *Global Changes: History, Climate, and Culture.* New York: Oxford University Press, forthcoming.

———. *Meteorology in America, 1800–1870.* Baltimore, Md.: Johns Hopkins University Press, 1990.

Forry, Samuel. "Researches in Elucidation of the Distribution of Heat over the Globe, and Especially of the Climatic Features Peculiar to the Region of the United States." *American Journal of Science* 47 (1844): pp. 18–50, 221–241.

Glacken, Clarence J. *Traces on the Rhodian*

Shore: Nature and Culture in Western Thought from Ancient Times to the End of the Eighteenth Century. Berkeley: University of California Press, 1967.

Goldberg, L. "The Absorption Spectrum of the Atmosphere." In *The Earth as a Planet,* edited by G.P. Kuiper, pp. 434–490. Chicago: University of Chicago Press, 1954.

Handel, M.D., and J.S. Risbey. "An Annotated Bibliography on the Greenhouse Effect and Climate Change." *Climatic Change* 21, no. 2 (June 1, 1992): pp. 97–255.

Hunt, Garry E., Robert Kandel, and Ann T. Mecherikunnel. "A History of Presatellite Investigations of the Earth's Radiation Budget." *Reviews of Geophysics* 24 (1986): pp. 351–356.

Imbrie, John, and Katherine Porter Imbrie. *Ice Ages: Solving the Mystery.* 2d ed. Cambridge: Harvard University Press, 1986.

International Geographical Union, Commission of Climatic Variations. *A Bibliography of Scientific Papers on Climatic Variations,* compiled by Henryk Arctowski. Lwów: IGU, 1938.

Martin, Paul Edmund. "Infrared Absorption Spectrum of Carbon Dioxide." *Physical Revue* 41 (1932): pp. 291–303.

Thompson, Kenneth. "The Question of Climatic Stability in America before 1900." *Climatic Change* 3 (1981): pp. 227–241.

See also Agricultural Meteorology; Atmosphere, Chemistry of; Atmosphere, Structure of; Climate, Pleistocene and Recent; Climate, Ancient Ideas; Climate Change, since 1940; Evolution and the Geosciences; Greenhouse Effect; Ice Ages; International Geophysical Year; International Polar Years; Meteorological Observing Systems, Early History; Meteorological Services, National and Regional; Meteorology; Ocean-Atmosphere Interactions; Solar Constant; Solar-Terrestrial Relations; Storms and Cyclones; Weather Modification

Climate Change, since 1940

A complex history of new kinds of data, computer-aided analysis, and new theories.

In 1940 climate was generally treated as a set of statistics about "normal" temperatures, precipitation, and other weather conditions, which were expected to undergo only mod-

est and temporary excursions. A half-century later climate was viewed as a planetary system, driven in alarmingly large variations by a multitude of internal feedbacks and external forces—not least human activity.

Well into the 1950s climatology remained much as it had been for the previous half-century and more: a scientific backwater, almost entirely descriptive, serving agriculture and the like. The usual assumption was that climate conditions of recent decades could be used to predict what to expect. If a region was subject to droughts and other transient changes, it was hoped they could someday be predicted through analysis of regular cycles, linked for example to sunspots.

It was known that there had been radical variations in the past, such as the warm epoch of the Middle Ages and the still warmer Carboniferous era. Above all loomed the ice ages as a central challenge to the few who attempted to explain climate change. Most believed that such major transformations were most likely caused by slow geological upheavals, especially the raising or lowering of continental areas, and perhaps by variations in the opacity of the atmosphere because of gas and dust from volcanoes and other sources. Nobody could specify just how these mechanisms operated, or even whether in fact they did.

More speculative were suggestions that climate was affected by periodic variations in the Earth's orbit, as calculated by Milutin Milankovitch (1879–1958). The slight variations in solar input seemed insufficient to transform climate over the entire globe. Variations in the radiation because of interstellar dust or changes in the Sun itself might do the trick, but these hypotheses lacked any observational basis whatsoever. Still less did scientists give much credence to the long-standing calculation by Svante Arrhenius (1859–1927) that humans themselves, by burning fossil fuels, were significantly augmenting the greenhouse effect produced by carbon dioxide together with water vapor.

Climatology began to change in the 1950s as it became apparent that the laboriously compiled tables of historical data were not applicable to recent years. Prominent climatologists such as Helmut E. Landsberg (1906–1985) increasingly agreed that the past half-century had seen a pronounced warming trend in the North Atlantic region or even worldwide. The news became familiar to the science-attentive public as they read reports about schools of codfish found north of their former habitats and the retreat of mountain glaciers. Melting of ice implied rising sea level, and some warned that coastal cities might someday be flooded. But most writers preferred an edenic vision of desolate northern tundra opened to agriculture. Whether the trend would continue, nobody could say, for its cause was unknown. The most common explanations invoked obscure and presumably cyclical processes involving volcanoes or the Sun.

The public, however, increasingly suspected that human technology could alter the globe, and not necessarily for the better. Many became convinced that nuclear bomb tests were already altering the climate, bringing unseasonable droughts or floods. Scientists added to the excitement with visions of deliberately altering weather patterns, for example by "seeding" clouds. John von Neumann (1903–1957) warned that future "climatological warfare" could become more dangerous than nuclear war itself.

Von Neumann himself founded a group, with military funding, that attempted to use electronic computers for long-range weather prediction. Work on climate change was to follow. Climate could never be understood until the general circulation of the Earth's atmosphere was explained, and attempts to find closed mathematical solutions had failed miserably. Theory could give no satisfactory explanation even for such simple facts as the trade winds. Numerical calculations offered a way forward. By the mid-1950s Jule Charney (1917–1981), Norman Phillips (b. 1923), and others had opened up the field with computer models that gave realistic weather patterns. These models could hardly be applied to studying climate change, however, in the absence of solid facts about what the significant forces were.

The first thing needed was an account of the actual history of the Earth's climate. Up to the 1950s scientists possessed only a few tools, from random remarks in ancient chronicles to the width of rings in well-preserved logs, all of debatable value. In the 1950s these tools were reinforced by more powerful ones backed up by carbon-14 dating. Most useful were ancient coral reefs, pollen in ancient lake beds, and, best of all, foraminifera shells in cores of clay drilled up from the ocean floor. The way forward was demonstrated in the late 1940s when Harold C. Urey (1893–1981) measured ancient ocean temperatures from oxygen isotope ratios in foraminifera.

In the following decade such tools, in the hands of Cesare Emiliani (b. 1922), Hans Suess (1909–1990), Wallace Broecker (b. 1931), and their collaborators brought surprising results. For one thing, carbon-14 dating showed that recent glacial periods seemed to accurately follow Milankovitch's orbital cycles. Equally strange, the last glacial period had ended around eleven thousand years ago with an episode of remarkably rapid climate change. The significance of these discoveries was recognized only gradually over the next two decades. These were the first solid signs that the climate system could be greatly affected by feedbacks, poised to flip abruptly from one state to another, with the feeble Milankovitch variations stimulating the flips and setting their schedule.

Pointing in the same direction were experiments by a group at the University of Chicago, who rotated a dish pan filled with water and heated at the edge. The resulting model of the atmosphere was complete with a miniature jet stream and tiny storms. The circulation in this simulacrum did not have a unique, steady state for its average behavior, but could lurch from one "climate" state to a very different one. Increasingly over the next decades, Edward N. Lorenz (b. 1917) and others warned that climate, like the dish pan, might vary in a way beyond our ability ever to predict or even to explain.

Meanwhile in 1956 William Maurice Ewing (1906–1974) and William L. Donn (b. 1918) caught attention with a theory that ice ages could be initiated when an open polar ocean fostered precipitation that would rapidly accumulate as ice. They suspected that just this might befall the world within the next few centuries. The cycle would be completed with falling sea levels, refreezing of the polar ocean, and retreat of the ice caps. While the theory was not generally accepted, it provoked thinking about delicate geophysical feedbacks and abrupt alterations.

Some claimed that nations might deliberately initiate such changes with titanic engineering projects in the Arctic. That was popular speculation rather than real science, but the idea that humans could alter climate was becoming acceptable. A pioneering advocate was Gilbert N. Plass (b. 1920). Using improved (although still far from perfect) calculations of radiation absorption, supported by advances in spectroscopic techniques, he predicted that by doubling carbon dioxide, human industry would cause a 3.6°C (6.5°F) average global temperature rise in the next century.

Most scientists supposed that such warming would be long delayed, because as carbon dioxide is added to the atmosphere the oceans would absorb it. In 1957 Suess and Roger Revelle (1909–1991) showed that in fact the oceans would absorb new carbon dioxide only very slowly and incompletely. The authors remarked that "human beings are now carrying out a large scale geophysical experiment" (Revelle and Suess, p. 19).

Much would depend on whether the level of carbon dioxide in the atmosphere was in fact increasing. Measurements were hopelessly inaccurate, and confused by irregular variations of carbon dioxide with the winds and seasons. Charles Keeling (b. 1928) attacked the problem with improved instrumentation and International Geophysical Year funding, monitoring carbon dioxide in the pure air on top of Mauna Loa in Hawaii. In 1961 he announced that the level was rising regularly, year after year (see Keeling).

Largely because of Keeling's curve, authoritative groups began to publish warnings of a future greenhouse effect warming. The sea level would rise, they said, and patterns of rainfall would change. Important examples were a 1963 report from the U.S. National Science Foundation and a 1965 report from the President's Science Advisory Committee. None of the panels demanded any change in industrial policy, but all called for more research effort on global climate change.

However, there were scarcely a hundred scientists in the world contributing regularly to climate change research, and they were too scattered among disciplines, from paleoceanography to solar physics, to exert organized pressure. Funding agencies responded with only modest increases.

Official concern nevertheless kept rising, particularly as numerical models produced convincing warnings. Building on the meteoric rise in computer power, groups at several locations greatly increased the spatial resolution and introduced a number of other elements that made their models more realistic. By the late 1960s these models could in some sense explain—or at any rate reproduce—the chief features of climate in most regions. Much was left out, with the oceans in particular barely represented, but the modelers could detect gross effects of changed boundary conditions.

In the forefront was an effort led by Syukoro Manabe (b. 1931) to produce the first full-scale calculation that accounted not only for radiation exchanges but also for convection and even some of the effects of water vapor. That turned out to be crucial: water would increasingly evaporate into the air as the world warmed, bringing a stabilizing feedback through greater cloud cover. The model predicted a rise of perhaps 2° or 3°C (3.6° or 5.4°F) if carbon dioxide doubled (Manabe and Wetherald). By itself this work would have been met with deep skepticism, but the number fell in the same general range as one-dimensional models based on simple radiation equations. As decades passed, increasingly sophisticated models would add confirmation.

This was no proof that the world would actually grow warmer, for other forces might swamp the effects of adding carbon dioxide. A number of scientists announced they had detected solar or terrestrial cycles that would make the next century not warmer, but colder. Others said that the observed warming trend was merely an artifact of measurements made in urban "heat islands," where local temperature increased with the population. Moreover, it seemed that since about 1940 the world had been growing cooler. Just at the time scientists had become confident that a rise was underway, global temperatures had perversely begun to turn back down, although the shift was so irregular that it was not apparent until the 1960s. The public became confused. Magazines sometimes predicted a balmy globe with cities flooded as the ice caps melted, and sometimes instead a catastrophic new ice age.

The uncertainties of the later 1960s grew when an increase in atmospheric particles was detected. Human agriculture and industry were pouring into the atmosphere not only carbon dioxide but also a variety of dust, smog particles, and chemical vapors. Similar material from volcanoes had long been known to cause temporary global cooling, and eminent climatologists such as J. Murray Mitchell, Jr. (1928–1990) and Hubert H. Lamb (1913–1997) felt that volcanic activity could explain much of the historical variation in global temperature. Then Reid A. Bryson (b. 1920) calculated that what he called the "human volcano" would rapidly cool the Earth by blocking sunlight; it might even precipitate a new ice age (see Bryson and Murray). These ideas were controversial, for only a minority of experts thought that aerosols from human activity could scatter enough radiation to matter. But with atmospheric pollutants rapidly increasing, studies on the effects were pressed. By the late 1980s these effects, notably an indirect one of increasing cloud opacity, were widely considered significant.

The Earth's albedo had always been recognized as an important element in climate change, but in the late 1960s it was getting increased attention. For example, simple calculations by Mikhail I. Budyko (b. 1920) and others suggested that the albedo of snow and ice brought feedbacks to a precarious point. The system could run away catastrophically, making the Earth a permanent ball of ice, or if things flipped the other way, a deathly furnace. Observations in these same years found that Venus was precisely a carbon-dioxide greenhouse hell and Mars a frozen desolation.

With different factors like dust and snow pushing this way and that, grave surprises might be in store. For example, beginning in the late 1960s several scientists hypothesized that with additional warming, part of the Antarctic ice sheet might surge into the ocean. This might happen within decades, they suggested, bringing both coastal flooding and sudden cooling. The first major public television special ever dedicated to climate warned that a "snowblitz" might pounce on the planet at any time (see Calder). Additionally, in the early 1970s disastrous droughts and crop failures in Africa and elsewhere focused public attention on climate change. Desertification seemed to be rushing out of control and the entire world food supply system looked precarious.

Few believed any longer that climate was static or, at worst, subject to gentle and regular cycles. Massive variation now seemed the rule, driven by human activity and many other forces. Some of these forces, such as volcanoes, could never be anticipated. As for the rest, there was increasing recognition in all the sciences that some systems—and the atmosphere was already the most famous example—are inherently chaotic. Their behavior, then, might be too complex and delicately balanced to define with even the most elaborate calculation. Thus while theoretical work on climate change had now become fully respectable as science, its predictive value was more in doubt than ever.

Help would have to come from data, and programs on an unprecedented scale were getting underway. Cooperating in complex social systems, geophysicists launched a Deep Sea Drilling Project (DSDP), an International Satellite Cloud Climatology Project (ISCCP), a Global Atmospheric Research Program (GARP), a Tropical Ocean and Global Atmosphere (TOGA) program, a World Ocean Circulation Experiment (WOCE), and various other programs whose acronyms stood for confederations of hundreds of workers measuring variables at a great many sites.

Still more costly and impressive were the satellites that for the first time allowed uniform and truly global data gathering. Even the International Geophysical Year of 1957 and 1958 had accumulated scarcely enough data to accurately characterize the general circulation of the atmosphere, while crucial information such as heat transport in the oceans had been wholly out of reach. But from the 1960s forward, satellites like *Landsat, Nimbus,* and their successors poured down worldwide data on temperatures, cloud cover, radiation balance, and so forth.

Other methods of data gathering in the 1970s were putting together the first accurate and reasonably complete pictures of past climate, covering many (but not yet all) regions of the globe. Along with traditional work using tree rings, pollens, loess beds, and the like, came numerous new methods. For example, isotope dating of coral reefs yielded a superb timetable of past sea level change. Meanwhile John Imbrie (b. 1925) and others pinned down ocean-core chronology by tying it to the record of geomagnetic reversal. They demonstrated irrefutably that the Milankovitch cycles show up strongly in a temperature record covering many millennia (Hays et al.). The unexpected dominance of a weak orbital cycle of about one hundred thousand years was convincing evidence that slow nonlinear feedbacks are crucial in climate change.

Equally striking were oxygen isotope records from ice cores drilled through the great ice sheets at Camp Century in Greenland and later at the Vostok Station in Antarctica and elsewhere. These nailed down both the long-term temperature cycles and the disconcertingly rapid changes at the end of the last glacial period. Around 1980 scientists learned how to extract air from the cores, and showed that radical fluctuations in carbon dioxide level somehow accompanied the temperature shifts.

All these data pouring in from satellite monitors, ocean sediments, and everything between, gave essential checks on the computer models. In the 1980s these models were emerging from infancy into the turmoil of adolescence. Modelers could now take into account many additional features, for example the effects of water vapor at different levels of the atmosphere. Better still, computer power had increased enough to allow crude calculations of the transport of energy in the oceans—an even tougher problem than atmospheric circulation, but of comparable significance for climate change. Models and ocean core data converged to assign particular significance to a gigantic but fragile cycle driven by water that sank in the North Atlantic.

Much in the models remained problematic, such as the crucial feedback from clouds. Thunderstorms were not easily modeled in cells that covered a million square miles. But confidence was gained when models that handled such things by different methods showed a rough consistency in the most important overall results. This consistency did not extend to the regional level. For a specified change in boundary conditions, at a given spot on the globe one model might predict higher precipitation, another lower.

As a separate check, in the 1980s modelers began to reconstruct past climates such as the recent glacial period. They could compare their results with figures compiled by the massive CLIMAP project of the 1970s. The reconstructions gave insights into radically different weather patterns, but they were inaccurate in significant ways. Thus the old central test of climate change theory—the onset and ending of ice ages—still had to be addressed with largely qualitative and debatable explanations, lacking the quantitative results that would demonstrate full understanding.

The history of these recent events is complex and confusing. That is partly because of historiographic difficulties discussed below, but partly because the trend of the science itself was precisely toward complexity and confusion. One reason was that old factors that had been considered merely speculative were reasserting themselves. For example, in the late 1970s John A. Eddy (b. 1931) showed that there had been a dearth of sunspots in the seventeenth century, and he argued that this was connected with the "Little Ice Age" of those years. Intrinsic solar variability, along with volcanism and other fundamental geophysical forces, would remain a joker in the pack for anyone who sought to read the future of climate change.

The difficulties redoubled as more and more new factors stepped forth as potential influences on the climate. For example, measurements in the early 1980s showed that methane and other gases besides carbon dioxide were rapidly increasing in the atmosphere, and might bring equivalent greenhouse effects. That suggested a prominent role for organic sources of gases such as sediments, northern bogs, perhaps even termites. The most crucial and unpredictable species was humanity, adding sources of methane as it planted ever more rice paddies and bred ever more cows.

Speculation about the impact of life on the physical state of the planet prompted strong feelings. The "Gaia" hypothesis that James E. Lovelock (b. 1919) propounded in 1973 argued that life had evolved interactively with the atmosphere, in such a fashion as to automatically regulate the climate system— or at least so long as the system was not stressed beyond some limit. Many nonscientists took up this viewpoint as a romantic teleology. Most scientists found Lovelock's hypothesis dubious, but it proved fruitful in directing attention to unexpected ways that biological systems could affect albedo, precipitation, and so forth.

Nothing was harder to unravel than biological interactions. An example of the difficulties was a controversy that began in the mid-1970s over the fate of the carbon dioxide added to the atmosphere. How much of it went into stimulating the growth of new plant matter and how much of it was dissolved into the oceans? Considering tropical deforestation in particular, was the terrestrial biota a net source of carbon or a sink? Whenever climatologists, ecologists, and oceanographers met they would get into vigorous and even angry arguments. Any conclusion about global warming would have to be tentative if, as many believed, a quarter of the carbon dioxide added each year was missing and unaccounted for.

The need for understanding came to seem more pressing during the 1980s, for statistics indicated that the rise in global temperature of the early decades of the century, which had reversed about 1940, had now resumed. More and more reports from authoritative groups (such as the National Academy of Sciences) insisted that the world should prepare for future harm from greenhouse warming. In 1985 the World Meteorological Organization came out for active policy changes to reduce the danger. In the summer of 1988, the hottest on record until then, James E. Hansen (b. 1941) testified to the U.S. Congress that global warming was already detectible. Attention rose sharply in both the scientific press and popular media. A poll in 1989 found that 80 percent of Americans had heard or read of the greenhouse effect. Most had some idea of what the phrase meant, although many got it confused with a different problem: the Antarctic ozone hole.

It had been noted in the 1970s that industrial expansion was rapidly adding chlorofluorocarbons (CFCs) to the atmosphere, and these would contribute to global warming. More immediately, the CFCs affected the atmosphere's protective ozone layer; public concern for this overlapped with worries about the greenhouse effect. By driving home how sensitive the atmosphere can be to human emissions, ozone depletion was probably a main reason for the increased prominence of greenhouse warming. Climate instability was also underlined at this time by warnings that a "nuclear winter" could result from dust lofted into the atmosphere by a nuclear war. Meanwhile the success of international negotiations to restrict CFC production seemed to provide a model for restraining other human impacts. The public, which tended to lump every potential insult to the atmosphere into a sort of all-inclusive pollution, pressed for something to be done to avert possible catastrophe. Science policymakers responded with expanded and reorganized research plans, notably in a program under U.N. auspices, the International Geosphere Biosphere Program.

While a few sociologists and political scientists have begun to study the social context of these recent developments, historians have not addressed modern climate research as such. An objective history of recent decades will not come easily. Study could begin with the accounts of scientist-participants sketched in review articles, some textbooks, and historically oriented books (such as Lamb; Schneider and Londer; Imbrie and Imbrie; Handel and Risbey). Of course scientists are liable to argue that the contributions of their own group should receive prominence. The historian cannot reply with the ideal of treating the past on its own terms, if that would mean giving equal space to each of the numerous research programs. Among the thousands of scientific papers scattered like seeds in the past, we are naturally most interested in those that have borne fruit. That approach is thwarted by current uncertainty about just which forces are most important for climate change and which approaches point toward the best explanations. Some controversies have remained unresolved for decades; matters now considered minor (as carbon dioxide once was) may eventually loom large, and vice versa.

The historian must also deal with fears that a wrong answer could bring a human catastrophe. Since the late 1980s there has been vigorous debate around the world, extending into electoral politics, over whether to impose such measures as a "greenhouse tax" on fossil fuels. Conservatives, always skeptical of environmental activism and governmental intervention, have insisted that such policies would be premature given the scientific uncertainties. They have argued against any interference with industry or agriculture, holding that a strong economy makes the best insurance against future shocks. Activists have replied that despite disagreements over detail, scientists generally agree that the greenhouse effect must inevitably produce global warming with severe consequences for many regions. Action to retard the damage should begin as soon as possible, they have maintained, and especially policy changes that they believe desirable anyway on such grounds as environmental protection.

These attitudes have been entangled with scientific arguments over, for example, the importance of solar variations in recent climate changes or the validity of numerical models. Historians who study the background of such debates must be wary of how their own political orientation is bound up with their attitude toward the plausibility of catastrophic global warming, and thereby with their reading of past scientific work.

Spencer R. Weart

Bibliography

Bryson, Reid A., and Thomas J. Murray. *Climates of Hunger: Mankind and the World's Changing Weather.* Madison: University of Wisconsin Press, 1977.

Calder, Nigel. *The Weather Machine.* New York: Viking, 1975.

Handel, Mark David, and James S. Risbey. "An Annotated Bibliography on the Greenhouse Effect and Climate Change." *Climate Change* 21 (1992): pp. 97–255.

Hays, James D., John Imbrie, and N. Shackelton. "Variations in the Earth's Orbit: Pacemaker of the Ice Ages." *Science* 194 (1976): pp. 1121–1132.

Imbrie, John, and K.P. Imbrie. *Ice Ages: Solving the Mystery.* Rev. ed. Cambridge: Harvard University Press, 1986.

Keeling, Charles D. "The Carbon Dioxide Cycle: Reservoir Models to Depict the Exchange of Atmospheric Carbon Dioxide with the Ocean and Land Plants." In *Chemistry of the Lower Atmosphere,* edited by S.I. Rasool, pp. 251–329. New York: Plenum Press, 1973.

Lamb, Hubert H. *Climate: Past, Present and Future.* 2 vols. New York: Barnes and Noble, 1977.

Manabe, Syukoro, and Richard T. Wetherald. "Thermal Equilibrium of the Atmosphere with a Given Distribution of Relative Humidity." *Journal of Atmospheric Science* 24 (1967): pp. 241–259.

National Academy of Sciences. Carbon Dioxide/Climate Review Panel. *Carbon Dioxide and Climate: A Second Assessment.* Washington, D.C.: National Academy Press, 1982.

Revelle, Roger, and Hans E. Suess. "Carbon Dioxide Exchange between Atmosphere and Ocean and the Question of an Increase of Atmospheric CO_2 during the Past Decades." *Tellus* 9 (1957): pp. 18–27.

Schneider, Stephen H., and Randi Londer. *The Coevolution of Climate and Life.* San Francisco: Sierra Club Books, 1984.

See also Agricultural Meteorology; Atmosphere, Chemistry of; Atmosphere, Structure of; Climate, Ancient Ideas; Climate Change, before 1940; Climates, Pleistocene and Recent; Evolution and the Geosciences; Greenhouse Effect; Ice Ages; International Geophysical Year; Meteorological Observing Systems, Early History; Meteorological Services, National and Regional; Meteorology; Ocean-Atmosphere Interactions; Solar Constant; Solar-Terrestrial Relations; Storms and Cyclones; Weather Modification

Climates, Pleistocene and Recent

Climates of the last 1.6 million years, if the base of the Calabrian formation in Italy is used as the Plio-Pleistocene boundary (Berggren and van Couvering).

Recent or Holocene climates date from the end of the Pleistocene at ten thousand radiocarbon years ago (Bowen, p. 106). The Quaternary Period (named by J. Desnoyers in 1829) encompasses both the Pleistocene and Recent (or Holocene) epochs (Berggren and van Couvering; Berry). But West *(Pleistocene)* and Flint (p. 384) have argued that the designation of the Holocene as separate from the Pleistocene is unwarranted because it is just another interglacial interval like so many previous interglacials (Bowen, p. 5). Instead of Holocene, West *(Pleistocene,* pp. 224–225) uses the term *"Flandrian,"* which in the hierarchy of stratigraphic nomenclature is a stage or age name, and West designates it as the most recent temperate or interglacial stage of the Pleistocene in which it follows other glacial and interglacial stages or ages. Such usage has not caught on, however, and Flandrian as a stratigraphic name is used only in Britain.

In 1839, Charles Lyell (1797–1875) assigned the term "Pleistocene" to what he had called Newer Pliocene deposits in 1833 and defined those deposits biostratigraphically as containing 90 to 95 percent modern species of marine mollusks (Berggren and van Couvering, p. A507). In 1846, Edward Forbes (1815–1854) recognized the Pleistocene mollusk deposits as representing colder climates than those from the Pliocene and proposed a new definition for the Pleistocene as a time marked by severe climatic conditions (Berggren and van Couvering). Forbes made the Pleistocene "synonymous with the *Glacial Epoch,* with postglacial time being designated *Recent*" (Bowen, p. 5). In 1873 Lyell accepted Forbes's definition, and the Pleistocene came to be defined climatostratigraphically as the Glacial Epoch rather than being biostratigraphically defined (Berry, p. 111). The idea that Pleistocene climates were colder than both Tertiary climates and recent climates therefore dates from Forbes (1846), who published his definition within a decade of 1838, when J. Louis R. Agassiz (1807–1873) first publicized the idea of a glacial period (Flint). Evidence that the most recent Glacial Epoch, or *Eiszeit,* began early in the Tertiary has forced stratigraphers to abandon Forbes glacial climatostratigraphic definition for the Pleistocene, but consistent with his idea of the Pleistocene being a cold time, the Eighteenth International Geological Congress in 1948 designated the base of the Calabrian section of marine sediments in Italy as the beginning of the Pleistocene because they contained marine fossils indicative of colder conditions than those occurring earlier in the Mediterranean (West, 1968; Berggren and van Couvering, p. A508).

Initially, the "Glacial" period, or *Eiszeit,* was seen as a single event that had caused species to migrate (see chap. 11 in Charles Darwin's *Origin of Species),* but in the 1840s and 1850s evidence for multiple tills was discovered (Flint, p. 17; Bowen, p. 2), first in France, then Wales, Scotland, and East Anglia. In 1858, Oswald Heer (1809–1883), working in Switzerland, was the first to identify sediments with a fossil flora indicative of a previous interglacial period like that of today (Flint, p. 17). By 1877, James Geikie (1839–1915) had interpreted four glaciations based on the East Anglican sequence of sediments and in 1895 proposed a system of glacials and interglacials for Europe. But it was the interpretation of Alpine river terraces in 1909 by Friedrich Karl Albrecht Penck (1858–1945) and Eduard Bruckner (1862–1927) that publicized the idea of four glaciations most widely (West, p. 217). According to Flint (p. 17), in 1882 Penck identified three layers of glacial drift in the northern Alps; Bowen (pp. 10–19) describes how Penck in 1885 used three river terraces to establish three glaciations for Bavaria and then expanded the scheme to four glaciations in 1909 by dividing the oldest terrace sequence in two. Both Bowen and Imbrie and Imbrie describe the rise and demise of the Alpine terrace data as a source of information on the timing of glacial and interglacial periods. Supporting evidence for four glacial advances for the Laurentide and Scandinavian ice sheets was worked out by 1900 and by the 1920s respectively (Flint, p. 17; West, 1968, pp. 217–219). This view of the Pleistocene as an ice age containing four episodes of glaciation has prevailed in textbooks up to recently despite abundant published evidence for an earlier initiation of ice age conditions and for many more than four glacial episodes within the Quaternary (Bowen).

The separate designation of the Recent or postglacial time dates from Forbes in 1846 (Flint, p. 382) and is an artifact of the concept then of there being just one glacial period or ice age that was followed by the warm climates of today. Gervais introduced the term Holocene ("wholly recent") in 1869, and in 1885 the term was accepted by the International Geological Congress (Bowen, p. 5; Roberts, p. 219). In 1969 the Holocene Commission for the International Union for Quaternary Research (INQUA) defined the Holocene as representing the last ten thousand radiocarbon years (with the Libby half life of 5,570 years) (West, 1989, p. 5), even though deglaciation was far from complete then and the Laurentide ice sheet did not disappear until about six thousand years ago.

The stratigraphic nomenclature for the Pleistocene and Holocene epochs remains burdened with multiple definitions and implications. Both of these terms and subunits within them have bio-, litho-, morpho-, chrono-, and climato-stratigraphic definitions (Berggren and van Couvering, pp. A506–509). Such a mixture of definitions can only lead to confusion because units that correlate by one set of criteria may not be synchronous or may not correlate by other criteria. Watson and Wright describe why this lack of correlation is expected, and Bowen (p. 79) notes that the choice of subdividing the Quaternary on the basis of climatic change means that "classification is based not so much on the rocks [fossils, moraines, etc.] themselves, but on climatic inferences drawn from them," which leads to problems of definition. The high temporal resolution and generally good time control for Quaternary deposits raises major problems for stratigraphic methods developed for pre-Quaternary deposits (Bowen, pp. 78–80).

As an example, within the Holocene, the warmest period has been designated as the climatic optimum (a value-laden term inappropriate to climatology), xerothermic (in 1942 by Paul Sears), altithermal (in 1947 by E. Antevs), or hypsithermal (in 1957 by Edward Deevey and Richard Foster Flint). The formal definition for the hypsithermal by Deevey and Flint mixes climatostratigraphic, biostratigraphic, and chronostratigraphic definitions under the implicit assumption that the biostratigraphic pollen assemblage zone inferred to be warmest in Denmark was globally synchronous with the warmest periods elsewhere (Kutzbach and Webb, p. 187).

Imbrie and Imbrie (1986) describe the evolution in understanding of Quaternary climates from the point of view of the influence of the Earth's orbital variations: tilt, precession, and eccentricity. They show how the theory develops and changes from Joseph Adhemar's initial formulation in 1842 to the 1863 version by James Croll (1821–1890) and finally to the version by Milutin Milankovitch (1879–1958) in 1920. They also record how each version of the theory was rejected and how even the data in support of the theory were rejected. (See also Kutzbach and Webb, pp. 179–187, for a discussion of developments since 1920.) Imbrie and Imbrie then describe how data from deep-sea cores provided support for the version of the theory that has wide acceptance today. They also discuss the development from the 1872 H.M.S. *Challenger* expedition until modern times of deep-sea data on past climates and how the continuous records of these data displaced the discontinuous records of moraines on land to show many more glacial periods than the four classically defined periods. Key to this development has been the use of oxygen isotope records from the deep-sea cores, which Harold Clayton Urey in 1947 theorized would record past temperatures and Nicholas Shackleton later in 1967 showed mainly provide a record of global ice volume (Imbrie and Imbrie, pp. 135–140).

One of the earliest sources of evidence about former cold climates was the description of mammoth fossils and carcasses in Siberia by Johann Georg Gmelin (1709–1755) in 1751 and Peter Simon Pallas (1741–1811) in 1773 (Sher). Guthrie (pp. 1–3) describes the debate between "floaters and sinkers," including Charles Lyell, who interpreted the carcasses and bones of mammoths and rhinoceroses as having floated from warm climates into the Arctic in floods, and Georges Cuvier, who in 1825 challenged this idea. The issue led to Russian and American expeditions to Siberia and was not fully resolved until the early 1900s. A second debate concerned how the carcasses of the mammoths that perished had been preserved.

On land, paleobotanical evidence has long been in the forefront for climatic inferences, since Heer in 1858 and Archibald Geikie (1835–1924) in 1863 used such evidence to infer that warm climates intervened between glacial periods (Imbrie and Imbrie, p. 57). West reviews the history of such evidence when used to describe previous interglacial periods and features the key contribution of K. Jessen and V. Milthers in 1928 in using palynological data to illustrate the sequence of vegetational changes during the last (Eemian) interglacial, which is now correlated with oxygen isotope stage 5e and dated to about 125,000±5000 years ago. Manten describes the history of Quaternary pollen studies that began in 1887 and gives a brief biography of Ernst Jakob Lennart von Post (1884–1951), who in 1916 introduced pollen percentages and made pollen data useful for climatic studies. In 1967 Margaret Bryan Davis published an English translation in *Pollen et Spores* (vol. 9, pp. 375–401) of part of von Post's 1916 lecture, and Magnus Fries published the pollen diagram that accompanied Von Post's original lecture in the *Review of Palaeobotany and Palynology* (vol. 4, pp. 9–13). Sharma and Chauhan describe early pollen studies in India and note the 1906 study by Ellsworth Huntington (1876–1947) of Pangong Lake. In another example of the belief in globally synchronous climate change, von Post in 1946 in *New Phytologist* (vol. 45, pp. 193–217) used regional parallelism to correlate postglacial pollen diagrams from around the world and to draw climatic inferences. From Holocene and previous intergla-

cial pollen records from Denmark, Johannes Iversen in 1958 developed an oversimplified three-stage model for the development of interglacial vegetation that still receives attention (Roberts, pp. 42–45), in part because it fits in with the biostratigraphic definition of interglacials (Bowen, p. 102). The records of other terrestrial data are described in West; Flint; Butzer; Bradley; and Roberts.

According to Flint (p. 16), Timothy A. Conrad, who was the first American to accept the glacial theory, was also the first in 1839 to describe evidence of frost wedges. Later in 1909, W. Lozinski introduced the term "periglacial" to be applied to the climates and features such as frost wedges induced by the climates near to ice sheets.

Climate changes in low latitudes were initially indicated by evidence both for glacial activity on tropical mountains and for high stands of dry lakes in arid regions. John Walter Gregory (1864–1932) was the first to record evidence of past glaciation on Mount Kenya in 1894, but a conference on tropical geomorphology in Dusseldorf in 1927 still concluded that tropical climates, at least those of tropical rain forest regions, had not changed during the Quaternary (Douglas and Spencer, p. 5). In 1884, "E. Hull first postulated that the Pleistocene Ice Age—considered as a single unit—corresponded to a period of moist climate, a 'Pluvial Age,' in the Palestinian desert" (Butzer, p. 312). Later, M. Blanckenhorn in the Nile Valley and J.W. Gregory in the Kenya Rift Valley extended the evidence for pluvials in the early 1900s. Speculation about tropical climates, which had begun with von Humboldt in 1811, continued with linkages of glacial climates with pluvial conditions in the tropics and culminated in 1947 at the first Pan-African Congress of Prehistory in the defining of four pluvials for the Pleistocene to match implicitly the four glacial periods (Butzer, p. 312), even though J.D. Solomon had already criticized the correlation of pluvials and glacials in 1939 (Bishop; see also Bowen, p. 54). Later radiocarbon dating helped convince Quaternary scientists that pluvials did not correlate with glacial periods (Butzer, pp. 350–351; Roberts, pp. 88–89). In 1921 R. Spitaler had proposed that orbital variations would influence tropical climates, but it took the climate modeling work of John E. Kutzbach (b. 1937) in 1981, time series analysis of marine data, and data compilations of F. Alayne Street-Perrott to show how the influence worked (Kutzbach and Webb, p. 179). Ironically, orbital forcing of monsoonal climates is much more direct than that for glacial climates, which orbital theory was originally to explain.

Climate modeling of Quaternary climates began in 1920 with Milankovitch's use of a zonal average energy budget model and was quickly followed by Spitaler's use of an empirical model (Kutzbach and Webb, p. 180). In 1974 Jill Williams, Roger G. Barry, and Warren Washington were the first to use a general circulation model to simulate climatic patterns for the last glacial maximum twenty thousand years ago (Bradley, p. 410).

Thompson Webb III

Bibliography

Berggren, William A., and J.A. van Couvering. "Quaternary." In *Treatise on Invertebrate Paleontology,* edited by Richard A. Robison and Curt Teichert, pp. A505–A543. Boulder, Co.: Geological Society of America, 1979.

Berry, William B.N. *Growth of a Prehistoric Time Scale Based on Organic Evolution.* Palo Alto: Blackwell Scientific, 1987.

Bishop, Walter William. "The Late Cenozoic History of East Africa in Relation to Hominoid Evolution." In *Late Cenozoic Ice Ages,* edited by Karl K. Turekian, pp. 493–527. New Haven: Yale University Press, 1971.

Bowen, David Q. *Quaternary Geology: A Stratigraphic Framework for Multidisciplinary Work.* Oxford: Pergamon Press, 1978.

Bradley, Raymond S. *Quaternary Paleoclimatology Methods of Paleoclimatic Reconstruction.* Boston: Allen and Unwin, 1985.

Butzer, Karl W. *Environment and Archeology: An Ecological Approach to Prehistory.* Chicago: Aldine Atherton, 1971.

Darwin, Charles. *On the Origin of Species by Means of Natural Selection, or the Preservation of Favoured Races in the Struggle for Life.* London: John Murray, 1859.

Douglas, I., and T. Spencer, eds. *Environmental Change and Tropical Geomorphology.* London: Allen and Unwin, 1985.

Flint, Richard Foster. *Glacial and Quaternary Geology.* New York: John Wiley and Sons, 1971.

Guthrie, Dale. *Frozen Fauna of the Mammoth Steppe.* Chicago: University of Chicago Press, 1990.

Imbrie, John, and Katherine Porter Imbrie.

Ice Ages: Solving the Mystery. 2d ed. Cambridge: Harvard University Press, 1986.

Kutzbach, John E., and Thompson Webb III. "Late Quaternary Climatic and Vegetational Change in Eastern North America: Concepts, Models, and Data." In *Quaternary Landscapes,* edited by Linda C.K. Shane and Edward J. Cushing, pp. 175–217. Minneapolis: University of Minnesota Press, 1991.

Manten, A.A. "Lennart von Post and the Foundation of Modern Palynology." *Review of Palaeobotany and Palynology* 1 (1967): pp. 11–22.

Roberts, Neil. *The Holocene: An Environmental History.* New York: Basil Blackwell, 1989.

Sharma, Chhaya, and M.S. Chauhan. "Palaeoenvironmental Inferences from the Quaternary Palynostratigraphy of Himachal Pradesh and Kumaon, India." In *Palaeoclimatic and Palaeoenvironmental Change in Asia during the Last 4 Million Years,* edited by D.P. Agrawal, P. Sharma, and S.K. Gupta, pp. 178–191. New Delhi: Indian National Science Academy, 1988.

Sher, A.V. "Pleistocene Mammals and Stratigraphy of the Far Northeast USSR and North America." *International Geology Review* 16 (1974): pp. 1–284.

Watson, R.A., and Herbert E. Wright, Jr. "The End of the Pleistocene: A General Critique of Chronostratigraphic Classification." *Boreas* 9 (1980): pp. 153–163.

West, Richard G. *Pleistocene Geology and Biology.* New York: John Wiley and Sons, 1968.

———. "The Use of Type Localities and Type Sections in the Quaternary, with Especial Reference to East Anglia." In *Quaternary Type Sections: Imagination or Reality?,* edited by Jim Rose and Christian Schluchter, pp. 3–10. Rotterdam: A.A. Balkema, 1989.

See also Age of the Earth, before 1800; Age of the Earth, since 1800; Atmosphere, Chemistry of; Atmosphere, Structure of; Climate Change, before 1940; Climate Change, since 1940; Dendrochronology; Ecology; Evolution and the Geosciences; Ice Ages; Mass Extinction and the Impact-Volcanic Controversy; Paleoecology; Paleontology; Stratigraphy

Colonialism and Imperialism

The relationship of the geosciences to colonization and the building of empires.

Formal and informal Western expansion have been intimately connected with activities of geologists, geographers, and geophysicists, among others, who often played an important role in the exploration, mapping, resource evaluation, and settlement of colonial acquisitions. The connection of geography in particular with imperialism has been sufficiently close to prompt the argument that the field owes its emergence as a modern scientific discipline to the European imperial endeavor of the late nineteenth century (Hudson, pp. 12–19). This is probably overstated, but the growth of Western colonies and imperial power undoubtedly proved a boon to the geosciences in the metropolitan lands in Europe, North America, and Japan (see Takeuchi). Apart from histories of geographers involved in surveying and mapping in specific expeditions, however, the role of the geosciences in the service of colonialism and imperial expansion has only recently become the object of any significant critical historical scrutiny, in works such as Trevor Levere's *Science in the Canadian Arctic: A Century of Exploration, 1818–1918* (1993) or the collection of essays edited by Anne Godlewska and Neil Smith entitled *Geography and Empire* (1994).

The "great man" theory of historical change dominated interpretations of the interaction of the geosciences and imperialist activities into the 1970s. Works like William Goetzmann's *Exploration and Empire: The Explorer and the Scientist in the Winning of the American West* (1966) or the essays edited by Robert I. Rotberg in *Africa and Its Explorers: Motives, Methods, and Impact* (1970) concentrated on examining the geosciences and imperialism through the careers of notable and influential individuals. Occasional efforts were also made to place geographical institutions in the larger context of modern Wester imperial expansion (McKay, pp. 214–232).

A new focus on the social and political context of the geoscientific interaction with the cultures that produced imperialism began to supplement the "great man" view beginning in the 1970s. With particular reference to the period of the "new imperialism" that began in the nineteenth century, many studies began to emphasize the symbiotic relationship between geographers and other scientists who benefited from the new jobs and public interest created by imperial expansion, and who at the same time helped by their scientific activities to legitimate colonialist regimes. The relationship of the geosciences to both formal and informal German imperialism is comparatively well covered. In *Studien zur politischen Wissenschaftsgeschichte der deutschen Geographie im Zeitalter des Imperialismus* (*Study Toward Political Science-History of German Geography in the Time of Imperialism,* 1971), Franz-Josef Schulte-Althoff has examined at length the role played by geography in German imperialism from 1870 to 1914. And Lewis Pyenson's works on German and Dutch geophysicists give sensitive interpretations of their cultural impact in the subjected societies. Elspeth Nora Lochhead has treated some aspects of this issue for Great Britain within a broader context in her detailed work on the emergence of the geographic discipline there.

Pyenson's judgment that the imperial role of the sciences in general has received far too little scholarly examination is applicable a fortiori to the geosciences. While the movement toward embedding the consideration of the geosciences and imperialism in a broader framework than that offered by an exclusive concentration on outstanding individuals or geographic societies is to be welcomed, a great deal of work remains to be done. Only in the case of Germany is there anything approaching a "literature" on the topic, and much work remains to be done on the role of the geosciences in the imperial histories of other nations. Research on the impact of the Western geosciences on the indigenous scientific traditions of the colonized cultures would not only deepen our understanding of the history of science, but also contribute to the understanding of the dynamics of cultural imperialism. Comparative studies that attempt to discover common elements in the experience of the geosciences in imperialism, as well as to point out unique elements of a particular nation's imperial history, would be especially productive.

David T. Murphy

Bibliography

Godlewska, Anne, and Neil Smith, eds. *Geography and Empire.* Oxford: Blackwell, 1994.

Hudson, Brian. "The New Geography and the New Imperialism: 1870–1914." *Antipode* 9 (1977): pp. 12–19.

Lochhead, Elspeth Nora. "The Emergence

of Academic Geography in Britain in Its Historical Context." Ph.D. diss., University of California, Berkeley, 1980.

McKay, Donald V. "Colonialism in the French Geographical Movement, 1871–1881." *Geographical Review* 33 (1943): pp. 214–232.

Pyenson, Lewis. *Cultural Imperialism and Exact Sciences: German Expansion Overseas 1900–1930.* New York, Berne, and Frankfurt am Main: Peter Lang, 1985.

———. *Empire of Reason: Exact Sciences in Indonesia 1840–1940.* Leiden, New York, Copenhagen, and Cologne: E.J. Brill, 1989.

Reingold, Nathan, and Marc Rothenberg, eds. *Scientific Colonialism: A Cross-Cultural Comparison.* Washington, D.C.: Smithsonian Institution Press, 1987.

Takeuchi, Keiichi. "The Japanese Imperial Tradition, Western Imperialism and Modern Japanese Geography." In *Geography and Empire,* edited by Anne Godlewska and Neil Smith, pp. 188–206. Oxford: Blackwell, 1994.

See also Cartography: Disciplinary History; Environmental History; Exploration, Age of; Geographical Societies; Geography and Imperialism; Geography; Geography, Elizabethan; Geopolitics; Humboldtian Science; Jesuits and the Earth; Masons and the Earth; Meteorological Observing Systems, Early History; Oceanographic Expeditions up to H.M.S. *Challenger;* Paleontology in Australia; Paleontology in the Antebellum American South; Polar Exploration

Computers and Meteorology

An essential tool in twentieth-century meteorology.

The electronic computer has had a profound effect on the evolution of meteorology since 1950, owing mainly to its very high speed and large capacity. Indeed, since it often provides the only practicable means of applying the basic theory of atmospheric motion, it has been a key element in the emergence of meteorology as a mature branch of physical science, on a par with astronomy, acoustics, and aerodynamics.

The other essential element in this advance was the body of physical laws that govern the behavior of any fluid, such as the atmosphere. Those are the second law of mo-

tion of Isaac Newton (1642–1727), relating the change of velocity of a unit mass of fluid to the gravitational, pressure, and viscous forces acting on it; the law of mass conservation, relating the change of density of the fluid to the net transport of mass; and the second law of thermodynamics, relating the rate at which heat energy is added to a unit mass of fluid to the change in its internal energy and the rate at which it does work in expanding against pressure forces. Each of these laws is expressed as a partial differential equation, involving the dependent variables pressure, density, absolute temperature, and the three components of velocity. Together with the equation of state, relating the pressure, density, and temperature, these equations compose a complete system, in the sense that there are just as many equations as there are variables if the rate of heating is regarded as known. In principle, those equations—the so-called hydrodynamical equations—determine the structure and behavior of the atmosphere everywhere and at all times.

The equations of motion and mass conservation were formulated by Newton in his famous *Principia Mathematica* (1687), and the thermodynamic energy equation was enunciated by Hermann von Helmholtz (1821–1894) in 1844. In view of the completeness and great generality of these equations, one might wonder why the theory of atmospheric motions had not been developed in the intervening century and a half to explain all meteorological phenomena. Simply stated, the reason is that it was so difficult to deduce the full consequences of the theory—that is, to solve the hydrodynamical equations subject to known boundary conditions and initial conditions imposed by the current state of the atmosphere. In their general form, those equations are nonlinear and thus do not possess families of elementary solutions that may be superposed to build up solutions that satisfy given initial conditions.

To be sure, many important results have been established by artificially simplifying the equations or by specializing them to apply to small departures from an equilibrium state. In those cases, the resulting linear equations may often be solved analytically in terms of previously tabulated functions, such as trigonometric and exponential functions or Bessel functions. An early example is Helmholtz's treatment of internal gravity waves, manifested by "billow clouds"—long parallel bands of cloud lying along the wave-crests. Others are the theory of "frontal" waves on the interface between a cold polar air mass and a relatively warmer subtropical air mass; the theory of Bernhard Haurwitz (1905–1985) of long waves in the predominantly horizontal flow of air in mid-troposphere (1940); and the theory by Jule Charney (1917–1981) of the vertical structure and stability of long waves (1947).

Significant as they were, these exact solutions of linearized equations did not lead much closer to the solution of the central problems of meteorology, such as the problem of predicting day-to-day changes of weather, that of explaining the "general" or average state of the atmosphere, or the problem of calculating the climatic response to changes in solar radiation, changes in atmospheric composition, or changes in the character of the underlying land- or sea-surface. To a large extent, this failure was the result of the inability of linear equations to describe the essentially nonlinear processes of energy transfer between different scales of motion. At the turn of the twentieth century, further progress toward the solutions of the fundamental problems of meteorology appeared to lie beyond our limited mathematical means.

The alternative possibility—that of finding approximate solutions of the hydrodynamical equation by purely numerical methods—was evidently explored first by Lewis Fry Richardson (1881–1953) in the closing months of World War I, in connection with the prediction problem. Briefly, Richardson proposed to represent a variable by its values at a regular array of discrete points and at discrete times. The derivative of a variable he approximated as the difference between its values at two adjacent points in the array, or at two successive times. With such approximations, the hydrodynamical equations reduced to a set of algebraic equations, involving only the numerical operations of addition, subtraction, multiplication, and division. The predicted value of each variable at an instant slightly later than initial time was calculated from these equations in terms of the variables' values at initial time. Thus, regarding the predicted values as new initial values, Richardson repeated the process to build up a prediction over any length of time.

Richardson carried out a single test calculation by hand between stints of driving an ambulance to the Front. His results, reported in his book *Weather Prediction by Numerical Process* (1922) were disappointing; the predicted changes of pressure were far greater than those observed to occur. Even more discouraging was Richardson's estimate that it would take a team of sixty-four thousand people, operating mechanical calculators, just to predict weather as fast as it actually happens. Interest in numerical solution of the hydrodynamical equations withered rapidly and lay dormant for twenty-five years. What was clearly needed were computing machines that operated ten thousand times faster than human computers.

The first electronic computers were designed and built by J. Presper Eckert (b. 1919) and John W. Mauchly (1907–1980) in the mid-1940s. These machines could perform about one thousand operations per second, primarily through the use of vacuum tubes as switching elements, rather than cogged wheels or electromechanical relay switches. Another major advance came with the realization by John von Neumann (1903–1957) that machines of this class must be self-programming, to avoid the human bottleneck of writing out the machine's instructions in full. Von Neumann and his associates designed a stored-program machine, in which the operands (numbers to be operated on) are stored at addressable locations in its memory, along with instructions containing the addresses of the operands. Thus, if a cycle of instructions is to be repeated, the machine is instructed to change the addresses of the operands where they enter into the basic cycle of instructions. This feature of the "stored-program" machine makes it ideal for large hydrodynamical calculations, in which a small number of operations is typically repeated on many different sets of numbers.

Seeking the most difficult problem that might conceivably be solved, Von Neumann singled out numerical weather prediction for special attention and established a small group for this purpose at the Institute for Advanced Study (IAS) in 1946. By 1949 this group had derived a special form of the hydrodynamical equations that was free of the difficulties encountered by Richardson, but retained the essential features of the atmosphere's large-scale motions. Using this formulation, the IAS group carried out the first successful numerical prediction on the computer ENIAC (Electronic Numerical Integrator and Calculator) at Aberdeen Proving Ground in April of 1950. The results, reported by Jule Charney, R. Fjortoft, and von Neumann (1950), showed that simple numerical prediction methods were comparable in accuracy with those of a skilled weather forecaster and could be expected to lead to considerably better methods.

These developments did not go unnoticed by the community of theoretical meteorologists. By 1953, no fewer than six new research groups—in the United States, Great Britain, Germany, Sweden, Japan, and the U.S.S.R.—had been established for the specific purpose of applying and extending the methods developed by the IAS group. As a direct result, numerical predictions were soon produced daily from current weather observations by U.S. and European weather services.

Owing to the necessity of producing a one-day forecast in less than twenty-four hours and the still rather limited capabilities of electronic computers, the earliest schemes of numerical prediction did not include the effects of atmospheric heating by convection, release of latent heat, absorption of solar radiation, or dissipation of kinetic energy by turbulence and viscosity. It was also realized that numerical prediction methods could not generate the correct "general circulation" or average state of the atmosphere unless they included those effects, simply because they are the ones that drive the atmosphere toward a definite average state. The effects of heating and dissipation were first included in a general circulation model by Norman Phillips (b. 1923) in 1956. His calculations, carried out on the IAS machine MANIAC (Mathematical and Numerical Integrator and Calculator), approximately reproduced the observed equator-to-pole decrease of temperature, the great westerly jet stream in the temperate latitudes, and the wavelength and intensity of large-scale disturbances in the flow of the atmosphere. Even though it was crude and lacking in vertical resolution, Phillips's model opened the way to extended- and long-range prediction of weather and climate.

With the adoption of the newly invented transistors as switching elements around 1960, the speed of electronic computers was rapidly increased to about one hundred thousand operations per second. Capitalizing on the great speed and capacity of the CDC 7600, Cyber 205, and other machines in that class, Cecil Leith (b. 1923) in 1965, Joseph Smagorinsky (b. 1924) in 1963, Yale Mintz (b. 1916) and Akio Arakawa (birth date unknown) in 1964, and Akira Kasahara (b. 1926) and Warren Washington (b. 1936) in 1967 designed and tested a succession of gradually improved general circulation models, with increasing spatial resolution and more refined treatment of thermodynamic processes. By now, calculations from these

models agree remarkably well with the observed features of the atmosphere's average state—even to details such as the double-jet structure of the westerly flow.

The step from general-circulation models to climate models was primarily to increase the averaging period from months or years to decades or centuries, and to take account of the effects of human and other biological activities on correspondingly long timescales. Thus, although the development of climate theory has not led to fundamental changes in the methods of calculation, it has required a ten- or hundredfold increase in the total volume of computation. Nevertheless, progress in this field has been rapid, owing mainly to the recent availability of electronic computers in the class of the Cray XMP and Cray YMP, multiprocessor machines that can carry out several different (but structurally similar) calculations in parallel. Over the past decade, numerous experimental calculations have been made to isolate the effects of deforestation, increased production of carbon dioxide and its absorption by plant life and oceans, and the effects of chlorofluorocarbons released as refrigerants or spray propellants. The results are still inconclusive, indicating that the average temperature of the troposphere is likely to increase, but at an uncertain rate. This question awaits further refinements of climate models.

At the other extreme, the advent of ever-faster machines has led to the development of methods for calculating short-range high-resolution forecasts of such medium-scale features as fronts, squall lines, and families of large thunderstorms. In the mid-1990s, these forecasts are computed at the points of a dense array, embedded in a much sparser array over which a low-resolution prediction is previously computed to provide boundary conditions around the dense array. Such limited-area predictions were introduced into the routine of local weather forecasting by the U.S. National Weather Service in 1985.

By now, numerical methods and the technology of computing have permeated virtually all branches of meteorology. Other problem areas in which they have been applied include the onset and structure of sea-breeze circulations and katabatic winds (cold air flowing down valleys); the formation and structure of lee-waves, manifested by lenticular clouds lying along the wave-crests in the lee of a mountain range; the growth and movement of hurricanes and tornados; heating by absorption of solar and infrared radiation by water vapor, clouds, and carbon dioxide; and formation of clouds by diffusion of water vapor and coalescence of water droplets. These and other applications discussed earlier do not constitute a complete catalog, but they may be sufficient to indicate that meteorology in the twentieth century has become a science of computing. Another indicator is the fact that over half of the original research papers now published in meteorological journals deal with the methods and results of numerical computation.

The face of meteorology has been changed forever by the computing machine. This is a multifaceted history waiting to be written.

Philip D. Thompson

Bibliography

Charney, Jule G. "The Dynamics of Long Waves in a Baroclinic Westerly Current." *Journal of Meteorology* 4 (1947): pp. 135–164.

Charney, Jule G., R. Fjortoft, and J. von Neumann. "Numerical Integration of the Barotropic Vorticity Equation." *Tellus* 2 (1950): pp. 237–254.

Haurwitz, B. "The Motion of Atmosphere Disturbances on the Spherical Earth." *Journal of Marine Research* 3 (1940): pp. 254–267.

Kasahara, A., and W. Washington. "NCAR Global Circulation Model of the Atmosphere." *Monthly Weather Review* 59 (1967): pp. 389–402.

Leith, C.E. "Numerical Simulation of the Earth's Atmosphere." In *Methods of Computational Physics,* edited by B. Adler, pp. 1–27. New York: Academic Press, 1965.

Mintz, Y., and A. Arakawa. "Very Long-term Global Integration of the Primitive Equations of Atmospheric Motion." *World Meteorological Organization Technical Note* 66 (1964): pp. 141–55.

Phillips, N.A. "The General Circulation of the Atmosphere." *Quarterly Journal of the Royal Meteorological Society* 82 (1956): pp. 357–361.

Richardson, L.F. *Weather Prediction by Numerical Process.* London: Cambridge University Press, 1922.

Smagorinsky, J. "General Circulation Experiments with the Primitive Equations." *Monthly Weather Review* 91 (1963): pp. 99–174.

See also Bergen School of Meteorology; Climate Change, before 1940; Climate Change, since 1940; Greenhouse Effect; Mathematics and Meteorology; Meteorology; Storms and Cyclones

Conservation of Natural Resources

Those living and nonliving, perpetual, renewable, or nonrenewable commodities gained from the physical environment to meet human wants and needs.

The issue of conservation has had a history of divisive disagreement. Public and private opinion over the appropriate development, protection, preservation, and rehabilitation of natural resources has differed in time, place, and culture. With the increasing burden of world population growth, intensive management of the natural environment will be required to maintain sustainability of life on the planet.

While some scholars consider aboriginal civilizations to be the "first ecologists," living in harmony with the land, examples, especially the use of fire, demonstrate that native cultures often altered the natural landscape to their perceived benefit. Limited population, however, appears to have been a more important factor than any well-defined, low-impact, indigenous land ethic. Nonetheless, traditional conservation techniques might prove useful for resolving contemporary resource management problems (Cronin, chap. 3; Klee, pp. 189–216; Ponting, pp. 1–7, 68–87).

As European-styled land use spread throughout much of the world following the Age of Discovery and resource consumption increased with the needs of the Industrial Revolution, naturalists began to voice their concerns for prudent management. Among them were William Bartram in his *Travels* (1791), Thomas Malthus in *Essay on the Principle of Population* (1789), Alexander von Humboldt in his *Essays on the Geography of Plants* (1807), and Thomas Jefferson, who practiced crop rotation and other innovative conservation techniques (Nash, *Wilderness,* pp. 54–55; Worster, *Ends of the Earth,* chap. 4).

While John James Audubon's magnum opus, *Birds of America* (1826–1838), visualized one aspect of the seemingly unlimited cornucopia of natural resources, perceptive thinkers encouraged the development of an American environmental consciousness in an era of manifest destiny. Ralph Waldo Emerson brought man and God together through *Nature* (1834), while Henry David Thoreau's "experiment in simplicity" (*Walden,* 1854) has endured and gained in influence (Cronin, chaps. 1–2).

As the exploitative resource practices of entrepreneur, speculator, and even homesteader continued unabated during the last half of the nineteenth century, conservationists stressed careful use of the seemingly infinite natural wealth. George Perkins Marsh, often called the "father" of the conservation movement in the United States, wrote the classic *Man and Nature: Or, Physical Geography as Modified by Human Action* (1864) in response to the despoliation of Vermont's virgin forests, and set the stage for further reaction (Cronin, chap. 6).

An active minority increasingly sought political redress and succeeded, for example, in the establishment of Yellowstone National Park in 1872. John Wesley Powell, famous for his exploration of the Colorado River, called for improved federal land-use patterns in his *Report on the Lands of the Arid Region of the United States* (1878), while the most revered of American naturalists, John Muir, found great audience for his wilderness preservation ethic through magazine articles and books such as *My First Summer in the Sierra* (1911) and *The Yosemite* (1912). He also used political agitation and founded the Sierra Club in 1892. In 1903 Muir entertained President Theodore Roosevelt in his beloved Yosemite Valley (Fox; Nash, *Wilderness,* pp. 108–121).

Although the preservation-minded Roosevelt was also a wilderness enthusiast and doubled forest areas under federal protection, he also advocated the need for rational development of natural resources. Creating the U.S. Forest Service in 1905 and naming Gifford Pinchot its first director demonstrated such beliefs. Pinchot was a utilitarian of the Progressive Era who believed that forest resources were to be managed for the greatest good for the greatest number. He expressed this position in *The Fight for Conservation* (1910). His multiple-use rationale remains central, although polemic, to twentieth-century American conservation thought (Nash, *American Environment,* part 2; Worster, *Ends of the Earth,* pp. 230–239).

With the onset of world depression and the American Dust Bowl years of the 1930s, resource conservation took on a dramatic urgency. Franklin D. Roosevelt created the Civilian Conservation Corps in 1933 and took measures to reduce overgrazing and soil erosion. The Tennessee Valley Authority (TVA), though controversial as a conservation project, brought a watershed approach to a regional

hydrological problem. The New Deal administration created the U.S. Fish and Wildlife Service in 1940 after intense lobbying by Jay Norwood "Ding" Darling, former director of the Biological Survey and president of the National Wildlife Federation, and others concerned with the apparent lack of governmental interest in wildlife conservation (Fox, chap. 6; Nash, *American Environment,* pp. 127–139, 147–151; Worster, *Ends of the Earth,* pp. 239–248).

Such renewed concern for wildlife and wilderness was particularly brought about through the actions of Robert Marshall, who became known as the founder of the wilderness preservation movement with his "Problem of the Wilderness" (*Scientific Monthly,* 1930), *The People's Forest* (1933), and his role in establishing the Wilderness Society in 1935. Aldo Leopold, schooled in the Pinchot forestry philosophy, applied the utilitarian approach to wildlife in *Game Management* (1933) but shifted focus when he asserted the existence of a land ethic in *A Sand County Almanac* (1949) (Nash, *Wilderness,* chaps. 11–12).

As the post–World-War-II Cold War and economic boom forced the United States into adopting a world outlook instead of isolation, an environmental consciousness slowly developed that went far beyond traditional conservation considerations. Rachel Carson's *Silent Spring* (1962) provided the impetus for grassroots political activism, while Secretary of the Interior Stewart Udall focused attention from the top down for the urgent development of a national environmental policy in *The Quiet Crisis* (1963). With growing popular support, the federal government passed air, water, waste disposal, and wilderness acts during the 1960s, while the decade of environmental awakening was capstoned with the passage of the National Environmental Policy Act (NEPA) in 1969 (Nash, *American Environment,* part 4).

Scientists reaffirmed the need for increased environmental concern. Paul Erhlich's *Population Bomb* (1968) warned the world that the postwar population boom could go beyond sustainable levels if it remained unchecked. The global society, but especially industrialized nations, needed to reduce consumption of energy and goods. Barry Commoner argued in *The Closing Circle* (1971) that technology was the prime cause of environmental degradation through the increased use of synthetic products. Regardless of the cause, sustainability of resources, both human and natural, has become the concern of contemporary global society (see Erhlich and Erhlich).

Environmental issues can no longer be confined to national borders. Overpopulation, rain forest destruction, desertification, the greenhouse effect, acid rain, and the disposal of nuclear and toxic wastes are but a few of the difficult problems facing the world. International efforts under the direction of the United Nations, most notably its Conference on Environment and Development, the so-called "Earth Summit" held in Rio de Janeiro in 1992, have begun to address the global sustainability question. Solutions, in part, will require a concerted cross-cultural effort to suitably manage the Earth's natural resources (Wilson, chaps. 14–15; Worster, *Ends of the Earth,* chap. 12).

The history of debates over conservation of natural resources is part of a lively emerging scholarship, often termed environmental history. While environmental history, environmentalism, and ecology are related, they are not identical. Scholars need to distinguish carefully among these as they write further histories.

William E. Fischer, Jr.

Bibliography
Cronin, William. *Changes in the Land: Indians, Colonists, and the Ecology of New England.* New York: Hill and Wang, 1983.
Erhlich, Paul, and Anne Erhlich. *The Population Explosion.* New York: Simon and Schuster, 1990.
Fox, Stephen. *The American Conservation Movement: John Muir and His Legacy* [1981]. Madison: University of Wisconsin Press, 1985.
Klee, Gary A., ed. *World Systems of Traditional Resource Management.* London: Edward Arnold, 1980.
Nash, Roderick. *Wilderness and the American Mind* [1967]. New Haven: Yale University Press, 1982.
———, ed. *The American Environment: Readings in the History of Conservation.* 2d ed. New York: McGraw-Hill, 1976.
Ponting, Clive. *A Green History of the World: The Environment and the Collapse of Great Civilizations.* London: St. Martin's Press, 1992.
Wilson, E.O. *The Diversity of Life.* Cambridge: Harvard University Press, 1992.
Worster, Donald, ed. *The Ends of the Earth: Perspectives on Modern Environmental History.* New York: Cambridge University Press, 1988.
———, ed. *Nature's Economy: A History of Ecological Ideas* [1977]. 2d ed. New York: Cambridge University Press, 1985.

See also Agriculture in the 17th and 18th Centuries; Desertification; Ecology; Economic Geology; Environmental History; Environmentalism; Greenhouse Effect; Mining Academies; Mining and Knowledge of the Earth; Pedology; Petroleum Geology to 1920; Petroleum in America; Soil Conservation; Soil Science; Water Quality; Wilderness

Contemporary Use of Historical Data

Addresses a characteristic of many geosciences, namely their occasional reliance on historical data.

Analyses of long-term phenomena in the geosciences require time series of sufficient duration for adequate resolution of these phenomena. Historical data provide just such time series and can be used successfully in fields such as geomagnetism, tectonics, seismology, earth orientation, climate, and in studies of the Sun.

This article is restricted to the uses of actual observations taken in the past, and omits inferences that can be made regarding the past through contemporary measurements of natural recording media (such as magnetization of rocks, growth rates of plants, and varves). Modern scientists interpreting historical data face an obstacle in that the conditions under which the observations were made are often unknown. Therefore the reliability and the realistic size of error of an observation are frequently difficult to determine. For example, before the invention of the marine chronometer by John Harrison (1693–1776) and others in the 1770s, longitude at sea was very difficult to determine (Malin). Measurements of the declination of a compass taken by mariners, which have been of great use in the field of geomagnetism, are thus subject to large uncertainties in longitude. Modern studies have found discrepancies during the seventeenth and eighteenth centuries of up to 20°. Nevertheless, plotting the data on a modern chart, accompanied by examination of the original ship's logs for recordings of wind speeds and place names, can often bring great rewards.

Consider as an example the current utility of historical magnetic data. The main geomagnetic field has its source in the fluid outer core of the Earth, and its change with time—the secular variation—is one of the few ways of investigating the dynamics of the outer core. Typical time scales for the secular variation range from decades to centuries, and studies of the evolution of the field demand data that extend over time intervals that are at least as long. It is thus fortunate that geomagnetism is one of the oldest branches of the exact observational sciences: theoretical and observational aspects were discussed as long ago as 1600, as discussed by S.R.C. Malin in "Historical Introduction to Geomagnetism" (pp. 1–49).

In addition to the theoretical interest in geomagnetism, it was the practical aspects of the Earth's magnetic field, in particular the use of the magnetic compass in navigation, that resulted in the wealth of historical data that has been accumulated since the end of the fifteenth century. As soon as it was realized that the magnetic compass did not everywhere point true north, it became necessary to make observations to enable corrections to be made from magnetic to true north. As noted above, one of the largest sources of error in early magnetic data was in the longitude of the observations, although latitude was measured with adequate accuracy throughout the period in question. Catalogs and collections of historical geomagnetic data have been compiled almost since the start of systematic observations, but the most recent and comprehensive is that made by Jeremy Bloxham, David Gubbins, and Andrew Jackson (1989). To avoid the danger of transcription errors, original sources of observations were consulted where possible. This collection was made primarily to provide a data-base from which to produce global mathematical models of the geomagnetic field and its secular variation from the earliest possible time to the present. Such models can then be used to study processes in the Earth's core and lower mantle. The models so far produced give a remarkably detailed picture of how the Earth's main magnetic field has evolved over the past three hundred years.

We now understand that short-period phenomena of geomagnetism (with periods of a few minutes to several hours) are caused by electric currents flowing in the Earth's upper atmosphere and that the influences controlling them originate in the Sun. In particular, many of these phenomena exhibit time changes that are connected with the sunspot cycle, the approximately eleven-year pe-

riodicity shown by the number of spots visible on the surface of the Sun. Since observations of sunspots date back to soon after Galileo's first use of the telescope in astronomy in the early years of the seventeenth century, there exists another geophysically important data set that covers, at least potentially, several centuries. The qualification is necessary because systematic sunspot counts date only from the mid-nineteenth century. However, inferences concerning the sunspot cycle can be made from historical records of auroras (northern lights) and of magnetic disturbances (magnetic storms), and a reasonably detailed description of the cyclic behavior of the Sun has been produced back to the time of the first telescopic observations and even beyond.

There are few areas of geophysics in which historical data, both instrumental and documentary, are so critically important as in seismology. Earthquakes pose a severe hazard to human life, the worst earthquake disasters having caused fatality figures in excess of five hundred thousand. Such destructiveness is unequalled by other types of disaster, natural or manmade. It is therefore one of the principal objectives of seismology to do what is possible to minimize the risk to human society from earthquakes. This can be done most effectively by studying the level of earthquake hazard at a particular place and recommending the appropriate engineering provisions to help ensure that buildings will be safe in any future earthquake.

Because of the complexity of the causes of earthquakes and the fact that they occur deep underground where direct physical observation is impossible, the only way to study the processes that govern earthquake occurrence is by examining the records of past earthquakes. And since the time cycles of individual earthquake-producing faults are often measured in hundreds of years, this means that historical research is essential.

Such research takes two forms. In the first case, instrumental records of historical earthquakes recorded on early seismometers are of great value. These are available back to about 1900, and enable us to make direct measurements of earthquake magnitude (a value proportional to the energy release of the earthquake, used as a measure of earthquake "size"). For seismically active areas, this period may contain enough earthquakes to make meaningful statistical analyses of earthquake probabilities possible. Usually that is not the case, and studies of twentieth-century earthquakes are undertaken in such a way as to enable a calibration of earthquake magnitude and earthquake effects to be made. It is then possible to collect historical descriptions of earlier earthquakes and use the calibration derived from twentieth-century data to estimate magnitudes for those earlier quakes. The result is a consistent catalog of earthquakes spanning several hundred years that can be used for statistical analyses of patterns of earthquake hazard. A good example is the study of Persian earthquakes made by Nicholas N. Ambraseys and Charles P. Melville in 1982.

A third area of the geosciences partially reliant on historical data concerns the angular velocity of the Earth's rotation (or, equivalently, the length of day), which undergoes small but detectable changes on a range of time scales. Changes on the shortest time scale, which are predominantly the result of exchange of angular momentum between the solid Earth and the atmosphere, can be measured accurately by the technique of Very Long Baseline Interferometry using radio telescopes. Changes on the time scale of decades, and the slow secular change in the rotation rate (attributable primarily to tidal friction) can be deduced only from historical measurements. A most valuable data set has been compiled by Francis Richard Stephenson and Leslie V. Morrison, encompassing data stretching back to Babylonian times. Telescopic observations of transits, eclipses, and occultations have been taken from the seventeenth century onwards. The accuracy of the measurements clearly decreases with their age, though even nineteenth-century observations are of sufficient quality to show unequivocal variations on a decadal time scale. Very early data serve to constrain the secular decrease in rotation rate. It is possible to predict this decrease from measurements of changes in the angular momentum of the Moon deduced from variations in its orbit, and from measurements of the changes in the Earth's moment of inertia by using the principle of conservation of angular momentum. The historical estimates are found to compare very favorably.

A similarly valuable collection exists of polar motion data (the components of displacement perpendicular to the rotation axis), though not as far back in time as for the length of day. The most reliable observations are for the twentieth century, made by the International Latitude Service and described in Kurt Lambeck's book. These data clearly show the existence of the Chandler Wobble, a free nutation of the Earth. The data have been valuable in determining the period of the wobble, which is significantly modified from that which would occur in a rigid oceanless Earth. As yet, excitation mechanisms for the wobble have not been established.

Finally we mention some other important areas of application of historical data. In climatology, Charles Keeling's measurements since the late 1950s of carbon dioxide concentrations in the atmosphere at Mauna Loa Observatory in Hawaii have established without doubt a monotonic increase in concentration superimposed on the seasonal variations. In geodesy, historical triangulation surveys have been compared with modern surveys, often performed using the satellite-based Global Positioning System, to calculate to high accuracy deformation in tectonically active regions. Surveys dating from the mid-nineteenth century have been used in California, and similar exercises have been carried out in the Aegean and New Zealand. Long time spans are needed, because even in very active areas strain rates may be only one part in ten million per year. Triangulation results can often be accompanied by an analysis of the fault-plane solutions of historical earthquakes; these give independent checks on the directions of compression and dilatation deduced from the triangulation.

Clearly, historical data are a valuable resource in the geosciences. Often, valuable data have been lost over time, and they cannot be re-created; and today's current data are tomorrow's historical data. It is therefore essential that the data we have are properly preserved and archived, for who is to say that future analyses of as yet unstudied phenomena may not require them?

Andrew Jackson
David Barraclough

Bibliography

Ambraseys, Nicholas N., and Charles P. Melville. *A History of Persian Earthquakes.* Cambridge: Cambridge University Press, 1982.

Bloxham, Jeremy, David Gubbins, and Andrew Jackson. "Geomagnetic Secular Variation." *Philosophical Transactions of the Royal Society* 329 (1989): pp. 415–502.

Guidoboni, Emanuela, Alberto Comastri, and Giusto Traina. *Catalogue of Ancient Earthquakes in the Mediterranean Area up to the Tenth Century.* Rome: Istituto Nazionale di Geofisica, 1994.

Lambeck, Kurt. *The Earth's Variable Rotation.* Cambridge: Cambridge University Press, 1980.

Malin, S.R.C. "Historical Introduction to Geomagnetism." In vol. 1 of *Geomagnetism,* edited by J.A. Jacobs, pp. 1–49. London: Academic Press, 1987.

Stephenson, Francis Richard, and Leslie V. Morrison. "Long Term Changes in the Rotation of the Earth: 700 B.C. to A.D. 1980." *Philosophical Transactions of the Royal Society* 313 (1984): pp. 47–70.

See also Climate Change, since 1940; Earthquakes, Historic; Earthquakes, Prediction; Geomagnetism, Theories before 1800; Geomagnetism, Theories since 1900; Geomagnetism, Theories between 1800 and 1900; Seismology, Historical

Continental Drift and Plate Tectonics

Among the most important collections of events in the geosciences in the twentieth century.

The earth sciences underwent a conceptual revolution during the 1960s, which ended nearly sixty years of controversy over the reality of continental drift. Before 1966 only a few workers accepted continental drift as a working hypothesis. Those who worked upon large-scale questions concerned with the evolution of the Earth's surface features mostly supported some sort of fixist theory. Fixist theories maintain that the continents and oceans have not appreciably changed their position relative to each other, whereas theories with the continental drift tradition (hereafter, the mobilist tradition) maintain that they have done so. Included among those theories within the mobilist tradition are the theories of continental drift or continental displacement proposed by Alfred Wegener, Frank Taylor, Alex du Toit, and Reginald Daly; theories of sea-floor thinning proposed by Arthur Holmes and H.W. Menard; theories of sea-floor spreading proposed by Harry Hess and Robert Dietz; theories of earth expansion proposed by Bruce Heezen, and S.W. Carey; and the theory of plate tectonics proposed by H.W. Morgan and Dan McKenzie. There was, in the earth science community, a general if unspoken commitment to fixism. Then in 1966 came the splendid confirmation of sea-floor spreading, and within a year the revolution was completed with the development of a mobilist theory of plate tectonics. Plate tectonics is now the reigning theory in the earth sciences, and continues to pro-vide a comprehensive and fruitful framework for investigating many problems.

Within the overall controversy there are two conceptually and temporally overlapping controversies: classical and modern. The classical controversy began around 1910, and had for the most part run its course by 1950, although it meandered through the fields of paleontology and paleoclimatology until the early 1960s. Every mobilist theory that received serious attention during the classical period gained support from physical geography, paleoclimatology, paleontology, geodesy, and other traditional areas of the earth sciences. The modern controversy began around 1950, and came about because of rapid developments in paleomagnetism and studies of the ocean floor. The paleomagnetic case for continental drift was in full swing by the late 1950s. Although former proponents of continental drift welcomed these new findings, most earth scientists found them insufficient to change their minds. Ocean floor studies underwent a tremendous growth during the 1950s, and, in the late 1950s and early 1960s, a few oceanographers solved several new problems by invoking either continental drift or earth expansion. However, other oceanographers offered fixist solutions to these same new problems. This debate was resolved in 1966 when most researchers accepted sea-floor spreading (a mobilist theory that did not involve earth expansion), and the controversy between mobilism and fixism ended. The end came from new discoveries about the sea floor that depended upon the development and use of geophysical techniques, including those that had been developed by paleomagnetists. Most of these new converts to mobilism quickly familiarized themselves with and made use of the classical case for mobilism, but the latter played, with one notable exception (namely, a 1965 computer-generated fit of the continents around the Atlantic), at most a minor role in the rapid acceptance of plate tectonics.

The aims of this essay are to outline the overall controversy over the reality of continental drift, and to address the question of why continental drift theories were rejected by most earth scientists until the confirmation of sea-floor spreading but were largely accepted with the confirmation of sea-floor spreading. This latter aim has been the focus of several historians and philosophers of science during the last fifteen years. (See Frankel, "Reception and Acceptance of Continental Drift" and "Vine-Matthews-Morley Hypothesis"; Glen; Hallam, *Revolution* and *Great Geological Controversies;* R. Laudan, "Recent Revolution"; Le Grand; Menard; Nunan; Oreskes; Stewart.) Indeed, this long-standing controversy in the earth sciences about the reality of continental drift is of special interest since it is one of the most important major revolutions in the sciences that has occurred in the twentieth century. In order to answer the question about why no theory of continental drift was accepted until the confirmation of sea-floor spreading, it is necessary to draw a distinction between two basic types of scientific problem, introduce the notion of a difficulty-free solution, and suggest what is involved in the acceptance of a scientific theory. Once those ideas are introduced, the history of the controversy will be presented in terms of those ideas.

There are two basic kinds of scientific problems that arise during a scientific controversy. There are explanation-seeking problems (ESPs) and explanation-difficulty problems (EDPs). Explanations for ESPs are attempted by proposing solutions or theories. EDPs take the form of objections that are raised against proposed solutions to ESPs. Without ESPs and their proffered solutions, there can be no EDPs. ESPs arise when scientists are puzzled by some phenomenon they cannot explain. Sometimes more data is gathered to determine whether the problem is legitimate. A solution is then offered. EDPs arise when someone raises an objection to the proposed solution. EDPs are usually raised as objections by scientists in opposing traditions, but they may be raised as objections by proponents within the same tradition. They may even be encountered by scientists while proposing their solutions. EDPs are solved through elimination of the particular difficulty either by altering the flawed solution or by showing that the raised difficulty is itself unfounded. In the controversy over continental drift, difficulties were always raised against proffered solutions. There are first- and second-order ESPs. First-order ESPs arise through the discovery of a puzzling phenomenon or thing whose existence, characteristics, or behavior is deemed puzzling in light of one's background knowledge and expectations. Suppose a scientist offers a solution to a first order ESP, proposing that the puzzling phenomenon can be explained by postulating some sort of hypothetical process. For instance, the scientist notices and is intrigued by the similarity in shape between the Atlantic coastlines of South America and Africa, proceeds to explain the

similarity by suggesting that the two continents were once united into a single landmass that subsequently split apart and drifted. The scientist then wonders how the single landmass split into two continents. This new ESP brought about by the solution to the first-order ESP is defined as a second-order ESP. Second-order ESPs have, as their subject matter, entities or processes that are invoked to solve first-order ESPs. Second-order ESPs cannot arise unless a solution has first been proposed to a first-order ESP.

Scientists present solutions to provide answers to ESPs. Although it is no small accomplishment to construct solutions to ESPs, it is a far greater achievement to construct solutions that are free from difficulties. Indeed, a major claim of this analysis of the controversy over the reality of continental drift is that EDPs play a central role within the controversy. To think (as some might) that scientists view the raising of EDPs as silly polemics and their removal as a mopping up exercise left to the ungifted but hardworking scientists is to completely misunderstand what occurs during a scientific controversy; participants engaging in a controversy expend considerable effort raising difficulties against solutions proffered by their opponents and removing those raised against their own.

The types of EDPs that occurred during the controversy over continental drift fall into two main categories—namely, data-difficulties and theoretical difficulties. Data-EDPs arise when part of the data or its relation with the solution is found to be suspect. They may pertain to the use of unreliable data, the discovery of anomalous data, or the failure to uncover data relevant to confirmation of the solution. Theoretical difficulties arise when a proposed solution to an ESP is plagued with internal inconsistencies or ambiguities; where the inconsistencies or ambiguities may arise within a given solution or among two or more solutions that are combined to form a single theory; or where a solution to an ESP is found to have undesirable relations with other noncompeting solutions, theories, or methodological doctrines.

Difficulty-free solutions to an ESP do not contain any recognized difficulties. They explain what they are supposed to explain without creating known difficulties. Difficulty-free solutions are taken to be empirically sound; they are believed to be based upon reliable data, face no anomalies, and lack no important supportive data. They are taken to be theoretically sound; there is good reason to believe that they do not clash with well-founded theories or methodological doctrines, do not utilize tenuous assumptions, and are internally consistent. Of course, it is easier to develop non-difficulty-free solutions than difficulty-free ones. More important, however, it is much harder to develop a solution that remains difficulty free after it is scrutinized by members of the appropriate scientific community.

During a scientific controversy, participants devote considerable time and energy trying to show that their solutions and theories are more effective problem solvers than those proposed by their opponents. To this end they attempt to increase the problem-solving effectiveness of their solutions and theories, to decrease the problem solving effectiveness of their competitors' solutions and theories, and to emphasize through direct comparison advantages possessed by their theories or solutions. They attack their opponents' view by raising difficulties against them to decrease their problem-solving effectiveness. They defend their own views by trying to increase both their explanatory scope through the elimination of anomalies and their explanatory effectiveness through removal of nonanomalous difficulties.

It is reasonable to accept a solution to an ESP if the solution satisfies the following two conditions:

S1. The solution is difficulty-free and remains difficulty-free after scrutiny by opponents.
S2. Of those available solutions the solution is the only difficulty-free solution.

If a solution satisfies S1 and S2 it clearly has a decided advantage in problem-solving effectiveness over the competition. If proponents of a solution are able to produce a difficulty-free solution, opponents are unable to raise difficulties against the solution, and opponents are unable to develop their own difficulty-free solution, the respective subcontroversy is resolved. Failure to accept the difficulty-free solution becomes irrational. Of course, many opponents do not accept the solution until they attempt to raise difficulties against it and remove difficulties facing their own solution. However, if they are unable to change the status of their solution to a difficulty free one or raise difficulties with the competing difficulty-free solution, but refuse to accept the competing solution, then they may be judged as having behaved irrationally.

It is reasonable to accept a theory within a controversy if it satisfies the following conditions:

T1. The theory possesses a solution to an ESP that satisfies conditions S1 and S2.
Restrictions: (a) If the theory contains more than one difficulty-free solution, the solutions have to be consistent with each other. (b) Satisfaction of T1 by a theory allows only for the acceptance of those aspects of the theory that are essential to the difficulty-free solutions.
T2. The theory has no theoretical difficulties.
T3. The theory solves more problems than any other competing theory that satisfies T1 and T2. Although these additional solutions do not have to be difficulty-free, they have to be consistent with the difficulty-free solutions, and, where appropriate, they have to accord to a degree appropriate to the standards of the subdisciplines with the difficulty-free solutions.

If a theory satisfies condition T1, it has a solution to an ESP worthy of acceptance in light of the above hypothesis about the acceptance of solutions. In order for a theory to possess a solution, key elements of the theory must entail the solution. The major role of T1 is the elimination of theories not containing difficulty-free solutions from the realm of acceptable theories. T1 requires two restrictions. First, if there is more than one difficulty-free solution, the solutions must be consistent with each other. Second, even if only one theory satisfies T1, it does not follow that all aspects of the theory ought to be accepted. Rather, satisfaction of T1 by a theory allows for acceptance of only those aspects of the theory needed for the deduction of the difficulty-free solutions.

Satisfaction of T1 is not sufficient for acceptance of those elements of the theory needed to deduce the difficulty-free solutions. Suppose a difficulty-free solution and a theory from which the solution may be deduced. If those elements of the theory needed to deduce the difficulty-free solution face a theoretical difficulty, there is good reason not to accept the theory. T2 is introduced to avoid such a possibility.

The combination of T1 and T2 is still insufficient to explain why a theory ought to be accepted. Suppose there are two or more theories from which a difficulty-free solution may be deduced, and the members of the relevant scientific community overwhelmingly accept one of the theories. If such a situation arises, T1 and T2 would not explain why one theory is accepted and the others are rejected. T3 is introduced to explain what happens in such a situation. Of course, if T3 is not satisfied, if the competing theories that satisfy T1 and T2 have the same problem-solving effectiveness, then none of the theories ought to be accepted.

To address the classical stage of the mobilist controversy, from Alfred Wegener to the end of World War II, requires some knowledge of the state of geological theory at the beginning of the twentieth century. The prospect of finding an overall theory to a common nest of ESP problems looked excellent to many earth scientists during the 1880s, for they believed that Eduard Suess (1831–1914), the great Austrian geologist of the late nineteenth century, had provided them with the basic framework for solving them. His theory, a version of contractionism, the reigning tradition of the time, was a fixist theory. Suess's most important work, *Das Antlitz der Erde,* an extensive presentation and defense of his secular (or long-term) contractionism, began in 1878, took thirty-six years to complete. (See, Greene, *Geology in the Nineteenth Century,* for an excellent account of the development and reception of Suess's secular contractionism.)

There are three major aspects of Suess's secular contractionism. Suess concentrated upon the major trends of large-scale geological structures. The proper objects of study were mountain systems, whole continents, and oceanic regions. In making broad-scale comparisons, he noticed that there are two types of continental margins, argued that they present two unsolved ESPs concerning their origin, and offered two different solutions, which were united into an overall theory. There is the fractured type of coastline where the geological features of the continents appear to be abruptly cut off by the adjacent ocean basin. Fractured coastlines owe their origin to the partial collapse of a formerly larger continent. The collapsed part of the continent becomes a new ocean basin, and the resulting coastline represents the location of the fracture. He designated this type of coastline as "Atlantic-type" since the continental margins surrounding the Atlantic Ocean are typically fractured, and he claimed that the Atlantic basin formed with the collapse of continental material that had once united the continents surrounding the Atlantic. He argued that mountain ranges on both sides of the Atlantic had been severed with the formation of the Atlantic basin. The other type of coastline, characterized by marginal folds, he labeled "Pacific-type," since the coastlines bounding the Pacific basin are made up of folded chains running parallel to the continental margins. Because these folded chains, expressed as mountain ranges or island arcs, are of relatively recent age and do not appear to be cut off by the Pacific Ocean, Suess argued that they determined the shape of the coastlines, and that the Pacific basin predated the surrounding coastlines. Suess thought the Pacific Ocean was the oldest existing ocean—perhaps formed by the ripping away of the moon.

The next major aspect of Suess's view was his adoption of the idea that the Earth has been contracting since its initial formation. He hypothesized that tensions are produced in the crustal layer because the inner layers contract more rapidly than the crust. Analogies were typically drawn between the wrinkling skin of a drying apple and the folding crust of a cooling Earth. Tensions are relieved by horizontal thrusting and folding, which result in the formation of mountain systems and island arcs. Other tensions are relieved by vertical faulting and large-scale subsidence, which in extreme cases cause the foundering or collapse of former continents into present-day oceans. Thus, Suess's theory offered a solution to the ESPs concerned with the origin of mountain ranges, island arcs, and the sinking of paleocontinents, which, in term, solved the problem about the origin of "Atlantic-type" coastlines. Suess, following other contractionists in his explanation of how the Earth contracts, a second-order ESP for contractionists, attributed the Earth's contraction to its continual cooling from its earlier molten state, which made perfect sense since it fit with Laplacian cosmogonies.

The last major aspect of Suess's contractionist theory is his hypothesis about the existence of paleocontinents that had sunk into present-day oceans. According to Suess, the present arrangement of continents and oceans is not a permanent feature of the Earth. Past continents had stood where present-day oceans reside and future oceans might appear, although Suess maintained that the present-day continents all contained ancient regions, or cratons, that have remained continental throughout geological times. Such massive collapses occurred with the resolution of radial tensions brought about by contraction of the

Earth. In light of his analysis of Atlantic and Pacific types of coastlines, he developed an extensive paleogeographic reconstruction. He argued that the Atlantic Ocean had formed with the collapse or foundering of two massive paleocontinents—northern and southern Atlantic paleocontinents separated by an ancient Mediterranean-type sea. This ancient sea, the Tethys, extended from the present-day Gulf of Mexico through the present-day Mediterranean Sea into the older part of the Indian Ocean. Gondwanaland, the southern continent, was made up of part of South America, much of the south Atlantic, most of Africa, Madagascar, Arabia, peninsular India, the younger part of the Indian oceanic basin, New Guinea, Australia, and Antarctica. The northern paleocontinent, Atlantis, spanned across the present-day north Atlantic connecting North America with Europe via Greenland. Suess supported the former existence of these paleocontinents with structural and paleontological arguments. The most important structural argument depended upon the fractured coastlines, which suggested young ocean basins and sunken paleocontinents coupled with the intercontinental correlations between European and North American mountain chains. These mountain ranges had formed as single chains but subsequently broke apart with the collapse of the paleocontinent. The major paleontological match-up involved the Permo-Carboniferous flora *Glossopteris,* a fernlike flora whose fossil remains had been found in India, South Africa, South America, and Australia. Gondwanaland was named after Gondwana, a region in India where abundant deposits of *Glossopteris* had been discovered.

Although many European paleontologists agreed with Suess, the assessment of Suessian contraction began to take a turn toward the worse at the end of the nineteenth century. When Wegener and Taylor introduced their mobilist theories, a number of geophysically minded earth scientists already had raised EDPs with Suess's contractionism. Opponents raised two theoretical EDPs. These EDPs arose through two discoveries about the Earth's interior. First, there was the initial substantiation of the idea that major features of the Earth's crust tend to remain in isostatic equilibrium with the denser, fluidlike interior. Second, there was the discovery of abundant amounts of radioactive material in the Earth's crust. The discovery of isostasy created a theoretical EDP with Suess's solutions that involved the sinking of former land bridges or paleocontinents (figure 1). Isostasists argued that the tendency of continents to maintain isostatic equilibrium required continental permanency, for they could not conceive of how former land bridges or continents could have sunk into a denser sea floor—it was as inconceivable as supposing that a piece of wood or block of ice could sink to the bottom of a pool. The other find, the discovery of abundant amounts of radioactive material within the crust, created an external theoretical EDP with the contractionists' solution to the second-order ESP about the mechanism responsible for the continued contraction of the Earth, for it called into question the assumption of a cooling Earth. With the discovery of radioactivity, the assumption of a cooling Earth became dubious, and opponents of Suess's theory argued that the problem-solving effectiveness of his contractionism had decreased.

Other geologists raised two anomaly EDPs with Suess's account of mountain building. They argued that his contractionist model would not lead to a restriction of crustal folding to a few major places upon the Earth's surface. Mountain belts are not evenly distributed throughout the Earth's surface. However, using the Suessian analogy of a drying apple to represent a shrinking Earth, opponents noted how the wrinkles of a drying apple's skin are equally distributed throughout rather than concentrated into a few regions. Others argued that the success in tracing the spectacular overthrusts in the Alpine system led to another anomaly EDP. Because of the length of some of the Alpine overthrusts and the amount of crustal folding involved, much larger than former estimates, critics argued that the amount of radial contraction needed to "unfold" the mountains of the Alpine system, not to mention all of the other mountain systems that had appeared upon the face of the Earth during its geological past, was much greater than allowed for by Suessian contractionism.

This multifaceted assault upon Suess's theory did not lead to its worldwide dismissal. The overwhelming majority of Continental European geologists who cared about large-scale questions continued to support contractionism—even with its postulation of collapsing paleocontinents. Other earth scientists rejected Suessian contractionism. But, rather than reject contractionism in general, they developed new contractionist theories that avoided the theoretical EDP faced by Suessian contractionism brought about by the discovery of isostasy and radioactivity. Earth scientists presented new versions of contractionism

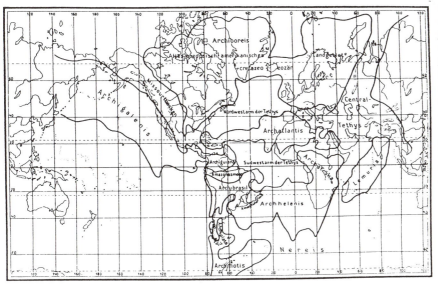

Figure 1. Hermann von Ihering (1850–1930) proposed that a series of landbridges could explain plant and animal distribution. Illustrated here are landbridges that he suggested existed in the Eocene. Source: H. von Ihering, Archhelenis und Archinotis, Gesammelte Beiträge zur Geschichte der neotropischen Region. *Leipzig: Engelmann, 1907.*

which, they argued, were consistent with isostasy and the presence of radioactive material. In fact, various new forms of contractionism were maintained until the acceptance of seafloor spreading during the 1960s.

Although several highly speculative views of continental drift appeared in the literature before 1900, they attracted little attention, and the dominant large-scale geological theories were articulated within a fixist framework. The first mobilist theories to receive attention were those of Alfred Wegener (1880–1930), a German meteorologist and geophysicist, and Frank Taylor (1860–1938), an American geologist. Taylor presented his idea at a meeting of the Geological Society of America in 1907 (figure 2). Wegener presented his version of continental drift in two articles that appeared in 1912. Wegener came up with the idea of continental drift before learning of Taylor's work, and he developed his more detailed and extensive theory independently of Taylor. Because Taylor's theory was generally ignored and played a small role within the overall controversy, it will not be discussed. (See, Laudan, "Taylor's Theory," for a discussion of the theory and its reception.)

Wegener came up with the idea of continental drift in December of 1910 upon studying a bathymetric world map that illustrated the congruency of the continental margins as well as the shape of the shorelines. He thought that the congruency, especially between Africa and South America, was sufficiently good that it needed an explanation. Thus, Wegener came up with continental drift as a solution to the ESP concerned with the congruency of the continental margins. This problem could not be solved by any other theory. At first, Wegener did not pay attention to the idea because he regarded it as improbable. However, he did not wait very long before giving it proper attention, for by January of 1911 he already understood both the paleontological need to postulate former land connections between South America and Africa, and the geophysical difficulty facing their postulation brought about by its inconsistency with the principle of isostasy.

Wegener's 1912 explication of his theory of continental drift is essentially a comparative evaluation of the problem-solving effectiveness of continental drift, Suessian contractionism, and the theory of oceanic and continental permanency. (See Greene, "Alfred Wegener," and Hallam, *Great Geological Controversies,* for accounts of Wegener's early work on continental drift.) The major steps of his comparative evaluation were as follows:

(1) Defense of the claim that Suessian theories of contractionism postulating the existence of former land bridges face geophysical external theoretical EDPs and anomaly EDPs.

Among the difficulties he singled out were the following: The discovery of radioactive material in the Earth's crust, lack of deep-sea sediments upon continental platforms, indicating that the continents had never been oceanic basins, and the establishment of isostasy. He took the last difficulty to be the most important, arguing that there was just no way to

Figure 2. Frank Taylor, an American geologist, also proposed a theory of continental drift in 1907, a few years before Alfred Wegener's 1912 proposal. Taylor argued that the continents had moved away from the North Pole, as shown by the arrows. Source: F.B. Taylor, "Bearing of the Tertiary Mountain Belt on the Origin of the Earth's Plan." Bulletin of the Geological Society of America *21 (1910): p. 209. With permission from Geological Society of America.*

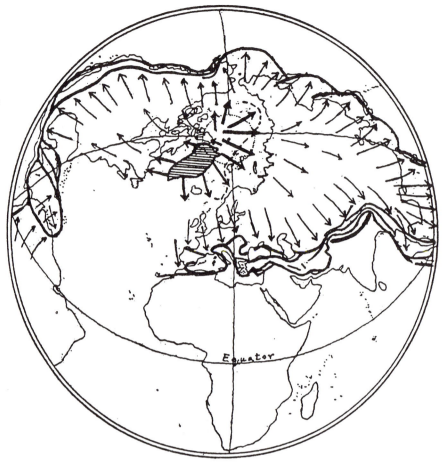

sink a less dense land bridge or paleocontinent into the denser sea floor consistent with the principle of isostasy.

(2) Dismissal of any theory that postulated the permanency of ocean basins.

Although Wegener agreed with those fixists who argued that the sinking of paleocontinents or former land bridges was inconsistent with isostasy, he thought little of their replacing sinking land bridges with permanently positioned ocean basins, for such a move led to theories with decreased problem-solving effectiveness. Such a replacement left unexplained two ESPs: the geological match-ups between the continents surrounding the Atlantic, and the disjunctively distributed past- and present-day life forms.

(3) The need for a new global hypothesis, which solves the ESPs addressed by the idea of sunken land bridges but is consistent with isostasy and thereby avoids the theoretical EDP faced by Suessian

contractionism, is satisfied by the new theory of continental drift.

Wegener argued that his theory could solve those problems solved by Suess's theory, but, unlike Suess's contractionism, it offered solutions that took into account the recent discovery of isostasy and was unaffected by the discovery of radioactivity. According to Wegener, the need for a new alternative followed from (1) and (2). Given (1), sinking land bridges were unacceptable. But, because of (2), the substitution of permanent ocean basins for sinking land bridges or paleocontinents was inadequate. What was needed was a way to postulate previous land connections among existing continents without supposing the existence of former land bridges.

Of course, continental drift was the answer. Wegener sketched out the breakup of his primordial continent, substituting partition and drift whenever and wherever Suess had postulated former paleocontinents. He supposed the formation of the Atlantic in place of Suess's northern and southern Atlantic paleocontinents, and replaced Suess's Gondwanaland with the breakup and drifting of India and the continents in the southern hemisphere to their present positions. He stressed the geological and paleontological matchups on both sides of the Atlantic, the need for a Mesozoic connection between Africa and Brazil in order to account for the paleontological similarities, and emphasized the need for several land connections between Australia and other fragments of Gondwanaland.

(4) Expansion of the drift theory's problem-solving effectiveness by providing solutions to other ESPs solved by Suessian contractionism.

Wegener also linked his hypothesis with the formation of mountain belts. They form on the leading edge of a drifting continent as it displaces itself through the simatic ocean floor—the Andes served as his primary example. Wegener suggested that his theory could account for the difference between Atlantic- and Pacific-type coastlines that had been identified and differentiated by Suess. Atlantic types were typically located on the trailing edges of drifting continents, and their fractured condition was caused by the suturing of the original land mass rather than the collapse of a paleocontinent. The typical folds of Pacific-type coastlines were either located on the leading edges of drifting continents, as are the Andes, and were caused by the crumbling of continental sial, or, as is the case of island festoons, were located on the trailing edge and formed as bits of sial broken off from the drifting continent. Thus Wegener expanded the overall problem solving effectiveness of his mobilist theory so that it solved three other problems that Suess's theory had been able to solve.

(5) The hypothesis of continental drift solves problems that Suess's theory is incapable of solving.

Wegener expanded the range of his theory to solve three problems which were unsolved by Suessian contractionism. There was the problem of why the continental margins on both sides of the Atlantic were congruent.

Wegener considered another ESP about why there are two preferred elevations of the Earth's surface: one representing the elevation of the continental plateaus and the other corresponding to the depth of the ocean basins. Wegener was quite impressed with this preference of the Earth's surface for only two elevations—recall that the title of both his 1912 articles was "The Origin of Continents" rather than, say, "The Horizontal Displacement of the Continents." Wegener's theory provided a solution—namely, that the two preferred elevations of the Earth's surface were a reflection of the fact that the ocean basins and continental platforms were in isostatic equilibrium. The sialic continents remain higher than the simatic ocean basins because sial is lighter than sima. Once the continental plateaus and oceanic basins became isostatically adjusted, they remained at their preferred elevations. Because Wegener appealed only to large-scale horizontal movements rather than major vertical changes, there would be no reason for continents and ocean basins to alter their elevation. The third problem Wegener's theory solved was the formation of an extensive ice cap in the Southern Hemisphere. This ice cap existed throughout the Permian, and probably began to form during the Carboniferous. Not only did Wegener claim that he had a solution, he was emphatic in his insistence that his was the only adequate one.

(6) The hypothesis of continental drift should be treated as a serious working hypothesis.

Wegener argued for (6) on the basis of (1) through (5). According to Wegener, continental drift solved the following ESPs: coastline congruency problem, the geological matchups between the continents surrounding the Atlantic ocean, the origin of Atlantic- and Pacific-type coastlines, the origin of the most recent mountain ranges, the origin of island arcs, the disjunctive distribution of many life forms, the origin of the Permo-Carboniferous ice cap, and the two basic elevations of the Earth's surface. Suessian contractionism offered solutions to the geological matchups, the disjunctive distribution of life forms, the two kinds of coastlines, and the origin of mountains and island arcs. However, its solutions faced recognized EDPs, and it had no solution to the congruency of the coastlines or the two preferred elevations. Oceanic permanency offered no solution to the disjunctive distribution of life forms, the geological matchups, the different kinds of coastlines, and the congruency of the coastlines. Nor could either of the competing views, even if coupled with polar wandering, offer a solution to the origin of the Permo-

Carboniferous ice cap that was as effective as Wegener's solution. Thus, Wegener argued that his theory was worthy of serious attention.

However, he did not argue for outright acceptance of continental drift but claimed that more work was needed to establish his theory, arguing that he needed a decisive test. He needed a difficulty-free solution to a problem that none of the competing theories could solve. Although drift theory offered the only solution to the coastline congruency problem, the fit between the northern continents surrounding the Atlantic was not very good. From where could such a solution arise? Suppose one obtained data that indicated a continuing displacement of one landmass relative to another in a direction and at a rate consilient with Wegener's paleogeographical reconstruction of the continents based upon the matchup of the coastlines, and his solutions to the problems concerned with the disjunctive distribution of life forms, geological matchups, and formation of mountain ranges at the leading edge of drifting continents. If Wegener could obtain the data, he would have a problem solution that fixists could not have, that would be anomalous for fixists, and would be consilient with many of his other solutions. If Wegener were able to develop such a difficulty-free solution, the solution remained difficulty-free after scrutiny by his opponents, and his opponents were unable to offer their own solution, he would have a solution worthy of acceptance. If the direction and rate of relative movement were consilient with his paleogeographical reconstruction of the continents, and his theory had no outstanding theoretical EDPs, he would be able to argue for the outright acceptance of continental drift. Such a test, he suggested, could be done using the techniques of astronomical position-fixing, for it could be used to gather data indicative of horizontal displacement of one landmass relative to another. No such measurements existed in 1912 that were reliable enough to eliminate any doubt. There were a few measurements that Wegener thought worth discussing even though he admitted they were unreliable. However, he thought they were a step in the right direction. What he wanted were additional and more reliable determinations; what he hoped for was the development of a difficulty-free solution based upon reliable geodetic measurements.

There was one problem that he acknowl-edged he could not solve: The question of what forces or mechanisms were responsible for the displacement of the continents. This second-order ESP—the so-called "mechanism" problem—was an obvious one for him to address. Because he had criticized the contractionist mechanisms for the collapse of paleocontinents and the formation of mountain ranges, he had to say something about the mechanism for continental drift. Wegener showed himself to be an excellent tactician in his treatment of this problem. He first claimed that horizontal displacement of drifting continents is not physically impossible so long as there are enduring forces that propel the sialic continents through the simatic sea floor. He appealed to the action of steady, long-term forces instead of impulsive, short-term ones because he realized that sima was more resistant to the latter type of forces than sial. Sima has greater rigidity than sial. Consequently, the sea floor would not make way for the continents if the propelling forces were impulsive. However, Wegener suggested that sial has greater residual rigidity than sima, and therefore it would yield to very slow movements of sial brought about by the action of mild and steady forces. Wegener likened sima to pitch. Pitch is highly resistant to rapidly acting forces. A piece of pitch will shatter when smashed by a hammer. But pitch yields to less powerful, long-term forces. A piece of pitch changes its shape if merely left alone for a few days through the action of gravitational forces. Then Wegener frankly admitted that he did not have a solution to the problem. To be sure, there were a number of possibilities, and Wegener referred to several of them: flight from the poles, tidal forces, meridional rifting, processional forces, polar wandering, or some combination of them. However, he bracketed his brief discussion of these possibilities by wisely pointing out that any serious attempt to answer this question would be premature since little was known about such forces or even the precise nature of continental drift.

Wegener expanded his account in his *Origin of Continents and Oceans*. The first edition appeared in 1915, and it was followed by new editions in 1920, 1922, and 1929. The 1922 edition probably was the most important, as it was the most frequently translated edition. During the classical stage of the controversy, English-speaking earth scientists most frequently cited the 1922 edition, which was translated into English in 1924. Wegener died in 1930. Wegener continued to enlarge the evidential base for his theory in ensuing editions, paid special attention to geodetic studies that appeared to indicate a westward drift of Greenland relative to Europe, and attempted to remove difficulties that opponents raised against his theory. Nevertheless, the fundamentals of his theory failed to undergo any substantial change from their initial development in his 1912 articles. (For discussions about the development of Wegener's ideas in various editions of *The Origin of Continents and Oceans,* see Hallam, *Revolution* and *Great Geological Controversies;* Le Grand; Marvin.)

Reactions to Wegener's theory were of three types. First, his theory spawned a number of subcontroversies within different disciplines of the earth sciences in which Wegener had offered a solution to an ESP. In each case, both fixists and mobilists raised EDPs with the competing solutions. Because neither of them were able to remove all of the EDPs, neither of them had a recognized difficulty-free solution. Consequently, no fixist or mobilist theory gained anything approaching universal acceptance among earth scientists. Consider, for example some of the EDPs raised by fixists. They raised EDPs with Wegener's solution to the ESP about the matchup of continental margins, arguing that the fit between Europe and North America was not nearly as good as the one between Africa and South America, that Wegener had overestimated the similarity between the two southern continents, and therefore that the amount of similarity was simply an accident. (For discussions about the reception of Wegener's fit of the continents, see Hallam, *Revolution*; Marvin; Le Grand.) Although many paleontologists welcomed Wegener's theory and argued in favor of its solution to the disjunctive distribution of life forms, other paleontologists such as G.G. Simpson, the most prominent American vertebrate paleontologist of the period, raised several EDPs with the mobilist solution throughout the 1940s, arguing that Wegener had greatly overestimated the number of disjunctively distributed life forms because of his appeal to unreliable data. Simpson argued that if mobilism were correct, there should be many more cases of disjunctively distributed life forms, and claimed that the few cases could be explained in terms of island-hopping and fortuitous rafting. (For accounts of the paleontological and biogeographical controversy, see Frankel, "The Paleobiogeographical Debate"; Hallam, *Revolution;* Le Grand; Laporte.) The controversy in paleoclimatology over Wegener's

solution to the Permo-Carboniferous ice cap underwent a similar evolution. Several eminent paleoclimatologists supported continental drift, including Wladimir Köppen, Wegener's father-in-law. Köppen co-authored a work in 1924 with Wegener, *Die Klimate der geologischen Vorzeit,* in which they expanded the paleoclimatological support for continental drift. However, throughout the 1920s and 1930s, fixists raised EDPs with Wegener's solution. Among other things, they argued that the existence of glaciated regions during the Permo-Carboniferous in the United States was anomalous with Wegener's theory since, according to Wegener, the United States had been tropical. Although Wegener and Alex du Toit altered the mobilist solution to avoid some of the EDPs raised by fixists, they were unable to produce a recognized difficulty-free solution. In addition, Charles Schuchert and Bailey Willis, two American fixists, developed an alternative solution to the problem in the early 1930s. (For accounts of the paleoclimatological controversy, see Frankel, "The Permo-Carboniferous Ice Cap"; Hallam, *Revolution;* Le Grand; Marvin.) A similar controversy arose in geodesy over the apparent westward drift of Greenland relative to Europe. Initial results during the 1920s, made by the Danish Geodetic Survey, offered support for mobilism. Wegener hailed the results as offering a potentially difficulty-free solution. However, new and more reliable results by the Danish Geodetic Survey in the 1930s, as fixists predicted, failed to support Wegener's theory, and led to the conclusion that the previous measurements were unreliable. (For discussions about the geodetic evidence for mobilism, see Hallam, *Revolution;* Le Grand; Menard.)

Second, the mechanism of continental drift proposed by Wegener was regarded as a weak link in his theory. Fixists such as Harold Jeffreys, the most important British geophysicist during this period, and many North American geologists and geophysicists argued that the particular forces that Wegener had invoked to move continents were inadequate. Jeffreys raised these objections in various editions of his very influential work in geophysics, *The Earth: Its Origin, History and Physical Constitution* (first edition, 1924), and at various symposia on continental drift during the 1920s and 1930s; many North American geologists and geophysicists raised their objections at a 1926 symposium on continental drift sponsored by the American Association of Petroleum Geologists. In addition, several fixists argued that even if Wegener's forces were to propel the continents through the sea floor, the continents would be unable to survive such a voyage because the crust beneath the sea floor is more rigid than continental material. Others argued that Wegener's solution to the mechanism problem was incompatible with his solution to the origin of mountains. In the former he needed to maintain that the ocean floor was weaker than the continents, but in the latter he maintained that the ocean floor was stronger than the continents because the resistance of the ocean floor causes the leading edge of drifting continents to crumble and fold into mountains. These EDPs raised against Wegener's mechanism affected every other solution of Wegener's theory that depended upon drifting continents, and therefore many specialists in paleoclimatology and paleontology who favored continental drift tempered their support. (For discussions of the mechanism objection see Frankel, "Reception and Acceptance of Continental Drift" and "The Paleobiogeographical Debate"; Hallam, *Revolution;* Le Grand; Marvin; Menard.)

Third, Wegener's theory, however, attracted the attention and support of several influential earth scientists whose interests cut across several fields within the earth sciences. These researchers presented their own theories of continental drift. Among them were Émile Argand, Alex du Toit, J. Joly, Arthur Holmes, and Reginald Daly. Argand was a leading Alpine geologist from Switzerland who greatly expanded drift's solution to the problem of the origin of mountains. In 1923, Argand wrote an extensive monograph in which he argued that such a solution was superior to contractionist theories of mountain building. John Joly, an Irish geophysicist, suggested a new solution to the mechanism question during the 1920s. (See, especially, his 1925 *Surface-History of the Earth.*) Alex du Toit, a renowned field geologist and one of the few South African geologists elected to the Royal Society, began defending continental drift in the 1920s and continued to support it until his death in 1949. After Wegener's death in 1930, du Toit became the torchbearer for drift theory. Du Toit, concentrating upon the geology of southern Africa and South America, garnered much additional support, and he presented his own version of continental drift in his 1937 *Our Wandering Continents.* (Discussions of Argand, Joly, du Toit, Holmes, and Daly may be found in Hallam, *Revolution;* Le Grand; Marvin; Menard.) The British geologist and geophysicist Arthur Holmes was probably the most

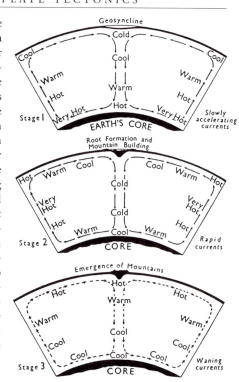

Figure 3. Arthur Holmes proposed in the 1920s that convection currents fueled by radioactive decay in the Earth's interior drive continental drift. Source: Arthur Holmes, Principles of Physical Geology. London: Thomas Nelson and Sons, 1944, p. 411. With permission from Van Nostrand Reinhold.

generally respected earth scientist to defend continental drift. During the 1920s he supported the contractionist theory of mountain building, but by the end of the decade he had rejected contractionism and, around 1930, began arguing in favor of continental drift. Holmes defended continental drift's solution to a number of problems and developed a new solution to the mechanism question, and he offered an improved mobilist solution to the origin of mountains. Holmes's solution to the mechanism problem replaced Wegener's forces with convection currents fueled by radioactive decay within the Earth's interior, and supposed that the continents ride passively atop the convection currents rather than plow their way through the sea floor (figure 3). Although vehement fixists such as Harold Jeffreys agreed that Holmes's new mechanism made mobilism no longer impossible, Jeffreys argued that Holmes's mobilism was extremely improbable. Moreover, there were many who questioned the plausibility of positing large-scale convection currents, and some, such as the Dutch geophysicist Vening Meinesz, who were willing to suppose that there was large-scale convection did not endorse mobilism, and posited a very different pattern of convection. In addition, Holmes's hypothesis was beyond the limits of testing because it depended upon unearthing data about the sea floor that was beyond the existing capabilities of geophysicists until the 1950s. Consequently, Holmes's mobilism faced both theoretical and missing data EDPs. (Detailed accounts of the development of Holmes's ideas may be found in Allwardt's dissertation; Frankel's "Arthur Holmes and Continental Drift"; Oreskes.) With a few notable exceptions, such as Beno Gutenberg and Reginald Daly, continental drift gained little support in North America. Gutenberg, born and trained in Germany, immigrated to the United States, where he became director of the Seismological Laboratory at the California Institute of Technology. (For a brief but interesting account of Gutenberg's endorsement of mobilism, see Menard.) Daly, born in Canada, began teaching at Harvard University in 1912, where he became one of the most eminent geologists in North America. During the 1920s he defended continental drift, offering a new solution to the mechanism problem. (See, especially, his 1926 *Our Mobile Earth*.) However, both fixists and mobilists raised EDPs with Daly's and Gutenberg's theories.

Most earth scientists, however, remained fixists. Although the classical arguments for mobilism continued to attract attention during the late 1940s and 1950s, and symposia were held from time to time to consider the merits of continental drift, the classical stage of the controversy had stagnated. Little new material and few new arguments were presented at these meetings. The case for continental drift was simply restated, and mobilism gained few converts.

The modern controversy over continental drift began with the rise of paleomagnetism. At the beginning of the 1950s, when the mobilism versus fixism controversy had lost steam, with neither side making progress, this little-known study became important for global tectonics. However, its application to global tectonics was not premeditated. Indeed, paleomagnetists who eventually developed a new case for continental drift were attracted to paleomagnetism, not because of continental drift, but because they thought it could help them solve problems concerning the origin and history of the geomagnetic field. They did not recognize, at least at the beginning, that their work would have any bearing on the question of continental drift. Some had never even thought about continental drift when they began their studies. However, it did not take them long to realize that paleomagnetism could be used to test fixist and mobilistic hypotheses.

The two major groups of paleomagnetists who developed a case for continental drift were from the United Kingdom, and were initially housed at the universities of Manchester and Cambridge. The Manchester group, headed by P.M.S. Blackett and John Clegg, began working at the end of 1952. It moved to Imperial College in 1953. The other and eventually more influential group began to form in Cambridge in the summer of 1950 when Jan Hospers, a new Ph.D. student, went to Iceland to collect lava samples for paleomagnetic investigation. This group coalesced under the general leadership of S.K. Runcorn in 1951. Various members of the group continued working at Cambridge until the end of 1955. Runcorn went to what was then the University College of the University of Durham (later the University of Newcastle), taking several paleomagnetists with him, including Kenneth Creer and Neil Opdyke. The major members of the Cambridge/Newcastle group included Kenneth Creer, R.A. Fisher, Jan Hospers, Edward Irving, Neil Opdyke, and Runcorn. Irving left Cambridge in 1954 for the Australian National University (ANU) to start his own group. The London, Newcastle, and ANU groups argued in favor of continental drift throughout the late 1950s and early 1960s. They began collecting rock samples first from the United Kingdom and then from various continents, initially testing reconstructions of the continents offered by Wegener and du Toit. Eventually, they attempted to develop their own reconstructions based upon paleomagnetic data. Their work reactivated the stagnating controversy of mobilism versus fixism. Their results were welcomed by those who were already in favor of continental drift. However, the land-based paleomagnetic evidence itself was insufficient to change the attitude of most earth scientists. Some geophysicists questioned the reliability of the paleomagnetic data supportive of mobilism, and even some paleomagnetists such as Cox and Doell argued that polar wandering without continental drift could explain the paleomagnetic data. (For a discussion about the rise of paleomagnetism, see Hallam, *Revolution;* Le Grand.)

Oceanography expanded rapidly during the 1950s (see Frankel, "Vine-Matthews-Morley Hypothesis"; Le Grand; and Menard). Oceanographic research was well funded, and geophysicists developed a variety of remote-sensing techniques to study the sea floor. By 1960 the combined efforts of several research teams at institutions and agencies such as Lamont-Doherty Geological Observatory at Columbia University, Scripps Institution of Oceanography, Cambridge University, Woods Hole, the U.S. Coast and Geodetic Survey, and the U.S. Office of Naval Research had transformed the sea floors from areas of deep mystery about which little or nothing was known into places of comparative familiarity. Paramount among their many discoveries was the worldwide network of oceanic ridges. Finding a solution to the origin of these, often located in the middle of existing oceans, became a major concern of marine geologists and geophysicists. Both fixist and drift solutions were offered. For example, Maurice Ewing, head of Lamont-Doherty Geological Observatory, H.W. Menard, one of the major figures at Scripps, and Harry Hess, a leading geologist at Princeton University, offered differing fixist solutions. Menard and Hess also proposed mobilist solutions. Bruce Heezen, an oceanographer at Lamont, presented a solution to the problem that invoked the idea of earth expansion.

In retrospect, nature turned out to be on the side of Hess's mobilist hypothesis, which was labeled "sea-floor spreading" by Robert Dietz, another supporter of the hypothesis. First presented in the form of a pre-print in December of 1960, it proposed that the sea floor is created along ridge axes by material forced up from the mantle by rising convection currents, and that the material spreads out perpendicularly from the axes creating new ocean basins. The next year Hess added the idea that horizontally moving sea floor eventually sinks into the mantle, forming oceanic trenches along the periphery of the basins. Sea-floor spreading offered a solution to the origin of oceanic ridges. In addition, Hess realized that if a ridge were created within a landmass, the landmass would split apart, a new ocean basin would form between the separated continental masses, and the continental masses would continue to move away from one another so long as the ocean basin continued to grow. Thus, if a new sea floor were to form within a continental land mass, continental drift would occur. Hess also realized that his version of mobilism offered a solution to the mechanism

problem that had plagued other versions of continental drift, for, in Hess's model, continents do not plow their way through existing sea floor, but simply passively ride upon the backs of convection currents as they move horizontally. Hess's idea was somewhat similar to Holmes's older idea of sea-floor thinning. (For detailed discussions of the development of Hess's mobilism, see Allwardt; Frankel, "Hess's Development.")

When Hess proposed his hypothesis, it was just one of several interesting solutions to the origin of mid-ocean ridges. Its importance lay in the fact that it spawned two important corollaries—corollaries that soon proved testable. The first was independently proposed by Fred Vine and Drummond Matthews, and by L. Morley. Vine, a Cambridge graduate student working under the supervision of Matthews, came up with the idea in 1963. Morley, a Canadian geophysicist, developed the idea in the same year. However, Morley's account was twice rejected before Morley added it onto a lengthy piece that he and a co-worker published in 1964. (For detailed accounts of the development and reception of the Vine-Matthews-Morley hypothesis, see Frankel, "Vine-Matthews-Morley Hypothesis"; Glen.) Although there were subtle differences between the Vine-Matthews, and Morley versions, both maintained that if sea-floor spreading has occurred and the Earth's magnetic field has undergone repeated reversals in its polarity as land-based paleomagnetic studies had indicated, then the sea floor should be composed of alternating strips of normally and reversely magnetized material, the strips should run roughly parallel to the ridge axis, and this pattern of magnetic anomalies should be approximately symmetrical on either side of the ridge.

The other hypothesis, invented by the Canadian geophysicist J. Tuzo Wilson, was presented in 1965. (For accounts of the development of Wilson's idea of transform faults, see Glen; Laudan, "The Method of Multiple Working Hypotheses"; Menard.) Wilson postulated a new class of faults, which he called transform faults. He argued that such faults would exist if sea-floor spreading occurred. Wilson explained how seismological data could be used to detect their existence. Both corollaries were confirmed in 1966. Vine and Wilson found confirmation of the Vine-Matthews hypothesis through examination of paleomagnetic sea-floor data that had been collected by workers at Scripps Institution of Oceanography. Further confirmation of the hypothesis

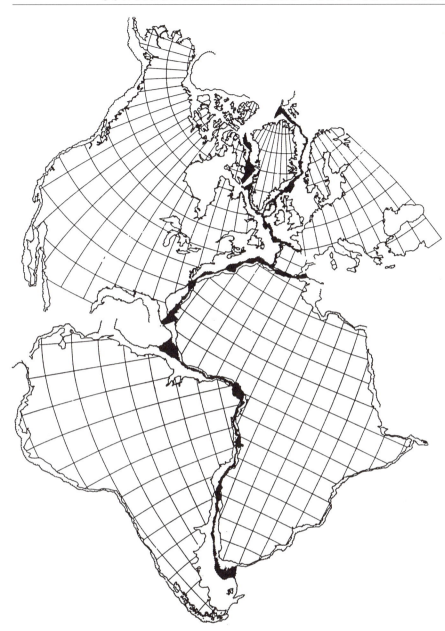

Figure 4. In 1965, Edward Bullard and his colleagues used a computer to match the coastlines of the Americas with those of Europe and Africa. Many found the "Bullard Fit," although problematic, convincing. Source: Bullard, E.C., J.E. Everett, and A. Gilbert Smith. "The Fit of the Continents around the Atlantic." In A Symposium on Continental Drift, *edited by P.M.S. Blackett, E. Bullard, and S.K. Runcorn, pp. 41–51. London: Royal Society, 1965. Map on pp. 48–49. With permission from Royal Society of London.*

came from the analysis by Walter Pitman, a graduate student at Lamont-Doherty Geological Observatory working under J. Heirtzler, of several magnetic profiles over the Pacific-Antarctic Ridge. L. Sykes, a seismologist also at Lamont-Doherty Geological Observatory, detected the existence of Wilson's transform faults by analyzing seismological data from the mid-Atlantic Ridge. With the confirmation of both these corollaries, most of the active researchers who had not been in favor of continental drift immediately accepted mobilism because of the explanatory advantages offered by sea-floor spreading when coupled with its two corollaries (figure 4).

Although the general acceptance of sea-floor spreading ended the mobilist controversy, the revolution in the earth sciences was not completed until the development of plate tectonics. Plate tectonics was independently conceived by Jason Morgan, a physicist turned geophysicist at Princeton University, and Dan McKenzie, a geophysicist at the Department of Geodesy and Geophysics at Cambridge University. Morgan presented his initial version in April of 1967 at a meeting of the American Geophysical Union, but he did not submit it for publication until August. After revision, it appeared in March of 1968. Morgan, originally scheduled to speak about trenches at the AGU meeting, decided instead to present his more recent work on plate tectonics. McKenzie, who attended the meeting, decided he had heard enough about trenches, and skipped Morgan's talk. As a consequence he had the chance to invent plate tectonics for himself. He conceived of it while visiting Scripps during the summer of 1967. Afterward he asked R.L. Parker, a fellow student at Cambridge now employed at Scripps, for some technical advice about data presentation. Parker obliged with a computer program he had designed for plotting maps on any projection, and their work was published at the end of 1967.

Plate tectonics grew out of the application of sea-floor spreading and its two corollaries to a spherical surface. Central to its development was the realization that Euler's theorem (which says that any movement of a point on the surface of a sphere can be described by rotation about a point, or "Euler" pole) could be used to describe the relative movements of ten or so rigid plates that make up the Earth's outer layer, the lithosphere.

Things moved rapidly after the innovation of Morgan and McKenzie. X. Le Pichon, a geophysicist and oceanographer at Lamont who had been an ardent fixist until 1966 but was one of the few who understood Morgan's talk at the spring meeting of the American Geophysical Union, used the extensive database at Lamont to extend Morgan's analysis to other areas of the world. Three other Lamont scientists, B. Isacks, J. Oliver, and L. Sykes, wrote an extensive summary paper in which they marshaled a tremendous amount of seismological support for plate tectonics. These five contributions led to the quick acceptance of plate tectonics by almost all earth scientists, including those who did not even understand, or perhaps appreciate, the differences between sea-floor spreading, continental drift, and plate tectonics (figure 5). (For a detailed discussion about the development of plate tectonics, see Frankel, "Development of Plate Tectonics.")

Mobilism was accepted in the form of sea-floor spreading with the confirmation of its two major corollaries, the Vine-Matthews-Morley hypothesis and Wilson's idea of transform faults. This happened because of the difficulty-free status of the ideas of Vine-Matthews-Morley and Wilson. As put forth above, it is reasonable to accept a solution to an ESP if the solution satisfies the following two conditions:

S1. The solution is difficulty-free and remains difficulty-free after scrutiny by opponents.
S2. Of those available solutions the solution is the only difficulty-free solution.

By 1966 both conditions were satisfied by the Vine-Matthews-Morley hypothesis and Wilson's idea of transform faults.

When the Vine-Matthews-Morley hypothesis was first proposed in 1963, it faced several EDPs. There were three anomaly EDPs and an important theoretical EDP. The theoretical EDP was as follows: the assumption of the Vine-Matthews-Morley hypothesis that the Earth's magnetic field undergoes repeated geopolarity reversals was still considered highly controversial in 1963. The first anomaly difficulty raised against the Vine-Matthews hypothesis concerned its apparent inability to account for the magnetic pattern immediately surrounding ridges. Although the intensity of magnetic anomalies was extremely high at the center of a ridge axis and gradually tapered off along the periphery of the axial zone, the amplitude of magnetic anomalies abruptly decreased outside the ridge flanks. Opponents claimed that this abrupt increase did not agree with the hypothesis. In the original presentation of the hypothesis, Vine and Matthews admitted that they had failed to account for the abrupt increase. However, their opponents claimed that this failure was very serious because their hypothesis not only failed to account for the increase, it could not do so. Indeed, opponents argued that the increase indicated that the magnetization of the ridge and its outer flanks did not have a common cause. The other anomalous difficulties were directed against the implied association between ocean ridges and a surrounding pattern of alternating normal and reversed strips of sea floor. First, the one clear example of the striped pattern, in the northeastern Pacific, surrounded no known ridge. Second, the few detailed magnetic surveys of ridges then available did not reveal the predicted pattern of magnetic anomalies. Thus, according to critics, the one clear-cut case in which a striped magnetic pattern occurred had no associated ridge, and ridges that had been surveyed were not flanked by the zebra pattern of magnetic anomalies.

By 1966 all of the difficulties were removed from the Vine-Matthews-Morley hypothesis. The assumption of repeated

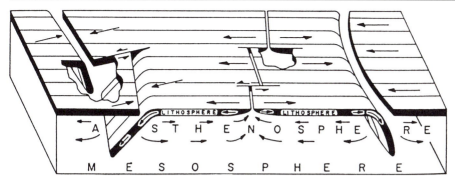

Figure 5. Plate tectonics, which began to emerge in the 1960s, explained the new phenomena revealed by geomagnetism and marine geology in terms of processes at plate boundaries: mid-ocean spreading, subduction, transform faulting, and so on. Source: Bryan Isacks, J. Oliver, and L.R. Sykes, "Seismology and the New Global Tectonics." Journal of Geophysical Research 73 (1968): pp. 5855–5899. Reproduced from p. 5857. Copyright by the American Geophysical Union.

geopolarity reversals was considered to be well founded by 1966. First, both major groups of paleomagnetists working on unearthing the geopolarity reversal time scale began to endorse it around 1964. Secondly, in 1965, the American group made up of Cox, Doell, and Dalrymple was able to construct an accurate time scale extending back several million years. The key to its development was their discovery in 1965 of the Jaramillo event, the most recent reversal of the geomagnetic field. In addition, this event was independently discovered through the examination of deep sea sediment cores by Opdyke and his co-workers at Lamont-Doherty in 1966. (For a detailed account of the development of the geopolarity reversal time scale, see Glen; for a detailed account of the reception of the Vine-Matthews-Morley hypothesis, see Frankel, "Vine-Matthews-Morley Hypothesis"; Glen; Menard.) In 1964, the anomaly about the decrease in the intensity of the magnetic anomalies beyond the flanks of a ridge were explained away as the result of the older age of the anomalies. The second anomaly was removed with the discovery of two ridges, the Juan de Fuca Ridge and the Gorda Ridge, which were shown to be associated with the magnetic anomalies in the northeastern Pacific. Indeed, Vine and Wilson (1965) showed that the zebra pattern of magnetic anomalies on both sides of the ridges was symmetrical. The last anomaly was removed through new magnetic surveys of known ridges. The two most important surveys, both undertaken by researchers at Lamont, were those over the Reykjanes Ridge and the Pacific-Antarctic Ridge. Both surveys revealed the predicted pattern of

magnetic anomalies, and led to the acceptance of the Vine-Matthews-Morley hypothesis by many of the paleomagnetists at Lamont. Walter Pitman's *Eltanin-19* profile of the Pacific-Antarctic Ridge was particularly convincing. Moreover, the Lamont paleomagnetists who had developed an alternative solution to the origin of the magnetic anomalies gave up their solution because they realized that the new data, data that they had collected, was anomalous with their solution.

The confirmation of Wilson's idea of transform faults provided mobilism with its second difficulty-free solution. When Wilson proposed his idea, there was little data to support it. One kind of transform fault Wilson proposed in 1965 is called a ridge-ridge transform fault. These faults connect ridge offsets. Wilson predicted that if such faults are transform faults, the direction of the fault should be opposite to that of the other possibility, a transcurrent fault, and he argued that the fault should be active only between ridge offsets. In 1966, L. Sykes, through a study of seventeen earthquakes, primarily located between offsets of the Mid-Atlantic Ridge, confirmed both of Wilson's predictions. The quality of Sykes's data as well as his techniques for analyzing the mechanism of earthquakes were not seriously questioned. Thus, mobilism had its second difficulty-free solution, and fixists did not even bother to attempt to develop their own difficulty-free solution.

The next stage in the modern controversy is from the acceptance of the Vine-Matthews-Morley hypothesis and Wilson's idea of transform faults to the acceptance of sea-floor spreading. It was put forth above that it is reasonable to accept a theory within a controversy if it satisfies the following conditions:

T1. The theory possesses a solution to an ESP that satisfies conditions S1 and S2.
Restrictions: (a) If the theory contains more than one difficulty-free solution, the solutions have to be consistent with each other. (b) Satisfaction of T1 by a theory allows only for the acceptance of those aspects of the theory that are essential to the difficulty-free solutions.
T2. The theory has no theoretical difficulties.
T3. The theory solves more problems than any other competing theory that satisfies T1 and T2. Although these additional solutions do not have to be difficulty-free, they have to be consistent with the difficulty-free solutions, and, where appropriate, they have to accord to a degree appropriate to the standards of the subdisciplines with the difficulty-free solutions.

The theory of sea-floor spreading gained acceptance with the confirmation of the Vine-Matthews-Morley hypothesis and Wilson's idea of transform faults, its two difficulty-free solutions. In particular, what gained acceptance were those parts of sea-floor spreading needed to deduce the Vine-Matthews-Morley hypothesis and Wilson's account of faulting between ridge offsets: that sea-floor material is created at ridge axes and spreads out along the horizontal. However, some aspects of the original idea of sea-floor spreading were generally ignored. For example, Hess's petrological account of the formation of different layers of oceanic crust was not accepted. Although many researchers simply stated that they had accepted sea-floor spreading, they usually had in mind only those parts of sea-floor spreading that were needed to derive the Vine-Matthews-Morley hypothesis and Wilson's analysis of faulting between ridge offsets. Moreover, Vine's and Wilson's hypotheses gave consistent results after the discovery of the Jaramillo event. In fact, both were used by Vine and Wilson in accounting for the behavior of the Juan de Fuca Ridge, which is located in the Pacific basin off the coasts of Oregon, Washington, and Vancouver. Thus the importance of T1 and its two restrictions.

Sea-floor spreading, however, was not the only mobilist theory from which the two difficulty-free solutions could be derived, for there were several versions of earth expansion.

Expansionists grafted the two solutions onto their theories, since they believed that new sea floor was created at ridge axes and spread out along the horizontal, creating new ocean basins. But most earth scientists paid little attention to expansion. Why? Expansion failed to satisfy T2. It had a nest of serious theoretical difficulties pertaining to what could cause the Earth to increase its radius at rates required to explain the formation of ocean basins and the drifting of the continents. That, of course, is not to say that sea-floor spreading, with its postulation of convection currents, was accepted as providing the correct mechanism for the creation and horizontal movement of sea floor, for many earth scientists were undecided about the role and behavior of convection in sea-floor spreading. However, most rejected expansionism as a possible answer because of its failure to satisfy T2.

Hess's and Dietz's versions of sea-floor spreading included the idea that sea-floor material is subducted at trenches. Wilson's overall account of transform faults also contained an analysis of the behavior of faulting at trenches, and he supposed that the horizontal motion of sea-floor material was transformed to the vertical as sea-floor material descended back into the Earth's interior at trenches. Seismologists found support for Wilson's account. Although this seismological data didn't eliminate the possibility of earth expansion, given the theoretical EDPs facing expansionism, they were what would be expected if sea-floor material were subducted at trenches.

Hess and Dietz also linked together sea-floor spreading and continental drift; Vine, Matthews, Morley and Wilson viewed their hypotheses as part of an overall theory that included continental drift. Moreover, I know of no earth scientist who accepted sea-floor spreading without accepting continental drift. Nevertheless, it was possible to envision sea-floor spreading without continental drift by postulating a decoupling between the moving sea floor and the continents. In fact, some researchers at least entertained the question of sea-floor spreading without continental drift. Thus, why did every earth scientist who accepted sea-floor spreading accept continental drift?

The answer is T3. Continental drift brought to sea-floor spreading a tremendous increase in problem solving effectiveness. By grafting continental drift onto sea-floor spreading, the combined theory offered solutions to the problems solved by continental drift during the classical stage of the mobilist controversy, the problems addressed and solved by the British paleomagnetists during the late fifties and early sixties, plus those problems solved by sea-floor spreading and its difficulty-free solutions. However, this is not to maintain that the classical solutions were without difficulties, for questions still remained about the overall quality and completeness of the data used to support them. But T3 does not require that every solution of an acceptable theory be difficulty-free.

Although the solutions offered by continental drift were not difficulty-free, they were either consistent with sea-floor spreading's non-difficulty-free solutions or, when appropriate, gave results that accorded with sea-floor spreading and its difficulty-free solutions. Some of the continental drift reconstructions offered by classical drifters and further refined by directional paleomagnetic studies of continental rocks coincided with the paleogeographical reconstructions of the ocean basins based upon the record of marine magnetic anomalies. There was a consilience, for example, between the timing of the Atlantic basin as determined by studies based upon an analysis of marine magnetic anomalies, and those based upon paleomagnetic analysis of continental rocks, and upon paleoclimatology, paleobiogeography, coastline and geological match-ups. Oceanographers used the marine magnetic anomalies and the geopolarity reversal timescale to establish the rates of sea-floor spreading, and to determine when the existing ocean basins formed. They and other earth scientists, many of whom were former proponents of continental drift, bootstrapped continental drift and its classical solutions onto the theory of sea-floor spreading. The age of the ocean basins gave earth scientists a secure footing for bootstrapping the solutions offered by directional paleomagnetism and classical theories of continental drift. Before the confirmation of sea-floor spreading and its difficulty-free solutions, classical drifters pointed to a consilience among many of their solutions, and those working in directional paleomagnetism also argued that their various paleogeographical reconstructions roughly coincided with some of the classical paleogeographical reconstructions of the continents. What they lacked, however, was a solid footing, for none of their solutions were difficulty-free.

Fixists who had supported fixist solutions during the classical stage of the overall controversy began to dismiss their former so-lutions in terms of a mobilist framework once they became aware of the success of sea-floor spreading and its two difficulty-free solutions. Moreover, they switched to mobilism because of the triumph of sea-floor spreading, its difficulty-free solutions, the removal of the theoretical difficulty over how the continents could plow their way through the sea floor, and the consilience between many of drift's classical solutions and the results of the Vine-Matthews-Morley hypothesis. These fixists often reexamined their data, reinterpreting it in terms of mobilism.

Henry Frankel

Bibliography

Allwardt, Alan. "The Roles of Arthur Holmes and Harry Hess in the Development of Modern Global Tectonics." Ph.D. diss., University of California, Santa Cruz, 1990.

Frankel, H. "Arthur Holmes and Continental Drift." *British Journal History of Science* 11 (1978): pp. 130–150.

———. "The Development of Plate Tectonics by J. Morgan and D. McKenzie." *Terra Nova* 2 (1990): pp. 202–214.

———. "The Development, Reception, and Acceptance of the Vine-Matthews-Morley Hypothesis." *Historical Studies in the Physical Sciences* 13 (1982): pp. 1–39.

———. "Hess's Development of His Seafloor Spreading Hypothesis." In *Scientific Discovery: Case Studies,* edited by Thomas Nickles, pp. 345–366. Boston Studies in the Philosophy of Science, vol. 60. Dordrecht: D. Reidel, 1980.

———. "The Paleobiogeographical Debate over the Problem of Disjunctively Distributed Life Forms." *Studies in History and Philosophy of Science* 12 (1981): pp. 211–259.

———. "The Permo-Carboniferous Ice Cap and Continental Drift." *Compte rendu de Neuvieme Congres International de Stratigraphe et de Geologie du Carbonifere* 1 (1979): pp. 113–120.

———. "The Reception and Acceptance of Continental Drift Theory as a Rational Episode in the History of Science." In *The Reception of Unconventional Science,* edited by S.H. Mauskopf, pp. 51–90. Boulder, Colo.: Westview Press for AAAS, 1979.

Glen, William. *The Road to Jaramillo:*

Critical Years of the Revolution in Earth Science. Stanford: Stanford University Press, 1982.

Greene, Mott T. "Alfred Wegener." *Social Research* 51 (1984): pp. 739–761.

———. *Geology in the Nineteenth Century: Changing Views of a Changing World.* Ithaca, N.Y.: Cornell University Press, 1982.

Hallam, A. *Great Geological Controversies.* Oxford: Oxford University Press, 1983.

———. *A Revolution in the Earth Sciences.* Oxford: Oxford University Press, 1973.

Laporte, Leo F. "Wrong for the Right Reasons: G.G. Simpson and Continental Drift." *Geological Society of America: Centennial Special* 1 (1985): pp. 273–285.

Laudan, R. "Frank Bursley Taylor's Theory of Continental Drift." *Earth Sciences History* 1 (1985): pp. 118–121.

———. "The Method of Multiple Working Hypotheses and the Discovery of Plate Tectonic Theory in Geology." In *Scientific Discovery: Case Studies,* edited by Thomas Nickles, pp. 331–343. Boston Studies in the Philosophy of Science, vol. 60. Dordrecht: D. Reidel, 1980.

———. "The Recent Revolution in Geology and Kuhn's Theory of Scientific Change." In *Paradigms and Revolutions,* edited by Garry Gutting, pp. 284–296. South Bend, Ind.: Notre Dame University Press, 1980.

Le Grand, H.E. *Drifting Continents and Shifting Theories.* Cambridge: Cambridge University Press, 1988.

Marvin, U.B. *Continental Drift: The Evolution of a Concept.* Washington, D.C.: Smithsonian Institution Press, 1973.

Menard, H.W. *The Ocean of Truth: A Personal History of Global Tectonics.* Princeton: Princeton University Press, 1986.

Nunan, Richard. "The Theory of an Expanding Earth and the Acceptability of Guiding Assumptions." In *Scrutinizing Science,* edited by A. Donovan, L. Laudan, and R. Laudan, pp. 289–314. Baltimore, Md.: Johns Hopkins University Press, 1992.

Oreskes, Naomi. "The Rejection of Continental Drift." *Historical Studies in the Physical Sciences* 18 (1988): pp. 311–348.

Stewart, John A. *Drifting Continents and Colliding Paradigms: Perspectives on the Geoscience Revolution.* Bloomington: Indiana University Press, 1990.

See also Convection within the Earth; Expanding Earth Theories; Figure of the Earth in the Satellite Era; Geology; Geophysics; Hypotheses, Method of Multiple; Lakatos's Idea of Scientific Research Programs; Mohorovicic Discontinuity; Novel Facts; Paleomagnetism; Paleontology; Plate Tectonics and Space-based Platforms; Popper's Ideas on Falsifiability; Radio Astronomy and the Earth; Radioactivity in the Earth; Shifting Crust Theory

Convection within the Earth

The transfer of heat by fluid circulation, which is triggered by an unstable density distribution related to initial differences in temperature.

Although convection is usually associated with highly fluid liquids and gases, it can occur in solids exhibiting sluggish, fluidlike behavior at high pressures and temperatures. A crucial theme in the history of the geosciences was the growing awareness in the twentieth century that some form of convection, rather than simple heat conduction, must have controlled the thermal evolution of the Earth. This reorientation had profound implications for theories of mountain-building, global tectonics, and the origin of the geomagnetic field.

Despite the fundamental importance of convection, historians of the geosciences have barely begun to address it as a topic in its own right. Instead, references to convection have appeared almost exclusively in histories devoted to other subjects, most notably continental drift and plate tectonics. Although this approach has proved relatively informative, it has also led to a somewhat skewed view of convection research. In the mid-twentieth century, for instance, there was considerable work on convection with little relevance to the continental drift question, which historians have generally ignored. Granted, such selectivity may be defensible in the case of any individual author whose primary focus is continental drift. Nevertheless, when considering the historical literature as a whole, the treatment of convection might be described as Presentism by default, because continental drift has become a favored topic in recent years. Although the existing historical work on convection is selective, it does represent a sound beginning—the remaining task will simply be one of filling in the gaps.

For this historical review, the nineteenth and twentieth centuries can be treated separately because of three developments around 1900 that profoundly altered our thinking about the interior of the Earth. First, the discovery that radioactivity is a major source of heat within the Earth would cast serious doubt on the efficacy of heat conduction as the primary means of escape. Second, the seismological evidence for the core implied a fundamental density stratification within the Earth that would have to be accommodated by any subsequent model of convective circulation. Third, the planetesimal hypothesis for the origin of the solar system seriously undermined the traditional nebular hypothesis, which had been the cosmological foundation for geological speculation throughout the nineteenth century. The nebular hypothesis is a convenient starting point for this review.

Stephen Brush, in his "Nineteenth-Century Debates about the Inside of the Earth," has set the stage for understanding the secondary yet crucial role of convection in nineteenth-century theories about the interior of the Earth. Early in the century geologists generally subscribed to the doctrine of central primitive heat, whereby the interior of the Earth had supposedly remained very hot after condensing from a gaseous nebula. Going a step further, if the Earth's interior were still molten, with only a thin crust floating on the surface like slag, then one could easily explain phenomena such as mountain-building, vulcanism, and the temperature increase in deep mines.

In the mid-1800s, physicists concerned with planetary problems (there were no "geophysicists" as such) raised forceful objections to the idea of a molten interior. Led primarily by William Thomson (Lord Kelvin, 1824–1907), these physicists argued that the Earth as a planet behaves as if it were completely solid or nearly so (Brush, pp. 231–242). If the Earth were still largely molten, for instance, then huge lunar tides generated on the nonrigid interior would almost certainly break up the thin crust. By equating solidity with rigidity, Thomson set a precedent that would persist well into the next century.

Although he advocated a completely solid Earth, Thomson by no means rejected the doctrine of central primitive heat or the nebular hypothesis. He simply believed that the Earth has already passed through the molten stage and is now cooling according to established conduction theory. And here Thomson made a crucial assumption that allowed him to complete, in the 1860s, his famous calculation of the Earth's age. If, during the primordial molten stage, vigorous convection stirred the Earth's interior to a uniform temperature near the freezing point (about 7,000°F, according to Thomson), then the entire globe might have solidified in a geological instant. This assumption of a uniform initial temperature greatly simplified Thomson's task of calculating back from current conditions to the time of solidification. The results indicated that the Earth is probably one hundred million years old or less, an estimate that stood until the discovery of radioactivity decades later (see Burchfield).

Of course, Thomson's calculation has been remembered primarily for the fatally flawed assumption that primitive heat is the only significant heat source. Yet the assumption of convective stirring early in the Earth's history, although generally overlooked, was no less crucial to Thomson's temporary influence over the geological community.

Brush (pp. 242–245) has also reviewed the role of convection in the backlash against Thomson's restrictive timescale. The Reverend Osmond Fisher (1817–1914), author of a well-known textbook in geophysics, argued around the tidal objection to internal fluidity and noted that any sort of convection within the Earth would convey heat to the surface much faster than conduction, thus invalidating Thomson's age calculation. Fisher developed a speculative model of subcrustal convection based on extreme fluidity, for which (argues Brush) he has been mistakenly recognized by some historians as anticipating modern tectonic theory.

With the discovery of radioactivity around 1900, Thomson's arguments concerning the Earth's age and thermal evolution quickly lost currency. On the issues of internal solidity and rigidity, however, he maintained considerable influence over geological thinking for the first two decades of the new century (Brush, pp. 252–254).

Arthur Holmes (1890–1965) was representative of the new order that began exploring the many implications of radioactivity for geology. Although the main focus of his career was the development and application of radiometric dating techniques, Holmes also devoted considerable energy to reformulating the thermal history of the Earth in light of the new-found heat source and dramatically lengthened timescale (about two orders of magnitude longer than Thomson had imagined).

Henry Frankel (pp. 137–148) has reviewed this secondary aspect of Holmes's career and how it eventually led him to postulate subcrustal convection as the mechanism for continental drift. (In the summary below, some additional detail has been provided to clarify Frankel's account.) At first, Holmes simply attempted to reconcile the physical aspects of Thomson's system with the reality of radioactive heating. In 1915 and 1916, therefore, he sought a hypothetical but plausible distribution of radioactivity within the solid globe that would merely retard Thomson's steady conductive cooling. Through this exercise he realized that the radioactive content of rocks would have to decrease exponentially within the first hundred kilometers of the surface, or conduction alone would be unable to convey the heat to the surface. This distribution, moreover, seemed entirely reasonable, provided that convection within the molten primordial Earth had managed to "sweep" the interior free of radioactivity. Although it was difficult to imagine how convection could have been so efficient, the fact that the Earth had solidified at all seemed to demand it. With this line of reasoning Holmes appealed to the nebular hypothesis of the origin of the Earth, which had recently fallen into disfavor among astronomers because of the rival (but short-lived) planetesimal hypothesis. Indeed, Holmes still attributed a fourth of current heat flow to central primitive heat.

By 1925 Holmes had detected a fatal flaw in his model, because the demands of steady conductive cooling implied a radioactive distribution and temperature gradient that were inconsistent with the existence of igneous activity. Within three years he concluded that the Earth's once-molten interior must have retained enough radioactivity to prevent any solidification in the normal sense (that is, crystallization). Lacking a better term, Holmes described the noncrystalline material of the substratum (mantle) as a "stagnant glass," which was extremely viscous by virtue of the enormous pressure. A glassy substratum, he argued, could easily dispose of its excess radioactive heat by sluggish convection. And glass, it seemed, had the distinct advantage of responding like a rigid solid in the short term while exhibiting viscous behavior in the long term, as required by convection.

As Frankel has stressed, Holmes arrived at this stage in his thinking solely through a careful consideration of the Earth's thermal evolution. Now, however, he saw that convection within the viscous substratum might be an acceptable way of "engineering" continental drift. Convection currents rising beneath a continent would diverge at the base of the crust, he argued, and exert a horizontal viscous drag sufficient to rupture the continental mass and carry the fragments apart.

Mantle convection, if not continental drift, received additional support in the late 1930s from David T. Griggs (1911–1974), who demonstrated in the laboratory that pseudo-viscous flow occurs in crystalline rocks subjected to small stresses for long periods of time. Henceforth it was no longer necessary for proponents of convection to postulate a glassy mantle, with all of its cosmological baggage, as Holmes had done. Also in the 1930s, Felix A. Vening Meinesz (1887–1966) proposed subcrustal convection currents as the cause of the huge negative gravity anomalies he had discovered in the East and West Indies. Vening Meinesz's work was the basis of the downbuckling (or tectogene) hypothesis for the origin of island arcs and mountains, which gained additional support from Philip H. Kuenen (1902–1976) and Harry H. Hess (1906–1969), among others.

Despite these achievements, mantle convection failed to gain widespread support in the 1930s and 1940s. Although there are a number of plausible explanations for this lukewarm response, Alan O. Allwardt, in "Working at Cross-Purposes," has suggested that fragmentation within the convection camp itself may have been a contributing factor. Taking Holmes and Vening Meinesz as examples, he shows that the two men differed on almost every important aspect of subcrustal convection. Although they agreed that ascending currents would probably be initiated beneath the continents because of the thermal blanketing effect, only Holmes thought the resulting viscous drag would be powerful enough to rupture the crust and cause wholesale continental drift. Thus Holmes's ascending currents could ultimately be found in the middle of new rift oceans, while Vening Meinesz's ascending currents remained fixed beneath the continental blocks.

In the early 1950s evidence from an unexpected source raised the possibility of ascending convection currents being initiated beneath the ocean basins rather than the continents. Edward C. Bullard (1907–1980) and others conducted the first direct measurements of heat flow on the ocean floor and found the average value about equal to that of continental heat flow. This result was perplexing because continental heat flow could be attributed to highly radioactive crustal rocks of granitic composition, which were not present in the ocean basins. The explanation, it seemed, was that the continents had formed early in the Earth's history by vertical differentiation, leaving the mantle below relatively depleted of radioactivity. In the ocean basins, crustal differentiation had been much less complete, and the same initial amount of radioactivity remained distributed at depth in the mantle.

Ursula B. Marvin (pp. 140–141) was the first historian to stress that this explanation of the heat flow enigma precluded continental drift. If the continents had in fact drifted away from their initial positions they would now overlie mantle material that had not lost its initial complement of radioactivity, and the equality of continental and oceanic heat flow would be lost. Bullard, however, went even further with this argument than Marvin has indicated. He realized that limited convection in the suboceanic mantle was a distinct possibility if conduction alone could not cope with the heat produced by the deeply distributed radioactivity.

In the mid- to late-1950s, the discovery of the median rift and anomalously high heat flow along the oceanic ridge system seemed to pinpoint the location of the ascending currents. Even before these discoveries, mantle convection had been employed in several models for the origin of oceanic ridges, but without continental drift as an expected consequence. W. Maurice Ewing (1906–1974), for instance, believed that oceanic ridges were formed by the injection of basaltic magma into the crust, having been supplied by rising convection currents in the mantle. Hess, alternatively, proposed that oceanic ridges were underlain by welts of altered mantle rock, the product of hydration reactions triggered by the hot fluids accompanying convection currents. He envisioned oceanic ridges as ephemeral, with life cycles of about one hundred million years representing a single convective overturn of the mantle. The sequential development of ridges was also pursued by H. William Menard (1920–1986).

Such hypotheses were decidedly ad hoc in nature because they treated ridges as relatively isolated features. Several historians, including Homer Le Grand (chaps. 8 and 9),

have commented on the lack of a unifying theme in marine geology and geophysics during the 1950s. Oceanic ridges, trenches, and fracture zones had reasonable but separate explanations, with little attempt at integration even though they all incorporated convection. Perhaps this situation could have been expected, given the daunting task of sorting through the voluminous data collected from the ocean basins after World War II.

Menard's recollections, *Ocean of Truth* (especially chaps. 5 and 8) reinforce this historical view of the 1950s, although he implies that the absence of a unifying theme was less of a handicap than it might appear in retrospect. Granted, Menard must be interpreted with caution, like any participant-historian, but one episode is particularly revealing in this context. After considerable work on the great fracture zones of the eastern Pacific, he concluded that they might be attributed to an extensive convection cell in the mantle: "I distinctly remember thinking some time late in the evolution of these ideas that somewhere in discoveries of this scale there must be a Penrose Medal waiting. . . . I was right. Tuzo Wilson received it 15 years later for his insight in converting fracture zones into transform faults" (Menard, *Ocean of Truth,* p. 66). In the 1950s, however, Menard was dreaming of a Penrose Medal for solving a problem of regional significance to the eastern Pacific. J. Tuzo Wilson (1908–1993) actually won the award for solving a problem of global significance.

In 1960 Hess developed the much-needed unifying concept in the form of sea-floor spreading (Le Grand, chap. 9). Sea-floor spreading explained the history of ocean basins in terms of large convection cells in the mantle with rising currents beneath the ridges and descending currents beneath the trenches. New sea floor created at the ridges would be transported passively on the backs of the convection cells and then destroyed at the trenches. One important consequence of this "conveyer belt" model was continental drift.

In many respects, Hess's sea-floor spreading bore a superficial resemblance to the model Holmes had developed thirty years earlier from an entirely different set of data. From the perspective of this review, one important difference is worth mentioning. Hess envisioned the ocean basins as being essentially "crustless," with little more than a thin alteration rind on top of the mantle. Whereas Holmes had argued with Vening Meinesz about the magnitude of viscous drag exerted on the crust, Hess eliminated the concept of viscous drag altogether. This innovation paved the way for corollary theories concerning magnetic stripes and transform faults, which ultimately led to the plate tectonic revolution.

There are numerous opportunities for additional research on the topic of convection. With the exception of Rachel Laudan's brief overview, little has been written on twentieth-century models of convection during the initial differentiation of the Earth. Vening Meinesz, for instance, envisioned a simple, two-cell convective overturn forming the core, mantle, and a single supercontinent. Once the core had formed, convection in the mantle would have broken up to several smaller cells, thereby disrupting the overlying supercontinent and forming, in his view, the basic pattern of land and sea observed today (Laudan, p. 663). In the 1950s Vening Meinesz backed his arguments with a sophisticated, spherical harmonic analysis of the Earth's topography.

The accepted theory for the Earth's magnetic field involves a convective dynamo in the liquid outer core, probably driven by the latent heat of the solidifying inner core. The history of this theory, which dates to the mid-1940s, is considered elsewhere in this volume. Two side issues merit historical investigation in their own right. In the early 1950s Hess noted that explaining the magnetic field by convection in the core virtually guaranteed convection in the mantle as well, or the required temperature gradient in the core would be destroyed and convection would stop. And William Glen (p. 99) has briefly suggested that the initial difficulties of modeling magnetic field reversals in terms of the convective dynamo drove many paleomagnetists to the concept of self-reversing rocks in the 1950s.

The broad topic of mantle convection would benefit from a series of detailed historical studies, each treating a different aspect of the problem. The impact of scale modeling and experimental rock mechanics, for instance, has barely been touched by historians. On the theoretical front, the concept of viscous drag and the arguments about whether phase transitions would stop convection need more attention. And finally, historians should address the changing role of convection in the "postrevolutionary" period of plate tectonics, which has yielded several alternatives to the simple convection cells envisioned by Hess and his contemporaries.

Alan O. Allwardt

Bibliography

Allwardt, Alan O. "Working at Cross-Purposes: Holmes and Vening Meinesz on Convection." *Eos, Transactions, American Geophysical Union* 69 (1988): pp. 899–906.

Brush, Stephen G. "Nineteenth-Century Debates about the Inside of the Earth: Solid, Liquid or Gas?" *Annals of Science* 36 (1979): pp. 225–254.

Burchfield, Joe D. *Lord Kelvin and the Age of the Earth.* Chicago: University of Chicago Press, 1990.

Frankel, Henry. "Arthur Holmes and Continental Drift." *British Journal for the History of Science* 11 (1978): pp. 130–150.

Glen, William. *The Road to Jaramillo: Critical Years of the Revolution in Earth Science.* Stanford: Stanford University Press, 1982.

Laudan, Rachel. "Oceanography and Geophysical Theory in the First Half of the Twentieth Century: The Dutch School." In *Oceanography: The Past,* edited by Mary Sears and Daniel Merriman. New York: Springer-Verlag, 1980.

Le Grand, Homer E. *Drifting Continents and Shifting Theories.* Cambridge: Cambridge University Press, 1988.

Marvin, Ursula B. *Continental Drift: The Evolution of a Concept.* Washington, D.C.: Smithsonian Institution Press, 1973.

Menard, Henry W. *The Ocean of Truth: A Personal History of Global Tectonics.* Princeton: Princeton University Press, 1986.

See also Age of the Earth, since 1800; Continental Drift and Plate Tectonics; Geomagnetism, Theories since 1900; Gravimetry; Gravity since 1800; Heat, Internal, Twentieth Century; Isostasy; Matter, Properties at High Pressure and Temperature; Nebular Hypothesis; Paleomagnetism; Presentism; Radioactivity in the Earth; Seismology, Marine

Cosmic Rays, Early History

Radiation from beyond the Earth's atmosphere.

By 1900, scientists were aware that gases, including the atmosphere, are always slightly ionized. In the next few decades, the search for the sources of this ionization led to the realization that the Earth is constantly bombarded by radiation having enormous penetrating power originating in the reaches of outer space. From the perspective of the history of the geosciences, the studies making up this search are important not only because they uncovered the existence of a hitherto unknown "cosmic" radiation but, also, because they provided important insights into other geophysical phenomena such as atmospheric conductivity and terrestrial radioactivity. This review focuses on these studies and the protracted process of experimentation and interpretation that constituted the discovery of cosmic rays.

There has been relatively little commentary on this process by historians of science, since they have tended to address the topic of cosmic rays in works devoted primarily to other fields, such as high-energy physics, that focus on studies conducted after 1930. Hence, most of what has been written about early cosmic ray research has been authored by scientists either as review articles or introductory chapters in books on cosmic ray physics.

It is noteworthy that a few scientific texts on modern physics treat the discovery of cosmic rays as a discrete event with a discoverer, Victor Hess (1883–1964), and a discovery date, August 7, 1912. This unit-event model of the discovery process, with its focus on Hess, has led the authors of these texts to overstate his accomplishments and to ignore the work of others. For example, the notion that the Earth might be subjected to a highly penetrating extraterrestrial radiation was not, as these authors would have it, a revolutionary new concept put forth by Hess. In fact, this idea was first posited in 1899 and discussed in the literature during the decade preceding Hess's work by a number of eminent scientists including three who became Nobel laureates.

By the turn of the century, scientists had concluded that gases are readily ionized by X rays and the radiation from radioactive substances like radium. W.F.G. Swann (pp. 811–813) provides an overview of the experiments that led to this conclusion. To the English scientist Charles Wilson (1869–1959), the finding that the atmosphere and other gases are always feebly ionized, even in the absence of x rays and the then-known sources of radioactivity, suggested that ionizing radiation from an extraterrestrial source might be responsible. His experiments, conducted in 1901, failed to confirm this hypothesis—a not surprising result in view of how little was then known about environmental sources of ionizing radiation.

Continuing the search for the source of ions in the atmosphere, investigators made measurements on mountains, in caves, and over lakes and oceans. Their findings contributed to what was then known about radioactivity by showing that radioelements are widely distributed in soil, rocks, air, and water. Qiaozhen Xu and Lauria M. Brown (pp. 23–26) review this work and they describe related experiments on the conductivity of the atmosphere that advanced this field as well. By 1908 such studies had led scientists to conclude that about half the ionizing radiation they were observing came from radioelements in the materials of their instruments and half was from sources outside the instruments which, because it passed through lead shields, was called penetrating radiation. A small part of this radiation was attributed to gaseous radioelements, chiefly radon, in the air and the remainder to radioelements in the Earth's crust.

However, the concept that some fraction of the ambient penetrating radiation was extraterrestrial in origin did not die. Despite the negative results obtained by Wilson in 1901, scientific luminaries like Pierre Curie (1859–1906) and Owen Richardson (1879–1959) continued to entertain this idea. But most scientists assumed that terrestrial radioactivity accounted for the weakly ionized state of the atmosphere and other gases. In 1909, several investigators independently suggested a way to test the assumption that ambient penetrating radiation, except for the small component from airborne radioactivity, was the product of earthbound radioelements. They argued that, by taking instruments aloft in a balloon, radiation intensity measurements made at successively greater heights should diminish in a manner predicted by air absorption calculations indicating that the radiation came from the Earth below.

The first such flight was made in the fall of 1909 in Germany. It produced data that seemed to show the expected diminution of radiation with altitude, but these results were flawed by instrument malfunction. Data obtained on a second flight a few months later in Switzerland displayed a much smaller decrease, and that finding seemed confirmed by measurements made atop the Eiffel Tower. Further flights by Albert Gockel (1860–1927) in 1910–1911 provided data that appeared to indicate a slight increase in the radiation intensity with altitude. Gockel speculated that this phenomenon might be due to unexpectedly high levels of airborne radioactivity.

In 1911, Austrian scientist Victor Hess pondered these results. According to a memoir he wrote in 1940 (Hess, "Discovery," p. 229), he decided that Gockel's data was "influenced by instrumental defects" and that he would "attack the problem by direct experiments of [his] own." Hess's carefully thought out research program, involving ten balloon flights in 1911–1913 with improved measuring apparatus, produced data showing that at an altitude of 5,350 meters (17,553 feet) the intensity of penetrating radiation is over six times greater than that near the ground. These data led him to conclude that a hitherto unknown highly penetrating radiation of extraterrestrial origin is bombarding the Earth.

Hess's assertion that a component of penetrating radiation is of cosmic origin met with criticism in the scientific community on the grounds that it was more probable his data were attributable to radioactivity in the upper atmosphere or to instrument error than to some incredibly energetic radiation from outer space. In 1913, balloon measurements to 6,300 meters (20,670 feet) by Werner Kolhörster (1887–1946) confirmed Hess's data, but that did not silence the critics. Indeed, the possibility of instrument error was given credence by Gockel and other investigators who published the results of tests showing that the type of measuring instruments used by Hess and by Kolhörster could have produced biased readings at high altitudes.

In 1922, Robert Millikan (1868–1963) attempted to confirm Hess's data with balloonsondes equipped to measure the intensity of penetrating radiation to altitudes of 15,000 meters (49,215 feet). But Millikan found a much smaller increase of intensity with altitude than that reported by Hess and Kolhörster. This finding, together with other experiments he made in 1923, convinced him that an extraterrestrial component of penetrating radiation does not exist. He implied that the data of Hess and Kolhörster may have been flawed by instrument error and that his own balloonsonde data could be attributed to radioactivity in the upper atmosphere. In response, Hess (*Electrical Conductivity*, p. 134) pointed out that Millikan had admitted that the response of his balloonsonde was adversely affected by temperature.

In 1925, Millikan performed an ingenious experiment involving underwater measurements of penetrating radiation at two California lakes. The results convinced him that penetrating radiation does have an extraterrestrial component of extremely high energy. Bruno Rossi, in his *Cosmic Rays* (pp. 8–10), describes the lake experiments that led to Millikan's conversion. Millikan's experiments and his conclusions were accepted by those scientists who had continued to doubt the findings of Hess and Kolhörster. Thus, it was not until the mid-1920s that the existence of what were by then called cosmic rays was fully accepted by the scientific community.

But the question of their "discoverer" remained. If the data of Hess and Kolhörster were primarily the reflection of an instrumental bias, then Millikan's lake experiments would represent the first unequivocal evidence for the existence of cosmic rays. If, however, Hess's data were correct, then Millikan's lake experiments merely confirmed the existence of the cosmic rays discovered by Hess and verified by Kolhörster.

In the late 1920s the discovery of the latitude dependence of cosmic ray intensity resolved much of the discrepancy between the findings of investigators in the United States and in Europe. In 1931–1932, data on the variation of cosmic ray intensity with altitude obtained by Erich Regener (1881–1955) and Millikan using balloonsondes, and by the manned balloon flights of August Piccard (1884–1962), validated Hess's 1912 findings. Thus, after two decades of uncertainty the discoverer of cosmic rays was identified and the time of the discovery established.

In 1936, Hess received the Nobel Prize for his 1912 work on cosmic rays. A significant factor in the delayed recognition of Hess's achievement, according to Charles A. Ziegler (pp. 741–963), was the fact that the balloon ascents in 1909–1911 by Gockel and others produced data that was subsequently recognized as erroneous because of the inability of the instruments used to withstand the rigors of flight. Although Hess and later investigators used instruments designed to eliminate those problems, doubts about the reliability of data they obtained at high altitude lingered on and were only slowly dispelled by advances in instrument technology.

After the existence of cosmic rays became generally accepted, research on them increased significantly to yield important insights in other geosciences and astrophysics, in addition to initiating new subdisciplines such as elementary particle physics.

Charles A. Ziegler

Bibliography
Hess, Victor F. "The Discovery of Cosmic Radiation." *Thought: Fordham*

University Quarterly 25 (1940): pp. 225–366.

———. *The Electrical Conductivity of the Atmosphere and Its Causes.* London: Constable and Co., 1928.

Rossi, Bruno. *Cosmic Rays.* New York: McGraw-Hill, 1964.

Swann, W.F.G. "The History of Cosmic Rays." *American Journal of Physics* 29 (1961): pp. 811–819.

Xu, Qiaozhen, and Lauria M. Brown. "The Early History of Cosmic Ray Research." *American Journal of Physics* 55 (1987): pp. 23–33.

Ziegler, Charles A. "Technology and the Process of Scientific Discovery: The Case of Cosmic Rays." *Technology and Culture* 30 (1989): pp. 939–963.

See also Atmosphere, Chemistry of; Atmosphere, Structure of; Chemistry, Terrestrial and Cosmical; Geophysics; Instruments, Upper Atmosphere and Near Space; Radioactivity in the Earth; Solar Wind; Solar-Terrestrial Relations

Cosmology and the Earth in Antiquity

Views of the relation of the Earth to the cosmos.

Babylonians, Egyptians, Hebrews, and other early peoples around the Mediterranean have left us poetry, psalms, and other interesting writings, including tax lists and royal mandates. But none of them described the Earth or the Heavens. Nor did the Greek poetry of Hesiod and epics of Homer. Sources for the cosmology of Ionian philosophers may suggest geophysical ideas, but they are fragmentary phrases that were often revised, updated, and thus contaminated by many later commentators who preserved the fragments. Clear ideas about the *Kosmos* before the fourth century B.C.E. are not in evidence.

Astronomical data gathered by Babylonian priests and astrologers provided them with periodicity tables from which they made arithmetical formulae in order to predict the appearances of Sun, Moon, conjunctions, and oppositions. Those data series became especially useful when expressed in terms of the standard divisions of the zodiac about 450 B.C.E., with further calculations (to base sixty) of hours, minutes, and seconds. Whether the zodiacal band was conceived in Egypt, Babylonia, or Ionia is unknown, but it assumed the regularities of a celestial sphere. The *longitudo* (length) of the zodiac was divided into twelve sections identified by stargroups (signs) named Capricorn, Aquarius, Pisces, Aries, Taurus, Gemini, Cancer, Leo, Virgo, Libra, Scorpio, and Sagittarius. For more precision each sign could be divided into four or five or thirty parts. Then one could say that the Sun is in the third part of Aries, the Moon in the fifth part of Taurus, Mars is in the 24th part of Pisces, and so forth. Apparently, division of each sign into thirty parts and thus division of the zodiac into 360° (12 x 30 parts) was especially useful for observing the movements of seven planets along the central lines of the zodiac, the ecliptic.

Latitudo (breadth) within the zodiac was determined by the course of the Moon, which not only moves from east to west nightly with the stars but also falls behind them slightly every 24 hours; thus the Moon can be said to have moved slowly back from west to east each month. Those movements are *in longitudo* (length). In addition, the Moon wanders *in latitudo* (laterally) to the north and to the south as it circles the Earth. The custom was to speak of eight parts of latitude above the ecliptic (to the north) and five parts below (to the south). Within that range of about thirteen parts, all seven planets moved east to west with the stars, but three (Mars, Saturn, and Jupiter) also gradually slipped back from west to east periodically. Their separate courses were complicated, as they appeared to stop, reverse direction, stop, and hurry on. All seven planets seemed to move laterally to the northern and to the southern parts (*latitudines*) of the zodiac. The Sun was the most regular, and its daily path from east to west was seen to vary only slightly (one or two parts) from the ecliptic. Venus on the other hand sometimes wandered beyond the extremes of the zodiac by one or two parts.

Wandering motions of the planets led to many speculations about their relations to each other and to the Earth. It was probably the sixth-century Pythagoreans who first expressed the concept of the heavens as an outer sphere carrying the stars from east to west. The astronomer and geometer Eudoxos of Cnidos (fl. ca. 370 B.C.E.) conceived of imaginary lines on that sphere defined by seasonal movement of the Sun, which was seen to be in the sign of Cancer at its extreme in summer, or in Capricorn at its extreme in winter. Thus, the tropics of Cancer and of Capricorn divided large parts of the sky. Most stars could be seen only in season during half of the year. However, there were stars in the north whose circles were always visible at night. Their circular motions allowed a theoretical pole to be defined; no star was actually at that geometric center, and those near it have changed from century to century. The lower limit of the stars that were always visible in the Mediterranean from Rodos served to define the Arctic Circle (at 23°51' north latitude, in modern terms); the Antarctic Circle was assumed to be its southern equivalent. The result was a schema of great circles by which one's mind could control data concerning heavenly phenomena—the *zonal rota* (see figure on p. 95 in "Climate, Ancient Ideas"), a concept that would be useful to astronomers and cartographers for more than two thousand years, and is still assumed for the language of latitudes today.

Distances of the planets from Earth and the periods of their courses were also estimated and studied: Mercury varied from 355 to 365 days, Venus from 365 to 485 days, but more regular were Mars 683, Jupiter 4,331, and Saturn 10,752 days. This led to a series of proposals: obviously, it could not be true that planets actually stopped and reversed, as we see them. Perhaps that could be explained if the Earth also turned on its own axis (Herakleides of Pontos, d. ca. 310 B.C.E.), or moved either around the Sun (Aristarchus of Samos, fl. 281 B.C.E.), or both (Aristarchus?). The periods of Venus and Mercury varied from year to year, but they could be seen only near the Sun. What if they circled the Sun while the group of three circled the Earth in conjunction (Ecphantos of Syracuse, fl. ca. 400; Plato, d. 347 B.C.E.; Chalcidius, fl. 400 C.E.)? Then, it was possible that the Sun moved on a circle eccentric to the Earth (Apollonios of Perga, d. ca.190, Hipparchos). There was no evidence to confirm such speculations, and few Greek and Roman astronomers and philosophers took them seriously. Aristotle of Stagira (384–322 B.C.E.) and Ptolemy of Alexandria (100–170 C.E.) specifically rejected all such ideas and preferred combinations of circles and predictive formulae concerning various kinds of planetary motions. Medieval scholars, however, such as François de Marchia (fl. ca. 1300), Jean Buridan (1275–1358), Nicole Oresme (1325–1382), Nicholas of Cusa (1401–1464), and Celio Calcagnini (1479–1541) lectured often on the relative motions of Sun and Earth, including the possible course of the Sun about the Earth, long before Nicholas Copernicus (1473–1543) and Johannes Kepler (1571–1630) published their works, redefining astronomy.

Within the scope of Hellenistic cosmology it was normal to think of the Earth as a sphere, but not at the beginning. In fifth-century Ionia, Anaxagoras of Clazomenae (ca. 450 B.C.E.), Anaximenes of Miletos (fl. 545), and Democritos of Abdera (fl. 410) may have thought of the Earth like a kneading trough if one may believe the reports by Aristotle. Other sources thought that those three Ionians, along with Leucippos of Miletos (fl. 440), had conceived of the Earth as drumshaped. However the Sun does not rise or set at the same time in all regions, as it should if the surface were flat; thus Archelaus, a student of Anaxagoras, would lower the center and raise the edges of the surface. The opposite approach may have been taken by Diogenes of Apollonia (fl. 450) if he spoke of the Earth as round. Yet, the sources for such contradictory ideas were written six, eight, and twelve hundred years after the pre-Socratics and usually cannot be accepted as reliable. (On three levels of evidence, see Dicks, pp. 39–42; on Thales, see Lindberg, pp. 27–29.) Any attributions today of "flat" or "disk" or "drum" concepts to Babylonian or Milesian philosophers must be dubious.

For example, Socrates (d. 399 B.C.E.) read the works by Anaxagoras to discover whether there was any reason to suppose the Earth to be flat, according to Plato's *Phaedros*. The Earth as a globe was accepted and taught by Plato (d. 347), Eudoxos of Cnidos (d. ca. 347), and Aristotle, and all Hellenistic writers thereafter. Two arguments were based upon observations of gravity and curvature. Firstly, as explained by Aristotle, earth and water are heavy elements and have a natural motion towards the center of the *Kosmos;* therefore the weight of all things composed of those elements cause them to press against each other, and they become evenly distributed around the center, resulting in a sphere which is the Earth. Secondly, during every lunar eclipse, the Earth's shadow falls upon the Moon from one side or the other, revealing Earth's curvature and thus its spherical shape. Additional support was given by Isidore of Seville (d. 636 C.E.), the venerable Bede (d. 735), Johannes de Sacrobosco (d. 1240), and many other medieval scientists.

All models of the Earth corresponded with the spherical heavens, but during the Middle Ages new thoughts were given by Jean Buridan (1286–1340) and many others to questions of gravity. The elements *terra* and *aqua* have weight, yet they have different abilities to move. What if the weight of *terra* (earth) moves its pieces into its own sphere, while the weight of *aqua* (water) moves its drops more freely into its own sphere? Each sphere would have its own center; but where then was the center of the *Kosmos?* Major movements of land brought about by earthquakes or avalanches would shift the center of the earthly sphere, raising a difficult question about the stability of the whole *Kosmos* (see Vogel). It may be this difficulty to which Copernicus referred in the introduction to his book *De revolutionibus* (1543) when he proposed that, by explaining the motion of the Earth around the Sun, his model of the planets would bring all elements into harmony—a view that was only gradually accepted.

Unfortunately, nineteenth- and twentieth-century classical scholars, historians of science, and art historians have generated a large and unreliable literature about this topic.

Wesley M. Stevens

Bibliography

Dallal, Ahmed. "Al-Biruni on the Climates." *Archives Internationales d'Histoire des Sciences* 34 (1984): pp. 3–18.

Dicks, D.W. *Early Greek Astronomers to Aristotle.* London: Thames and Hudson, 1970.

Jensen, P.J., and J.H. Waszink, eds. *Plato Timaeus: A Calcidic Translatus.* London and Leiden, E.J. Brill. 1962.

Laserre, François, ed. *Die Fragmente des Eudoxus von Knidos.* Berlin, 1966.

Lindberg, David. *The Beginnings of Western Science.* Chicago: University of Chicago Press, 1992.

Lloyd, G.E.R. *Early Greek Science: Thales to Aristotle.* London: Chatto and Windus, 1970, chap. 1.

Stevens, W.M. "A Double Perspective on the Middle Ages." In *Non-Verbal Communication in Science prior to 1900,* edited by R.G. Mazzolini, pp.1–28. Florence: Leo S. Olschki Editore, 1993.

———. "The Figure of the Earth in Isidore of Seville's De natura rerum." *ISIS* 71 (June 1980): pp. 268–277.

Vogel, Klaus. A. "Das Problem der relativen Lage von Erd- und Wassersphäre im Mittelalter und die kosmographische Revolution." *Mitteilungen der Osterreichischen Gesellschaft für Wissenschaftsgeschichte* 13, nos. 1–2 (1993): pp. 103–143.

See also Climate, Ancient Ideas; Cosmology and the Earth; Earth, Models of before 1600; Earthquakes, Theories from Antiquity to 1600; Flat Earth Models; Meteorological Ideas; Seismology, Historical

Cosmology and the Earth in Medieval Europe

A geocentric universe, inherited from the Greeks and refined by Christian theologians to include its creation by God. Changes in the period include the shift from Platonic to Aristotelian philosophy in the thirteenth century and the beginnings of observational science.

The cosmology of the Middle Ages was inherited from Greek natural philosophers, and interpreted and modified by editors and encyclopedists of the late Roman empire. Some of these, being Christian, studied to adapt pagan philosophy to the new religion. This process was made easier by the strong neo-Platonist strain in Christianity that was due to the influence of St. Augustine (354–430 C.E.). During the first part of the Middle Ages thinking about the cosmos was profoundly deductive: its exponents being churchmen rather than scientists, their main concern was to explain natural phenomena in terms of the truth of the revealed Scriptures and the orderliness and beneficence of the divine plan. Indeed, commentaries on the first chapter of Genesis were the vehicle for a number of early medieval works on cosmology.

Briefly described, the Earth was the unmoving center of a spherical universe, everywhere filled with matter and flooded with light. Surrounding the Earth were eight transparent spheres, one for each of the seven "planets" (in this order: Moon, Mercury, Venus, Sun, Mars, Jupiter, Saturn) and one for the stars. Beyond these was a "primum mobile," a sphere that transmitted motion to the rest. Various arrangements were proposed for the outer spheres, including a crystalline or aqueous sphere ("the waters above the Earth" from Genesis), and an empyrean, the heaven that existed from the first day and was inhabited by the angels. The spheres were spaced in perfect mathematical intervals in relation to one another and, as they revolved, produced celestial music.

The motive power of celestial rotation was the love that heavenly bodies, conceived of as divine intelligences, bore toward God. This was not Aristotle's concept, but it was easily compatible with Christian theology. The stars and planets yearned to be united with the divine mover and thus circled endlessly. The force of gravity was also described as an emotional inclination, in this case, for like to be united with like. For example, heavy, earthy objects fell to Earth, while fiery objects tended upwards.

All matter was composed of five elements, and these were arranged with ether in the spheres beyond the Moon, and fire, air, water, and earth in descending order and in combination in the sublunar realm. Change and decay occurred only in the sphere below the Moon, while above all was perfection, and the heavenly bodies moved in continuous, circular, or perfect motion. (Disturbing events like comets were thought to occur between the Earth and the Moon.) God was the designer, animator, and preserver of this harmonious and orderly universe.

The Greeks had thought the universe to be eternal, but Christian philosophers, following the Bible, believed it to be created from nothing by God and destined to end.

Within this general schema were various refinements and points of discussion. For example, the Heraclidean theory that Mercury and Venus revolved around the Sun survived into the medieval period through the works of Macrobius (early fifth century C.E.) and Martianus Capella (fl. 410–439?), and coexisted with the more conventional view of a completely geocentric universe. The concept of planetary epicycles devised by Ptolemy and the complex system of concentric spheres for each planet postulated by Aristotle were both known in the Middle Ages, and their usefulness in accounting for the vagaries of planetary motion were appreciated. By the end of the thirteenth century Ptolemy's system had won out, because of its practical superiority, but only after much serious debate.

As for the Earth itself, it was generally conceived to be spherical, although some writers such as Isidore of Seville (ca. 560–636) seem unclear on this point and use the word "sphere" when they appear to mean "disk." The inhabited world, or *oecumene*, occupied one-third of the surface of the globe and was composed of three continents: Asia, the largest; Europe; and Africa or Libya. The boundaries dividing them were the Mediterranean, the River Don (Tanais), and the Nile. This tripartite division corresponded neatly with the division of the Earth between the three sons of Noah: Ham in Africa, Shem in Asia, and Japhet in Europe. The great ocean surrounded the oecumene. The idea of other worlds and peoples in the Southern or Western hemispheres was condemned by the Church, but speculation about the Antipodes continued, and a fourth, southern continent even appeared on maps in the works of the Spanish saints Isidore (ca. 560–636) and Beatus (ca. 730–798).

The Earth was divided into five climatic zones, and it was agreed that the frigid and torrid zones were uninhabitable and probably unexplorable. Adventuring to the Southern Hemisphere was thus impossible, but the way to the west was left provisionally open, and indeed Irish monks under St. Brendan (484–570) were thought to have journeyed there and found land as early as the sixth century.

The Middle Ages inherited two estimates of the size of the Earth from Greek writers, and for some time was at a loss as to how to verify or improve upon them. The estimate by Poseidonius (135–51 B.C.E.) of 180,000 stades for the Earth's circumference was passed on through Strabo (ca. 63 B.C.E.–23 C.E.) and Ptolemy (fl. 150 C.E.) to Roger Bacon (ca. 1220–ca. 1292), eventually to reach Columbus (1446?–1506), while the more correct figure by Erastosthenes (fl. 235 B.C.E.) of 252,000 stades appears in the work of Macrobius and Martianus Capella. Related to these were estimates of the sizes of the Sun and Moon and the distances in the universe. In general the Middle Ages estimated the solar system to be much smaller than modern measurements indicate—for example, they thought the Earth's shadow extended as far as Venus—but still it was vast enough to produce humility in the thoughtful observer.

The natural philosophy of classical antiquity reached the Middle Ages through works by the encyclopedists and commentators of the fourth and fifth centuries. For the Middle Ages, the most important pagan authors were Calcidius, Macrobius, and Martianus Capella. To Calcidius (late fourth century C.E.) the medieval period was indebted for what it possessed of Plato—the first part of the *Timaeus*—accompanied by the translator's commentary. Macrobius (fifth century) preserved the last part of *De Re Publica* (known as *Scipio's Dream*) of Cicero (106–43 B.C.E.). His commentary, illustrated with helpful diagrams (climate zones, the heavenly spheres), passed on the general structure of the cosmos as seen by the Platonists, as well as digressions on the mystical force of numbers and the interpretation of dreams. Like other late Roman writers on nature, Macrobius seems to have repeated received notions without fully understanding them. His readers did likewise until some classical ideas became hopelessly muddled. The wave of new translations from Greek originals that appeared in the thirteenth century came as a breath of fresh air.

Martianus Capella's allegorical presentation of the seven liberal arts in *De Nuptiis Philologiae et Mercurii* contained a review of the state of knowledge in astronomy and geography. This work, along with that of Macrobius, is usually credited with keeping the idea of the spherical Earth alive during the early Middle Ages.

These three works were copied and recopied throughout the medieval era, but of even greater importance were the works of great churchmen, whose comments on scientific matters were usually peripheral to their major concerns. St. Augustine, in *The City of God*, praised Platonism for its correct concept of God as the true author of the universe, but he admired the Platonists more for turning from the study of "obscure and inconclusive subjects," such as natural science, to the more important topic of morality (Book VIII.3). He condemned the idea of people living on the other side of the Earth in a passage that cast doubt on the Earth's sphericity ("even if the world is supposed to be a spherical mass. . ." Book XVI.9). Clearly an offhand remark, it had a great impact because of Augustine's enormous prestige.

Even more influential in scientific matters was St. Isidore of Seville. His *Etymologiae* or *Origines* was a sort of dictionary, covering all of human knowledge from grammar to the harnesses of horses. "When you see where a name has come from," wrote Isidore, "you understand its significance more quickly." He drew on a tremendous range of classical authors, though not all in their original state, and retailed their ideas for many successive generations of Europeans. His shorter work, *De Natura Rerum,* contained so many illustrative diagrams that it was nicknamed *Liber De Rotarum* (the book of circles). Although Isidore is often criticized for his uncritical acceptance of misinformation from Roman sources, his attitude toward the study of the natural world was positive. In his dedication of *De Natura Rerum* to King Sisebut of Spain, he wrote: "It is God himself who has given me true science so that I may understand the harmonious order of the heavens and the specific qualities of the various elements, the successive phases of the astral revolutions and the divisions of the seasons" (quoted by Bréhaut, p. 28).

In England, Bede (673–735) contributed to the survival of scientific ideas by his works *De Natura Rerum* and *De Temporum Ratione.* These were essentially further repetitions of Pliny the Elder, but unlike his predecessor, Isidore, Bede's work is a miracle of clarity. "A regard for evidence, a love of mathematical and verbal refinement, a determination to achieve truth by the best methods of his day, and a refusal to copy without understanding mark him as a scientist" (Jones, p. 129). Writing about the phenomenon of the ocean tides, he even added contemporary, local observations. His computus, or construction of tables for calculating Easter, was based on a nineteen-year lunar cycle, and they continued to be consulted well into the early modern era.

Bede, however, like most early medieval scholars, was primarily interested in biblical exegesis. Science was useful for understanding the word of God, for use in allegorical interpretation (such as bestiaries), but there was little attempt to add to or test inherited wisdom. The first glimpse of creative scholarly work in cosmology comes with the school of Chartres in the twelfth century. The scholars were Platonists, but the first translations from the Arabic editions of Ptolemy and Aristotle began to be made in this century, and speculation on basic cosmological questions, such as the existence of matter prior to the Creation, was rife. Bernard Silvester (fl. 1147–1177) in his *Cosmographia* constructed a myth of the cosmos similar to that in the *Timaeus,* and further rationalized the idea of man as microcosm of the universe. The close connection between heavenly and earthly events had long been an accepted truth. Even though astrology had been formally condemned by the Church, this prohibition extended only to the influence of the stars over human free will. Medieval thinkers firmly believed that planetary motion affected the weather, one's health and temperament, and major events such as wars and social upheavals. This all-embracing harmony was part of the unified view of the cosmos. In addition, the Arabs, whose work now began to enter Western Europe through the gates of Sicily and Spain, were great adepts at astrology and had no compunctions about fatalism. The famous tables of coordinates of latitude and longitude compiled by Arabic astronomers were made for casting horoscopes, and for the next several centuries, astronomy and astrology were to remain synonymous.

The permeation of Western European thought by the newly available works of Aristotle was complete by the mid-thirteenth century. The principal cosmological works, *De Caelo* and *Meteorologica,* were available after 1160. Although Aristotle and Plato differed little on the general structure of the cosmos, Aristotelian thought brought a new questioning attitude toward scientific theories and an experiential approach to natural phenomena. The impact can be seen on the mind of a man like Robert Grosseteste (1169–1253), who wrote that science begins with the observation of natural events, and from them hypotheses are constructed. It was to be several centuries before systematic experimentation began to be the basis of science and even longer before the geocentric universe was seriously challenged, but the groundwork was clearly being laid.

The condemnation of Aristotle's scientific works by ecclesiastical authorities in Paris in 1210 caused a serious flutter in the new university. The ban was revoked in 1234, but in 1277 the bishop of Paris denounced a series of propositions, including the eternity of the universe and its inevitable operation according to natural law. The latter was thought to restrict unduly the absolute power of God. By this time, however, Aristotelian science was solidly established in the massive *Summae* of St. Thomas Aquinas (1225?–1274). Called simply "the Philosopher," Aristotle was the most powerful single force in science for the next four hundred years.

The most comprehensive treatment of medieval cosmology is still that of Pierre Duhem, whose ten-volume work appeared beginning in 1913, with the last volumes published posthumously in 1959. He was the first to look at medieval science as a creative enterprise in its own right, not merely a trough of ignorance between the Greeks and the revolution of the seventeenth century. His coverage of individual thinkers is very complete, but in some cases now needs to be modified in the light of more recent research. Histories of science necessarily deal with cosmology briefly, and the medieval period, especially before 1200, is often slighted. An important exception is A.C. Crombie, whose treatment of this period is commendably full. Most modern studies are on individuals, such as W.H. Stahl on Macrobius, or Lynn Thorndike on Sacrobosco. A collection of articles edited by David Lindberg includes "Cosmology" by Edward Grant and "The Philosophical Setting of Medieval Science" by William A. Wallace. Lindberg also published, in 1992, an overview of ancient and medieval science, with over half the book devoted to

the Middle Ages. He includes much general information about the intellectual and institutional history of the period, as indicated by his lengthy subtitle.

The medieval cosmos survived until the seventeenth century, dominating the western mind for two thousand years. Its definition of the relationship between humanity and the larger world of Earth and stars was profoundly satisfying, and still leaves many traces in our culture. Its grandeur is best summed up by Dante's description in the *Divine Comedy.* After descending to the depths of the Inferno in the Earth's core, he and his guide, Vergil, go through the center and out the other side. Dante describes vividly the moment when "down" becomes "up." They voyage to Mount Purgatory in the forbidden Southern Hemisphere, a place not usually attainable by mortals. Then after climbing to view the Earthly paradise at its summit, the poet ascends sphere by sphere into the realms of increasing light until, in the utmost sphere, he is in the presence of God, invoked as the supreme light. Here he reaches the conclusion of his voyage, where "my desire and will, like a wheel that spins with even motion, were revolved by the Love that moves the sun and the other stars" (*Paradiso,* XXXIII, ll. 142–144. Sinclair's translation).

Evelyn Edson

Bibliography

Bréhaut, Ernest. *An Encyclopedist of the Dark Ages: Isidore of Seville.* New York: Columbia University Press, 1912.

Claggett, Marshall. *The Science of Mechanics in the Middle Ages.* Madison: University of Wisconsin Press, 1959.

Crombie, A.C. *Augustine to Galileo: The History of Science, A.D. 400–1650.* London: William Heinemann, 1957.

Duhem, Pierre. *Le système du monde: histoire des doctrines cosmologiques de Platon à Copernic.* 10 vols. Paris: A. Hermann, 1915. Reprint. *Medieval Cosmology: Theories of Infinity, Place, Time, Void, and the Plurality of Worlds.* Abridged. Translated and edited by Roger Ariew. Chicago: University of Chicago Press, 1985.

Jones, Charles W. *Bedae opera de temporibus.* Cambridge: Medieval Academy of America, 1943.

Lindberg, David. *The Beginnings of Western Science: The European Scientific Tradition in Philosophical, Religious, and Institutional Context, 600 B.C. to A.D. 1450.* Chicago: University of Chicago Press, 1992.

———, ed. *Science in the Middle Ages.* Chicago: University of Chicago Press, 1978.

Murdoch, John E. *Album of Science: Antiquity and the Middle Ages.* New York: Scribners, 1984.

See also Climate, Ancient Ideas; Cosmology and the Earth; Earth, Size of; Earth, Models of before 1600; Flat Earth Models; Mappaemundi; Meteorological Ideas; Tides before Newton

Cosmology and the Earth in Pre-modern Orient

A culture of natural knowledge centered on China and independent until the last several centuries of science based on ancient Babylonian and Greek traditions.

Orient as defined here is non-Western, a word frequently employed in the nineteenth century. The vague but long-standing dichotomy between Orient and Occident, or East and West, has generated much shallow debate and confusion. In order to avoid them in what follows, when I speak of Eastern and Western sciences, I refer to two complementary traditions, well defined as follows.

The historical center of Western science moved from Babylonia to classical Greece to Hellenistic Egypt, India, and the Arabic-speaking lands, and thence to Renaissance Europe, thus to the modern-day Western world. In the East the center stayed on in China until the period of European expansion; Korea, Japan, and Vietnam remained cultural satellites. Hence, unlike Indian and Arabic sciences, in which the main current of Western scientific thought flowed and developed, China and East Asia provide us with an independent counterculture of science.

Morphological cosmology was represented by *Kait'ien* theory. The first scientific cosmological treatise—scientific in the sense of being divorced from poetic fantasy and local folklore, and in the sense of being mathematical—is found in the *Choupei suanching* (the arithmetical classics of the Chou gnomon). The extant text may go back to the fourth century B.C.E. and was based on observational data of the sixth century B.C.E. *Kait'ien* (literally, "the sky as a cover") cosmology is generally identified with the content of the *Choupei suanching* and is closely linked with the use of the gnomon. A consideration of elements of the theoretical and empirical knowledge available at the time this treatise was compiled enables us to analyze its cosmology.

This theory entailed technical knowledge of the following:

1. The use of the gnomon and gnomon-shadow template.
2. The time of the solstices, also available from gnomon observations. The time of the equinoxes was determined by simple linear interpolation.
3. The belief in a "polar region" centered on the North Pole, defined as a region constantly illuminated during the summer and dark during the winter.

It also assumed preconceived notions, as follows:

1. The *yin-yang* principle.
2. The concept of *t'ienyuan tifang* (literally, "the sky is circular and the Earth square"). It was probably a metaphorical statement, founded on the idea of *yin-yang* dichotomy, with the sky characteristically moving and the Earth characteristically at rest.
3. The idea of the parallelism of sky and Earth. They were considered to be either both flat or both convex, and parallel.
4. Polar centricity. The North Pole was given the most venerable place in the firmament. In contrast to the zodiacal framework of the Western cosmos, the East Asian maintained a polar-equatorial coordinate system.
5. The correspondence hypothesis of *its'un ch'ienli*—that is, 1 *ts'un* (about an inch) to 1,000 *li* (1 *li* is approximately half a kilometer). Shadow length was believed to increase 1 *ts'un* for every 1,000 *li* north of the "center of the universe," and to decrease by the same amount for every 1,000 *li* south. The idea was based on the notion of the parallelism of Earth and sky and is obviously a simple and crude hypothesis.
6. The hypothesis that the distance between sky and Earth is 80,000 *li*.

With the elements enumerated above and with limited mathematical tools, including the Pythagorean theorem, they created an elaborate, quantitative world picture. In ancient China, where the armillary sphere and angular measurement had not yet developed, it was necessary for the elaboration of a cosmological system to depend solely upon linear distance, projected from the terrestrial onto the celestial region.

Much has been said about two rival cosmological theories in ancient China, *Kait'ien* (flat or curved heavens) and *Hunt'ien* (spherical heavens). One can say for sure that both theories had close association with the astronomical instruments in use. The original *Kait'ien* of flat heavens and Earth theory was put forward when only measuring sticks for gnomon shadow-length observations were available, while the *Hunt'ien* theory of spherical heavens was introduced when angular measurement was made possible by using armillary spheres around the first century C.E.

The focal point of the *Hunt'ien* theory is simply recognition that the shape of the sky is spherical. Its associated armillary sphere proved extremely useful to astronomers of this era, for example in the determination of the lengths of day and night. According to the *Kait'ien* model, the length of a day in any season of the year is determined by linear interpolation between the summer and winter solstices, a method that obviously gives incorrect results. But the only other feasible method was day-to-day observation. Once the *Hunt'ien* model was accepted and the armillary sphere employed, the movement of the Sun on the ecliptic became graduated and the length of a day in an intermediate season was measurable—for instance, by applying a measuring cord to the instrument—with no observation or calculation required. There was no necessity for speculation as to the height of the sky or for use of the hypothetical 1 *ts'un* to 1,000 *li* correspondence.

Thus, the association of the armillary sphere with the development of astronomical technique resulted in the firm establishment of the *Hunt'ien* school. Cosmological controversy died out as astronomers lost interest and came to occupy themselves solely with routine observations and calendar-making. The later dynastic histories repeated the cosmological discussions of the *Chinshu* (the official history of the Chin dynasty) without substantial change. According to the new standard history of the T'ang dynasty, the concern of astronomers was "exclusively calendrical calculations and observations, in order to provide the people with the correct time. Whether the *Hunt'ien* or *Kait'ien* cosmology is the true one is no concern of the astronomer." Despite the extensive foreign contacts made by the Chinese during the medieval period, a general lack of interest in cosmol-

ogy prevented Indian and Islamic theories from having much lasting influence.

In Greek antiquity, the spherical Earth theory was necessarily associated with the spherical heavens to form a concentric universe. One wonders why the spherical Earth theory never appeared in the Chinese and East Asian tradition, in which a sophisticated technology had been developed, before the arrival of Western missionaries in the sixteenth and seventeenth centuries.

There was empire-wide land surveying conducted during the T'ang period. They had clearly recognized the curvature of the Earth and indeed developed a "curved Earth" theory. Nevertheless, they had not fully extended to a full-curved Earth—namely, a spherical Earth theory.

My conjecture is that they placed "the center of the Earth" near the capital and that it played the role of what we call today the reference point for land-surveying and mapmaking. In view of their China-centered thought, it might have been difficult to accept the spherical Earth theory, which located the center of the cosmos in the dark, unreachable underside of the Earth.

Eastern astronomers must have known the cause of eclipses. Then, lunar eclipses must have been interpreted as the shadow of the Earth projected on the Moon, but they avoided such a schematic representation. They might have drawn it in private notebooks for eclipse calculation but it was not their style to publish any illustration officially, as their treatises were expressed only numerically, not geometrically.

The traditional ideology of Chinacenteredness precluded the value of circumnavigation. Those people of inferior cultures were seen as coming to pay tribute to China from all over the world. The Chinese must have tried circumnavigation, but it was excluded from their cultural value system and hence not proclaimed.

Later, when Jesuits came to East Asia in the seventeenth century and conveyed the idea of spherical Earth theory, Japanese Confucian scholars said that "we are not aggressive and hence we do not try invasion overseas. Hence, we have not employed a spherical Earth theory."

In the West, until the time of Copernicus, cosmological speculation in the Aristotelian tradition and practical astronomy in the Ptolemaic heritage were two virtually separate fields. An analogous bifurcation was maintained in East Asia, perhaps more thoroughly.

It seemed that while the discussion and debate on the morphology of the universe had stagnated and nearly terminated among the professional astronomers' community, the interest in what is going on and how it came to being inside the universe—namely, the dynamism and natural philosophy of world-formation and world-running—occupied the minds of Chinese and East Asian intellectuals.

Beginning in the tenth century, the neo-Confucian movement attempted to revive the older classical Confucianism by incorporating it in a systematic philosophy. Old ideas about the origin, formation, and shape of the universe were reexamined, and although the basic mathematical and astronomical tenets were not disturbed, attempts were made to rationalize them.

The neo-Confucians favored the *Hunt'ien* theory. Chi Hsi (1131–1200), the chief figure of the school, argued that the *Kait'ien* theory could not explain how the sky kept in consonance with the Earth. That his quasi-mechanical model derived from the *Hunt'ien* theory is apparent from the following oft-quoted statement: the shape of the sky and Earth is as if somebody joins two bowls with water inside. So long as he constantly turns them around with his hands, the water remains inside and is not spilled, but no sooner does he stay his hands for a moment than it runs out.

Chi Hsi's concept of the world was rooted in his materialistic cosmogony, the origin of which can be traced back at least as far as the *Huai-nan tzu* (Book of the Prince of Huai-nan, about 120 B.C.E.). This work is based on the behavior of the cosmic protyle, *ch'i.*

Heaven and Earth were in the beginning nothing but the *ch'i* of *yin* and *yang.* This single *ch'i* was in motion, turning around, and after the turning had become very rapid, there was separated out a great quantity of sediment. There being no way by which it could escape from within, it coagulated and formed an Earth in the center. The purest elements of *ch'i* became the sky, the Sun, the Moon, and the stars.

Chi Hsi goes on to state that the rotation of the sky keeps the Earth in equilibrium, just as the turning bowls do the water: thus the heaven moved unceasingly, turning round day and night. Should heaven stop only one instant, the Earth must fall apart. But the gyration of the heaven was so fast that a great amount of sediment was amassed in the middle. This sediment of the fluid is the Earth. Therefore it is said that the purer and lighter parts became heaven, the grosser and more turbid, the Earth.

The sky now is no longer a surface, but a whirling space of graduated fluidity extending from the sphere of stars to the Earth. The uppermost part contains the purest *ch'i* and rotates most rapidly, whereas the *ch'i* nearer the Earth is more turbid and revolves more slowly. The starry sphere is purely *yang;* the earthly, purely *yin,* is at rest. The planets in between are partly *yang* and partly *yin.* They turn with less speed than the starry sphere because they are retarded by the *yin* influence that emanates from the Earth. The Sun is more *yang* than the Moon and therefore rotates more rapidly.

Shizuki Tadao (1760–1806) was the first scholar in East Asia to undertake the transmission of Isaac Newton's doctrine. In his *Rekisho shinsho* (New treatise on Calendrical Phenomena, 1798–1802), he raised the question of why all the planets rotate and revolve in the same direction, in planes not greatly inclined to the ecliptic. He then presented a hypothesis concerning the formation of the planetary system. It resembled the hypothesis of Kant and Laplace. In view of the relative inaccessibility of Western treatises, it is unlikely that Tadao borrowed his idea from anyone else. His hypothesis, considering his background in neo-Confucian ideas, was not a titanic leap. Many aspects of it were already present in the neo-Confucian vortex cosmogony, which claims that beginning with primordial chaos the light fluid tends to float to the surface and heavy matter to precipitate at the center in the course of one-way revolution. Hence, a small portion of the ideas of attraction and centrifugal force provided Tadao with a more elaborate mechanical hypothesis, formulated in accordance with the heliocentric system.

Tadao is also the man who translated Western heliocentrism into the moving-Earth theory. This translation is still prevalently employed in East Asia. The moving Earth implies both the rotation and revolution of the Earth and hence it is a rather inarticulate term to adopt as a scientific vocabulary. Then, a question remains why philosophically oriented Tadao employed such a term uncritically and why it was widely accepted among East Asians. It must be due to the difference of their interest in natural philosophy from that of Westerners.

In the genuine East Asian tradition, there were no morphological or geometrical arguments as to the position of the center and shape of the cosmos. In that respect, they remained relativistic: whether the center of the cosmos is located in the Sun or in the Earth was no essential question for them. Their interest was focused on the dynamic nature within the cosmos, what force is at work to move things. The *yin-yang* dichotomy of Heavens or Earth and of movement or rest was also their major concern. Whether the Earth moves or is at rest was for them the basic doctrine, and hence the title moving-Earth theory was commonly used for Copernicanism.

Although Buddhism originated in India, it came to East Asia and exerted a dominating influence, especially on Japan. The Japanese had a notion of the universe as a limitless void, with no bounds being even conceivable. They also had a cosmology that originated in Jaina cosmography, in that it set at the center of the Earth Mount Sumeru, around which the Sun, the Moon, and the stars revolve. In the unlimited universe, purely a product of contemplation, the existence of an infinitely great number of worlds was quite possible. In Buddhist terms, a hierarchy of a thousand worlds, each containing its own Mount Sumeru, formed a "medium world," a thousand of which constituted in turn a "great world." Since the sky was seen as a void in which celestial bodies could move about freely, there could be no rigid crystalline orbs. Because the universe was seen as infinitely extended, it could not possibly rotate. During the eighteenth and nineteenth centuries, when Western science infiltrated into Japan, some Buddhist priests opposed the incoming Aristotelian cosmos and Copernican heliocentrism in order to defend Buddhist doctrine, which lasted even to the twentieth century.

Serious historical attention to these issues has been sporadic. It is hoped that more investigations will be undertaken.

Shigeru Nakayama

Bibliography
Forke, Alfred. *The World Conception of the Chinese.* London: A. Probsthain, 1925.)
Major, John S. *Heaven and Earth in Early Han Thought.* Albany: State University of New York Press, 1993.
Nakayama, Shigeru. *A History of Japanese Astronomy: Chinese Background and Western Impact.* Cambridge: Harvard University Press, 1969.
Needham, Joseph. *Science and Civilisation in China.* Vol. 3. Cambridge: Cambridge University Press, 1959.

See also Cosmology and the Earth; Earth, Models of before 1600; Meteorological Ideas in Pre-modern Orient

Cosmology and the Earth in the Renaissance

Views on the place of the Earth in the cosmos, based on philosophical reappraisal of ancient and medieval scientific philosophy and on a new trust in empirical data.

Generally, the Renaissance (roughly 1400 to 1600) has been simplistically labeled as a rebirth of ancient Greek and Roman culture on the one hand, and as the transition from medieval to modern society on the other. The complexities of the period are not so easily bounded, but a useful key to a contextual perspective of the Renaissance and the roles of the Earth in its cosmology is to view it with a sympathy to its unique transitional factors. The Renaissance served as a clearinghouse of ideas, reestablishing a critical awareness and reassessment of ancient thought. Meanwhile, new independent perspectives emerged, alongside new views of humanity and nature. The process was documented by the fecundity of the printing press (see Wightman).

Renaissance science reflected a greater knowledge of the world, but it was uncertain of a systematic theory of nature. The Renaissance cosmos was organized predominantly within the framework of Aristotle (384–322 B.C.E.), based on the long process of medieval philosophical and theological compromise and assimilation. This had started with a patchwork of Christianized, ancient Platonic fragments. This view included a geocentric universe with an immobile Earth. It was expanded and rendered more complex by Aristotelian medieval Islamic and European commentary. The dramatic arrival in the thirteenth century of Aristotle's apparently thorough, rationalist philosophy was attractive to European natural philosophers and enjoyed preeminence during the rise of high medieval scholasticism (see Wightman).

In fifteenth-century Italy, the humanistic philosophy turned to ancient Greece to revitalize the integral relation of humanity to the cosmos. The humanists looked upon the medieval corpus as so much adulteration of ancient thought, rendered sterile by inferior translation and hair-splitting commentaries. The early agenda of humanism became the purification of the ancient corpus by critical retranslation, a task meant to introduce original ancient texts as a touchstone of knowledge and as a cultural model. The emphases on an ordered delineation of the Earth and Heavens and on Platonic cosmic infinitude and mathematical certainty, as adopted by such important thinkers as Nicholas of Cusa (1401–1464), encouraged flexibility in the reappraisal of nature and bolstered the tenuous medieval mathematical and empirical legacy. Incomplete and unknown ancient sources on physical nature—particularly Greek—were rediscovered. Ancient science, including a more comprehensive interpretation of Aristotle, stimulated a secular emphasis, as did humanist-influenced scholarly printing. One effect of this was a wider enthusiasm for science.

Aristotle's cosmology was synthesized in the Eudoxian cosmos. Seven geocentric spherical orbs rotated in circular perfection at appearance-saving different rates around the immovable Earth, with rotational motion transmitted successively from an initial mover, *primum mobile,* the all-encompassing eighth sphere. Aristotle had also proposed that the celestial spheres were composed of a solid, crystalline, transparent, ethereal element. The Earth, the imperfect terrestrial sphere, encompassed inferior sublunar spheres, based on the four elements of Empedocles (ca. 444 B.C.E.), fire, air, water, and earth, which Aristotle had developed at length (see Schmitt).

Whereas Aristotle's views on the Earth remained relatively intact by the Renaissance, views on the Heavens had been significantly modified through the centuries. Claudius Ptolemy (fl. 139–161 C.E.), illustrated the tension between the practical needs of the astronomer and the systematic ones of the philosopher. He restructured the Aristotelian cosmos because of the more exact astronomical observations of Hipparchos (fl. 130 B.C.E.). These indicated that the planetary movements conformed to eccentric orbits around the Earth. Through the Middle Ages the geometric models of the cosmos became more complicated in the effort to account for the appearances of irregularity in angular velocity, retrograde motion, and the precession of the equinoxes. Ultimately, the Renaissance cosmos needed a total of eleven spheres (see Grant; Wightman).

Renaissance nature was interpreted by a diverse authorship, uneven in systematic acumen but largely free of medieval formalistic scholarship. Specialized study of physical nature was an evolving characteristic of the sixteenth century, a part of the redefinition of cosmography as a delineation of the cosmic order. Astronomy, still influenced by its counterpoint, astrology, lay at one end of the scale of disciplines of cosmography; geography and its applications lay at the other. The remaining middle ground of natural philosophy concerned the terrestrial sphere, where nature's proximity allowed fruitful close inspection, as the concise depictions of terrestrial nature by Leonardo da Vinci (1452–1519) revealed.

The sixteenth century brought a high awareness of observation, the key to a systematic overhaul of the cosmographical scheme. Ancient example and the humanistic insistence on truth inspired a century of data-recording, cataloging, and classification. This effort was applied literally worldwide in the voyages of exploration. These in turn stimulated new interest in delineating the extension of land and sea and even the atmosphere and the celestial region. Though not always steered by improved instrumentation as in the case of astronomical observation, terrestrial data spanned meteorological phenomena, tides, earthquakes, and a complement of anomalies designated as "prodigies" of nature (see Thorndike). Systemization at the microcosmic scale through descriptive classification was pursued with fervor in numerous studies on minerals and the earthly constituents, the most famous being the systematic mineralogy of Georgius Agricola (1494–1555).

Though often discontinuous with the inductive insights of medieval predecessors, Renaissance thinkers provided important glimpses of experimental method. The diversity included the application of statics in evaluation of atmospheric moisture by Nicholas of Cusa and the measurements of the extent of the atmosphere with timed rockets and of the ocean with timed, weighted floats by Giovanni da Fontana (fl. ca. 1410–1449). The appeals to experiment included the sixteenth-century landmark magnetic investigations of Robert Norman and the proposed theoretical applications of magnetism to Earth's rotation of William Gilbert (1540–1603); Agricola's geological and hydrological theory; simulations by Francis Bacon (1560–1626) of wind by heating air; and development of and experiments with the first glass bulb thermometer by Galileo Galilei (1564–1642).

Observations began to blur and redefine the boundaries between the terrestrial and celestial realms in the late sixteenth century. Part of a vigorous English Copernicanism,

Ideas about the nature of the Earth and its place in the cosmos were in transition around 1600, as shown by this illustration from Thomas Digges's Perfit Description of the Caelestiall Orbes of 1576. *Digges placed Earth among the planets, in motion around the Sun, but he retained the Aristotelian spheres of earth, water, air, and fire. Source: Kuhn, Thomas.* The Copernican Revolution. *Cambridge: Harvard University Press, 1957. With permission from Harvard University Press.*

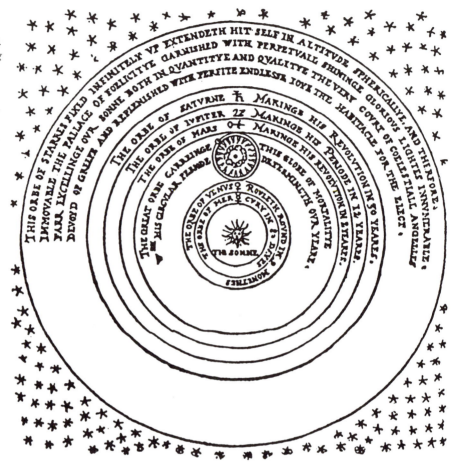

Thomas Digges (1543–1595) called for proving Earth's rotation by study of annual parallax (see figure). Moreover, propitious celestial events provided fundamental physical contradictions of Aristotle's science. Accurate observations of a supernova and several late-century comets, particularly by Tycho Brahe (1546–1601), shook the tenets of celestial immutability, ethereal composition, elemental boundary limits, and tempted cosmological restructuring. Already earlier in the century fundamental and growing criticism of elementary legitimacy of fire, then air, by Girolamo Cardano (1501–1576), and then all the elements, was providing a case that the sphere of fire at the top of the terrestrial sphere does not exist, and that comets and the Milky Way, previously defined by Aristotle as terrestrial meteorological phenomena, are in fact celestial in origin (see Thorndike).

The fundamental Aristotelian system was at risk. The degree to which Renaissance thinkers accepted Aristotelianism was bounded by a complex web of qualifications reflecting their own comprehension of the necessity of modification of cosmographical order. At one end, conservative scholars explained physical discontinuities as anomalies and as speculative uncertainties. At the other end were provincial, characteristically subjective, cosmological alternatives, based on the traditions of ancient occult philosophies, such as Cabbalism, Pythagoreanism, Hermeticism, and Neo-Platonism. The middle ground included a wide spectrum of intellects ranging from observationally theoretically vital to amorphously uncommitted. Appraisal of most Renaissance thinkers suspends the urge to polarize their thought. Rather, their subtlety and reservations reflect the latitude available in systematic uncertainty, a vacillation therefore suspending a plausible resolution to cosmological definition during the Renaissance. Resolution could only come with time. Generalities of natural philosophy had to be tested against the emerging exactitude of the celestial and terrestrial sciences.

The traditional historiography of Renaissance cosmology has entailed philosophical as well as intellectual and scientific issues. In nineteenth and turn-of-the-century historical appraisals, the place of the Earth in renaissance cosmologies was secondary to greater cosmological relationships. Encyclopedic, multi-volume historical surveys of science began with Pierre Duhem's history of cosmology from Plato to Copernicus in *Le systeme du monde* (System of the World, 1919–1959). A thorough, terrestrially oriented balance came in Lynn Thorndike's later *History of Magic and Experimental Science* (1923–1966), a comprehensive appraisal of the influence of both science and pseudo-science on celestial and terrestrial conceptualization. Fruitful as an exhaustive data-base for textual and contextual analysis, it remains a most useful springboard to the pertinent bibliography.

Renaissance cosmological analysis also benefited from the subsequent tighter focus of scholars on this period and topic. The result has been a wide variety of interpretations of Renaissance cosmology, balancing conventional and occult perspectives of nature. Proceeding from the familiar biographical fare, such as J.L.E. Dreyer's *Tycho Brahe: A Picture of Scientific Life and Work in the Sixteenth Century* (1890) and useful translations like P. Fleury Mottelay's edition of Gilbert's *De magnete* (1893), more analytical treatment of the cosmographical views of seminal Renaissance thinkers followed. One example is Ernst Cassirer's *Individuum und Cosmos in Philosophie der Renaissance* (1927). Well integrated biographies have included thoughtful reappraisal of Brahe in Victor E. Thoren's *Lord of Uraniburg* (1991), and new studies of lesser known personalities, such as of Brahe's associate Paul Willich in *The Willich Connection: Conflict and Priority in Late Sixteenth Century Cosmology* by Owen Gingerich and Robert Westman (1988). Other historians have emphasized regional spheres of Renaissance intellectual and scientific influence. F.R. Johnson's *Astronomical Thought in Renaissance England* (1937) focused on the English endorsement of the physical fact of the rotation and revolution of the Earth rather than of saving the appearances. Johnson also discussed the uniquely English debate over magnetic force as an agent of the Earth's rotation,

a position advocated by Gilbert. R.J.W. Evans's *Rudolf II and His World: Study in Intellectual History 1576–1612* (1973) provided a much-needed reappraisal of central and eastern European speculations about the Earth and the Cosmos in both conventional and occult cosmologies. Evans provides access to a wide and neglected literature.

A distinct departure in presentation has been interpretations of nonverbal media. These provide yet another means of conveying the complexity of Renaissance cosmological thought. Though analysis was peripheral and sometimes too generalized, S.K. Heninger's *Cosmographical Glasse* (1977) presented Renaissance cosmographical diagrams as a survey of cosmological preferences. An intriguing look at artistic and practical mechanism was presented by Otto Mayr and Klaus Maurice in the catalog *The Clockwork Universe: German Clocks and Automata 1550 to 1650* (1980). This book presented the depth of cosmological reflection and the wide definition of technology that inspired northern European patrons and artisans to produce mechanical models and instruments indicating both conventional and occult interpretations of nature. Similarly, Evans, bowing to Frances Yates, Allen Debus, and others, analyzed the organismic interpretations of mechanism influenced by late Renaissance occult cosmology and philosophy.

A deeper understanding of Renaissance cosmological thought, particularly in respect to the Earth, might prosper further with broader efforts in textual and contextual readings of printed and manuscript primary cosmographical sources. Many thinkers and the depth of their personal perspectives remain for closer inspection. For instance, the English polymath John Dee (1527–1608) has been contextually reinterpreted in *John Dee's Natural Philosophy: Between Science and Religion* (1988) by Nicholas Clulee, who convincingly interprets more traditional and particularly medieval physical influences on Dee than his occult veneer has portrayed, thereby questioning recent theories of occult and inductive linkage.

The rise in the late twentieth century of both scholarly and popular interest in interrelationships of the Earth and the cosmos have proceeded from both new scientific knowledge of that interaction and from a more emotional environmental awareness. New historiographical approaches have appeared, ranging from constructivism to feminist/gender studies. In the final analysis such approaches will rise or fall depending on their scholarly usefulness and on how well they measure up during contextual analysis. Excessive ideology, speculation, and particular agendas must be of a qualified, secondary importance.

William J. McPeak

Bibliography

Cassirer, Ernst. *Individuum und Cosmos in Philosophie der Renaissance.* Leipzig: n.p., 1927.

Grant, Edward. *Planets, Stars, and Orbs: The Medieval Cosmos, 1200–1687.* Cambridge: Cambridge University Press, 1992.

Johnson, Francis R. *Astronomical Thought in Renaissance England.* Stanford: Stanford University Press, 1937.

Schmitt, Clarence. *Aristotle and the Renaissance.* Cambridge: Harvard University Press, 1983.

Thorndike, Lynn. *History of Magic and Experimental Science.* 8 vols. New York: Columbia University Press, 1964–1966.

Wightman, William F.D. *Science and the Renaissance.* 2 vols. Edinburgh: University of Aberdeen Press, 1962.

See also Atmosphere, Structure of; Atmospheric Optics to 1600; Cosmology and the Earth; Earth, Models of before 1600; Earthquakes, Theories from Antiquity to 1600; Exploration, Age of; Geography and Renaissance Magic; Geomagnetism, Theories of before 1800; Meteorological Ideas; Minerals and Crystals, Fifteenth to Eighteenth Centuries; Mining and Knowledge of the Earth; Occult Philosophy and the Earth in the Renaissance

Cosmology and the Earth in the Scientific Revolution

Involved change of cosmology from Earth-centered to Sun-centered, which resulted in increased focus on Earth, including its magnetism, age, and formation; greatest criticism of period concerns claims of loss of control, subjectivity, and the death of nature.

The period of the Scientific Revolution has been the focus of major historical investigation. Although historians do not agree about the duration, content, or revolutionary nature of this era, all would acknowledge that the period from 1500 to 1700 witnessed great changes in the content, context, and status of science. This was particularly true for the study of cosmology, since much of the investigatory work of the period involved astronomy, cosmology, and the geosciences.

Most histories of the Scientific Revolution begin with Nicholaus Copernicus (1473–1543), who developed a new model of the universe. This model had important implications for Earth studies as well, since Copernicus claimed that the Earth revolved around the Sun and was therefore a planet rather than the center of the universe. This position directly contradicted the cosmology of Aristotle (384–322 B.C.E.), both in terms of the placement of the Earth and for explanations of movement on the Earth and in the universe. Aristotle had maintained that the two types of motion, perpendicular on Earth and circular in the heavens, were a direct result of the Earth's central and distinct position. By removing the Earth from the center of the universe, Copernicus destroyed the physics that had explained the heaviness of objects on the Earth and the motion of the heavens, without supplying an alternative explanation. It is not surprising, therefore, to find cosmologers hesitant to take up Copernicus's model. Indeed, many historians today would argue that the Copernican system gained few adherents before 1600, when Johannes Kepler (1571–1630) declared himself to be a Copernican. As well, despite Copernicus's innovations, Aristotle's cosmology lasted well into the seventeenth century. Still, the shift of the position of the Earth from center to periphery began a process that somewhat ironically focused more attention on the Earth itself.

Both Tycho Brahe (1546–1601) and Kepler occupied themselves with the shape and makeup of the universe and therefore with the Earth's position in that universe. Brahe produced his own planetary model with the Earth in the center, the Sun revolving around the Earth, and the other planets revolving around the Sun. This hybrid model had few supporters, with the exception of the Jesuits, but the extremely accurate astronomical observations made by Brahe were employed by Kepler after Brahe's death. As a Copernican, Kepler did not follow the model created by Brahe. He believed the Sun to be in the center of the universe; in attempting to develop a mathematical analysis of the harmony of the spheres based on neo-Platonism and number magic, he advanced his first law, which states that the paths of the planets, including the Earth, are elliptical rather than round. Kepler's most significant contribution to the study of the Earth was his attempt to develop a new celestial mechanics to replace the now defunct Aristotelian schema. Kepler claimed that there is a relationship between magnetism on Earth and the force emitted by the Sun to keep the Earth in orbit. The Earth is thus pulled around its elliptical path by this solar vortex of unseen power. Although this idea was not directly followed, Kepler thus began the unification of celestial and terrestrial mechanics that was completed under Sir Isaac Newton (1642–1727).

Investigations of motion on the Earth were carried out by other major natural philosophers of the period, such as Galileo Galilei (1564–1642), René Descartes (1596–1650), Christiaan Huygens (1629–1695), and Newton. Galileo's experiments with falling bodies, Descartes's with elastic collisions, and Galileo's and Huygens's examination of pendulums resulted in a growing awareness of the attractive power of the Earth and its mathematical formulation. Newton united these theories with the astronomical investigations of Kepler in his theory of universal gravitation. Newton claimed that an apple falling to the Earth was compelled by the same force that kept the Moon in orbit around the Earth, and that these two events were mathematically equivalent. In other words, he had employed Copernicus's claim that the Earth is a planet and had substituted a new and complete mechanics for Aristotle's now moribund system.

The story of these new developments in cosmology has long interested historians of science. Indeed, this period has attracted more historians of science than almost any other area. Until recently, however, most historians of the Scientific Revolution have focused more on the stars than on the Earth, and so the development of the sciences of the Earth as part of the changing cosmological picture has remained less well understood. Historians of geography and geology have also been responsible for this relative lack of knowledge, since until recently they have seen only the prehistory of these disciplines when they have examined the sciences of the Earth during the Scientific Revolution. Looking for the rise of the modern disciplines of geography and geology, they have denigrated the achievements of pre–eighteenth-century practitioners and have praised seventeenth-century accomplishments only insofar as they have pointed the way to more recent developments.

This has been particularly true among historians of geology. The period of the Scientific Revolution has been viewed as important insofar as practitioners have foreshadowed the accomplishments of the eighteenth and especially nineteenth centuries. This has been the emphasis of both Roy Porter, in *The Making of Geology* (1977), and Rachel Laudan, in *From Mineralogy to Geology* (1987). Both trace the development of modern geology, claiming that it developed from a rather undifferentiated study in this early period (mineralogy for Laudan and cosmology for Porter) into a discrete discipline of geology. Laudan does an admirable job of setting out the "common sense" notions of seventeenth (and therefore eighteenth) century mineralogists. These included a classification system based on natural kinds (earths and stones, metals, salts, and sulfurs) and arranged by shape (crystals, figured stones or fossils, and strata). Recently, Yushi Ito, in his Ph.D. thesis "Earth Science in the Scientific Revolution, 1600–1728" (University of Melbourne, 1985) and later in "Hooke's Cyclic Theory of the Earth" (1988), has taken Porter and Laudan to task for this presentist view, claiming that the accomplishments of the seventeenth century must be understood in their own right and that the formation of the Royal Society of London in 1660 helped the geological interests of the scientific community to coalesce. In other words, those with interests in studies of the Earth had already begun to establish a separate group well before the work of Vulcanists and Neptunists in the eighteenth century.

Likewise, historians of geography have for too long ignored the study of the Earth in the period before Nathanael Carpenter (1589–1628?) and Bernhardus Varenius (1622–1650), or have relegated it to a position of infancy. J.N.L. Baker, for example, articulated this view in *The History of Geography* (1963), seeing Varenius's *Geographia generalis* (1650) as the formative study for the modern discipline of geography. Baker's was by no means an isolated voice, since most historians of geography have cited Alexander von Humboldt (1769–1859) as the father of modern geography. History of geography, less fashionable than that of geology, has been slower to resist this presentist tendency. Indeed, there remains a great gap in the history of geography in the period of the Scientific Revolution, although Norman J.W. Thrower's "Edmond Halley and Thematic Geo-Cartography" (1978) does begin to assess the cartographic innovations of Edmond Halley (1656–1742).

As historians interested in the study of cosmology and the sciences of the Earth in the period of the Scientific Revolution have begun to evaluate this study in its own right, rather than merely as a prologue to a later story, a number of important areas of investigation have emerged. Probably the most significant, both for contemporary natural philosophers and for modern historians, is the emphasis on an investigation of magnetism, especially as it related to navigation. Because the sixteenth and seventeenth centuries were the era of great expansion for most European powers, an understanding of the magnetic nature of the Earth was fundamental. Historians have also begun to examine changing views of the age and formation of the Earth. Natural philosophers in the seventeenth century began to move away from literal biblical accounts of earthly beginnings and to look instead to the Earth itself for its history. In part because this development presages the emergence of eighteenth- and nineteenth-century schools of Neptunism and Vulcanism, historians of geology have found this area important. Finally, some historians, especially Carolyn Merchant and Margarita Bowen, have begun to look at the study of the Earth in this period and noted with concern the increasing stress on the objectivity of knowledge and of the Earth itself. This has been one of the strongest critiques of the period, coming from a feminist and ecological point of view.

Magnetism had long fascinated natural philosophers, in part because the magnetic compass had been in use by navigators from and the twelfth century C.E. in Europe. Indeed, the study of the Earth's magnetism was almost directly related to navigational needs, and so it is not surprising to see a huge increase in interest in geomagnetism in the period of the great European voyages of exploration. During the Scientific Revolution probably the most important theoretical statements were made by William Gilbert (1540–1603), who claimed in *De Magnete* (1600) that the Earth is a giant magnet. Stephen Pumfrey, in his article "'O tempora, O magnes'" (1989), demonstrates that the adoption of Gilbert's theories was not a straightforward affair and that national pride, patronage, education, and networks of knowledge were of more significance than falsifiability or predictive powers. Indeed, problems of magnetic declination and secular variation plagued magnetic investigators for most of the seventeenth century, shown, for example, in the correspondence on magnetic topics between Marin Mersenne (1588–1648) and Athanasius Kircher

(1602–1680). The question of secular variation (long-term change of the magnetic directions over the globe's surface), battled out on national lines as Pumfrey shows, achieved some closure with Halley's chart of isogonic variation (1701). This latter story is told, with less sociological clarity, by Thrower (pp. 195–228).

While this interest in magnetic phenomena had ancient roots, an interest in the age of the Earth and in how the geological history of the Earth had unfolded was of more recent origin. The question of the age and history of the Earth was probably the most important topic for seventeenth-century natural philosophers interested in the Earth, and therefore historians have correctly put great emphasis on this issue. As Martin Rudwick has shown in *The Meaning of Fossils* (1977), discussions about fossils hung on the relative weight given to the Genesis creation story. Such natural philosophers as Thomas Burnet (1635–1715), John Aubrey (1626–1697), John Wallis (1616–1703), Robert Hooke (1635–1703), Robert Boyle (1627–1691), Nicholas Steno (1638–1686), and John Woodward (1665–1728) debated the meaning of fossils, largely arguing that these figured stones were organic in origin and therefore implied that the oceans and mountains of the world had once been in a very different configuration. Rudwick traces the changing opinions of the origins of fossils, beginning with natural philosophers holding them to be jokes of God and therefore of inorganic origin, to a belief that they were the remains of once-living animals and plants. This, of course, involved some explanation as to why fossils of sea creatures were to be found deposited on the highest mountains, and therefore natural philosophers posited a series of floods covering much of the Earth. Burnet argued in *The Sacred Theory of the Earth* (1691) that the Great Flood of biblical times had caused the originally smooth crust of the Earth to crack and develop uneven mountains and oceans, thereby depositing these fossils and causing other geological phenomena. Yushi Ito has shown that this theory was contested during the Scientific Revolution, especially though not exclusively by Hooke. In his lectures to the Royal Society in the 1680s and 1690s, Hooke argued that the history of the Earth was cyclical, with countless instances of subsidence and elevation, caused by earthquakes and underground fires. This view of the Earth's history, "with no vestige of a beginning," predates the cyclical theory of James Hutton (1726–1797) by a hundred years. Ito does not argue that Hutton was influenced by Hooke, whose ideas fell into disrepute because of Newton's and Woodward's control of the Royal Society in the early eighteenth century. On the other hand, Ito insists that we cannot say Hooke was a man ahead of his time, but rather we must see that this cyclical theory was one of a number of choices in vogue from the seventeenth century.

Probably the most telling critique of the study of the Earth in the period of the Scientific Revolution has concerned the development of objectivity in Earth studies and, with it, the death of nature. Margarita Bowen, in *Empiricism and Geographical Thought* (1981), argues that geography (and in this context all geosciences) surrendered too much when it gave up the concept of the Earth as a coherent and living organism and instead strove to make its discipline objective and mathematical. This trend, she argues, developed from the methodology of Francis Bacon, whose message of destroying the Idols destroyed as well the subjective conversation between the observer and the thing observed. Bowen has been deeply influenced by ecological concerns of the twentieth century, but persuasively argues for the world we have lost. In a similar vein, Carolyn Merchant evaluates studies of the Earth in the sixteenth through eighteenth centuries in her book *The Death of Nature* (1980). Merchant contends that in this period the image of the Earth underwent a startling transformation. Where the Earth had traditionally been a good mother, to be nurtured and supported, during the Scientific Revolution that picture changed. First philosophers bemoaned and then condoned the abuse of mother Earth, gradually transforming this abuse into the just punishment and taming of a wild temptress, and finally seeing nature as dead, inert matter. When nature became lifeless, contends Merchant, men were able to exploit it without remorse. This is a strong feminist critique of the positive "master narrative" of the Scientific Revolution, and one that needs to be carefully assessed.

The historical investigation of cosmology and the Earth during the Scientific Revolution is an enormous undertaking. Historians began looking at cosmology from the point of view of astronomy and the heavens and have only recently begun to lower their sights to the Earth. While many interesting studies of the Earth in this period have now been undertaken, tremendous numbers of issues remain untouched or unresolved. Especially, this period needs to be examined in its own right, as Ito has begun to do, rather than using the seventeenth century as a springboard to the putatively more interesting community of the eighteenth. The study of the Earth in the seventeenth century was a rich and multifaceted study and deserves much more investigation than has hitherto been performed.

Lesley Cormack

Bibliography

Baker, J.N.L. *The History of Geography.* Oxford and New York: Basil Blackwell, 1963.

Bowen, Margarita. *Empiricism and Geographical Thought: From Francis Bacon to Alexander von Humboldt.* Cambridge: Cambridge University Press, 1981.

Ito, Yushi. "Hooke's Cyclic Theory of the Earth in the Context of Seventeenth Century England." *British Journal for the History of Science* 21 (1988): pp. 295–314.

Laudan, Rachel. *From Mineralogy to Geology: The Foundations of a Science, 1650–1830.* Chicago: University of Chicago Press, 1987.

Merchant, Carolyn. *The Death of Nature. Women, Ecology and the Scientific Revolution.* San Francisco: Harper and Row, 1980.

Porter, Roy. *The Making of Geology. Earth Science in Britain 1660–1815.* Cambridge: Cambridge University Press, 1977.

Pumfrey, Stephen. "'O tempora, O magnes': A Sociological Analysis of the Discovery of Secular Magnetic Variation in 1634." *British Journal for the History of Science* 22 (1989): pp. 181–214.

Rudwick, Martin. *The Meaning of Fossils: Episodes in the History of Palaeontology.* London: Macdonald, 1977.

Thrower, Norman J.W. "Edmond Halley and Thematic Geo-Cartography." In *The Compleat Plattmaker. Essays on Chart, Map, and Globe Making in England in the Seventeenth and Eighteenth Centuries,* edited by Norman J.W. Thrower, pp. 195–228. Berkeley and Los Angeles: University of California Press, 1978.

See also Age of the Earth before 1800; Cosmology and the Earth; Deluge; Earthquakes, Theories from Antiquity to 1600; Earthquakes, Theories from 1600 to 1800; Elizabethan Geography; Exploration, Age of; Geomagnetism, Theories before 1800; Gravity, Newton, and the Eighteenth Century; Occult Philosophy and the Earth in the Renaissance; Plutonists, Neptunists, Vulcanists; Sacred Theory of the Earth

Cycle of Erosion

A term commonly believed to stem from the "cycle of erosion" or the "geographical cycle."

The term was formally introduced by William Morris Davis (1850–1934) in a famous paper of that title in the 1899 issue of the *Geographical Journal* following earlier papers in which the idea was hinted at and then used to analyze the landscapes of Appalachia. Initially it was a deductive scheme that set down the "normal" evolution of a rapidly uplifted landscape, eroding slowly through geological time in a humid temperate climate, under the influence of subaerial processes. It is still described in introductory textbooks of physical geography and geology and is variously termed the river cycle, normal cycle, landscape cycle, or erosion cycle. It is best to have the definition of "The Complete Cycle of River Life: Youth, Adolescence, Maturity, and Old Age" in Davis's own words:

A river that is established on a new land may be called an original river. . . . It must at first be of the kind known as a consequent river, for it has no ancestor from which to be derived. . . . Once established, an original river advances through its long life, manifesting certain peculiarities of youth, maturity, and old age, by which its successive stages of growth may be recognized without much difficulty. . . . In its infancy the river drains its basin imperfectly, for it is then embarrassed by the original inequalities of the surface, and lakes collect in all the depressions. . . . As the river becomes adolescent, its channels are deepened and all the larger ones descend close to base-level. . . . With the deepening of the channels, there comes an increase in the number of gulleys on the slopes of the channel. . . . With their continued development the maturity of the system is reached; it is marked by an almost complete acquisition of the original constructional surface by erosion under the guidance of the streams. The lakes of the original imperfections have long since disappeared; the waterfalls of adolescence have been worn back. . . . In the later and quieter old age of a

river system, the waste of the land is yielded more slowly by reason of the diminishing slopes of the valley sides. (Davis in "Rivers and Valleys of Pennsylvania," *National Geographic Magazine* 1 (1889).

The common assertion that the *Origin of Species* (1859) of Charles Darwin (1809–1882) was the stimulus to the use of the "age" terms and indeed to the appearance of the Cycle itself can be disputed. Most of the Cycle's elements had been deduced or discussed as far back as the literature of the Classical world. The idea of a cycle of landscape change connected to schemes of global geological change that restore the landscape to its original form can be traced back to the seventeenth century, as for example described in Ito's paper on "Hooke's Cyclic Theory of the Earth." *Theory of the Earth* (1795) by James Huttons (1726–1797) is a very late manifestation of the idea. Similar notions are found in the Greek literature to Aristotle and beyond. The notion of attaching terms for age to parts of a landscape, especially to the crucial element of rivers, far predates any Darwinian influence, as John Robison (1739–1805) testifies. Writing of historical views in the introduction of his 1797 hydraulic article on "Rivers" in the *Encyclopædia Britannica*, he says:

But in general their origin and progress . . . bear some resemblance (as . . . observed by Pliny) to the life of man. . . . Its beginnings are insignificant, and its infancy frivolous. . . . Gathering strength in its youth it becomes wild and impetuous. Impatient of the restraints which it still meets in the hollows among the mountains, it is restless and fretful. . . . It comes into the world with more prudence and discretion . . . yielding to circumstances. . . . Now increased by numerous allies . . . it becomes grave and stately. . . . till it is laid to rest in the great abyss.

One may debate the exact meanings of terms in old texts, but little of the Cycle was strictly new—most especially with respect to rivers. Davis's immediate inspiration came from landscape exploration in the American West and his need for a research paradigm for Appalachia. The cyclic notion was extended from rivers to landscape by Davis and by him and others to almost every imaginable landscape type from glacial to arid. Awkward exceptions to the rule were categorized as "accidents"—for example earthquakes, volcanism, and short-term climatic changes such as glaciation. Davis's own writings on the Cycle, climatic variants, modifications and defenses of it in response to criticisms, and its applications in pedagogy can be found in his *Geographical Essays,* edited by Douglas Wilson Johnson (1878–1944) in 1909. Robert Beckinsale (1976) has described the subsequent spread of the Cycle. With various local modifications it took hold quite strongly in France, as evidenced by Pierre Birot's 1960 summary *Le cycle d'érosion sous les différents climats,* and in Great Britain and the former British Empire. It was never popular in Germany and countries with academic connections to Germany, where a preference for climatic geomorphology prevailed. Ironically the fullest statement of the cycle by Davis is available only in his 1912 book *Die Erklärende Beschreibung der Landformen* (Explanatory description of landforms), which was never translated into English, although an English manuscript must surely have existed. *The Physical Geography (Geomorphology) of W.M. Davis*—a set of notes taken from Davis's lectures in California long into his retirement—shows significant modifications in his thinking.

The influence of the Cycle as a driving paradigm for landscape research began to wane after World War II when interests in quantitative landform analysis and present-day landscape processes developed, and when the Cycle's simplistic diastrophic (that is, pertaining to movement of the Earth's crust) underpinnings were increasingly undermined by developments in global tectonics—plate tectonics, as it eventually became. The most enduring aspect of the cycle has been the terminology it supplied for stages of river and landscape evolution: "youth," "maturity," and "old age" for landform characteristics and "consequent" and "subsequent" for stream systems are prime examples. This persistence is probably because of continual use in elementary pedagogy. No first-year text in earth science omits it, although they often damn with faint praise.

Despite much published opposition to the Cycle, deliberately acyclic alternative schemes are hard to find, apart from those of Nevin Melanchtan Fenneman (1865–1945) in 1936 and John Tilton Hack (1913–1991) in 1960, both of which applied to exactly the area for which Davis devised the cycle. Bishop (1980) argues that the Cycle endured for so long because it was unfalsifiable in Popperian terms. Further historical analysis of cyclic thinking in earth science is required, especially in regard to the nuanced meaning of terms in pre-nineteenth-century literature.

Keith J. Tinkler

Bibliography

Beckinsale, Robert P. "The International Influence of William Morris Davis." *Geographical Review* 66 (1976): pp. 448–466.

Bishop, P. "Popper's Principle of Falsifiability and the Irrefutability of the Davisian Cycle." *Professional Geographer* 32 (1980): pp. 310–315.

Chorley, R.J., R.P. Beckinsale, and A.J. Dunn. *The History of the Study of Landforms.* Vol. 2 of *The Life and Work of W.M. Davis.* London: Methuen, 1973.

Davis, W.M. "The Geographical Cycle." *Geographical Journal* 14 (1899): pp. 481–504.

———. *Geographical Essays.* Edited by Douglas Wilson Johnson. Boston: Ginn, 1909. Reprint. New York: Dover, 1954.

———. *The Physical Geography (Geomorphology) of W.M. Davis.* Edited by P.B. King and S.A. Schumm. Norwich: Geo Books, 1980.

Fenneman, N.M. "Cyclic and Non-cyclic Aspects of Erosion." *Science* 83 (1936): pp. 87–94.

Hack, J.T. "Interpretation of Erosional Topography in Humid Temperate Regions." *American Journal of Science* 258A (1960): pp. 80–97.

Ito, Y. "Hooke's Cyclic Theory of the Earth in the Context of Seventeenth-Century England." *British Journal for the History of Science* 21 (1988): pp. 295–314.

See also Actualism, Uniformitarianism, and Catastrophism; Climates, Pleistocene and Recent; Diluvialism; Geology; Geomorphology: Disciplinary History; Hydrologic Cycle; Ice Ages; Pedology; Soil Science; Soil Conservation

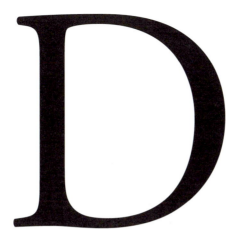

Deluge, The

Also known as the Flood, Noah's Flood, and the Noachian Deluge.

One of the most influential of all geological theories associated fossils with a vast inundation, which was long identified as being that described by Moses in Genesis. Christian writers from Josephus (ca. 80 C.E.) to Martin Luther (1544) combined biblical, classical, and geological evidence to substantiate the reality of the most momentous geological event in the history of humanity. Such theorizing became particularly common in the later seventeenth century as writers like Nicolaus Steno (1669), Agostino Scilla (1670), and Robert Plot (1677) all accepted the reality of the Deluge but refused to consider it the sole agency of geological change.

Clearly the most influential of deluge speculations was Thomas Burnet's *Sacred Theory of the Earth* (1684–1690), which appeared in a series of Latin and English editions, dominating the topic for about seventy years. Combining Genesis and other biblical sources with classical and more recent authorities, Burnet reasoned that the Earth had originally consolidated from a shapeless fluid mass, forming concentric strata around an aqueous core. The surface of this new planet was smooth, regular, and uniform, without either mountains or sea. But solar heat dried out the Earth's fragile crust and boiled its trapped waters underneath. Eventually, the crust gave way and internal waters surged forth over the great plain of the world, causing the universal flood reported by Moses. After a time, these flood waters withdrew into a broken Earth, leaving behind the varied landscape of continents, seas, and mountains familiar to us. Burnet's eloquent descriptions of this new Earth coincided with a new cultural awareness of landscape, as manifested in art and poetry.

For both religious and scientific reasons, Burnet's colorful theory aroused more opposition than support. Among those who proposed scenarios contrary to his were John Woodward, William Whiston, Erasmus Warren, and John Beaumont. Though none of these alternative theories much resemble modern geology either, the discussions as a whole were increasingly scientific rather than theological. As a result, writers became progressively more skeptical of the ability of the Deluge to explain geological phenomena. Throughout the eighteenth century, other explanations became not only possible but necessary. These explanations often presupposed a timescale far beyond the advent of humanity.

Major theories in the latter part of the eighteenth century often failed to acknowledge the Deluge at all. It plays no role, for example, in the theories of Georges Louis Buffon (1749, 1779), Abraham Gottlob Werner (1770s), or James Hutton (1785), and none of these three ever took biblical evidence seriously. Even so, the idea of vast inundations (one or more) continued to appeal, and therefore reappeared in theories by Peter Simon Pallas (1778), John Williams (1789), Richard Kirwan (1799), and even the Huttonian Sir James Hall (1812). Its final major supporters were Georges Cuvier (1813) and William Buckland (1823). In 1831, however, Adam Sedgwick publicly abjured his previous belief in the Deluge as a geological agency and Buckland himself followed in 1836. It was no longer a respectable concept after that.

Dennis R. Dean

Bibliography
Dean, Dennis R. "The Rise and Fall of the Deluge." *Journal of Geological Education* 33 (1985): pp. 84–93.

See also Actualism, Uniformitarianism, and Catastrophism; Age of the Earth before 1800; Cosmology and the Earth in the Scientific Revolution; Diluvialism; Earth in Decay; Evolution and the Geosciences; Fossilization; Geological Time; Geology; Geomorphology; Masons and the Earth; Paleontology; Plutonists, Neptunists, Vulcanists; Popper's Ideas on Falsifiability; Sacred Theory of the Earth; Stratigraphy

Dendrochronology

Study of annual growth rings of trees, with primary emphasis on archaeology and climatology. Recognition of the annual nature of tree rings may be traced at least back to the work of Leonardo da Vinci (1452–1519), who also suggested that ring widths indicated past climatic conditions. Naturalists such as Georges Louis Leclerc de Buffon (1707–1788) and Carl Linnaeus (1707–1778) employed this technique to estimate the ages of trees, as did foresters in the nineteenth century who wished to determine the dates of injuries to trees from insects, fires, and climatic conditions.

The development of dendrochronology into an organized science, however, was the work of astronomer Andrew Ellicott Douglass (1867–1962) of the University of Arizona. During the first quarter of the twentieth century, Douglass perfected the crucial technique of cross-dating. Because the trees of the arid Southwest were particularly sensitive to changes in rainfall, ring widths varied widely from year to year. The resulting characteristic patterns of narrow and wide rings appeared in specimens of different age, allowing Douglass to create a chronology based on overlapping patterns. This technique led to the construction of chronologies much longer than would have been possible with the use of a single tree, providing a Ponderosa pine sequence of nearly five hundred years and a Sequoia sequence of more than three thousand years.

Douglass's initial goal in creating the new science of dendrochronology stemmed from his interest in the variability of the Sun. Convinced of the close relation between ring width and precipitation, Douglass saw in these patterns a possible means to test the influence of sunspots on terrestrial climate. By the early 1920s, he had found several cyclical patterns in tree-ring records, one of which corresponded closely to the eleven-year sunspot cycle. More dramatic confirmation of his theory came from the work of British astronomer E. Walter Maunder (1851–1928), who discovered in various records a prolonged sunspot minimum between 1645 and 1715 (the so-called Maunder Minimum). Douglass's tree-ring records showed an absence of the eleven-year cycle during the same period, convincing the Arizonan that he had found a significant relationship. Although later studies brought this connection into doubt, the search for a climate/sunspot connection guided much of Douglass's work for the rest of his life (Webb, *Tree Rings and Telescopes,* pp. 101–130, 179–188; Eddy, pp. 11–21).

The use of tree-ring records as evidence for past climatic change also led Douglass toward his most dramatic contribution to science. Even with the cross-dating technique, the record from living trees proved limited. Within a decade after beginning his dendrochronological research, Douglass perceived that the tree-ring record could be expanded through analysis of archaeological material, especially from ruins in desert climates such as Egypt and the American Southwest. During the 1920s, Douglass worked closely with the National Geographic Society, which supported archaeological expeditions to the pueblo ruins of Arizona and New Mexico. Beams from the ruins proved particularly valuable, although charcoal specimens soon emerged as equally reliable sources of data. Employing his cross-dating technique to these specimens, Douglass constructed a series of floating chronologies that allowed him to trace past climatic fluctuations and to assign relative dates to the various ruins. By the summer of 1929, these various chronologies had been grouped into two long sequences, one based on living trees and extending to around 1300 and the other a floating chronology of more than 580 years based on pueblo ruins. A charcoal specimen unearthed at the Show Low Ruin (Arizona) in July of 1929 bridged the gap between the two sequences, allowing a precise dating of the various ruins and providing archaeologists with specific dates for placing pueblo developments in historical perspective. By the mid-1930s, Douglass had integrated many more specimens into the known chronology, extending the record back to 11 C.E. and establishing dendrochronology as a central tool for archaeologists (Webb, *Tree Rings and Telescopes,* pp. 131–151).

Douglass's success in creating this new science attracted attention and support, notably from the Carnegie Institution of Washington and the University of Arizona. After several years of Carnegie funding, which included the loan of much equipment, the university established the Laboratory of Tree-Ring Research in December of 1937, with facilities concentrated in the new football stadium on campus. Although assuming emeritus faculty status, Douglass served as director of the Tree-Ring Lab for the next two decades, coordinating the institutional growth of the facility. The laboratory soon became involved in various research projects tracing climatic fluctuations in the Southwest, as well as in archaeological research throughout the region. Douglass himself spent the last years of his life attempting to establish a connection between his tree-ring records and various astronomical phenomena, but with little success.

Perhaps the most dramatic expansion of dendrochronological research took place in the 1950s, through the work of Edmund Schulman (1908–1958). One of Douglass's principal associates since the 1930s, Schulman began studying the bristlecone pine of California in 1953, soon finding an exceptionally long tree-ring record in this species. By the time of his death, Schulman had measured several specimens more than four thousand years old, providing yet another long chronology with which to record climatic fluctuations. This research has continued as one of the major functions of the Tree-Ring Lab, which now has a complete North American bristlecone chronology extending back to 6700 B.C.E. (Webb, *Tree Rings and Telescopes,* pp. 186–187; Fritts, *Tree Rings and Climate,* pp. 22–23). The existence of this long chronology led to another significant archaeological contribution in the 1960s, when the bristlecone pine record was used to correct the radiocarbon dating method developed a decade earlier. Discrepancies had been discovered between radiocarbon dates and established historical dates for Egyptian artifacts, leading archaeologists to consider the need for recalibration. The Tree-Ring Lab worked with various radiocarbon laboratories during the 1960s to create a calibration curve to correct the radiocarbon dates and to expose the systematic fluctuations in the amount of carbon-14 in the atmosphere over time (Hitch, pp. 303–305).

Although dendrochronology continues to be an important adjunct to archaeology, since the 1960s its principal function has been to reconstruct past climates on the basis of the tree-ring record. Working with meteorologists, dendrochronologists have attempted to coordinate tree-ring widths with climatic records from the western United States for the past century. With records from nearly one thousand trees from sixty-five sites in western North America, dendroclimatologists have reconstructed a series of maps for the region's pressure, temperature, and precipitation for much of the twentieth century, charting seasonal changes as well as long-term fluctuations. Having established the correlation between climate and tree-ring characteristics for the recent period, these scientists have reconstructed past climates for the region from 1600 to the present, constantly refining their models of long-term climatic conditions (Fritts, *Reconstructing Large-scale Climatic Patterns,* pp. 12–19, 29–57, 118–162). Such studies may ultimately provide a means to predict more accurately the region's weather patterns, and they have already disclosed that certain political decisions concerning water resources (such as the Colorado River Compact of 1922) were based on inaccurate data about river flow and long-term supply problems.

Because of the greater sensitivity shown by western North American trees, dendroclimatologists continue to emphasize these specimens. Expansion of the geographical range of tree-ring studies, however, remains an important goal. Studies of conifers in northern Mexico have proceeded since the late 1960s, but they have been made especially difficult by a lack of knowledge of the details of tree growth in this region. Beginning in the mid-1970s, research in Argentina, Chile, Australia, and New Zealand has attempted to establish chronologies for those areas to provide a more complete picture of world climatic conditions ("Tales the Tree Rings Tell," p. 7). Expansion of dendrochronology into the Eastern United States has been limited by the complacent nature of the ring records, indicating that eastern and northern trees are less clearly influenced by climatic fluctuations than trees in the arid west. Nonetheless, in 1975 the National Science Foundation assisted in the establishment of a tree-ring laboratory at Columbia University's Lamont-Doherty Geological Observatory to begin the creation of chronologies for Eastern forests. Although based on less sensitive species, some Eastern chronologies have been extended to five hundred years in the past, providing significant knowledge of past climatic conditions in New England and the Hudson River valley (Trefil, p. 49). The geographical expansion of tree-ring studies represents an important step toward a global perspective on past climates.

Although tree-ring widths continue to be the primary data for dendrochronological analysis, other techniques emerged in the 1980s as important additions to the discipline. Ratios of hydrogen, oxygen, and carbon isotopes in tree wood provide useful information concerning past conditions, as relationships between various growth characteristics and isotopic ratios have emerged from research. The biological explanation for these relationships remains unclear, however, restricting the application of this technique. The analysis of wood density through low-level x-ray studies adds detailed knowledge of growing conditions to complement that obtained from ring widths, which record only average conditions ("Tales the Tree Rings Tell," p. 9). Equally important, density measurements may prove useful in deciphering tree-ring records in humid climates, where traditional dendrochronological methods have enjoyed only mixed success. As these and other techniques are refined, the study of the annual growth rings of trees will find application in an even broader spectrum of research programs.

George E. Webb

Bibliography

Eddy, John A. "Historical and Arboreal Evidence for a Changing Sun," In *The New Solar Physics,* edited by John A. Eddy, pp. 11–33. Boulder, Colo.: Westview Press, 1978.

Fritts, Harold C. *Reconstructing Large-scale Climatic Patterns from Tree-Ring Data.* Tucson: University of Arizona Press, 1991.

———. *Tree Rings and Climate.* London: Academic Press, 1976.

Hitch, Charles J. "Dendrochronology and Serendipity." *American Scientist* 70 (1982): pp. 300–305.

"Tales the Tree Rings Tell." Mosaic 8 (September/October 1977): pp. 2–9.

Trefil, James S. "Concentric Clues from Growth Rings Unlock the Past." *Smithsonian* 16 (July 1985): pp. 47–54.

Webb, George E. "Solar Physics and the Origins of Dendrochronology." *ISIS* 77 (1986): pp. 291–301.

———. *Tree Rings and Telescopes: The Scientific Career of A.E. Douglass.* Tucson: University of Arizona Press, 1983.

See also Age of the Earth since 1800; Climates, Pleistocene and Recent; Climate Change before 1940; Climate Change since 1940; Conservation of Natural Resources; Ice Ages; Radioactivity in the Earth; Solar Constant; Solar-Terrestrial Relations

Desertification

Land degradation in dry to subhumid areas resulting from various factors, including human activities and climatic variations.

The term "desertification" was apparently first publicized by the Frenchman A. Aubréville in his monograph *Climats, Forêts et Désertification de l'Afrique Tropicale,* published in Paris in 1949. Phrases like "man-made deserts," used by Walter C. Lowdermilk in 1935 and by E.P. Stebbing in 1938, and "desert encroachment," by H. Klintworth in 1948, had already been mentioned earlier this century. Aubréville, who was Inspecteur Général des Eaux et Forêts des Colonies (Colonial Inspector General of Waters and Forests), distinguished two major causes of desertification: first, destruction or degradation of the soil; second, the action of climatic factors.

In relation to the first cause, Aubréville considered man the main culprit for the degradation of African forests into savannah. Thus he used the phrase savannization as a form of desertification. Aubréville also included climatic variations as a cause for desertification, as shown by his expression *désertification climatique* (p. 140). Aubréville coined the term "desertification" to describe deterioration of vegetation and soil conditions in a rather wide sense, not just restricted to arid zones.

Human perception of the impoverishment of fertile areas into waste lands or deserts dates back to the distant past. Desertification, therefore, is neither a new development nor a new concept, apart from the term as such. Ancient expressions of the phenomenon are conveyed to us in various parts of the Bible, for example Psalm 107:33–34 (Revised Standard Version): "He turns rivers into a desert, springs of water into thirsty ground, a fruitful land into a salty waste, because of the wickedness of its inhabitants." The text presents desertification, in this case, as a castigation from the Creator. The word *desert*—that is, *midbar* in Hebrew—is specifically used, while salinization of the soil is also indicated. Quite famous are the historic problems of desertification related to the ancient irrigation agriculture of Mesopotamia, where salinization and siltation (river silt) posed major problems. The town of Ur was abandoned by its citizens, when the Euphrates changed its course and the intricate irrigation system became useless as a result, overtaken by the desert (Whyte, p. 94).

An ancient text highlighting human causes for desertification is Jeremiah 12:10–11 (New International Version): "Many shepherds will ruin my vineyard and trample down my field; they will turn my pleasant field into a desolate wasteland. It will be made a wasteland, parched and desolate before me; the whole land will be laid waste because there is no one who cares." The Hebrew word *midbar* is translated here as wasteland. Human factors, like carelessness, were emphasized vis-à-vis natural factors by the classical author Columella regarding agricultural degradation. Columella was born in southern Spain, but spent most of his life in Italy during the first century C.E. In his treatise *De re rustica (On Rustic Matters,* I.1.18ff), Columella discussed "the bad state of agriculture in contemporary Italy. But he refuses to side with the pessimists who blame the climate or the exhaustion of the soil instead of the carelessness, ignorance and lack of skill of those who till it" (White, p. 34).

This tension of who is to blame, climate (nature), man, or both, is still very much debated in the modern perception and interpretation of the concept of desertification. Land degradation in the Mediterranean lands during historical times was viewed by Ellsworth Huntington (1876–1947) in *Civilization and Climate* (1924) as the result of adverse climatic changes, in the framework of his hypothesis of climatic determinism. The human factor as a cause for desertification (as well as the reverse process of land reclamation) was eloquently emphasized by Lowdermilk in his *Palestine: Land of Promise* in 1944 (p. 1): "By neglect, ignorance and suicidal agriculture, peoples have bequeathed to their descendants *man-made deserts* of sterile, rocky and gullied lands." Documented examples of human influence on desertification in Near-Eastern history are presented by A. Reifenberg in his classic work *The Struggle between the Desert and the Sown* (1955), as well as by R.O. Whyte (1961).

The more restricted term "desertization" has been advocated since 1959 by Henri N. Le Houérou (p. 364) to describe "the extension of desert landforms and landscapes to areas where they did not occur in the recent past." In his opinion, "The term desertification has been misused for decades to describe the degradation of vegetation and soil conditions in arid, semi-arid and even humid zones. In many cases these processes have nothing to do, scientifically, with the desert. The regression of tropical forest into savanna and that of Mediterranean forest into steppe are examples of this. Neither climatically, geomorphologically nor biologically can savanna and steppe be classified as deserts."

The tragic drought in the Sahel, which began in 1968 and lasted through most of the 1970s and early 1980s, induced the General Assembly of the United Nations in 1974 to adopt resolutions that led to the U.N. Conference on Desertification held in Nairobi in 1977, organized by the United Nations Environment Program (UNEP). Representatives of ninety-four countries discussed the issue and a lengthy definition of desertification was formulated, commencing as follows: "Desertification is the diminution or destruction of the biological potential of the land, and can lead ultimately to desert-like conditions. It is an aspect of the widespread deterioration of ecosystems, and has diminished or destroyed the biological potential of the land, i.e., plant and animal production, for multiple use purposes at a time when increased productivity is needed to support growing populations in quest of development." The above definition ended with a call for action: "Action to combat desertification is required urgently before the costs of rehabilitation rise beyond practical possibility or before the opportunity to act is lost forever" (UNCOD, 1977).

Many publications about desertification began to appear since the UNCOD conference. Almost four thousand annotated publications are listed in the *World Desertification Bibliography* (Summers et al.). The concept and definitions of desertification were reviewed by Michael H. Glantz and Nicolai Orlovsky in 1984. Scientific views still range between man-induced desertification on the one hand and climate-induced desertification on the other. Human perception has not really changed since the days of Columella.

At the 1992 Earth Summit in Rio de Janeiro, a concise definition of desertification was formulated: "Desertification is land degradation in arid, semi-arid and dry subhumid areas resulting from various factors, including climatic variations and human activities." The United Nations General Assembly adopted a UN Convention to Combat Desertification in 1994, which went into force in 1996 after ratification by fifty nations (Bruins and Berliner).

Hendrik J. Bruins

Bibliography

Bruins, Hendrik, J., and P.R. Berliner. "Bioclimatic Aridity, Climatic Variability, Drought and Desertification: Definitions and Management Options." In *The Arid Frontier: Interactive Management of Environment and Development,* edited by H.J. Bruins and H. Lithwick, pp. 97–116. Dordrecht: Kluwer Academic, 1997.

Glantz, Michael H., and Nicolai Orlovsky. "Desertification: A Review of the Concept." In *Encyclopedia of Climatology,* edited by J.E. Oliver and R. Fairbridge. Stroudsburg, Pa.: Hutchinson and Ross, 1984.

Klintworth, H. "Desert Encroachment over the Karoo." *Farming in South Africa* 23 (1948): pp. 723–728.

Le Houérou, Henri Noël. "Man and Desertization in the Mediterranean Region." *Ambio* 6 (1977): pp. 363–365.

Lowdermilk, Walter C. "Man-Made Deserts." *Pacific Affairs* 8 (1935): pp. 409–419.

Stebbing, E.P. "The Man-Made Desert in Africa." *Journal of the Royal African Society Supplement* 37, no. 146 (1938): 13.

Summers, Ken, Barbara Hutchinson, Robert Varady, Carla Casler, and Deirdre Campbell. *World Desertification Bibliography.* Nairobi: United Nations Environment Program (UNEP). Tucson: Office of Arid Land Studies (OALS), University of Arizona, 1991.

UNCOD, Secretariat United Nations Conference on Desertification. *Desertification, Its Causes and Consequences.* New York: Pergamon Press, 1977.

White, K.D. *Roman Farming.* London: Thames and Hudson, 1970.

Whyte, R.O. "Evolution of Land Use in South-western Asia." In *A History of Land Use in Arid Regions,* edited by L. Dudley Stamp, pp. 57–118. Paris: UNESCO, 1961.

See also Climate Change before 1940; Climate Change since 1940; Conservation of Natural Resources; Environmental History; Hydrologic Cycle; Pedology; Soil Conservation; Soil Science; Water Wells in Antiquity

Deutsche Seewarte (German Naval Observatory)

An early and prominent institution promoting hydrographic, oceanographic, and other geophysical research.

The roots of the institute reach back to 1865 when, at the *Erste Versammlung Deutscher Meister und Freunde der Erdkunde* ("First Assembly of Masters and Friends of Geography"), Georg Neumayer (1826–1909), a natural scientist with a navigator's patent and strong interest in geosciences, pleaded for the establishment of a nautical and geosciences center in northern Germany. However, it was not Neumayer but Wilhelm von Freeden (1822–1894), director of a nautical school, who took the first practical step in that direction. Assisted by the chambers of commerce in Hamburg and Bremen, as well as by a number of shipping companies, he opened the Norddeutsche Seewarte (North German Marine Observatory) in Hamburg in 1868. His aim was to contribute to the safety and economy of navigation through individual sailing directions based on the evaluation of observations by German seafarers. The foundation of the German *Reich* in 1871, however, called for a greater solution, and in 1875 the Deutsche Seewarte was established in Hamburg as an institution under the German Admiralty.

Neumayer, since 1872 Hydrographer of the Admiralty, was appointed director, and he held that office for twenty-eight years. Under his capable leadership, the Seewarte succeeded in building up a highly competent staff of scientists and captains and gained a guiding position with regard to nautical affairs and geosciences in Germany, as well as a worldwide reputation in those fields. Neumayer was one of the initiators of the First International Polar Year of 1882 and 1883 and of the Antarctic International Cooperation from 1900 to 1905.

A man whose education was similar to Neumayer's was Carl C. Koldewey (1837–1908). After several years as navigator on sailing ships he studied mathematics and was an excellent captain of the German North Polar expeditions of 1868 and 1869/1870. He served as head of the Nautical Department. Wladimir Köppen (1846–1940), head of the

Meteorological Department, became widely recognized for his contributions to climatology and marine meteorology. His successor in office was Alfred Wegener (1880–1930), famous meteorologist, geoscientist, and Arctic explorer, who perished in 1930 during his Greenland expedition. His hypothesis of continental drift at last found confirmation by the concept of plate tectonics. Gerhard Schott (1866–1961) was the first oceanographer of the Seewarte. After taking part in voyages of sailing ships and in the German *Valdivia* expedition of 1898 and 1899, he presented the wealth of his marine experience in two big volumes on the geography of the oceans.

Those four leading experts stand for the many eminent scientists and captains who, through their achievements and publications contributed to the glory of the Seewarte. The directors, after 1911 called presidents, of the Deutsche Seewarte were retired admirals, even after World War I, when the institute was placed under the German Ministry of Transportation. The last president, from 1934 to 1945, was Fritz Spiess (1881–1959), held in high esteem for his leadership of the *Meteor* Expedition of 1925 to 1927.

The successful Deutsche Seewarte, with its characteristic building at the port of Hamburg, was destroyed by bombs at the end of World War II. New structures began to develop. For the hydrographic, geophysical, and oceanographic tasks of the former Deutsche Seewarte, of the Marine Observatory at Wilhelmshaven, the Deutsche Hydrographische Institut (DHI), was formed in Hamburg in December 1945. The meteorological functions of the former Deutsche Seewarte were first taken care of by the Meteorologische Amt für Nordwestdeutschland (Meteorological Office for North-Western Germany) established in Hamburg. In November 1952 this office was named Seewetteramt (SWA, Sea Weather Office), as the marine part of the federal agency Deutscher Wetterdienst (DWD, German Weather Service) created by law of the Federal Republic of Germany. DHI and DWD became "Superior Federal Authorities" within the jurisdiction of the Federal Ministry of Transportation.

The DHI was charged with the management of ships for surveying, wreck searching, monitoring marine pollution, and marine research. Further, it had become responsible for the drawing, printing, and issuing of all German sea charts and nautical publications. To its duties belonged the type-testing, licensing, and checking of all navigational instruments on German ships. Further, hydrographic services concerning tidal motion, wind effect on sea level, storm-surge warnings, sea-ice distribution, and nautical warnings had to be carried out. The DHI was charged to watch over the sea with regard to radioactive and other noxious substances. A special laboratory was installed. Thus, a scientific and administrative center for hydrography, geosciences, and marine research was created that served the safety of navigation, the protection of the marine environment, as well as scientific requirements.

The president of the DHI during the initial phase until 1960 was Günther Böhnecke (1896–1981), former director of the Marine Observatory Wilhelmshaven and scientist on board the research vessel *Meteor* during the Atlantic Expedition of 1925 to 1927. The ships of the DHI, apart from their hydrographic duties in home waters, took an active part in numerous international cooperative investigations. The DHI played a prominent role in the endeavors to advance marine research in Germany that began in 1960. In cooperation with the Deutsche Forschungsgemeinshaft (DFG, German Research Association), a new research vessel, *Meteor,* was planned and put into service in 1964. The DHI served as owner of the *Meteor* and used 50 percent of her time for its own research. The operating costs of the ship were carried in equal parts by DHI and DFG. This cooperation proved to be successful and lasted until 1985, when the *Meteor* was put out of service. During those twenty-one years, *Meteor* undertook seventy-three research cruises and covered a distance of 650,000 nautical miles (1.2 million kilometers).

In the following years the DHI continued its scientific investigations in physical oceanography, marine chemistry, marine geology, and geophysics, and, in particular, proved its ability to act as connecting link between pure and applied research. In response to the growing public awareness and sensibility regarding the health of the ocean, the research directed toward the protection of the marine environment and related administrative activities increased. A major change occurred in 1990 when the DHI and the Bundesamt für Schiffsvermessung (Federal Office for Tonnage Measurement of Ships) in Hamburg merged to form the Bundesamt für Seeschiffahrt und Hydrographie (BSH, Federal Maritime and Hydrographic Agency).

Following the German unification at that time, the authority of the BSH was extended to the relevant installations in the eastern part of Germany.

Hans Ulrich Roll

Bibliography

Deutsches Hydrographisches Institut. *Das Deutsche Hydrographische Institut und seine historischen Wurzeln.* Hamburg: Deutsches Hydrographisches Institut, 1979.

Roll, Hans U. "On the Roots of Oceanography in Germany." *Deutsche Hydrographische Zeitschrift* Reihe B, no. 22 (1990): pp. 3–19.

Roll, Hans U., and Erich Süssenberger. "Die Deutsche Seewarte—historiche und wissenschaftliche Aspekte." *Annalen der Meteorologie* (Neue Folge) no. 4 (1969): pp. 7–12.

Schott, Wolfgang. *Early German Oceanographic Institutions, Expeditions and Oceanographers.* Hamburg: Deutsches Hydrographisches Institut, 1987.

Voppel, Dietrich. "Das Deutsche Hydrographische Institut an der Schnittstelle zwischen Grundlagen- und angewandter Forschung." *Deutsche Hydrographische Zeitschrift* 43, no. 4 (1990): pp. 195–205.

See also Hydrography; International Oceanographic Commission; International Council for the Exploration of the Sea; International Organizations in Oceanography; Meteorological Services, National and Regional; Meteorology, Marine; Oceanography, Physical; Woods Hole Oceanographic Institution

Dew

Explained for centuries as rising vapor until experimental research revealed unexpected factors in the nineteenth century.

Aristotle's account was an early attempt at explaining the nature of dew. However, it was the American-born physician William Charles Wells who correctly explained its origin. In his *Meteorologica,* Aristotle had proposed that dew forms from vapor. Some of the day-formed vapor does not rise high, Aristotle explained, because of the small ratio of the fire raising the vapor to the water being raised. From this occurrence, vapor cools and descends at night to form either dew or hoarfrost. Aristotle concluded that dew forms when the vapor condenses into water and when neither the heat is great enough to dry the water, nor the cold great enough to cause the water to freeze (book I, chaps. 9–11). William Charles Wells, through observations and experiments, concluded that dew is condensed from air in contact with cooled objects that have lost their heat to the night sky. His detailed and methodical work led him to win the Royal Society's Rumford Medal.

In *An Essay on Dew, and Several Appearances Connected with It,* Wells described the phenomenon of dew, the theories of dew (both former and new), and appearances connected with dew. Wells began his investigations in the autumn of 1784. His early notion that dew is "attended by the production of cold" (p. 2) was later replaced with his understanding that dew is formed by a "preceding cold in the substances upon which it appears" (p. 28).

Wells acknowledged the work of some of his predecessors in *An Essay,* including the work of Aristotle. He noted that Aristotle's theory of dew was still entertained by many, as were other, more contemporary theories. He also observed that although investigations on the cause of dew could have been carried out since the invention of the thermometer, a complete understanding was impossible before the discoveries on heat made by John Leslie and Benjamin Thompson, Count Rumford (Wells, p. 34). Wells's work was later followed by the investigations of John Aitken, who contributed to an understanding of the dew found on plants.

John Herschel paid tribute to Wells in his *Preliminary Discourse* (1830) by praising Wells's work "as one of the most beautiful specimens we can call to mind of inductive experimental enquiry lying within a moderate compass" (p. 162). Wells's account of dew was also included in Herschel's *Meteorology,* an essay that originally appeared as an article in the *Encyclopædia Britannica* (1861, pp. 46, 91). *An Essay* is important to the history of science in that Wells provided a thorough historical account of the people and events leading to his discovery.

There are no known discussions of this topic by science historians.

Valerie N. Morphew

Bibliography

Aristotle. *Meteorologica.* In *Great Books of the Western World,* translated by E.W. Webster, vol. 8, pp. 445–494. Chicago: William Benton, 1952.

Herschel, John F.W. *Meteorology.* Edinburgh: Adam and Charles Black, 1861.

————. *A Preliminary Discourse on the Study of Natural Philosophy.* London: Longman, Orme, Brown, Green, and Longmans, and Taylor, 1830.

Wells, William Charles. *An Essay on Dew, and Several Appearances Connected with It.* Philadelphia: Haswell, Barrington, and Haswell, 1938.

See also Atmosphere, Chemistry of; Atmosphere, Structure of; Atmosphere, Discovery and Exploration of; Hydrologic Cycle; Instruments, Meteorological before 1800; Instruments, Meteorological since 1800; Meteorological Ideas in Europe, Fifteenth to Eighteenth Centuries; Meteorology; Precipitation, Theories of

Diluvialism

A nineteenth-century geological theory.

Although sometimes applied to earlier theories affirming the reality of the Flood of Noah on the basis of geological evidence, the term "diluvialism" more properly applies to geological theories of the 1820s that interpreted what we now regard as glacial phenomena as the residue of one or more recent but transient inundations. The general idea of periodic catastrophes was popularized by the French comparative anatomist Georges Cuvier in 1813, but we associate diluvialism more particularly with William Buckland, who championed it in a series of works, including *Vindiciae Geologicae* (1820) and *Reliquiae Diluvianae* (1823). In presenting his evidence, Buckland emphasized bone deposits in caves and the formation of valleys. Fluvialist interpretations of the latter were not then generally accepted. Under the influence of Louis Agassiz (1840), Buckland abandoned diluvialism in favor of the glacial theory.

Dennis R. Dean

Bibliography

Dean, Dennis R. "The Rise and Fall of the Deluge." *Journal of Geological Education* 33 (1985): pp. 84–93.

See also Actualism, Uniformitarianism, Catastrophism; Deluge; Geology; Ice Ages; Plutonism, Vulcanism, Neptunism; Stratigraphy

Disciplinary History

Considers scientific disciplines as historical phenomena. Such histories examine the intellectual, social, and institutional factors that contribute to and characterize the processes of discipline formation, definition, and possible dissolution.

Significant events in these processes may be the appearance of a name for an activity, a professorship, a university department or institute, or a journal dedicated to the subject. Degree programs, especially Ph.D. programs, point to critical periods in disciplinary development. Some historians have portrayed this development as inherent in the nature of science, or have argued that a series of necessary steps must be followed. Others have argued that disciplines are much more contingent on social factors, and that intellectual relations among sciences may take many different forms.

Disciplinary history may appear presentist in its assumptions. Specifically, it might assume that the currently accepted disciplines of science (such as geology or meteorology) exist somehow in nature itself. It might assume that these inevitably had to come into existence in their current form, and that the story of their development has always been directed toward this goal. Based on such an assumption, a disciplinary history would search for foreshadowings of the current disciplines.

This approach to disciplinary history is fatally flawed. Natural knowledge and the organization of its understanding and pursuit are much more complicated. Historians investigating the histories of scientific disciplines must be prepared to accept that the boundaries between disciplines have been subject to continuous negotiation among scientists with differing interests and emphases. Some might stress research methods, others willingness to speculate, and others the goals of research. Some scientists might be especially interested in building the institutional support structure that allows research of a certain kind to be undertaken. Others might emphasize clarification of the foundational principles of a field. All of these factors indicate how complicated and various the stories of scientific disciplines can be.

Disciplinary history discusses how the social, institutional, and intellectual landscapes of disciplines have changed over time. In what scientific and extra-scientific contexts was such research conducted and discussed? How did these contexts change over time? What were the major problem areas? How did they change? Disciplinary history may even legitimately question whether X constitutes or ever did constitute a discipline. Historical research related to disciplines may also discuss research styles, schools, programs, and so on.

Disciplinary histories in this volume include Agricultural Chemistry, Agricultural Geology, Cartography, Ecology, Geodesy, Geography, Geology, Geomorphology, Geophysics, Meteorology, Mineralogy, Oceanography (Physical), Pedology, Planetary Science, Seismology, Soil Science, and Space Science.

A selection of secondary literature on disciplinary history appears in the bibliography.

Gregory A. Good

Bibliography

Barkan, Diana Kormos. "A Usable Past: Creating Disciplinary Space for Physical Chemistry." In *The Invention of Physical Science: Essays in Honor of Erwin N. Hiebert,* edited by Mary Jo Nye et al., pp. 175–202. Dordrecht: Kluwer Academic, 1992.

Bechtel, William. "Integrating Sciences by Creating New Disciplines: The Case of Cell Biology." *Biology and Philosophy* 8 (1993): pp. 277–299.

Buntebarth, Günter. "Zur Entwicklung des Begriffes Geophysik." *Abhandlungen der Braunschweigischen Wissenschaftlichen Gesellschaft* 32 (1981): pp. 95–109.

Frängsmyr, Tore, ed. *Solomon's House Revisited: The Organization and Institutionalization of Science.* Nobel Symposium 75. Canton: Science History Publications, 1990.

Geison, Gerald L. "Research Schools and New Directions in the Historiography of Science." *Osiris* 2d series, no. 8 (1993): pp. 227–238.

Good, Gregory A. "Geomagnetics and Scientific Institutions in 19th-Century America." *EOS: The Transactions of the American Geophysical Union* 66 (1985): pp. 521–526.

Hufbauer, Karl. "Solar Physics' Evolution into a Subdiscipline (1945–1975)." In *New Trends in the History of Science,* edited by R.P.W. Visser et al., pp. 73–91. Amsterdam: Rodopi, 1989.

Kertz, Walter. "Die Entwicklung der Geophysik zur eigenständigen Wissenschaft." *Mitteilungen der Gauss-Gesellschaft E.V. Göttingen* 16 (1979): pp. 41–59.

Kushner, David. "Sir George Darwin and a British School of Geophysics." *Osiris* 2d series, 8 (1993): pp. 196–223.

Mills, Eric L. "The Historian of Science and Oceanography after Twenty Years." *Earth Sciences History* 12 (1993): pp. 5–18.

Paffen, K., and G. Kortum. *Die Geographie des Meeres. Disziplingeschichtliche Entwicklung seit 1650 und heutiger methodischer Stand.* Kieler Geographische Schriften, 60. Kiel, 1984.

Schröder, Wilfried. *Disziplingeschichte als wissenschaftliche Selbstreflexion Wissenschaftsforschung: Eine Darstellung unter Heranziehung von Fallstudien der Wissenschaftsgeschichte der Geophysik.* Frankfurt am Main and Berlin: Peter Lang Verlag, 1982.

Stichweh, Rudolf. *Zur Entstehung des modernen Systems wissenschaftlicher Disziplinen: Physik in Deutschland, 1746–1890.* Frankfurt: Suhrkamp, 1984.

———. "La Structuration des disciplines dans les universités allemandes au XIXe siècle." *Histoire de L'Éducation* 62 (1994): pp. 55–73.

Woodward, William R., and Robert S. Cohen, eds. *World Views and Scientific Discipline Formation: Science Studies in the German Democratic Republic.* Boston Studies in the Philosophy of Science, vol. 134. Dordrecht: Kluwer Academic, 1991.

See also Agricultural Chemistry; Agricultural Geology; Cartography; Ecology; Geodesy; Geography; Geology; Geomorphology; Geophysics; Meteorology; Mineralogy; Oceanography, Physical; Pedology; Planetary Science; Seismology; Soil Science; Space Science

Dowsing

The locating of water or minerals with a forked stick or other simple device.

Georgius Agricola, in his description of mining in the Harz Mountains of Germany in his *De re metallica* (1556), was the first to note the supposed ability to locate minerals by means of a forked stick. Around 1630 the practice was being used to locate mineral water in France, and after that dowsing has been applied almost exclusively to groundwater. Dowsing or water witching (water divining in Britain and Australia) is unknown outside countries connected with northern Europe. Arthur Ellis of the U.S. Geological Survey comprehensively reviewed the subject in 1917, and no new historical information has been published since then. Although numerous tests have failed to achieve more than statistically random results, the belief is still widely held today.

D. Philip Commander

Bibliography

Ellis, Arthur J. "The Divining Rod: A History of Water Witching." U.S Geological Survey Water-Supply Paper 416 (1917).

See also Artesian Water; Drilling; Drilling, Scientific; Geysers; Hydrologic Cycle; Mineral Waters; Precipitation, Theories of; Water Quality; Water Wells in Antiquity

Drilling

The driving of a hole into the Earth.

The earliest known drilling seems to have been hand-operated rotary coring, to a depth of 6 meters (20 feet), used in Egyptian quarry operations about 3000 B.C.E. However this appears to have had no influence on later developments, and it was the production of brine for salt that was the main stimulus for the development of drilling techniques.

Deep drilling was developed in China, but there is no unanimity on the date. According to Confucius (around 600 B.C.E.), brine wells were in existence in the early part of the Chou dynasty (1122–256 B.C.E.), but these were probably hand dug. Some authors have assumed that they were drilled, because of the considerable depths, although according to J.E. Brantly (p. 48) wells were apparently dug by hand for oil (Brantly) in Japan to depths of 180 to 270 meters (600 to 900 feet) by about 600 C.E. Yang Wenheng (1983, pp. 266–267) is clear that the drilling of the first small diameter deep brine bore in China was between 1041 and 1053 C.E., during the Song dynasty, and Marco Polo mentioned that these reached depths of 458 meters (1,500 feet). The Chinese drilling was carried out with bamboo rods or bamboo fiber ropes. The drill bit was alternately raised and lowered by a team of men jumping on and off a lever, while the rope was turned to maintain a straight hole. Chinese wells were lined with bamboo tubing, and those producing gas were known as fire wells. The deepest recorded well drilled in Szechuan by these traditional means was 1.5 kilometers (4,800 feet).

Artesian wells in the western desert of Egypt (fifth century B.C.E.) and Artois (eleventh century C.E.) were probably hand dug, with the necessity for the well digger to make a hasty exit when the artesian strata were reached. The artesian wells in Modena, Italy, were sunk by hand until the artesian strata were approached; then the remaining thickness of the confining bed was pierced with an auger. According to Bengt B. Broms and Nils Flodin, augers were sketched by Leonardo da Vinci around 1500 C.E. and were in use with connected rods in the 1700s for site investigation of bridges and large structures (pp. 160–165).

Drilling with rods was further developed in France during the 1700s, mainly for water (Brantly, p. 59). By the end of the century a depth of 330 meters (1,083 feet) had been reached, and the results of boring were being systematically recorded with the emerging interest in stratigraphic geology.

Reports of Chinese drilling probably reached Europe in the seventeenth century, but the first full account was sent by a French missionary called Imbert, and discussed by an incredulous French scientific society in 1829. The European experience of drilling with linked rods had not been particularly successful, and the Chinese techniques led to significant improvements. The subsequent completion of the Grenelle artesian bore near Paris in 1841 to a depth of 548 meters (1,798 feet) was a great stimulus to further drilling.

In North America, the spring pole percussion method, developed by David Ruffner for brine wells in western Virginia in 1806, and the walking beam variant, were in use throughout the 1800s. After the first bore drilled specifically for oil by Edwin Drake in Pennsylvania in 1859, the oil industry took the lead in development of drilling. Bores were carried deeper with the availability of iron, starting in 1849 and later steel pipe for casing. Steam power began to replace human and horse power after the 1850s.

Diamond bits were first used for drilling rock in 1863, and were in general use in mineral exploration and in mines by the turn of the century. The Frenchman Fauvelle had used water circulation with either rotary or percussion techniques in 1845, but rotary drilling involving a mud circulation, either inside or outside the rods, was not in wide use until after 1895. Rotary drilling became established in the oil industry after the success in 1900 of the Lucas well at Spindletop, Texas.

Drilling for oil was extended offshore first from floating platforms, and in 1933 the first submersible rig was used. Deep-sea drilling was tested off California in 1960 in preparation for the Mohole Project and was soon able to provide important new stratigraphic data on the oceanic crust.

The history of drilling provides an opportunity for exploring an example of how technology has affected our knowledge of the Earth. It has not been thoroughly examined.

D. Philip Commander

Bibliography

Bowman, Isaiah. "Well Drilling Methods." U.S Geological Survey Water-Supply Paper 257 (1911).

Brantly, J.E. *History of Oil Well Drilling.* Houston, Tex.: Gulf Publishing Co., 1971.

Broms, Bengt B., and Nils Flodin. "History of Soil Penetration Testing." In *Penetration Testing 1988, ISOPT-1,* edited by De Ruiter, pp. 157–220. Balkema, 1988.

Yang, Wenheng. "Rocks, Mineralogy and Mining." In *Ancient China's Technology and Science.* Beijing: Institute of the History of Natural Sciences, Chinese Academy of Sciences Foreign Language Press, 1983.

See also Artesian Water; Dowsing; Drilling Techniques; Geysers; Hydrologic Cycle; Mineral Waters; Precipitation, Theories of; Water Wells in Antiquity

Drilling, Scientific

Drilling for specifically scientific purposes.

Geologists and oceanographers have used drilling to investigate the deep layers of the Earth's continental and oceanic crust. Scientific studies of continental rock layers have been made as part of exploratory drilling to locate buried petroleum hydrocarbon deposits, but much of the proprietary data have remained unpublished. Drilling techniques have been modified from those used on land for hydrocarbon exploration, in order to obtain sediment cores and rock samples from underwater strata. Initial ocean drilling programs began on the continental shelves, with subsequent operations attempting to drill through in progressively deeper water, including sediments and basement rocks in the deepest abyssal plains of the oceans.

In 1957, two American oceanographers came up with the idea of drilling a borehole through the entire crust to the Mohorovicic Discontinuity, in deep-sea waters where the crust is thinnest. They felt that drilling such a borehole would enable geologists and oceanographers to better understand the processes by which seafloor crust was initially formed and later buried by sediment layers. Coordinated by scientists in the loosely organized American Miscellaneous Society (AMSOC), the Mohole Project successfully developed the techniques for drilling in the deep ocean. In 1961, Phase I of the Mohole Project obtained cores of sediment layers and seafloor basalts, by a dynamically positioned drilling ship floating in 3,350 meters (11,000 feet) of water off Guadalupe Island, Mexico. Drilling operations aboard *CUSS I* were praised by President John F. Kennedy, and the project gained national attention through articles written by John Steinbeck for *Life* magazine, and an article by Samuel W. Matthews in the *National Geographic* magazine in 1961. The AMSOC technical director for Phase I of the Mohole Project, Willard Bascom, wrote *A Hole in the Bottom of the Sea* in 1961, a book outlining for the general public the scientific rationale for proposing to drill a borehole to the Mohorovicic Discontinuity.

Despite the success of the initial phase of drilling, the AMSOC scientific staff responsible for Mohole Phase I decided not to continue in direct supervision of Phase II drilling (which was to culminate in the ultimate Mohole), but to act as advisors to a prime drilling contractor selected by the National Science Foundation, the agency that had funded Phase I operations. Controversy over the Mohole began with the selection of a Texas engineering firm, Brown and Root, as the drilling contractor. Debate over possible political influence in the choice of Brown and Root caused Congress to investigate the project. In 1966, the Mohole Project was canceled by Congress because of five years of expenditures with only limited results, ever-increasing estimates of drilling costs, and continuing disagreement between the AMSOC scientists and Brown and Root engineers over proposed plans for drilling Phase II of the project. National notoriety for the project was fostered by the debate on whether to use an intermediate-sized drill ship to perfect drilling techniques for the Mohole (favored by the AMSOC advisory group), or Brown and Root's plan to design an enormous drilling platform in a single "go for broke" attempt to drill the Mohole. Ultimately, congressional action canceling the project caused it to be ignored by most oceanographers as an embarrassing scientific fiasco (Munk, p. 3).

Out of the failure of the ill-fated Mohole Project came a successful ocean drilling program that has obtained seafloor samples from all the ocean basins of the Earth in a twenty-five year effort (Davies, pp. 384–385). In 1963, while testifying before a congressional subcommittee investigating the Mohole Project, the director of the National Science Foundation announced his decision to start a national program for deep-ocean sediment coring (the "intermediate ship" approach favored by AMSOC). One year later, four oceanographic institutions (the Institute for Marine Sciences of the University of Miami, Lamont Geological Observatory of Columbia University, Scripps Institution of Oceanography of the University of California, and Woods Hole Oceanographic Institution) formed a group called JOIDES (Joint Oceanographic Institutions for Deep Earth Sampling) to coordinate drilling plans. In May 1965, six holes were drilled on the continental shelf and slope off Jacksonville, Florida, in water depths of up to 1,032 meters (3,385 feet), with subbottom coring to depths of 320 meters (1,050 feet), as described by JOIDES in 1965.

Based on the success of the Blake Plateau drilling program, Scripps Institution of Oceanography, with assistance from JOIDES, proposed an eighteen-month drilling program in the Atlantic and Pacific oceans, the Deep Sea Drilling Project (DSDP). Global Marine Drilling Company constructed a vessel, *D/V Glomar Challenger,* specifically designed for drilling operations in water depths of up to 6,100 meters (20,000 feet), with penetration of 760 meters (2,500 feet) into the seafloor. DSDP was arguably the most cost-effective program funded by the National Science Foundation; it was extended beyond its initial eighteen-month venture for another fourteen years! DSDP was noteworthy for international scientific participation beginning with two non-American scientists aboard *Glomar Challenger* on the second DSDP cruise, and postcruise scientific studies of DSDP materials were made by international oceanographers and geologists beginning with the publication of volume 1 of the *Initial Reports of the Deep Sea Drilling Project* in 1969. The ninety-three volumes of this series contain the drilling results, descriptions of the recovered seafloor cores, and postcruise scientific studies performed on sediments and rocks recovered by each cruise. In 1975, the International Phase of Ocean Drilling began, when foreign partners in JOIDES were accepted, with partial financial support for drilling provided by France, Germany, Great Britain, Japan, and the Soviet Union. Between 1968 and 1983, *Glomar Challenger* success-

fully drilled 1,092 seafloor boreholes at 624 sites, in all oceans of the world except the Arctic. The American Geological Institute printed brief summaries of each DSDP leg in *Geotimes* magazine, and articles covering the first sixty-two legs were reprinted in three volumes by the institute in 1975, 1976, and 1979.

In 1981, after thirteen years of DSDP operations, JOIDES convened a "Conference on Scientific Ocean Drilling" (COSOD) in Austin, Texas, to discuss plans for future scientific drilling with a newer drillship to replace the aging *Glomar Challenger.* JOIDES's plans for continued drilling were contained in the "COSOD Report" in 1981, predicated on financial and technical support by American petroleum companies for an "Ocean Margin Drilling Program" (OMDP). This project proposed to modify the giant Howard Hughes vessel *Glomar Explorer* for drilling in areas that had been inaccessible to *Glomar Challenger,* such as high-latitude areas in the Arctic Ocean and close to Antarctica, in greater water depths close to continents, and in nearshore areas with possible buried hydrocarbon deposits, which required "blow-out" prevention on the drillship (Davies and Hay). Although declining oil prices forced the oil companies to withdraw from this project, in 1983 the Ocean Drilling Program (ODP) began, with a new drillship (the Sedco/BP 471, or *JOIDES Resolution*) and a new scientific operator, Texas A&M University (Davies, pp. 436–437). ODP continued the accomplishments of its predecessor, DSDP into the mid-1990s and produced new scientific results and successful deep-ocean drilling. The results of scientific ocean drilling by Project Mohole, the Deep Sea Drilling Project, and the Ocean Drilling Program were highlighted by a 1989 publication by the Ocean Studies Board of the National Research Council, *Symposium Commemorating the 25th Anniversary of the Demonstration of the Feasibility of Deep Ocean Drilling,* and were also summarized in a 1993 issue of *Oceanus* magazine.

Other noteworthy offshore drilling has been performed by the U.S. Geological Survey on the continental shelf and upper continental slope of the United States, to obtain data on the stratigraphy of seafloor sediment layers, and their engineering properties for seafloor structure emplacement. In 1967, the Geological Survey's Atlantic Stratigraphic Project (ASP) drilled twenty-four wells on the outer continental shelf from Maine to South Carolina. In the mid-1970s, planned lease sales of offshore drilling rights along the East Coast of the United States required the Geological Survey to estimate the value of petroleum hydrocarbon reserves buried in offshore lease blocks. The Geological Survey drilled several Continental Offshore Stratigraphic Test (COST) wells to provide estimates of the potential value of hydrocarbon deposits buried along the Atlantic and Gulf coasts of the United States, as reported in two works edited by Peter A. Scholle. Also, in 1976 the USGS Atlantic Margin Coring Project (AMCOR) drilled twenty stratigraphic wells along the U.S. East Coast, using the drillship *Glomar Conception* to drill in water depths between 20 and 300 meters (66 and 984 feet). This project was designed to obtain information on stratigraphy and mineral resources other than petroleum hydrocarbons along the Atlantic coastline. Results of the AMCOR drilling were outlined by John C. Hathaway and others in 1979.

On-land drilling for scientific purposes was stimulated by the early successes of Phase I of the American Mohole Project. Drilling techniques adapted from those used for hydrocarbon exploration have enabled earth scientists to better understand the physical processes and the principles controlling the formation and alteration of continental crust. For a time, there was the potential of a "race to the Moho" rivaling the "space race" of the Cold War era. Russian scientists were interested in drilling the deep continental crust, to understand processes by which ophiolitic rocks and their underlying metalliferous strata were formed. Between 1960 and 1962, the combination of economic interest and national pride during the Space Race period inspired scientists of the Soviet Union to plan drilling a "Russian Mohole" whose objective was to reach the Mohorovicic Discontinuity before the American drilling program (Bascom, p. 50). The Soviet Inter-Departmental Scientific Council for the Study of the Earth's Interior and Superdeep Drilling planned an ambitious continental drilling program, which included deep boreholes in productive oil and gas regions (the Dnieper-Donetsk, Caspian Sea, and Timan-Pechora basins), and ore-bearing regions (the Muruntau, Norilsk, and Krivoi Rog areas), along with two superdeep wells to reach the Mohorovicic Discontinuity (Kozlovsky, p. 11).

Only limited results of the Soviet drilling program have been published in English. The Krivoi Rog well in Precambrian iron-ore deposits of the Ukrainian Shield had been drilled to 3,648 meters (11,965 feet) by July 1990, but continued drilling to its ultimate target depth of 11–12 kilometers (6.8–7.5 miles) was made uncertain by the breakup of the Soviet Union. Another superdeep well targeted a gravity maximum in the Kura Depression of Azerbaijan (Kozlovsky, pp. 4–12), assumed to be locally thinned continental crust or an uplift of the underlying basaltic layer, with a planned total depth of 13 kilometers (8.2 miles). The best-reported superdeep well planned to penetrate 15 kilometers (9.4 miles) of metal-bearing Precambrian strata on the Kola Peninsula, east of northern Finland. Kola Peninsula drilling began in 1967, using rotary drilling to penetrate shallow sedimentary rocks and the uppermost copper-nickel deposits of Precambrian Shield rocks near Polyarny, 60 kilometers (38 miles) southwest of the Barents Sea coastline. Using the results obtained by this upper crustal drilling, Soviet engineers designed a new "superdeep" drilling rig (Kozlovsky, p. 514) to penetrate deep crystalline rocks to a total depth of 15 kilometers (9.4 miles). The superdeep well was begun in May 1970, and fourteen years of drilling resulted in a total penetration of 12,063 meters (39,565 feet) by August 1984, when the Kola borehole was visited by American members of the Continental Scientific Drilling Committee (Behr et al., p. 165). A 1987 Yevgeny Kozlovsky volume (originally published in Russian in 1984) summarized the results of drilling the first 12 kilometers, when drilling was suspended to allow logging and seismic studies using borehole recording instruments (Shirley). The Kola superdeep well provided some surprises: a seismic discontinuity at 7 kilometers (4.4 miles), first believed to be caused by basaltic rocks, turned out instead to be Archean age gneiss. According to Shirley, after the logging program, drilling was continued on the Kola superdeep well to the depth of 12,262 meters (40,220 feet) by the mid-1990s, but the well probably would be halted at a total depth of 13 kilometers (8.2 miles) because of the economic problems caused by the break-up of the Soviet Union.

Deep continental drilling has also been an ongoing scientific project in Germany. Deep drilling was discussed by German geologists beginning in 1977, and the KTB *(Kontinentales Tiefbohrprogram der Bundesrepublik)* was allocated half a billion Deutsch-marks (about U.S. $300 million) by the German Ministry for Research and Technology, for an ultradeep drilling program (Shirley). Forty proposed drilling sites were narrowed to two in the early

1980s (Raleigh, p. 8), and in 1986, the Oberpfalz site near the Bavarian village of Windischeschenbach on the Czechoslovakian border was chosen for drilling a scientific borehole to depths of 10–12 kilometers (6.2–7.5 miles). Between 1987 and 1989, a pilot hole was drilled to a depth of 4,000 meters (13,120 feet) in basement rocks of the Variscan Shield, with exceptional core recovery (3,594 meters, or 11,790 feet). The pilot hole was to acquire information on shallow continental layers, to obtain maximum core recovery in shallow layers so they could be drilled through without core recovery by the ultradeep well, to take borehole temperature profiles for estimating temperatures to be experienced in the deep hole, and to refine techniques for drilling, coring, and logging in the ultradeep hole. The pilot hole produced some surprises (Shirley), such as the presence of open, fluid-filled fractures at a depth of 3.4 kilometers (2.1 miles), and unexpectedly high borehole temperatures, which forced reduction of the planned total penetration in the ultradeep well from 12 kilometers (7.5 miles) to 10 kilometers (6.2 miles). The deep borehole was started in September 1990, using the largest drilling rig in the world, developed and built specifically for the ultradeep well. By spring 1992, total penetration of 6 kilometers (3.7 miles) was achieved in the ultradeep well, when further drilling was suspended to allow borehole logging, and to set casing to enable drilling to greater depths (Shirley). Drilling was continued, with hopes of reaching the total depth of 10 kilometers (6.2 miles) sometime in the mid-1990s.

Based on the successes of scientific ocean drilling, many American geologists have proposed a coordinated continental drilling program to study the rocks of North America. Several small-scale experimental continental drilling projects were proposed in 1975, when Eugene Shoemaker of the U.S. Geological Survey convened a Continental Scientific Drilling Committee sponsored by the National Research Council. In 1978, this committee made proposals for a number of drilling programs to study various continental rock types and geologic provinces (Raleigh, pp. 1–4). In the mid-1980s, a group of geologists at the University of Tennessee proposed a deep drilling project in the Appalachian Mountains, called ADCOH (Appalachian ultraDeep COre Hole), as a counterpart to the German KTB drilling program. The ADCOH project performed seismic surveys and surficial geological examinations, selected a drilling site (Ra-leigh, pp. 343–354), and did preliminary shallow drilling in the southern Appalachians, but after this initial study, the National Science Foundation failed to provide further funding for drilling the ultradeep borehole. Two other noteworthy American continental drilling programs have been the Cajon Pass well (Raleigh, pp. 132–140) and the Valles Caldera drill site (Raleigh, pp. 273–307). The Cajon Pass area was selected for drilling to obtain further knowledge of the nature of continental rocks near the southern terminus of the 1857 Tejon Pass earthquake, the last major seismic event on the southern section of the San Andreas Fault. This well, located 4 kilometers (2.5 miles) north of the San Andreas Fault near the town of Pearblossom in southern California, was drilled through 700 meters (2,300 feet) of sandstones atop 1,100 meters (3,600 feet) of igneous granodiorite. Plans for continued drilling of deeper boreholes in this region are being made. The Valles Caldera well was drilled near Fenton Hill, New Mexico, 32 kilometers (20 miles) west of the Los Alamos National Laboratory. This region, a "hot dry rock" geothermal site, has been used for energy production, by pumping fluids down wells, and using the heat of a cooling magma body to produce steam. Between 1981 and 1983, several large-diameter boreholes were drilled, with spot coring to establish the nature of the penetrated rock units. Two wells were drilled to 3,065 meters (10,050 feet) and 4,398 meters (14,430 feet) through Precambrian metamorphic rocks with granodiorite intrusive rocks.

Historians have yet to examine the history of scientific drilling. Several perspectives could readily be pursued. How did the expectations of the researchers and the results fit with geological and geophysical theories current in the different periods? On what assumptions about the Earth's structure were these researches based? What do these episodes reveal about the interaction of scientists, national governments, international organizations, petroleum companies, and Cold War politics? How was this research related to the attitudes evidenced in the International Geophysical Year, the Space Race, and the Plate-Tectonic Revolution? All of these offer rich possibilities for future historical analysis.

Dean A. Dunn

Bibliography

American Geological Institute. *Deep Sea Drilling Project, Legs 1–25*. AGI Reprint Series 1. Falls Church, Va.:

American Geological Institute, 1975.

———. *Deep Sea Drilling Project, Legs 26–44*. AGI Reprint Series 2. Falls Church, Va.: American Geological Institute, 1976.

———. *Deep Sea Drilling Project, Legs 45–62*. AGI Reprint Series 4. Falls Church, Va.: American Geological Institute, 1979.

Bascom, Willard. *A Hole in the Bottom of the Sea*. Garden City, N.Y.: Doubleday, 1961.

Behr, Hans-Juergen, Francis G. Stehli, and Helmut Vidal, eds. *Observation of the Continental Crust through Drilling II*. New York: Springer-Verlag, 1987.

Davies, Thomas A. "Deep Ocean Drilling." *Ocean Science and Engineering* 9, no. 4 (1984/1985): pp. 381–446.

Davis, Thomas A., and William W. Hay. "Ocean Margin Drilling Program." *EOS, Transactions of the American Geophysical Union* 61 (1980): pp. 712–713.

Hathaway, J.C., C.W. Poag, P.C. Valentine, R.E. Miller, D.M. Schultz, F.T. Manheim, F.A. Kohout, M.H. Bothner, and D.A. Sangrey. "U.S. Geological Survey Core Drilling on the Atlantic Shelf." *Science* 206 (1979): pp. 515–527.

Joint Oceanographic Institutions for Deep Earth Sampling (JOIDES). "Ocean Drilling on the Continental Margin." *Science* 150 (1965): pp. 709–716.

———. *Report of the Conference on Scientific Ocean Drilling, November 16–18, 1981*. Washington, D.C.: Joint Oceanographic Institutions, Inc., 1981.

Kozlovsky, Yevgeny A., ed. *The Superdeep Well of the Kola Peninsula*. New York: Springer-Verlag, 1987.

Matthews, Samuel W. "Scientists Drill at Sea to Pierce Earth's Crust." *National Geographic* 120 (November 1961): pp. 686–697.

Munk, Walter H. "Affairs of the Sea." In *A Celebration in Geophysics and Oceanography—1982, In Honor of Walter Munk*, pp. 3–23. San Diego: Scripps Institution of Oceanography, Reference Series 84–5, March 1984.

Raleigh, C.B., ed. *Observation of the Continental Crust through Drilling I*. New York: Springer-Verlag, 1985.

Scholle, Peter A., ed. "Geological Studies on the COST No. B-2 Well, U.S. Mid-Atlantic Outer Continental Shelf Area." *U.S. Geological Survey Circular* 750, 1977.

———, ed. "Geological Studies of the COST No. B-3 Well, United States Mid-Atlantic Continental Slope Area." *U.S. Geological Survey Circular* 833, 1980.

Shirley, Kathy. "Drillbit Still Turning in Germany." *AAPG Explorer* (January 1993): pp. 20–21.

"25 Years of Ocean Drilling." *Oceanus* 36, no. 4 (Winter 1993/1994): p. 136.

See also Artesian Water; Dowsing; Drilling; Geysers; Hydrologic Cycle; Mineral Waters; Mohole; Precipitation, Theories of; Water Wells in Antiquity

Earth in Decay

An idea prevalent until the beginning of the eighteenth century, and used by Gordon L. Herries Davies for the title of his 1969 book about the history of British geomorphology before 1878.

After the Renaissance the Earth was presumed to have been created by God in a state of perfection, subsequent to which it had decayed. Initially, decay was thought to be because of the Fall, and ensuing sin in the world. Later, everyday erosion and more specific causes and catastrophes were believed to contribute to the decay, such as earthquakes, eruptions, hurricanes, tidal waves, and particularly Noah's Flood. Under this view, primarily driven by theology in various guises, the world consisted of ugly boils, warts, and excrescences—mountains and volcanoes in particular—and as such is thoroughly reflected in literature as described in Marjorie Hope Nicolson's *Mountain Gloom and Mountain Glory: The Development of the Aesthetics of the Infinite.* A changing worldview, which was to replace this perspective, was partly encouraged by attempts in and outside the Royal Society of London (after 1670) to explain landscape features, such as glacial erratics, and even the supposed remnants of large-scale floods, as the result of natural processes and to render them susceptible to rational explanation. The growth of Newtonian science in the late seventeenth century, and the principle of universal gravitation—that everything attracts every other thing—led to attempts, for example by Edmond Halley (1656–1742) and William Whiston (1666–1753), to explain floods by the passage of comets. Sudden variations in the position of the Earth's axis, such as promoted by Robert Hooke (1635–1703), were also held to be responsible for floods, and for the stranding of fossil bodies in locations far removed from the sea.

This close attention to description of the landscape in all its physical features, and a growing familiarity with what we now call the rock or geological cycle, tended to distance teleological explanations to larger-scale aspects of the terraqueous globe. In parallel, a changing aesthetic with a new attraction to the beauty of the natural landscape, allied with new theologies such as deism (the acceptance of a God without the benefit of a revealed religion), claimed the globe as a place designed expressly for human habitation.

The changing attitudes placed an intellectual price on the interpretation of ordinary processes of denudation. If the world, as it was seen to be, was created as an express design for humans, why then was it so obviously subject to erosion or decay? Gordon L. Herries Davies has called this problem the "denudation dilemma." Various attempts were made to resolve it. The reality of erosion could be questioned or denied; its role could be trivialized as insignificant within the timespan of five thousand years since the Creation—commonly regarded as realistic in the eighteenth century—and in view of the forthcoming End of the World; or, its effect could be said to be that of a short-term cleansing agent revealing the perfect form beneath. It was also suggested, for example by the Scottish naturalist John Walker (1731–1803) in the lecture notes that Harold Walter Scott published (1966) as "John Walker's Lectures on Geology," that minute particulate impurities discovered by evaporating rainwater might be a restorative element, replacing the mass lost by denudation.

A much more radical solution was envisaged by the end of the century, and it also entailed a conceptual restructuring of the time spans involved for the age of the Earth. James Hutton (1726–1797) developed *A Theory of the Earth* (1795) in which the restorative process was that of mountain-building, in which the ruins of this world—the sediment carried to the oceans—became the basis of the next world when it was uplifted out of the sea. In this way the Earth stayed in a long-term balance, and because the processes were so slow, it remained at all times a globe perfectly habitable for humans.

By the beginning of the nineteenth century practical concerns associated with the Agricultural and Industrial revolutions focused attention on more specific activities: the nature of fossils, the character of minerals, the interpretation of particular rock types such as granite, and field studies of specific localities. In addition, the concept of an extremely long time scale for geological processes was becoming acceptable. In consequence, overriding teleological concerns with theological overtones were put aside. However, although the teleology of Earth science changed in the two centuries after 1800, the pragmatic elements of slow change over enormous time spans remained an essential part of what later became the geological cycle.

Keith J. Tinkler

Bibliography

Davies, Gordon L. Herries. *The Earth in Decay.* London: MacDonald, 1969.

Nicolson, Marjorie Hope. *Mountain Gloom and Mountain Glory: The Development of the Aesthetics of the Infinite.* New York: Norton, 1963.

Scott, Harold Walter. *John Walker's Lectures on Geology, including Hydrography, Mineralogy, and Meteorology, with an Introduction to Biology.* Edited with notes and an introduction by Harold W. Scott. Chicago: University of Chicago Press, 1966.

See also Age of the Earth, before 1800; Age of the Earth, since 1800; Cycle of Erosion; Deluge; Diluvialism; Geography; Geological Time; Geology; Geomorphology; Sacred Theory of the Earth; Volcanoes, Theories before 1800

Earth, Figure of in the Satellite Era

A period of rapid change in methods of determining the Earth's figure.

Ancient Greek philosophers had already concluded that the Earth is spherical. The pioneering theoretical and observational work done during the seventeenth and eighteenth centuries showed that the figure of the Earth approximates that of an oblate ellipsoid. In more recent times, the figure has been defined as a biaxial ellipsoid of rotation, cocentered with the Earth, which best fits the global geoidal surface. Thus, by definition, the knowledge of the global geoidal surface has become a prerequisite to determine the figure of the Earth. The figure so determined is sometimes called the real figure of the Earth to distinguish it from the figure determined on the basis of hydrostatic equilibrium theory. The figure based on the hydrostatic equilibrium theory is generally called the hydrostatic or equilibrium figure of the Earth. As the name implies, this is the figure the Earth would have had if it were in a state of hydrostatic equilibrium. The distinction between the real figure of the Earth and its equilibrium figure is a development of the satellite era.

Before artificial satellites, geometric and surface gravimetric methods were used to determine the geoidal surface. But these methods by their very nature could yield only small portions of the geoidal surface in limited areas. These local or regional geoids were so few that it was difficult to integrate them into a credible global geoid. The figure of the Earth determined from these, therefore, had limited accuracy on a global basis, although it fitted quite well the local or regional geoid on which it was based.

This led an influential group of theoreticians to argue that the method of the hydrostatic equilibrium theory for determining the figure of the Earth yielded more accurate results than the other methods then available. Harold Jeffreys argued for this in *The Earth* in 1962 (pp. 127–157). These developments led to the presumption that there is no difference between the hydrostatic and real figures of the Earth. We now know that the two are not the same. Before satellites, however, there were no data to demonstrate the distinction. As a result, the distinction between the real and equilibrium figures was lost in the historical usage and the term "figure of the Earth" became a generic term.

The satellite era began with the launch of *Sputnik* in 1957 by the Soviet Union. *Sputnik* was quickly followed by satellites launched by the United States. As the orbital data of the artificial satellites were analyzed, it soon became clear that such analyses provided by far the most accurate knowledge of the long wavelength components of the Earth's global gravity field. This knowledge came in the form of coefficients of low-degree terms in the spherical harmonic expansion of the Earth's gravity field. Initially, the best determined of these coefficients was J_2, the coefficient of the second-degree term.

The satellite-determined value of J_2 derived from orbital data of *Explorer I* and *Sputnik II* was used to determine a highly accurate value of the Earth's flattening by a number of investigators, including J.A. O'Keefe et al. in 1958, Desmond King-Hele and R.H. Merson in 1959, and E. Buchar in 1958. At the same time, the satellite determinations of the long-wavelength components of the global geoid, along with other geopotential data, made it possible for the first time to determine the size of the Earth's ellipsoid that best fit the geoid. These values improved as more satellite data became available. The satellite-derived results were so much better than any ever available or even imaginable during presatellite times that the International Union of Geodesy and Geophysics replaced its long-reigning (since 1924) International Reference Ellipsoid with the satellite-determined Geodetic Reference System 1967 (GRS 67). This was subsequently revised to GRS 80. The GRS 80 values for the figure (real) of the Earth are, according to B.H. Chovitz in 1981:

semimajor axis   a = 6,378,136 meters
                      (20,920,286 feet)
flattening   f = 1/298.257

Determination of a highly accurate value of J_2 from satellites also made it possible for the first time to apply the hydrostatic equilibrium theory to determine the hydrostatic flattening of the Earth directly. The geopotential coefficient J_2, coupled with the Earth's precessional constant H, already known to a fairly high degree of accuracy, yields quite precise values of Earth's polar moment of inertia. This, in turn, has been used to determine the hydrostatic flattening of the Earth as distinct from its actual flattening. The difference between the hydrostatic flattening and actual flattening of the Earth gives a measure of the stresses pertaining in the Earth.

Satellite-determined J_2 and the precessional constant H were used to derive hydrostatic flattening in 1960 by, among others, S.

Henriksen. These values were improved and refined by M.A. Khan in 1967. Since the pre-satellite applications of the hydrostatic theory did not make any distinction between the hydrostatic and real figures of the Earth, there were certain ambiguities in the presatellite formulation of the theory that presented problems for postsatellite applications. Consequently, the hydrostatic theory was reformulated to remove these ambiguities and was revised and extended to adapt more readily to the new postsatellite applications and data types (see Khan, "General Solution," passim). The most current value of the flattening of the hydrostatic or equilibrium figure of the Earth is

hydrostatic flattening, f_h = 1/299.75

The size of the equilibrium Earth ellipsoid is generally computed by assuming that it is volumetrically equivalent to the real Earth reference ellipsoid. Based on this assumption, Khan reported in 1989 ("Equilibrium Figure) the value of the semimajor axis of the equilibrium figure to be

semimajor axis, a = 6,378,101 meters

The hydrostatic or equilibrium figure of the Earth implies a state of zero stress in its interior. The departure of the Earth from this state reflects that state of stress. This is particularly interesting to geophysicists as such stresses can be invoked to explain a geophysical mechanism that may be found or assumed to exist in the Earth's interior. Apart from its traditional historical appeal, it is for this reason that the equilibrium figure of the Earth is of special interest to geophysicists in the late twentieth century.

The problem of determining the figure of the Earth had occupied the central attention of geodesists and other scientists for many, many centuries. The data from artificial Earth satellites solved this problem, and many other problems, with such finality during the first few years of the satellite era that after centuries of being at or near the top of the list of the hottest research problems, the figure of the Earth is now a routinely known fact about our planet. This has enabled geodesists and geophysicists to move on to other problems, many of which were not even regarded within the realm of possibility prior to the satellite era.

This is a brief historical note confined to a summary version of the advances in our knowledge of the figure of the Earth in the postsatellite era. Satellite data solved the problem of the real and equilibrium figures of the Earth in such a rapid succession of developments that this satellite era history is packed in an almost single though giant leap. Consequently, it is brief. History tends to accumulate only when the scientific discovery and progress toward a goal are incremental.

M.A. Khan

Bibliography

Buchar, E. "Motion of the Nodal Line of the Second Russian Earth Satellite and the Flattening of the Earth." *Nature* 1982 (1958): pp. 198–199.

Chovitz, B.H. "Modern Geodetic Earth Reference Models." *EOS, Transactions of the American Geophysical Union* 62 (1981): pp. 65–67.

Henriksen, S. "Hydrostatic Flattening of the Earth." *Annals of the International Geophysical Year* 12 (1960): pp. 197–198.

Jeffreys, Harold. *The Earth.* Cambridge: Cambridge University Press, 1962.

Khan, M.A. "Equilibrium Figure of the Earth." In *The Encyclopedia of Solid Earth Geophysics,* edited by D.E. James, pp. 378–385. New York: Van Nostrand Reinhold Co., 1989.

———. "General Solution of the Problem of Hydrostatic Equilibrium." *Geophysical Journal of the Royal Astronomical Society* 18 (1969): pp. 177–188.

———. "Some Parameters of a Hydrostatic Earth." *EOS, Transactions of the American Geophysical Union* 48, no. 1 (1967): p. 56.

King-Hele, Desmond, and R.H. Merson. "New Value for the Earth's Flattening Derived from Satellite Orbits." *Nature* 183 (1959): pp. 881–882.

O'Keefe, J.A., et al. "Oblateness of the Earth by Artificial Satellites." *Harvard Announcement Card* 1408. Cambridge: Harvard Astronomical Observatory, 1958.

See also Cosmology and the Earth; Earth, Models of before 1600; Earth, Size of; Expanding Earth Theories; Geodesy; Gravimetry; Gravity, Newton, and the Eighteenth Century; Instruments, Upper Atmosphere and Near Space; Planetary Science; Plate Tectonics and Space-based Platforms; Radio Astronomy and the Earth; Scientific Rocketry to *Sputnik*; Space Sciences

Earth, Models of before 1600

Dominant views of the Earth before the Scientific Revolution.

Since about 400 B.C.E. the Earth has always been spoken of as a sphere, depicted in four different models. The Earth as a globe and the heavens as a sphere were notions of the Pythagoreans in the sixth and fifth centuries B.C.E. that were then given descriptive rationality by Plato (427–347 B.C.E.) and Aristotle (384–322 B.C.E.). Subsequently, all descriptive literature in both Greek and Latin was consistent only with these concepts and expressed them clearly.

Drawings of the Earth took the forms of four basic models, each representing the Earth as a globe. The Earth as a whole was drawn on papyrus or parchment with lines and circles in four figures: *orbis quadratus, orbis terrae,* the *zonal rota,* or two interactive spheres of *terra* (earth) and *aqua* (water). Each model of the spherical Earth was projected onto a page as a *rota* (circle), divided into parts by simple lines; and each *rota* could be elaborated into larger and more detailed representation of the Earth and its parts (Harley and Woodward, vol. 1, pp. 286–370).

The *orbis quadratus* (shown in figure 1) was a diagram used to describe both the spherical heavens and the spherical Earth. This is a neglected classical model of the Earth. Within a circle it displays the heavens as four continents of stars divided by bands of water (*colures*), or the Earth as four continents of land divided by great oceans. The bands of water are shown as running north/south and east/west, so that one may speak of hemispheres, but the principal hemispheres of Earth were the east and the west. Some Pythagoreans thought that people in their *oikoumené* were "the upper ones in the right-hand part" while others in the south were "the lower ones in the left-hand part." On the contrary Aristotle asserted that "we are in the lower hemisphere and on the right" of the model (*De caelo* II.2). Each perspective assumed a four-part model, such as was found in ornamental designs of many Mediterranean peoples (Szabó, pp. 160–169; Stevens, pp. 269–270).

Following the Pythagorean orientation of this figure, the *sunoikoi* lived in the great northern land masses of the Eastern hemisphere around the middle sea and *antoikoi* lived to the south; but in the western hemisphere *perioikoi* lived in the northeastern quarter and *antipodes* (Latin: *antipodae*) in the southeastern quarter. The quarters of the globe were like slices of an apple, and the

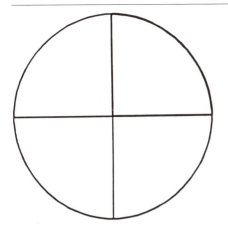

Figure 1. Orbis quadratus, Hellenic.

sunoikoi lived diametrically opposite to the *antipodes:* if each entered the inner caverns of Tartarus and slid down toward the center, they would meet foot to foot.

This model may have been inspired by the idea of celestial *colures,* two great circles drawn through the north/south poles and the east/west equinoctial points. They are perpendicular to one another and divide the heaven into quarters (Aujac, in Harley and Woodward, vol. 1, pp. 140–143, figure 8.8). One of these *colures,* together with the celestial equator, could be projected onto the Earth and produce the *orbis quadratus,* as shown on the Farnese Atlas in Naples, Museo Archeologico (Harley and Woodward, vol. 1, pp. 142–143, figs. 8.10 and 8.11).

This model of the Earth was explained by Krates of Mallos in his *Geographia* during the mid-second century B.C.E., when he taught at Pergamum in Asia Minor, and at Rome and by Strabo (d. ca. 20 C.E.). It was used more fully both for the heavens and for the Earth by Geminos of Rhodes, who may have lived about 50 B.C.E., in his *Astronomia* (date and location uncertain). It was often assumed in Latin lit-erature and influenced early Latin cartography. It was displayed on a coin of 44 B.C.E. (Harley and Woodward, vol. 1, p. 64). A simple *orbis quadratus* may be seen in the margin of Lucan's *Pharsalia* (written ca. 62/63), copied in ms. Bern, Burgerbibliothek 45 (ca. 900 C.E.), fol. 41, probably as a teaching device. The concept of the equatorial ocean in the torrid zone was also transmitted by Macrobius (ca. 400) in his *Commentary on the Dream of Scipio.* It is ig-nored in modern literature (for example, Lloyd; Lindberg), but it was often assumed in Greek and Latin literature. Ideas about the people called *antipodae* required it, and almost every allusion to "quarters of the Earth" from which winds blow or strangers arrive referred to quar-ters of *orbis quadratus* (Aujac; Stevens; Stevenson; Szabó).

The *orbis quadratus* also influenced early Latin cartography, especially the *Macrobius mappaemundi.* There was a variation of the *zonal rota* in manuscripts of the works of Macrobius that turned its east/west orienta-tion toward north/south. In the attempt to display habitable lands on both sides of the middle torrid zone, these drawings of the

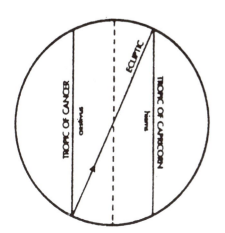

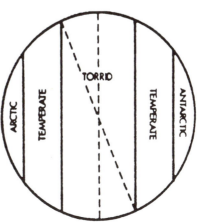

Figure 2. Eudoxian Schemata for Heavens and Earth, known as zonal rota.

sphere sometimes presented land masses around the south pole (see Gauthier Dalché), but the notion that antipodae lived at or near the Arctic pole is entirely modern (Harley and Woodward, vol. 1, pp. 243–244; Stevens, pp. 269–270).

A second model is shown in figure 2, the *zonal rota*. Essentially astronomical, it nevertheless was easily adapted to represent the spherical Earth. It may have been created by Eudoxos of Cnidos (fl. 370 B.C.E.), friend of Plato. Diagrams of the *zonal rota* usually show lines for the extreme northerly and southerly reach of the Sun's seasonal path but also a diagonal line from the one extreme of the ecliptic to the other. This diagonal could be drawn from the easternmost interception of the Tropic of Cancer with the horizon in summer to the westernmost intersection of the Tropic of Capricorn with the horizon in winter (or vice versa for astronomy). Normally the equator was not shown, but the Arctic and Antarctic circles often were drawn, as projected from the schools of Rodos, Kos, or Cnidos (in modern terms: 23°51' north latitude). Those four imaginary lines for dividing and studying the heavens were commonly projected onto the Earth to indicate bands of climate: temperate, torrid, cold. (Dicks, pp. 17–21; Aujac, pp. 196–205; Harley and Woodward, vol. 1, pp. 140–147).

Orbis terrae became more widely used in classical and medieval science. It is one quarter of the *orbis quadratus* and is represented on wall or parchment as a *rota terrarum* (figure 3) in three parts. From this perspective the globe is represented by dividing a circle into the upper half for Asia and the lower half for Africa and Europe. The line dividing the latter two continents is the middle sea, whereas the Nile River (or sometimes the Red Sea) separates Africa from Asia, and the River Tanais (Don?) indicates very roughly the land change between Europa and Asia. Outside the circle there is usually nothing of concern, and sometimes it is designated simply Ocean. Nevertheless, other lands were known, but were simply out of sight.

The tripartite *orbis terrae* was used in Greek, Roman, and medieval schools to teach about the globe of Earth and its parts. Its earliest representation is in a Latin manuscript, El Escorial R.II.18, the seventh-century schoolbook by Isidore of Seville (d. 636) called *De natura rerum* (On the Nature of Things) (Stevens, pp. 268–277). It took many forms and accompanied many texts that explained it. Usually, it was oriented to *oriens*

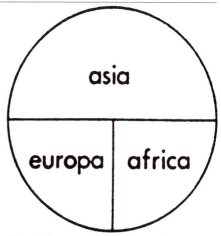

Figure 3. Rota terrarum *with three continents,* Hellenistic.

(east). The lower quarters were called Europa and Libya (or Africa). The part called Libya by the Greeks came to be known as Africa in Latin writings by extension of the Roman term for *Africa nova* (Tunisia). The horizontal line could be pushed higher to give more room to Europa and Africa; and the vertical half-line separating those two could slip to the right or to the left for different purposes.

The tripartite *rota terrarum* design of this *orbis terrae* was flexible and could be adapted to emphasize cities, islands of the Mediterranean, rivers of Africa and Asia, and the great peninsula of Europa. It was also expanded about 800 C.E. for use as a *periplous* to identify regions and peoples, as one traveled the shores of the middle sea. One series of *mappaemundi* based upon this *Orbis terrae* projected the oceans from the back side of the globe at top and bottom of the *rota* and displayed many distant islands in those oceans, such as the Azores, Canaries, and Madeiras in the North Atlantic, Taprobane (Sri Lanka) in the Indian Ocean, and a huge unnamed land mass in the Pacific, possibly the Philippines or Japan. In ms. Vat.Lat.6018 from about 800 C.E. (figure 4), extensions and curvature in projections of those islands provide further confirmation that this model represented the Earth as a globe (Destombes and Almagià, pl. 19; Stevens, pp. 271–274).

Krates of Mallos (fl.150 B.C.E.), Strabo (fl.150 B.C.E.), and Ptolemy (fl.150 C.E.) used the *orbis terrae* model, and variants of it appeared with the works of Sallust (40 B.C.E.) and of Lucan (60–64 C.E.), though its earliest surviving representation was in a manuscript of seventh century Spain. It was explained by Isidore of Seville in his *De natura rerum* (621), the venerable Bede (d. 735) in his *De natura*

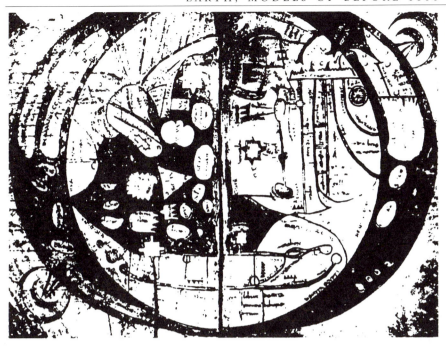

rerum (701), Hrabanus Maurus (d. 856) in his *De computo* (820), Abbo of Fleury (d. 1004) in his *Quaestiones* (986–988), and Johannes Sacrobosco in his popular *De sphera* (1230), and many other scholars described the globe in terms of this model (Destombes and Almagià, chap. 2; Harley and Woodward, vol. 1, pp. 296–304). Medieval cartography probably stemmed from use of this model because of its flexibility.

Apparently in ignorance of those models of the Earth as a globe, a Syrian merchant in the sixth century tried to select passages from Hebrew and Christian scriptures, in order to create a new cosmology, formed from elements of a tent. His name, Cosmas Indicopleustes, dates, locale, and religion are all uncertain. If he was a Christian in some sense, he was obviously antagonistic to orthodox teaching and wanted to discredit Christian philosophers teaching in Alexandria. His work included interesting drawings of the Earth as a tent with a flat floor, upright walls, and two levels of covering. For art historians this is an important document of early Byzantine book illustration (Wolska-Conus). But it stands alone and does not represent either common or sophisticated Christian thinking about Earth or Heavens or Scriptures. It was unknown in Western Europe until the fifteenth century and had no influence on medieval cosmology or cartography.

Two independent but interactive spheres of *terra* and *aqua* are shown in figure 5. Earth

can be thought of as a ball or globe, but it is also one of the four basic elements of Hellenistic science: earth, air, fire, and water. During the fourteenth to sixteenth centuries some scholars tried to unify these concepts by speaking of *terra* as a sphere of the element earth and the surrounding *aqua* also a sphere of the element water. The sphere of earth rose partly out of the water, as an explanation of how the continents were above the ocean by which they were surrounded.

Interest in the question of what happened to the center of the globe when there were large land shifts, such as would result from earthquakes and avalanches, may also have led Jean Buridan (1295–1358) to express this idea and to speculate further about the center of the universe *(Kosmos, mundus)*. Cartographical drawings of the Earth with three continents often showed them slightly off-center, relative to the surrounding waters, as seen in figure 6. This aspect of medieval *mappaemundi* had gone unnoticed until it was recognized and explained by K. Vogel (1994).

Each model of the Earth as a globe could be studied as a *rota* drawn on a page with any orientation, but they were usually drawn with *oriens* (east) toward the top of the page. Terminology was provided however from all sides, so that each model would be turned as it was being studied. All surviving diagrams that display the Earth depict it as a globe throughout the Middle Ages and thereafter, supported by

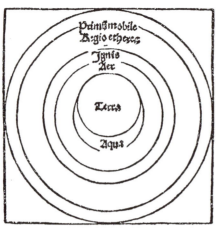

Figure 5. Spheres of terra *and* aqua, *from a fifteenth-century edition of Sacrobosco's* De sphaera mundi. *Source: A.E. Nordenskiöld,* Facsimile Atlas to the Early History of Cartography with Reproductions of the Most Important Maps Printed in the XV and XVI Centuries. *Stockholm, 1889. Translated from the Swedish original by Johan Adolf Ekelöf and Clements R. Markham, with a new introduction by J.B. Post. New York: Dover, 1973, p. 71. With permission of Dover publications.*

the texts that accompany those diagrams.

Historians of cartography have often attributed "flat earth" or "disk" concepts to early Mediterranean peoples, for example Bunbury, Beazley, Tozer, Taton, Bagrow, Kimble, and others. Because Greeks and Romans used the *zonal rota* it was said that they believed in a spherical Earth, but the "flat earth" was supposed to be assumed by "Church fathers" and most medieval scholars before Columbus. The writings of John K. Wright have often been cited for this notion in the Middle Ages. Manuscript drawings of the *orbis terrae* and the *rota terrarum,* called the T-O map, were disconcerting to those who did not read the texts that accompanied them.

Nevertheless, the *zonal rota* had also been used by "Church fathers." Readings of the evidence in context by F.S. Betten in 1923, C.W. Jones in 1934, and W.M. Stevens in 1980 have required a reassessment of both texts and diagrams, with the result that it is now widely known that all models and diagrams assumed and all texts taught the spherical Earth at all times, as well as that early Christians and Church fathers accepted it without difficulty (see Stevens; Lindberg; Harley and Woodward; Von den Brincken). Final efforts to say that someone in the "Dark Ages" must have been wrong about this and should have taught that the Earth was flat, disk-shaped, or like a wheel have turned to

Isidore, bishop of Seville (d. 636), and his *Etymologiae,* whose only English translator, E. Brehaut, had simply asserted in 1912 that it was so. Stevens, however, has shown that Isidore also taught that the Earth is a globe, as did everyone else, and that there is no contrary evidence (Harley and Woodward, vol. 1, pp. 319–321). Introduction of a medieval "flat earth" notion into American social imagination in connection with Columbus by the fiction writer Washington Irving has been debunked by Jeffrey B. Russell, *Inventing the Flat Earth: Columbus and Modern Historians* (1991). Old prejudices die hard, especially if they are not old.

In the meantime new evidence has been introduced about *orbis quadratus* by Stevens and about interactive spheres of *terra* and *aqua* by Vogel. They help to clarify the ideas of Aristotle and of medieval philosophers who used his work, *De caelo* (On the heavens), as well as the figures of speech, such as "from that quarter" or "the four quarters" of the Earth or the "surrounding waters," which were used by ancient and medieval writers on all subjects. Modern writers tend to generate new, quite different assumptions that they suppose are behind such phrases. From these assumptions many misunderstandings about the past arise.

The older histories of cartography can scarcely be used for the ancient peoples around the Mediterranean Sea, including their speculations about Greek cosmology; and those histories are positively misleading about the Middle Ages and Renaissance, particularly the oft-cited work of John K. Wright (1925). However, the numerous authors who participated in *The History of Cartography,* edited by J.B. Harley and David Woodward (1987), are usually instructive and reliable. Unfortunately, they fail to notice the *orbis quadratus* and its influence.

Wesley M. Stevens

Bibliography
Aujac, Germaine. "L'image du globe terreste dans la Grèce ancienne." *Revue d'Histoire des Sciences* 27 (1974): pp. 193–210.
Destombes, M., and R. Almagià, eds. *Mappemondes, A.D. 1200–1500.* Amsterdam: N. Israel, 1964.
Dicks, D.W. *Early Greek Astronomers to Aristotle.* London: Thames and Hudson, 1970.
Gauthier Dalché, Patrick. "Les représentations géographiques." *Testo e Imagine nell'alto medioevo: ATTI delle SETTIMANE DI STUDI* 41 (Spoleto

Figure 6. Continents were sometimes represented slightly off-center in medieval maps. From Andreas Walsperger, ms. Vat. Pal. Lat. 1362b.

1994): pp. 693–764 and plates I–XV.

Geminus. *Gemini elementa astronomiae.* Edited and translated into German by Karl Manitius. Leipzig: Teubner, 1898.

Harley, J.B., and D. Woodward, eds. *The History of Cartography.* 2 vols. Chicago: University of Chicago Press, 1987.

Lindberg, David C. *The Beginnings of Western Science.* Chicago: University of Chicago Press, 1992.

Lloyd, G.E.R. *Early Greek Science: Thales to Aristotle.* London: Chatto and Windus, 1970.

Romm, James S. *The Edges of the Earth in Ancient Thought: Geography, Exploration, and Fiction.* Princeton: Princeton University Press, 1992.

Russell, Jeffrey B. *Inventing the Flat Earth: Columbus and Modern Historians.* New York: Praeger, 1991.

Stevens, Wesley M. "The Figure of the Earth in Isidore's *De natura rerum.*" *ISIS* 61, no. 2 (1980): pp. 268–277.

Stevenson, Edward Luther. "Reconstruction of the Globe of Crates of Mallos, ca.

150 B.C." In vol. 1 of *Terrestrial and Celestial Globes.* 2 vols. New Haven: Yale University Press, 1921. See esp. fig. 5.

Szabó, Arpád. "Roma quadrata." *Rheinisches Museum* 87 (1938): pp. 160–169.

Vogel, Klaus A. "Das Problem der relativen Lage von Erd- und Wassersphäre im Mittelalter und die kosmographische Revolution." *Mitteilungen der Österreichische Gesellschaft für Wissenschaftsgeschichte 13,* nos. 1, 2 (1993): pp. 103–143.

Von den Brincken, Anna-Dorothee. *Fines Terrae. Die Enden der Erde und der Vierte Kontinent auf mittelalterlichen Weltkarten.* Hannover: MGH Schriften 36, 1992.

Wolska-Conus, Wanda. *La topographie chrétienne de Cosmas Indicopleustès: Théologie et science au VIe siècle.* Paris: Presses Universitaires de France, 1962.

Wright, John K. *Geographical Lore of the Time of the Crusades.* New York: American Geographical Society, 1925, 1965.

Earth, Size of

Scientifically determined for the first time by Eratosthenes (276–195 B.C.E.) in the third century B.C.E. Before that, there were only fanciful speculations; and after that, there were imitations of Eratosthenes' method with increasing refinements up to modern times, when satellite techniques replaced Eratosthenes' method.

Prescientific speculations ranged from an infinite size of a flat Earth suggested in the five-thousand-year-old Sumerian-Babylonian epic *Gilgamesh;* to a finite size combined with fanciful shapes as described by the Ionian philosophers of the sixth century B.C.E.; to an aesthetically and philosophically pleasing spherical shape without definite numerical size, proposed by the Pythagorean school of the sixth century B.C.E.; to Aristotle (384–322 B.C.E.), who mentioned the first numerical estimate of 400,000 stadia for the length of the Earth's circumference, probably by the Pythagorean Archytas of Tarent (ca. 400 B.C.E.). Then Archimedes (287–212 B.C.E.) mentioned 300,000 stadia, probably proposed by Dikaiarch (fourth century B.C.E.), a student of Aristotle's.

Eratosthenes' milestone achievement of actually measuring two pertinent phenomena—namely the length of the longest meridional arc available, stretching along the Nile from Alexandria to Syene, paired with the length of the Sun's shadow cast by a gnomon in Alexandria on the day of the summer solstice—is fortunately described in detail by Strabo (64–21 B.C.E.). Eratosthenes' writings are lost.

Strabo was interested as a geographer in Eratosthenes' systematic collection of geographic data, but did not much appreciate his theoretical conclusions about the size of the Earth, which he considered extraneous to the task of a geographer and of which he, Strabo, did not understand too much, by his own repeated admissions. Ironically, however, it was an isolated brief remark of his—". . . of the more recent measurements of the Earth, the one which makes the Earth smallest in circumference . . . I mean that of Posidonius

who estimates its circumference at about 180,000 stadia . . ." (in lieu of Eratosthenes' 252,000 stadia)—that had an unbelievable impact on general knowledge, literature, encyclopedias throughout the centuries, and even helped Christopher Columbus (1451–1506) to get financial support for his westward exploration plans (see Russell).

Yet, from bits and pieces of other ancient literature it appears that Posidonius (ca. 135–51 B.C.E.), whose writings are lost, never made such a competing calculation, which in any case would have included a circular error and a substandard procedure. As Hugo Berger (1836–1904) put it bluntly in 1903 (p. 582): "It would have marked Posidonius as an idiot for all times. Strabo, who did not understand a thing of all this, as any Roman, just copied it out of context from Posidonius' notes." Nonetheless, an emotional controversy about Posidonius' alleged correction of Eratosthenes has been kept up among historians, some eager to rescue Posidonius' good name by suggesting explanations: different stadia had been used in getting such seemingly contradictory results, or it was just a very simplified classroom example, or it was the inexcusable fault of Marinus of Tyre (first and second century B.C.E.) and Ptolemy (ca. 100–178 C.E.) to have picked up this canard uncritically and transmitted it as correct to posterity. On the other hand, Ptolemy's writings make quite clear what he and Marinus were doing. They were continuing Eratosthenes' collection of geographic information into a map by adding to the well-known, because well-traveled, European part what they heard about the Asian part. Here Ptolemy disagreed with Marinus' overestimate of the longitudinal extent of Asia as he described it; Marinus' own writings are lost. This did not affect the size of the Earth as such, and there is no indication whatsoever that their literary accusers in that respect had a point. Even so, Hugo Berger (pp. 592–593) maintains the accusation of technical incompetence, not realizing that the shoe is on the other foot.

By mere authority of the printed word, the literature perpetuated both negative and positive corrections to Eratosthenes' result, whether substantiated or not. Some of the critics were not even substantive enough to make it explicitly into print, with the exception of Hipparchus (ca. 160–125 B.C.E.) in the second century B.C.E. Pliny the Elder (23–79 C.E.) wrote: "Hipparchus . . . added a little less than 26,000 Stadia" to Eratosthenes' result. Why would he have done that? Berger and others are quick to blame the incompetence of the ancient writer and to judge his remark "a confusion and egregious blunder," as evidenced by his alleged sudden change of subject and his assumed misunderstanding of the material. A careful reading of Pliny shows, however, no such confusion at all, but on the contrary a logical exposition leading to the 26,000 stadia. Retracing Hipparchus' probable computation considering what was available to him at his time, Irene K. Fischer ("Another Look," pp. 155–156) shows that Hipparchus should have arrived at a theoretical correction of 15,900 stadia for the Earth's circumference, which would be too small for technical significance, but interesting in the context of the historical and literary dispute. The recomputed result is a little less than 16,000 stadia or, in Roman numerals, XVI M. Pliny's original quote is "*stadiorum paulo minus XXVI M.*" It could well be that an accidental duplication of the Roman numeral X by the scribe could have caused this whole story.

At the time of Columbus, reports on his travels to Cathey (China) and Cypango (Japan) by Marco Polo (1254–1324) had enlarged the geographical knowledge toward the Orient. The notion that Ptolemy had used a smaller Earth was part of the general consciousness. It did not focus, however, on a new arc measurement to deduce from it the size of the terrestrial sphere, but on the distribution of land and water on the surface—that is, Ptolemy's reduction of Marinus' overlong extent of Asia. The world geography *Imago Mundi* of 1410 by Pierre d'Ailly (1350–1420?) sided with Marinus' longer Asian extent, which left less for the sea to complete the global circuit along a latitude circle through Athens. Thus, "The ocean . . . between Spain and India . . . is of no great width. It is evident that this sea is navigable in a very few days if the wind be fair," quoting from Aristotle and Pliny. This idea was reinforced by the well-known apocryphal book *Esdras* II, 6:42: "The waters to be gathered together in the seventh part of the Earth, but six parts you dried up."

Samuel Elliot Morison (1887–1976) tells in great detail in his *Admiral of the Ocean Sea* (1942) how Columbus culled from this background information a proof that his plan to reach India by westward navigation from Spain would be much shorter than the land route eastward and thus would deserve royal financial support. In his demonstration he also took advantage of the confusion of different kinds of miles, specifically switching Arabic miles (2,160 meters, or 7,085 feet) for the much shorter Roman miles (1,485 meters or 4,871 feet) so that he came up with a sea distance of only 4,400 kilometers (2,732 modern miles). We know of this difference in miles from the fact that the Arabic mile, used in the ninth-century arc measurement by Caliph al-Mamun (ca.? 813–833) still exists on a nilometer near Cairo, where it was identified, measured, and described by Wilhelm Jordan (1842–1899) in his *Handbuch der Vermessungskunde* (Handbook of measurement, 1888–1890).

Confusion about measurement units of the same name existed all along, today as well as in antiquity. Thus the often discussed and disputed question whether Eratosthenes' size of the Earth compared well to modern results, or was somewhat too large or too small, is moot, since it is still argued which of several stadia of his time he actually used. It is moot also because the concept of the spherical Earth to compare it with has changed to that of an ellipsoidal Earth through the famous French measurements in the seventeenth and eighteenth centuries. Louis XIV (1638–1715) wanted an exemplary map of France, based on arc measurements after the well-known Eratosthenes model but using modern techniques such as triangulation. Famous names are connected with these measurements such as l'Abbé Jean Picard (1620–1682), Philippe de La Hire (1640–1718), Jean-Dominique (1625–1712) and Jacques Cassini (1677–1756), and others. As a great and unsettling surprise it appeared that the length of a 1° meridional arc seemed to decrease toward north, not permitted to a well-behaved spherical Earth. It suggested that the Earth was pointed toward the poles. But Isaac Newton (1642–1727) deduced from his theory of universal attraction that a rotating Earth would have to be flatter at the poles. The Académie Royale des Sciences coped with this literally Earth-shaking conflict between geometric and dynamic theory, between Earth-elongators and Earth-flatteners, between the French and the British, in a magnificently simple manner by sending out two expeditions far apart in latitude, one to Peru (now Ecuador) led by Charles-Marie de la Condamine (1701–1744), and the other to Lapland in 1736, led by Pierre de Maupertuis (1698–1759), to find out who was right. If the 1° arc in Lapland was shorter than the Peru arc, the French would be right, otherwise the British. And the British were right. The notion of a terrestrial sphere changed to the notion of an oblate ellipsoid of revolution.

The outside world took quite an interest in this basically technical yet internationally exciting event. Voltaire (1694–1778) caught the mood with his comments. He praised Maupertuis for having "flattened the Earth and the Cassinis" and he made fun of de la Condamine, whose assignment was more strenuous and took much longer: "You have found by prolonged toil, what Newton found without leaving his home."

Now an international game developed to determine the correct dimensions of such an ellipsoidal Earth—that is, the length of the major and minor axes (or, as technically preferred, the major axis and the flattening, which is the ratio of the difference between the axes to the major axis). Different results were obtained, however, in different regions, which gradually led to the unsettling suspicion that there may not be a unique Earth-ellipsoid.

Also unsettling was the possibility suspected on the Peru expedition by Pierre Bouguer (1698–1758) that the attraction of high mountain masses on the geodetic measurements may distort the results. Moreover, a theoretical calculation of such an effect did give an even much larger distortion than was observed, which in turn suggested less density in the mountains than was assumed or some balancing mass deficiencies underneath. Such speculations cast a shadow of doubt on the validity of all geodetic measurements. Jean-Baptiste-Joseph Delambre (1749–1822) wrote in *Grandeur et Figur de la Terre* (1822) in a rather pessimistic mood that such possible falsifications besides the unavoidable observational errors in all field work would seem to make everything unsure; one may have to be resigned to choosing some practically convenient numbers for the length of the Earth's axes and give up the search for precision.

The disillusionment about these uncertainties was overcome in time by a change of concept. Instead of searching for an illusive ellipsoid by trying to explain away the disturbing deviations, these were accepted as realities, as evidence of a very irregular Earth surface, called the geoid. The various ellipsoids derived in different areas were now seen as mere practical devices for these specific areas, with no implications for the rest of the Earth. The focus of studies was the meaning of the deviations in terms of geophysical forces, relegating the ellipsoid to a technical reference surface. Changing from one ellipsoid to a more suitable one became a mere mathematical transformation.

In 1924 the General Assembly of the International Association of Geodesy (IAG) in Madrid adopted the so-called International Ellipsoid with semimajor axis a = 6,378,388 meters (20,921,113 feet) and flattening f = 1/297 as an International Model of the Earth. By 1956 this was known to be too big. Two superlong meridional arcs had been measured by Eratosthenes' method, one reaching from Canada into Chile, and the other from Scandinavia to South Africa. The resulting model had a semimajor axis of only 6,378,260 meters, holding the flattening fixed at 1/297. Then came the surprise of the unprecedented satellite technique, changing the flattening to a smaller value of 1/298.3, which had an impact on the semimajor axis by reducing it to 6,378,160 meters. In 1967 the XIVth General Assembly of the IAG in Lucerne decided to acknowledge the developments since the adoption of the now obsolete International Ellipsoid of 1924. It recommended instead an Earth model with semimajor axis of 6,378,160 meters and flattening of 1/298.25, but refrained from calling it another International Ellipsoid. More modestly, it was designated as part of the 1967 Reference System, acknowledging the connection with other geophysical numbers and the advisability of consistency. Also, the continued use of the old International Ellipsoid was noted where data collections had been assembled on it, as well as further derivations of reference ellipsoids for specific studies.

One may wonder: was Delambre correct after all in his pessimistic judgment that one would have to adopt convenient numbers in lieu of a precise size of the Earth? Yes and no. Yes, because now international agencies adopt numbers by vote. No, because the focus of interest has shifted to the implications of the irregular geoid available with unprecedented precision, robbing the ellipsoid of its previous cosmological significance.

The geoid had been visualized and vaguely defined in 1837 by Friedrich Wilhelm Bessel (1784–1846) as mean sea level, continued into land by a net of channels filled with calm water. With the modern capability of extending geodetic activities into the oceans, marine geodesy was added to the scope of geodesy and promptly collided with oceanography. A dispute whether mean sea level slopes toward north or south as measured geodetically or oceanographically along the north-south coasts was called "one of the most puzzling problems of recent years" by Harald U. Sverdrup (1888–1957) in 1942. An analysis by Irene K. Fischer in 1977 revealed the culprit to be a difference in basic concepts and reference systems. This example also highlights the increasing interconnection of the geosciences. The function of geodesy in the late twentieth century has remained the basic determination of location, but with increasing precision and ease in procedures through continuous updating of instruments and procedures, including satellite techniques.

Irene K. Fischer

Bibliography

Berger, E. Hugo. *Geschichte der wissenschaftlichen Erdkunde der Griechen.* Leipzig: Von Veit, 1903.

Fischer, Irene K. "Another Look at Eratosthenes' and Posidonius' Determinations of the Earth's Circumference." *Quarterly Journal of the Royal Astronomical Society* 16 (1975): pp. 152–167.

———. "The Figure of the Earth—Changes in Concept." In *Geophysical Surveys,* edited by William Markowitz, vol. 2, no. 1, pp. 3–54. Dordrecht and Boston: D. Reidel, 1975.

———. "Mean Sea Level and the Marine Geoid—An Analysis of Concepts." *Marine Geodesy* 1, no. 1, (1977): pp. 37–59.

Jordan, Wilhelm. *Handbuch der Vermessungskunde.* Stuttgart: J.B. Metzler, 1888–1890.

Morison, Samuel Elliot. *Admiral of the Ocean Sea: A Life of Christopher Columbus.* Boston: Little, Brown and Co., 1942.

Russell, Jeffrey B. *Inventing the Flat Earth: Columbus and Modern Historians.* New York: Praeger, 1991.

Sverdrup, Harald Ulrich, M.W. Johnson, and R.H. Fleming. *The Oceans, Their Physics, Chemistry, and General Biology* New York: Prentice Hall, 1942.

See also Atmospheric Optics to 1600; Cosmology and the Earth; Earth, Figure of in the Satellite Era; Earth, Models of before 1600; Expanding Earth Theories; Geodesy; Gravity, Newton, and the Eighteenth Century;

Earthquakes, Historic

Among the earliest geological phenomena to be recognized, together with volcanic eruptions and floods.

Because of the frequency, uncertainty, and destructiveness of earthquakes, major ones have been chronicled from very early times. Among the purely naturalistic explanations of their occurrence, that proposed by Aristotle—that they are due to subterranean winds—remained foremost until the seventeenth century. A series of alternative explanations then followed, but earthquakes were not described and explained from a modern point of view before the twentieth century.

Among the many earthquakes noticed by historians and religious writers in antiquity, a particularly well attested one took place at Alexandria in 365 C.E. and was recorded by St. Jerome; another, which destroyed the city of Antioch in 526, provided the first good record of aftershocks. Toward better understanding, the time of day, the prevailing weather, and eventually the duration of quakes were increasingly recorded.

The Jamaican earthquake of 1688 was the first in which wavelike undulations of the ground were specifically mentioned. A second Jamaican earthquake of 1692 at Port Royal and the famous Lisbon quake of 1755 were very widely reported. Lisbon 1755 is often regarded as the first earthquake to have been investigated scientifically. The Calabrian earthquake of 1783 (with aftershocks lasting four more years) was at the time the best reported earthquake in history. Though the New Madrid earthquakes of 1811–1812 were the most powerful in the history of the United States, fewer persons were affected, and the subsequent fieldwork was of lower quality.

A Neapolitan earthquake of 1857 was notable because of the thorough investigation of it made single-handedly by Robert Mallet, an engineer-scientist who had already published extensively on seismology. His recognition of earthquakes as waves and his techniques for the analysis of structural damage have continued to be influential. They were used, for example, by Charles Dutton in his report on the Charleston, South Carolina, earthquake of 1886 and by later investigators in Japan and California. Our modern understanding of earthquake phenomena, or at least the beginning of it, derived from the extensively studied San Francisco earthquake of 1906, was explained in a classic publication in two volumes in 1908 and 1910: *The Californian Earthquake of April 18, 1906: Report of the State Investigation Commission.* The second volume, written almost entirely by H.F. Reid, expounded the elastic rebound theory.

Other twentieth-century earthquakes since that of 1906 have been more powerful and more destructive, but one may cite the

A view of the San Francisco City Hall after the 1906 earthquake. From Hugo Bennioff's glass slide collection. Courtesy of the Archives, California Institute of Technology.

1989 Loma Prieta (San Francisco area) quake as being among the first to be explained by a developed understanding of plate tectonics and as having taken place in a densely populated area whose previous seismic history was already well known.

Dennis R. Dean

Bibliography

Dean, Dennis R. "Robert Mallet and the Founding of Seismology." *Annals of Science* 48 (1991): pp. 39–47.

Lyell, Charles. *Principles of Geology.* Vol. 1. London: John Murray, 1830.

Ward, Kaari, ed. *Great Disasters.* Pleasantville, N.Y. and Montreal: Reader's Digest, 1989.

See also Actualism, Uniformitarianism, and Catastrophism; Earthquakes; Historiography, Eighteenth-Century England; Seismology

Earthquakes, Prediction

The advance establishment of certain parameters that define a seismic event in time and space, as well as in its physical dimensions: the position of its epicenter, the moment when it commences, and its magnitude.

The essential characteristics of the principle lines of past research into earthquake prediction are to be found in two different approaches to the problem: statistical and deterministic prediction. Statistical prediction means calculating the probability that an earthquake of a certain magnitude will occur in a given zone within a certain period of time.

Seismic phenomena have been researched over a span of about twenty-five centuries. So far, however, encouraging results have been obtained only in a few test areas where research has been carried out in considerable depth and breadth. If assessments of this kind are to produce tangible results, it is necessary not only to study the historical seismicity of the area under investigation, but also to evaluate geological factors on a regional and local scale, as discussed in a 1990 special issue of the journal *Physics of the Earth and Planetary Interiors.* Such an approach is particularly useful for seismic zoning studies and for estimating seismic hazard.

Deterministic prediction, on the other hand, is based on the understanding of the deterministic physical laws that relate the measurement of those physical parameters that are defined as precursors to the actual occurrence of the seismic event. The empirical approach to the problem of earthquake prediction—that is to say, the attempt to establish phenomenological laws—has led many scholars and researchers to suggest relationships between precursors and earthquakes over a historical time span that already covers about twenty-five centuries and is still in progress. This study began in the Mediterranean area and spread into Central Europe, the Euro-Asian Continent, the Far East, and America in ways and at times that parallel those found in the history of earthquake theories and seismic instruments. Bruce A. Bolt reviews ongoing research on "Forecasting Earthquakes" in *Earthquakes and Geological Discovery* (chap. 8).

The study of earthquake precursors in fact goes back a long way. Many examples of earthquake prediction occur in ancient literature, but the writer concerned very often did no more than adopt divinatory practices in order to make general disaster predictions. Only in a few cases is it possible to identify an intention to establish a causal natural relationship between a phenomenon that is defined as "precursory" and an earthquake. An early notable example is Pherecydes, who is thought to have been a teacher of Pythagoras. Cicero mentions the case in his *De fontibus librorum Ciceronis qui sunt de divinatione:* "Pherecydes . . . predicted an earthquake when he saw that the water from a well which was usually well filled had disappeared." According to T. Schinche, who published an edition of Cicero's work in 1875, however, Pherecydes should be regarded as a diviner rather than a physicist. Current research into water level changes in aquifers prior to earthquakes shows nevertheless that Pherecydes had identified a phenomenon that still plays a useful part in earthquake prediction studies (see Roeloffs). Later on, and indeed throughout the Middle Ages, philosophers and scientists turned their attention to investigating the causes of earthquakes rather than trying to predict them. There were occasions, it is true, when phenomena now considered to be precursory were observed and recorded, but the essential reason for doing so was to provide evidence in support of some general theory of the origin of earthquakes. In line with the philosophical and religious attitudes of the time, scholars turned their attention to other phenomena, such as different kinds of disasters, miracles, and so on, which accompanied earthquakes and seemed to be linked to them. The predominant theory throughout the Middle Ages was that put forward by Aristotle, according to whom earthquakes were generated by air pressure that gave rise to subterranean winds. In Renaissance times, a new attitude toward the direct observation of natural phenomena became very important. Antonio Jacopo Buoni, a doctor from Ferrara, referred to bubbling gas and the clouding of water in wells before and during the earthquake of 1570 at Ferrara. He reported this in his treatise *Del terremoto: Dialogo di Jacopo Antonio Buoni medico ferrarese distinto in quattro giornate* (Modena, 1571), which contained much observational and historical information, including a reference to Nicolò Cardano's having observed

similar phenomena. Anomalous gas emissions and the occurrence of geophysical anomalies in subterranean water are in the late twentieth century the subject of intense research activity (see H. Wakita et al.).

In the sixteenth and seventeenth centuries, the circulation of scientific theories became more intensive and influential, partly as a result of printing and the abandonment of the Aristotelian theory of earthquakes; historical records of earthquakes reflect this more favorable cultural situation. The seventeenth century notably saw a substantial exchange of scientific information between the Jesuit fathers and China, especially Father Matteo Ricci, who traveled there for cultural and scientific purposes. He established a good diplomatic relationship with the Chinese authorities, and brought into being active cultural exchanges. He designated as his successor Father Nicola Longobardi, whose name was adapted by the Chinese to Long Huamin. Longobardi was a native of Caltagirone in Sicily who in 1597 arrived in Peking, where he died in 1655. His work on *The Interpretation of Earthquakes* was published there in Latin in 1626 (translated into Italian by G. Matteuci, *Interpretazione del terremoto,* Naples, 1988). Longobardi set out clearly precursor phenomena such as anomalous emissions of gas from the Earth, the clouding of water in wells, and a change in the taste of water before earthquakes—phenomena now held to be indicators of geochemical changes in ground fluids. He also mentioned exceptionally high tides, which are now held to be indicators of probable crustal deformations. Longobardi attributed precursor phenomena to subterranean gas pressure, and he also considered certain meteorological conditions and the appearance of certain cloud formations to be seismic precursors, stressing the importance of Aristotle's *Meteorologica.* All the phenomena he lists have been the subject of earthquake prediction research in the late twentieth century, as are discussed in, for example, T. Rikitake's *Earthquake Forecasting and Warning* (Tokyo, 1982) and in *Earthquake Prediction: Proceedings of the International Symposium on Earthquake Prediction* (Paris, 1984). Modern Chinese earthquake prediction research also considers meteorological phenomena to be important. Lu Dajiong's *Impending Earthquake Prediction* (Nanjing, 1988) clearly demonstrates the survival of traces of Aristotelian thought, as brought to China with great effect by the Jesuit missions.

Antonio Prati e l'ultima sua scoperta

Until around 1800, however, theories about the causes of earthquakes still could not include precursor studies in proper research programs. Hence precursor phenomena remained little more than curiosities of nature. At the end of the nineteenth century, an Italian chemist, Demetrio Lorenzini, published detailed information and careful measurements concerning the behavior of water in a well (see D. Albarello et al.). His aim was to devise an observational system that could be used for predicting earthquakes, as is also clear from his correspondence with M.S. De Rossi.

Partly because of the 1909 Messina earthquake, scholarly activity on the subject became more intense in the early twentieth century. Guido Alfani reported that Father Atto Maccioni had twice succeeded in detecting radio signals as precursors of earthquakes by using a "coherer"—an instrument capable of detecting electromagnetic emissions that had been devised by Temistocle Calzecchi-Onesti in 1887. In 1909 Father A. Maccioni published the first impressive results of experiments to predict earthquakes using slightly modified versions of the coherer. In 1909 the Italian engineer Antonio Prati improved the device and patented a version intended for commercial use (figure 1). This is probably the first attempt to produce a practical device for studying precursory phenomena to predict earthquakes. In 1924 E. Ungania suggested in *Presismofono Ungania. Unico apparecchio*

preavvisatore dei terremoti, segnalatore delle perturbazioni elettromagnetiche (Bologna, 1924, pp. 1–34) that information about impending earthquakes obtained with the coherer should be broadcast in Italy. Similar investigations are in progress in the 1990s, for example that of A.C. Fraser-Smith et al.

At roughly the same period, similar researches were being carried out in Japan, involving a network of observatories for monitoring electromagnetic emissions. Particularly important was the founding of the Japanese Seismological Society after the Yokohama earthquake of 1880. British interest in this kind of research—an example is Robert Mallet's fundamental *Great Neapolitan Earthquake of 1857. The First Principles of Observational Seismology* (London, 1862)—was "exported" to Japan, since that country had more to offer for experiments. The man responsible for this transfer was John Milne, who from 1876 to 1895 worked in Japan and actively supported earthquake precursor research.

After the 1891 Mino Owari earthquake, the Imperial Earthquake Investigation Committee was set up to investigate seismic and volcanic phenomena and to limit their effects. After the earthquake (7.9 on the Mercalli scale) that destroyed the Kanto region in 1923, the Earthquake Research Institute was founded. In 1927, K. Shiratoi first detected radon changes in hot springs in Japan before certain earthquakes (see Shiratoi). Reports of seismic precursor monitoring also appeared in the 1940s and 1950s by G. Imamura (on hot springs), Z. Hatuda (on radon in the soil), and S. Okabe (on radon in the air). Japanese interest in this sphere increased after the publication of *Prediction of Earthquakes—Progress to Date and Plans for Further Development. Report of the Earthquake Prediction Research Group of Japan* (Earthquake Research Institute of Tokyo, 1962) by C. Tsuboi, K. Wadati, and T. Hagiwara, which provided guidelines for modern research programs involving the observation and analysis of many different precursor parameters, such as crustal deformation, changes in ratios of velocities of primary (P) and secondary (S) seismic waves, and electrical and magnetic anomalies. Most encouraging results have been obtained since 1980, as reviewed in *Evaluation of Proposed Earthquake Precursors* (Washington D.C., 1991), edited by M. Wyss.

Many earthquake prediction research projects in the late twentieth century are based on the dilatancy theory worked out by C.H. Scholtz et al. in the important article "Earthquake Prediction: A Physical Basis" in *Science* in 1973, or on modified versions of it. These theories attempted to provide an organic explanation of the contemporaneous occurrence of a number of precursory phenomena (see Sobolev and Dietrich).

Soviet research into earthquake prediction began in the 1960s and involved the study of numerous geochemical and geophysical factors, the most interesting results of experiments being obtained above all in test areas in central Asia (see I.G. Kissin et al.). A recent review of this work is K.N. Abdullabekov's *Electromagnetic Phenomena in the Earth's Crust* (Rotterdam, 1991). Characteristic of the former Soviet Union's researches on earthquake prediction was the strong, competent, multidisciplinary approach. In fact the entire Academy of Sciences of the USSR actively cooperated in this topic, a continuing characteristic of Russian geophysicists, geochemists, mathematicians, seismologists, and so on. The geochemical approach generally has produced in the former Soviet Union very interesting results; such results have not always been evident in countries where the simple seismological approach has been more prevalent (see M. Dall'Aglio). G.A. Mavlianova also discussed this approach in *Hydrogeoseismological Precursors of Earthquakes* (Tashkent, 1983), as did V.L. Barsukov and his colleagues in *Earthquake Prediction, Proceedings of the International Symposium on Earthquakes Prediction* (Paris, 1984, pp. 169–180).

In the People's Republic of China, a massive earthquake prediction research program was launched in the 1960s, and it has produced encouraging results (figure 2). Characteristic of the Chinese research program is the particular attention paid to the empirical observation of natural phenomena, including macroscopic ones, such as animal behavior and meteorological phenomena. Alongside this, Chinese scientists have continued advanced automatic instrumental measurement of a variety of parameters (see Wan).

Earthquake prediction studies began in the United States in the late 1960s. Certain test areas, such as Parkfield in California, have recently been provided with sophisticated equipment for monitoring precursory phenomena, as discussed by W.H. Bakun.

In the European and Mediterranean areas, important results have been obtained in Turkey, where a joint Turkish-German project is being carried out. This project involves the simultaneous observation and analysis of multiple precursors. The results achieved so far have confirmed the suitability of this approach, and it has been largely approved by the scientific community (see C. Schindler et

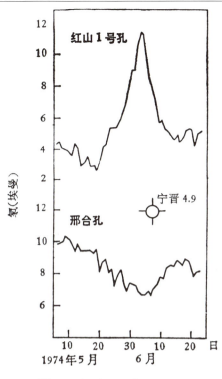

Figure 2. Example of prediction of a 4.9 magnitude earthquake that occurred in Hebei Province, China, on June 6, 1974. The anomalous behavior of Rn222 with respect to the average level in water wells located in Jiangshan (upper part) and in Xinghe (lower part) allowed Chinese researchers to forecast the seismic event one week before. Reproduced from Hydrochemistry Group, Seismological Brigade of Hebei Province. "Studies on Forecasting Earthquakes in the Light of the Abnormal Variations of Rn Concentration in Ground Water." Acta Geophysica Sinica 18 (1975): pp. 279–283.

al.). This example has influenced other projects that are now under way in Greece, southern Italy, Germany, India, New Zealand, and South Africa.

Since the late 1980s the scientific debate concerning earthquake prediction has been strongly affected by advances in Greece, Japan, and France in deterministic earthquake prediction through the study of electrical precursory phenomena. This has been reviewed in a 1993 issue (no. 2/3) of *Tectonophysics,* edited by P. Varotsos and O. Kulhànek. Seismologists, as a scientific class, have been skeptical of this approach (see P.W. Burton), drawing attention to the apparent fortuitousness of the predictions and arguing that these were actually guesses. The total denial of the validity of this type of research may invalidate earlier analogous work, or it may prove to be widely accepted and representative of a consolidated state of the art (see Sobolev). Contributions to the debate have come from G. Di Bello et al. and L. Jouniaux et al. in 1994, who clearly proved the nonfortuitousness of the occurrence of electrical signals and plausibly related their deterministic structure to earthquakes.

The intense scientific discussion about electrical precursory phenomena is actually only one of the many episodes of debate associated with earthquake prediction in the late twentieth century. These debates arise partly from a strong specialization of experiences and methodologies between seismometric seismology and the geophysics of nonseismometric phenomena. Such divisions have involved many contemporary seismologists and geophysicists.

Such tensions have been partly the result of the need for mutual seismic monitoring by the superpowers after World War II. During the Cold War this monitoring proved very important for distinguishing between subterranean nuclear explosions and actual earthquakes. If the efficiency of knowledge transfer from seismic research to the engineering of buildings is regarded as a scientific indicator, some conclusions are possible about the effects of the organization of seismic research on the prediction of seismic events. Modern engineering has long had an answer to the problems connected with earthquakes: in highly economically developed and seismically active areas like California and Japan, research on earthquake prediction does not have high priority. In those countries, protection from earthquakes is entrusted to an advanced engineering know-how, because predictions of

individual events do not seem profitable. Such considerations are not valid for developing countries, where it is possible to foresee potential applications of research on earthquake prediction if only owing to the excessive cost of the buildings resistant to seismic events. Military agencies such as the U.S. Navy, U.S. Air Force, and NATO have supported and controlled applications in other areas. Hence, most immediate application of research on seismic precursors concerns small regions that are exposed to strong seismicity, that are densely populated, or that are areas of particular strategic interest.

Although systematic historiographic material is lacking, the rich scientific literature on earthquake prediction suggests several paths of historical investigation. One critical topic concerns the links between scientific research on earthquake prediction and the theory of decision-making in policy. Carl-Henry Geschwind has provided one case study of this type in his analysis of reactions to the 1906 San Francisco earthquake. Furthermore, it is essential to remember that, politically, earthquake prediction has been considered in completely different ways in countries with different forms of government, such as China compared with the United States or Japan with Europe. Moreover, the different human experiences of earthquakes in different regions requires historical examination. Such considerations can also be seen in the cases of other natural disasters. Any further historical work on this topic must rely heavily on close examination of scientific publications, together with related materials on economic history and the history of political organization or public policy.

Giovanni Martinelli

Bibliography

Albarello, D., G. Ferrari, G. Martinelli, and M. Mucciarelli. "Well-level Variation as a Possible Seismic Precursor: A Statistical Assessment from Italian Historical Data." *Tectonophysics* 193 (1991): pp. 385–395.

Bakun, W.H. "The Parkfield, California Earthquake Prediction Experiments." In *Prediction of Earthquakes, Occurrence and Ground Motion, Proceedings of the ECE/UN Seminar,* edited by C.S. Oliveira, pp. 681–693. Lisbon, 1990.

Bolt, Bruce A. *Earthquakes and Geological Discovery.* New York: Scientific American, 1993.

Burton, P.W. "Electrical Earthquake

Prediction." *Nature* 315 (1985): pp. 370–371.

Dall'Aglio, M. "Earthquake Prediction by Hydrogeochemical Methods." *Società Italiana di Mineralogia e Petrologia—Rendiconti* 32 (1976): pp. 421–436.

Di Bello, G., V. Lapenna, C. Satriano, and V. Tramutoli, V. "Self Potential Time Series Analysis in a Seismic Area of Southern Italy: First Results." *Annali di Geofisica* 37 (1994): pp. 1137–1148.

Fraser-Smith, A.C., A. Bernardi, P.R. McGill, M.M. Bowen, M.E. Ladd, R.A. Helliwell, and O.G. Villard, Jr. "Low-frequency Magnetic Field Measurements near the Epicenter of the Ms. 7.1 Loma Prieta Earthquake." *Geophysical Research Letters* 17 (1990): pp. 1465–1468.

Geschwind, Carl-Henry. "Earthquakes and Their Interpretation: The Campaign for Seismic Safety in California, 1906–1933." Ph.D. Diss., Johns Hopkins University, 1996.

Jouniaux, L., S. Lallemant, and J.P. Pozzi. "Changes in the Permeability, Streaming Potential and Resistivity of a Claystone from the Nankai Prism under Stress." *Geophysical Research Letters* 21 (1994): pp. 149–152.

Kissin, I.G., W.M. Belikov, G.A. Ishankuliyev, Wang Chengmin, Zhang Wei, Dong Shouyu, Jia Huazhou, and Wan Dikun. "High Amplitude Hydrogeologic Precursors of Earthquakes in Seismic Regions of the Former Soviet Union and China: A Comparative Analysis." *Journal of Earthquake Prediction Research* 2 (1993): pp. 89–103.

Maccioni, Atto. "Nuova scoperta nel campo della sismologia." *Atti della R. Accademia dei Fisiocritici in Siena* 1 (1909): pp. 435–444.

Milne, John. "Earthquakes in Connection with Electric and Magnetic Phenomena." *Transactions of the Seismological Society of Japan* 15 (1890): pp. 135–163.

Roeloffs, E.A. "Hydrologic Precursors to Earthquakes: A Review." *Pure and Applied Geophysics* 126 (1988): pp. 177–209.

Schindler, C., W. Balderer, W. Gerber, and E. Imbach. "The Marmara Poly-Project: Tectonics and Recent Crustal Movements Revealed by Space-geodesy and Their Interaction with the Circulation of Groundwater, Heat Flow and Seismicity in Northwestern Turkey." *Terra Nova* 5 (1993): pp. 164–173.

Shiratoi, K. "The Variation of Radon Activity of Hot Springs." *Sciences Reports of the Tohoku Imperial University* series 3, no. 16 (1927): pp. 614–621.

Sobolev, G.A. "Application of Electric Method to the Tentative Short-term Forecast of Kamchatka Earthquake." *Pure and Applied Geophysics* 113 (1975): pp. 229–235.

Sobolev, G.A., and J.H. Dietrich. "Two Models for Earthquake Forerunners." *Pure and Applied Geophysics* 113 (1975): pp. 169–181.

Wakita, H., Y. Nakamura, and Y. Sano. "Short-term and Intermediate-term Geochemical Precursors." *Pure and Applied Geophysics* 126 (1988): pp. 267–278.

Wan, Dikun. "China's National Seismic Well-Network for Observation of Groundwater Behavior (Water Level and Hydrogeochemistry) and Typical Earthquake Cases." *Journal of Earthquake Prediction Research* 2 (1993): pp. 1–16.

See also Contemporary Use of Historical Data; Earthquakes, Theories from 1600 to 1800; Instruments, Seismic; Jesuits and the Earth

Earthquakes, Theories from Antiquity to 1600

Theories that explained earthquakes on either supernatural or naturalistic grounds.

There was never a clear dividing line in the ancient world between religion and the observation of nature. Naturalistic interpretations of earthquakes are therefore not to be taken as examples of "rational" thought, by contrast with those others that had their origin in the religious mentality which, we must always remember, was a fundamental aspect of all ancient and medieval culture. Despite our unwillingness to consider such beliefs as belonging to the interpretation of nature, we really cannot ignore them. The religious tradition concerning great seismic events in the Mediterranean basin goes back more than three, or even four, millennia: linguistic traces and dialectical substrata can be found in place names, and they are the material of myths and lore gathered and written down much later.

Seismic phenomena were attributed to divinities such as Poseidon or Zeus, or to mythological figures such as the Giants, or even to heroes and "holy men," in a tradition that led right up to the legends of the Christian saints. In ancient Greece, the phrase "the god shook . . ." was used to indicate an earthquake in exactly the same way as was "divine wrath" in Byzantine chronicles.

In archaic times, as discussed by Bruno Helly, the observation and prediction of earthquakes was the province of very holy philosophers, who tried to forecast disasters such as seismic events. The Ionian thinkers of the sixth century B.C.E. were busy carrying out a process of rationalization, and they were also recorded as making responses and predictions about earthquakes. In the sixth and fifth centuries B.C.E., certain earthquakes had already occurred (such as the one at Sparta in 464 B.C.E.) that were to stimulate reflection on seismic phenomena and provide material for the earliest treatises on the subject.

Ancient earthquake theories were much affected by the particular image of the Earth created by natural philosophers. Whatever the school of thought, the cause of the shaking of the Earth was always considered to be an element. It might be water, fire, air (Aristotle worked out a subterranean wind theory), or a combination of elements. The view that the cause lay in the elements sometimes led to explanations involving the aging of the Earth and the collapse of subterranean caverns within it. There were also pluralist theories based on an analogy with the human body. The Aristotelian theory of earthquakes held sway for seventeen hundred years, a record in the history of scientific theories. What hindered the development of new theories in the West was the preponderant influence of theology rather than natural philosophy up to the sixteenth century.

Contrary to common belief, it is characteristic of the ancient world that there were many different interpretations of seismic phenomena, as we can see from the works of Aristotle, Pliny the Elder, and Seneca. Even a brief review of these theories requires a survey of the principal developments in the history of ancient and medieval philosophy.

The earliest theory of the causes of earthquakes was attributed by Seneca (*Naturales Quaestiones*, 6.6.1) to Thales of Miletus (ca. 624–ca. 545 B.C.E.), whom Aristotle (384–322 B.C.E.) identified as the initiator of philosophical enquiry into the principles of nature. According to him, the cause of earthquakes is to be found in the principle (or material cause) of all things, namely water or the humid element, on which the Earth floats like a vast ship. This theory was supported by the observation that new springs gush from the Earth when it is struck by an earthquake—a phenomenon that is again explained by comparison with a ship, which takes in water when it rolls (Seneca, 6.6.2). The importance of Thales is that he abandoned the cosmogonies of the time and was the first thinker to discuss the importance of physical reality as the principle of things.

Unlike Thales, Anaximenes (586–528 B.C.E.) saw the cause of earthquakes as lying not in a first principle of corporeal elements preceding water, but in the original element air. It is the rarefaction and condensation of air, he held, that give rise to all the elements (fire, wind, clouds, water, and so on). He tackled the problem in terms of efficient cause: even if air or water are the prime elements of things, once things in the world have taken their being, they have an autonomous existence. His interpretation was thus different from the others, and he used a strange simile to illustrate how earthquakes occur: the Earth is like an old house in which the lower parts suddenly give way, thereby undermining the upper parts or causing them to collapse (Seneca, 6.10.2). Seneca's image fit what Aristotle told us about Anaximenes: it is the internal workings of the Earth, subject as they are not only to aging but also to a lack or excess of water, that produce shaking at the Earth's surface.

Closely linked to Thales's theory is another mentioned by Seneca, which explains earthquakes as deriving from the spontaneous movement of subterranean waters: rivers on the Earth swell, flood and violently wash away everything they encounter, and the waters that lie in great basins under the Earth behave similarly. Democritus of Abdera (late fifth century B.C.E.), as reported by Aristotle, adopted a similar position. The Earth, he argued, is full of water, and when it receives an excessive extra quantity after torrential rain, it moves. The mass of water that the Earth is no longer able to retain bursts out and so produces earthquakes.

Aristotle and Seneca apparently disagreed about Anaxagoras (499–428 B.C.E.) as well as Democritus. Aristotle attributed to Anaxagoras the theory that earthquakes occur when the ether, which has a natural tendency to rise, is imprisoned in subterranean cavities and cannot escape because the Earth's pores are blocked by rain. Aristotle rejected this explanation in the *Meteorologica* (2.7.365a) as overly simplistic, because it assumes that the Earth is a flat object floating on ether, and especially because it does not explain the particular circumstances (time and place) in which earthquakes mostly occur. As Costantino Marmo ("Aristotle to Seneca," p. 172) points out, Seneca presented Anaxagoras' theory in his *Naturales Quaestiones* (6.9.1) as an attempt to provide a unified explanation of both celestial and subterranean phenomena in terms of the action of fire. However, ether was considered to be a "fiery" substance, and Seneca (6.9.3) also mentioned other natural philosophers who, like Anaxagoras, thought instead that combustion within the Earth causes collapses and hence cracks in the Earth's crust.

This theory and the one involving subterranean water were probably also linked to that which saw the prime cause of earthquakes as the action of subterranean vapors released by water under the Earth. The metaphor used to illustrate this theory was quite original and closely echoed those used in medical treatises: water boiling in a pan on the fire.

A number of largely similar theories explained seismic phenomena in terms of the "force of the air" (pneuma). The natural philosopher Diogenes of Apollonia (fifth century B.C.E.), a pupil of Anaxagoras, first put forward this theory. Aristotle associated it in the *Metaphysica* (1.3.984a) with Anaximenes, whose disciple he was according to Diogenes Laertius (9.9.57), as the proponent of the doctrine that air is the first principle of things. Where he apparently parted company with his master was in making air responsible for earthquakes. Air, he thought, penetrates into the bowels of the Earth through the pores that either appear in its surface naturally or are created by the erosive action of rivers and tides. But when the pores are blocked, the air finds that its exit is barred and it begins to move violently. Since it cannot follow its natural rectilinear movement, it turns upward and shakes the Earth (Seneca, *Naturales Quaestiones,* 6.15.1).

Although Diogenes of Apollonia (or rather Seneca in reporting him, 6.12.1–2) did not clarify the nature of the *spiritus* whose thrust shook the Earth, it seems clear that the prime element in this case clearly was not the air but rather its most natural manifestation, the wind. However, it was Archelaus (fifth–fourth century B.C.E.)—the presumed master of Socrates and pupil of Anaxagoras—who

specified that the wind is responsible for earthquakes. The view of Aristotle was that winds and earthquakes have common elements. In his *Meteorologica* (2.7.365a), he dealt with earthquakes immediately after winds precisely because they have the same kind of cause.

According to Aristotle's *Meteorologica* (2.4), there are two types of exhalation: one is damp and is called vapor, while the other is dry and has no specific name, but is commonly called by the name of a subspecies "smoky exhalation" (2.4.359b). The latter is the origin and natural substance of the wind (2.4.360a), which is therefore more than just air in movement. This dry exhalation, called *pneuma,* is the common factor in earthquakes and winds. Thus when the Earth is warmed by the Sun and its own internal fire, it produces a large quantity of *pneuma,* both internally and externally (see Oeser, passim; Chatelain, passim). When the *pneuma* comes out of the Earth it gives rise to winds; but when it travels downward into the Earth, it collects and so causes earthquakes (2.8.365b). The relationship between the damp and dry exhalations of the Earth also explains the climatic conditions in which, according to Aristotle, earthquakes usually occur: at night and at midday, because of the absence of wind and exhalations; and in spring and autumn, because they are times of heavy rain and drought. In the *De mundo,* which some scholars attribute to Aristotle, four types of earthquake are listed: they may be tilting, shaking, collapsing, or splitting (4.396a).

In their interpretations of earthquakes, Theophrastus (373/370–287 B.C.E.) and his pupil Strato of Lampsacus (328–270/278 B.C.E.) developed certain aspects of Aristotle's theory. Theophrastus added subterranean collapses to *pneuma* as causes of earthquakes, while Strato of Lampsacus brought in the dynamic relationship between *pneuma* and heat and cold, whose continually changing state in the bowels of the Earth was held to account for the movement of the *pneuma* and its action at the Earth's surface (Seneca, *Naturales Quaestiones,* 6.15.2–6). Strato stressed the importance of the Aristotelian view concerning the importance of empirical observation and experimental research. This attitude led him to add new earthquake subtypes, divided according to the accompanying phenomena (the emission of blasts of wind, stones or mud, or subterranean noises), or on the basis of the type and number of shocks ("strike earthquakes" if there is a single shock,

"vibrational earthquakes" if they produce oscillations in opposite directions).

In addition to those we have already
dealt with, there are theories that we can describe as "pluralist." Democritus had thought
that wind and water in subterranean cavities
act similarly. The same dynamics applied to
both fluids (compression, search for a way
out, and outburst), though it was sometimes
the wind that pushed the water (6.20.1–4).

According to Epicurus (341–270 B.C.E.),
an earthquake could be produced by all the
causes mentioned (which can be reduced, in
accordance with the scheme of things set out
in Seneca's work, to the four original elements:
water, earth, fire, and air) and by others as
well. He criticized all those who had done no
more than indicate a single cause (Seneca,
Naturales Quaestiones, 6.20.5), the reason for
his attitude being that the causes of earthquakes belong to a category of objects—those
that are "obscure of their own nature"—which
can be known only by inference or conjecture
based on signs. Marmo has recently argued
("Aristotle to Seneca," p. 176) that we can
read these assertions by Epicurus as an invi-
tation to construct explanatory models via
systematic use of analogy deriving from what
is perceived by the senses. We have to recognize the profound ethical motivation underlying his choice of methodology: the plurality
of explanations for phenomena such as earthquakes, which go beyond all human possibility of direct observation, helps to preserve the
unperturbed tranquillity of mind that is held
to be the ideal state for the man of learning.

The old Stoa (third–second century
B.C.E.) has not left us any specific contributions to the interpretation of earthquakes.
Chrysippus (281/277–208/204 B.C.E.)
thought the world is a living, rational, and
animate being. His general attitude can be
deduced from the later reworking of the
pneuma theory by Posidonius (135–51 B.C.E.),
who belonged to the middle Stoa (Diogenes
Laertius, 7.1.142). The use of the analogy
with the functioning of the human body here
acquired even greater significance. Like
Aristotle, Posidonius suggested a classification
of earthquakes into four types: "undulatory,
catastrophic, whirling, and shaking" (Diogenes Laertius, 7.1.154). Closely connected
to the Stoic view was the theory of vital breath
which, according to Seneca (6.16.1), was "accepted by many writers."

Roman culture inherited a great deal
from the classical Greek world, and it took
over ancient thinking about earthquakes almost without modification. Lucretius (98–54
B.C.E.) in his *De rerum natura (On the Nature
of Things),* Seneca (4 B.C.E.–65 C.E.) in his
Naturales Quaestiones, and Pliny the Elder
(23–79 C.E.) in his *Naturalis historia* are the
principal cultural links through which classical earthquake theories have come down to
us. They did not work out new theories, but
described traditional interpretations, often
placing them beside descriptions of earthquakes and other geodynamic phenomena of
their own day. Seneca's treatise was written
after the famous eruption of Vesuvius in 79
C.E., which buried the cities of Pompeii and
Herculaneum under a 6-meter thick layer of
pumice. The works of these writers acquired
a great reputation and were known and
quoted throughout the Latin Middle Ages.
Pliny in particular provides us with a *summa*
of the whole breadth of ancient learning.

Toward the end of antiquity, the religious
and naturalistic interpretations of earthquakes
tended to come together where empirical
practice and religious ideas met, as in the case
of astrology. Pausanias, an important Greek
writer of the second half of the second century C.E., ignored previous writers of a rationalistic tendency and attributed earthquake
effects entirely to Poseidon, in accordance
with the earliest tradition. Earthquakes became part of that group of disturbing phenomena that led to what has been described
as the late antique "age of anxiety." As far as
natural phenomena are concerned, Christian
culture did not break away from that of the
ancient world. It apparently simply transformed content and expectations, in some
cases doing little more than superimposing
new values on those handed down from the
classical world, accepting and stressing the
importance of earthquakes as signs. As Christianity established itself as the dominant culture, religious thought tended to become
more radical, and discouraged rationalistic
interpretations of seismic activity. In the *Liber
de haeresibus* (Book of heresies), written between 383 and 391 by Philastrius, bishop of
Brescia (he died between 391 and 397), the
belief that earthquakes have a natural origin
is listed as heresy 102 (Migne, p. 12, col.
1216). The coexistence of the religious and
naturalistic theories within the same cultural
context (even when the former lost its rigid
formulation) led to the view that there are two
kinds of earthquake: the natural and the non-
natural. This belief persisted almost into modern times, with direct consequences for the
development of new earthquake theories.

Constantino Marmo discusses theories of earthquakes in the early medieval West. One noteworthy passage on earthquakes was written by that great heir of ancient learning, Isidore of Seville (560–636), one of the earliest and most famous medieval encyclopedists. In his *Etymologiae,* Isidore made only a few brief observations on earthquakes, mentioning the opinions of Sallust, Lucretius, and other authors whom he did not identify. Although these comments were expressed in general terms, one can clearly detect traces of classical explanations of earthquakes. In the *De natura rerum liber,* however, Isidore's attitude was different, since his preference here was for Aristotle's theory. In this second text, the fundamental clash was rather between worldly learning, which provided a causal and rational explanation of seismic and other phenomena, and scriptural learning, which interpreted events on Earth as signs of an otherwise inscrutable divine will. Isidore seemed to be trying to consider the opposed theories of internal collapses and subterranean water movements as corollaries of the theory of trapped winds (46.2, p. 76). Certainly, internal collapses and subterranean water movements could both be conceived as consequences of the movement of winds, which was capable of producing earthquakes by itself. Another aspect of Isidore's—and what was effectively the medieval—view of earthquakes, took its inspiration from the Scriptures, and found its most appropriate allegorical expression in the theory of winds. The wind that blows violently from the bowels of the Earth was a symbol of the spirit of God that will come to judge the world at the end of time. About a century later, the Venerable Bede (ca. 672–735) returned to the subject in his *De natura rerum liber* (Migne, 90, cols. 187–278). In effect he repeated the theory of winds, presenting it in the same form as Isidore, but adding a new element by drawing a parallel between the production of earthquakes and that of thunder and sea floods (tsunami). Despite the immense force of attraction exerted by the earthquake image used in the Revelation of John—the sixth seal before the end of time—medieval Latin thought, at least in its most elevated expression, made a distinction between naturalistic and allegorical thought, thus displaying a rational awareness of the way different means of expression could be used (Marmo, "Isidoro di Siviglia," pp. 326–327). Nevertheless, it was the religious rather than the naturalistic view of the world that increasingly held sway, and for many centuries religious thought dominated the interpretation of all natural phenomena.

Alongside this Christian thought we find Islamic thought, as expressed in the Koran (seventh century). The only occasion when the image of the earthquake appears in the Koran is in the title and opening lines of Sura XCIX, 1, where it is not a forewarning of the end of the world, but a representation of that end itself. Islamic religious thought does not appear to involve a nature-culture polarity, such as one finds becoming codified in the Latin West. In Islamic religious thought, everything is or belongs to or is represented within culture, for everything has a meaning that can be deciphered through the workings of a world made to suit humanity. The Islamic view of the world is substantially anthropocentric, and the concept of a law of nature does not exist, being replaced by a concept of habitualness observed by the elements of nature, in conformity with the progress of a continuing process of creation. The speculations of Islamic philosophy have grappled with this concept, taking as their starting point an atomistic theory of never-ending creation. Creation is uninterrupted and, as observed by man, generates a limitless process of semiosis.

Arab natural philosophy did not invent new interpretative theories about earthquakes, but rather added new empirical observations to support them. In any case, this was the way theoretical progress was made in the Middle Ages, and "inventions"—which were generally improvements to already well known theories—never took the form of revolutions. The observation of earthquakes, and of nature in general, received a new stimulus from the works of Avicenna (Ibn Sina, 980–1037), for whom volcanic and seismic activity were evidence of the existence of winds imprisoned in the bowels of the Earth. Avicenna's translation and commentary on Aristotle's *Meteorologica* became well known at the height of the Latin Middle Ages and exerted an influence on the whole of medieval thought about the Earth in the West. His treatise *De mineralibus* became the basis for later treatises on nature. F.E. Peters discusses these questions in his *Aristotle and the Arabs* (1968).

Averroes (Muhammad ibn Ahmad ibn Muhammad ibn Rushd, 1126–1198) rejected Avicenna's view that the world derives from God, and held that matter is eternal. His argument that it is science and not a mystical relationship that puts man in communion with God was an attack on the all-embracing

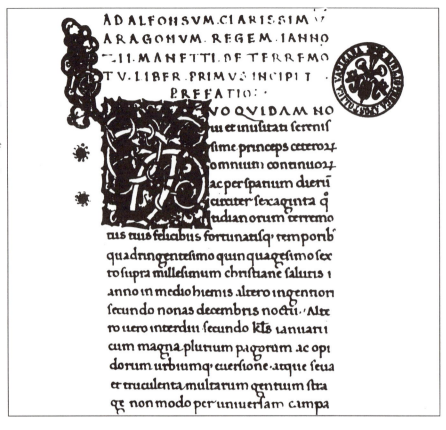

mysticism of al Ghazali. His theories caused him to be condemned and exiled in 1195, and he exerted a profound influence on culture in the Latin West. The Averroists overturned certain arguments of Averroes, going so far as to maintain that there is a separation between the truth of faith and the truth of reason, thus upsetting the primacy of religious thought over naturalistic thought. Bonaventura and Thomas Aquinas later opposed them, for fear that a kind of double truth might become established.

These philosophical diatribes had a direct influence on the development of theories about earthquakes and the nature of the Earth generally. One philosopher who was deeply influenced by Avicenna was Albertus Magnus (1206–1280). His thought was widely known, particularly in the fourteenth and fifteenth centuries, and his treatise *De mineralibus et rebus metallicis* (On minerals and metals, ca. 1260, published in *Physicorum Libri octo* in 1494) is a point of reference for all Western "seismological" thought up to the beginning of the sixteenth century. Albertus Magnus maintained that natural sciences (which he defined as profane) must be cultivated in different ways from those that are

proper to theology, and he also held that research inspired solely by reason is valid. But the many problems raised by the clash between religious interpretations of the world and theoretical models acquired a new and solid philosophical treatment only in the works of Thomas Aquinas (1221–1274). In his interpretation of earthquakes, which formed part of a cosmogony based on Aristotelian geocentrism, Aquinas established a hierarchy of values that nevertheless did not resolve the conflict between religious ideology and a rationalist model in the interpretation of natural phenomena. He saw God as the prime cause and material as a secondary cause.

This conviction that there are two kinds of earthquake, the natural and the prodigious, weaved its way through medieval culture in the West and became explicit in the "seismological" thought of the Italian Renaissance. It was elaborated on by Giannozzo Manetti (1369–1459), a Florentine humanist and politician, in his treatise *De terraemotu libri tres* (Three books on earthquakes, 1457), in which one finds a blend of ancient learning and contemporary theology (figure 1). In the late fifteenth century, Leonardo da Vinci (1452–1519) produced a theory that seemed to look forward to the next stage in research, though he still used the classical language of philosophy. He was probably influenced by his experiments with firearms and mines in suggesting that there exist subterranean fires (the theory had already been put forward in ancient times) that have a complex relationship with masses of water: "the heat at the core of the world is the fire which is spread through the earth and the seat of its vegetative core is the fires which in various parts of the earth breathe in pools and in sulphur mines and in volcanoes" (*Codex Hammer,* 3B, 34v). What he expressed here involves an ancient anthropomorphic view of the Earth.

Experiments in metallurgy and new techniques of warfare, with gunpowder, mines, and bombs (already in occasional use at the end of the fifteenth century) encouraged a new attitude toward seismic phenomena. From the mid-sixteenth century onward, classical theories were undermined by new observations, in which empirical observation and analogical argument took precedence over grand philosophical and theological constructions, as in *De la Pirothecnia,* (Venice, 1540) of Vannuccio Biringuccio (1480–1538/1539), a work on metals, smelting, and related topics.

The first new developments in earthquake theory were worked out by the German scholar Georg Bauer (known by the latinized name Agricola, 1494–1555), who was a pupil of Francesco Vicomercato's in Turin. His critique of Aristotelianism almost constituted a secondary confutation in his *De re metallica* (On metals, published posthumously in 1558) and also appeared in his *De natura fossilium* (1558). It was characteristically terse in expression and based on a new and exclusively "naturalistic" logic. Leaving on one side any philosophical or religious concerns, Agricola rejected the Earth-Sun relationship that had been considered the sole source of the Earth's heat since the time of the earliest philosophers. The view that the Sun directs its heat inside the Earth (which was thought to be a cold body) had already been propounded in Aristotelian theory, to account for the production of subterranean vapor and wind from the clash of heat-dryness with cold-dampness. A single empirical observation allowed Agricola to turn the problem on its head: one only needs to look at furnaces to see that heat does not descend. He worked out a coherent theory based on internal fire as the cause of volcanoes and earthquakes, without any

need to bring in the heat of the Sun. This assertion was sufficient to allow him to refute Aristotelian semiology about signs forecasting earthquakes (related to meteorological states) and to maintain that the occurrence of earthquakes has nothing to do with the seasons or the time of day. From this he deduced that earthquakes cannot be predicted. He did not refer specifically to fire, but rather to inflammable materials; the cause of the combustion was to be found in specific chemical substances: bitumen, nitre, and sulphur. The "fuse" could take the form of compression or overheating of the external air. On a number of occasions he explained seismic phenomena by means of a comparison with mines and the relationship between the mass of gunpowder used and the size of the explosion chamber. He was the first to trace a relationship between "hot" zones in the Earth (thermalism) and earthquake frequency. The great volcanic explosion at Pozzuoli (near Naples) in 1538 and the creation of Mt. Somma played an important part in the history of volcano and earthquake theory. The spread of news of these events throughout Europe was facilitated by the availability of the printed word and the fact that Latin was still the international language of science. Despite the striking novelty of Agricola's treatise, however, his views were considered no more than a curiosity even twenty years after their publication.

In the late sixteenth century, a sort of think tank on the causes of earthquakes was set up at the court of Ferrara, Italy, partly as a result of the strong earthquake of November 1570. A number of rationalizing treatises about that earthquake were published by Jacopo Antonio Buoni (*Del terremoto. Dialogo di Jacopo Antonio Buoni medico ferrarese distinto in quattro giornate,* Modena, 1571), Lucio Maggio (*Del Terremoto Dialogo del Signor Lucio Maggio gentil'homo bolognese,* Bologna, 1571), Alessandro Sardo (*Discorso del Terremoto,* 1587), and others, bringing to a close a period of crisis and opposition to Aristotelianism that is typical of the scientific unrest of Renaissance times (figure 2).

Toward 1600, earthquake interpretive models therefore appeared between new scientific perspectives and old prejudices. Kepler's interpretation is typical of this situation. His *Harmonice mundi* (1619)—an eclectic blend of the theories of Agricola and Aristotle—was modified by reference to Tycho Brahe's new astronomical theories about comets. Kepler's conception of the

Figure 2. Detail of the Libro or Trattato di diversi terremoti (1570–1574), a manuscript by Pirro Ligorio (Archivio di Stato di Torino, Antichità Romane, vol. 28, f. 61). It is the first known Western plan of an antiseismic building. The famous architect based this design on a keen analysis of seismic effects observed on buildings in Ferrara in 1570.

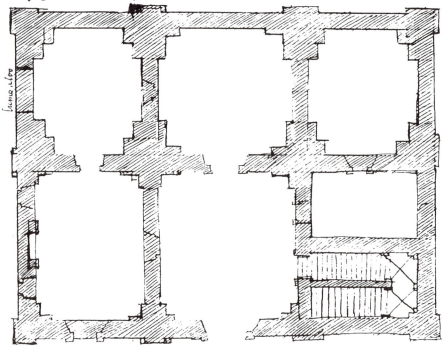

Earth was of an ancient anthropomorphic kind, and he interpreted earthquakes as a "panic" reaction of the Earth to the approach of a comet. He saw comets, however, not as meteoric bodies forming part of the atmosphere, as had Aristotle, but as celestial bodies. The link between comets and earthquakes had been upheld by a number of Aristotelian writers in the late Middle Ages and Renaissance, and was still in fashion. The view was held that since comets were atmospheric meteors of a hot-dry type, they could set off earthquakes when they approached a cold-wet body such as the Earth. It was hence commonly believed that comets are precursors of earthquakes and can warn of their occurrence. Kepler took the partly different view that while comets are the primary "cause" of earthquakes, the earthquake phenomenon itself occurs "within" the Earth.

Emanuela Guidoboni

Bibliography

Boschi, Enzo, Graziano Ferrari, Paolo Gasperini, Emanuela Guidoboni, Giuseppe Smriglio, and Gianluca Valensise. *Catalogo dei forti terremoti in Italia dal 461 a.C. al. 1980.* Rome: Istituto Nazionale di Geofisica, SGA, 1995.

Chatelain, Louis. "Théories d'auteurs anciens sur les tremblements de terre." *Mélanges d'archéologie et d'histoire* 29 (1909): pp. 87–101.

Guidoboni, Emanuela, Alberto Comastri, and Giusto Traina. *Catalogue of Ancient Earthquakes in the Mediterranean Area up to the 10th Century.* Rome: Istituto Nazionale di Geofisica, SGA, 1994.

Helly, Bruno. "Observations et théorie sur les séismes dans les sources historiques grecques." In *Tremblements de terre, Histoire et Archéologie,* edited by Bruno Helly and Alex Pollino, pp. 63–71. Antibes: Association pour la promotion et la diffusion des connaissances archéologiques, 1984.

Isidore of Seville [Isidorus Hispalenses]. *De natura rerum liber.* Edited by Gustavus Becker. Amsterdam: A.M. Hakkert, 1967.

Isidorus Hispalenses. *Etymologiarum sive originum libri XX.* [Scriptorum Classicorum Bibliotheca Oxoniensis]. 2 vols. Edited by W.M. Linsday. Oxford: Oxford University Press, 1985.

Leonardo da Vinci. *Il Codice Hammer e la Mappa di Imola presentati da Carlo Pedretti.* Florence: Giunti Barbèra, 1985.

Marmo, Costantino. "Le teorie del terremoto da Aristotele a Seneca." In *I terremoti prima del Mille in Italia e nell'area mediterranea,* edited by Emanuela Guidoboni, Istituto Nazionale di Geofisica, pp. 170–181. Bologna: SGA, 1989.

———. "La teoria del terremoto da Isidoro di Siviglia alla rinascita carolingia." In *I terremoti prima del Mille in Italia e nell'area mediterranea,* edited by Emanuela Guidoboni, Istituto Nazionale di Geofisica, pp. 323–335. Bologna: SGA, 1989.

Migne, J.-P. *Patrologia Latina.* Paris: Apud editorem, 1845, 1850.

Oeser, Erhard. "Historical Earthquake Theories from Aristotle to Kant." In *Historical Earthquakes in Central Europe,* edited by Rudolf Gutdeutsch, Gottfried Grünthal, and Roger Musson, pp. 11-31. Vienna: Abhandlungen der Geologischen Bundesanstalt, 1992.

Peters, F.E. *Aristotle and the Arabs. The Aristotelian Tradition in Islam.* New York and London, 1968.

See also Cosmology and the Earth; Earthquakes; Meteorological Ideas in Folklore and Mythology; Meteorological Ideas in Classical Greece and Rome; Seismology

Earthquakes, Theories from 1600 to 1800

A transitional period in ideas about earthquakes.

The seventeenth century was very important in the history of earthquake theories; mechanistic interpretations of natural events became established, covering everything from the origin of the solar system to the structure of the Earth. This was a striking innovation, and marks a fundamental change in thinking about terrestrial phenomena; but an attempt was also made in the seventeenth century to harmonize religious and providential thinking with mechanistic philosophy. Science had not yet become separated from philosophy, and earthquake theories still formed part of philosophers' cosmologies.

Theories about the causes of earthquakes were to be found as part of those major scientific and philosophical questions that are characteristic of seventeenth-century thought: the origin and age of the Earth, the Flood, and the interpretation of fossils. New geological discoveries, especially in sedimentology and petrography, drew attention to matters that aroused anxiety in the religious and biblical consciousness of the time, and that became separated from science only after mid-century.

The publication of the great *Principia philosophiae* of René Descartes (1596–1650) at Paris in 1644 opened the period of mechanistic interpretations of the Earth. According to Descartes, every phenomenon, from the creation of the world to its extinction, is to be explained as the effect of the motion of the "elements" of which all matter was made. His conception of the Earth as a luminous star that had become a cold planet involved the presence of a central fire with various other fires. The unevenness of the Earth's crust was explained as deriving from landslides and internal splits that had occurred during the process of cooling. In paragraphs 76, 77, and 78 of Part IV of his *Principia,* Descartes set out how earthquakes are generated: exhalations from within the Earth combine in various ways to form sulphur, bitumen, oil, and clay, the particular combination depending on whether the motion of the particles involved is fast or slow. When these exhalations become lodged in the cracks and cavities of the Earth's uneven surface, they form "dense and thick fumes, similar to those which are given off by a recently extinguished candle." Descartes held that just as a candle is rekindled when another candle flame is placed close to it, so "when any spark of fire is struck in these cavities, all the fumes are immediately ignited," bursting into flame and exerting violent pressure against the sides of the cavity. This explosion causes an earthquake at the surface, its degree of violence depending on the quantity of inflammable exhalations and the extent of the unevenness of the Earth's surface.

A few years before Descartes's work, Athanasius Kircher (1602–1680), a German Jesuit, witnessed the violent earthquake that struck Calabria in March 1638. What he saw and reported in his treatise *Mundus subter-*

raneus (Amsterdam, 1665) seemed to him to support the theory that earthquakes have a fiery cause and are related to volcanic activity. He had witnessed the first violent tremors from a boat, and had watched the sea "boiling"—a phenomenon he thought to be indicative of the release of heat from nearby volcanic complexes, which he claimed to have seen erupting during the first shocks. Kircher maintained that there is a great fire at the center of the Earth that is connected to smaller fires through a complex network of underground channels and tunnels, and he published an intriguing representation of these. This *Systema ideale pyrophilactorum subterraneorum,* as he called it, accounted for earthquakes and volcanoes within a single, unitary model, which used earlier theories about inflammable materials (figure 1).

The concept of nature as a combination of material and motion governed only by laws tended to be accepted by philosophers and criticized by naturalists, and it had difficulty in gaining overall acceptance. Many seventeenth-century geologists agreed with Descartes's hypothesis about the structure and strata of the Earth but rejected his naturalist philosophy and attempted to find confirma-

Figure 1. Athanasius Kircher's 1665 "Philosopher's Model" of the fiery system of the Earth, which explained seismicity and volcanic activity. From Mundus subterraneus *Amsterdam, 1665.*

tion of their views in the Bible. Among these writers were Thomas Burnet (*Sacred Theory of the Earth,* London, 1684), John Ray (*The Wisdom of God,* London, 1691), John Woodward (*An Essay Toward a Natural History of the Earth,* London, 1695), and William Whiston (*A New Theory of the Earth,* London, 1696).

In 1683, six years before the publication of Burnet's sacred theory of the Earth, Martin Lister (1638–1712) had published in the *Philosophical Transactions* of the Royal Society of London a theory that earthquakes are caused by the decomposition of pyrites. This chemical theory of earthquakes was destined to enjoy great success, and it provided a number of ideas for Woodward, who thought that sulphur and nitre are the cause of volcanic eruptions. What happened in this view was that subterranean fire controls the entire flow of terrestrial waters. This flow might be disturbed by an "obstruction," leading to abnormal pressure at some point in the waters contained within the Earth's internal abyss. The obstruction concerned could press against and split open the surface, thereby causing an earthquake. According to Woodward, that could also explain the frequent occurrence of observable hydrogeological disturbances at the Earth's surface during earthquakes.

The creationists, who upheld the sacred theory of earthquakes, thought that earthquakes are not primary dynamic elements to be understood as forming part of a general model; with the exception of Whiston, they did not work out any original contribution to earthquake theories. According to Erhard Oeser (p. 25), Whiston supposed that the Flood was caused by a comet plunging into the bowels of the Earth, and imagined the Earth coming to an end in a great earthquake, also caused by a comet.

Alongside these philosophical disquisitions, there were also minor contributions of a less theoretical and more empirical kind, which nevertheless made an important contribution to the success of the naturalistic interpretation of earthquakes by helping to consolidate the process of rationalization. After the Ragusa earthquake of 1667, for example, the Italian physicist Francesco Travagini published his *Super observationibus a se factis ultimorum terraemotorum ac potissumum Ragusani, Physica disquisitio seu gyri terrae diurni indicium* (Venice, 1673). In this work Travagini applied certain experimental methods to the question of the direction of the earthquake, and used the way

building materials were thrown about and suspended bodies moved, to help him understand the effects of earthquakes on buildings (figure 2).

The theory of the explosion of inflammable substances in contact with fire in the center of the Earth predominated in the late seventeenth and early eighteenth centuries, even though it found its place in different cosmological systems. Lazzaro Moro (1687–1764) and Antonio Vallisneri (1661–1730) both upheld the theory of continuous strata in the Earth, and used the fire theory to explain geodynamic phenomena. Moro thought that effective proof of this theory was provided by the sudden "appearance" of a new island in the Aegean, near Santorini, on March 23, 1707. On the basis of Newton's axiom that *effectuum naturalium eiusdem generis eadem sunt causae* (natural effects of a single kind have the same causes), he asserted that all islands and mountains are of fiery and volcanic origin. Earthquakes, therefore, were another manifestation of the same dynamics. Bernhard Varen (Varenius, 1622–ca. 1650), who wrote a treatise entitled *Geographia generalis* (Naples and Leyden, 1715), was another supporter of the fire theory, maintaining that earthquakes were caused by the combustion of sulphurous and bituminous substances. The fire theory was adopted by many physicists and naturalists with certain variations, often within a system in which God was the prime mover of all phenomena.

While some based their ideas on recent theories and experiments, there were also writers of culture and reputation whose ideas were expressed in terms of a widely diffused culture based on ancient classical thought—particularly that of Aristotle and Seneca. An example is Giorgio Baglivi (1668–ca. 1707), who provided a worthwhile description of the great earthquake that struck central Italy in 1703. Since, however, he was an anatomist with an anthropomorphic conception of the Earth, he indulged in a profusion of medical comparisons to account for the endless sequence of shocks during that period of seismic activity. The fact that his work was very successful is evidence that no single earthquake theory was generally accepted: there coexisted a variety of different interpretations, based on different epistemological systems.

Descartes's theory was a basic point of reference for the rationalists, and it was used in the cosmology of Gottfried Wilhelm Leibniz (1646–1716) in an attempt to reconcile mechanistic and creationist theories.

Figure 2. Drawings from a 1673 work by Franciscus Travagini, in which he inquired into the transmission of seismic motion on the Earth's surface and into the pendular movements of buildings in relation to the distance of major effects. His observations have never been used.

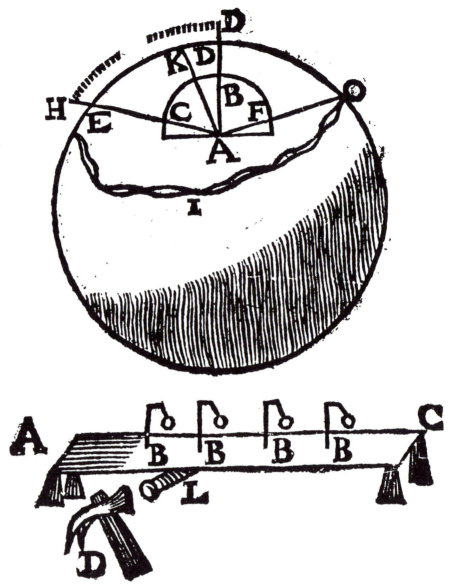

His *Protogaea sive de prima face telluris* was published posthumously in 1749, but had been completed by 1690. He accepted the idea of central fire, but did not exclude the possibility that water might be a cause of major transformations in the Earth's crust.

When Georges Louis Leclerc de Buffon (1707–1788) published his first work, *Histoire et théorie de la Terre,* in Paris in 1749—more than a century after the publication of Descartes's *Principia*—the compromise between Genesis and the natural sciences was brought to an end, though not without certain ambiguities remaining. At this early stage, Buffon upheld the theory that earthquakes are caused by the explosion of flammable materials set off by the fire at the center of the Earth. Later, in 1780, however, he redefined his position within the great dispute between Neptunists, Vulcanists, and Plutonists, and underlined the importance of water as a factor in transformations of the Earth and as a cause of earthquakes.

In the mid-eighteenth century, a new stage in the development of earthquake theory began, as a result of experiments in electricity and terrestrial magnetism. The discovery by Benjamin Franklin in 1750 that atmospheric electricity is exactly the same as that obtained using a Leyden jar opened up new theoretical possibilities. A consideration of the causes of earthquakes was also stimulated by the occurrence of a close sequence of seismic events. There was an earthquake at Callao and Lima in Peru in 1746 (a summary report was published by Franklin and Hall in 1749), and then two occurred in England in 1749 and 1750, disconcerting the English, because it was commonly believed that the British Isles were more or less aseismic. An earthquake at Perugia in central Italy in 1751 provided an occasion for further observations. And a few years later, in 1755, came the great earthquake catastrophe that destroyed Lisbon. About thirty years later still, in 1783, Calabria was reduced to a heap of rubble by as many as five disastrous earthquakes within the space of a few weeks. Thus, within a few decades, seismological thought was placed with its back to the wall, so to speak, and it underwent rapid theoretical changes of both a scientific and philosophical nature.

The intensification of theoretical study is illustrated by the chronology of publications on the subject. In 1750, William Stukeley (1687–1765) published *The Philosophy of Earthquakes, Natural and Religious,* in which he expressed the opinion that earthquakes were caused by an electrical discharge between the Earth and the atmosphere and that seismic motion was due to the interference of vibrations similar "to that of an instrument string or a glass when the edge is rubbed with a finger." Stukeley suggested that vibratory motion could lead to the vibration of a substantial mass, which would be capable of producing considerable mechanical effects. He used Lister's chemical theory of earthquakes (1683) to account for the explosion.

A year later, in 1751, a monk named Andrea Bina (1724–1792) from the monastery at Montecassino published his *Ragionamento sopra la cagione de' terremoti* at Perugia (it was republished in 1757 with additional material on the Lisbon earthquake). He supported the view that earthquakes are caused by electricity, and refuted earlier theories. Like most supporters of the electrical theory at that time, Bina tried to show that "everything" was electricity. He maintained that the shock felt by a human being from a Leyden jar discharge was exactly the same as an earthquake shock; and he also maintained that the "electrical fluid" in the bowels of the Earth was excited by the explosion of combustible materials existing beneath the surface, and that this caused violent shaking of the Earth's crust.

The electrical theory was also supported by important scientists who studied electricity quite independently of earthquakes. Some of them could not resist the temptation to extend the scope of their considerations to that field. Giovanni Battista Beccaria (1716–1781) wrote the first rigorous treatise in Europe on electricity. He was made a fellow of the Royal Society in 1755, had corresponded with Benjamin Franklin, and was an authority on electrical experiments. In his *Dell'elettricismo artificiale e naturale, libri due,* 1753, Beccaria expressed quite different opinions from those of Stukeley, maintaining that the interior of the Earth is soaked in "electrical vapor," which is in some way a source of atmospheric electricity. Like Benjamin Franklin, Beccaria thought that this electricity is seeking a state of equilibrium: if the imbalance, as he called it, occurs in the atmosphere, the result is lightning, whereas within the Earth it causes earthquakes. Beccaria thought of electricity as a kind of "elastic vapor," capable of massive expansion and of transmitting energy at high speed. More than twenty years later, however, he retracted that interpretation, after becoming acquainted with the observations and records made by the Bolognese physicist Alfonso Malvezzi Bonfiglioli in connection with the Bologna earthquakes of 1779–1780.

Apart from the fire and electricity theories (with all their variations), there was also a third theory, based on the view that the cause of earthquakes might be compressed air, especially if it is hot. In 1703, Amonton published a dissertation in the *Mémoires de l'Académie des Sciences* suggesting that the cause of earthquakes is air at high pressure and temperature trapped under the Earth's surface. This idea of sudden thrust may have been connected in some way to contemporary experiments with compressed air rifles. In the 1752 *Philosophical Transactions,* Stephen Hales (1677–1761) used recent experiments on the velocity and elasticity of air to support his suggestion that air pressure is capable of producing the thrust that then causes an earthquake. This coexistence of a variety of interpretations, experiments, and theories about the causes of earthquakes typified the whole eighteenth century.

In these same years, the great *Encyclopédie* of Diderot and D'Alembert (1755)—one of the most important repositories of contemporary learning—offered an earthquake theory within a complex and somewhat eclectic vision involving the combined action of fire, air, and water. The presence of inflammable materials (bitumen, sulphur, alum, and pyrites), together with a central fire, could give rise to great conflagrations when in contact with air. If the heat then came into contact with subterranean water, a large quantity of steam would be produced: it would be like an immense furnace, in which water could stimulate the fire and hence produce steam again. And if the steam were under pressure in tunnels, it could lead to explosions similar to those caused by mines. Mention was made not only of the experiment carried out by Nicolas Lemery (1645–1715), who succeeded in reproducing "seismic explosions" by mixing sulphur and iron filings, but also of the criticisms of M. Rouelle, a chemist who claimed that the experiment was not valid because iron is not found in a pure state in nature.

An Italian *Ciclopedia,* published in Naples in 1754, propounded the fire theory, but added a curious paragraph entitled "Artificial earthquakes," in which the reader was offered an earthquake recipe: the homemade explosive (20 pounds of iron filings and 20 of sulphur, with water) buried 3 or 4 feet deep in the Earth, would produce a spectacular explosion after 6 or 7 hours.

The great earthquake at Lisbon in 1755 had a very disturbing effect on European culture at the time, and immediately afterward the scientific debate was seen to reach new conclusions.

The German philosopher Immanuel Kant (1724–1804) wrote three studies on the interpretation of earthquakes in 1756, namely *Von der Ursachen der Erdeschütterungen, Geschichte und Naturbeschreibun,* and *Forgesetze Betractung.* Kant followed Buffon's geology, was a Newtonian, and believed in the fire theory. He did not work out a new theory on the origin of earthquakes, but concentrated his attention on a few key ideas that were basic to rationalist thought. These concerned: (1) the propagation of seismic effects over long distances; (2) the immediate cause of earthquake shocks; and (3) the temporal behavior of large seismic periods. In connection with (1), Kant maintained that there are subterranean channels and tunnels that run parallel to mountain chains and the course of great rivers (he thought that the principal propagation direction in Italy is north-south, whereas he believed that in Portugal it is east-west). As regards (2), he accepted the chemical explanation, in accordance with the experimental chemistry of his day. He thought the seismic "explosive mixture" to consist of two parts vitriol oil, eight parts water, and two parts iron. According to Oeser (p. 28), Kant accepted the mechanical hydro-

dynamic experiments of Carré, and maintained "that even water can react like a solid body when suddenly compressed. Thus it can transmit shocks almost without softening them." As regards (3), he thought that earthquakes result from hot air compressed within subterranean cavities under high mountains. He thought that both the intervals between shocks and their recurrence are determined by a "chemical respiratory process" that also governs the emission of this hot air from the mouths of volcanoes. Kant considered electricity to be a marginal curiosity, and declared that too little was known about magnetism to permit theorizing.

A year later, in 1757, Elie Bertrand, a Swiss geologist and a pastor at Berne, published a little book entitled *Mémoires historiques et physiques sur les tremblements de terre.* The work included a catalog of historical earthquakes felt in Switzerland from the sixth century to his own day, together with his own earthquake theory (derived from Buffon and Stukeley) and, in particular, certain doubts and observations. He expressed his conviction that many aspects of earthquakes could still not be explained, such as the high speed at which seismic effects are propagated and the enormously large areas that can be involved (he had observed the effects of the Lisbon earthquake in Switzerland). Bertrand's doubts and detailed observations were important to John Michell (1724–1793), as he himself pointed out. Michell was a fellow of Queens' College, Cambridge, and published his "Conjectures concerning the Cause and Observations upon the Phaenomena of Earthquakes" in the 1761 *Philosophical Transactions.* This article left a deep impression. Michell drew attention to the similarities between seismic and volcanic phenomena, deducing from this that they have a common origin. His theory subsequently became known as Vulcanism. He made a detailed study of the direction, force, and amplitude of ground movements, as well as their propagation time, and he was the first to apply wave theory in this field. By applying this method, he was able to establish that the earthquake's source was 10 to 15 leagues out to sea between the latitudes of Lisbon and Oporto. He tried to show that the motive source of seismic vibrations, as well as of volcanic eruptions, is water vapor, produced by contact with incandescent earth-masses. There can be no doubt about the modernity of his approach, as Charles Davison points out in *The Founders of Seismology* (pp. 18–24), but his contemporaries were often still accustomed to metaphysi-

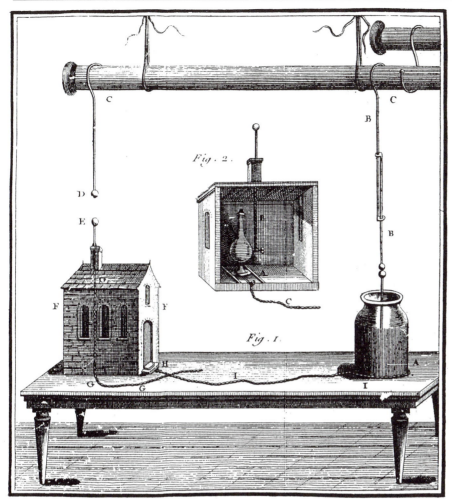

Figure 3. Design of the demonstrative table planned by F. Bertholon in 1787 to demonstrate the electrical origin of earthquakes. The device triggered an electrical discharge, which caused the paper houses to burn out; it met with remarkable success. From De l'éléctricité des météors. Lyon, 1787.

cal and deductive reasoning, and they had difficulty in understanding him.

The great fire theory was now in decline. After the Lisbon earthquake, scientific argument produced, alongside the volcanic theory, a radical version of the electrical theory, with numerous experiments to illustrate it. At this time the famous Joseph Priestley (1733–1804) also accepted the electrical theory. Then a young man, he carried out various laboratory experiments in support of electricity as the cause of earthquakes, which he reported in *The History and Present State of Electricity* (1766). Tiberio Cavallo (1749–1809) also supported the electrical theory. He was a prominent member of the Royal Society, and published *A Complete Treatise on Electricity in Theory and Practice, with Original Experiments* in London in 1777. But the most vigorous, indeed almost fanatical, proponent of the electrical theory of earthquakes was Pierre Bertholon (1741–1800), a priest at the Ora-

tory of St. Lazare in Paris. In his *De l'éléctricité des météores* (Lyon, 1787), he supported this theory with some "experiments" that aroused great curiosity because they were thought to reproduce the real dynamics of earthquakes on a small scale. He placed some cardboard houses, resting against a small pile of paper and wood shavings, on an electrical square, and then set off an electrical discharge, which produced a jolt and usually set fire to the objects on the square (figure 3). He also designed some "earthquake protectors" in 1779 as a defense against seismic shocks. This "protection" involved inserting into the earth at places where earthquakes were frequent long iron bars with divergent points called *verticilli* at their ends. The points at the lower end were intended to absorb the "electric fire," while those at the top were to disperse it. It was in effect a kind of inverted lightning arrester.

The question of protection against earthquakes was also dealt with by Giuseppe

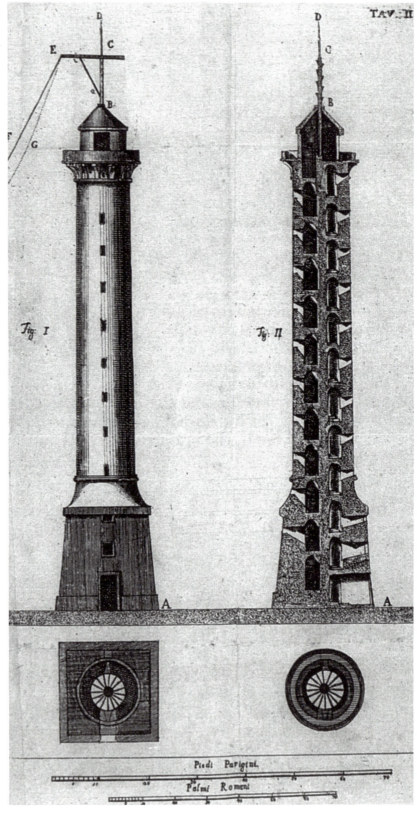

Figure 4. Earthquake-guard towers planned by Roman architect Giuseppe Valadier in 1787 to protect Rimini against future earthquakes. Based on Bertholon's theories, they were conceived as overturned lightning arresters. They were never built. From A. Comastri, p. 163.

Vannucci, another minor proponent of the electrical theory. In 1787, he suggested building two antiearthquake towers, which were subsequently designed and drawn by the papal architect Giuseppe Valadier, who was then very young and unknown (figure 4). These towers were to be placed along the Adriatic coast to protect Rimini from future earthquakes (Comastri, p. 163).

According to Timoteo Bertelli (p. 489), both Luigi Galvani (1737–1798) and Alessandro Volta (1745–1827) opposed the electrical theory. According to Dennis R. Dean (pp. 481–495), Benjamin Franklin (1706–1790) was another scientist who made no specific contribution to this area and avoided direct debate with electricity supporters, though they all used him as an important point of reference.

Reactions within European culture to the Lisbon earthquake had stimulated an enormous theoretical debate. The great earthquakes of 1783 in Calabria, on the other hand, tended rather to lead to new scientific observations. For many years, there was a strange and almost endless succession of publications in which famous and not so famous authors compared facts and opinions, serious theories and more modest interpretations. Three schools of thought emerged, and they represent the stage reached by earthquake theories in the late eighteenth century. These schools were composed of (1) the supporters of the fire theory—a minority who had points of contact with the Vulcanists; (2) the pure Vulcanists and those who had points of contact with the supporters of the electrical theory; and (3) the supporters of the pure electrical theory and those who had points of contact with the supporters of fire or with Vulcanists.

According to Augusto Placanica (pp. 75–76), one of the supporters of the fire theory who deserves to be remembered for the originality of his ideas is Benvenuto Aquila (1784). In his vision, when the seismic shock is released from the central fire in the Earth, there is an immense movement of rock masses toward each other, leading to the breakdown of their static equilibrium. Among the most important of the Vulcanists were William Hamilton (1730–1803) and Déodat G.S. Dolomieu (1750–1801). The latter worked out some interesting ideas on the relationship between seismic effects and the nature of the ground. One of a group of well-known supporters of the electrical theory was Giovanni Vivenzio, a physicist at the court of Naples, who wrote a very detailed description of the effects and sequence of the thousands of aftershocks at the time of the Calabria earthquakes. He published *Istoria e teoria de' tremuoti in generale ed in particolare di quelli della Calabria e Messina del 1783* (1783). As evidence of the validity of the electrical theory, he had Bertholon's experiment with cardboard houses carried out in the presence of the queen of Naples in 1785. The "great and marvelous" device prepared by Vivenzio was supposed to convince everyone of the correctness of the electrical theory. He also designed an antiseismic cottage—a sort of hut made with a wooden truss—wood being known as a poor conductor of "electrical fluid" (one of these constructions survived the 1908 Messina earthquake) (figure 5). Among the well-known supporters of the electrical theory at that time was Andrea Gallo, who kept a "meteorological diary" at the time of the Calabria earthquakes. And then there was Cristofano Sarti, a professor at the University

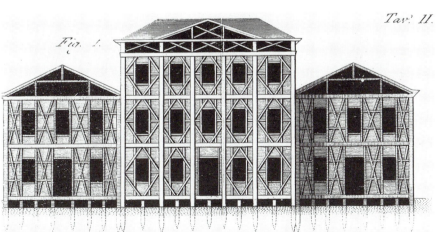

Figure 5. The casa baraccata *was an application of the theory of electricism: wood, as a poor conductor, should have insulated the building from electro-seismic discharges. Some of these small houses were built in Calabria after the 1783 earthquakes. From G. Vivenzio, table 2, p. 59.*

of Pisa, who compared the movement of houses to that of a pendulum and wrote a number of suggestions for constructing anti-seismic buildings in his *Saggio di congetture su i terremoti* (Lucca presso Francesco Bonsignori, 1783).

An important new contribution was made by the scientists of the *Reale Accademia delle Scienze e Belle Lettere* in Naples, led by Michele Sarconi. The originality of their work lay in their making detailed records of earthquake damage to buildings (150 villages were visited) and earth surfaces, and illustrating their findings with seventy plates, in *Istoria de' fenomeni del tremoto avvenuto nelle Calabrie, e nel Valdemone nell'anno 1783* (1784). A highly skilled cartographer, Father Eliseo della Concezione, accompanied the expedition and drew a large map of the earthquake's effects, adopting a simple and effective 4° scale. Data collected in the field were particularly important, and are currently being analyzed by historical seismologists. The central point around which general discussion circulated was "the conservation of the principle of continuity" in nature—a subject that preoccupied natural philosophers almost to obsession. It had to be shown that a continuous cause (fire or water) was producing a discontinuous effect (an earthquake). Electricity, however, seemed to lend itself to a discontinuous cause theory, and that may be one of the reasons why it appealed so much. The ideas of natural philosophers and naturalists seemed to have become locked in attempts to solve this problem.

From an epistemological perspective, deductive logic was still the main procedure adopted, using analogical axioms and procedures. By comparison with other contemporary scientific disciplines—especially chemistry, but also late eighteenth-century geology—seismological thought still seemed to be floundering in metaphysical questions in those years, as well as under the spell of cosmological ideas, with the result that it was prevented from developing an "experimental" dimension. Nevertheless, as the eighteenth century came to a close, naturalistic thought as applied to the interpretation of earthquakes had on the whole been consolidated and freed from religious pressure.

The electrical earthquake theory continued to exist into the late nineteenth century, and was definitively confuted by Timoteo Bertelli only in 1887; but the volcanic theory enjoyed a great deal of success in the nineteenth century. Earthquake theory was now firmly established in geological thought and physical conceptions of the Earth.

Emanuela Guidoboni

Bibliography

Bertelli, Timoteo. "Di alcune teorie e ricerche elettro-sismiche antiche e moderne." *Bollettino di bibliografia e di storia delle Scienze matematiche e fisiche* 20 (1887): pp. 481–542.

Comastri, Alberto. "Un terremoto in cerca di spiegazione: la teoria elettricista di Giuseppe Vannucci." In *Il terremoto di Rimini e della costa romagnola: 25 dicembre 1786,* edited by E. Guidoboni and G. Ferrari, pp. 157–165. Bologna: Storia Geofisica Ambiente, 1986.

Davison, Charles. *The Founders of Seismology.* Cambridge: Cambridge University Press, 1927.

Dean, Dennis R. "Benjamin Franklin and Earthquakes." *Annals of Science* 46 (1989): pp. 481–495.

Oeser, Erhard. "Historical Earthquake Theories from Aristotle to Kant." In *Historical Earthquakes in Central Europe,* edited by Rudolf Gutdeutsch, Gottfried Grünthal, and Roger Musson, pp. 11–31. Vienna: Abhandlungen der Geologischen Bundesanstalt, 1992.

Placanica, Augusto. *Il filosofo e la catastrofe.* Milan: Einaudi, 1985.

Tobriner, Stephen. "La Casa Baraccata: Earthquake-resistant Construction in 18th Century Calabria." *Journal of the Society of Architectural Historians* 42, no. 2 (1983): pp. 131–138.

Vivenzio, Giovanni. *Istoria e teoria de' tremuoti in generale ed in particolare di quelli della Calabria, e di Messina del 1783.* Naples: Nella Stamperia regale, 1784, 1993.

Woodward, J. *Essay Toward a Natural History of the Earth.* In *Geografia fisica,* edited by J. Woodward. Venice: Giambattista Pasquali, 1739.

See also Actualism, Uniformitarianism, and Catastrophism; Earthquakes; Geodesy; Geology; Gravimetry; Historiography, Eighteenth-Century England; Instruments, Seismic; Plutonists, Neptunists, Vulcanists; Seismology; Volcanoes, Theories before 1800

Earthquakes, Theories since 1800

A period of transition in the explanation of earthquakes.

Research into the physical causes of earthquakes began to assume its modern form around 1800. By the late eighteenth century, a relative consensus had been reached among those interested in geology that earthquakes are the result of natural forces being unleashed within the ground, rather than acts of God. With the rise of new and more rigorously researched geological theories during the early part of the nineteenth century came the desire to develop more sophisticated understanding of seismic processes.

There have been two schools of historiographic interpretation regarding the development of the modern theories of earthquakes. Members of the first school, composed in general of those who come to the history of seismology from within geology, are usually not concerned with theories that have subsequently been shown to have little merit. Thus, seismologist Benjamin F. Howell, Jr., opens his history of the field with a very brief examination of the reputedly mythological age of earthquake explanation, which he contends lasted until the early twentieth century (pp. 5–6). Using only visual observation and without the aid of sensitive seismographs, he argues, earthquake researchers prior to 1900 had little means to explore the phenomena of earthquakes. For Howell, seismology did not exist until scientists developed modern equipment and began to record and analyze seismic activity in an objective manner.

The second school, composed of historically minded seismologists and more recently of historians of science, takes a greater interest in early theories of earthquakes. Authors in this camp seek to explore the development of theories of earthquakes within specific historical milieus, and to relate these views to the changing intellectual contexts as well as to new empirical observations and theoretical advances. Studies in this school tend to explore the development of seismic theories in richer detail, and without regard to the accuracies of the theories themselves. Bruce Bolt, for example, opens his popular account of the field of seismology with an entire chapter devoted to tracing the development of the study of earthquakes from the earliest times to the present (Bolt, pp. 1–23).

Similarly, Charles Davison's classic work on the rise of the discipline of seismology provides a rich historical account of seismic theories from the period of the Enlightenment onwards. Davison sees the modern study of earthquakes commencing with the work of John Michell in the late eighteenth century.

Michell's work was reviewed in the 1818 edition of the *Edinburgh Review,* reflecting the fact that his work was still considered the definitive study of earthquakes into the early nineteenth century. Michell argued that earthquakes are the result of the release of large quantities of gases beneath the Earth's surface, the same phenomenon (he wrote) that also gives rise to volcanic activity. Michell argued that these gases push on the surface from below and cause the wavelike deformations of the crust associated with earthquakes.

So Michell had established general foundations of seismic theory late in the eighteenth century. In the early nineteenth century, however, the occurrence of a series of large earthquakes helped to pave the way for more detailed studies of seismic phenomena. The first of these took place in the vicinity of Valparaiso, Chile, in 1822. Several accounts of this quake were recorded, including one that was transmitted to the Geological Society of London by Maria Graham in 1824. According to Davison, Graham's account represents a detailed and thoroughly considered set of observations of the effects of the Chilean quake. Davison, for example, notes her observations of the swelling of rivers and lakes that followed the temblor, as well as the effect of soil condition on the structural damages of various buildings (pp. 34–35).

A second great quake in this region occurred in February 1835, at the time that the H.M.S. *Beagle* and its renowned naturalist, Charles Darwin, were in the area. Both Darwin and the *Beagle*'s captain, Robert FitzRoy, recorded their observations of the after-effects of the quake. They noted in particular the large uplift on the island of Santa Maria, where between 8 and 10 feet of seabed became exposed after the quake (Davison, p. 37).

These new observations of the effects of earthquakes helped to push forward theories regarding their origin. In developing his comprehensive treatise on the *Principles of Geology* published in successive volumes in the early 1830s, Charles Lyell considered the relationship of earthquakes and volcanoes to other geological phenomena (Rudwick, pp. 15–18). Lyell concurred with Michell that there is a direct relationship between the phenomena of earthquakes and volcanoes, and that the causes of both are deeply interrelated with the nature of the Earth's core. Evidence suggested that these phenomena are connected to the passage of heat from the Earth's interior to its surface. Lyell concluded, therefore, that at some distance below the surface, the interior of the Earth consists of a great quantity of intensely heated material, some of which is in a constant state of flux.

The question of the origin and persistence of this internal heat was a problem for Lyell's larger argument regarding the steady state in geology. For the more limited purpose of this essay, however, the important conclusion reached by Lyell was his determination of the connection between the internal conditions within the Earth and external results of these conditions observable on the surface. Lyell repeated approvingly Michell's theory that a rolling motion in the surface takes place in an earthquake. Michell had likened this movement to a bubble of air moving beneath a carpet: the ultimate cause of earthquakes is therefore the release of a large quantity of gas within the Earth's core. Lyell agreed that large quantities of gas might exist in a liquefied form under great pressure within the core. The sudden release of this gas, he argued, could cause both the wavelike motion of earthquakes and the upheaval and depression of land associated with them.

This theory, held by Michell and Lyell, was gradually discredited during the nineteenth century, as controversies over the composition of the interior of the Earth threw into question some of its basic assumptions. Both Lyell and Michell had based their reasoning on the belief that the globe consists of a thin surface shell surrounding a great quantity of liquid matter in the core. Later in the century, however, the evidence for the solidity of the Earth's interior grew with the work of William Hopkins and William Thomson (Lord Kelvin), who both argued strongly in favor of a much thicker crust, if not a completely solid planet (Brush, pp. 231–242). This made the notion of the release of gas an unlikely cause for earthquakes, since the crust would be too thick to be tossed about like a carpet. No other mechanism, however, was suggested to replace this theory. As a result, investigations into earthquakes took on a much more empirical character in the middle and late nineteenth century.

Two of the most prominent of these empirical investigators were Alexis Perrey in France and the Englishman Robert Mallet. Perrey compiled extensive annual lists of earthquakes around the globe, concluding that earthquakes are more prevalent in the winter months; he also attempted to correlate seismic activity with the lunar period. Working independently, Mallet also compiled a comprehensive earthquake catalog, one that attempted to list every earthquake ever recorded. He relied extensively on previously published catalogs and travel literature, as well as newspapers and scientific journals. Mallet also undertook extensive research on the great Neapolitan quake of 1857, initiating the tradition of detailed empirical studies of large-scale earthquakes. His varied researches made him a great influence on the next generation of seismologists who came of age in the latter part of the nineteenth century (Dean, pp. 64–65).

Mallet's arguably most significant work was on the dynamics of ground tremblors published in the *Transactions of the Irish Academy* in 1848. There, Mallet defined an earthquake as "the transit of a wave of elastic compression in any direction, from vertically upward to horizontally, in any azimuth, through the surface and crust of the Earth." (Davison, p. 68). Mallet considered earthquakes to be the effect of the passage of such a wave of motion through the Earth. He recognized the complexities that were introduced into this motion by "movements of permanent elevation or depression," and by the dependence of the waves' velocity on the density of the rock through which the wave passed. As to the causes of earthquakes, Mallet suggested that earthquakes result from the sudden flexure or rupturing of the crust, resulting in the release of massive forces.

Davison gives this memoir a fundamental place in the development of the science of seismology (Davison, p. 70). Howell's modern assessment, however, which reflects the perspective of a practicing seismologist, criticizes Mallet for not appreciating the full significance of faulting in the genesis of earthquakes (Howell, p. 7). Still, Howell lauds Mallet for coming within "a very short step" of realizing that faulting is the source of seismic vibrations. This step was first taken, according to Howell, by Bunjiro Koto after the 1891 Mino-Owari earthquake in Japan. In his discussion of this event, Koto concluded firmly that earth movement along a fault was the cause, rather than a mere effect, of this quake. While Howell gives primary credit to Koto for this discovery, he also traces the gradual emergence of an awareness of the relationship between faulting and earthquakes throughout the latter part of the nineteenth century. In this context, Howell mentions Josiah D. Whitney, Edward Suess, Grove K. Gilbert, and James D. Dana as theorists whose work contributed to the eventual development of a theory of faulting (Howell, pp. 7–10).

Figure 1. A view of the surface rupture near San Francisco after the 1906 earthquake. From the glass slide collection of Hugo Benioff. Courtesy of the Archives, California Institute of Technology.

Seismologists such as Howell interested in modern theory rather than historical development tend to give the most credit for this realization to Harry F. Reid's study of the great San Francisco quake of 1906 (figure 1). In his work, Reid suggested that the crust bends elastically under some form of stress. When this stress exceeds the breaking point of the rocks involved, they fracture. The resulting movement causes a sudden release of energy that is propagated as seismic waves and is felt as an earthquake. Although this so-called elastic rebound theory was not new, Howell gives Reid most of the credit for this insight since he elaborated his idea more fully than previous authors, and provided a more quantitative analysis of the theory.

By the early twentieth century, then, the study of earthquakes had begun to achieve its modern form. With the increasing realization that earthquakes are caused by fault ruptures, investigators interested in the origin and effects of earthquakes began to look for ways to measure both the actual intensity of the shaking and to pinpoint its origin. This brought on the development of new instruments to aid in the recording and categorizing of earthquakes. Increasingly, this pursuit took on an international character, as investigators across Europe and in the United States and Japan took up the question of how

to rigorously measure earth movement and its effects.

Mallet had been the first to suggest that scientists set up a series of observational stations around the world to monitor seismic activity (Bullen and Bolt, p. 2). In order for this venture to be useful, however, an instrument that could accurately record ground motion was needed. During the second half of the nineteenth century, the first such seismographs were developed in Europe and Japan. In 1855, Italy's Luigi Palmieri developed an electro-magnetic seismograph, probably the first instrument invented for seismic research that was capable of detecting earth tremors imperceptible to human beings. In the decades that followed, more sensitive seismometers were developed that transformed the study of earthquakes from a largely observational study of the effects of earthquakes into a more precise science concerned with the study of seismic waves. In particular, seismographs became a critical means for understanding the interior of the globe, and in turn the underlying causes of seismic activity.

Although debates over the interior of the Earth had been raging during the nineteenth century, the development of the seismometer provided new insights into the exact composition of the core. In the 1890s, a group of British scientists working in Japan determined

that the energy released by earthquakes passes through the interior of the Earth. The study of these waves, they determined, could provide the first direct evidence regarding the ratio of elasticity and density within various regions of the Earth's core (Brush, pp. 250–251). By analyzing the information from these waves, Andrija Mohorovicic determined in 1909 that there exists a sharp transition between the "crust" and the "mantle." In 1913, Beno Gutenberg made the first accurate estimate of the location of this transition, pinpointing the boundary at a depth of around 2,900 kilometers (1,800 miles) (figure 2).

During the subsequent decades, productive studies of the nature, location, and propagation of earthquakes combined increasingly accurate and sensitive seismometers, the new understanding of the Earth's interior, and the growing worldwide network of earthquake observatories. Together, these tools helped scientists to construct a more complete picture of the Earth's interior, and of the locations and effects of earthquakes. Two of these developments are particularly noteworthy. Working with this new data, in 1936 Inge Lehman first produced evidence of the existence and nature of the core. Extrapolating from this development, K.E. Bullen classified the interior of the Earth into a series of shells based upon the depth and elasticity of each

layer. Around the same time, Charles Richter developed a magnitude scale for earthquakes in collaboration with Gutenberg that allowed seismologists to classify the relative size of earth tremors. This scale has passed into common parlance as the Richter scale of earthquake magnitude (Goodstein, pp. 222–226).

In the past three decades, new insight into the underlying causes of earthquakes has resulted from the acceptance of the theory of continental drift and the rise of plate tectonics. The theory that the continents are not fixed in place but subject to a kind of drift was first proposed in the early part of this century by Alfred L. Wegener. Although earlier geologists had suggested that such movements might have taken place, Wegener outlined his theory in greater detail, and his work sparked a lively debate within the geological community.

In general, Wegener's theory received a negative reception until after World War II, when new seismological data, together with more extensive knowledge of the sea floor, made continental drift look more plausible (Le Grand, pp. 170–181). During the course of the last three decades, a combination of discoveries from various fields of research, including seismology, oceanography, and geomagnetism, have led to the widespread establishment of the theory of continental drift. It is now well accepted that the combined forces generated by tectonic movement and subcrustal convection are the ultimate cause of seismic activity. In the last few years, therefore, attention within the field of seismology has turned from an attempt to understand the forces causing earthquakes toward attempts to understand the rate of recurrence of temblors and to predicting future earthquakes. These fields, however, are still in their infancy, and it is not clear what the results of these investigations may turn out to be (Howell, p. 45).

Historians of the geosciences are just beginning to investigate many of the developments that were critical in the transformation of earthquake research during the past two centuries. Many areas, as a result, are yet to be explored, such as the varied development of seismic theories in particular national contexts, the rise of seismic study institutions, and the critical role of instrumental advances in the rise of seismology as a scientific field. Exploring these areas, as well as the relationship of earthquake research to the more general study of the geosciences, will provide historians with fertile ground in the coming years.

David A. Valone

Bibliography

Bolt, Bruce. *Earthquakes and Geological Discovery.* New York: Scientific American Library, 1993.

Brush, Stephen G. "Nineteenth-Century Debates about the Inside of the Earth: Solid, Liquid, or Gas?" *Annals of Science* 36 (1979): pp. 225–254.

Bullen, K.E. and Bruce A. Bolt. *Introduction to the Theory of Seismology.* 4th ed. Cambridge: Cambridge University Press, 1985.

Davison, Charles. *The Founders of Seismology* [1927]. Reprint. New York: Arno Press, 1978.

Dean, Dennis R. "Robert Mallet and Seismology." *Annals of Science* 48 (1990): pp. 39–67.

Goodstein, Judith R. "Waves in the Earth: Seismology Comes to Southern California." *Historical Studies in the Physical Sciences* 14 (1984): pp. 201–230.

Howell, Benjamin F., Jr. *An Introduction to Seismological Research.* Cambridge: Cambridge University Press, 1990.

Le Grand, H.E. *Drifting Continents and Shifting Theories.* Cambridge: Cambridge University Press, 1988.

Rudwick, Martin. "The Strategy of Lyell's *Principles of Geology.*" *ISIS* 61 (1970): pp. 5–33.

See also Actualism, Uniformitarianism, and Catastrophism; Earthquakes; Geodesy; Geology; Gravimetry; Instruments, Seismic; Modeling and Inversion in Oceanography; Seismology; Tides, Earth; Tsunamis

Ecology: Disciplinary History

The study of the interrelations between organisms and their environment—that is, their physical surroundings and relations with other organisms.

The term "ecology" was not in wide use before the twentieth century. Its broad scope blurs the boundaries of the discipline historically. Persistent concepts of ecology are the sense of suitable place for an organism, its functional role in the operation of the world, and a balance of nature achieved through interaction. More modern additions to this core are the ideas of ecosystems and material and energy flow. The appropriate picture of nature as a whole has been a perennial debate. Depending on analogies to other coherent entities, ecologists have described the world as an organism, a community, or a machine. Each analogy includes a role for interacting components but carries unique implications for the ultimate meaning of natural order.

Despite the fact that the modern environmentalist movement increased interest in ecological science in the 1960s, ecology is not environmentalism. After 1900 ecologists modeled themselves after the hard sciences and usually attempted to separate their discipline professionally from conservationism. Nor is ecology a philosophy of nature and humanity's place in nature. Because it creates models of how the world works, however, ecology has always been entwined with its moral and political implications. Ecologists drew heavily upon analogies between the human and natural worlds, leaving the language of ecology rich in social and economic metaphors.

By 1900, the central organizing themes were already part of a scientific view of nature. Their roots are in professional and amateur natural history. The origins of ecology lie in the goals of Enlightenment science of the mid-1700s. Naturalists thought that their proper Newtonian goal was to find rational patterns and order in the diversity of nature, and derive the laws of its processes.

Carl Linnaeus (1707–1778), leader of the reorganization of taxonomy, was an early exponent of ecological interlinkage. Nature was an orderly pattern, divinely provided through well-designed parts and laws. In 1751, Linnaeus described a managed "economy of nature." Each species fit a particular physical habitat. Each preserved the whole, for it both ate and was eaten by some other. The maintenance of balance integrated the well-being of the individual, the species, and the whole world.

The ecological meaning of the world, in addition, was anchored in natural theology. Linnaeus meant to show God's benevolence and wisdom in the design of nature. Species were unchanging and closely governed. In the late 1700s, naturalists turned to cataloging adaptations, infusing their descriptions with references to the Creator's designs. Although the message was the purposeful structure and harmony of the world, Linnaeus raised questions about biogeographic distribution, food chains, competition, and starvation as a population limiter.

Donald Worster in his 1985 *Nature's Economy* (chaps. 1–2) argues that classical ecological ideas were determined by perceptions of humanity's place in nature. He portrays the history of ecology as a struggle between the two human feelings toward nature. Linnaeus embodies the "imperialist" view, characterized by mechanistic science and the desire to master and manage resources rationally (Worster, pp. 33–53). The Selbourne naturalist Gilbert White (1720–1793) is "arcadian," finding value in nature's harmony. The arcadian seeks to preserve, and to make humanity a part of nature (Worster, pp. 7–11).

Worster's dichotomy misses the way naturalists saw no conflict between a providential harmony and human needs. The imperialist economy of nature, no less than arcadian harmony, was a holistic vision of humanity in nature. Despite their managerial role, humans lay within the constraints of inexorable natural laws. In Linnaeus's "mechanical" model, nature was an economic community, following laws of exchange. It was a "polity" or system of governance. In parallel, political economists developed similar models of equilibrium maintained by the interaction of parts fulfilling discrete functions.

In addition, identifying White as arcadian obscures just how managed his agrarian landscape was. The idyllic and pragmatic visions fused. Alexander von Humboldt (1769–1859) embodied the union of science, exploi-

tation, and love of nature. His explorations of the American tropics from 1799 to 1804 served both theoretical geography and economic goals. He wrote stirringly of the beauties and wonders of raw nature. Few naturalists before the late 1800s considered that humans could disrupt the balance. Without a sense of destructive impact, moral concern and the spiritual drive to conserve nature had little prominence until the mid-1900s.

Not included in the Linnean model of nature's economy were extinction and dynamically changing biogeographic distributions. Humboldt made the break with static distribution in his 1805 treatise on plant geography. He pioneered the descriptive tools of plant zones and isotherms of climate, seeking the causes beneath such regular patterns. Janet Browne, in her *Secular Ark* of 1983 (pp. 47–52), suggests that the linkages and comparisons of natural groups were modeled on nations. The shared interest with political science was the effect of a few essential, underlying physical conditions upon the character of a region's inhabitants.

Extending Humboldtian ideas on the effect of the environment on distribution, Augustin de Candolle (1778–1841) made explicit the influence of other individuals or species. Despite the avowed benevolence of nature's economy, nature was harsh. Using a common metaphor, Candolle in the 1820s developed the notion of a warfare for resources, a struggle for existence among individuals with unique physical requirements. Browne (pp. 54–55) considers ecology, distinct from global and historical biogeography, to stem from Candolle's interest in physical factors and habitats. Followers developed methods for numerical data on patterns of occurrence and regional diversity of species. Plant sociology or statistics became a dominant European tradition, and ecological surveys received the first academic and governmental support.

More interested in processes, geological naturalists added the historical dimension (Browne, pp. 102–110). They were driven by the need to explain extinctions and obvious distribution changes. Charles Lyell (1797–1875) in 1830–1833, followed by Charles Darwin (1809–1882), merged the historical geography of species with the ecological struggle. They stressed competition and equilibrium, but with changeable circumstances allowing a more dynamic balance. Darwin and Alfred Russel Wallace (1823–1913), in the 1850s to 1870s, completed the synthesis by adding evolution to the factors of distribution and removing the linkage to natural theology (Bowler, chap. 6).

By the late 1800s, ecological naturalists had three avenues for research: studies of adaptations, botanical statistics on assemblages and physical conditions, and historical accounts of the spread of species. In this climate, the German evolutionist Ernst Haeckel (1834–1919) in 1866 coined the word *Oecologie,* declaring that the Darwinian theory required a new science of the relationship of organisms to the conditions of existence. He defined it as a branch of physiology, intending ecology to be the broad study of the structure and function of nature as a whole. Even Haeckel himself, however, worked primarily on reconstructing evolutionary trees. Darwinism actually inspired little ecological work, despite its emphasis on the struggle for existence.

Eugene Cittadino, in his *Nature as the Laboratory* of 1990 (pp. 82–115) identifies the one school that followed Haeckel's suggestion. The German botanists Ernst Stahl (1848–1919) and A.F. Wilhelm Schimper (1856–1901), working in the colonial tropics in the 1880s, developed Darwinian adaptation studies of plant physiology and anatomy. They integrated it with detailed knowledge of environmental conditions, forming a foundation of modern physiological ecology. Schimper's 1898 text announced a program to derive plant geography in principle from studies of individual adaptations to environments. This, however, was not the program that created the emergence of ecology.

A durable theme in the history of ecology, outlined most broadly by Robert P. McIntosh in his *Background of Ecology* in 1985, has been the organization of a self-conscious discipline around 1900. The precipitating text was an 1895 Danish book on plant geography, later published as *Oecology of Plants,* by Eugenius Warming (1841–1924). Its orientation was explicitly toward plant associations with one another. American and British plant ecologists led the flowering of ecology from 1900 through the 1930s. They benefited from the trend toward specialization in the sciences and the explosive growth of research universities. The model of science for the new ecologists was physiology: rigorously empirical and experimental. Led by Frederic Clements (1874–1945) at Nebraska and Henry Cowles (1869–1939) at Chicago, they succeeded by capturing research support, and by elaborating a powerful integrating paradigm (Cittadino, pp. 146–155). They also created courses and wrote textbooks. Clements's *Research Methods in Ecology* (1905) was the first. In Britain, the leader was Arthur G. Tansley (1871–1955), influential in founding the British Ecological Society, and its *Journal of Ecology,* in 1913. The Ecological Society of America followed in 1915, its journal *Ecology* appearing in 1920. The different research programs all declared ecology to be defined by its attention to the community level of organization.

Warming and Clements in the early twentieth century postulated a climax formation as the inevitable culmination of a succession of species in each climate or habitat. It was a stable, typical assemblage of interdependent species. Thus the vegetation type became a whole, like an organism. Considering it to have a functional physiology and a development made the analogy even deeper.

Although widely shared, the organism image had differing implications. Like Warming, Cowles was a materialist. He emphasized the competitive dynamics that maintain a community's organized uniformity. Clements developed a philosophical view more dependent on Herbert Spencer's model of society as a social organism. For Clements, the community was a superorganism. The climax was equivalent to both mature development and homeostasis, another powerful concept derived from recent physiology. Such traits of the whole were emergent, at a level transcending individual organisms.

The historian Donald Worster sees the organismic holism as a part of the arcadian sentiment (pp. 20–21, 212). But Clements was no romantic environmentalist. He intended to provide Midwestern farmers with knowledge for practical management. As Cittadino points out (pp. 149–154), the principle of a higher level of organization was a physiological ideal. Supporters and opponents of the superorganism split along the deep philosophical division found throughout biology, between materialist mechanism and organicist vitalism. Nature as an organism was meant to capture both self-maintenance and a purposive, even progressive, order. Competing with mechanism, such views were widely shared at the time in physiology, embryology, and non-Darwinian evolutionary theories. The debate over what causes regulation and order would continue to divide ecology into the late twentieth century.

The organismic paradigm held sway at

first in animal ecology as well. It emerged through the stimulus of Victor Shelford (1877–1968) at Chicago. He began, in the years following 1910, by emulating the work of Clements and Cowles on physical conditions and distribution. The Chicago school came to be defined during the 1920s to the 1940s by the group led by Warder Clyde Allee (1885–1955), which produced the influential textbook *Principles of Animal Ecology* (1949). In tracing their history, Gregg Mitman in his 1992 *State of Nature* (pp. 72–88) shows that Allee explicitly drew parallels to human society. Not only did sociology influence his view of nature, but he also was willing to draw political and moral lessons from biology to society. Mitman (pp. 158–201) sees Allee's biology shaped by the social values of pacifism and cooperation instead of competition. However, Allee's interest in the integrated community as a cooperative entity was also consistent with the organism metaphor.

Meanwhile, a distinct strain of animal ecology had begun to dominate ecology by the 1930s. Coming out of an analysis of the community's interactions, *Animal Ecology* (1927) by Charles Elton (1900–1991) turned theory toward predator-prey relationships and the factors governing population size. Doubtful of a stable balance of nature, Elton rejected the integrated superorganism in favor of a dynamic model. He went back to economic metaphors, capturing the sense of ecological roles and interaction in terms like "niche" and "food chain."

Other ecologists were coming simultaneously to population regulation. Sharon Kingsland traces in her 1985 *Modeling Nature* the complex web of influences from models of society, insect population control, and desires to emulate physicists' laws. Raymond Pearl (1879–1940) in the 1920s extended statistics on the human population to a general mathematical model of exponential growth, the S-shaped logistic curve. Developing a mathematical theory also appealed to Alfred Lotka (1880–1949). Trained as a physical chemist, he attempted in *Elements of Physical Biology* (1925) a grand derivation of general laws of populations and systems out of principles of thermodynamics, energy exchange, and action-reaction equilibria. Universal laws would make systems comparable from chemistry to human society to the whole Earth. As Kingsland (pp. 26–27, 82–87) shows, he made Pearl's equations useful, and captured ecologists' interest with a two-species predation model. Simultaneously, and also drawing from physics, Vito Volterra (1860–1940) developed a similar model for predation and competition. Derived for fisheries problems, Volterra's work carried mathematical equations to ecologists interested in population and resource management. In Australia, entomologist Alexander J. Nicholson (1895–1965), aided by a physicist, produced in 1933–1935 an elaborate model incorporating predation, competition, and reproduction. The machine became the dominating analogy for balance. Competition was the controlling factor, responsive to population density and able to maintain the oscillating equilibrium.

Mathematics received a boost from tests of the models in simplified laboratory environments made in the mid-1930s by Georgii Gause (b. 1910). Although Elton distrusted the models, he agreed with the perception of dynamic order and the emphasis on competition, predation, and coexistence. Population ecologists debated heatedly about the usefulness of mathematical models and lab experiments, and about how regulation works. The historian Kingsland shows how the models succeeded in bringing an eagerly desired dose of simple rules, numerical data, testability, and prediction to the complexities of a young science. She sees the debates as a competition among ecologists for their own scarce resources. But given the complex network of agendas and supports, perhaps the heat over regulation is as usefully seen as a struggle for intellectual authority in a rapidly growing discipline.

By the 1940s, plant and animal and aquatic ecology had become almost distinct disciplines. One tie among them was the demotion of climax and superorganism as the central paradigm. From 1917 to 1939 Henry Gleason (1882–1975) argued for communities as summations of individual interactions. His doubts about the organism analogy were joined in 1935 by Tansley, who coined the term "ecosystem" from the language of physics to imply a more materialist, less teleological view. Plant ecology lost its dominance with the shift away from the superorganism.

An emerging potential unifier was an alternative holistic approach growing out of biogeochemistry, and developed most strongly in aquatic ecology (limnology). The Russian mineralogist Vladimir Ivanovich Vernadsky (1863–1945), in his *La Géochimie* (1924) and *La Biosphère* (1926 in Russian, 1929 in French), defined the biosphere as the thin layer of life on Earth that ties the land surface, water, and atmosphere into a system interactive with its living components. The ecological environment is a global whole, a system in which chemical elements cycle between the parts, integrating living and nonliving. The species, as a population, has its role as the component that moves material and energy through the system.

Douglas R. Weiner in his 1988 *Models of Nature* (pp. 64–70) describes an independent Russian tradition that developed a thriving, innovative ecology in the early 1900s. In parallel with European and American science, phytosociology flourished first. Russian romanticism of the land led to a far greater emphasis on mutually dependent relationships. Vernadsky elevated this approach, presenting the physical environment as an interacter. The Clementsian school had made biotic relations the primary interest, with physical conditions a substrate for communities. Vernadsky in the 1920s added the idea that the biotic can in turn influence the physical world, not just locally but even globally. He suggested that the Earth's atmosphere of oxygen, nitrogen, and carbon dioxide had an organic origin. Ecology became part of the new biogeochemical history of the Earth.

American animal ecologists pursuing mathematical models little noticed Lotka's similar vision of the organic world as a single biophysical system. Rather than social interactions, the system had kinetics, or energetics and motion, seen in food webs and in the great cycling of the Earth's water, nitrogen, phosphorus, and carbon dioxide. Vernadsky had much greater impact within the U.S.S.R. During the 1920s to 1930s, he led young Soviet ecologists to field and theoretical work on systems, geochemistry, and energetics. Their goal was a mathematically exact and quantitative science. Vernadsky also came to see humans as a new large-scale geochemical force, leading him to conservationist programs. The historian Weiner (pp. 125–133) sees this as the source of conflict with Stalinist politics, which killed Soviet ecological science in the 1930s.

Despite the numbers of students, including Gause, that he influenced, Vernadsky thus had little impact outside the Soviet Union, until his ideas were rescued and elaborated on by G. Evelyn Hutchinson (1903–1991) and his group at Yale University. Associated there with a circle of emigré Russian intellectuals, and long interested in geochemistry, Hutchinson in the 1930s became acquainted with Vernadsky's ideas and promoted them. He also knew of the pioneering field work of the Norwegian geochemist Viktor Moritz Goldschmidt (1888–1947), who concentrated on the integration of material cycles. Hutchinson

assimilated biogeochemistry into his work, to try to relate the structure of planktonic communities to competition and chemical changes.

In his *Entangled Bank* of 1992, Joel B. Hagen calls this making biogeochemistry more biological, by taking its insights down to the single pond and answering traditional questions about species distribution (pp. 63–65). Aquatic ecologists had never had much interest in tracing individual organisms. They followed the seminal insight of "The Lake as a Microcosm" (1887) by Stephen A. Forbes (1844–1930), one of the first explicit treatments of a system and its circulation of matter balancing production and consumption. They measured lake populations in terms of productivity, and paid more attention to the chemical environment. Also trained in embryology, Hutchinson in the 1930s used the superorganism metaphor to treat the "metabolism" of matter and energy by a community. With parallels to Elton's thinking about interlinkage through feeding, Hutchinson's biogeochemistry implied maintenance of a steady state of balance of the essential chemicals, processed in the environment by organisms. Integrating Elton and Vernadsky, biogeochemical nutrient cycling provided a way to move beyond Shelford's law of limiting requirements that determine where a species lives, to a larger view of physical processes operating throughout a system. Lake population dynamics became a problem of energy transfer. But to Hutchinson's group after 1940, the organismic analogy was merely heuristic, a way to mathematical theory.

Thus in another sense, Hagen argues (pp. 98–99), this was a new biology, less tied to the natural historical interest in species and less divided between zoologist and botanist. These scientists saw themselves as addressing properly the role of chemistry in biological systems. Like Vernadsky, they viewed biogeochemistry as a way to see the sum of all living matter, in operation across physical space and boundaries. They were more attracted to a set of black boxes operating in delimited systems, accessible to quantification, experimentation, and modeling as in physics.

Modeling and experimentation were the appeal of this new ecology. Through students and leadership, Hutchinson molded much of the post-1945 research agenda. Ever sensitive to other sciences, the Hutchinson school turned to the models of mechanical organization in economics and cybernetics. The Russian view had made energy the key to writing mathematical equations. Hagen (pp. 62–77) traces Hutchinson's transformation of ecosystem into an economic metaphor of producers and consumers of matter and energy, a biogeochemical system of budgets and exchanges, with formal mathematical parallels to population dynamics. From cybernetics came feedback loops. Hutchinson's colleague Raymond Lindeman (1915–1942) produced an immensely influential study in 1942 relating community structure to productivity and energetics. He made the ecosystem the centerpiece concept, defining its central problems as biogeochemistry, energy flow, and succession.

The *Fundamentals of Ecology* (1953) of Eugene Odum (b. 1913), destined to become the leading text through several editions, provided the unifying ecosystem paradigm. It combined Lotka's physicalist approach, the Russian school of biogeochemistry, the modeling of energy flow and material cycles, and an emphasis on landscape features that define natural systems. Comparative and experimental studies of particular habitats, such as lakes, forested watersheds, and estuaries, exemplified the new ecosystem approach of the 1950s and 1960s. It confirmed biogeochemistry as a key to ecology. It avoided vitalism because cybernetics showed the possibilities of machines that regulate themselves. Ecosystem ecology captured the unique, emergent level of organization, depicted as a machine. Hagen shows (pp. 100–121) that it emulated physics, and it attracted enormous funding from governments interested in management.

The ecosystem concept flourished after World War II, in a boom time for ecology. As in its first phase, ecology again benefited from increased funding, university positions, and specialization. What had been a small discipline grew with public awareness of threats to the environment. Mitman stresses (pp. 143–195) the social causes for the diminution of the superorganism and the Allee school after 1950, seeing ecologists move from interest in social insights to environmental engineering. But there had also been a conceptual destruction of organism and group analogies. Quantitative community studies supported Gleason. Supporters of the superorganism had often been Lamarckians, opposed to the Darwinian emphasis on struggle. That view lost definitively in the 1930s synthesis of genetics and natural selection theory. Darwinian principles argued against such teleology, and the debate over population regulation effectively debunked organicist harmony. The new focus was on competition and individualist interaction. With support and insight from evolutionary

theory, population and adaptation studies rose to new prominence in the 1950s. Hutchinson and his student Robert MacArthur (1930–1972) stimulated the hope for a science using mathematical models to unify Darwinism, individual competition, and community structure into a general theory. The ecosystem concept succeeded because it was able to encompass competitive interaction as a controlling process at the individual level. Nonetheless, an enduring split with population ecology arose because of the accent on feedback and self-regulation of ecosystems.

Attempts to revive a vision of communities or ecosystems as actual self-controlling, purposeful entities have met the enduring modern rejection of teleology and of superorganism as anything more than a heuristic metaphor. The Gaia hypothesis (1979) of James Lovelock (b. 1919) was such an effort to view the Earth with organicist holism, seeing the biosphere controlled by organisms for the purpose of maintaining a global balance. The idea is dependent on the elaboration by Lynn Margulis (b. 1938) of Vernadsky's idea that the atmosphere evolved, changing as a result of biological processes. Stripped of Lovelock's controversial teleology, this historical biogeochemistry is a part of ecologists' models of global pollution and warming.

From its multiple lineages early in the 1900s, ecology continued to fragment into a sprawling, complex set of subdisciplines with their own journals and funding avenues. Specialization grew out of pragmatic interests in groups of organisms or particular habitats, such as fisheries and tropical ecology. The major branches more generally reflected broader conceptual and methodological camps, relevant to each level of the natural world. Kingsland and Hagen have also noted the competition for support and intellectual authority.

Future historical work will need to continue exploring the connections of ecologists' theories and practices to other sciences, and among their own subdisciplines. Among social factors, environmentalism appears to have had little influence on the development of ecology, but historians are just beginning to produce close case studies.

William Kimler

Bibliography

Bowler, Peter J. *Evolution: The History of an Idea.* 2d ed. Berkeley: University of California Press, 1989.

Browne, Janet. *The Secular Ark: Studies in the History of Biogeography.* New

Haven: Yale University Press, 1983.

Cittadino, Eugene. *Nature as the Laboratory: Darwinian Plant Ecology in the German Empire, 1880–1900.* Cambridge: Cambridge University Press, 1990.

Hagen, Joel B. *An Entangled Bank: The Origins of Ecosystem Ecology.* New Brunswick: Rutgers University Press, 1992.

Kingsland, Sharon E. *Modeling Nature: Episodes in the History of Population Ecology.* Chicago: University of Chicago Press, 1985.

McIntosh, Robert P. *The Background of Ecology: Concepts and Theory.* Cambridge: Cambridge University Press, 1985.

Mitman, Gregg. *The State of Nature: Ecology, Community, and American Social Thought, 1900–1950.* Chicago: University of Chicago Press, 1992.

Weiner, Douglas R. *Models of Nature: Ecology, Conservation and Cultural Revolution in Soviet Russia.* Bloomington: Indiana University Press, 1988.

Worster, Donald. *Nature's Economy: A History of Ecological Ideas.* San Francisco: Sierra Club Books, 1977; Cambridge: Cambridge University Press, 1985.

See also Climates, Pleistocene and Recent; Conservation of Natural Resources; Dendrochronology; Disciplinary History; Environmental History; Environmentalism; Evolution and the Geosciences; Fossilization; Geochemistry: The Word and Disciplinary History; Geography and Natural Theology; Geography; Humboldtian Science; Ice Ages; Iso-Lines; Mass Extinction and the Impact-Volcanic Controversy; Paleoecology; Paleontology; Preface; Soil Conservation; Wilderness

Economic Geology

The application of the principles of the geosciences to the study of the origins, occurrence, and utilization of mineral deposits of economic importance.

The term "economic geology," originally applied to the study of metallic ore deposits and their origin, now often includes fuels, nonmetallic minerals, building materials, and ground water. Petroleum geology, for example, is considered to be a subdivision of economic geology.

An early attempt to develop a theory of ore genesis based on direct observation was made by Georg Bauer, better known as Georgius Agricola (1494–1555), whose *De re metallica* (1556) drew on his extensive knowledge of the mines of his native Saxony. An important stimulus to economic geology as a profession was the establishment of the mining academy at Freiberg, Saxony, in 1765, which attracted a great number of students from many countries throughout the world during the nineteenth century when growing industrialization was creating a demand for scientifically trained experts in mining geology. The school's most famous professor was Abraham Gottlob Werner (1749–1817), who applied his neptunist theories to the study of vein formation. His theory that veins were formed in previously existing fissures by descending waters contrasted with the plutonist ideas of James Hutton (1726–1797), who held that veins were filled by molten material that arose from deep in the Earth.

The debate over the genesis of ores continued throughout the nineteenth century and into the twentieth, stimulating research that contributed to the development of economic geology. Geologists from various countries proposed theories involving ascending, descending, or lateral secretion of ore-bearing solutions. Carl Bernhard von Cotta (1808–1879), who taught at Freiberg from 1842 to 1874, developed a systematic treatment of ore deposits in his widely used textbook *Die Lehre von den Erzlagerstätten* (1859, translated into English in 1870 as *A Treatise on Ore Deposits*), which exerted an enormous influence on the scientific study of ore deposits throughout the world (Jensen and Bateman, p. 37). One of the foremost economic geologists of the United States was Waldemar Lindgren (1860–1939), a Freiberg graduate who served for many years as mining geologist for the U.S. Geological Survey and professor of economic geology and head of the geology department at the Massachusetts Institute of Technology. As author of an influential textbook and founder and first editor of the *Annotated Bibliography of Economic Geology,* Lindgren was instrumental in developing the field of economic geology in the United States.

In 1905 Lindgren, Josiah Edward Spurr (1870–1950), Frederick L. Ransome (1868–1935), and other economic geologists founded the journal *Economic Geology* to provide a forum for the discussion of new ideas on the genesis of ore deposits. In an article in the first is-sue, Ransome pointed out that the periodicals devoted to general geology seldom published articles on economic geology, even though ge-ologists working in industry, on railroads, and on state and federal geological surveys were doing important scientific research related to their practical work. *Economic Geology* was patterned on the German *Zeitschrift für Praktische Geologie,* published in a country where applied geology had a long and respected history, unlike England and America, where it was regarded, Ransome thought, "as occupy-ing a somewhat lower plane," perhaps because it involved "descent into the gloom and grime of mines" rather than research in attractive sur-roundings (Ransome, p. 2).

In 1920 some of the same people orga-nized the Society of Economic Geologists, which adopted *Economic Geology* as its offi-cial publication in 1922 (Bateman, pp. 7–8). The society was instrumental in advancing the status of economic geologists, defining pro-fessional standards, and drawing up a code of ethics for a large group of geologists who had been contributing to the scientific aspects of applied geology for many years.

Economic geology retains its close ties to general or theoretical geology because the eco-nomic geologist draws from all of the earth sciences, including stratigraphy, petrology, mineralogy, and geomorphology. Today, as the need for new mineral resources grows, geo-physics, geochemistry, and laboratory experi-ment play an increasing role in determining the conditions under which useful mineral deposits form and in prospecting for the source and extent of these deposits.

There are almost no comprehensive his-tories of economic geology, its development as a science, or the role that the geosciences have played in a nation's economic develop-ment. An exception is Mary C. Rabbitt's his-tory of the U.S.G.S., which provides a chronological account of the founding and growth of the national survey, paying particu-lar attention to work bearing on the "general welfare" of the country and the contributions of its geologists to the science of economic geology.

Peggy Champlin

Bibliography
Bateman, Alan M. "Economic Geology." *Economic Geology* 50 (1955): pp. 1–37.
Jensen, Mead L., and Alan M. Bateman. "Brief History of the Use of Minerals and the Development of Economic Geology." In *Economic Mineral Deposits,* pp. 32–40. 3d ed. New York: John Wiley, 1979.
Rabbitt, Mary C. *Minerals, Lands, and Geology for the Common Defence and General Welfare.* 3 vols. Washington, D.C.: Government Printing Office, 1979–1986.
Ransome, Frederick L. "The Present Standing of Applied Geology." *Economic Geology* 1 (1906): pp. 1–10.

See also Geological Maps; Geological Surveys; Geological Surveys, U.S. State; Matter, Prop-erties at High Pressure and Temperature; Mineralogy; Mining Academies; Mining and Knowledge of the Earth; Ore Formation, Theories since 1800; Petroleum Geology to 1920; Petroleum in America; Petrology

Environmental History

The role of humans in changing the environ-ment in historical time and the effect of the environment on human history.

Environmental history is one of history's newer fields, having become a recognized branch only since the 1970s. This occurred partly as a response to a developing interest in ecology and environmental issues at that time. Although contemporary environmental history has its roots in political activism, the field has developed, with contributions from the history of technology and the economy, into a separate scholarly enterprise that owes few remaining debts to political agendas.

While environmental history was at first concerned with North American topics, a more global perspective emerged in the 1980s. Because this is a fairly new field, the connection between environmental history and the history of science has not been fully developed. One of the most comprehensive points of intersection between the two fields is in the history of the geosciences. This in-tersection has two aspects. The influence that humans have over the environment gener-ally does not result directly from science, but from the application of science in efforts to improve technology. The use of geosciences from stratigraphy to seismology has contrib-uted greatly to the environmental effects of industry, as have the application of chemis-try and physics. In addition, the geosciences have often been instrumental in identifying and investigating more subtle indicators of environmental change, from air and water pollution to climate change and the degra-dation of soils.

Some aspects of environmental history are well explored by existing literature, while others have not been addressed. This essay focuses on four representative examples of environmental history. Firstly, a synopsis of the development of environmental history is presented. This includes the multidisciplinary components that have been combined with social, technological, and economic history. Secondly, it addresses the scope of human knowledge of the Earth. The ability of a culture to adapt to its environment and to turn the environment to its own purposes is explored. Thirdly, a brief account is given of the literature describing the impact of industrialization on the Earth. Environmental decay due to human activities reflects the level of understanding that cultures have of their environments. Finally, the transition from local and regional to global environmental history is explored.

Until the last decades of the twentieth century, most historians considered the natural environment as a function of local, social, or even diplomatic history without diverging greatly from an emphasis on human accomplishments and events. The environment was often seen only as background for human endeavors or as an obstacle for humans to overcome.

One early example of a historical work that acknowledged, and indeed celebrated, the local environment was *The Mediterranean* (1949, English translation 1972) by Fernand Braudel (1902–1985). It quickly became a classic. Beginning with a comprehensive geography of the Mediterranean basin, Braudel examined the influence that the topography and climate of the area had on the growth of civilization there. The book focused on the human events of the sixteenth century while giving due regard to the stress that a growing population had on the sea and land. In addition, Braudel saw the Mediterranean as an avenue for trade as well as conquest and warfare.

Other historians have seen the need to address the environment as part of human history. Richard White's 1985 historiographical essay delineates the development of American environmental history. White (b. 1947) describes the writings of Frederick Jackson Turner (1861–1932), Walter Prescott Webb (1888–1963), and James Malin (1893–1979) as developing the connection between humans and the environment as part of their work. Unfortunately, as White notes, these scholars did not look closely at human effects

on their surroundings (White, p. 297).

A number of ostensibly unrelated fields make invaluable contributions to understanding environmental history. The natural sciences give a multidisciplinary perspective for historians. Anthropologists study past cultures. Geographers, geologists, and meteorologists can describe weather and geological events that have had an impact on the survival of past populations. Historians of ancient civilizations can simultaneously provide information for environmental historians and derive perspectives that can be helpful to understanding their own fields. Finally, human reproduction must also be taken into account as a factor affecting the way humans influence the environment.

The disposition of humanity to alter its surroundings is pervasive. Human cultures have all made changes in their environments, most to the best of their technical abilities. Only with the advent of industrialization, however, has that propensity for adaptation shifted from demands upon local environments to global effects.

In ancient times, the use of water ranked among the most important aspects of life. In *Man and Water* (1976), Norman Smith places drinking water and agricultural irrigation systems into historical context by looking at hydraulic engineering over time. While Smith carries the discussion of hydraulics into the modern age, he begins with a look at the great engineering works of Mesopotamia (chap. 1). Despite a professional admiration for the technical abilities of the Mesopotamians, Smith notes that their irrigation systems failed because they could not overcome the problem of siltation. Recently, archaeologists have investigated the possibility that an abrupt climate change had occurred around 2200 B.C.E. that caused a desertification process in northern Mesopotamia, aggravating water shortages (Weiss et al., passim).

On the African continent, human-induced environmental changes had been occurring for many millennia. In *Environmental History of East Africa* (1982), A.C. Hamilton examines equatorial east Africa beginning 2.5 million years before present. Hamilton reviews the history of the landscape, plant life, climate, and humans of that area. Humans influenced the environment through both agriculture and expanding population, and were affected by weather patterns, water availability, and insect-borne diseases.

Much later, in the second and third millennia B.C.E., Egyptians took both a passive and an active role in their environment each spring with the flooding of the Nile River (Smith, chap. 1). This caused new soil that had been washed from higher ground to be deposited upon the fields depleted by the crops of previous years. The resulting nourishment not only replenished the soil, but also gave assurance that nature had again been reborn in realization of age-old patterns.

As noted by Clarence J. Glacken in *Traces on the Rhodian Shore* (1967), the Egyptians participated in nature by manipulating plants and other vegetation to meet their own designs and purposes (chap. 3). This practice had an influence on the ancient Greeks. Generally, this involved improving existing plants to provide greater yields of food. The fortuitous crop excesses resulting from this pursuit could be used for trade. Sometimes these botanical efforts were successful, often they were not. In any case, the roots of human-induced change in the environment could clearly be seen.

The Egyptians also deified the land, the water, and all of nature. For example, the act of planting trees was considered the same as an act of penance for the soul (Hughes, chap. 3). Like earlier civilizations, Egyptians relied on the environment for the raw materials of construction, though possibly on a larger scale than ever before. The great pyramids, palaces, and tombs built in Egyptian times did more; than express concepts of religious grandeur; they also rendered a sense of control over the environment.

In later times the Greeks and Romans had no less impact on their environments. The Earth yielded the same wood and stone for construction, but an expanding population and inattention to preservation of resources combined to make forest-depletion a problem described by Plato in the fourth century B.C.E. With the disappearance of the forests came erosion of the soil. As noted by Glacken (chap. 3) and J. Donald Hughes (chap. 11), the barren and rocky landscapes familiar in modern Greece were not always that way. They were once as rich as any other areas bounding the Mediterranean Sea. However, an understanding by the ancients that the land was unchanging led ultimately to its degradation.

Glacken and Hughes both note, however, that many ancient Greeks and Romans were well aware that the flora was steadily disappearing from the landscape, but there was little interpretation applied to this phenomenon (Hughes, chap. 11). Despite the fact that, like the Egyptians, the Greeks and Romans assigned a sense of deity to their natural surroundings, wood was still needed for ships and fuel. In addition, the growth of the city-states had a detrimental environmental effect. Greek and Roman societies were not deliberately destructive, but they caused harm to their natural surroundings because of the demands they placed on their resources. They were, however, sensitive to the fact that some atonement had to be made for the destruction being caused. Efforts were commonly made to balance the natural world by planting trees, designing parks and gardens, and by marking some areas as protected from development (Hughes, chap. 10).

One of the first major actions of land transformation in Europe was seen in the western Netherlands. In *Medieval Frontier* (1985), William H. TeBrake focuses on human manipulation of the Rijnland between 950 and 1350 C.E. The story of Dutch efforts to claim land from the sea is marked by a rapidly expanding population and subsequent demands on agriculture of that period.

In *Medieval Religion and Technology* (1978), Lynn White, Jr., focuses on Medieval technology in a series of essays on the connection between the teachings of Latin Christianity and European social value systems. He argues that Christianity changed the symbolism of God from a power present in all of nature to the spiritual entity that created the Earth. This fostered the attitude that humans needed to control nature as a duty to God. Modern ecological problems, he argues, can be traced to the relationship between the teachings of Christianity and the human conquest of nature.

White notes that Western Christianity encouraged gathering information about the world through the scientific explorations of natural philosophers. Science and Christianity embraced the doctrine that nature is an incomplete creation meant to be dominated by human effort and intelligence. This mandate called for nature to be understood, and it greatly encouraged European assimilation of the recently rediscovered knowledge of the ancient Greeks and of medieval Arabs.

Robin Attfield in *The Ethics of Environmental Concern* (1983) and Clarence Glacken both take exception to White's thesis that human supremacy over the environment was espoused by the Christian church. Attfield notes that early Medieval Europeans viewed themselves as little different from the natural world surrounding them. He advances references in the Old Testament that issued God's decree that animal, bird, fish, and people alike were participants in the Creation (chap. 2).

Glacken places a more pastoral and benign connotation on God's instructions to humans than does White (Glacken, chap. 5). The Bible, the conscience and blueprint for the Judaeo-Christian tradition, encouraged humans to use the resources and sustenance that nature presents, and to coexist with the other creatures to carry out the completion of God's creation. This did not necessitate ascendancy over nature, Glacken argues, rather it required mutually beneficial existence.

As Western civilization pushed into the Americas, the concept of human dominance over the land was a powerful stimulus. In order to open new avenues of commerce, and with a rather sardonic eye toward human destiny to master nature, Europeans began to colonize foreign lands.

In *Ecological Imperialism* (1986), Alfred W. Crosby writes that the "Neo-European" colonies in America were formed to provide commodities in short supply for the mother countries, such as beef, wheat, wool, hides, and coffee. This necessarily required that lands with temperate climates be colonized and turned over to agriculture. Colonists were motivated not only by the prospect of financial gain but also by the promise that the new lands would bear a more bountiful harvest than had the lands they were leaving. Famine was a regular occurrence in Europe and Asia, and the new colonies were, as much as anything else, intended to overcome that problem. But the spread of European populations led to widespread unintended environmental ramifications.

Because Europe, Asia, and Africa are connected by land, the indigenous cultures maintained some contact with one another. After people crossed the Siberian land bridge approximately twelve thousand years (or more) before the present, however, and began their southward trek, the bridge was lost and they were isolated on a different continent. From that time until around 1500 C.E. the two branches of humanity had almost no contact. With the beginning of the sixteenth century, the two civilizations were locked into an ever-widening cycle of encounter and subjugation.

In *Changes in the Land* (1983), William Cronon studies not only the impact of Western settlement on the American landscape, but also the changes wrought by Native American cultures. The Naragansetts, Pequots, and Mohegans in eastern New England, like Na-

tive Americans elsewhere, used fire to clear land and as a tool for hunting (chap. 3). The Micmacs, of present-day Nova Scotia, were hunter-gatherers, using the bounty of the land to supply their yearly food stocks. While this interaction with the environment may have been subtle, it was no less tangible. Fishing nets and weapons were produced from the raw materials supplied by nature, as were the necessities for making clothing and shelter. Taking naturally occurring objects to satisfy survival needs is, in itself, a method of manipulating the environment.

While the Massachusetts Bay colonies were established as an escape from religious tyranny in England, they also lay in a bountiful land that could furnish much needed timber and foodstuffs for Europe. With the invaluable help of local Indians, the colonists began to fish, trap for furs, and farm as part of a growing commerce with England.

In *The Middle Ground* (1991), Richard White renders a history of Native Americans around the Great Lakes that focuses on relationships both among the various tribes and with the encroaching Europeans. Like Cronon's, White's astute presentation includes descriptions of how local environments were used to advantage by Native Americans. As trading liaisons were established with Europeans, food and wildlife became items of commerce. Even though Europeans viewed the Native Americans around the Great Lakes as alien and culturally incomprehensible, they cooperated with the Algonquians, Iroquois, and others to secure furs for trade on the European market. This caused a depletion of many wildlife populations.

Timothy Silver examines the Indians and European colonists in America's Southeast before the formation of the United States in *A New Face on the Countryside* (1990). Silver notes that the impact of Native American civilizations upon the environment was greatly limited by their technology. The stone axes used by the Indians were ineffective for cutting down large trees. But with the metal axes used by colonists, the methods of clear cutting the forests were introduced. The growing population of Europeans who cleared the land for farming, combined with the overhunting of local fur-bearing animals, greatly changed America's environment.

In colonizing the Americas, Europeans entered a land that was strange to them. They largely chose to ignore the model of adaptation practiced by Native Americans and instead endeavored to transform the land into something they understood. This involved the practice of clearing large tracts of land for agriculture. European farming methods changed forever the environment and the life styles that Native Americans had known.

During the early seventeenth century, English settlers discovered the tobacco native to North America and soon established a lucrative market between England and the Chesapeake colonies. Tobacco was so easy to grow and profitable to sell that farmers of the American Southeast had to be compelled by law to set aside a portion of their lands expressly to be used for growing food for their families and slaves. Primary sources related to this, as well as T.H. Breen's "Planter's Minds," are included in Carolyn Merchant's *Major Problems in American Environmental History* (chap. 4).

In his 1926 *Soil Exhaustion as a Factor in the Agricultural History of Virginia and Maryland, 1606–1860,* Avery O. Craven (1886–1980) examined the high toll wrought upon the land by repeatedly growing a single crop until the soil yielded no more nutrients. Driven by high profits, farmers generally grew tobacco to the exclusion of all other commercial crops. Because tobacco quickly drains the nitrogen and potassium from the soil, farmers found that they had to abandon depleted fields for fresh land. In the process, extensive forests were cleared for the cultivation of tobacco. The demands placed upon the colonies by England combined with poor agricultural practices led to abuse of the land.

In the mid-eighteenth century, Europeans were entering a period of technological advances known as the Industrial Revolution. While pollution did not begin with modern industrialization, and has always been a byproduct of human manufacturing endeavors, it was greatly intensified by the proliferation of factories. This third section examines the impact of industrial pollution on the environment, the effects of over-use of resources, and questions these developments raise in environmental history.

The reliance on machinery to perform tasks that had previously been preformed by human or animal power, or at best, water power, unwittingly caused great stress on the natural environment. Steam engines that burned wood or coal to create their power not only tapped those natural resources from the Earth, but also expelled noxious gasses into the atmosphere. It was often felt that the sheer size and volume of the air and waters could absorb and dissipate these discharges.

With industrialization of the United States in the nineteenth century, the country faced the same dilemma of how to use its natural resources as did European governments during America's colonial period. According to Joseph M. Petulla in *American Environmental History* (1977, Introduction), the history of the United States has many examples of leaders struggling to place natural resources into the context of market capitalism and free enterprise—premises that lay at the heart of American democracy. America's vastness and the illusion of inexhaustible resources justified exploitation of the land. After America gained its independence, support for entrepreneurialism only validated this attitude.

The industrial use of resources expanded unchecked through the late nineteenth century until the conservationist movement began in earnest. Beginning with a small, disjointed effort by scientists, naturalists, and transcendentalists to conserve America's dwindling wilderness and resources, the movement grew to governmental proportions under President Theodore Roosevelt. Federal legislation was ultimately passed to protect and manage millions of acres of forest preserves and national parks (Petulla, chap. 11).

Writing as an environmentalist, Petulla notes that American concepts of democracy favor industry and enterprise at the expense of the environment when the two conflict. This is reinforced by America's system of politics and jurisprudence. The technological abilities and business imperatives of modern America increased the degree of natural resource exploitation.

Arguably, one of the most influential books regarding humans and the environment has been *Silent Spring* (1962) by Rachel Carson (1907–1964). Carson chiefly focused on the harmful effects of pesticides used in modern agriculture. Referring to mounting scientific evidence, Carson told of a world in which widespread pesticide use had destroyed virtually all lower forms of life on Earth. The spring was silent because the living creatures had all died off from consuming food contaminated with DDT, BHC, ATP, and other recently introduced chemicals.

Many of Carson's critics contended that she had exaggerated the dangers of pesticide use and had sensationalized its impact upon birds, fish, and other animals. However, those who supported the contentions in *Silent Spring* applauded it as a work that made our industrial society reconsider the connection between pesticides and the natural world. Carson pointed out that the Earth's atmosphere and oceans have limits as to how much pesticide they can dilute. This theme is echoed in *DDT: Scientists, Citizens, and Public Policy* (1981) by Thomas R. Dunlap. Dunlap investigates efforts by scientists and the public to influence policy regarding pesticides and the environment.

In *The Recurring Silent Spring* (1989), H. Patricia Hynes celebrates Carson as a pioneer woman scientist and author. Hynes notes that *Silent Spring* encouraged ordinary people to question whether material and economic progress should be pursued at the expense of the environment. Hynes also partly credits *Silent Spring* with fostering the creation of the United States Environmental Protection Agency.

The end of the 1960s marked a time of increased awareness of the human impact on the natural world. One book that helped to put environmental issues into perspective was *Nature's Economy* (1979) by Donald Worster. In it, Worster examines the history of the science of ecology through scientific debate and governmental policy decisions from the initial appearance of the term in 1866. This book provides one of the best examples of the relevance of history of science to environmental history. Worster, however, places ecology as much in philosophical and social terms as in scientific by noting that the goals of science are always open to interpretation by cultural interests. Worster makes plain the idea that the popular understanding of ecology is often not reflected within scientific models.

Population growth and urbanization placed special stresses on the environment. In America, population increases resulting largely from immigration quickly overwhelmed many municipal systems. Because America lagged behind England and Europe in embracing industrialization, the successes and failures in constructing various waste disposal systems could be evaluated.

Waste disposal within urban centers has been a problem concerning societies since ancient times. With industrialization the problem increased dramatically. In *Garbage in the Cities* (1981), Martin V. Melosi points out that while many people appreciated the link between filth and disease in the nineteenth century, and laws were passed to address those problems, the laws were often ignored or poorly enforced. As a result, epidemics caused by poor sanitary conditions in American cities were not uncommon as late as the 1940s.

The strain on barely adequate waste disposal plans was exacerbated by the ominous flow of industrial waste being pumped into the air and water. By 1900 the problems of polluted water, sewage and garbage disposal, and smoke and noise abatement were perceived as serious by many. During the 1960s and 1970s, some Americans began to realize the link between garbage generation and the profligate consumption inherent in affluence (Melosi, chap. 7).

The problem of waste disposal is common to industrialization regardless of the location. In the mid-nineteenth century, Germany's Ruhr River basin was converted into an industrial system. While the factories in the area were pouring pollution into the air and water, German governments were concerned only with the condition of the economy. German courts favored industrial interests over protecting the environment or the people living within the Ruhr basin (Brüggemeier, pp. 37–51).

German governments in the late nineteenth and early twentieth centuries looked upon the growing pollution problem as a nuisance to be endured by the local inhabitants. However, by the 1960s the population of the Ruhr River basin began to press for political and legal solutions. By the 1990s, technological remedies have helped to curb air pollution, but the rivers of the area are still used to carry industrial waste, and soil contamination has been widely discovered (Brüggemeier, pp. 51–52).

Although environmental historians have not yet given adequate attention to industrial air pollution, Lynne Page Snyder makes a significant contribution in her study of atmospheric discharges in the steel industry. In 1948, a weather anomaly caused pollution from a zinc smelter to form a debilitating smog that lasted for several days over two steel-mill communities in southwestern Pennsylvania. Hundreds became ill and a number of deaths resulted. This incident caused the public and the federal government to view air pollution as a health issue, where previously the reduction of air pollution had been seen as a means of reducing waste through efficient consumption of resources (Snyder, pp. 125–133).

Scientists of many fields have investigated global air quality. In *Atmospheric Pollution* (1981), Alfred R. Meetham addresses a wide-ranging audience including engineers, scientists, politicians, and concerned citizens to describe the ill effects of air pollution and what can be done to combat the problem. While keeping the book's language as non-technical as possible, Meetham covers fuel and energy sources for home and industrial use and the measurement, spread, and prevention of atmospheric pollution.

Human intervention in the environment is certainly not limited to the land or the air. In *The Fisherman's Problem* (1990) Arthur F. McEvoy describes the ecosystems of California's rivers and ocean shores. His focus rests on the point that those who fish for a living must range upon the free ocean in search of common resources. Because this must be profitable, and because of keen competition for dwindling resources, voluntary limitations on catches are very difficult to guarantee. While most commercial fishers have understood the dangers in not sustaining fish populations, the over-harvesting of fish has become more problematic and pervasive through new technologies. An environmental history of the technological impact on sea life is much needed.

Many of the same problems seen in the oceans of the world are common to smaller bodies of water. In *The Late, Great Lakes* (1986), William Ashworth provides an environmental history of North America's mid-continental lakes. Ashworth looks at the water- and land-borne resources of the Great Lakes both before and after industrialization. Human settlement, the toxic effluent of the timbering, mining, and shipping industries, and pesticides disruptive to the natural environment, brought the lakes' ecosystem near death by the late 1950s and early 1960s.

Fish populations that had once sustained the Chippewas and astounded the first Europeans in the area had been reduced to the point that few fisheries could be kept in business by the 1960s. Lamprey eels, competition from alewife fish, and toxic industrial wastes had reduced Great Lakes commercial fish yields to less than 10 percent of the numbers known during the 1920s (Ashworth, chap. 11).

The Aral Sea in the former Soviet Union has also been subjected to human intervention that has caused its surface area to be reduced by more than 40 percent since the 1960s. As a shallow terminal lake, the Aral relies on an inflow from rivers and groundwater to counter the lake's losses to evaporation. The lake has been decreasing in size because of a decade of low rainfall levels in the 1970s and the diversion of tributary waters for agricultural irrigation (Micklin, pp. 1170–1171).

The reduced volume of the lake has had correlate effects on the fishing industry of the region, and has initiated a desertification process in the surrounding area. The change in this landscape feature has also had a dramatic impact on local weather patterns. While some scientists believe that the problem can be resolved if immediate action is taken, others believe that the damage is irreparable (Micklin, pp. 1172–1174).

The global problem of deforestation has been considered in a number of works since the 1980s. The loss of forest ecosystems is examined in *Tropical Rain Forests and the World Atmosphere* (1986) by Ghillean T. Prance, *World Deforestation in the Twentieth Century* (1988), edited by John F. Richards and Richard P. Tucker, and *Deforestation of Tropical Rain Forests* (1992) by Torsten Amelung and Markus Diehl. While each of these works has a slightly different focus, they all agree that destruction of the Earth's forests will have a serious negative effect on global climate and ecological balance.

One scientific study that examines human influence on the Earth can be found in Neil Roberts's *Holocene: An Environmental History* (1989). Roberts focuses on an interdisciplinary approach covering several regional examples of human ecology and the influence that the environment has had on humans. Beginning at ten thousand years before present, Roberts carries his study through modern times, and even takes a brief look at what the future may hold regarding human interaction with the environment.

In *Preserving the Global Environment* (1991), Jessica Tuchman Mathews has edited several essays describing the most pressing modern environmental issues ranging from population growth to the economic policies that drive the demand for resources. In addition to the problem of deforestation, this work addresses ozone-layer depletion, climate change, and the need for international cooperation to resolve environmental problems.

Until recent years the field of environmental history has been dominated by an American perspective. The March 1990 issue of the *Journal of American History* presents a series of articles relating to several broader aspects of environmental history. *The Norton History of the Environmental Sciences* (1992), edited by Peter J. Bowler, offers a wide range of global and historical issues. The bibliographical essay in this work is especially helpful in identifying many sources covering environmental history from antiquity to the present. Moreover, new articles and books relating environmental history to the geosciences appear or are reviewed every year in *Environmental History Review,* or are indexed in the *ISIS Current Bibliographies* under the physical, earth, and biological sciences.

Industrialization on the scale known in the twentieth century was made possible through technology informed by science. Much of the environmental history of the late 1980s and 1990s has been driven by economic interests and governmental policy concerns. Population growth, technology and industrialization, spreading consumerism, and human impact on the world ecosystem are global in scope. They require recognition from the world community as problems that affect everyone regardless of political boundaries. Local environmental problems, moreover, have a cumulative effect that contributes to global warming, ozone depletion, air and water pollution, and desertification. Environmental history, relying on multidisciplinary contributions from both the sciences and humanities, can provide interpretation of human interaction with the environment, broadening perspective on these issues.

Scott W. Daley

Bibliography
Ashworth, William. *The Late, Great Lakes: An Environmental History.* New York: Knopf, 1986.
Brüggemeier, Franz-Joseph. "A Nature Fit for Industry: The Environmental History of the Ruhr Basin, 1840–1990." *Environmental History Review* 18 (Spring 1994): pp. 35–54.
Craven, Avery O. *Soil Exhaustion as a Factor in Agricultural History of Virginia and Maryland, 1606–1860.* Urbana: University of Illinois, 1926.
Hughes, J. Donald. *Pan's Travail: Environmental Problems of the Ancient Greeks and Romans.* Baltimore, Md.: Johns Hopkins University Press, 1994.
Melosi, Martin V. *Garbage in the Cities: Refuse, Reform, and the Environment, 1880–1980.* College Station: Texas A&M University Press, 1981.
Merchant, Carolyn, ed. *Major Problems in American Environmental History.* Lexington, Ky.: D.C. Heath, 1993.
Micklin, Phillip P. "Desiccation of the Aral Sea: A Water Management Disaster in the Soviet Union." *Science* 241 (September 2, 1988): pp. 1170–1176.
Petulla, Joseph M. *American Environmental History: The Exploitation and Conservation of Natural Resources.* San Francisco: Boyd and Fraser, 1977.
Snyder, Lynne Page. "'The Death-Dealing Smog over Donora, Pennsylvania': Industrial Air Pollution, Public Health Policy, and the Politics of Expertise, 1948–1949." *Environmental History Review* 18 (Spring 1994): pp. 117–139.
Weiss, H., M., A. Courty, W. Wetterstrom, F. Guichard, L. Senior, R. Meadow, A. Curnow. "The Genesis and Collapse of Third Millennium North Mesopotamian Civilization." *Science* 261 (August 20, 1993): pp. 995–1003.
White, Richard. "Historiographical Essay on American Environmental History: The Development of a New Historical Field." *Pacific Historical Review* 54 (August 1985): pp. 297–335.

See also Agriculture in the Seventeenth and Eighteenth Centuries; Climate Change, since 1940; Conservation of Natural Resources; Exploration, Age of; Ecology; Earth in Decay; Environmentalism; Geography and Imperialism; Geography and Natural Theology; Geography; Geopolitics; Greenhouse Effect; Humboldtian Science; International Organizations in Oceanography; Meteorology, Medical; Mining and Knowledge of the Earth; Ozone; Soil Conservation; Soil Science; Water Quality; Wilderness

Environmentalism

Political activity relating to ecology or the natural environment.

Historians have produced an enormous amount of scholarly work devoted to environmental activism. These scholars have addressed a myriad of issues. Many have studied particular organizations created to defend the environment; others have considered the roots of environmental activism by studying the religious and philosophical origins of the movement. Some scholars have focused on the fundamental question of preservation versus conservation, while others have studied the political and social contexts in which environmental movements have emerged. These traditional perspectives, as well as new analyses that consider the importance of gender, race, and class in environmentalism, add to our understanding of the factors that influence people to agitate for the protection of the natural world.

Some historians argue that humans have exhibited an awareness of the natural world and a determination to protect it for centuries. Robert Alison's article "The Earliest Traces of a Conservation Conscience" examines early examples of environmental awareness. Published in *Natural History* in 1981, Alison's piece describes conservation efforts during the Roman occupation of England and across the Middle East. In *Historical Ecology* (1980), Lester Bilsky has collected essays documenting environmental awareness in a number of cultures across the centuries, including early Greece, Rome, and China. In all of these countries, historians have noted individuals who sought to protect the natural world for either economic or spiritual reasons.

Religious factors have certainly shaped human attitudes toward the physical world and have encouraged many to work actively to protect the environment. Essays compiled by J. Ronald Engel and Joan Gibb Engel in *Ethics of Environment and Development* (1990) document the various perspectives of traditional religions toward the environment.

In addition to examinations of more traditional religious tenets, scholars have also studied the contradictions that mark Christian attitudes toward environmental protection. Controversial new works by feminist scholars have addressed the issue of gender and the unique relationship of women to the Earth. Writing in the wake of the women's movement of the 1960s, feminist scholars have demanded a new examination of traditional conceptions about nature. In *Gyn/ecology* (1978) by Mary Daly and in the various works of Carolyn Merchant, especially *The Death of Nature* (1980), the singular connection between women and the natural world has been articulated and a new approach, often labeled eco-feminism, has been explored.

While spirituality has transcended temporal and geographical constraints and has promoted environmental activism in communities around the world, environmentalism in the Western world has also been shaped by other unique factors. The origin of contemporary Western environmental awareness may be located in the romantic movement of the nineteenth century. Influenced by trends in art and literature, intellectuals increasingly recognized the significance of the natural world for its aesthetic value alone.

Encouraged by the advancements in scientific thought initiated during the Enlightenment, scientists during the romantic era joined thinkers like Lord Byron (1788–1824) in their celebration of the natural environment. In England, this aesthetic movement influenced young men like Charles Darwin (1809–1882), who wrote in 1838 that "I Was Born A Naturalist," a quote that provided Ralph Colp, Jr., with the title of an article he wrote on Darwin in 1980 for the *Journal of the History of Medicine*. Less famous men than Darwin studied and sought to protect the natural environment they came to treasure. Many of these enthusiasts channeled their energies into naturalist clubs. A plethora of studies of specific clubs have been written by both professional and amateur historians. Broader studies of this phenomenon include John Ranlett's article "'Checking Nature's Desecration': Late Victorian Environmental Organizations," published in *Victorian Studies* in 1983. David Elliston Allen offers a synthesis for one country with his *Naturalist in Britain: A Social History* (1976, second edition 1994).

By the mid-nineteenth century, these developments spread to the United States and were quickly wedded to the transcendentalist philosophy of Henry David Thoreau (1817–1862) and Ralph Waldo Emerson (1803–1882). The international importance of the transcendentalists' ideals and their impact on naturalists has been evidenced in articles like "Emerson's Natural Theology and the Paris Naturalists: Toward a Theory of Animated Nature," published in *Journal of Ideas* in 1980. Painters, influenced by the Romantics and the Transcendentalists, also promoted the beauty of the natural environment. "Ecological Vision and Wildlife Painting toward the End of the Nineteenth Century," written by Allen Ellenius and published in *The Natural Sciences and the Arts* (1985) depicts the growing interest expressed by some painters in the outside world.

While these writers gave voice to the intellectual facets of the growing naturalist movement, others like John James Audubon (1785–1851) and his predecessor John Bartram (1699–1777) explored and documented the American wilderness. Audubon, perhaps the most famous of the naturalists who traveled the United States, enjoyed a career that has been chronicled in a number of publications; among the best of the recent works on Audubon is *On the Road with John James Audubon* (1980), written by Mary Durant and Michael Harwood. Audubon and his fellow travelers provided widely viewed illustrations and accounts, promoting the ideal that nature is uniquely beautiful and should be valued. *City of Nature: Journeys to Nature in the Age of American Romanticism* (1980), describes this phenomenon.

All of these factors contributed to the birth of the contemporary environmental movement, a movement that dates from the late nineteenth century and that was born from a unique combination of intellectual trends and social and economic factors. During the last few decades of that century, intellectuals and naturalists responded to the environmental devastation wreaked by the massive industrialization of the period. Sparked by the destruction of natural resources they saw around them and made aware by the closing of the frontier around 1890 of the growing need to preserve the environment, many individuals began to articulate the need to conserve natural resources.

Perhaps the most famous of the early professional conservationists was Gifford Pinchot (1865–1946), an American who enjoyed the benefits of a Yale education, wealth, and subsequent training in forestry in Germany. Pinchot was a champion of the philosophy of sustained-yield management, arguing that lumbermen should always plant more trees than they cut, ensuring timber for the future and minimizing loss of topsoil and the siltation of waterways. Pinchot was influential in guiding President Theodore Roosevelt toward the doctrine of conservation.

Along with protecting the American forest, efforts were also undertaken to protect the arid lands of the American West and the water systems of that same region during the Progressive Era. In 1902, the federal government enacted the Reclamation Act, which provided funding for the construction of dams and irrigation systems across the western United States. This policy, which had originally been proposed by explorer-geologist John Wesley Powell (1834–1902) in his 1878 *Report on the Lands of the Arid Region of the United States,* proposed that the natural limitations of the land be recognized when settlement was initiated.

U.S. President Theodore Roosevelt (1858–1919) embraced the arguments proposed by Pinchot and Powell and, in 1908, presented the concept of conservation to the American people in a speech he made to a meeting of the governors of the various states. Roosevelt argued in this speech that it is morally necessary to protect the wilderness from overdevelopment in order to guarantee that later generations will have an opportunity to continue its use. His goal was to provide the greatest good for the largest number of people; Roosevelt, like Pinchot and other progressive reformers, sought to ensure resources for future generations, demonstrating a willingness to sacrifice nature in order to fulfill the perceived needs of humanity. *Conservation and the Gospel of Efficiency,* written by Samuel Hays and originally published in 1959, offers a critical appraisal of these early conservationists.

The anthrocentric position espoused by Roosevelt and his colleagues did not go unopposed. In *Man and Nature,* published in 1864 by George Perkins Marsh (1801–1882), the question of humanity's ethical obligation to the natural world was addressed. Marsh looked beyond the economic value of nature and chronicled the devastation man had wrought on the environment from ancient times through the present. According to Marsh, humanity was obligated to repair its damage of the natural world; his biocentric perspective acknowledged the inherent inviolate characteristics of nature and demanded that a new respect for the Earth be exhibited.

John Muir (1838–1914), a naturalist and writer who was fundamental in articulating the preservationists' creed, espoused many of Marsh's ideas. His biocentric perspective proposed that the interests of nature equal those of man. Preservationists sought to protect certain natural regions from development; unlike the conservationists who saw protected land as reserved resources awaiting later development, the preservationists demanded that these ecological systems be protected in perpetuity.

The most famous debate in the Progressive Era conflict over conservation versus preservation took place over the Hetch-Hetchy Valley, an area in Yosemite National Park in California. During the first decade of the twentieth century, San Francisco sought permission from the federal government to build a reservoir in the valley for its water supply. Muir and his supporters in the Sierra Club, an organization that he had helped create in 1892, vehemently fought the city. Both Muir and Pinchot attempted to use their influence to convince President Roosevelt of the merit of their positions. Roosevelt, at heart a conservationist rather than a preservationist, was convinced by Pinchot to support the city's goal. Ultimately, the city succeeded in its campaign. Details of this debate and of other confrontations that occurred during the Progressive Era are discussed in: *John Muir and His*

Legacy: The American Conservation Movement (1981), by Stephen R. Fox; *The Politics of Wilderness Preservation* (1982), by Craig Allin; *The Pathless Way: John Muir and the American Wilderness* (1984) by Michael Cohen; and Robert Ben Martin, *The Hetch Hetchy Controversy: The Value of Nature in a Technological Society* (1982).

While the conservationists won in the Hetch-Hetchy conflict, the preservationists were successful in convincing the American Congress to pass a National Parks Act in 1916; this bill created a separate National Park Service whose primary goal was to protect national parks and wilderness areas. This story is told in great detail in *The Birth of the National Park Service* (1985), an account by participant Horace Albright as told to Robert Cahn, and in John Ise's *Our National Park Policy: A Critical History*, published in 1961 but still a valuable source.

The United States was not alone in establishing national parks. In New Zealand, the Maori people acted to protect their native homelands by placing them under the protection of the English crown; their efforts led to the establishment of the Tongariro National Park in 1894. South Africa followed in 1898 by creating the Sabie Game Reserve, a facility to protect the unique wildlife. Max Nicholson examines conservation and preservation movements in the former British Empire in *The Environmental Revolution* (1970), and in *The New Environmental Age* (1987).

Progressive Era campaigns to protect the environment also addressed the changes occurring in the growing cities. Urban reformers, too, sought to preserve and protect what remained of the natural world around them. Frederick Law Olmstead (1822–1903), the landscape architect who designed New York's Central Park, argued that urban dwellers need access to open spaces in order to preserve their mental health. Jane Addams (1840–1935), best known for her work with Hull House in Chicago, actively fought to protect the urban poor from the filth of city life. The historian Martin Melosi addresses these themes in *Garbage in the Cities: Refuse, Reform, and the Environment, 1880–1980* (1980); he has also edited a collection of essays, *Pollution and Reform in American Cities, 1870–1930* (1980), which considers environmental decay in the urban setting. Perhaps the best, most recent, description of the environmental consequences of urban life is William Cronon's *Nature's Metropolis* (1991).

The debate between American preserva-tionists and conservationists continued through the Progressive period and into the Depression. During the 1930s, however, faced with economic devastation and fearful of a challenge to the capitalist economic system, conservationists directed their attention toward improving agriculture and promoting economic stability. At times, these programs sacrificed natural resources in order to preserve the larger social order; at other times, New Deal projects like the Civilian Conservation Corps actually engaged in creating and protecting natural resources. Contemporary accounts of the struggles that occurred over these matters within Franklin Roosevelt's administration can be found in a number of primary sources. Robert Marshall (1901–1939), an ardent supporter of expanding the National Forest system, wrote his plea for conservation in his book *The People's Forest* in 1933. *The Secret Diaries of Harold Ickes,* secretary of the interior during the New Deal, discuss a number of issues including the internal discussions that shaped federal policy toward the environment during the 1930s. T.H. Watkins's recent biography of Ickes (1874–1952), *Righteous Pilgrim: The Life and Times of Harold Ickes* (1990), offers a briefer, more analytical study of Secretary Ickes's policies; Barry MacKintosh's 1985 article "Harold Ickes and the National Park Service" focuses specifically on Ickes's attitudes toward natural resource preservation.

The contemporary environmental movement, while shaped by early-twentieth-century debates over preservation and conservation, may be said to have had its origins in the post–World War II world. Shaken by the devastation of the war, and particularly by the environmental threat of atomic weaponry, citizens around the world began to discuss the fragility of the natural world. In 1949, Aldo Leopold's *Sand County Almanac* echoed the plea of George Perkins Marsh in *Man and Nature* and called for the creation of a new land ethic. Leopold (1886–1948), like Marsh, argued that humanity has a natural obligation to protect the environment and that by violating that obligation, we disobey the natural order of the universe.

While Leopold couched his argument in philosophical terms, Rachel Carson (1907–1964) drew a frightening portrait of life in a postnuclear, pesticide-laden world in *Silent Spring* (1962). Carson's dramatic style and meticulous argument convinced many Americans that the world around them was seriously imperiled. Publication of *The Quiet Crisis* by

U.S. Senator Stewart Udall (b. 1920), with an introduction by President John F. Kennedy (1917–1963), further legitimized the growing concern many felt about this issue. In the wake of these publications, and bolstered by the social unrest of the 1960s, a number of local, as well as national and international, organizations sprang up to protest environmental destruction.

One of the best known environmental organizations to emerge has been Greenpeace. Born in British Columbia, Canada, in 1969, Greenpeace initially worked to stop American nuclear weapons testing. Nurtured by the antigovernment, antibusiness attitudes of the day, Greenpeace quickly found itself gaining notoriety. Along with Greenpeace, associations like Earth First!—a loose organization advocating ecotage, the nonviolent destruction of industrial equipment used to assault the land—came to represent the most radical of the environmental action groups. More accepted were the traditional organizations like John Muir's Sierra Club and the Audubon Society; both groups saw their membership rolls expand significantly since the 1960s.

These organizations, as well as most other environmental groups, have published accounts of their histories and their ambitions. These works include *Warriors of the Rainbow: A Chronicle of the Greenpeace Movement* (1979) by Robert Hunter; *The History of the Sierra Club, 1892–1970* (1988), written by Michael P. Cohen; and *Ecodefense* (1987) by Dave Foreman and Bill Haywood. Edward Abbey's novel *The Monkeywrench Gang* reflects the social currents that produced these environmental organizations.

Despite the relative success of preservationist associations, mainstream environmental policy in the United States still reflects conservationist traditions. While some progress was made during the 1960s and 1970s with the passage of bills such as the National Environmental Policy Act of 1969, the nation endured a retrogressive environmental policy under the administrations of presidents Ronald Reagan (b. 1911) and George Bush (b. 1924). As Samuel P. Hayes documented in his recent book *Beauty, Health, and Permanence: Environmental Politics in the United States, 1955–1985* (1987), Reagan appointees such as James Watt (b. 1938) and Anne Gorsuch Burford (b. 1942) attempted to use their offices to undermine the advances that had been made during previous decades.

Environmentalists in the United States have tended to stay within the traditional two-party system or to eschew party politics all together, concentrating their efforts, instead, in direct-action campaigns aimed at the grassroots. In other parts of the world, however, activists have formed their own parties, usually calling themselves Greens. Beginning in New Zealand in 1972 and in Europe a year later, these organizations sought support from citizens who believed the environment to be as significant an issue as the economy or the military. By the early 1990s, Green parties had gained representation in parliaments across Europe.

Green parties have not enjoyed unbridled success, however. Like all political parties, they have faced both internal and external conflicts. In Germany, where the Greens have possessed significant popular support, the party has had difficulty in protecting itself from internal divisions over economic issues; in other words, some members see the goal of their party as fundamentally altering the nation's economic system, while other members are strictly focused on natural resource preservation. An analysis of the history of the various Green parties is found in *The Green Wave: A Comparative Analysis of Ecological Parties* (1992) by Wolfgang Rudig and P. Lowe. *Green Parties: An International Guide,* published in 1991, also provides an introduction to the history of Green politics.

Green parties have also been influential in Eastern Europe and in countries of the former Soviet Union. During the last years of the Soviet Union's hegemony over Eastern Europe, a number of Green movements emerged to advocate improvements in the Soviets' notoriously poor natural resource management programs. In the wake of the Soviet collapse, independent Green parties have sought to help shape the cleanup of the extensive environmental damage done by the old regimes. "The Emergence of Soviet Environmental Studies" by Blair Ruble, published in *Environmental History Review* in 1980, is one of the earliest works devoted to these issues.

While the Green parties may be the most visible symbol of environmental activism around the planet, other, less public transformations may actually indicate the depth of the environmental movement. The growing popularity of recycling, the increased attention being given to the need for sustainable growth based on the least environmental damage, and the growing concern for the loss of nonrenewable resources suggest that, increasingly, individuals are focusing on the need to limit their consumption and to protect the natural world around them.

The history of environmentalism is an important area of consideration for historians of the earth sciences. Because environmentalists and earth scientists interact on so many levels, a conception of the historical trends that shape each of these areas is imperative for both. In addition, the history of environmentalism reminds us of the intersection of social and political history and the history of science.

Sandra Barney

Bibliography

Alison, Robert. "The Earliest Traces of a Conservation Conscience." *Natural History* 90 (1981): pp. 72–77.

Bilsky, Lester, ed. *Historical Ecology.* Port Washington, N.Y.: Kennikat Press, 1980.

Cohen, Michael. *The History of the Sierra Club, 1892–1970.* San Francisco: Sierra Club Books, 1988.

Hays, Samuel P. *Beauty, Health, and Permanence: Environmental Politics in the United States, 1955–1985.* New York: Cambridge University Press, 1987.

———. *Conservation and the Gospel of Efficiency.* New York: Atheneum, (1959) 1974.

Hunter, Robert. *Warriors of the Rainbow: A Chronicle of the Greenpeace Movement.* New York: Holt, Rhinehart and Winston, 1979.

Muller-Rommel, F. ed. *New Politics in Western Europe: The Rise and Success of Green Parties and Alternative Lists.* Boulder, Colo.: West View Press, 1989.

Nicholson, Max. *The New Environmental Age.* Cambridge: Cambridge University Press, 1987.

Norton, Bryan G. *Toward Unity among Environmentalists.* New York: Oxford University Press, 1991.

Pepper, David. *The Roots of Modern Environmentalism.* London: Croom Helm, Ltd., 1987.

Ranlett, John. "'Checking Nature's Desecration': Late Victorian Environmental Organizations." *Victorian Studies* 26 (1983): pp. 197–222.

Rubin, Charles. *The Green Crusade: Rethinking the Roots of Environmentalism.* New York: Free Press, 1994.

Ruble, Blair. "The Emergence of Soviet Environmental Studies." *Environmental History Review* 5 (1980): pp. 2–13.

Rudig, Wolfgang. "Green Party Politics around the World." *Environment* 33 (1991): pp. 7–31.

Scheffer, Victor. *The Shaping of Environmentalism in America.* Seattle: University of Washington Press, 1991.

Worster, Donald, ed. *American Environmentalism: The Formative Period, 1860–1915.* New York: John Wiley and Sons, 1973.

See also Climate Change; Conservation of Natural Resources; Ecology; Earth in Decay; Geography and Imperialism; Geography and Natural Theology; Geography; Geopolitics; Greenhouse Effect; Humboldtian Science; International Organizations in Oceanography; Meteorology, Medical; Mining and Knowledge of the Earth; Ozone; Soil Conservation; Soil Science; Water Quality; Wilderness

Evolution and the Geosciences

The theory of historical change in the forms of life, having major implications for the scientific view of the Earth and the conditions of life.

Evolutionary ideas have shaped the development of the geosciences in two prominent areas. First, changes in life implied a past Earth with a different natural order and physical conditions. Prehistoric climates and even biogeochemical processes, such as in the atmosphere, became open questions for field research and theory. With geophysical change thought to be a stimulant for evolution, events of climatic change took on new significance. Second, biological history demanded a long timescale, which prompted earth scientists into dating geological eras and the age of the Earth.

Evolution was brought into scientific respectability by *On the Origin of Species* (1859) by Charles Darwin (1809–1882). Darwin connected ideas about geological history, the fossil record, biogeographic distribution, anatomical relationships among species, ecological interaction, and heredity. His theory of natural selection made transformation an inevitable consequence of ecological pressures and adaptive hereditary variation, assuming that geophysical conditions also changed (Ruse, chap. 7). This promoted geology to great scientific importance as a foundation of Darwinism, one of the most famous, revolutionary, and significant ideas in science.

In the years since, the word "evolution" has come to encompass far more than a theory about biological species. Modern treatises in geology frequently treat the evolution of a formation, without intending actual similarity with biological processes. From rocks to societies to ideas, the term captured the language of historical change. This casual usage obscures the different implications the term has carried.

The first question is how to talk about evolution before Darwin. The word itself was not in existence, at least for species transformation. In the 1700s, evolving meant an unrolling of biological structure, as the embryo grows into the adult form (Bowler, chap. 9). This orderly process of hidden parts became a metaphor for chemical release of gases. The social philosopher Herbert Spencer (1820–1903) knew this when he popularized the term "evolution" for Darwin's theory. He incorporated Darwinism into his own theory of inevitable cosmic progress, in which life is a trend of increasing organization and complexity. The origins and popular success of evolutionism lie in theories of progress as much as ideas about biological species (Bowler, pp. 8–25).

Theories about changes in species had been proposed before 1859, but they did not prompt schools of radical research or find scientific acceptance. Older histories found precursors of evolution in materialist theories and in philosophical opposition to Christian interpretations of the world. Thus the eighteenth-century Enlightenment seemed the source of evolutionism. Its Newtonian science fostered naturalistic schemes for the origin and development of life. Darwin, this interpretation implied, simply fleshed them out and fitted them with an acceptable mechanism.

Modern historians distrust such presentist glimpses of ideas that developed in separate contexts. A provocative thesis has been Michel Foucault's conclusion that Enlightenment scientists framed their ideas on organic change within a static vision of natural order. Developmental theories by G.L. Leclerc, comte de Buffon (1707–1788) and Jean-Baptiste de Lamarck (1744–1829) were shockingly materialistic, but not evolutionist in the modern sense. Change meant the filling in of God's created, rationally constructed order. The dramatic shift to a dynamic, open-ended nature, as Darwinism proposed, came in the 1800s. The two world views are so different that materialism is but a minor continuity from the Enlightenment to Darwin.

Peter Bowler's *Evolution: The History of an Idea* (1989) provides the most complete review of the history of evolutionism. He argues (pp. 50–89), with more detail about the biological theories, that Foucault's thesis helps somewhat to see what Darwin did. Adopting open-ended development was crucial. But the dichotomy facing naturalists was between created order and random disorder. That did not preclude theories of historical change, and indeed naturalists devoted much attention and effort to the evidence of change during the 1700s.

Earlier evolutionism is not a direct precursor, but for complex reasons. Darwinism was founded in a climate of reaction against Enlightenment materialism; natural theology was dominant. But most historians agree that Newtonian theories of mechanistic dynamics, from ecology and economics, played a great role in Darwin's thinking (Bowler, chap. 6). Those theories had roots in the Enlightenment and ties to natural theology.

Darwinism appeared in an intellectual climate receptive to historical theorizing. Progressive views of human history provided metaphors for change in the natural world. Although ideas of social progress arose in the 1700s, they did not at that time inspire evolutionism. They did not expand the timescale beyond the six thousand years of biblical chronology. Geological discovery and interpretation did.

As Martin Rudwick reveals in his 1976 *Meaning of Fossils*, reformulating the nature of fossils came first. Nicholas Steno (1638–1686) in 1669 had made the connection to once-living creatures. At first, discovery of novel forms was not surprising, because naturalists recognized that much of the world's diversity was not cataloged. Better collections forced the question of why fossils were different from contemporary species in size and form. More problematic were those found in the wrong environment, such as marine fossils on mountaintops. Various theories of sedimentation and deposition found the answer in past events.

That the Earth had a history was understandable. Time in the Judeo-Christian view was a narrative with beginning and ending (Rudwick, pp. 68–75). The history of rocks was fit into a prevailing frame of natural theology, to preserve the sense of design, despite a distinctly secular mood growing in Newtonian science. Naturalists connected the Earth's past to biblical chronology. Marine fossils were a result of the Deluge. Science and empiricist religion shared a faith in order and regular causes. Rational history and laws of processes were the goal, and science also discovered God's designs.

A deeper dilemma arose when naturalists tied assemblages of fossils to emerging ecological ideas about the cohesion of the economy of nature. Species interact in an orderly set of roles and connections. Past lives must have been in such an economy. When the fossils were unique, it implied that the organization and structure of the Earth had been different. Rudwick intentionally emphasizes the interaction of data and theorizing, because this was a period of accumulation. The types of fossils available, meaning the kinds of evidence, had great influence on the ideas that developed. Ever richer evidence suggested many past assemblages, which could be arranged as strata into a sequence of eras. The history of life gave the names to geological periods. Each needed time to exist, be destroyed, and be replaced. Information about biological fossils pushed naturalists toward a historical geology, with its implied deep time.

Leading figures in the establishment of deep time were James Hutton (1726–1797) and Charles Lyell (1797–1875). From a textual analysis, Stephen Jay Gould argues in *Time's Arrow, Time's Cycle* (pp. 3–19) for a role of metaphor over empirical observations in their work. They recognized the debate to be about the nature of time and change. The choices were history as a linear narrative or a nature of immanent laws. Gould (chap. 4) has made sense of Lyell's commitment to uniformitarian principles and opposition to evolutionism. It was a rejection of progressive history with its unique events and unpredictability. Lyell drew on the appeal of simple Newtonian systems with universal physical laws and regularity, thus in one sense rejecting history's narrative despite the fossil evidence.

Noting the simultaneous rise of self-conscious history, archaeology, and philology, Paolo Rossi argues in *The Dark Abyss* in 1984 that these parallels were as important as geology in the discovery of deep time. But the historical thinking was usually, for Victorians, progressive. It stemmed from another deep tradition for the language and meaning of change. Aristotelian organic philosophy saw historical change as a development, like the growth of a body. It is purposeful, aimed at an end like the mature organism. This was the metaphor for history in the nineteenth century. Whether change is in fact so teleological became a central part of the debate over geological and biological history (Rudwick, *Meaning of Fossils,* chap. 4). Progressive development was not the answer for Lyell, who thought Newtonian mechanism eliminated organicism.

Darwin subverted Lyell's vision of history as a nonprogressive state of balanced physical forces, by seeing the history of fossil life as a uniquely sequential story. Darwin drew upon evidences from embryology to make his argument for a sequence of forms, and yet he rejected the implicit purposeful development common to that subject. His synthesis was novel, deriving the origins of order from mechanistic processes, eliminating the need for design or direction (Ruse, pp. 188–201). Although the historian Bowler has pointed out how progressivist views persisted and returned in later evolutionism, Darwin provided a model for all the historical sciences. He made available a science with principles of historical contingency, with mechanistic laws, and without religious language.

The classic account of the importance of his work as a geologist to Darwin's theorizing is Michael T. Ghiselin's 1969 *Triumph of the Darwinian Method.* Darwin developed a hypothetico-deductive method that he applied with consistency to geological and evolutionary problems. Fieldwork led to a crisis, demanding explanations of extinction, distribution, variation, and relationships. The conclusion was that small local causes operate over long time, accumulating and dynamically producing the arrangement of the world. A naturalistic evolution of new species was a rejection of natural theology's principles of design. Both uniformitarianism and natural selection were appealing because they seemed properly scientific.

Certainly, like Darwinism, other disciplines appealed to the methodological standards of physical causes, consistency, and connections to the evidences from other sciences. Geophysical views of the origin of the Earth itself grew out of mathematical astronomy and dynamics, but may have prospered from the imagery of evolution, if not its data. Historians have barely begun the deep cross-disciplinary work to follow Ghiselin's suggestion that Darwin's success provided a method and legitimized other historical geosciences.

Rudwick's 1992 *Scenes from Deep Time* (pp. 247–251) emphasizes to the contrary the continuity of visual imagery of the past.

Darwinism fit right into the already popular constructions of past ages with their own climates and species. Evolution did provide a new language and scientific verification, but the message that persisted was one of progress to the present higher state of nature, including humanity as the goal.

Evolutionary theory did have one effect on chronological constructions from fossil data. Having given up the restrictive human chronology, geologists in the mid-1800s were prone to assume any time necessary. Fossiliferous eras were dated only with relative time, but geologists talked casually of hundreds of millions of years, or even of a limitless expanse's being available (Burchfield, p. 10). Darwinism confirmed this tendency: natural selection works slowly and thus it demands a long timescale. With evolution demonstrated, geologists could defend extended age.

Their ideas were already under assault from the physicist William Thomson, Lord Kelvin (1824–1907). Attracted to the physics of heat and models of a cooling Earth, Kelvin in 1852 began research and publication on the age of the Earth from physical calculations. In the standard account of the great debate over the age of the Earth that sprang up in the late 1800s, Joe Burchfield says in his 1975 *Age of the Earth* that Darwin enforced geologists' awareness of time and increased interest in the topic, but Kelvin introduced rigor and a quantitative, absolute timescale. In 1862, Kelvin restricted the age to less than four hundred million years. By 1868, he was leaving less than one hundred million years for the geological history of life. The estimates grew more restrictive, until by 1897 he had arrived at an age of twenty-four million years.

Kelvin was certainly aware of the implications of his limits for natural selection theory. He grudgingly accepted evolution, but only if it were directed by divine supervision. Pure Darwinism seemed morally and physically in error, an impossible theory of order arising out of randomness. He ignored geologists' historical fossils to embrace a model from physics.

Geologists were pulled in two directions. Evolution had provided an organizing theory for their subject, but physics was the prestigious ideal. Evolution threw geology and physics into a sharp conflict over proper methods and evidences. Burchfield shows that Kelvin's physics carried the day. Despite a diversity of approaches to dating the Earth, almost all agreed to Kelvin's limit of one hundred million years. A few strong Darwinians insisted that biological evidence should take precedence over calculation. But, as Bowler (chap. 9) explains, natural selection was in decline as the accepted mechanism of evolution. Alternative theories did not demand such extreme gradualism. Geologists turned to determinations from physical phenomena, never to turn back to the direct use of evolutionary sequences for absolute dating.

Too severe an assault on their uniformitarian gradualism was resisted. Geology and physics stayed in tension, with geologists not willing to completely give up their use of evolution (Burchfield, pp. 96–117). The vast age of the Earth came back dramatically after 1896 with the discovery of radioactive heat. Although some defenders of Darwinism crowed triumphantly about having been right all along, it was still an innovation from physics. Physicists, not paleontologists, pushed the startling estimates of age into the billions of years with the new radioactive decay estimates after 1908. Geologists who derived their interest in the question still from evolution, and depended on fossil markers, actually ignored and resisted the radiometric techniques (Burchfield, pp. 171–189). By then, most geologists had accommodated to theories of more rapid evolution, and were not demanding extreme age.

The only remaining opposition to radiometric dating came from another view of evolution theory, or rather antievolutionism. Ronald Numbers's 1992 *Creationists* provides the most detailed internal analysis of the arguments made by the movement calling itself scientific creationism. Such creationists recognized a historical truth, that Darwinism destroyed the role of religion in a scientific world view. In general, they denied an ancient Earth and the process of evolution. Their campaign, originating in the 1960s and flourishing in the 1980s, assailed geology as a support for evolution. Geology was caught up with philosophical and religious disapproval of evolution as dangerous to moral order. Numbers recognizes that consistency required their complaints against the validity of geological dating. Still controversial, creationist ideas have had little success within science but have had some political effect in the United States.

Besides an old age, evolutionists in the late 1800s had few suggestions for how the Earth had changed. One problem facing them was the origin of life, for spontaneous generation of life from nonliving matter was definitively disproved experimentally during this time (Farley, pp. 121–150). Most biologists were content with Darwin's own conclusion that the problem lay outside the realm of science, inaccessible to data or experimentation. Biologists constructed the tree of life with origins in unicellular creatures (Bowler, pp. 199–205). Thomas Huxley (1825–1895) caused a brief sensation in 1868 when he thought he had found the first step in seabed samples. It turned out not to be, but the idea that the ocean depths were old, unchanging, and likely to still hold primitive forms encouraged oceanographic exploration.

The chemical idea of the origin of life revived in the 1920s in the Soviet Union. Vladimir Ivanovich Vernadsky (1863–1945), developing biogeochemical ideas, held that life originated in a different atmosphere, and that later oxygen, nitrogen, and carbon dioxide had organic origins. Aleksandr Ivanovich Oparin (1894–1980) in *The Origin of Life* (1936) made the innovative insight that a single step to life was not needed. He postulated a series of increasing chemical organization, a continuity from inorganic to organic to organized life. Then in 1953 Stanley L. Miller (b. 1930) experimentally confirmed the first step. Re-creating Oparin's postulated early atmosphere, he produced a spontaneous formation of organic molecules. The experiment created sensational interest in the possibilities of discovering and replicating the conditions of life's origin (Farley, pp. 176–179). The geochemistry and atmosphere of ancient times became important new subjects of the geosciences.

Another evolutionary problem that inspired geoscientific ideas was peculiar biogeography, such as a single species found on opposite sides of the ocean. Data on the biogeographic distribution of modern and fossil species helped Darwin and Alfred Russel Wallace (1823–1913) arrive at the theory of evolution. Lyellian geology saw the Earth as a balance of building and decay processes, altering slowly. Darwin had used the relationships of animals on young islands to those on nearby older continents to argue for evolution. Wallace in particular saw evolution as a law explaining the replacement of species in time and space, and he continued to pioneer historical biogeography in the late 1800s. Darwinians stressed dispersal and isolation as the key to the patterns of species on Earth. Wallace actively promoted the theory of land bridges to connect areas with the same or similar species. The bridges, he argued, had

formerly connected land masses, then disappeared. This idea, made necessary by evolution, was the geoscientific paradigm for historical connections between continents until the mid-1900s, when continental drift replaced it.

A more general effect of evolutionism on theories of geology was Darwin's dependence on gradualism, or slow accumulations of small changes. Biologists and geologists saw this as a triumph against catastrophism, which had to be abandoned as too nearly invoking the miraculous to be science. Evolutionists almost universally supported a gradualist dogma for geology (Gould, pp. 174–176). Then in 1977, Niles Eldredge (b. 1943) and Stephen Jay Gould (b. 1941) introduced their theory of punctuated equilibrium. Even though their bursts of evolutionary change were still slow compared with biological lifetimes, they were rapid for geological time. The still controversial theory directed a great deal of attention to rates of change, and reopened the possibility of catastrophism.

At the same time, controversy developed over the theory of asteroid impact and mass extinction by Luis Alvarez (1911–1988) and his colleagues. The fossil assemblages define distinct eras, with occasional sharp boundaries where an entire biota disappeared. The end of the dinosaurs captured public attention, but there are several other important extinction events in Earth's history, as William Glen has discussed in his 1994 *Mass-extinction Debates*. The history of these debates is just beginning to be written. They represent at the least a repercussion for the geosciences of thinking about change and the demands of evolutionary theory.

William Kimler

Bibliography

Bowler, Peter J. *Evolution: The History of an Idea,* 2d ed. Berkeley: University of California Press, 1989.

Browne, Janet. *The Secular Ark: Studies in the History of Biogeography.* New Haven: Yale University Press, 1983.

Burchfield, Joe D. *Lord Kelvin and the Age of the Earth.* New York: Science History Publications, 1975.

Farley, John. *The Spontaneous Generation Controversy: From Descartes to Oparin.* Baltimore, Md.: Johns Hopkins University Press, 1977.

Foucault, Michel. *The Order of Things: The Archeology of the Human Sciences.* London: Tavistock, 1970.

Ghiselin, Michael T. *The Triumph of the Darwinian Method.* Berkeley: University of California Press, 1969.

Glen, William, ed. *The Mass-extinction Debates: How Science Works in a Crisis.* Stanford: Stanford University Press, 1994.

Gould, Stephen Jay. *Time's Arrow, Time's Cycle: Myth and Metaphor in the Discovery of Geological Time.* Cambridge: Harvard University Press, 1987.

Numbers, Ronald. *The Creationists: The Evolution of Scientific Creationism.* New York: Alfred A. Knopf, 1992.

Rossi, Paolo. *The Dark Abyss of Time: The History of the Earth and the History of Nations from Hooke to Vico.* Chicago: University of Chicago Press, 1984.

Rudwick, Martin J.S. *The Meaning of Fossils: Episodes in the History of Palaeontology.* 2d ed. Chicago: University of Chicago Press, 1976.

———. *Scenes from Deep Time: Early Pictorial Representations of the Prehistoric World.* Chicago: University of Chicago Press, 1992.

Ruse, Michael. *The Darwinian Revolution: Science Red in Tooth and Claw.* Chicago: University of Chicago Press, 1979.

See also Age of the Earth; Climates, Pleistocene and Recent; Climate Change; Deluge; Ecology; Foucault's Order of Things; Geography and Natural Theology; Geography; Geological Periodization; Geological Time; Geology; Humboldtian Science; Mass Extinctions and the Impact-Volcanic Controversy; Paleontology; Plutonists, Neptunists, Vulcanists; Stratigraphy

Expanding Earth Theories

Family of twentieth-century theories based on the premise that the Earth has expanded over time from a smaller globe, perhaps as little as 55 percent of the Earth's present diameter. First developed in detail during the 1920s and 1930s, expansion theories enjoyed a revival in the 1950s and 1960s and continue to sustain a modest but persistent research program. Although sometimes motivated by other concerns, the chief historical significance of expansion theories has been their potential to accommodate the evidence for continental displacement and provide at least a partial account of the underlying mechanism.

William Lowthian Green (d. 1890) probably deserves credit as the first serious proponent of Earth expansion, introducing the idea initially in 1857. I.O. Yarkovski advocated expansion in 1899 as a consequence of the transformation of weightless ether into matter. Several more theorists proposed some form of expansion during the first quarter of the twentieth century, but their work went largely unnoticed.

Credit for the first sustained focus on Earth expansion's potential as a mechanism for explaining the movement of the continents relative to each other goes to Bernhard Lindemann (b. 1871–?) in 1927 and Otto C. Hilgenberg in 1933, two German scientists working independently in Göttingen and Berlin, respectively. Unlike most of their contemporaries, both Lindemann and Hilgenberg were completely persuaded by the empirical arguments for continental displacement compiled by Alfred Wegener in *Die Entstehung der Kontinente und Ozeane* (The origin of continents and oceans, 1915). But like most of their contemporaries, they found Wegener's account of the possible mechanisms for moving the continents completely implausible. Instead of requiring the continents to plough through the ocean floor, as Wegener did, Lindemann and Hilgenberg suggested that the continents were driven apart from each other as the ocean floors expanded to accommodate a growing Earth.

Hilgenberg deserves special mention for three reasons. He was the first to attempt to fit the continents together in a continuous sialic shell, using the continental shelf outlines on a modern dimension globe as templates for papier-mâché continents that he then transferred to a globe 60 percent the size of his reference globe. Moreover, by conceiving of expansion on such a scale from the early Mesozoic, Hilgenberg was also the first to suggest a rapid expansion model. And finally, his model of expansion was radial: the continents should be conceived as conic wedges anchored in the Earth's core, being driven apart from each other in all directions by expanding oceanic crust (Hilgenberg, *Vom wachsenden Erdball,* pp. 2–9, 22–29). In all three respects Hilgenberg anticipated rapid expansion models developed in the 1960s and 1970s.

Hilgenberg's notion of a contiguous globe-encircling continental crust also provides an elegant explanation of the Earth's dual hypsometric curve. In this view, as our planet cooled and stabilized, the lighter sialic material rose to the surface and was evenly distributed across the Earth's face. Subsequently, as this continental shell was rifted apart in various places by expansionary forces within the Earth, a second layer of crustal material was created to fill the expanding rifts, but at a much lower elevation than the original continental shell. This two-stage process of crustal development would correspond naturally to the dual mean elevations of the continental plateaus and the ocean floors (see Carey, *The Expanding Earth,* p. 31).

In addition, the sialic shell has been cited, at least by the advocates of rapid expansion, to explain the otherwise statistically odd fact that all the continents could accrete on one side of the globe to form Pangaea, Wegener's super continent. If the Earth was once completely covered by a sialic shell, then Pangaea did not accrete at all. The emergence of the Pacific at the beginning of the Mesozoic "created" the other side of the globe, and Pangaea was merely the intact residue of the original sialic shell.

The work of the early expansionists, including Hilgenberg's, failed to generate any real interest, and was completely forgotten by the time a second wave of expansion theorists reinvented the tradition, and subsequently rediscovered Hilgenberg and his predecessors. This second wave emerged during the late 1950s, matured in the 1960s and 1970s, and has been fighting an uphill battle against skeptics in the dominant plate-tectonics research tradition ever since.

There are actually three distinct subspecies of modern expansion theories, distinguishable both by the rate of expansion and by what they are designed to explain. *Slow expansion,* the first to emerge, was developed by Lazlo Egyed (b. 1914) at Eötvös University in Budapest. In 1956 Egyed began publishing a series of papers arguing that paleoclimatic evidence suggests gradually diminishing cycles of marine transgression on continental areas during Phanerozoic time—that is, a net decrease in sea level. But Egyed also calculated that the volume of seawater had increased during this period by at least 4 percent. To explain this apparent paradox, he suggested that the Earth's radius has been undergoing gradual expansion at a constant rate of less than a millimeter a year, which translates into less than a 3 percent increase in the Earth's diameter over the past two hundred million years. He also argued that expansion would explain the fossil evidence for a secular decrease in the Earth's rotational speed. Devonian and Carboniferous corals exhibit alternating sequences of minute ridges and furrows that are assumed to constitute daily growth lines (as they do in modern corals). This record suggests that 350 million years ago the terrestrial year was 400 days long, gradually diminishing to 365 days as the Earth completed progressively fewer revolutions during its annual orbit around the Sun.

Egyed's arguments for slow expansion were subsequently advocated by the English geologist Arthur Holmes (1890–1965) in the final (1965) edition of his influential textbook *Principles of Physical Geology* (pp. 702–707). At that time a variant of slow expansion was also defended by the English geophysicist Ken Creer, who was influenced not only by Egyed's views, but also by the speculation of physicists Paul Dirac (1902–1984) and Robert Dicke (b. 1916) concerning the possibility of gradual diminution in g, the value of the universal gravitational constant. Similar speculation motivated Canadian geologist J. Tuzo Wilson (b. 1908) to entertain slow expansion briefly during the early 1960s.

Creer was also influenced by goodness-of-fit arguments propounded by fast expansion advocate S. Warren Carey (b. 1911) (see below). In the early 1960s Carey met Creer while on a lecture tour in England. Observing Creer's efforts to reconstruct Pangaea on a modern dimensions globe, Carey said: "Oh, you'll never fit the continents together on a globe of the present size; you'll have to go to a smaller globe." Carey's remark convinced Creer to try what Hilgenberg had done: to reconstruct a sialic shell by fitting the continents on a smaller globe. But Creer never assumed that expansion could be used to explain post-Pangaea continental displacement. Unlike Hilgenberg (and Carey), who thought the rate of expansion has been exponentially increasing over time, so that its most dramatic geological effects weren't evident until the breakup of Pangaea, Creer took the opposite view, assuming that most of the expansion took place during the Archeozoic. Creer held that the Earth had achieved about 94 percent of its present diameter by the early Paleozoic, and 96 or 97 percent by the end of the Paleozoic. With only 3 or 4 percent of the expansion occurring during the Mesozoic and Cenozoic, expansion could be no more than a background phenomenon to the dispersal of Pangaea.

Fast expansion is based on the idea that the Earth was almost entirely covered by a sialic shell as recently as two hundred million years ago, and that this shell, broken only along one hemisphere by a narrow Eo-Pacific ocean, constituted Pangaea before its decomposition. In this view, the Earth's radius is currently increasing at a rate of 2 to 4 centimeters a year, but really significant expansion didn't begin until the Jurassic dismantling of Pangaea, when the Earth's diameter was still not much more than 60 percent of its present size. Exponentially increasing expansion was virtually imperceptible throughout the Precambrian, and still very gradual for most of the Paleozoic, with the first true oceanic crust emerging in an Eo-Pacific rift during the early Permian, 260 to 280 million years ago.

Although Hilgenberg anticipated this view, the earliest of the second wave of fast expansion theorists were the Australian geologist S. Warren Carey and the American oceanographer Bruce Heezen (1924–1977). Carey came to this idea after convening a continental drift symposium at his home institution, the University of Tasmania, in 1956. He was struck then by the inability of the conferees (himself included) to achieve a really good fit of the continents to improve on Wegener's sketchy outline of Pangaea. All more precise reconstructions on a globe of modern dimensions left ineliminable triangular gores of varying sizes between neighboring continental masses, the most dramatic of which was the putative Tethys Ocean separating Australia, India, and Antarctica from the Asian cratonic block—6,000 kilometers across at the broad end of the triangle. (See the shaded areas in figure 1.) Carey subsequently realized that these gores could be eliminated by reconfiguring the Pangaea jigsaw on a much smaller globe. (Compare figure 2 with figure 1.) The gores, in this view, are just cartographic anomalies that would not exist but for the misguided attempt to fit the continental "skin" of a smaller Earth on a sphere too large to accommodate it. An appropriate metaphor would be the prospect of trying to fit the intact peel of an orange over a grapefruit.

As information about the constitution of oceanic crust accumulated in the 1960s and 1970s, the gore argument has been elaborated further, especially by Hugh Owen, a stratigrapher and cartographer at the British Museum. Owen has pointed out ("Constant Dimensions," pp. 180–182) that there is no sea-floor material old enough to occupy the space where the Triassic gores supposedly exist. This lacuna might be explained if there were any evidence of ancient subduction trenches along the margins of these gores that might have consumed the missing crust or, alternatively, if there were evidence of compression at those margins, in which case the missing crust might have been pushed up against the adjacent continents. But Owen argues that neither of these is the case, that the putative gore separating Argentina from Angola, for example (see figure 1), was passive-margined all the way back to the Triassic.

Carey also concluded that expansion was dictated by geological evidence that the Pacific perimeter had been growing rather than shrinking since the Jurassic. On a constant-dimensions Earth the Mesozoic and Cenozoic growth of the Atlantic can be accommodated only if there is a compensating diminution of the Pacific. Carey presented these ideas for the first time in the 1958 published revision of his presentation to the 1956 symposium "The

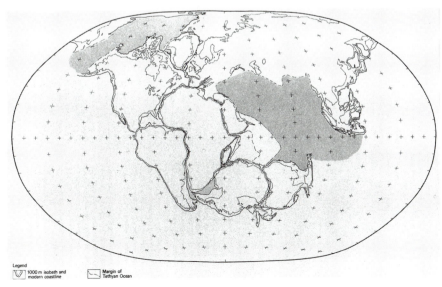

Figure 1. Standard reconstruction of Pangaea about 180 million years ago, assuming an Earth of modern dimensions. Oceanic crust required to be present in the reconstruction, but of which no evidence exists (Paleozoic Arctic and Tethys oceans, and the triangular gaps between Africa and South America, Africa, and Antarctica), is shaded. From Owen, 1981, p. 184, courtesy of The Natural History Museum, London.

Legend

1000 m isobath and modern coastline

Margin of Tethyan Ocean

*Figure 2. Expansionist
reconstruction of Pangaea
about 180 million years
ago, assuming an Earth
with a diameter 80 percent
of modern value. Shaded
oceanic crust present in
reconstruction no longer
exists, but could
theoretically have been
subducted during the
intervening period at the
trenches inserted off the
Pangaean continental shelf
(of which there is still
evidence in the present
distribution of subduction
trenches). From Owen,
1981, p. 185, courtesy of
The Natural History
Museum, London.*

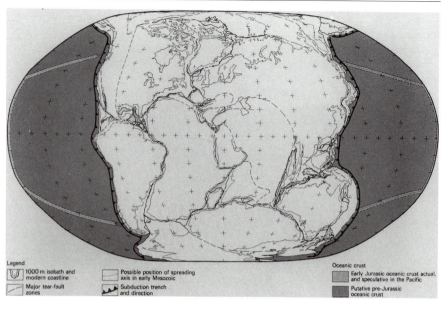

Figure 2. Expansionist reconstruction of Pangaea about 180 million years ago, assuming an Earth with a diameter 80 percent of modern value. Shaded oceanic crust present in reconstruction no longer exists, but could theoretically have been subducted during the intervening period at the trenches inserted off the Pangaean continental shelf (of which there is still evidence in the present distribution of subduction trenches). From Owen, 1981, p. 185, courtesy of The Natural History Museum, London.

Tectonic Approach to Continental Drift" (pp. 311–319). Since that time he has lectured and written extensively on the subject, and arguably deserves credit as the Alfred Wegener of this tradition.

Carey's version of fast radial expansion is just one of several that have been developed in the second wave of expansion theories. It is not really even a pure version of radial expansion, for Carey is willing to countenance rotation of continental blocks (although not subduction; see *The Expanding Earth,* pp. 54–79, 390). A purer version of the theory, closer to Hilgenberg's initial conception of radial expansion, has been developed by Klaus Vogel, a retired concrete engineer and amateur geologist living in the town of Werdau, in southeastern Germany. Like Hilgenberg, but initially unaware of his predecessor's work, Vogel began by experimenting with the task of reconstructing Pangaea on small-earth globes in the early 1970s. To demonstrate the nature of radial expansion, Vogel came up with the idea of inserting his mesozoic globe reconstruction inside a transparent modern dimensions globe. Unlike Carey's model, the relative positions that Vogel's Triassic continents bear to one another are basically the same as the relative positions of the continents today (with the exception, of course, of the distance between them).

Bruce Heezen came to embrace fast Earth expansion as a result of his familiarity with the newly emerging data about the existence of a worldwide belt of oceanic ridges. Working at the Lamont Geological Observa-

tory of Columbia University, Heezen discovered in 1953 that a deep rift valley runs down the center of the mid-Atlantic ridge, and he recognized subsequently that other ocean floor ridges also possess rift valleys, and that most seismic activity on the ocean floor appears to be restricted to the immediate vicinity of these rifts. As data from ocean floor exploration accumulated in the late 1950s, it also became apparent that the entire ocean floor is relatively young, with no core samples predating the Jurassic, and that the age of oceanic crust increases with distance from oceanic ridge lines. Based on this information, Heezen reasoned that the oceanic ridges are zones of crustal creation, with new crust emerging from the rift valleys and then spreading out across the ocean floors. On the assumption that all the ocean basins must be growing to accommodate this new material, Heezen argued verbally for fast expansion in 1958 and in print by 1960.

Although Heezen introduced a novel set of reasons for accepting expansion, his account was never as elaborate as Carey's. Moreover, he gave up the idea in the late 1960s, having become convinced that Harry Hess's 1960 model of sea-floor spreading was basically correct, whereby crustal growth at the oceanic ridge lines might be offset by crustal destruction in subduction trenches, primarily around the Pacific margin. Nonetheless, Heezen's temporary advocacy of expansion was historically significant because, in the North American geoscience community, he had a higher professional profile than Carey.

Heezen's sympathy for the view gave fast expansion enough visibility to encourage scientists to take note of Carey's more detailed account as well. Between Heezen's prestige and Carey's energy for proselytization, fast expansion became, for a few years in the early 1960s, a serious (although never popular) candidate for explaining the mounting evidence for continental displacement.

Unlike Heezen, Carey has never accepted the subduction hypothesis, and consequently rejects all plate tectonic accounts of continental displacement. Subduction is indeed incompatible with radial expansion models of the sort advocated by Carey, Hilgenberg, and Vogel. If continental blocks sit atop wedges of material being simultaneously driven apart from each other by newly emergent oceanic crust, then they can never meet again once oceanic rifts have separated them. If, on the other hand, subduction has occurred, then continental blocks may have repeatedly met, separated, and met again throughout the Phanerozoic, as subduction trenches gradually closed ancient oceans and brought the bordering continents into collision to create new suture zones of compressional orogenesis. The Himalayan mountain ranges are often cited as a recent example of this phenomenon, the result of the Indian subcontinent's colliding with Asia during the Paleocene. The Urals and the Appalachians are regarded as Paleozoic instances of the same phenomenon. The Appalachians, for example, are widely assumed to be the product of a Devonian collision between North America, Europe, and Africa, after a subduction-induced closure of the Iapetus Ocean, an Ordovician proto-Atlantic.

Fast expansionists like Carey are not especially impressed with compressional accounts of orogeny, because they can offer alternative accounts of Paleozoic orogenic "sutures" as predominantly extensional rather than compressional phenomena. In Carey's view, the Appalachians and the Urals are the product of diapiric uplift, accompanied by gravity-driven lateral flow of extruded material ("Tectonic Approach," pp. 322–338; *Theories of the Earth,* pp. 205–250).

In the case of India, Carey explains the unusually massive uplift and clear evidence of compression by suggesting that, while ancient India was never separated from the rest of Asia, the subcontinent was spread out clockwise in the direction of Arabia and Africa, and connected to Asia by a triangular block of continental material that became compressed

by India's Cenozoic rotation into its present position, around a hinge located at the apex of the Arabian Sea ("Tectonic Approach," pp. 264–271). Alfred Wegener also assumed that India was attached to Asia since the Triassic. He labeled the conjoining continental crust the *Lemurian zusammenzog* (Lemurian compression).

Ancient faunal distribution patterns may provide a greater challenge. J. Tuzo Wilson pointed out in 1966 that the suture-zone account of the formation of the Appalachians would also serve to explain the otherwise anomalous distribution of shallow-water Ordovician marine fossils. Distinctive species of trilobites from that period have been found to predominate on opposite sides of the Atlantic. But those found primarily on the North American side ("Pacific province" trilobites) are also found in Norway, Scotland, and the northern half of Ireland, while "Atlantic province" trilobites, found mainly in Europe and Africa, are also found in southern Newfoundland, Nova Scotia, coastal New England, and southern Florida. Wilson suggested in "Did the Atlantic Close and then Reopen?" that the distribution could easily be explained if residual bits of proto–North America and proto–Africa/Eurasia, with their previously embedded Ordovician fossils, became attached to opposite shores during the putative Devonian collision, and were then left behind when the continents broke apart again during the Atlantic rifting of Pangaea.

Carey and other expansionists have, however, exhibited considerable ingenuity in addressing such anomalies. In the case of the Ordovician trilobite distributions, Carey has argued that the pattern can be explained in terms of separation along the axis of the Appalachian and Caledonian orogeny rather than across it—north/south faunal distribution rather than an east/west one, provided that we recognize that this mountain belt underwent a massive sinistral shear during the Devonian. Scandinavian and Scottish trilobites would then match trilobites found in Pennsylvania because the regions would have been adjacent during the relevant period in the Ordovician, before Scandinavia, Britain, and Ireland were shifted 3,000 kilometers to the north along this Devonian megashear (*Theories of the Earth and Universe,* pp. 180–184).

In some cases paleontology and paleogeology actually work to the advantage of expansionists. Many specialists of the Himalayan region, for example, are convinced that there never was a wide separation between India and the rest of Asia (See Gansser). Nonetheless, evidence of subduction continues to remain a potential source of embarrassment for fast-expansion theories, and certainly undercuts prospects for reconciliation between the expansion and the plate tectonics research programs.

To take just one illustration, consider the magnetic anomaly lineations produced in alternating parallel bands on each side of active oceanic ridge lines. This pattern is now widely understood to be the effect of periodic polarity reversals in the geomagnetic field, imprinted on new oceanic crust as it emerged from an oceanic rift valley, cooled past the Curie point, and gradually flowed away on each side of the ridge line. But while the pattern is completely symmetric across the mid-Atlantic ridge, the corresponding Pacific pattern is severely truncated in the eastern Pacific, where polarity reversals extend back only as far as the Eocene. In the western Pacific, oceanic crust dates back to the Jurassic.

Plate tectonics accommodates this asymmetry by assuming that the missing portions of the eastern South Pacific have been subducted down the Peru-Chile trench, and those in the eastern North Pacific have been subducted and overrun by the western lateral motion of North America. Carey suggests instead that the Pacific simply grew asymmetrically. Advocates of plate tectonics, of course, are likely to dismiss such an explanation as an ad hoc device to circumvent uncooperative facts.

Primarily to deal with the evidence for subduction, and to secure an even better fit of the pieces composing the Pangaean supercontinent, some recent expansion theorists, like Hugh Owen, have advocated a third class of theories, which we might call *moderate expansion*. Instead of assuming that Pangaea constituted an almost completely unbroken sialic shell covering a sphere less than two-thirds of the Earth's present diameter, Owen argues that the early Jurassic Earth must have been at 80 percent of its present diameter. He speculates that the sialic shell started to break up much earlier, at the beginning of the Paleozoic. Of course at that rate, expansion can explain only a portion of the Phanerozoic continental displacement for which we now have evidence. But advocates of moderate expansion do not deny the occurrence of subduction, which they take to explain the balance of the displacement. Owen's only quarrel with plate tectonics is the assumption that the rate of subduction in the oceanic trenches is equal to the rate of crustal creation at the oceanic ridges. Like Carey, he regards this assumption as an unexamined dogma of plate tectonics, and one that is not supported by the evidence. (The nature of that evidence is beyond the scope of this essay, but it is cataloged in detail in Carey, *The Expanding Earth* [pp. 39–79], and summarized more informally in his *Theories of the Earth* [pp. 150–189]).

Owen arrived at the conclusion that the Earth was roughly 80 percent of its present size, rather than the 60 percent figure of fast expansionists, as a consequence of meticulous map reconstructions employing traditional cartographic methods rather than commonly used computer programs. Most computer-generated cartography fails to reproject continents after they have been rotated or shifted with respect to the projection pole used in the original map construction. Without reprojection, a rotated or shifted continent has been distorted from its original shape, reducing the accuracy of the fit. With appropriate reprojections incorporated, Owen concluded that the gores of missing Triassic crust would be completely eliminated on an 80 percent globe (*Atlas*, pp. 3–5, 8–11, 15). (Figure 2 actually depicts Owen's model of Pangaea, with a large Paleozoic Pacific. Hilgenberg, Carey, and Vogel would have at most a narrow Eo-Pacific lune separating Pangaea's western and eastern extremities.)

No expansion theories enjoy widespread support in the 1990s. Although empirical arguments against moderate and fast expansion were offered in the 1960s and 1970s, they are of debatable merit (see Carey, *The Expanding Earth*, pp. 16–22; *Theories of the Earth*, pp. 190–201). The real reasons for current indifference to this research tradition seem to be more theoretical in nature.

Ken Creer, for example, gave up pursuing the idea of expansion when he realized how much distortion had to be accommodated in the continents if they were to be molded onto a globe of smaller dimensions. Unlike Hilgenberg, who worked with the malleable medium of papier mâché, Creer was forced to contend with the problem when he used fiberglass to construct his continents. In order to bend these less flexible puzzle pieces to a smaller globe, he simply took up the distortion in the center of his continents. Recognizing later that this was an arbitrary assumption on his part, and that the distortion might have as easily affected continents at their edges, he gave up the project as a hopeless enterprise. (For the same reason, Owen refuses to speculate about the precise fit of the continents during the Paleozoic era. But he thinks that, while this distortion makes the expansion reconstruction project untenable on a 60 percent globe, distortion is still minimal at 80 percent.)

The absence of a physical mechanism to explain why expansion should occur is a problem more often cited by detractors. Indeed, expansion advocates concede that they can offer nothing more than speculation on this issue. Some of the speculation has been pretty implausible. Hilgenberg, like Yarkovski, relied on the idea of transforming massless ether into matter, so that the Earth would have increased in mass as well as volume (*Vom wachsenden Erdball*, pp. 29–35). The most widely shared explanation entertained today seems to be the hypothesis that the Earth's core consists of disassociated and densely packed subatomic particles that are undergoing a phase change and assuming atomic structure at the core/mantle boundary. In atomic form, these particles occupy more volume, thus exerting expansionary pressure on the Earth as a whole. This idea was proposed first by Lindemann, and by South African astronomer J.K.E. Halm (1866–1944) in 1935 in "An Astronomical Aspect of the Evolution of the Earth," writing apparently in ignorance of both Lindemann's and Hilgenberg's work. But here again, there is no developed physical theory to explain why the core should be so constituted, and in standard views it is not.

Ultimately, the problem with expansion for most Earth scientists may be Ockham's razor: they are convinced that, in the lateral convection belt models associated with plate tectonics, they already have a reasonably plausible explanation of continental displacement. Why then should they rely on two distinct mechanisms, when one may suffice, and especially when the other seems so bizarre? There is, at the level of theory at least, a lack of elegance and simplicity in moderate expansion in particular. Not only does it require two apparently independent engines of continental displacement, but it also lacks the internal aesthetic unity of pure radial expansion. Owen cannot appeal to his theory, for example, to explain why all the continents should happen to accrete into a single supercontinent at the end of the Paleozoic.

But such aesthetic judgments are a matter of degree. Plate tectonics cannot explain why all the continents should congregate on one side of the globe either. On the other end of the spectrum, while Carey's model of fast expansion would, if correct, require only one mechanism for continental displacement, even his theory is more complicated, and arguably less elegant, than the purely radial expansion proposed by Vogel.

In the final analysis, regardless of the aesthetic appeal of simplicity, expansion's prospects for supplanting plate tectonics, or even sharing the stage with it, will be determined by additional empirical tests. It may be that the Earth is a less tidy place than either expansion or plate tectonics purists would have us believe; it may be more like Owen's somewhat messier planet. Despite the current level of underexposure from which expansion theories suffer, the jury is still out on the question of their empirical validity. The fortunes of either moderate or fast expansion could improve during the coming decades, although moderate expansion looks more promising at present.

Richard Nunan

Bibliography

Carey, S. Warren. *The Expanding Earth.* Developments in Geotectonics 10. Amsterdam: Elsevier, 1976.

———. "A Tectonic Approach to Continental Drift." In *Continental Drift: A Symposium,* edited by S.W. Carey, pp. 177–355. Hobart: University of Tasmania, 1958.

———. *Theories of the Earth and the Universe.* Stanford: Stanford University Press, 1988.

Creer, Kenneth M. "An Expanding Earth?" *Nature* 205 (1965): pp. 539–544.

Egyed, Lazlo. "The Change in the Earth's Dimensions Determined from Paleogeographical Data." *Geofisica Pura e Applicata* 33 (1956): pp. 42–48.

Gansser, Augusto. "Facts and Theories on the Himalayas." *Eclogae Geologicae Helvetiae* 84 (1991): pp. 33–59.

Halm, J.K.E. "An Astronomical Aspect of the Evolution of the Earth." *Astronomical Society of South Africa* 4 (1935): pp. 1–28.

Heezen, Bruce C. "The Rift in the Ocean Floor." *Scientific American* 203 (October 1960): pp. 98–110.

Hilgenberg, Otto C. *Vom wachsenden Erdball.* Berlin: Giessmann and Bartsch, 1933.

Holmes, Arthur. *Principles of Physical Geology.* New York: Ronald Press, 1965.

Lindemann, B. *Kettengebirge, kontinentale Zerspaltung und Erdexpansion.* Jena: Fischer, 1927.

Owen, H.G. *Atlas of Continental Displacement, 200 Million Years to the Present.* Cambridge: Cambridge University Press, 1983.

———. "Constant Dimensions or an Expanding Earth?" In *The Evolving Earth,* edited by L.R.M. Cocks, pp. 179–192. London: British Museum and Cambridge University Press, 1981.

Vogel, Klaus. "The Expansion of the Earth—An Alternative Model to the Plate Tectonics Theory." In *Critical Aspects of the Plate Tectonics Theory, Volume II (Alternative Theories),* edited by S.S. Augustithis et al., pp. 19–34. Athens: Theophrastus Publications, 1990.

Wilson, J. Tuzo. "Did the Atlantic Close and then Reopen?" *Nature* 211 (1966): pp. 676–681.

See also Cartography; Continental Drift and Plate Tectonics; Earth, Size of; Oceanography, Physical; Paleomagnetism; Paleontology; Sea-Level; Shifting Crust Theory

Exploration, Age of

Critical period in the development of European consciousness. The study of the Earth was greatly affected by interest in navigation and cartography, the concept of the terraqueous globe was first discussed, effects of climate on human beings was investigated, and theories of ethnography were proposed.

The Age of Exploration (fifteenth through seventeenth centuries) was a critical period in the development of European consciousness. Although the Chinese had probably sailed farther and many fishing peoples had been traversing the Atlantic Ocean for centuries, the achievements of Vasco da Gama (ca. 1469–1524) and Christopher Columbus (1451–1506), as well as those who followed, fundamentally changed the way Europeans understood the Earth and their relationship to it. These early explorers, equipped with a Christian and imperial belief in the righteousness of their cause and the superiority of their understanding, challenged the authority of the ancients, especially Claudius Ptolemy (fl. second century C.E.). Columbus and those who came after demonstrated to Europeans the existence of a continent completely unknown to the ancients (though well known to its inhabitants). More important for Earth

In the sixteenth century, map and globe makers struggled to keep abreast of exploration. Johannes Schöner (1477–1547) produced a number of maps and globes that reflected his changing ideas. Source: A.E. Nordenskiöld, Facsimile Atlas to the Early History of Cartography with Reproductions of the Most Important Maps Printed in the XV and XVI Centuries. *Stockholm, 1889. Translated from the Swedish original by Johan Adolf Ekelöf and Clements R. Markham, with a new introduction by J.B. Post. New York: Dover, 1973, p. 83. With permission of Dover Publications.*

studies, these explorers disproved a number of ancient and medieval theories of the Earth, most particularly by demonstrating that the globe has a much larger proportion of dry land than had hitherto been suspected, that it is possible to sail through the equatorial regions without burning up, and that people can and did live south of that equatorial region in the lands known as the antipodes.

The "Voyages of Discovery" were not principally concerned with investigating the Earth, so it is not surprising that the geological information they collected was minimal. The prime motivating factor for these voyages was amassing great wealth, both for the individual and for the country sponsoring the enterprises. At first, the destination was the Far East—Cathay and the Spice Islands. The Portuguese were most successful at reaching these areas, setting up important trading depots in Goa (India), Malacca (Malaysia), and the Moluccas (Spice Islands). The Spanish, having reached the Americas by mistake, soon modified their mission, and although they continued to seek gold and especially silver, the *conquistadores* began to focus on colonization, seeing the natives as a useful slave population and one that could easily be converted to Christianity. Later, as the cultivation of sugar and cotton became more important to the Spanish, the African slave trade was introduced into this economic arrangement. And yet, it would be a mistake to separate these imperial and mercantile enterprises from the growing interest in and study of the Earth. As David Livingstone has pointed out, the study of geography was inexorably linked with religious and mercantile concerns. As early modern Europeans began to see the Earth as God revealed through His works, they began to treat the study of the Earth as a new and naturalistic path to spiritual knowledge.

While the primary impact of the Age of Exploration on Europe was economic, there were several ways in which this new development aided in the study of the Earth. The so-called discoveries encouraged innovations in cartography and navigation, led to a changing understanding of the terraqueous globe, spawned an interest in the effect of climates on human beings, and launched ethnographic investigations and debates concerning the peoples of the New World. While earlier historians of the Age of Exploration have concentrated primarily on the romantic and perilous adventures of the explorers themselves, as well as on the economic, social, and political consequences for Europe, in recent years more attention has been devoted to the developing picture of the Earth. While much work remains to be done, the emerging portrait of Earth studies in this period reveals the continual struggle on the part of the geographers and navigators to preserve some of the ancient knowledge of the Earth while acknowledging the new worldview they could see with their own eyes.

Questions of navigation were of most importance to explorers. It is not, therefore, surprising to find that the earliest historical work on the study of the Earth in this period was designed to explain navigational theories and techniques. D.W. Waters, in his *Science and the Techniques of Navigation in the Renaissance* (1976), described the trial-and-error methods and incremental accumulation of knowledge concerning longitude and latitude determination, magnetic variation, and wind and current theories. Waters's classic work had at its heart the contention that utility and socioeconomic circumstances had more to do with the development of astronomical and

geographical theories than did scholars and universities. While his work seems rather descriptive today, its lucid treatment of navigational techniques and theories, as well as its perceptive inclusion of practical application, make it a worthwhile introduction to the field. Connected with this development of navigation were the changes taking place in cartography. While historians of cartography have long admired the beauty and rarity of Renaissance maps, especially of the New World, it is only recently that these historians have begun to analyze these maps as cultural and intellectual artifacts. Probably the most innovative and successful of this new type of historian is J.B. Harley, whose *Maps and the Columbian Encounter* (1990) uses deconstructive and postmodernist analytical methods to claim that maps of the early first contacts tell us more about the society that produced them than they do of the objective world of the fifteenth century.

More important conceptually than improvements in navigational techniques or new map projections was the changing understanding of the relationship between the sphere of Earth that rested in the center of the universe and the sphere of water that surrounded it, as envisaged by Aristotle (384–322 B.C.E.). In the Middle Ages, scholars such as Johannes de Sacrobosco (fl. 1230) had suggested that these two spheres could not be precisely concentric (how else could any dry land exist above the outer sphere of water?) and that the earthly sphere emerges at one place only on the globe. This accounted for the seeming contradiction, according to W.G.L. Randles, between the flat picture of the *terra firma* or *oekemene* (the land mass of Eurasia) and the round sphere of the earth understood from astronomical and Aristotelian teaching. As explorers began to show that there is much more dry land than Ptolemy had suspected, Sacrobosco's compromise was no longer possible and natural philosophers were forced to rethink the relationship between earth and water. This led, argues Thomas Goldstein, to the unification of these two distinct spheres into one. Goldstein contends that when Nicholas Copernicus (1473–1543) argued in book 1, chap. 3 of *De Revolutionibus orbium coelestium* (On the revolution of the heavenly spheres) that the Earth is round and therefore subject to the same rules of physics as the round universe (that is, that it should share the circular movement of the universe), he was referring to a different spherical Earth than Sacrobosco had envisaged. Gone were the separate spheres of earth and water and in their place one unified terraqueous globe. This unification of water and earth was to prove essential to the new physics and astronomy of the next hundred years.

The third major concern to people studying the Earth during this period also had ancient roots. Explorers and scholars alike were concerned about the effect of climates on their ability to prosper in new parts of the world, and that concern could be traced back to the Greeks. From the Alexandrian Parmenides (b. ca. 515 B.C.E.) came the theory of the five climatic zones (which Ptolemy also used); the two polar zones were thought too cold to inhabit, and the torrid zone was likewise uninhabitable, leaving only the two temperate zones for human occupation. As the explorers discovered that people can and did live in all the zones, new theories began to develop, claiming that certain types of people are suited to specific climates and will not flourish elsewhere. This whole complex relationship between human beings and their environment was explored by Clarence Glacken in *Traces on the Rhodian Shore*. Glacken develops three themes: nature as designed creation; the influence of the environment on human beings; and the influence of human beings on their environment (that is, control over nature). He claims that these three attitudes to nature developed consecutively over time. The second development, the effect of climate on human beings, corresponds with the Age of Exploration.

The final theme of the Age of Exploration that has interested historians has been the question of first contacts between Amerindians and Europeans. This contact has had a long and critical history, beginning with the damnation by Bartolomé de las Casas (1474–1566) in 1522 of his Spanish countrymen's activities. More recently, Anthony Pagden, in *The Fall of Natural Man* (1982), has masterfully traced the debates among scholars at the University of Salamanca concerning the changing Aristotelian status of New World peoples. These intellectuals were divided as to whether the Amerindians could better be seen as natural slaves or natural children, and the rise of the latter opinion had serious ramifications concerning the morality of stealing their possessions, rather than caring for them until they came of age. Stephen Greenblatt tackles this question of possession as well, in his *Marvelous Possessions* (1991), in which he argues that the European explorers, beginning with Co-lumbus, used the concept of wonder as a medium through which to confront "the other," and that they really saw themselves rather than the natives who were there.

The Age of Exploration was a period of danger and adventure, as well as blind luck and willful ignorance. Much of the historical work that has been done to date has therefore looked at the political, economic, and social aspects, rather than at the ramifications for studies of the Earth. Although this is understandable, it has limited our picture of this vibrant age. Much work needs to be done on the geological understanding of the early explorers, navigators, and theorists. Why did they think there would be gold in the New World (aside from the fact that they at first thought they were in China)? How did concepts of magnetism change in those years before the important work of William Gilbert (1544–1603)? How did concepts of the terraqueous globe develop? As well, more sophisticated analysis is needed to understand the first encounters between Europeans and natives, if we are to develop a *modus vivendi* today. The Age of Exploration was created by its practitioners as an age of myth-making, and we must get beyond those myths if we hope to understand the events that were to prove so pivotal for most of the modern world.

Lesley Cormack

Bibliography

Glacken, Clarence J. *Traces on the Rhodian Shore: Nature and Culture in Western Thought from Ancient Times to the End of the Eighteenth Century.* Berkeley and Los Angeles: University of California Press, 1967.

Goldstein, Thomas. "The Renaissance Concept of the Earth in Its Influence upon Copernicus." *Terrae Incognitae* 4 (1972): pp. 19–51.

Greenblatt, Stephen. *Marvelous Possessions: The Wonder of the New World.* Chicago: University of Chicago Press, 1991.

Harley, John Brian. *Maps and the Columbian Encounter.* Milwaukee, Wis.: Golda Meir Library, 1990.

Livingstone, David. "Science, Magic and Religion: A Contextual Reassessment of Geography in the Sixteenth and Seventeenth Centuries." *History of Science* 26 (1988): pp. 269–294.

Pagden, Anthony. *The Fall of Natural Man: The American Indian and the Origins of Comparative Ethnology.* Cambridge:

Cambridge University Press, 1982.

Randles, W.G.L. *De la Terre Plate au Globe Terrestre: Une Mutation Epistémologique Rapide.* Paris: Librairie Armand Colin, 1980.

Waters, David Watkin. *Science and the Techniques of Navigation in the Renaissance.* London: Maritime Museum Monographs and Reports No. 19, 1976.

See also Ballooning; Cartography: Disciplinary History; Climate, Ancient Ideas; Colonialism and Imperialism; Cosmology and the Earth; Earth, Models of before 1600; Earth, Size of; Geographical Societies; Geography and Imperialism; Geography; Geography and Renaissance Magic; Geography, Elizabethan; Humboldtian Science; Jesuits and the Earth; Masons and the Earth; Oceanographic Expeditions up to H.M.S. *Challenger*; Polar Exploration

Facies, Sedimentary

Rock units distinguished by lithological, structural, and organic aspects in the field.

In sedimentary geology, the term "facies" is now commonly used in this way, as proposed by J.F.M. De Raaf et al. in 1965. These authors subdivided a group of three formations into a cyclical repetition of a number of units called facies, distinguished by the above criteria. Though this was by no means the first definition of facies, it has become widely accepted, in part because De Raaf's co-authors were Harold Reading and Roger Walker, who later went on to publish the now classic works *Sedimentary Environments and Facies* (Reading, 1978, 1986), and *Facies Models* (1979, 1984; Walker and James, 1992). In this interpretation, sedimentary facies are defined as far as possible on the basis of objective, descriptive criteria (largely those that can be determined in the field), though it is understood that the facies so defined will ultimately be given an environmental interpretation. Therefore the defining criteria generally do not include aspects of sedimentary rocks known to be produced by diagenesis (for example, degree of compaction, induration, cements, concretions) or diastrophism (for example, jointing, cleavage). The term "metamorphic facies" has also been applied, in quite a different context, to describe metamorphic mineral assemblages formed under similar conditions (such as pressure and temperature) of metamorphism. By extension, the same type of meaning has been applied to diagenetic facies: in this review we discuss only the application commonly used in sedimentary geology. Though the title of this article is sedi-mentary facies, the qualifier is commonly understood—and indeed the term "sedimentary facies" was actually first defined by Raymond C. Moore in 1949 (p. 32) as "any areally restricted part of a designated stratigraphic unit which exhibits characters significantly different from those of other parts of the unit." Though this definition was popular in the United States during the 1950s, it does not correspond to the original use of the term, and has now largely been abandoned in favor of the definition given by De Raaf and his colleagues.

The analysis of facies, though it was pioneered and practiced in continental Europe in the nineteenth century, did not become a major part of sedimentary geology, as practiced in anglophone countries, until the 1970s. It was, however, the dominant trend in sedimentary geology throughout the 1980s, and has only recently been supplanted in popularity by sequence stratigraphy (Walker and James).

The term "facies" comes from the Latin word meaning aspect, and it was used by geologists well before the nineteenth century. Nicholas Steno, in his *Prodromus* published in Latin in 1669, describes "six distinct origins for facies in Tuscany" and recognized the importance of sea-level changes in producing them: but it is clear that he was using the term in the sense of a formation (stratigraphic unit) and not in the modern sense of the word (see, for example, Hölder, pp. 27, 352–356). The modern concept of facies was first fully developed by Amanz (or Amand) Gressly (1814–1865). While Gressly was a student at the University of Strasbourg, under the direction of Jules Thurmann, he began to study the Jurassic rocks of the northwest part of Switzerland. In his first major publication, in 1838, he explained how he was led to develop the idea of facies, and explained: "There are two principal points that always characterize the group of modifications that I call *facies* or *aspects of stratigraphic units:* one is that *a similar petrographic aspect of any unit necessarily implies, wherever it is found, the same paleontological assemblage; the other, that a similar paleontological assemblage rigorously excludes the genera and species of fossils frequent in other facies"* (Gressly, pp. 10–11, translated from the French: the emphasis is Gressly's own).

Thus Gressly recognized the intimate relationship between lithologic and paleontologic aspects of facies, and did not attempt to separate the two, as some later authors have, into lithofacies and biofacies. Eugene Wegmann has reprinted part of Gressly's original paper.

Following Gressly, the next major development of the facies concept was due to Johannes Walther (1860–1937), a German geologist and paleontologist and author of several influential works (for his life see the biography by Ilse Seibold). Though his books were never translated into English, they influenced pioneer American sedimentologists such as Amadeus William Grabau and William H. Twenhofel. Many were translated into Russian, and their influence led to many studies of facies in that country, and to the use of Walther's term "lithology" in Russia to describe studies that focused on the environmental interpretation of sedimentary rocks. In the West, the term "lithology" is used instead to describe the simple description of rocks, rather than their genetic interpretation, which is called petrology. Walther's main contribution to the study of facies is found in his three-volume *Einleitung in die Geologie* (Introduction to geology as a historical science). Walther recognized that since facies are related to environments, progress in their study will be made using a comparison of the spatial relations exhibited by modern environments and the vertical relations that can more easily be studied in ancient stratigraphic successions. Walther referred to this as the ontological method (a use of the term "ontology" quite different from that found in metaphysics), or the method of comparative lithology. "Comparative lithology . . . makes genetic comparisons, and of all the qualities of a rock, gives those first place that the rock received when it was first formed. . . . [We

distinguish] primary and secondary qualities; and we understand under the first those qualities which a rock possessed when it was still subject [to its environment of deposition], while all those rock qualities acquired through diagenesis or metamorphism are considered secondary" (Walther, 1894, vol. 3, p. 976, translated from the German). He enunciated an important principle of this method, which has subsequently become known as *Walther's law:* If there is no stratigraphic break, only those facies can be superimposed in a section that were deposited beside each other.

Though modern use of the term "facies" varies somewhat, most writers follow either De Raaf or Moore, and do not concern themselves much about its historical usage or philosophical presuppositions. But such was not the case earlier.

Gerard V. Middleton

Bibliography
Gressly, Amanz. "Observations géologiques sur le Jura Soleurois." *Nouvelles Mémoires Société Helvétique des Sciences Naturelles* 2 (1838): pp. 1–349.
Hölder, Helmut. *Geologie und Paläontologie in Texten und ihrer Geschichte.* Freiberg-München: Verlag Karl Alber, 1960.
Middleton, G.V. "Johannes Walther's Law of the Correlation of Facies." *Geological Society of America Bulletin* 84 (1973): pp. 979–988.
Moore, Raymond C. "Meaning of Facies." *Geological Society of America Memoir* 39 (1949): pp. 1–34.
Nelson, C.M. "Facies in Stratigraphy: From 'Terrains' to 'Terranes.'" *Journal of Geological Education* 33 (1985): pp. 175–187.
Reading, H.G., ed. *Sedimentary Environments and Facies.* 2d ed. Oxford: Blackwell, 1986.
Seibold, Ilse. *Der Weg zur Biogeologie: Johannes Walther (1860–1937), Ein Forscherleben im Wandel der deutschen Universität.* New York: Springer-Verlag, 1992.
Walther, Joannes. *Einleitung in die Geologie als historische Wissenschaft: Beobachtungen über die Bildung der Gesteine und ihrer organischen Einschlüsse.* 3 vols. Jena: Fischer, 1893–1894.
Walker, R.G., and N.P. James, eds. *Facies Models: Response to Sea Level Change.* St. John's: Geological Association of

Canada, 1992.

Wegmann, Eugene. "L'expose original de la notion de facies par A. Gressly (1814–1865)." *Science de la Terre* 9 (1963): pp. 83–119.

See also Heavy Minerals; Paleontology; Sedimentary Geology; Sedimentology; Stratigraphy

Flat-Earth Models

An early view of the Earth.

Almost every person who has traveled away from his home or village perceives that the Earth is flat. Of the few writings that have survived from ancient times—Mayan, Chinese, Indian, Egyptian, Babylonian, Greek—many used mythology and religion to codify this view.

Twenty-six centuries ago, however, a small Mediterranean culture, the Greeks, started to use philosophy and science, instead of mythology and religion, as the main tools for trying to understand the world. They extended their minds beyond their own personal experiences and tried to deduce the nature of the Earth and the Heavens. The Greek Ionian philosophers from Miletus changed the interpretation of the sky from an astrological, calendar system to an astronomical, cosmological science.

Thales (ca. 640–562 B.C.E.) taught that the Earth is a circular disk floating on the ocean, while his student Anaximander (ca. 610–546 B.C.E.) said the Earth is a concave cylinder with a diameter three times the depth. His Earth was unsupported in the center of the universe. A third Ionian, Anaximenes (ca. 585–528 B.C.E.), said the Earth is flat like a table and supported by air. Other Greek writers that believed we live on a flat Earth include Xenophanes (ca. 570–478 B.C.E.), who described a flat surface that extends down without limit, and Anaxagoras (ca. 500–428 B.C.E.), who was the first to explain eclipses and to say that the Moon is lit by the Sun (see Dreyer; Heath).

Two contemporaries of Anaxagoras were the first writers to dispute the flat Earth models. Philolaus, the first writer in the Pythagorean school, described a spherical Earth. Pythagoras (ca. 580–500 B.C.E.), the founder of this secretive society, may have originated the spherical concept, but he and his immediate followers left no writings. It is not known why the Pythagoreans first proposed a spherical Earth, but Heath (p. 48) prefers a mathematico-aesthetical explanation. The only non-Pythagorean before Plato to write about a spherical Earth was Parmenides, a founder of the Eleatic school of philosophy. He did, however, have close ties with the Pythagorean school.

The Atomist school, well known for significant theories about the nature of matter, disputed the views of Parmenides and the Pythagoreans and continued the Ionian flat-Earth models. In the fifth century B.C.E., Leucippus taught that the Earth is like a tambourine and rides or floats on an airy vortex, while his follower Democritus said the Earth is a disk depressed in the middle, supported by air (see Heath).

Speculation about the shape of the Earth clearly ended with Aristotle (384–322 B.C.E.). In *De Caelo,* he used scientific reasoning to show that astronomical observations are more consistent with a spherical Earth model than with any flat-Earth model that had been proposed. Writers continued to give observational arguments against flat-Earth models; most notably Claudius Ptolemy in *Almagest* (ca. 150 C.E.) and Nicolaus Copernicus in *De revolutionibus* (1543 C.E.) (see Crowe).

No major writers after Aristotle have disputed the sphericity of the Earth, although a few writers and clerics continued to support the flat-Earth concept through the Middle Ages. Even though Aristotle supported the correct shape of the Earth, he did so inconsistently. The validity of the arguments that Aristotle, Ptolemy, and Copernicus used to compare flat and spherical model systems has been disputed (Neugebauer, pp. 576, 678, 1093). Although they invoked a pre-Newtonian view of gravity to prove the Earth's sphericity, they did not apply these same principles to alternative flat-Earth models. The proof of the Earth's sphericity was not as obvious as it is sometimes portrayed.

David Thorndill

Bibliography

Crowe, Michael J. *Theories of the World from Antiquity to the Copernican Revolution* New York: Dover, 1990.

Dreyer, J.L.E. *A History of Astronomy from Thales to Kepler* [1906]. New York: Dover Publications, 1953.

Heath, Thomas. *Aristarchus of Samos, the Ancient Copernicus* [1913]. New York: Dover Publications, 1981.

Neugebauer, Otto. *Studies in the History of Mathematics and the Physical Sciences Series: A History of Ancient Mathematical Astronomy.* 3 vols. New York: Springer-Verlag, 1975.

See also Cosmology and the Earth; Earth, Figure of in the Satellite Era; Earth, Models of before 1600; Earth, Size of; Gravity before Newton; Gravity, Newton, and the Eighteenth Century

Fossilization

The production of a fossil form from a living organism. Fossilization includes all processes from the death of an organism (necrolysis) and its final burial (biostratonomy or biostratinomy) to chemical and mechanical alterations within the sediment (fossil diagenesis).

The study of the fossilization process started only when the true nature of fossils was known. As early as 500 B.C.E. Xenophanos (570–480 B.C.E.) and Herodotus (500–424 B.C.E.) realized that fossils are remains of animals and plants, preserved in rocks on land as the result of natural catastrophes. The sea must have formerly been where marine shells were found on land. However, the idea by Aristotle (384–322 B.C.E.) that fossils are the result of a molding force *(vis plastica)* within the Earth, the same force that governs the growth of living organisms on the Earth, was generally accepted for almost two thousand years. Aristotle explained the "stoniness" of fossils as compared with living organisms by "vaporous exhalations." Avicenna (980–1037), Albertus Magnus (1192–1280), and Agricola (1494–1555) elaborated this into a theory of a petrifying fluid *(succus lapidescens)* present everywhere in water. Such petrification was also seen at work in the formation of stalactites, corals, calcareous algae, gall stones, pearls, and even in meteorites.

Diluvialists in the Middle Ages claimed fossils to be the remains of organisms drowned during the biblical deluge, a concept that remained popular until after the publication of Charles Darwin's *Origin of Species* (1859). Fracastoro (1483–1553) was one of the first to deny the Aristotelian *vis plastica.* He also denied that fossils originate with the Deluge: in that case they would have scattered over the surface and not been buried deep in the rocks. Also, Leonardo da Vinci (1452–1519) argued in his notebooks that fossil marine shells found in the mountains of Monferrato (near Turin), 400 kilometers (250 miles) from the Adriatic, could not be related to the Deluge: the fossil bivalves must have lived in Monferrato because they were still articulated. He had observed that living bivalves could travel only 3 to 4 ell per day, not fast enough to keep pace with the rising waters and traverse 250 miles in forty days, the duration of the biblical deluge. Fossil fish, da Vinci argued, were dead fish embedded in mud, the organic matter having decayed, leaving only the skeleton; marine bivalves could become buried under mud and fill with mud after decay of the organic matter. Da Vinci was an early advocate of the "actualistic principle" (or principle of uniformity), inferring the nature of past events by analogy with processes observable at present. Actualistic studies have since proven invaluable in understanding the fossilization process.

Paleontology as a science was founded at the end of the eighteenth century by Georges Cuvier (1769–1823) and Jean-Baptiste Lamarck (1744–1829), among others. In Germany contributions to the understanding of the fossilization process were made for instance by Leopold von Buch (1774–1853), who published on the silification process of fossils (1831), a process of gradual replacement (permineralization) by silica that makes possible preservation of fine structures.

Alcide d'Orbigny (1802–1857) illustrates the rapid progress in understanding fossilization in his *Cours élementaire* (1849). He probably gave the first definition of fossilization that "covers all processes related to the changes occurring after the death of an organism and leading to recognizable traces/remains in the sediment." To become fossilized, organic remains must be buried, preferably under water. D'Orbigny extended Cuvier's theory of revolutions, supposing twenty-seven revolutions during the history of the Earth, which destroyed life not locally, as Cuvier had suggested, but all over the world. This catastrophic killing, he argued, was due to rapid sedimentation (hence remains were fossilized), which killed not only benthic organisms (those living on or in the bottom), but also the pelagic organisms (those living in the water-column). D'Orbigny proved experimentally that pelagic cuttlefish, squid, and fish die rapidly when the suspended sediment load of the water is increased (a fine actualistic experiment to prove his anactualistic theory of catastrophes!).

Johannes Walther (1860–1937) contributed significantly to the interpretation of older deposits and the understanding of fossilization using the actualistic method (his "ontological method"). In 1883 Walther started studies of recent sediments and their organisms in the newly founded (1872) Stazione Zoologica at Naples, Italy. His work on the famous Jurassic Solnhofener lithographic limestone (1904) is a landmark in the study of the fossilization process. He considered the Solnhofen deposits a *Leichenfeld* (graveyard) in which most animals arrived dead except for a few benthic organisms that died at the end of "death marches." Absence of bacteria, scavengers, and waves, plus rapid burial acted to keep remains even of medusae intact. Walther was well aware of the limits of his ontological method: fauna and flora had changed with time, recent counterparts for fossil organisms could not always be found, and the recent environments were insufficiently studied. In his *Einleitung in die Geologie* (1893–1894) he devoted a chapter to the incompleteness of the fossil record: there is no quantitative correspondence between fossils and the once-living fauna, a topic studied in more detail in 1991 by Susan Kidwell and Dan Bosence (Allison and Briggs, pp. 115–209).

Othenio Abel, Erich Wasmund, Wilhelm Quenstedt, Rudolf Richter, Franz Hecht, and Johannes Weigelt continued this German line of studies on fossil preservation including actualistic studies. The monograph (1927) by Weigelt (1890–1948) on biostratonomy of vertebrates is an effort to document vertebrate death, decay, decomposition, putrefaction, disarticulation, transport, and burial in recent environments and to indicate their relevance to fossil preservation. The core of his study was formed by the description of the Smither's Lake *Leichenfeld* in Texas: a catastrophic death of many vertebrates resulting from a sudden sharp drop in temperature. Sediment coverage, he argued, might preserve such carcass concentrations. Later he did find a succession of carcass concentrations in the Eocene lignites of Geiseltal, Germany. A recent (1989) translation has made his work better known. Particularly vertebrate paleontologists continued this line of actualistic fossilization research (for example, Behrensmeyer and Hill). Comparisons between fossil assemblages using taphonomic data (numbers of specimens, relative abundance, size frequency, distribution, degree of bone breakage, abrasion, and so on) are now used to better explain how they were formed.

Franz Hecht in 1933 studied in detail the fate of organic material after burial. In field and laboratory experiments he followed decay (with oxygen) and putrefaction (without oxygen) processes using nitrogen-content as a measure of proteins. Proteins are organic compounds built up of amino acids; all of them contain nitrogen. Within weeks proteins rapidly decrease often even to zero levels. Of buried crabs and shrimps, after four months only chitin was left and shrimp skeletons had fallen apart. If buried deep enough in the layer lacking oxygen, part of the lipids of fish or shark was preserved. Lipids released at or near the surface during decay floated away. Thus absence of oxygen and burial in sediment are prerequisites for preservation of organic matter, and chitin and lipids had some preservation potential. Hecht also observed *Steinkerns* (sediment infillings, internal molds) of cockle shells in recent tidal flat sediments. The carbonate shells had disappeared due to H_2SO_4 (hydrogen sulphate) formation during decay of organic matter. In experiments with mussel shells and decaying mussel flesh, the chitinous outer layer (periostracum) disconnected from the partly dissolved shells; thin *Posidonia* shells of the Carboniferous period might also represent only the periostracum. There is a revival of such experiments to explain exceptionally preserved soft-bodied biota. New techniques such as gas chromatography, pyrolysis, and mass spectrometry now facilitate the study of biosynthetic molecules. This molecular paleontology has resulted in new information on decay and diagenis in the late twentieth century.

In his *Flachseebeobachtungen* (shallow-sea observations), Rudolf Richter (1881–1957) published numerous observations in the early twentieth century on embedding of shells, concerning their orientation, left/right sorting, and concave up or down position. He used these to interpret fossil deposits. He stimulated the foundation in 1928 of a special institute to study recent processes of sedimentation and fossilization: Senckenberg am Meer in Wilhelmshaven along the Wadden Sea. Wilhelm Schäfer reviewed much of the earlier work in the North Sea and Wadden Sea in his *Aktuo-Paläontologie* (1962), compiling data on death, disintegration, and embedding of corpses or parts of corpses for all taxonomic groups in this area. Much was based on his own experiments both in aquariums and in the field. Only after translation in 1972 did this rich source become known to a wider public.

North American research mainly followed lines developed by Ivan A. Efremov, particularly due to the support of Everett C. Olson. The incompleteness of the fossil record ("information loss") was the main reason for Efremov to advocate a better study of processes and principles governing the transition of organic remains from the biosphere to the lithosphere, rather than the elucidation of paleoenvironments, which was the main thrust of the German school. Efremov coined the word "taphonomy" in 1940 for the study of the fossilization process. Quantification of this incompleteness became a major goal in taphonomic studies. David R. Lawrence estimated in his "Taphonomy" that up to 75 percent of the species in the marine environment were soft-bodied and thus had little preservation potential. A new impetus was the understanding that taphonomic studies should deal not only with information loss, but that they can provide an information gain: Mark V.H. Wilson argued in 1988 that the study of transport and of burial and diagenesis, including the fate of the soft parts, allows a better understanding of sediment genesis. The German tradition in taphonomic studies is finally getting the appreciation it deserves. For instance, Wilhelm Quenstedt, inventor in 1927 of the word "taphocoenosis" (*Grabgemeinschaft,* what is buried together), had already hinted at this information gain. Gerhard C. Cadée deals in more detail with the history of taphonomy in his 1991 article. This can serve as an entrance point for those interested in pursuing this history further.

Gerhard C. Cadée

Bibliography
Allison, Peter A., and Derek E.G. Briggs, eds. *Taphonomy: Releasing the Data Locked in the Fossil Record.* New York: Plenum, 1991.

Behrensmeyer, Anna K., and Andrew P. Hill, eds. *Fossils in the Making.* Chicago: University of Chicago Press, 1980.

Cadée, Gerhard C. "The History of Taphonomy." In *The Processes of Fossilization,* edited by Steven K. Donovan, pp. 3–21. London: Belhaven Press, 1991.

Efremov, Ivan A. "Taphonomy: New Branch of Paleontology." *Pan-American Geologist* 74 (1940): pp. 81–93.

Hecht, Franz. "Der Verbleib organischer Substanz der Tiere bei meerischer Einbettung." *Senckenbergiana* 15 (1933): pp. 165–249.

Lawrence, David R. "Taphonomy and Information Losses in Fossil Communities." *Geological Society of America, Bulletin* 79 (1968): pp. 1315–1330.

Quenstedt, Wilhelm. "Beiträge zum Kapitel Fossil und Sediment vor und bei der Einbettung." *Neues Jahrbuch für Geologie und Paläontologie, Abteilung B. Geologie und Paläontologie* 58 (1927): pp. 353–432.

Schäfer, Wilhelm. *Aktuo-Paläontologie nach Studien in der Nordsee.* Frankfurt am Main: Kramer, 1962. Translated as *Ecology and Paleoecology of Marine Environments.* Edinburgh: Oliver and Boyd, 1972.

Weigelt, Johannes. *Rezente Wirbeltierleichen und ihre paläobiologische Bedeutung.* Leipzig: Weg, 1927. Translated as *Recent Vertebrate Carcasses and Their Paleobiological Implications.* Chicago: University of Chicago Press, 1989.

Wilson, Mark V.H. "Taphonomic Processes: Information Loss and Information Gain." *Geoscience Canada* 15 (1988): pp. 131–148.

See also Actualism, Uniformitarianism, and Catastrophism; Deluge; Evolution and the Geosciences; Facies, Sedimentary; Mass Extinction and the Impact-Volcanic Controversy; Paleoecology; Paleontology; Stratigraphy

Foucault's *Order of Things*

A late-twentieth-century author and work with relevance to the historiography of the geosciences. It may not be immediately obvious that the work of the distinguished French scholar Michel Foucault (1926–1984), whose ideas (which drew particular inspiration from Nietzsche) came to be so influential in the English-speaking world in the 1970s and 1980s, might have much to do with the history of the sciences of the Earth. Foucault wrote on topics like the histories of medical practice, madness, sexuality, power, language, and theories of wealth. But he also considered the history of systems of classification, and this hints at how his thought may be useful in the history of the geosciences.

The text of Foucault specially relevant for present purposes is his *Les Mots et les Choses* (1966), translated into English as *The Order of Things* (1970). His procedures and assumptions, initially misunderstood by many, were explicated in *L'Archéologie du Savoir* (1969), translated as *The Archeology of Knowledge* (1972). But this difficult book unfortunately failed to clear up all misunderstandings. Useful analyses of Foucault's thought are provided for English-language readers by, for example, Alan Sheridan, Barry Cooper, and Gary Gutting.

In *The Order of Things,* Foucault studied three areas of human thought or scholarly activity—that today might be called historical linguistics, economics, and biology—from the Renaissance to the nineteenth century. He argued that each went through two analogous transformations at about the same time, thereby giving a threefold periodization for each of the three areas. On this basis, he claimed there is a common *episteme,* or system of knowledge, underpinning the study of wealth, language, and living organisms in each of the three periods. Thus we have the following schema:

Renaissance	Classical Age	Nineteenth Century
"Histories" of animals and plants	Natural history	Biology
"Histories" of precious metals and coins	Analysis of wealth	Economics
Etymologies (which may confer power over nature, and so on)	General grammar	Historical linguistics (Philology)

The "Classical Age" (the meaning of which term is somewhat special to Foucault) was considered to run from about 1660–1670 to about the beginning of the nineteenth century. Thus Foucault's periodization seems to approximate to the better known categories of the Renaissance, the Enlightenment, and the period of the rise of historicism and romanticism.

It should be observed that Foucault did not propose that there is some overarching *Zeitgeist* (spirit of the age) or *Weltanschauung* (worldview) that characterized or "shaped" each of his three periods. Certainly, an *episteme* was not envisaged as having some kind of power that caused people to think the way they did at any given time. Foucault simply contended that in the studies of natural history, money, and language there were certain common features in the way these were thought about, studied, or understood. Similar features might or might not be found in other areas, such as psychology, political theory, or whatever. This was an empirical question, to be determined by the "archaeologist" (as Foucault liked to think of himself) excavating the "strata" preserved in libraries, art galleries, and so on. The *episteme* was the result of a common pattern of thinking, not a cause. Though Foucault refused the label of structuralist, he has often been regarded as such, for when it came down to it what he was

chiefly doing was looking for analogies and disanalogies—systems of relations between coexisting disciplines—revealed in texts or in cultural objects.

Considering the attention that has been bestowed on Foucault's ideas, it is surprising that so little has been written by historians of science from an avowedly Foucaultian perspective, though in the history of biology the work of François Jacob is a notable exception. We have, however, found it useful to examine the history of the study of minerals and strata with Foucault's periodization of the history of natural history in mind, and the results have been highly suggestive (Albury and Oldroyd).

Consider first the Renaissance scholar, giving an account of some plant or animal. He would (according to Foucault, and the claim seems warranted) endeavor to record all possible relevant information. This might include, then, not only the object's appearance or behavior but also its magical and medicinal powers, its uses in heraldry, its mention in mythology, its "sympathies" and "antipathies," its "correspondences" (which might be comprehended by the understanding of certain "signatures"); and moreover a summary of all that had previously been written or said about the object, which was, in effect, part of its being (Foucault, *Order of Things,* pp. 25–30). When all such matters were known, then the scholar would understand the nature of the plant or animal. The whole system may be understood as a network of resemblances or similitudes.

So it was with Renaissance writers on the mineral kingdom. Conrad Gesner, for example, in his *De Rerum Fossilium* (1565) considered resemblances between minerals and geometrical forms, celestial objects, animals, plants, and artifacts. In his posthumous *Musaeum Metallicum* (1648), Ulisse Androvandi treated minerals under the headings of synonyms, definitions, origins, nature and properties, varieties, mode and place of occurrence, uses, historical references, sympathies and antipathies, temperaments, mysteries, miracles, moralia, adages, epithets, mythologies, dreams, symbols, and *lapidati.* This suggests that the *episteme* for the Renaissance study of animals and plants was manifested equally in the discourse for the study of minerals.

But when we move into Foucault's Classical Age, the style changes radically, to yield what was called "natural history" (Foucault, *Order of Things,* pp. 128–132). Objects were collected as before, but they were now classified in such a way that their differences were more important than their similarities and analogies. Secret "virtues," literary and heraldic significances, and other associated forms of Renaissance lore were systematically excluded. Attention was focused on external features, for the purpose of naming and classification, arrangement, and display. In Foucault's words, a natural history was "provided by surfaces and lines, not by functions or invisible tissues. The plant and the animal are seen not so much in their organic unity as by the visible patterning of their organs. . . . Natural history traverses an area of visible, simultaneous, concomitant variables, without any internal relation of subordination or organization" (Foucault, *Order of Things,* p. 137).

The paradigm case of this kind of approach is furnished by the eighteenth-century Swedish naturalist Carolus Linnaeus. He developed a system for studying and classifying the many plants that he and his students collected. These were preserved as pressed specimens, or cultivated in Linnaeus's botanical garden, in beds laid out according to his classificatory system. Each plant was given a concise description according to its external, visible parts (considering their number, proportion, figure, and situation), and for shorthand naming just two words were used—for genus and species. The actual basis of the classification of plants was artificial but effective: one counted the number of male parts, and the number of female parts. On this basis, a kind of tabular grid could be constructed, and the different kinds of plants could be pigeonholed thus, according to the number of the sexual parts, either in a book or in a set of flower beds. The classificatory system can be thought of as a grid through which the natural historian looked at the world. Such a procedure typified the Classical natural historian, according to Foucault (*Order of Things,* p. 141).

As is well known, Linnaeus divided the natural world into three kingdoms: animal, vegetable, and mineral. It is not surprising, then, that his classificatory procedure for minerals was fundamentally the same as that used for plants. First the surfaces of a crystal were described and counted. Next one imagined the surfaces of the crystal folded out onto a plane. And then the resulting geometrical shapes were totted up. For example, a quartz crystal might be described as consisting of a hexagonal prism with a hexagonal-base pyramid at each end. When the faces were "unfolded," one would have eighteen joined figures: six rectangles, and twelve triangles. Crystals could thus be described and classified in a manner that was analogous to the procedure adopted for plants—by counting certain clearly determinable, external, visible features.

A somewhat similar procedure to that of Linnaeus was carried forward in France by Jean Baptiste Romé de l'Isle. In his *Essai de Cristallographie* (1772) he offered diagrammatic representations of crystals along Linnaean lines, and in his general crystallographic scheme different forms of crystals were construed by thinking of them as arising (mentally) from certain bevellings and truncations of a small number of simple geometrical solids. Hardness and specific gravity were also considered. Clearly, the procedure was based upon a contemplation of the features of crystals that could be determined without attempting to understand the internal constitution of the objects under study. This was as would be expected in Foucault's Classical Age.

In *The Order of Things,* Foucault does not argue for a total and immediate transition or rupture of the prevailing *episteme* of natural history between the Classical Age and the nineteenth century—with the emergence of a historical outlook and of "Man" as a new conceptual category (as Foucault controversially proposed). He cites investigators such as the botanist Antoine Laurent de Jussieu, the anatomist and physician Félix Vicq-d'Azyr, and the zoologist Jean-Baptiste Lamarck as transitional figures. In such authors, it is suggested, the visible is related to the invisible in some degree; "the more obvious signs displayed on the surfaces of bodies" indicate their "hidden architecture" (Foucault, *Order of Things,* p. 229).

Such considerations also seem to have applied in Romé de l'Isle's *Des Caractères Extérieurs des Minéraux* (1784) and in René Juste Haüy's *Essai d'une Théorie sur la Structure des Cristaux* (1784). But while Romé de l'Isle could only speculate on possible connections between external appearances and internal constitutions, Haüy developed a highly sophisticated method of crystallographic analysis, partly empirical and partly theoretical. Guided by visible cleavage planes, he sought to gauge the shapes of the building blocks of the different kinds of crystals, which he termed primitive forms. There were supposedly six such forms. Below this level he discussed three types of integrant molecules. Finally, one would reach to the several chemical constituents themselves—his constituent molecules, the nature of which might be revealed by chemical analysis. With remarkable success, Haüy showed how the vast array of different kinds of crystals might be built up (mentally) by suitable arrangements of the several different kinds of building blocks. The particular value of his method was that it offered some hope of making sense of the considerable variety of crystal shapes that might be exhibited by substances of the same chemical constitution. He could also explain how substances that were chemically different might nevertheless have the same crystalline form.

A more directly chemical approach was offered by the Swedish chemist Torbern Bergman in a paper published in 1777. His countryman Axel Cronstedt (and others) had already made progress in the use of fiery techniques (with the blowpipe) to characterize different kinds of minerals and rocks (Oldroyd, "A Note"). But such fiery methods were, we suggest, properly within the *episteme* of the Classical Age in that they simply provided some additional visible features whereby substances might be recognized and described. Bergman's procedure was different. He dissolved rocks or minerals in hot alkali, and then separated out their different constituent earths: "ponderous earth" (baryta), lime, magnesia, "argillaceous earth" (alumina), and "siliceous earth" (silica) were recognized. His standardized procedure used an ordered sequence of appropriate precipitating agents. The weights of the different constituent earths could also be determined and the total compared with the weight of starting material (Oldroyd, "Some Eighteenth-Century Methods"). The technical difficulties were hard to overcome at first, but analysts such as Nicholas Louis Vauquelin and Martin Heinrich Klaproth soon improved on Bergman's results.

Bergman (1784) also envisaged a hierarchical mineral classification, based on the "earthy" constituents determined by his humid (water-based) analyses. Higher categories of salts, earths, metals, and inflammables were also invoked. Such work was, we suggest, on a par with the analyses of organic structure that began to appear in the work of researchers like Vicq-d'Azyr toward the end of the Classical Age. However, unlike Haüy, Bergman was not able to establish a link between the internal constituents and the external forms.

For Foucault, the major figure in the transformation of Classical natural history to nineteenth-century biology was Georges Cuvier (Foucault, "La Situation de Cuvier"). As is well known, Cuvier saw animals as being constructed in such a fashion that they could function successfully in their environments, or according to what he called their conditions of existence. Their various parts formed an integrated whole. And if one dug down into their bodies by dissection one could discern a series of organs which, he said, exhibited a subordination of parts. The more peripheral, less fundamental, parts exhibited the greatest variation and variety; the more fundamental interior parts were more constant in form. Thus using the results of anatomical examination, one might, in principle, construct a hierarchical classification system that was not arbitrary (as had been the case in Classical taxonomy above the level of the biological species, since it dealt only with the similarities and differences of external visible characters). Also, Cuvier established a procedure for effecting comparisons between different kinds of animals, and he could use known living types to guide him in the reconstruction of fossil vertebrates. He envisaged four main *embranchements* of the animal kingdom, there being, it seemed, just four basic ways in which animals might be structured so as to meet the conditions of existence.

In Cuvier's view, if animals were properly adjusted to their conditions of existence, as appeared to be the case, any anatomical or physiological change could only be for the worse. However, the geological record did seem to indicate major changes in animal form. So Cuvier envisaged the globe as having undergone a series of major catastrophes, at each of which many organisms were killed off. He was somewhat ambivalent as to how they were replaced: perhaps by migration from areas not affected by the catastrophes; or perhaps (as some of his followers envisaged) by mysterious creation of new forms. While Cuvier's theory was profoundly antievolutionary, Foucault has asserted ("La Situation de Cuvier") that in fact it was a precondition for the emergence of Darwinian theory. Cuvier ruptured the old tabular grid of Classical taxonomy. In fact, we may conveniently regard the *embranchements* as a cross-section of an evolutionary tree; and if we add the dimension of time (Cuvier was more than willing to think of the Earth as immensely old) then the idea of the taxa splitting and diverging over time, yielding the Darwinian tree of life, became thinkable, as had not been the case in the Classical Age. The all-important point was the mesh between organisms and their environment; and the idea of their anatomical structures, both internal and external, revealed their taxonomic positions. Thus Cuvier offered the possibility of a history of life: this was thinkable in the nineteenth-century *episteme*.

Analogies for such conceptual changes may be found in ideas about the mineral kingdom, as mineralogy and crystallography gave way to the new science of historical geology. Through the Classical Age various theories of the Earth had been proposed—such as those of René Descartes, Gottfried Wilhelm Leibniz, William Whiston, George Louis Leclerc Buffon, and James Hutton. But apart from the last of these (which was proposed only toward the end of the eighteenth century), the theories were essentially extensions of astronomy and had rather little to say about the Earth's strata, the rocks, minerals, and fossils. It should be noted, however, that Buffon (1786) imagined that on the Earth's first formation (from a comet) five primitive "glasses" separated out (quartz, jasper, schorl, feldspar, and mica), and that by their weathering and chemical alteration five different series of minerals might be formed. Thus his mineralogy had a temporal dimension. So too did Lamarck's system (1786). He proposed that decayed matter from animals and plants had given rise to two chainlike sequences of mineral conversions, both ultimately leading to the formation of rock crystal (pure elementary earth). Thus there was a strong analogy between Lamarck's mineral theory and his well-known chain theory of living bodies.

But the theories of Buffon and Lamarck should be regarded neither as historical doctrines nor as evolutionary theories of minerals. In both systems, there was a supposed sequence of changes that a mineral would naturally follow after its formation. It was, so to speak, programmed to follow a predetermined sequence of changes. Such an approach to the past was very different from that of the nineteenth-century stratigrapher, who, by examining strata and their spatial relationships, along with their fossil and mineral contents, would endeavor to work out a contingent history of the globe, piecing together the items of stratigraphical information as would a historian working his way through archival records.

The chief transitional figure, leading to nineteenth-century historical geology, was probably the German mineralogist Abraham Gottlob Werner, well known for his teaching of mineralogy at the Mining Academy at Freiberg. In 1774, as a young man, he published a handbook on the identification of minerals by means of their external characteristics. This was entirely in keeping with the Classical *episteme* as conceived by Foucault. But Werner also developed an interesting and very influential theory of the Earth (1786), which offered a significantly different approach to the mineral kingdom. He envisaged an irregularly shaped primeval core to the Earth, and an immense primeval ocean containing much matter in solution or suspension. The ocean gradually disappeared (by an uncertain mechanism), and layers of crystalline, and then sedimentary, matter were deposited on the core in a clearly recognizable sequence. There was also a transitional category, consisting of matter that was partly crystalline and partly mechanical in origin.

We do not do justice to the subtleties of Werner's theory (cf. Laudan, chap. 5), but for the present purposes we may conceive that the result of his proposed sequence of events was a series of "formations" (his neologism) that could be found as layers round the core, rather like the layers of an onion. Werner worked out this sequence in Saxony, but his observations there were thought to be applicable generally. The layers of rocks manifested a discoverable time sequence: he was offering a temporalized natural history of the mineral kingdom. Thus the theory provided the basis of a definite research program—one examined rocks in different countries and saw them as exemplifications (with local variations) of the general pattern established in Saxony.

But this worldwide research program, carried out by Werner's many students such as Alexander von Humboldt, soon required modification. Instead of discovering a perfect set of onion skins, the researchers found that some were greatly expanded; or they might be attenuated or even missing. And sometimes formations equivalent to, rather than identical with, the Saxon exemplars were discovered. Nevertheless, the program proved workable up to a point; and in general the order of the mineral masses was preserved, even if items were sometimes missing or somewhat different from those that were expected according to the Saxon paradigm.

Certain interesting analogies, perhaps indicative of a common early-nineteenth-century *episteme,* can be seen in the work of von Humboldt, Haüy, and comparative anatomists such as Vicq-d'Azyr, Étienne Geoffroy St-Hilaire, and Cuvier. Vicq-d'Azyr (working in the late eighteenth century) made anatomical comparisons between quite closely related animals, so no particular difficulty was encountered, just as Werner's geognosy worked well enough within the confines of Saxony. Geoffroy St-Hilaire, taking a "transcendental" view of anatomy, envisaged a general animal archetype, the several component parts of which might be variously modified in the different animal types. This we may compare with von Humboldt's approach to Werner's geognosy. And in Haüy's crystallography, we find a constancy of angular relations between the molecular components of various crystals; also we can envisage the molecular layers being built up in a regular fashion rather like Werner's mineral formations.

In the case of Cuvier, however, the analogy breaks down. In Cuvier's anatomy, morphological comparisons operated only within a given *embranchement;* whereas between the *embranchements* the anatomical structures were fundamentally different and in consequence one had to think in terms of physiological functions that were performed by analogous (not homologous) parts—for example, lungs, gills, tracheae.

It may not be unexpected, then, that Cuvier (with the cooperation of Alexandre Brongniart) had effectively abandoned the Wernerian program, in favor of building up a stratigraphical column on the basis of both lithologies (that is, physical characters of the rocks) and organic fossils. He was a historical geologist in that a contingent sequential record of strata was sought in a given area (the Paris Basin as far as Cuvier was concerned), and lateral correlations were effected as far as that could be accomplished (say from France into southern England). It seemed that often there were substantial lithological differences from one area to another. On the other hand, it appeared that there was a general constancy in fossil forms in strata of a particular epoch. (This principle had previously been enunciated at the end of the eighteenth century in England by William Smith.) But Cuvier was not a thoroughgoing historical geologist, in that he thought that there were radical discontinuities from one epoch to the next. These discontinuities—indicative for Cuvier of grand catastrophes—may be paralleled by the radical discontinuities between his *embranchements,* as construed in his comparative anatomy. There was, therefore, epistemic coherence between Cuvier's anatomical and stratigraphic concepts, indicative of a common manner of thinking in the two aspects of his work.

For the principle of historical continuity in stratigraphy, we turn to the uniformitarian doctrines of Charles Lyell. But Lyell's historicism was consistently modulated by his methodological assumption of uniformity: in a sense he did not have a historical view of geology. Certainly there were endless changes, and a

historical record of these changes could be pieced together by the stratigrapher. But in the last resort, overall nothing really ever changed for Lyell, except for the emergence of humans.

The systematic geological mapping of the Earth's surface began in the first half of the nineteenth century. For a man such as Roderick Murchison, who was one of the most active in this endeavor, the task was to establish certain grand stratigraphical systems. He proposed the Silurian and the Permian, and he was also actively associated with the establishment of the Cambrian and the Devonian. Each system was characterized by a particular set of fossils, and the ground was mapped accordingly. For Murchison, any kind of rock type might turn up in any system. So far as he was concerned, a gneiss, for example, could just as well appear above as below limestone. So the universal lithological order of Werner was repudiated. On the other hand, there was seemingly a universal fossil order; and the history of the globe was supposedly interrupted by catastrophic episodes, as Cuvier had envisaged.

These several elements all came together in the work of Charles Darwin. The history of the globe, and its organic inhabitants, had been smooth and continuous, but was apparently discontinuous because of the incompleteness of the historical record. One dug in the Earth to find its fossils, rather than just examining its external lithological or mineralogical features. But while Lyell furnished the necessary continuities, and mysterious catastrophes seemed not to be required because of the immensity of geological time envisaged and the recognition of the incompleteness of the stratigraphical record, Darwin proffered the idea of biological progress, through constant adaptation of organisms to an ever-changing environment. (But Darwin himself was suspicious of the notion of biological progress.)

While Foucaultian parallels between geoscience, botany, and zoology are readily found for the Renaissance and the Classical Age, they are less satisfactory for the nineteenth century, though as mentioned Darwin succeeded in forging a convincing synthesis of geological and biological knowledge, and in that sense we might say that the separate disciplines evinced a common *episteme.* It may be, however, that we find in Foucault's notion of power a more clear-cut application of his concepts to geoscience in the nineteenth century.

As mentioned, geologists in the nineteenth century began the systematic process of mapping the globe. A nation's geology was disciplined by the mapping procedure, which made possible the accurate understanding of the internal, invisible, parts of the Earth, and their commercial exploitation. (We might even think, fancifully perhaps, of the Earth being punished too by the geologists' hammers, and by the mining operations that were so greatly increased as a result of the Industrial Revolution. And even today geologists talk of establishing stratigraphical control of a region.) A geological map served as a kind of panopticon of a country's mineral wealth. That the systematic compilation of geological maps should have emerged as and when it did, under the aegis of appropriate bureaucratic structures (geological surveys), seems highly congruent with the nineteenth-century *episteme,* as revealed in Foucault's studies of hospitals, asylums, and prisons. We may add that the notion of power and control over the geological systems was eagerly sought by prominent nineteenth-century geologists. That Murchison was called "King of Siluria," that he embraced this title, and that he did all in his power to expand "his" Silurian domain, would seem natural to someone attracted by Foucault's mode of analyzing the past (cf. Oldroyd, *The Highlands Controversy*).

We would insist, however, that while Foucault's analysis can provide numerous insights and suggestive hypotheses for the historian of geology it should not be thought of as universally applicable. For example, the theory of the Earth devised by Descartes in terms of the interaction of his hypothetical, metaphysically grounded corpuscles, does not seem to be a typical product of either Renaissance lore or Classical natural history, as described by Foucault. It was a product of the mechanical philosophy and was integrated with astronomical theory. As such, it does not seem to find a natural component of any of the epistemic systems discussed by Foucault; yet Descartes sought to give a theory of minerals and strata, along with everything else.

Moreover, Foucault's work leaves us with numerous queries. In particular, his readers are likely to want to know the causes of the grand epistemic shifts entertained in *The Order of Things*. Nevertheless, despite such seeming mysteries, Foucault's work may still hold out the possibility of interesting lines for future research. For example, was there something in nineteenth-century geology that pertained to Foucault's claimed emergence of the concept of "Man"? Lyell's *Antiquity of Man* could well be examined from that perspective.

David Oldroyd
William Randall Albury

Bibliography

Albury, W. Randall, and David R. Oldroyd. "From Renaissance Mineral Studies to Historical Geology in the Light of Michel Foucault's *The Order of Things*." *British Journal for the History of Science* 10 (1977): pp. 187–215.

Cooper, Barry. *Michel Foucault: An Introduction to His Thought*. Toronto: Edwin Mellen, 1981.

Foucault, Michel. *L'Archéologie du Savoir*. Paris: Éditions Gallimard, 1969.

———. *Les Mots et les Choses*. Paris: Éditions Gallimard, 1966. Translated as *The Order of Things: An Archaeology of the Human Sciences*. New York: Pantheon Books, 1970.

———. "La Situation de Cuvier dans l'Histoire de la Biologie." *Revue d'Histoire des Sciences et de leurs Applications* 23 (1970): pp. 62–69.

Gutting, Gary. *Michel Foucault's Archaeology of Scientific Reason*. Cambridge, New York, and Melbourne: Cambridge University Press, 1989.

Laudan, Rachel. *From Mineralogy to Geology: The Foundation of a Science 1650–1830*. Chicago and London: University of Chicago Press, 1987.

Oldroyd, David R. *The Highlands Controversy: Constructing Geological Knowledge through Fieldwork in Nineteenth-Century Britain*. Chicago and London: University of Chicago Press, 1990.

———. "A Note on the Status of A.F. Cronstedt's Simple Earth and His Analytic Methods." *ISIS* 65 (1974): pp. 506–512.

———. "Some Eighteenth-Century Methods for the Chemical Analysis of Minerals." *Journal of Chemical Education* 50 (1977): pp. 337–340.

Sheridan, Alan. *Michel Foucault: The Will to Truth*. London and New York: Tavistock Publications, 1980.

See also Earthquakes, Theories from 1600 to 1800; Evolution and the Geosciences; Geography in Enlightenment Encyclopedias; Historiography, Eighteenth-Century England; Humboldtian Science; Lakatos's Idea of Scientific Research Programs; Mineralogy; Minerals and Crystals, Fifteenth to Eighteenth Centuries; Popper's Ideas on Falsifiability; Presentism; Volcanoes, Theories of before 1800

Geochemistry: The Word and Disciplinary History

A borderline field between geology and chemistry, with roots in mid-nineteenth-century Germany.

Geochemistry established itself in America in the early twentieth century and became an independent enterprise several decades later, after successfully bridging several scientific disciplines. The historical development of geochemistry is divided into three distinct eras. The first era was created by the chemist Carl G. Bischof (1792–1870), the geologist Justus Roth (1818–1892), and the early American geochemist Frank W. Clarke (1847–1931), who collected analytical data on the chemistry of rocks, minerals, and waters. Modern geochemistry, with its emphasis on finding the laws governing the abundance and distribution of the elements in the crust of the Earth, coincides with the rise of two great research schools in the 1920s, one in Russia under Vladimir I. Vernadsky (1863–1945), and the other in Germany, led by the Norwegian mineralogical chemist Victor M. Goldschmidt, working partly in Oslo, partly in Göttingen. After 1945, the field entered a new era, ushered in by the work of isotope chemist Harold Urey (1893–1981) and his research team at the University of Chicago, working on studies that have since become classics of geochemistry. No full-length history of geochemistry exists. Its social structure, which would include institutions, education, funding, and publications, also merits study.

Judith R. Goodstein

Bibliography
Goldschmidt, Victor Moritz. *Geochemistry.* Oxford: Clarendon Press, 1958.

See also Chemistry, Terrestrial and Cosmical; Disciplinary History; Ecology; Economic Geology; Evolution and the Geosciences; Geology; Heat, Internal, Twentieth Century; Matter, Properties at High Pressure and Temperature; Mohole and Other Drilling Projects; Ore Formation, Theories since 1800; Petrology; Sedimentology; Stratigraphy

Geodesy: Disciplinary History

The science of measuring the size and shape of the Earth.

Apart from fulfilling the normal human curiosity to know ever more about the planet we inhabit, geodesy provides the critical controls needed to determine the position of a point (that is, the location of a place or person) on the Earth's surface. It, therefore, is the backbone of any location mapping, transportation (including marine and space navigation), and more recently, communication systems. It originally developed from land surveying methods and measurement techniques of geometry that were historically employed to prepare local or regional location maps or to demarcate boundaries. As early as 3500 B.C.E. Babylonians produced reasonably accurate maps indicating that field information was obtained by surveying and plotted to scale. Around 2900 B.C.E., Egyptians built pyramids with an accuracy that indicates application of surveying techniques. Such techniques were routinely used by 1400 B.C.E. to relocate boundaries wiped out by the Nile's flood waters. A preliminary effort is made by Volker Bialas to place some of this in historical context in his 1982 *Erdgestalt, Kosmologie und Weltanschauung* (Figure of the earth, cosmology, and worldview, pp. 9–18).

Eratosthenes (276–194 B.C.E.), however, is generally considered the first to have described and applied a scientific measuring technique for determining the size of the Earth. His method, a simple concept of basic geometry, was elegant and is still used today in principle. Knowing the length of an arc l and the corresponding central angle α that it subtends, one can find the radius R of the sphere or its circumference from the simple relationship: $l: 2\pi R = \alpha°:360°$. Eratosthenes assumed that a camel caravan could travel between Alexandria and Syene in fifty days at a fairly constant camel speed of 100 stadia/day. He further assumed that Syene and Alexandria were on the same meridian (which they are not) and that the sun shines vertically down a well at Syene at the summer solstice at noon (which it did not). He then measured the angle of sunbeams with the vertical at noon at the summer solstice in Alexandria and concluded that his measurement must be the central angle between Syene and Alexandria. Using this information in the above-noted relationship, he obtained a value of 250,000 stadia or 46,250,000 meters (using the then-current value of the stadium) for the circumference of the Earth. By definition, the modern value for the length of a meridian is 40,000,000 meters. Thus, his value was only 15–16 percent too large. This is remarkable considering the very crude approximations he had used in his measurements. Again, Eratosthenes' contribution is more in ushering in a scientific era for determining the size of the Earth than in the accuracy of his results.

These rapid and exciting developments in concept, method, and measurement of the size and shape of the Earth peaked in the third and second centuries B.C.E. The Western historical literature frequently states that there is no important advance or activity in the history of geodesy for the next almost eighteen centuries. That is incorrect. At best, it is an ethnocentric statement. There is indeed a relative lull of about eight centuries counting from the second century B.C.E. Then, the focus of activity seems to have shifted, for at least a few centuries, to Asia and the areas now known as the Middle East.

In 723–726 an arc surveyed by I-Hsing in China showed the Earth to be approximately spherical. In about 827, Al-Farghani, an Arab astronomer, carried out an arc measurement northwest of Baghdad under the Caliph Al-Mámûn. But these results, particularly those of the Chinese arc measurement, were not known in Europe. Had they been known, they would have led to a serious reconsideration of the early-eighteenth-century arc measurement results of Jean-Dominique Cassini, and Western science might perhaps have been spared a bitter controversy. Around 1529, a French physician, Jean François Fernel (1497–1558), carried out a meridian arc measurement between Paris and Amiens. Thus, it is clear that considerable, though sporadic, geodetic activity occurred during the period identified in the Western literature as a dormant era in geodesy.

A new era in geodesy began with the introduction of the method of triangulation. The basic idea of triangulation was initially applied by Gemma Frisius (1508–1555) in the Netherlands and by the Danish astronomer Tycho Brahe (1546–1601) in Denmark before the end of sixteenth century. Until that time, the term "geodesy" meant land surveying, in a more common sense. The method of triangulation was developed and introduced in the scientific literature by the Dutch mathematician Willebrord van Roijen Snell in 1615. It soon became one of the most powerful tools of geodesy. Snell used it to determine the size of the Earth. His results, however, showed the size 3.4 percent too small (see Bialas, pp. 84–91; Perrier, pp. 30–36).

The next few decades saw the development of the telescope and of logarithmic tables. Along with triangulation, these developments launched geodesy as a modern science. In 1669–1670, Jean Picard used these triple tools to measure the length of an arc extending from Paris 1.2° northward, to determine the size of the Earth. Picard's length of 1° meridian arc was used by Isaac Newton. In his epoch-breaking calculations of the law of gravitation, which he published in *Principia Mathematica* in 1687, Newton theorized that as the Earth rotates about its axis, the centrifugal forces acting on the particles in the equatorial plane should cause the equator to bulge and the Earth to assume the shape of an oblate spheroid of rotation. He found that the equatorial semiaxis of the Earth would thus be 1/230 (correct value: 1/298.25) longer than its polar semiaxis. At about the same time, Christian Huygens, a Dutch mathematician, showed that the Earth would be flattened at the poles. This ended the spherical era started by the early Greek thinkers and ushered in the ellipsoidal or spheroidal era (Bialas, chap. 4; Perrier, chap. 1).

Newton's findings helped to solve an enigma posed by a French expedition to Guiana in 1672. It had found that a pendulum clock that kept good time in Paris lost 2 1/2 minutes per day at Cayenne near the equator. Nobody knew how to interpret those observations at that time, but Newton's results provided the explanation: gravity would be stronger at the poles than at the equator.

The work of Newton and Huygens laid the foundation stone for expanding the scope of geodesy to include gravity-based methods to determine the size and shape of the Earth. This category of methods later became physical geodesy. The methods based on the arc measurement and the use of arc geometry would develop into geometric geodesy. Although the word "geodesy" continued to be applied to land surveying into the nineteenth century, its meaning was gradually reserved more for these scientific investigations.

The concepts of Newton and Huygens also infused new life into arc-measurement methods to verify the new theoretical predictions. The focus of these methods now shifted toward determining the oblate shape of the Earth. Astronomer Jean-Dominique Cassini and his son Jacques Cassini tried to measure the oblateness of the Earth by continuing Picard's arc north to Dunkirk and south to the boundary of Spain. It is interesting to note that the elder Cassini had argued since 1691 that since the telescopic observations of Jupiter showed it flattened at the poles and since the Earth also rotates on its axis as does Jupiter, the Earth should be flattened at the poles too. Thus, the Cassinis (father and son) had no intellectual predisposition to challenge Newton's results as is sometimes insinuated. Their results, published in 1720, showed, however, that the Earth is egg-shaped—that is, a prolate spheroid with its equatorial axis shorter than its polar axis, and not an oblate spheroid as theorized by Newton and Huygens. This started an intense controversy between the French and English scientists. To settle this controversy, the French Academy of Sciences sent one expedition in 1735 to Peru (close to the equator) under the leadership of Pierre Bouguer and Charles-Marie de La Condamine and another in 1736 to Lapland (close to the Arctic Circle) under Pierre-Louis Moreau de Maupertuis to measure the lengths of a meridian degree at each place. Results proved that the Earth is flattened at the poles, as predicted by Newton and Huygens. Later,

large errors were found in the measurements, but fortunately they did not change the results. These results gave a value of 6,397,300 meters for the equatorial radius and 1/216.80 for the flattening. These values are considerably different from the current values. Their real contribution lies in the fact that they settled the controversy about the shape of the Earth once and for all.

In 1740, Colin Maclaurin, a Scottish mathematician, showed that if the Earth were a fluid of uniform density rotating about a fixed axis, it would assume the shape of an oblate spheroid. But there was considerable evidence that the Earth's density increased greatly toward its center. In 1743, Alexis-Claude Clairaut, a French mathematician/physicist showed that whatever the internal constitution of the Earth, it would assume the shape of an oblate spheroid. He also deduced the relationship between the variation of gravity from equator to pole and the flattening in what is called Clairaut's theorem. It shows simply that one can determine the flattening of the Earth by measuring the force of gravity in two different latitudes.

In 1791, the French Academy of Sciences adopted the definition of a meter as 1/40,000,000th part of the meridian circle. Numerous arc measurements were made subsequently to tie in with this adopted definition. One such measurement was between Dunkirk and Barcelona, carried out between 1792 and 1798. These, combined with the Peruvian measurements, gave a semimajor axis a = 6,376,428 meters and flattening f = 1/311.5.

This era of mathematical advances and their subsequent observational confirmation in geodesy continued into the nineteenth century. The important work of the German mathematician Carl Friedrich Gauss and of his contemporary, the German astronomer Friedrich Wilhelm Bessel, provided the basis for adjustment computation, error estimation, and systematized triangulation. In 1841, Bessel also deduced the dimensions of an Earth ellipsoid from arc measurements he had conducted a decade earlier. In 1849, the British physicist George Gabriel Stokes published his formulation of the variations of gravity on the Earth's surface, providing a practical and convenient method of computing geoidal heights from gravity data (Bialas, chap. 6; Perrier, chap. 2).

As the various national geodetic groups launched their own efforts to compute the dimensions of an Earth ellipsoid, they realized that their arc measurements and astronomical observations needed to extend beyond several national boundaries to provide an adequate data base. This need for international cooperation in geodesy led to the founding of several international organizations in the nineteenth century. Friedrich Robert Helmert (1843–1917), an eminent geodesist, was a leader in these efforts. The present survivor of this historical process is the International Union of Geodesy and Geophysics (IUGG), founded in 1919. Its geodesy-related component is called the International Association of Geodesy (IAG). The stories of these and other national and international geodetic organizations are sketched in Bialas (chaps. 7–9, passim) and Perrier (pp. 159–183). At its second general assembly held in 1924, the IUGG adopted values for a and f for what was called the International Reference Ellipsoid as a = 6,378,388 meters and f = 1/297.0. At a subsequent meeting held in 1930 (the fourth IUGG general assembly), the formula for the determination and variation of normal gravity on the surface of this ellipsoid was adopted. This is known as the International Gravity Formula. These quantities constituted the first internationally endorsed geodetic reference model.

In spite of this international trend, many of the countries used their own ellipsoids primarily for reasons of national pride. Thus England used an ellipsoid computed by the British geodesist A.R. Clarke in 1880. The United States, because of its British affiliation, first used Clarke's 1866 ellipsoid, then changed to the international ellipsoid computed by the American geodesist J.F. Hayford in 1910. Germany and some other Continental countries used Bessel's 1841 ellipsoid. The Soviet Union used an ellipsoid derived by a Russian geodesist, F.N. Krassowski, in 1938. Not until quite recent times did the international community agree to standard dimensions of the Earth-ellipsoid.

In addition to using different ellipsoids, many countries used their own initial points to which they tied their national geodetic systems. In the beginning, of course, this was done out of sheer convenience. As the need for international standardization of geodetic quantities grew, attempts were initiated toward the mid-twentieth century to tie most of these systems together in a World Geodetic System network.

Such adjustments required knowledge of certain quantities, such as geoidal undulations

and vertical-deflection components. Determination of these quantities from gravimetric data had clear advantages over their determination by geometric means. The mathematical formulas for determining these quantities from gravity data were already available. Stoke's formula for determining geoidal heights had been known since 1849. In 1928, F.A. Vening Meinesz had developed related formulas for computing the vertical-deflection components. But these formulas could not be applied, as the gravity data were too sparse to provide any useful results. Consequently, in the second quarter of the twentieth century, a concerted international effort was launched by a group of leading geophysicists to standardize and expand the network of gravity observations, first by using pendulums and then gravimeters (see, for example, Heiskanen and Vening Meinesz, pp. 222–310). George P. Woollard, first at the University of Wisconsin and then at the University of Hawaii, Maurice Ewing and J. Worzel of Columbia University, F.A. Vening Meinesz at the University of Utrecht, W.A. Heiskanen at Ohio State University, and many others at several universities, the U.S. Department of Defense agencies, and the U.S. Coast and Geodetic Survey led their respective groups in the cooperative international effort to measure, collect, standardize, and archive gravitational data. The gravity anomalies derived from such data were used to compute the geoidal undulations and vertical deflection components wherever such data were available in the requisite density.

This ushered in what is called the geoidal era. In fact, the geoidal era had evolved gradually over a good part of the preceding century. As early as the first few decades of the nineteenth century, it was realized that if sufficient geodetic measurements were available, the ellipsoid would only approximate the actual shape of the Earth. Laplace, Gauss, and Bessel had pointed out the deviation of the plumb line, later termed as deflection of the vertical, in 1802, 1828, and 1837 respectively. In 1828, Gauss had talked of a surface "which intersects everywhere the direction of gravity at right angles and part of which coincides with the surface of the oceans." This level surface was called the geoid by J.B. Listing in 1873. But the paucity of geodetic and gravimetric measurements had delayed its determination, except its local component in limited areas. In the geoidal era, the focus of geodesy shifted to the shape, size, and other properties of the geoid, and the figure of the

Earth came to be defined as the best-fit figure of this geoidal surface.

The geoidal era was stimulated and financed primarily by the various agencies of the U.S. Department of Defense, as they needed the precise knowledge of the local geoid for weapon-launching and defense purposes. Over large areas of the Earth's surface, however, the gravity measurements had either not been made, or if made, were not available for various reasons, and thus the gravity data coverage did not meet the minimum density required for the application of Stoke's formula. Consequently, a number of statistical and geophysical techniques were developed to reduce, correct, and otherwise statistically manipulate these data to approximate the theoretical requirements as closely as possible. There was also a vast body of research on what type of gravity anomaly—that is, free air or isostatic—is most suited for geodetic applications.

With the development of these techniques and increasing amounts of gravity data, local geoids were computed for several areas. It became increasingly possible to visualize the availability of a global geoid at some point in the future, however distant, by the gradual integration of these local or regional geoids and by filling in the voids. Consequently, the debate about the Earth's figure shifted to finding an ellipsoid of revolution that would provide a best fit to the global geoidal surface. But the voids in the anticipated global geoid were numerous and vast. There were hardly any data over the vast oceans. Most of the land areas had either not been surveyed or were inaccessible. Political polarization impeded access to data for areas where gravity surveys had been conducted. Gravity data obtained by oil and mineral companies was hard to obtain because of their concern about competition. Further, the feeling, correct to some extent, that precise knowledge of the local geoid is important to an enemy for targeting its weapons made access to such data even more difficult, lest its unrestricted availability lead it into hostile hands (Heiskanen and Vening Meinesz, pp. 222–310).

Advances in electronic surveying equipment, in the meantime, improved significantly both the range and accuracy of distance-measurement methods. This led to significant improvements in the refinement of national geodetic systems. However, these advances could still not be used for measuring intercontinental distances needed to connect various national geodetic systems.

As these efforts progressed, yielding considerable dividends in terms of advances in classical geodesy, a new development, initially unrelated to the discipline of geodesy, took place. The Soviet Union launched its first artificial Earth satellite, named *Sputnik,* in 1957. The advent of the satellite age, aided by rapidly expanding computer technology, opened up a new satellite era in geodesy. This changed forever the scope and potential of the discipline of geodesy. The application of satellites to geodesy developed into a new subdiscipline called satellite geodesy. Even early satellite missions provided estimates of the long-wavelength components of the Earth's gravity field and therefore, its flattening and size, with an accuracy that had not even been imaginable with surface geodetic methods. By the mid-1960s, reasonably accurate long-wavelength components of global gravity and the geoid were achieved. In this early phase of geodetic research based on artificial Earth satellites, the Smithsonian Astrophysical Observatory (SAO) at Cambridge, Massachusetts, the Naval Weapons Laboratory (NWL) of the U.S. Department of Defense (DoD), the Applied Physics Laboratory (APL) of the Johns Hopkins University, and to some extent the Goddard Space Flight Center (GSFC) of the U.S. National Aeronautics and Space Administration (NASA) played leading roles. About a decade of research on the use of artificial Earth satellites for geodetic purposes yielded such excellent results that the IUGG, at its fourteenth general assembly in 1967, adopted the satellite-derived values for what is called the Geodetic Reference System 1967. This system was subsequently replaced at the seventeenth general assembly of IUGG by Geodetic Reference System 1980. The most current values adopted for this system are $a = 6,378,136 \pm 1$ meter and $f = 1/298.257$. The value of f is derived from satellite-determined J_2, the second geopotential coefficient in the spherical harmonic representation of the Earth's gravity field. As potential technological applications of satellites emerged beyond their preliminary political missions, specific geodetic mission satellites were launched. Because of the major financial, logistical, and personnel resources required on a long-term basis for such vast scale and multifaceted missions, it became more and more difficult for individual universities or other small research groups to handle such large-scale efforts, and the task fell inevitably to the Goddard Space Flight Center, the Jet Propulsion Lab (JPL), and Wallops Flight Center (WFC), from among the U.S. civilian agencies, and to the U.S. DoD's Defense Mapping Agency (DMA) to a principal degree. Later on, the U.S. Department of Commerce's National Ocean Survey (NOS) also became responsible for the scientific research aspects of some of the dedicated scientific mission satellites. Several other agencies and institutions played various roles.

The advantages of using artificial Earth satellites in geodetic applications had become so clear within a few years of the first satellite launch that in 1965 NASA initiated a major program in geodesy called the National Geodetic Satellite Program (NGSP). Although this program was a result of in part NASA's own needs for its future missions and in part the requirements of other groups both in the United States and abroad, the two major objectives of this program were stated to be the development of a unified world reference system and the determination of the gravitational field of the Earth. The major participants of the program were NASA's GFSC, SAO, DoD, National Geodetic Survey (NGS), and Ohio State University (OSU). Other organizations such as APL, JPL, WFC, and the University of California, Los Angeles (UCLA), also made important contributions to the program. University of Hawaii, Honolulu (UH), also contributed to the program through a National Academy of Sciences cooperative program.

NGSP achieved its main objectives by the mid-1970s. It was followed by a plethora of NASA programs intended to apply space-based techniques to the study of the Earth, such as the Earth Dynamics Monitoring and Forecasting Program. The principal element of this program was the Tectonic Plate Motion Project composed of the San Andreas Fault Experiment, the Pacific Plate Motion Experiment, Astronomical Radio Interferometric Earth Surveying, the Laser Earth Dynamic Project, Lunar Laser Ranging, and more. Later on, some of these programs were combined into the Crustal Dynamics Project. These programs overlapped with the emergence of yet another of NASA's major programs, the Earth and Ocean Dynamics Applications Program (EODAP). Subsequently, EODAP was split into two programs: the Ocean Processes Program and the Geodynamics Program. The Crustal Dynamics Program became a part of the Geodynamics Program. Although the Ocean Processes Program, as the name implies, was primarily to study the dynamics of ocean phenomena, and the Geodynamics Program was designed to investigate crustal and lithospheric processes, the division between them was sometimes more administrative than disciplinary. These two programs made critical contributions to geodesy. Radar altimeters in the Earth-orbiting satellites were used to determine the detailed geoid (in fact, sea-level heights) over the oceans. Most recent determinations of the global geoid, based on a combination of satellite orbital data, surface gravity data, and satellite altimetry data, claim accuracies of a few centimeters. Corresponding spherical harmonic representations of the Earth's gravity field have been developed to reflect mean gravity anomalies on a global basis over $5° \times 5°$ squares quite accurately and over $1° \times 1°$ squares nominally. Thus, the main problem of the determination of the global gravity field to the frequency resolution required by many classical geodetic applications has been nearly solved. These global gravity-field solutions are being constantly updated as more data become available. Detailed gravimetric surveys are still needed to measure the finer structures of the gravity field. Several summaries of the satellite contributions to the disciplines of geodesy, geophysics, and oceanography are available in scientific literature (see, for example, Khan, pp. 3–68).

In the area of crustal and lithospheric studies, the DoD's Global Positioning System (GPS) satellites, originally intended for accurate global navigational purposes, and the Satellite Laser Ranging (SLR) systems are being used for precise position locations and precise measurements of intracontinental and intercontinental scale baselines. The allied field of Very Long Baseline Interferometry (VLBI) using quasar sources has seen vast improvements over the last three decades. These developments, generally lumped under space geodesy, have opened up new possibilities in geodesy that were considered illusory even in the early satellite era. The techniques of space geodesy, combined with computer capabilities of truly vast capacity, have made it possible to make intercontinental and intracontinental baseline measurements to accuracies of a few centimeters. Potential accuracies of a few millimeters are a clear possibility in the near future. These capabilities have extended the reach of geodesy to such problems as dynamic ocean processes, plate collision tectonics, and earthquake prediction. Thus the traditional boundaries of geodesy, geophysics, and oceanography are extending and merging. It is already hard to categorize a geodesist in the classical sense anymore. The advances in satellite geodesy since its birth about three decades ago are so numerous as to need a separate disciplinary history.

There are a large number of individuals and institutions, both in the United States and abroad, who have made significant contributions to geodesy in the late twentieth century. They cannot all be listed here because our focus is on the generic disciplinary history, and not on the contributors.

There is also considerable emphasis on the early history. The more recent developments, which constitute the bulk of the scientific progress made to date in geodesy, deserve much greater historical scrutiny. The more recent disciplinary developments, nevertheless, need to be seen through the prism of time to maintain historical perspective. An integrated historical account of the older disciplinary developments also reassesses their contributions from the ever-changing perspective of a rapidly developing discipline, and prevents their fading with time.

Articles in recent editions of general encyclopedias offer basic outlines of this history. For example, the 1993 edition of *Encyclopedia Britannica* includes: "The Earth: Its Properties, Composition, and Structure," and "The Earth Sciences." *Grolier's* 1993 edition includes "Surveying," and *Encyclopedia Americana* has articles on "Earth" and "Geodesy." More careful scholarship, however, can be expected in books and articles based on detailed consideration of actual historical documents. Books by Georges Perrier, Volker Bialas, and John L. Greenberg are good starting points for further investigations. Recent textbooks such as Wolfgang Torge's *Geodesy* offer a useful guide to the scientific literature of the late twentieth century. Ultimately, closer examination of original documents is indispensable.

M.A. Khan

Bibliography
Bialas, Volker. *Erdgestalt, Kosmologie und Weltanschauung: Die Geschichte der Geodäsie als Teil der Kulturgeschichte der Menschheit*. Stuttgart: Konrad Witter, 1982.
Greenberg, John L. *The Problem of the Earth's Shape from Newton to Clairaut. The Rise of Mathematical Science in 18th-Century Paris and the Fall of "Normal" Science*. Cambridge: Cambridge University Press, 1994.
Heiskanen, W.A., and F.A. Vening Meinesz. *The Earth and Its Gravity Field*, pp. 222–310. New York: McGraw-Hill Book Co., 1958.
Khan, M.A. "Satellite Contributions to Geophysical Exploration at Sea." In *Handbook of Geophysical Exploration at Sea*, edited by Richard A. Geyer, pp. 3–68, Boca Raton, Fla.: CRC Press, 1983.
"National Geodetic Satellite Program," *NASA SP-365*. National Aeronautics and Space Administration: Government Printing Office, 1977.
Perrier, Georges. *Wie der Mensch die Erde Gemessen und Gewogen Hat. Kurze Geschichte der Geodäsie*. Translated by Erwin Gigas, with a new foreword and an appendix on international organizations. Bamberg: Meisenbach, 1949. Originally published as *Petite Histoire de la Géodésie. Comment l'homme a mesuré et pesé la Terre*. Paris: Alcan, 1939.
Torge, Wolfgang. *Geodesy*. Translated by Christopher Jekeli. Berlin and New York: Walter de Gruyter, 1980.

See also Climate, Ancient Ideas; Continental Drift and Plate Tectonics; Cosmology and the Earth; Disciplinary History; Earth, Figure of in the Satellite Era; Earth, Models of before 1600; Earth, Size of; Gravity before Newton; Gravity, Newton and the Eighteenth Century; Gravity since 1800; Instruments, Gravity; Isostasy; Latitude; Plate Tectonics and Space-Based Platforms; Radio Astronomy and the Earth

Geographical Societies

Formed as geography became a recognized science.

Geographical societies have played an important role in the organization of science for more than 150 years. During the Enlightenment, enthusiasm for travel, exploration, and amateur scholarship intensified among the European gentry and bourgeoisie. Governments also began to sponsor exploration on a large scale, notably into the "New World" of the Pacific. In 1782, Jean-Nicolas Buache was appointed geographer to the court of Louis XVI. With royal approval, Buache attempted unsuccessfully to launch a geographical society in 1785 to coordinate French exploration (Lejeune, pp. 21–22). Stung into action by this failed initiative, a group of London scientists and businessmen, led by Sir Joseph Banks (president of the Royal Society and a veteran of Cook's Pacific expeditions) and Major James Rennell (chief surveyor of the East India Company), launched the Association for Promoting the Discovery of the Interior Parts of Africa in 1788. Over the next decades, the African Association (its shorter title) sponsored several pioneering expeditions, including those of Mungo Park, Hugh Clapperton and Alexander Gordon Laing.

The Napoleonic wars gave a new impetus to strategically important geographical sciences like cartography and land surveying, particularly in France. By 1815, affluent, educated and well-traveled former soldiers were to be found in virtually every major European city. These men became the clientele for the first geographical societies. The earliest was the *Société de Géographie de Paris* (SGP), which held its inaugural *séance* in July 1821. The 217 founding members included Edme Jomard, Baron Degérando, Jean-Baptiste Say, Jean-Denis Barbié du Bocage, Charles Athanase Walckenaer, and the Marquis de Laplace (the society's first president). Twenty percent of the membership were foreigners, including the great Prussian explorer and polymath Alexander von Humboldt, and Conrad Malte-Brun, the society's first secretary-general, a republican who left his native Denmark to settle in revolutionary France. The SGP established a journal, the *Bulletin de la Société de Géographie de Paris,* and offered prizes for approved projects, including 9,000 F. to the first European to return from Tombouctou, which was awarded controversially to René Caillié in 1829 (Fierro, pp. 4–17). A second, more modest geographical society, the *Gesellschaft für Erdkunde zu Berlin* (Berlin Society for Geography, GEB), was established at the instigation of the cartographer Heinrich Berghaus in April 1828 with a foundation membership of just fifty-three, including von Humboldt and Carl Ritter, professor of geography at Berlin and the society's inaugural president and dominant personality until his death in 1859. The society's principal publication was the *Zeitschrift der Gesellschaft für Erdkunde zu Berlin* (Lenz, p. 218). Neither society possessed sufficient funds to sponsor large-scale overseas exploration, and their monies were dispersed instead across a bewildering range of smaller topics. Early SGP prizes included one for a statistical investigation of road and canal commerce between Paris and Le Havre and another for a linguistic survey of the Russian empire. This eclecticism, coupled with a post-Napoleonic hostility to "imperial" overseas scholarship, adversely affected the SGP, which had fewer than three hundred members in 1830 (Fierro, pp. 247, 287).

The establishment in that year of the Royal Geographical Society (RGS) of London, under the patronage of William IV, marked a significant new departure. Several London societies committed to fieldwork and overseas travel already existed, including the Linnean Society for natural history (1788), the Palestine Association (1804), the Geological Society (1807), the Zoological Society (1826), and the Raleigh Club (1826), the last-named being a boisterous dining club whose forty members claimed collectively to have visited every part of the known world. The RGS was to provide a clearer focus for those with an interest in travel and exploration. Even at its foundation, it was far larger than either of the continental societies. The 460 original fellows included John Barrow, the explorer of the African Cape, and Robert Brown, the pioneer student of Australian flora. Within a year it had taken over the Raleigh Club, the African Association, and the Palestine Association, to gain a virtual monopoly on British exploration. The dominance of the RGS increased over subsequent decades. By 1850 there were nearly eight hundred fellows, twice that of Berlin and eight times more than in Paris, where the membership had slumped. Its journal was the *Proceedings of the Royal Geographical Society.* Most fellows were amateur scholars, but a number of prominent scientists were also involved, including Charles Darwin, who was elected after his return from the voyage of the *Beagle* in 1838. The success of the RGS, which had nearly twenty-four hundred fellows in 1870, reflected the strength of natural science in Britain, the wealth of the country's upper middle class (which provided the bulk of the fellowship), and the confidence that a large navy and overseas empire gave to prospective British explorers (Cameron, passim; Kolm, pp. 411–413).

The dominant figure was Sir Roderick Murchison, foundation fellow, director of the Geological Survey, and RGS president 1843–1845, 1851–1853, and 1862–1871. A talented publicist and entrepreneur, Murchison advocated geological and geographical exploration as a precursor to British commercial and military expansion and promoted the RGS as the major British center of exploratory expertise (Stafford, passim). Using its substantial reserves, the RGS sponsored exploration in advance and on a large scale by providing money, setting precise objectives, lending equipment, and arbitrating on the innumerable ensuing disputes. It also published general advice through its *Hints to Travellers,* which began in 1854. The society's map collection was among the largest in the world. Other societies would normally offer only *post hoc* awards and medals for successfully completed voyages. By concentrating on exploration and discovery, the RGS exploited a vicarious national passion for muscular "heroism" in exotic places that was enthusiastically promoted by the British press. Africa loomed large in the public imagination and the exploration of the "Dark Continent," particularly the quest for the source of the Nile, provided an exciting and popular focus for the society's activities. All the major African explorers of the day—Burton, Speke, Livingstone, Stanley—were sponsored in some degree by the RGS, although their relationships with the society were not always cordial. As the blank spaces on the map were filled in, the RGS more than any other organization was able to bask in the reflected glory. A commitment to overseas exploration remained the society's central concern until well into this century. Of the 280 founder's and patron's medals awarded between 1832 and 1979, fewer than 15 percent were in recognition of nonexploratory work (Stoddart, p. 23).

Meanwhile, other societies were founded at Frankfurt (1836), Rio de Janeiro (1838), Mexico City (1839), St. Petersburg (1845), Darmstadt (1845), The Hague (1851), New York (1852), Geneva (1853), Constantine, Algeria (1853), Vienna (1856), Leipzig (1861), Dresden (1863), Munich (1869), Florence (1867, moving to Rome in 1872), and Bremen (1870) (Kolm, pp. 411–413). By the 1860s, most of these societies were expanding rapidly. In Paris, the city's increasingly affluent and internationally minded bourgeoisie and the openly imperialist aspirations of the Napoleonic Second Empire perfectly suited the ethos of the SGP. Under the able leadership of the Marquis de Chasseloup-Laubat (Napoleon III's former naval and colonial minister) and Charles Maunoir (a former civil servant in the war ministry), who became president (1864–1873) and secretary-general (1867 to 1897) respectively, the SGP began to attract a younger, more energetic membership (Fierro, pp. 51–87; Kolm, pp. 411–413). In 1870, it had 650 members. The GEB also became more active under the presidency of the influential African explorer Heinrich Barth in 1863–1865 (Lenz, p. 218).

The Franco-Prussian War of 1870 gave an unexpected boost to geography in both France and Germany. Military defeat and the loss of Alsace-Lorraine caused widespread dismay in France coupled with a concerted attempt to halt a perceived national decline.

The Prussian educational system was widely believed to have been the secret of Germany's success in 1870. France, in order to challenge German hegemony, needed to develop its own system of patriotic civic instruction as a route to national rejuvenation. A carefully constructed geography curriculum would introduce the next generation to the beauty, richness, and variety of France's *pays,* inform them of their nation's role and responsibilities in the world, and inculcate a much-needed sense of patriotic duty. By the end of the century a dozen new university chairs in geography had been established. Germany, eager to sustain its reputation as the intellectual center of the discipline, responded with a similar drive.

Membership of the SGP increased rapidly, reaching 1,353 in 1875 and 2,500 in 1885. In the GEB, membership also grew from 600 members in 1875 to 1,275 in 1900 under the presidency of Ferdinand von Richthofen, a leading geomorphologist and explorer of China (Lenz, p. 218). The number of societies also began to increase. In Germany, there were nineteen societies by World War I, including new associations in the former French towns of Metz (1878) and Strasbourg (1897). In France, geographical fever was even more acute. In 1870, the SGP was still the only French geographical society; by 1909, there were twenty-seven, one in virtually every French city and four in Algeria. A second geographical society—the *Société de Géographie Commerciale de Paris* (SGCP)—was established in Paris in 1876. As its name implies, this was a more commercial organization with a particular interest in promoting trade with France's burgeoning empire. It subsequently established provincial and overseas sections in Tunis (1896), St. Etienne (1899), Brive (1901), Hanoi (1902), and Constantinople (1904). The French provincial societies were, like the SGCP, especially committed to commerce and trade, particularly within the empire. By the turn of the century, total membership of the French societies exceeded 16,500, far in excess of the equivalent figures for Britain and Germany (fewer than 10,000 each). One third of the global membership of geographical societies was French (Schneider, pp. 99–112).

In Britain, the growth of the RGS continued on its majestic path. There were 3,500 fellows in 1885 and 5,300 in 1913. Provincial societies were established at Edinburgh (the Royal Scottish Geographical Society, or RSGS, 1884), Manchester (1884), Newcastle (1887), Liverpool (1892), and Southampton

(1897) (Mackenzie, passim). However the RGS retained its dominance of the British geographical movement, assisted by powerful and influential senior fellows such as Sir Clements Markham and Lord Curzon. Paradoxically, the success of the RGS in mid-century may explain why geography had no significant presence in British universities. The reputation of the RGS meant that geography was firmly associated with exploration, mapping, and the description of physical landscape features—hearty, unscientific, and outdoor activities that seemed out of place in the cloistered, contemplative worlds of Oxford, Cambridge, or the Scottish universities. A chair of geography had been established at University College, London, in 1833 and was filled by Captain Maconochie, the RGS president, but this lapsed almost immediately when its holder went overseas. A full-time British university position in geography was not created until 1887 when an Oxford University Readership was awarded to Halford Mackinder, partly paid for by the RGS (Stoddart, pp. 41–127).

Dozens of other societies were established between 1870 to 1914, the high point of global enthusiasm for geography, including Budapest (1872), Amsterdam (1873), Bern (1873), Lisbon (1875), Bucharest (1875), Cairo (1875), Antwerp (1876), Brussels (1876), Copenhagen (1876), Madrid (1876), Stockholm (1877), Buenos Aires (1879), Tokyo (1879), Naples (1880), San Francisco (1881), Sydney (1883), Melbourne (1883), Florence (1884), Neuchâtel (1885), Brisbane (1885), Adelaide (1885), Lima (1888), La Paz (1889), Kristiansand, Norway (1889), Genoa (1890), Moscow (1890), Philadelphia (1892), Prague (1894), Bahía Blanca (1894), Sao Paulo (1894), Uppsala (1895), Zurich (1896), Barcelona (1896), Seattle (1898), Chicago (1899), Minneapolis (1904), and Gothenburg (1908). By 1914, there were about 130 geographical societies around the globe, many running subsidiary branches in different locations. At the turn of the century, the larger geographical societies were probably ranked as follows (figures include all categories of member): RGS (London), 4031; Lisbon, 3283, including nearly 1,000 honorary and corresponding members; SGCP (Paris), 2935, including its provincial and overseas sections; Lille, 2,232; RSGS (Edinburgh), 2,070; SGP (Paris), 2,047; Vienna, 2,000; Rome, 1,560; New York, 1,358; St. Petersburg, 1,273; GEB (Berlin), 1258; Seattle, 1,200; Amsterdam, 1,185; Budapest, 1,142; Stuttgart, 1,127; Stockholm, 1,120 (Kolm, pp. 411–413).

The social and professional composition of these societies varied. In the older, capital city societies, the armed forces, the civil service, and the nobility were significant elements. In the RGS, a consistent 18 percent of fellows were active or former military officers. In the SGP, the equivalent group became increasingly significant, representing 7 percent of the membership in 1821 and nearly 20 percent on the eve of World War I. Parisian civil servants and diplomats represented nearly 30 percent of the foundation SGP membership and around 13 percent in 1913. The percentage involved in commerce, trade, and business in both the RGS and the SGP increased steadily, from less than 10 percent in the 1830s to between 15 and 20 percent in the early twentieth century. The importance of the nobility decreased in both societies, from up to a quarter of the original memberships to less than 5 percent by 1909. In the provincial French and British societies, local business communities provided the bulk of the membership (Fierro, pp. 271–276; Lejeune, pp. 25–33; Mackenzie, passim; Schneider, p. 95; Stoddart, p. 60).

Most societies experienced internal conflict about substantive geographical disputes (such as the debates about the source of the Nile in the RGS) and broader moral or ideological questions (such as the acrimonious RGS controversies surrounding Stanley's brutal methods, the desirability of big game hunting, and the admission of women fellows, which was fought off until 1913). There were also fierce debates in London, Paris, and elsewhere between traditionalists, committed to a "gentlemanly," amateur style of educated travel, and a more professional constituency who fought to increase the societies' scientific credibility. Unfortunately, hard-won scientific credentials sat uncomfortably alongside the increasingly political and ideological aspirations of many geographical societies. By the 1890s, and often before, the major European societies had become well-organized and influential pressure groups in support of colonial expansion. Outside of Europe, in the Americas and Australia, the major geographical societies were mainly involved in the exploration and mapping of uncharted continental interiors and hence in a critical element of the nation-building process.

During World War I, the resources of some of the larger societies were used for intelligence purposes, and in New York, the American Geographical Society (under the presidency of the geopolitical theorist Isaiah

Bowman) became the headquarters of the House inquiry into the future political order of the postwar world. By the interwar period, however, there were few blank spaces left on the map, and the process of empire- and nation-building was largely complete. The intellectual and political climate was therefore less conducive to the kinds of geographical societies that had developed over the preceding generation. The larger societies, like the RGS, remained powerful institutions, but the smaller societies began to fold. The older societies were also weakened by the growing suspicion of university geography teachers, frustrated by the continuing aura of Victorian amateurism. These professional, scientifically trained groups tended to establish their own, independent organizations like the Institute of British Geographers (IBG), created in 1933 as the United Kingdom's professional organization. (British geography schoolteachers also founded their own organization, the Geographical Association, as early as the 1890s for similar reasons.)

World War II spelled the end for many societies. In war-battered Berlin, the GEB's residence and invaluable collection were completely destroyed, although the society was relaunched after 1945. Other societies, in Germany and elsewhere, never recovered. Those that did survive were shadows of their former selves. Many had to sell impressive residences and dispose of map collections and libraries. The surviving societies have attempted, with varying degrees of success, to reflect new intellectual agendas and a post-imperial world order. The RGS is now a significant focus for research on environmental and conservation issues and, partly for this reason, is due to remerge with the IBG to create a unitary British association once again. It is undeniably true, however, that the heyday of geographical societies were the quintessential "imperial" years between the 1870s and the 1920s.

Michael J. Heffernan

Bibliography

Cameron, Ian. *To the Farthest Ends of the Earth: 150 Years of World Exploration.* London: Macdonald and Jane, 1980.

Fierro, Alfred. *La Société de Géographie de Paris (1826–1946).* Geneva and Paris: Librairie Groz and Librairie H. Champion, 1983.

Kolm, Georg. "Geographische Gesellschaften, Zeitschriften, Kongresse und Austellungen."
Geographisches Jahrbuch 19 (1897): pp. 403–413.

Lejeune, Dominique. *Les sociétés de géographie en France et l'expansion coloniale au XIXe. siécle.* Paris: Bibliothèque Albin Michel, 1993.

Lenz, Karl. "The Berlin Geographical Society 1828–1978." *Geographical Journal* 144, no. 2 (1978): pp. 218–222.

Mackenzie, John M. "The Provincial Geographical Societies in Britain, 1884–1894." In *Geographical Knowledge and Imperial Power,* edited by M. Bell, R.A. Butlin, and M.J. Heffernan, pp. 231–243. Manchester: Manchester University Press, 1994.

Schneider, William H. "Geographical Reform and Municipal Imperialism in France, 1870–80." In *Imperialism and the Natural World,* edited by John M. Mackenzie, pp. 90–117. Manchester: Manchester University Press, 1990.

Stafford, R.A. *Scientist of Empire: Sir Roderick Murchison, Scientific Exploration and Victorian Imperialism.* Cambridge: Cambridge University Press, 1989.

Stoddart, D.R. *On Geography and Its History.* Oxford: Blackwell, 1986.

See also Colonialism and Imperialism; Geography; Geological Societies; Geophysical Societies and International Organizations; Geopolitics; Humboldtian Science; International Organizations in Oceanography; Meteorological Societies

Geography: Disciplinary History

An enduring and pervasive form of knowledge of the Earth, and yet one still debated widely on basic disciplinary grounds.

Geography is a biform discipline that has been practiced by all human civilizations. First, humans have pragmatically described the regions of the world, and enumerated their contents in textual and cartographic "geographies," for the benefit of priests, bureaucrats, merchants, industrialists, politicians, military officers, diplomats, lawyers, and others. Second, humans have sought to explain the spatial structures of the world, especially as they concern the relations between humans and the natural environment. The distinction between the two aspects of geography is in large part the creation of specialized academic geographers who have sought since 1870 to define themselves as a legitimate, scientific, and explanatory discipline in contrast to the popular acceptance that geography is simply regional description. The history of geography is accordingly written as a history of discipline-defining individuals and "geographic thought" that largely ignores social conditions (Bowen; IGU). Livingstone's excellent history is far more open to social factors, although intellectual issues remain dominant. Geography's social history thus remains an open field of study (Driver; Dunbar, *History*, pp. xi–xii).

In traditional societies, geography was an inherently intellectual enterprise that was the preserve of the knowledge-based religious elites, in which respect it should more properly be considered as a major component of cosmography, the description of the created universe. In the various cosmographical *mappaemundi* constructed by medieval Christian, Hindu, and Buddhist clerics, for example, "factual description" was completely integrated with explanatory frameworks for the structure of the cosmos. The development of extensive networks of commodity exchange, coherent political states, and large secular elites led to the construction of less overtly cosmographical descriptions of the world. Greco-Roman society for example produced several geographies, notably those by Strabo (ca. 64 B.C.E.–ca. 21 C.E.) and Claudius Ptolemy (ca. 90–168 C.E.); Islamic scholars produced similar works, such as the *Nuzhat al-mushtāq* (*Book of pleasant journeys into faraway lands*) by al-Idrīsī (493–560 A.H.; 1100–1165 C.E.) or the 1598 *Ā'īn-Akbarī* (Institutions of Akbar) by Abū al-Fazl (958–1011 A.H.; 1551–1602 C.E.), which defined the Mughal empire in northern India. Such geographies and their maps feature prominently in the first two volumes of Harley and Woodward, *History of Cartography*.

Secular geographical texts were structured according to contemporary religious and cosmographical beliefs. In Renaissance Europe, geographical texts were written by general scholars and philosophers working within the overlapping institutions of the church, universities, and private scholastic patronage. The prominence of ecclesiastics in geographical writing steadily declined with the secularization first of knowledge and then, after 1700, of academia. They took the form of their texts from classical models. Ptolemy's *Geography* was translated into Latin ca. 1410, the first printed edition appearing in 1477. It provided the cartographic or mathematical model of geographical description in which

lists of places and basic descriptions of regions accompanied numerous maps. Ultimately, this form of geography evolved into the modern atlas. Strabo's *Geography* promoted a more textual form of description, liberally illustrated with maps and other graphics, to form compendia of geographical knowledge collected from numerous sources and organized by each region in turn, as for instance the *Cosmographia universalis* (1544) of Sebastian Münster (1489–1552). To structure the content of their works, Renaissance geographers consciously relied upon biblical authority (such as the postdeluge peopling of the world defining the current distribution of races), Platonic-medieval hermeticism (for example, the macrocosm-microcosm analogy), and astrology (such as by defining the character of regions and cities by their relation to the zodiac) (Livingstone, pp. 66–83).

The Reformation's shift from interpreted faith to revealed faith led to the proposition that the world ought to be actively investigated in order to reveal the divine hand of providence in its design, a position codified in the *Systema geographicum* (1611) of the Lutheran Bartholomäus Keckermann (1572–1609). The result was an empiricist view of the world, already exemplified in the great voyages of discovery, legitimated by linear perspective's mechanistic demarcation between the human observer and the observed world, and structured by teleological explanation: the world functions as it does because Providence designed it that way. A key theme of David Livingstone's *Geographical Tradition* (1992) is the reduction of teleological explanation to a vaguely expressed deism after 1700, in which form it remained a dominant thread in geographical writing until the later 1800s, when it was replaced by evolutionary schemes. Geography's empiricism has continued to the present, Stephen Toulmin argues, reinforced first by the mechanistic metaphor for the world and then, after 1750, by the popular scientism that replaced the Newtonian system in Western culture.

Geography's developing empiricism was cemented by the initial social institutionalization of professional geography within the European states. This process paralleled the centralization of each state's administration, its ability to control its own territories through military and financial coercion, the extension of the state's coercive capabilities overseas, its exploitation of natural resources and commodity creation, and the varying participation within its political hierarchy of the genteel, professional, and mercantile classes. The initial centralization of governments in the fifteenth and sixteenth centuries was manifested in a round of organized mapping and censuses that formed the domestic equivalent of the voyages of exploration to Africa, Asia, and the Americas. Geographical descriptions were used to define each country as a distinct entity, thereby reinforcing national and cultural distinctions and legitimating the new states. The religious wars of the seventeenth century and the subsequent intensification of the Western European states led to more detailed and structured surveys of home territories and colonies after about 1650, which continued with ever greater comprehensiveness and system into the nineteenth century.

The growth of the gentry and bourgeoisie concomitant to the sixteenth-century intensification of commodity exchanges steadily increased the market for geographical texts. Some authors claimed scholastic credentials and originality, such as *Geography Delineated* (1625) by Nathaniel Carpenter (1589–1628) or the influential *Geographia generalis* (1650) of Bernhard Varen (1622–1650). But in addition there were numerous strictly commercial works that did little more than summarize, copy, and rehash existing works. Following Keckermann, seventeenth-century geographical texts followed a basic pattern: they first proclaimed their empiricist foundations with explanations of the mathematical construction of global space and of the processes of map-making, then they described each region of the world in turn. Many geographical texts dealt only with cartography. The seventeenth-century works remained popular well into the eighteenth century: for example, the fourth English-language edition of Varen's text appeared in 1765. The huge quantities of information being produced under state auspices by the later eighteenth century led to a new genre of monstrous, multivolume geographic encyclopedias, such as the eleven-volume *Neue Erdbeschreibung* (1754–1792) of Anton Friedrich Büsching (1724–1793) or the eight-volume *Précis de la géographie universelle* (1810–1829) of Conrad Malt-Brun (1775–1826). At the same time, commercial publishers increasingly supplemented their texts with "geographical tables" listing facts (country size, river length, mountain height, and so on) to be memorized by school children (Bowen, pp. 144–173).

The geography of the 1700s and early 1800s reaffirmed the socioreligious values of its bourgeois practitioners and devotees. Their teleological assumptions promoted knowledge-acquisition as the preserve of the upper social classes. They celebrated a world designed by God for human habitation and use, representing North America as the virgin continent to be civilized by European culture as the manifest destiny of the United States (Livingstone, pp. 105–119, 142–155). They celebrated a world structured according to a rational and mathematical system that might be known through observations and measurements and distilled into truthful descriptions. For Immanuel Kant (1724–1804), Alexander von Humboldt (1769–1859), Karl Ritter (1779–1859), and others, geography was the discipline for synthesizing information about nature and its inhabitants (Livingstone, pp. 113–119, 134–142). Geography epitomized the encyclopedic ideal of the bourgeois Enlightenment, of bringing all knowledge together under one roof. And geographers celebrated an objectified and commodified world to be subdivided, appropriated, controlled, and exploited. That is, empiricist geography was not only an instrument of empire, it also served to legitimate Europe's overseas imperial ventures.

By 1800 geography was completely institutionalized as a profession within the capitalist European states. Geographers were directly employed within the civil and military bureaucracies; governments distributed information to favored publishers (for example, the *géographes du roi* in France); and the members of the states' elites formed the principal market for commercial products. Commercial geographical institutions were established by former or current state employees, such as the *Societas cosmographia* (fl. 1746–1754) in Nuremberg, which failed for lack of state support; the Justus Perthes Anstalt in Gotha, Thuringen, Germany (1785–present); and the African Association in London, England (1788–1830). The intimate ties between European states, their burgeoning colonial ventures, and geography were enshrined in the formation after 1820 of specialized societies in the capitals of the three most militaristic European states: the *Société de géographie de Paris* (1821); the *Gesellschaft für Erdkunde zu Berlin* (1828); and the Royal Geographical Society, London (1830). These societies—and later imitators in, for example, St. Petersburg (1845) and New York (1851)—provided a common meeting place for professional geographers, members of the industrial and financial elites, and officials of home and colonial governments. They coordinated and organized funding for expeditions to non-European areas; and they provided a clearinghouse for the resultant geographical information (Livingstone, pp. 156–172, 216–259).

Such was the system until 1870. Geography was a professional activity and an essential (if dry) subject in elite schooling. Its presence in universities still depended on the personal interests of faculty. The only significant variation was the replacement of teleological explanation with evolutionary schemes relating humans to the natural environment, even before Darwin. The dramatic expansion of European industrial militarism and imperialism after 1870 served to intensify professional geography in the active search for and exploitation of new resources, new markets, industrial investment, and in competitive territorial delimitation (Hudson; Livingstone, pp. 241–259). For example, the expeditions to China in the 1860s by Ferdinand von Richthofen (1833–1905) were sponsored by the Prussian government and the Bank of California; during the expedition Richthofen mapped the coal fields in the Shantung peninsula of China, which in turn induced the Germans to annex Qingdao (Tsingtao) in 1898 (Hudson). The Franco-Prussian War (1870–1871), characterized by the American Geographical Society's president as being fought "as much by maps as weapons" (Keltie, p. 473), led to renewed efforts in military academies to teach geography. European states with imperial pretensions that still lacked metropolitan geographical societies now founded them to encourage and legitimate their territorial expansion. The metropolitan societies began a series of quadrennial international geographical congresses in 1871. Simultaneously, provincial industrial elites created geographical societies aimed at expanding commerce and industry. About twenty of the thirty-eight geographical societies founded on the Continent between 1870 and 1880, and the six founded in Britain between 1885 and 1900, were established in industrial, provincial cities (MacKenzie). The two sets of societies were distinct. The metropolitan societies remained the meeting place of the established professional geographers, with large military and political memberships and a consciously territorial emphasis. The provincial societies were more overtly concerned with profit and possessed a more amateur (and less cartographic) composition.

Geography's practical and political uses were ultimately responsible for the establishment, again after 1870, of university programs

in geography (Dunbar, *Modern Geography;* Martin and James, pp. 162–386). The common recognition for the need to expand basic geographic education led most industrialized countries to establish teacher-training programs. In Germany, the need was political. The German Empire (founded 1871) forced geography into the curriculum of grade and high schools, both to impart basic information and to promote Germany as a coherent nation rather than the product of Prussian militarism. Between 1874 and 1885, twelve of twenty-one German universities created geography programs offering the *facultas docendi* (teaching degree) as well as the Ph.D. More effort was given by the professors to evening classes on teaching geography than to their general lectures (Keltie, pp. 475–497). Both Austria-Hungary and France quickly copied the German example and established national curricula and university chairs in geography during the 1870s. The forced industrial militarization after 1868 by Japan's Meiji government was modeled along German lines, using German capital, and not surprisingly, included the creation of German-style universities with geography programs. The less centralized education system in Britain meant that the establishment of geography in the schools and universities took longer. J. Scott Keltie's revelation in 1885 of the dismal state of British geographic education compared with that of France and Germany led to readerships in geography at Oxford and Cambridge (1887–1888), but university programs did not take off until after 1918. In the United States geography became a mainstay of the "normal" (teacher-training) schools; the first geography courses were taught at Harvard in 1878, but a separate program in geography was not established until 1903, at Chicago.

Academic geography grew steadily, if slowly, through the 1900s, as evidenced by the formation of explicitly academic geographic societies, such as the Association of American Geographers (founded 1904, initially as an educational lobby), the *Association de géographes français* (1920), and the Institute of British Geographers (1933). The big boom, however, came after World War II, when reconstruction, social compacts, and the Cold War caused a wholesale expansion of the universities in the industrial countries. For example, the 66 geography programs in the United States in 1943 rose to 89 in 1947 and then to 179 in 1972 (derived from the Association of American Geographers [AAG]), even as geography declined almost completely as a school subject. In Britain, secondary education was opened to all children after 1944, leading to substantial increases in university geography programs to provide the necessary teachers. The discipline was also well represented in the new universities created after 1963. Finally, the expansion of basic and secondary education, as early as the 1930s in Brazil, prompted university (teacher-training) geography programs throughout the developing/decolonizing world, as summarized in the short articles compiled by Gary Dunbar in his *Modern Geography*.

The institutional growth of academic geography was not, however, balanced by any coherent self-description as an intellectual discipline. Geography is essentially construed as regional description, and empiricist description has not been deemed sufficiently "scientific." Academic geography initially derived its intellectual legitimacy from the environmental sciences, notably geology and zoology, which provided its first professors. This reflects the later-nineteenth-century concerns for social Darwinism (or neo-Lamarckianism) which sought to integrate "man" with "environment," in particular through assumptions that human society and culture are plastic and susceptible to impression by the environment, so that the character of human existence is determined by physical conditions. William Morris Davis (1850–1934) at Harvard, Halford Mackinder (1861–1947) at Oxford, Friedrich Ratzel (1844–1904) at Leipzig, and their disciples accordingly sought general laws of the influence of environment on behavior, further underpinning the racist and imperialist ideologies of the period (Livingstone, pp. 177–215, 221–241). One reaction to environmental determinism adopted in Germany and France was to reject theory, acknowledge geography's practical roots, and pursue huge, highly detailed chorographic (that is, regionally descriptive) studies structured by an orderly sequence of topics for systematic description: geology first, then relief, climate, natural resources, zoogeography, and so on. This approach was adopted into English-language geography through *The Nature of Geography* (1939) by Richard Hartshorne (1899–1992). A later reaction to environmental determinism, increasingly apparent in the 1930s, was the adoption of the possibilist stance, which favored human agency, seen particularly in French social history and in the cultural geography of Carl Sauer (1889–1975) at Berkeley. After 1950, with pressure from physical geographers, academic geography in most countries turned away (again) from description in order to become a truly positive

"science of space," complete with laws, models, and certitude. The resultant "quantitative revolution" was dominant until about 1980, since which time geographers have followed a variety of humanistic, structuralist, poststructuralist, Marxist, realist, and feminist approaches to explain human existence in space (Livingstone, pp. 260–346).

After its overexpansion in the 1950s and 1960s, academic geography began to retreat. Its vehement rejection of regional description in the 1960s meant that governments (particularly that of the United States) and international agencies (such as the United Nations and the World Bank) have in the 1970s and 1980s increasingly turned to "area studies" programs for expertise. The decline of the formal empires and their associated ideologies has meant that the provincial societies are almost extinct and the metropolitan societies have been substantially weakened. Nevertheless professional geography has only continued to expand, with the rise of planning and environmental agencies in all the industrial nations. However, this is an inward-looking geography and has been further fragmented into numerous specialties. Geography as a professional discipline will continue (geography by any other name is still geography), but its long-term future as an academic discipline is perhaps in doubt. It is perhaps impossible to separate the writing of the history of geography from these ongoing debates and developments. Hence, scholars will continue to adopt new perspectives on the history of geography.

Matthew H. Edney

Bibliography

Association of American Geographers. *Guide to Programs in the United States and Canada, 1992–1993*. Washington, D.C.: AAG, 1992.

Bowen, Margarita. *Empiricism and Geographical Thought from Francis Bacon to Alexander von Humboldt*. Cambridge: Cambridge University Press, 1981.

Driver, Felix. "Geography's Empire: Histories of Geographical Knowledge." *Environment and Planning D: Society and Space* 10 (1992): pp. 23–40.

Dunbar, Gary S. *The History of Modern Geography: An Annotated Bibliography of Selected Works*. New York: Garland, 1985.

———, ed. *Modern Geography: An Encyclopedic Survey*. New York: Garland, 1991.

Harley, J.B., and David Woodward, eds. *The History of Cartography.* Chicago: University of Chicago Press, 1987– . 6 vols. in 8 books.

Hudson, Brian. "The New Geography and the New Imperialism: 1870–1918." *Antipode* 9, no. 1 (1977): pp. 12–19.

International Geographical Union, Commission on the History of Geographic Thought. *Geographers: Biobibliographical Studies.* T.W. Freeman, founding editor; Geoffrey J. Martin, current editor. London: Mansell, 1977– .

Keltie, J. Scott. "Geographical Education: Report to the Council of the Royal Geographical Society." *Supplementary Papers of the Royal Geographical Society* 1, no. 4 (1885): pp. 439–594.

Livingstone, David N. *The Geographical Tradition: Episodes in the History of a Contested Enterprise.* Oxford: Blackwell, 1992.

MacKenzie, John M. "Geography and Imperialism: British Provincial Geographical Societies." In *Nature and Science: Essays in the History of Geographical Knowledge,* edited by Felix Driver and Gillian Rose, pp. 49–62. Historical Geography Research Series 28. London: Historical Geography Research Group, 1992.

Martin, Geoffrey J., and Preston E. James. *All Possible Worlds: A History of Geographical Ideas* [1972]. 3d ed. New York: John Wiley, 1993.

Toulmin, Stephen. *Cosmopolis: The Hidden Agenda of Modernity.* New York: The Free Press, 1990.

See also Cartography; Colonialism and Imperialism; Exploration, Age of; Geographical Societies; Geography, Elizabethan; Geography and Imperialism; Geography and Natural Theology; Geography and Renaissance Magic; Historiography, Eighteenth-Century England; Humboldtian Science

Geography, Elizabethan

A critical period for geography in early modern England. Geography then divided into three areas: mathematical, descriptive, and chorographical. It provided a meeting place for theory and practice that helped to fashion the English people and develop proto-imperialism.

The Elizabethan world view encompassed an expanding globe and an enclosing nation. While more and more of the world lay within the grasp of those brave or foolhardy enough to venture forth, the English were increasingly defining themselves and their country as separate from the Continent and the rest of the terraqueous globe. This seemingly contradictory view of their world— at once expansive and exclusive—was developed by the English in the late sixteenth century through the study of geography.

During the late sixteenth century, the study of geography gained popularity in England (Cormack, passim). Geography was taught at the universities, geographical works were read by merchants, courtiers, and country gentlemen, as well as by investors and explorers, and it was practiced by academics, writers, and courtiers, as well as by those who ventured forth to see for themselves. In examining the people and ideas involved in the sixteenth-century study of geography, it becomes clear that in the course of this period, it developed into three related branches, mathematical, descriptive, and chorographical geography, each with distinct practitioners and different topics of investigation. Each branch helped develop the ideology of geography and the image of English men and women as unique and separate from other peoples.

Mathematical geography was most closely akin to the modern study of geodesy, that branch of applied mathematics that determines the exact geographical positions of places and the figures and areas of large portions of the Earth's surface, the shape and size of the Earth, and the variations of terrestrial gravity and magnetism. Elizabethan mathematical geographers spent much of their time devising means to determine longitude at sea and to navigate in northern waters. The greatest achievements in this area were made by William Gilbert (1540–1603), who claimed in *De Magnete* (1600) that the Earth is a giant magnet, and Edward Wright (1558–1615), who mathematically derived Mercator's projection in *Certain Errors of Navigation* (1599). Cartography, the study of maps and map-making, was related to mathematical geography, although cartography depended far more on guild methods of transfer of knowledge and less on any systematic development of theories or models. Studied by a small group of scholars who were also interested in other mathematical topics, this was the most rigorously theoretical form of geography.

The second branch, descriptive geography, portrayed the physical and political structures of other lands, usually in an inductive and relatively unsophisticated manner. Because of this relative lack of rigorous analysis, and because its primary goal was utility of knowledge, descriptive geography was the most easily accessible of the three geographical subdisciplines. It encompassed everything from practical descriptions of European road conditions to outlandish yarns of exotic locales, providing intriguing reading and practical information alike. It included analyses of Ptolemy's theory of climates, which explained the ability of different peoples to live productively in different climates, as well as convincing the English that they must remain in the northern regions.

The final type of geography, chorography, developed in the course of the late sixteenth century, combining a medieval chronicle tradition with the Italian Renaissance study of local description. Chorography was the most wide-ranging of the geographical subdisciplines, since it included an interest in genealogy, chronology (including the age of the Earth), and antiquities, as well as local history and topography. Chorography thus united an anecdotal interest in local families and wonders with the mathematically arduous task of genealogical and chronological research.

Modern interest in Elizabethan geography began with the pioneering work of E.G.R. Taylor, especially her *Late Tudor and Early Stuart Geography* (1934). Though Taylor's conclusions sometimes lacked sophistication, she was single-handedly responsible for the revival of twentieth-century interest in English geography and read or examined more geographical texts than any other historian before or since. Taylor stressed the practical impetus for geography, suggesting that the study of geography was stimulated because it provided necessary information and skills for exploration and oceanic voyages. Taylor saw geography as part of a rising middle-class assertion of independence from scholastic and university-dominated studies. She claimed that Elizabethan geography was stimulated and improved by practical craftsmen, motivated by practical concerns.

In the years following Taylor's pioneering effort, few geographical historians continued her project. Geography itself as a discipline was in a period of transition and this was reflected by the lack of innovation in the pursuit of its history. That began to change in the 1970s, however, first evidenced by the important work of John Shirley, concerning Thomas Harriot. With this publication, the history of British geography seems to have entered a new era.

Thomas Harriot (1560–1621), with the exception only of John Dee (1527–1608), was Elizabethan England's most famous geographer. In Shirley's 1974 anthology *Thomas Harriot: Renaissance Scientist,* Harriot's clientage, career aspirations, and mathematical ability were analyzed, showing a strong relationship between scholarship, court patronage, and geographical interest. Harriot's mathematical and geographical interests seem to have been directly affected by the patronage of Sir Walter Raleigh (1552?–1618), by his imperialistic interest in Virginia, and by his scientific training while a student at Oxford. Although Harriot did not publish extensively, he carried out active research sponsored by Raleigh in fields such as the problem of determining longitude at sea, the imperfection of the Moon, and the relationship between natives and settlers in the Virginia colony.

In the related field of the history of navigation, the definitive text is David W. Waters's *The Art of Navigation in England in Elizabethan and Early Stuart Times* (1958). Waters contended that the sixteenth century was a period of transformation for British navigation, emerging from the status of an immature art into a full-fledged science. This was made possible by the introduction of mathematics into navigation and the interplay between theoretical mathematicians (usually university-trained) and practical navigators. Thus, in navigation as in geography, we see a growing emphasis on the symbiotic relationship between mathematics and scholarly training, on the one hand, and practical concerns on the other.

Also related to the more general field of geography is that of cartography. Histories of cartography, like the older tradition of history of geography, have tended to remain fairly superficial, dealing more with details of individual maps and less with their theoretical foundations or social ramifications. More recently, however, Sarah Tyacke has investigated English cartography with more sensitivity and theoretical consideration, concentrating on the place of maps in society and demonstrating that the function of maps changed in the period from 1530 to 1590, as people began using them to settle court cases; maps "became an integral part of the way of thinking about the country" (Tyacke, p. 18). Richard Helgerson, in 1986, discussed county maps as literary texts, claiming a relationship between the iconography of the maps and the degree of county loyalty. Thus the trend in modern history of cartography begins to emphasize this relationship between the map and its social milieu.

In the 1980s interest renewed in Elizabethan geography. This resurgence of interest has sprung in part from the fact that geography provides an interesting site from which to study the convergence of interests of theoreticians and practitioners, as well as providing a window into early modern thought more easily accessible than other scientific endeavors. Helgerson's work on iconography and self-fashioning represents such a trend. So too does Stephen Pumfrey's work on magnetism. Pumfrey examines the work of William Gilbert (a figure deserving much more scholarly investigation) and demonstrates the sociological factors of scientific closure, including national pride, patronage, education, and networks of knowledge.

Indeed, it is clear that the study of Elizabethan geography is of vital importance as we try to understand the scientific and social changes of this period. Early modern geography grew from theoretical or classical foundations, it employed a methodology of incremental fact-gathering, and it helped promote an ideology of utility that encouraged the public use of scholarly knowledge for the good of the economic and political state. Within these three facets, not unique to geography, lies the key to the "new science" of the seventeenth century. Thus, by concentrating on intermediate disciplines such as geography, historians of science can begin a new analysis of just how and why science changed in the late seventeenth century.

Lesley Cormack

Bibliography

Cormack, Lesley B. "'Good Fences Make Good Neighbors': Geography as Self-Definition in Early Modern England." *ISIS* 82 (1991): pp. 639–661.

Helgerson, Richard. "The Land Speaks: Cartography, Chorography and Subversion in Renaissance England." *Representations* 16 (1986): pp. 51–85.

Pumfrey, Stephen. "'O tempora, O magnes': A Sociological Analysis of the Discovery of Secular Magnetic Variation in 1634." *British Journal for the History of Science* 22 (1989): pp. 181–214.

Shirley, John, ed. *Thomas Harriot: Renaissance Scientist.* Oxford: Clarendon Press, 1974.

Taylor, E.G.R. *Late Tudor and Early Stuart Geography 1583–1650.* London: Methuen, 1934.

Tyacke, Sarah, ed. *English Map-Making 1500–1650.* London: British Library, 1983.

Waters, David W. *The Art of Navigation in England in Elizabethan and Early Stuart Times.* London: Hollis and Carter, 1958.

See also Cartography; Colonialism and Imperialism; Cosmology and the Earth; Exploration, Age of; Geodesy; Geography; Geomagnetism, Theories before 1800; Hydrography; Occult Philosophy and the Earth in the Renaissance

Geography in Enlightenment Encyclopedias

The study of the Earth and its productions as part of useful knowledge, particularly during the eighteenth century.

Enlightenment knowledge is now seen more as a process, in which ideas of utility and rationality were undisputed arbiters of modernity and progress in social life, than as a strict period of time. Geography in its various forms—through discovery, listings of peoples, nations and productions, and in commerce—was an important part of enlightened interest in reason and useful knowledge. Historians of geography have only recently begun to focus in detail upon enlightenment geographies—for example, David Livingstone in *The Geographical Tradition*—and upon the relationship to other knowledges within encyclopedias and other Enlightenment attempts at ordering knowledge—for example, Charles Withers in "Geography in Its Time." Richard Yeo has shown in "Reading Encyclopedias" how the texts themselves have been social and intellectual enterprises, concerned to establish the importance of the producers as well as the knowledge.

It is important to recognize that geographical information has appeared in the earliest encyclopedias, in Western and non-Western scholarly traditions. In Pliny's 77 C.E. *Historia Naturalis,* for example, it is treated as listings of productions by place alongside ethnographic information. In early Arab and Chinese encyclopedias, geography figures as a major part of urban and political administration. In the texts of Western Renaissance humanism such as Honorius' *Imago Mundi* (translated by William Caxton in 1481 as *The Mirrour of the World*), geographical material is both regional description and listings of natural products by country. In this sense, then, as Robert Collison has shown in *Ency-*

clopedias: Their History through the Ages, geographical information has always figured in encyclopedic attempts at ordering the world of knowledge and has always, by the contexts of its time, been considered useful.

The beginnings of modern encyclopedism and the place of geography as part of wider concerns with social and intellectual improvement and enlightenment through reason and utility date from the early seventeenth century, notably though not alone in the work of Francis Bacon (1561–1626). In his incomplete *Instauritio Magna (Great Instauration)*, Bacon included an "Encyclopaedia of Nature and Art." Geography was allied to natural history in this project. In his scheme, geography sat between metaphysics, and was reckoned part of mixed mathematics, and history, itself divided into natural and civil. Geography was thus situated within the orbit of that empirical inductivism Bacon was more widely promoting. In its links to history, geography was part both of discourses of social meaning (civil history) and of what Michel Foucault has portrayed in the *Order of Things* (chap. 5) as the seeing and descriptive science of natural history, at a time when new visions of the world, new knowledges gained through geographical exploration, were so common. Bacon's classification of knowledge into three parts—history, poetry and knowledge corresponding to the faculties of memory, imagination, and reason, themselves partly drawn from Pliny and Aristotle—had lasting impact upon Enlightenment encyclopedias.

The major modern encyclopedic texts of the Enlightenment are considered to be Ephraim Chambers's *Cyclopedia, or Universal Dictionary of Arts and Sciences* (1728), and Denis Diderot and Jean d'Alembert's *Encyclopédie; ou Dictionnaire raisonée des sciences, des arts, et des metiers*, published in Paris in seventeen volumes between 1751 and 1765. The *Encyclopedia Britannica*, published by a society of gentlemen in Scotland in 1771, was much influenced by Chambers. There are three principal points to note in consideration of geography in these (and other) Enlightenment encyclopedias: the definition of the term itself; the relationship of geography as classified knowledge to all other knowledge within the world of learning; and the differing utility seen for the subject.

For Chambers (p. 140), geography was "the Doctrine or Knowledge of the Earth, both as in itself, and as to its Affections; or a Description of the Terrestrial Globe, and particularly of the known habitable Part thereof, with all its Parts." Geography was chorographic in intent and method, and a branch of mathematics "in that it considers the Earth, and its Affections, as depending upon Quantity, and consequently measurable." Geography was split into general or universal, which dealt with the Earth in general, and special or particular geography, which dealt with descriptions of countries. Geographical metaphors inform Chambers's work throughout: he talks of the "whole field of knowledge" having some parts more cultivated than others, of the mind being reclaimed "from its native Wildness" by learning and reason, and of his project as a means to chart *terrae incognitae* and, thus, improve world learning. In his chart of knowledge, geography has closest links with hydrography, the mathematical sciences, and through them, with navigation and commerce. This positioning in classificatory terms and viewed in utilitarian terms was mirrored in the *Encyclopédie* and in contemporary works of geography.

The principal entry on geography in the *Encyclopédie* appears in volume VII, published in 1757. Attention is given there to geography under three different period headings: ancient geography ("the description of the land from the time of the development of the Ancient peoples up to the fall of the Roman Empire"); geography of the Middle Ages; and modern geography ("from the rebirth of letters to the present day"). Modern geography was divided into natural, historical, civil and political, sacred, ecclesiastical, and physical. Each of these categories had particular definitions as branches of the discipline, just as the subject itself has been shown (Withers, pp. 257–260) to have been particularly situated as a branch on the Tree of Learning. Reference is made to geography and its relation to geometry and astronomy and its use in commerce and for the military. A detailed diagrammatic system of the parts of geography in a later supplementary volume principally divides the subject into universal and particular geographies in ways typical of the period. The measurable quantities of the Earth predominate, certainly in physical geography, and the categorization of human characteristics mirrors those of contemporary special geographies. The chorographic tradition within the discipline is strongly to the fore. But the idea of "a country considered of itself" is also to be understood as Enlightenment judgments on social quantity, national development as a measurable phenomenon. In these important senses, geography was part of a contemporary concern for useful knowledge. It was in these terms principally a practical discipline although, as has been shown by Livingstone (chap. 4), theoretical discussions on the discipline were current. But its practicality, its utility, was different according to the needs of its audience: to the merchant as navigation, to the military in the form of charts or topographic account, to the interested traveler, improving child, or auto-didact as new and distant worlds brought near through map and text. These differing utilities are implicit in the preface to the first edition of the *Encyclopaedia Britannica* (1771), which noted, "Utility ought to be the principal intention of every publication. Wherever this intention does not plainly appear, neither the books nor their authors have the smallest claim to the approbation of mankind."

The foregoing is to note the place of geography in Enlightenment encyclopedias per se. We should also note the role of dictionaries and universal grammars, especially from the later seventeenth century, as means of classifying and putting an order to things, and the production of geographical texts—universal geographies—on encyclopedic principles. Alan Downes has termed these latter works bibliographic dinosaurs (p. 380).

The growth in dictionaries and universal grammars from the seventeenth century was not only bound up with attempts to "fix" language by definition of meaning, but also to codify accepted practices between linguistic terminology, particular forms of knowledge, and social usage. Even earlier, works such as Charles Estienne's 1553 *Dictionarium, historicum, geographicum et poeticum* signified moves to encyclopedic dictionary-making in which the incorporation of a glossary of geographical terms was part of attempts to order the world of knowledge and to place that knowledge in the hands of an "enlightened" few. The publication of geographical works whose titles represent the idea of global learning as well as that of summarizing knowledge of the world signifies a developing relationship from the late seventeenth century between geography and the philosophy of encyclopedism. Thus we have an anonymous *Geographical Dictionary* (1662), Chamberlayne's *Compendium Geographicum* (1685), Bohun's *Geographical Dictionary* (1688), and a further work of the same title in 1693. Gordon's *Geography Anatomized: or, a Compleat Geographical Grammar* (1693) "reduced the whole body of Modern Geography to a true Grammatical Method" in order to promote what he termed "the great utility"

of that "most Pleasurable and Useful Science." In both his intent and in the title to his work, he may be considered one of the earlier advocates of that rhetoric of enlightened utility that both structured and informed the universal geographies of the eighteenth century.

These encyclopedic and Enlightenment geographies have been shown to increase in both number and size during this period by Francis Sitwell in *Four Centuries of Special Geography*, although the intent and format altered relatively little. Salmon's 1749 *New Geographical and Historical Grammar* claimed both in method (by being a "grammar" to label the discourse), and in content (the subtitle read *Wherein the Geographical Part Is Truly Modern*), to be "Entertaining and Instructive." His intention was utility and national progress, to see geographical knowledge as part of a new modernity. His view of the usefulness of geography echoes the several utilities claimed for the discipline in contemporary encyclopedias: "Here the Senator and Politician may view the Constitution, Forces, and Revenue of the respective Kingdoms and States; the Divine may observe the Religion and Superstition of the respective People; the Merchant, and Marine Officer, the Produce, Traffic, Periodical Winds and Seasons, in the various Climates" (p. i). These statements and intentions are replicated in French and German geographies as well as within the English-speaking geographical literatures. In Jedidiah Morse's 1789 *New Geographical Dictionary*, such enlightenment notions on geography were first widely established within the United States.

Much work remains to be done on geography in (the) Enlightenment. On one level, many of the texts of the time have been regarded as theoretically impoverished and the discipline to have been weak in consequence. This is to ignore the profound importance of practical knowledge as part of bourgeois interests in commerce, and to underplay, too, the ways in which eighteenth-century universal geographies were also disciplining texts, part of attempts to bring the world of learning and the learning of the world to order. More needs to be known on the different audiences for these enlightened geographies. Non-Western philosophies of encyclopedism and geography are underrepresented in our histories. Finally, this short discussion has pointed to the need to review the idea of the Enlightenment, or, at least, to consider the geographical texts of the time in context with earlier intellectual traditions.

Charles W.J. Withers

Bibliography

Collison, Robert. *Encyclopedias: Their History through the Ages.* New York: Hafner, 1964.

Downes, Alan. "The Bibliographic Dinosaurs of Georgian Geography (1714–1830)." *Geographical Journal* 137, no. 3 (1971): pp. 379–387.

Foucault, Michel. *The Archaeology of Knowledge.* London and New York: Tavistock, 1972.

———. *The Order of Things.* London and New York: Tavistock, 1974.

Livingstone, David. *The Geographical Tradition: Episodes in the History of a Contested Enterprise.* Oxford: Blackwell, 1992.

Sitwell, Francis. *Four Centuries of Special Geography.* Vancouver: University of British Columbia Press, 1993.

Withers, Charles. "Geography in Its Time: Geography and Historical Geography in Diderot and d'Alembert's Encyclopédie." *Journal of Historical Geography* 19, no. 3 (1993): pp. 255–264.

Yeo, Richard. "Reading Encyclopedias: Science and the Organization of Knowledge in British Dictionaries of Arts and Sciences, 1730–1850." *ISIS* 82 (1991): pp. 24–49.

See also Cosmology and the Earth, Scientific Revolution; Exploration, Age of; Foucault's *Order of Things;* Geography; Geography: The Word; Geophysics: The Word; Historiography, Eighteenth-Century England; Humboldtian Science; Presentism; Wilderness

Geography and Imperialism

A historiographical theme.

It is often suggested that the development of modern science has been intimately associated with the process of European imperial expansion that began in the fifteenth century. Certainly the construction of the great European colonial empires—first in the Americas and subsequently in the Pacific, Asia, and Africa—correlated with periods of dramatic scientific and technological development in the core areas of the imperial system. Some have argued that innovation in science, technology, and medicine effectively determined not only the growth of economic and commercial power within capitalist Europe but also the pace and direction of European imperial expansion outside the Continent. New shipping technology and navigation techniques together with a mastery of gunpowder and firearms, it is claimed, allowed a handful of conquistadors to control vast territories in the Americas, while the Gatling gun, quinine, telegraphs, and aviation served the same function for their Victorian and twentieth-century successors in tropical Africa and Asia (Headrick, passim).

Other writers have moved beyond the "hardware" of imperial authority to consider the more diffuse connections between different branches of European science and the process of imperial expansion. The histories of several disciplines—anthropology, archaeology, astronomy, history, philology, medicine, and the natural sciences—have all been recast in the light of the imperial assumptions and values underlying their origins and development. It has even been argued that the entire structure of European knowledge, the very epistemological foundations on which the modern academy has been erected, is largely the outcome of unexamined, universalist (and hence imperialist) preconceptions about the world and its inhabitants. Modern science is, some suggest, a fundamentally European and Eurocentric activity. Although European science represents only one, culturally specific route to understanding, it alone has claimed universal validity while conspiring in the forced imposition of its methods and philosophies in regions where knowledge and understanding had previously taken different forms. Science and empire-building thus marched arm-in-arm: both were supremely ambitious, universalizing projects concerned to know all, to understand all, and, by implication, to control all (Said, passim).

Geography illustrates better than most "imperial sciences" the soaring proprietorial ambition of the European imperial mind. Unlike other disciplines, particularly those in the pure sciences, geography's philosophical and epistemological status has always been vaguely defined. While other scientists claimed expert authority over particular areas of knowledge or theory, geography has traditionally (and immodestly) eschewed specialization and championed instead the cause of a general science of the Earth and its inhabitants. Geographers, particularly in the last century, often saw themselves as part of a "pan-discipline" whose self-appointed task it was to unite, partly for educational purposes, the otherwise disparate branches of the sciences and humanities. Geography's function was to bring together material from other disciplines and re-present it in neat, regionally specific digests.

A compelling case can therefore be made for interpreting geography as the practical and academic handmaiden of European imperial expansion. The navigational and cartographic skills of the geographer during the "heroic" age of exploration and discovery paved the way for European military and commercial colonization of the Americas, Asia, and Africa. The principal geographical "tool" was, of course, the map, an artifact that emerged in a recognizably modern form during the Renaissance. By representing the huge complexity of a physical and human landscape in a single image, geographers and cartographers provided the European imperial project with arguably its most potent device. European exploration and mapping of the coastlines of the Americas, Africa, Asia, and the Pacific and the subsequent terrestrial topographic surveying of these vast continents during the eighteenth and nineteenth centuries (generally with state support) was self-evidently an exercise in imperial authority. To map hitherto "unknown" regions (unknown, that is, to the European), using modern techniques in triangulation and geodesy, was both a scientific activity dependent on trained personnel and state-of-the art equipment and also a political act of appropriation that had obvious strategic utility to occupying imperial forces (Harley, passim). It was also an exercise that gripped the popular imagination in the imperial core regions. The twin process of exploration and mapping in the far-flung regions of the globe was a source of enormous public interest, particularly in the more literate eras of the eighteenth and nineteenth centuries. To many, the geographer-explorer was the ideal masculine hero (the notion of a female geographer seemed almost a contradiction in terms), selflessly pitting himself against the elements and hostile "natives" in remote regions for the greater glory of his country and race (Driver, passim).

Developing alongside geography as exploration and discovery from the middle decades of the nineteenth century was a more sedentary, theoretical, and academic version of the discipline. The map was equally important to this "new" geography but became an increasingly sophisticated image, capable of representing not only the material "reality" of the physical and human landscape but also the "hidden" features of a locality's economic, social, or political characteristics through the skillful deployment of cartographic symbols. The "new" academic geography, it has been argued, was even more of an imperial science than its practical predecessor (Hudson, passim). A cursory glance at the work of some of the dominant voices in the discipline during the late nineteenth century, men such as Sir Halford Mackinder in Britain (who occupied the first readership in geography at Oxford in 1887) and Friedrich Ratzel in Germany, makes this abundantly clear (Kearns, passim; Bassin, passim). Mackinder, Ratzel, and other leading university geographers provided a range of intellectual justifications for Europe's imperial role through their geopolitical theorizing, their detailed assessments of the commercial wealth of different overseas territories, and their often crude Darwinian or environmental theorizing about the relative merits of different races and the role of climate and environment on social development. For their part, geography schoolteachers in the same era did much to popularize and simplify these messages for each new generation. After examining geography textbooks from the late nineteenth and early twentieth centuries, it is indeed difficult to avoid the conclusion that the subject had become little more than a thinly disguised form of racial and imperial propaganda.

By the end of the nineteenth century, the "high water mark" of European imperial expansion, geography had become "unquestionably the queen of all imperial sciences . . . inseparable from the domain of official and unofficial state knowledge" (Richards, p. 13). For Sir Harry H. Johnston, explorer, African colonial administrator, and prominent fellow of the Royal Geographical Society, geography should have pride of place in the British educational system as "the eldest sister of the bunch." It should be made, he claimed, a compulsory subject for all aspiring British politicians, diplomats, and civil servants for it was only through detailed geographical description, complete with authoritative and regularly updated topographical and thematic maps, that a region could be known, understood, and therefore possessed by those in authority. By dividing the world into regions and ordering the burgeoning factual information about the globe into regional segments, geography offered one solution to the yearned-for objective of classifying and understanding the human and environmental characteristics of the entire globe. Through geography the world could, at last, be visualized and conceptualized as a whole (Heffernan et al., p. 5).

While there is plenty of irrefutable evidence to support this interpretation of geography's history, such a simple functionalist reading of the knowledge-power equation tends to gloss over the complex and contested nature of both sides in the relationship. As geography developed into a large and heterogeneous academic pursuit, so its connections within the politics of imperialism, itself a minefield of competing ideologies, became more elaborate. By the early decades of the twentieth century, it is difficult to interpret the geographical community, even within a single country, as a cohesive group. Various, often mutually exclusive, visions of the discipline coexisted and different forms of imperial engagement were advocated by different schools of geographical thought.

At the risk of erecting arbitrary categories, it is possible to identify at least four different, overlapping, and sometimes conflicting forms of "geo-imperialism." The relative importance of these variations on a theme changed over time and from place to place. For want of better terms, these can be identified as economic imperialism, environmental imperialism, cultural and religious imperialism, and political imperialism (Heffernan, pp. 100–108). Economic imperialism was a persistent element in the geographical discourse. European empires were presented as "natural" commercial units, engaging in interimperial trade but also offering an all-important intraimperial economic self-sufficiency and coherence. In this way, the economics of empire was depicted as a benign partnership between rich and poor, beneficial for colonizer and colonized alike.

This perspective overlapped with, but sometimes contradicted, a strong environmental imperial impulse. According to this argument, a coherent and planned policy of environmental management in the colonial periphery was an economic and commercial necessity in order to maximize mid- and long-term returns on investment. Colonial environmental management thus became a strong moral argument for a rational, technologically sophisticated imperial presence. While such a perspective obviously clashed with a more exploitative concern for quick commercial returns from the empire, the idea of environmental conservation, preservation, and management was a powerful element in the geographical rhetoric about the physical landscapes and resources of the non-European world.

In this guise, environmental imperialism sustained a form of patrician cultural and religious imperialism that saw empire as a conduit through which the self-evident benefits of European language and civilization could diffuse around the globe. Cultural imperialists, inspired by philanthropic or Christian motives, were often in direct conflict with the economic imperialists discussed above. For a cultural imperialist, empires were not primarily economic or commercial units; rather they were emerging cultural entities whose otherwise disparate regions and countries were linked together by a common set of values or principles derived from the metropolitan power. This position tended to celebrate the costs, responsibilities, and moral burdens of empire rather the likely commercial benefits.

This rhetoric was often expressed in a universalist, or at least pan-European, language that stressed the moral responsibilities of the civilized "white man" in a still uncivilized world. But these views could also be articulated in a more narrowly nationalist tone. Cultural imperialism was, in this latter mode, part of a broader nationalist geopolitical imperialism that stressed the need for empire as a makeweight in the balance of power between the major European powers. From this perspective, empire brought prestige and offered all the strategic advantages of a global territorial presence together with huge reserves of "manpower" that the "mother country" could draw upon if needed.

Toward the end of the nineteenth century, a few politically radical geographers, such as the Russian anarchist Petr Kropotkin, began to develop geographical critiques of European imperialism. But there seems to have been no coordinated, anticolonial lobby within the geographical movement. Other anarchists, such as the leading French geographer Elisée Reclus, were still willing to defend certain forms of imperial rule as necessary and desirable.

It is not suggested here that there were clearly defined schools of geographical thought in each of these cases. Rather, some if not all of these themes continually surfaced and resurfaced in the geographical literature, sometimes in the same text. Indeed, much of the intellectual power of European imperialism lay in the ability of its leading prophets to mobilize simultaneously distinct and even contradictory arguments to justify a European imperial presence in different regions. All of these geo-imperialist formulations were, however, informed by a common set of geographical theories about the relationship between human societies and their physical environments. For many, European imperial expansion—in whatever form—was linked to, even preordained by, notions of environmental determinism. The unique climatic and environmental circumstances in the imperial heartlands of Western Europe had created, it was claimed, energetic, expansive civilizations, just as the very different and less beneficent climates and environments of the colonial periphery had created inferior societies and weaker civilizations in need of an ordering and benign European presence. To a degree, this notion was connected to crude social Darwinian theories about the differential evolution of races, in turn linked to racial theories about the nature and characteristics of different peoples and their potential for development (Peet, passim).

While the various components in this pseudo-scientific geographical rhetoric overlapped and were mutually sustaining, they were also the sites of serious moral, philosophical, and scientific disagreement. For example, far from supporting racial interpretations of human development, environmental determinism was frequently deployed to counter the arguments of racial theorists. Environmental determinists stressed the overriding significance of "external" climatic and physical geographical factors on the process of social and economic progress. Through the judicious use of modern science and technology, it was sometimes argued, a colonizing power could overcome the worst aspects of a particularly challenging environment by draining the pestilential marsh or irrigating the barren desert and, in so doing, could free the local inhabitants from the pernicious influence of their surroundings. Physical and moral "improvement" were thus linked, and both were dependent on the benign intervention of a "superior" external force. In time, and if coupled with a wise cultural and educational policy, a colonized people would eventually be able to take control of their own resources and manage their own affairs. In this sense, environmental determinism was a direct continuation of the progressive humanism of the Enlightenment.

For many racial geographical theorists, on the other hand, the most important constraining influence on the development of different peoples were "internal," biological and physiological factors, usually connected with intelligence. Even if "internal" disadvantages were originally conditioned by "external" environmental factors, they had become, according to many commentators, immutable and permanent racial characteristics that defied an optimistic belief in the possibility of human improvement. This argument presupposed the need for a permanent imperial presence of intellectually and racially superior rulers in order to manage the people and environments of the colonial world (Livingstone, pp. 216–260).

Between World Wars I and II, the range of geographical writing was such that it is impossible to assert that geography was unproblematically a science of imperialism. This was partly because imperialism had itself become such a complex moral, political, and intellectual arena. Insofar as individual geographers remained committed to European empires, they were generally aligned with a liberal, benign, and developmental colonial ethos that emphasized the sacrifices and responsibilities of Western scientists and colonial administrators rather than the advantages that empire brought. After 1945, and the beginning of decolonization, some radical geographers began to champion the antiimperial cause on a variety of moral, political, and environmental grounds, a noteworthy example being the great French desert geomorphologist and North Africanist Jean Dresch, who worked hard to convince his reluctant comrades in the French Communist Party to support the Algerian cause during the war of independence. By the 1960s and 1970s, in a more-or-less conscious attempt to rid the discipline of its unsavory imperialist connotations and the resulting lack of academic rigor and respectability, geography lurched first into an abstract world of mathematical modeling and quantitative spatial science and then shifted again, particularly after 1968, toward a more politically engaged, radical orthodoxy in which the geographer's science was to be used to champion the rights of the world's poor and dispossessed. Hence, while European imperialism and European geography were chronologically and conceptually connected developments, the relationship between the two has always been complex and contested.

Michael J. Heffernan

Bibliography

Bassin, Mark. "Imperialism and the Nation-state in Friedrich Ratzel's Political Geography." *Progress in Human Geography* 11 (1987): pp. 473–495.

Driver, Felix. "Geography's Empire: Histories of Geographical Knowledge." *Environment and Planning D: Society and Space* 10 (1992): pp. 23–40.

Harley, Brian. "Maps, Knowledge and Power." In *The Iconography of Landscape: Essays in the Symbolic Representation, Design and Use of Past Environ-*

ments, edited by Denis Cosgrove and Stephen Daniels, pp. 277–312. Cambridge: Cambridge University Press, 1988.

Headrick, Daniel R. *The Tools of Empire: Technology and European Imperialism in the Nineteenth Century.* Oxford: Oxford University Press, 1981.

Heffernan, Michael. "The Science of Empire? The French Geographical Movement and the Forms of French Imperialism, 1870–1920." In *Geography and Empire,* edited by Anne Godlewska and Neil Smith, pp. 92–114. Oxford: Blackwell, 1994.

Heffernan, M., M. Bell, and R.A. Butlin. "Introduction." In *Geographical Knowledge and Imperial Power,* edited by M. Bell, R.A. Butlin, and M.J. Heffernan, pp. 1–7. Manchester: Manchester University Press, 1994.

Hudson, Brian. "The New Geography and the New Imperialism." *Antipode* 9 (1977): pp. 12–19.

Kearns, G. "Halford John Mackinder 1861–1947." *Geographers: Bio-bibliographical Studies* 9 (1985): pp. 71–86.

Livingstone, David N. *The Geographical Tradition: Episodes in the History of a Contested Enterprise.* Oxford: Blackwell, 1992.

Peet, Richard. "The Social Origins of Environmental Determinism." *Annals, Association of American Geographers* 75 (1985): pp. 309–333.

Richards, Thomas. *The Imperial Archive: Knowledge and the Fantasy of Empire.* London: Verso, 1993.

Said, Edward W. *Culture and Imperialism.* London: Chatto and Windus, 1993.

See also Climate Change, before 1940; Colonialism and Imperialism; Exploration, Age of; Geography, Elizabethan; Geography in Enlightenment Encyclopedias; Geography and Natural Theology; Geopolitics; Humboldtian Science

Geography and Natural Theology

An important context for geography in the seventeenth, eighteenth, and nineteenth centuries.

Natural theology is conventionally contrasted with "revealed theology" because its claims about God are constructed irrespective of "revelation." Typically, this has been taken to mean that the existence (and perhaps certain attributes) of the deity are believed to be discernible from a rational interrogation of the created order. Perhaps the most characteristic of natural theology's formulae has been the design argument, which postulates that from evidence of judicious planning in the world the existence of a superintending divine intelligence can reasonably be inferred. While the classical formulations of natural theology, such as that of Augustine, Aquinas, and Scotus, pre-date the Scientific Revolution, it was during the seventeenth century that empirical investigation of the natural world began to be drawn more centrally into the orbit of teleological confession. A major stimulus to this development were the Boyle Lectures—a series of sermons to vindicate Christianity "against notorious infidels"— provided for in Boyle's will; and beginning with the first lecturer, Richard Bentley, Newtonian science was deployed to serve this end. The connections between natural theology and science, particularly in the English tradition, have thus been deep and lasting, and have served a variety of both scientific and theological functions.

The idea of a designed Earth could and did promote a range of religious, scientific, and sociopolitical agendas. Even among Christian theologians it could be employed in various ways. Indeed two different versions of the design argument—the argument *to* design, and the argument *from* design—can readily be discerned (McPherson). The argument *to* design presupposes that the world is the creation of a supreme divine agent and that it will therefore provide evidence of his design. By contrast the argument *from* design constitutes a foundationalist argument postulating that instances of design in the world provide grounds for belief in the existence of God. The former is a confessional proclamation whereas the latter is a philosophical claim. Either way advocates mobilized the findings of science as resources to confirm teleology.

Within science, natural theology could meet a variety of needs. It could regulate scientific theorizing by disposing practitioners toward agreeable solutions to problems; it could help obviate the seeming conflict between believing piety and the infidelity of mechanical theories by projecting images of a divine mechanic or architect; it could facilitate the presentation of potentially seditious science in religious vocabulary thereby shielding scientists from suspicions of heterodoxy; and it could provide answers to specific problems—such as postulating creationist explanations for patterns of geographical distribution.

Natural theology had political and social uses as well. In the seventeenth century, for example, analogies between the laws of matter and the role of monarchy enabled particular political arrangements to be underwritten by both natural and divine law. Later parallels between political economy and the economy of nature, drawing on the metaphor of the divine economist, played a similar role.

Such conceptual elasticity reveals substantial variation in the natural theology tradition—a variation that itself has a geography. In Germany and in the Netherlands physico-theology survived much better than in France, where connections between Catholic orthodoxy and dissent were more polarized. In England it flourished best of all, perhaps because, as Brooke puts it, "there was no need for enlightened minds to overthrow religion itself because there was no pope, no inquisition, no Jesuit order, no comparable grip of the priesthood on families through the practice of confession" (p. 200).

We have then what we might call a geography *of* natural theology. We also have geography *in* natural theology. Physico-theology's engagement with geographical knowledge was wide-ranging and encompassed such themes as the Earth's surface features, its plant and animal life, its demographic characteristics, and its global regional character. We will examine first some of the ways such topics surface in the classic statements of physico-theology in the seventeenth and eighteenth century; then we will turn to the persistence of teleological modes of thought within geographical discourse throughout the nineteenth and even into the twentieth century.

In the wake of the Scientific Revolution, the features of the Earth's surface could be conscripted in a variety of ways to serve physico-theology. John Ray's *Wisdom of God Manifested in the Works of Creation* (1691) is a useful point of departure, because it sought to exemplify how the natural harmonies of nature evidenced divine beneficence. Among the diverse topics in which he exulted were the hydrological proportions of the globe, bird flight, human anatomy, and in particular the character of vegetation. Here he dilated on organic adaptability to environment and animal instinct, both of which illustrated how form and function expressed an overall harmony. In the *Sacred Theory of the Earth* by Thomas Burnet (1635–1715), by contrast, it was the *im*perfection of the Earth's features that revealed its appropriateness for sinful humanity. Throughout its history the planet had decayed from original perfection—a dissolution in which the deluge played a key role; but there was hope that the final conflagration would usher in a new heaven and a new Earth. This gloomy rehearsal of the global story, however, encouraged others to present a more flattering picture of the contemporary Earth and its suitability for humanity. John Woodward, for example, in his *Essay Towards a Natural History of the Earth* (1695) could see little evidence that the pre- and postdiluvial worlds were radically different. Certainly there were differences, but these only went to show that the postdiluvial Earth had a constitution more suited to humanity than its predecessor, which was really fitted only for unfallen humanity. The "world which emerged from the diluvial metamorphosis was a world perfectly adapted to the needs of fallen man" (Davies, p. 116). And in this world the close links between the accumulation of humus, soil erosion, and human agriculture tellingly revealed divine design.

William Derham's *Physico-Theology* of 1713 was devoted to his elucidation of the teleological significance of the "Terraqueous Globe." Here he surveyed the general figure of the Earth, and its constituent parts, together with its inhabitants, devoting considerable space to human and animal physiology. All these were designed to provide, as he put it in the subtitle of the work, "A Demonstration of the Being and Attributes of God from His Works of Creation." The detail of Derham's volume repeated many of the standard themes already rehearsed by Ray, but, according to Glacken, Derham's application of the design argument to population theory—a move about which Süssmilch enthused—constituted a significant development of the tradition. Certainly others had incorporated population statistics into the fabric of natural theology. John Graunt, for example, elaborated in his *Natural and Political Observations Made upon the Bills of Mortality* (1662) on how Christianity and the laws of nature alike endorsed the moral wisdom of monogamy. William Petty likewise connected up population growth and distribution with physico-theology by urging that an underpopulated Earth would provide unbelievers with grounds for doubting the purpose of creation. But Derham elaborated on the way in which demography evidenced how God had kept a *balance* of population. According to Glacken (p. 422), this "serious application of the design argument to population theory is one of the noteworthy developments of the seventeenth and early eighteenth centuries." Population stability, sex structure, and changing life expectancy were thus evidence of what Derham called "admirable and plain Management" and "Harmony in the Generations of Men."

The theme of the balance of nature was to play a prominent role in the writings of those like Gilbert White who wrote of the economy of nature. In *The Natural History of Selborne*, published in 1789, White recorded the natural order of his own parish, surveying everything from taxonomy and ornithology to seasonal change (see Worster). Throughout, there is a pervasive sense of the area's complex unity in diversity. And not surprisingly. For Providence had contrived to make "Nature . . . a great economist." Here was a political economy of nature; everything fitted together "economically." Similar sentiments are clearly discernible in the writings of Linnaeus, K.L. Willdenow, and Eberhard Zimmerman.

Despite a range of philosophical assaults during the Enlightenment, emanating from such thinkers as Kant and Hume, the use of geographical data in natural theological argument survived well into the nineteenth century. Much of it took as its point of departure William Paley's extraordinarily popular *Natural Theology* of 1802, a volume that Darwin had found inspirational in his early days. Geography's complicity in the natural theology enterprise can adequately be illustrated by reference to two discrete bodies of literature—namely, that of Christian apologists and that of practitioners of geographical science.

In his book *The Christian Philosopher or The Connection of Science and Philosophy with Religion*, published in 1825, Thomas Dick (1774–1857) devoted considerable attention to geography as one of the "Sciences which are related to Religion and Christian theology." Dick, a liberal thinker, impatient with theological technicalities, developed a natural theology that enjoyed a particularly large readership in the United States. Here he fastened upon such topics as the figure of the Earth, the natural and artificial divisions of the globe, the features of mountains, oceans, and rivers, and population size as indicative of the operations of divine providence. Such sentiments were, by now, conventional enough. But geography was of even more specific interest to religious believers because of its intimate connection with the missionary enterprise. As Dick put it: "In a religious point of view, Geography is a science of peculiar interest. For "the salvation of God," which

Christianity unfolds, is destined to be proclaimed in every land. . . . But, without exploring every region of the Earth . . . we can never carry into effect the purpose of God." Accordingly directors of missionary enterprises were advised to acquaint themselves with geographical knowledge in order that they would not "grope in the dark, and spend their money in vain." Christianity therefore had nothing but the most intimate interest in contemporary "voyages of discovery" because they were engaged in bringing to light the "moral and political movements which are presently agitating the nations." The moral diagnosis was particularly significant: for alongside its topographical disclosures, geography was engaged in nothing less than providing a moral inventory of the globe. In this way geography played its role in the cultivation of a moral teleology. Geographical knowledge was thus presented as the stimulus *par excellence* to embarking on a global moral crusade to bring benevolence and enlightenment to the ends of the Earth. Thus if geography could confirm faith through its elucidation of providential arrangements of the Earth's surface, it could also stimulate the faithful to remake the Earth through worldwide evangelization.

Geography thus had the capacity to serve the sentiments of Victorian Christian apologists. Indeed as late as 1883 the Edinburgh professor of divinity Robert Flint, for example, was still plundering the writings of such geographers as Carl Ritter and Arnold Guyot for what he called their rich store of teleological data. That such sources could be called upon, of course, itself bears witness to the continued vitality of teleological thinking within geography. This indeed was recognized by H.R. Mill, who, writing in 1929 on the development of the subject in the nineteenth century, commented, "Teleology or the argument from design . . . was tacitly accepted or explicitly avowed by almost every writer on the theory of geography, and Carl Ritter distinctly recognized and adopted it as the unifying principle of his system." In his Bridgewater Treatise on *Astronomy and General Physics* (1834), for example, William Whewell used the phytogeographical work of Humboldt to demonstrate how the Creator had adapted various plant forms to their regional climatic regimes. Again, Mary Somerville, in her *Physical Geography* (1858), argued that the patterns of human settlement demonstrated the arrangement of divine wisdom, while Arnold Guyot's ecological geography, drawing on Ritter's work, was built upon the providentially governed "grand harmonies" of nature. As for Matthew Fontaine Maury, author of the *Physical Geography of the Sea* (1855), it was the mechanistic operations of marine and atmospheric circulation systems and of energy transfers between land, sea, and air, that confirmed to him the wisdom of Paley's celebrated clock analogy.

Further instances of geographical teleology could be elaborated ad libitum. In this regard Victorian geographical writing is hardly exceptional. Reinforcement for what might be called doxological science was readily forthcoming from such members of the British scientific fraternity as David Brewster, William Buckland, James Hutton, Roderick Murchison, Richard Owen, Adam Sedgwick, and William Whewell, not to mention the diverse authors of the *Bridgewater Treatises,* and from such American figures as Louis Agassiz, Alexander Dallas Bache, James Dwight Dana, Asa Gray, Joseph Henry, Benjamin Silliman, and Alexander Winchell. That these writers deployed teleological principles in a wide variety of ways for a variety of different scientific and theological purposes scarcely needs comment; but that their science was domiciled within a natural theology framework confirms the significance of teleology as a common context for their scientific endeavors.

During the past two centuries, of course, natural theology as an enterprise has been the subject of attacks from philosophers, scientists, and indeed theologians themselves. Hume and Kant, for example, mounted their epistemological critiques on the limits of reason and on the deficiencies of analogical argumentation; Darwin's theory of natural selection subverted William Paley's schema by showing how organic adaptation to environment could have arisen by purely natural means; and in the twentieth century the Swiss theologian Karl Barth declared himself an avowed opponent of all natural theology. Despite such criticisms, the natural theological enterprise has cast a long shadow over the heritage of geographical thought and practice.

David N. Livingstone

Bibliography
Brooke, John Hedley. *Science and Religion: Some Historical Perspectives.* Cambridge: Cambridge University Press, 1991.
Glacken, Clarence J. *Traces on the Rhodian Shore: Nature and Culture in Western Thought from Ancient Times to the End of the Eighteenth Century.* Berkeley: University of California Press, 1967.
Herries Davies, Gordon L. *The Earth in Decay: A History of British Geomorphology 1578–1878.* London: MacDonald, 1969.
Larson, James. "Not without a Plan: Geography and Natural History in the Late Eighteenth Century." *Journal of the History of Biology* 19 (1986): pp. 447–488.
Livingstone, David N. *The Geographical Tradition: Episodes in the History of a Contested Enterprise.* Oxford: Blackwell, 1992.
———. "Natural Theology and Neo-Lamarckism: The Changing Context of Nineteenth Century Geography in the United States and Great Britain." *Annals of the Association of American Geographers* 74 (1984): pp. 9–28.
McPherson, Thomas. *The Argument from Design.* London: Macmillan, 1972.
Mill, Hugh Robert. "Geography." In *Encyclopaedia Britannica.* 14th ed. Vol. X. London: The Encyclopaedia Britannica Company, 1929.
Tuan, Yi-Fu. *The Hydrological Cycle and the Wisdom of God: A Theme in Geoteleology.* Toronto: University of Toronto Press, 1968.
Worster, Donald. *Nature's Economy: A History of Ecological Ideas.* Cambridge: Cambridge University Press, 1977.

See also Cosmology and the Earth; Earth in Decay; Ecology; Evolution and the Geosciences; Geography; Geological Surveys, U.S. State; Geological Time; Humboldtian Science; Hydrologic Cycle; Sacred Theory of the Earth; Sociological/Constructivist Approaches; Volcanoes, Theories before 1800; Wilderness

Geography and Renaissance Magic

An important context for geography in the fifteenth, sixteenth, and even seventeenth centuries.

Links between science and magic—to use two abstractions—have been the subject of numerous historical investigations (for example, Dobbs; Debus; Webster; Garin; Vickers). These studies have engendered considerable debate over the precise role, if any, that should be accorded to magical beliefs in the genesis of modern science. In general, magic can be considered "a system of beliefs underpinning a body of technical or craft knowledge and practice, which sought to capture and control the power and processes of nature for man's (or perhaps merely the individual adept's) advantage" (Henry, p. 583). The label "magic" of course is a singular term for a multiplicity of beliefs and practices such as astrology, alchemy, and natural and spiritual magic, with a host of minor deviations and variations like palmistry and geomancy. What united these diverse practices was a general assumption that their operations were occult or hidden and thus required seers skilled in a variety of relevant arts.

Despite the earlier attacks of Augustine and other church fathers, magical thought and practice blossomed during the Middle Ages and Renaissance especially in the wake of the unearthing of a range of ancient documents dealing with various magical arcana. Chief among these was a body of semireligious writings then believed to have originated in Egypt and allegedly the work of one Hermes Trismegistus. This hermetic tradition, according to writers like Frances Yates, played a crucial role during early modern science's gestation period. Certainly the details of such claims have been contested, but there is now a widespread recognition that a more general neo-Platonic movement did exercise a significant influence. As Keith Thomas writes (p. 264): "Until the later seventeenth century the work of the practising wizard was sustained by the parallel activities of many contemporary intellectuals. Indeed the possibility of certain types of magic was a fundamental presupposition for most scientists and philosophers."

Whatever precise role is to be accorded to magic in the development of modern science, there is no doubt that numerous key figures during the period of the Scientific Revolution involved themselves with various occult arts. Newton, for example, conducted secret alchemical experiments, maintained a lively interest in magic, and devoted much energy to elucidating the symbolic apocalyptic of the biblical books of Daniel and Revelation. Indeed it has been claimed that if Newton had not been steeped in the alchemical tradition, he would not have accorded the role he did to the force of gravitational attraction.

Consider also the impact of astrology. Kepler, for example, was a practicing astrologer and his scientific writings are suffused with what has been called "number mysticism." Tycho Brahe too, otherwise one of the founders of modern astronomy, did nothing to resist attributing astrological significance to the new star that appeared in the heavens in 1572; to him it presaged political turmoil in Northern Europe and ultimately a new world order.

Again Francis Bacon embraced aspects of astrology, as did his devotee John Bainbridge, who exploited to the full the comet of 1618 for anti-Catholic purposes. Later William Petty looked in 1647 for administrators "skilled in the best rules of judicial astrology" in order that they could "calculate the events of diseases and prognosticate the weather." Indeed in the wake of the Royal Society's investigation of comets during the mid-seventeenth century, detailed inventories were drawn up of correspondences between the appearance of comets and political events, natural disasters, and economic fortunes.

Also of considerable importance was the tradition of natural magic championed by Paracelsus (ca. 1493–1541), a polymath whose contributions to chemistry, medicine, and cosmology were all of a piece with his interest in theology and the occult arts. The belief that many secrets and mysteries, known to the ancient *magi* but long lost, lay hidden in nature and could be recovered, prompted an empirical approach to the natural world that rode in tandem with scientific advance. Paracelsus and his followers thus constantly opposed Aristotle on knowledge about everything from medicine to natural history. Many authentic chemical, pharmacological, and general medical findings were gained through the passion to release the magical properties buried in stones, herbs, and other plants. To many, natural magic had an important role to play in the new science, unlike demonic magic, which spawned esoteric sects and secret brotherhoods. The former, however, was seen to be fully consonant with the scientific outlook of men like Bacon and Samuel Hartlib (d. 1670?).

While the impact of magical discourse and craft on science was clearly multifaceted, several important trends are discernible. Henry identifies two in particular. First, the experimental method has been seen as embedded in magical traditions in which observation could uncover causal connections between phenomena. Second, the magicians' fascination with number and number mysticism encouraged the mathematization of the study of nature. In the magical writings of figures like Cornelius Agrippa, John Baptista Porta, John Dee, and Pietro Pomponazzi these motifs persistently reassert themselves.

In the light of these connections between magic and science it is no surprise that the study of geography did not remain immune to such hermetic influences. After all some of the problems with which geographers traditionally concerned themselves, such as regional variation, were not far removed from astrologers' efforts to connect up the history of nations and the history of the stars. For all that, historians of the subject with few exceptions have excised such considerations from the historical narratives they have produced. Here we briefly review the impact of hermeticism—particularly astrology—on chorography, terrestrial geometry, meteorology, and ethnology.

Chorography, or the study of the areal differentiation of the Earth's surface, was one of the subjects taken up in William Cunningham's *Cosmographical Glass* of 1559. In this work he surveyed numerous standard geographical principles—latitude and longitude, the globe's major climatic zones, and survey methods. But a significant part of the geographical enterprise dealt with the description of the various individual regions of the world. And here his astrological sympathies clearly revealed themselves (Livingstone, "Science, Magic and Religion"; *Geographical Tradition*). His visual representation of the globe was surrounded by the heavenly spheres, and he proceeded to outline "the Planets and signes governing every region" of the Earth and to supplement the Ptolemaic cosmological scheme by adding the locations of regions and cities unknown to, or omitted by, Ptolemy. Similar concerns are also evident in Thomas Blundeville's pedagogic survey of cosmography, astronomy, and geography in 1594. For him, too, knowledge of the world's regions was umbilically tied to "the motions, aspects, and influences of the starres." Moreover, his instructions on the use of Mercator's globes was all of a piece with his explanations of the use of the horoscope and his elucidation of the twelve houses of astrology (Livingstone, ibid.).

If some geographical practitioners were drawn to the significance of astrology for understanding regional variation, others found in numerology the key to measuring the Earth—*geo*metry. In Italy, for example, the practical geometry of the surveyor and cartographer was substantially informed by cabalistic number theory. Thus in the writings of Nicolo Tartaglia both geography and chorography, no less than astrology and geomancy, were portrayed as crucially dependent upon geometry. So far as geography was concerned, considerable significance was attached to "the idea of landscape symbolising an achieved harmony between human life and the hidden order of creation" (Cosgrove, "Geometry of Landscape," p. 265). This mathematical theme—intimately associated as it

was with microcosm-macrocosm schemata—is also particularly evident in the work of the English polymath John Dee. For it was in his 1570 *Mathematical Preface* to Euclid's *Elements of Geometrie* that Dee both defined what he took to be the scope of geography and chorography, and outlined the ways in which number provides access to the temporal and spiritual worlds (Cosgrove, "Environmental Thought"). Besides, Dee's compendious survey of the progress of the "voyages of discovery," written in 1577, was suffused with both political and hermetic ways of advancing the imperial interests of the British Empire.

Astrological principles similarly insinuated their way into the practices of meteorology. Like the other figures we have just been considering, Leonard Digges (ca. 1520–1559) was a mathematical practitioner specializing in surveying, navigation, and gunnery. His volume *A Prognostication Everlastinge of Righte Good Effecte,* subsequently augmented by his son Thomas, was a treatise on meteorology. Here he brought an astrological-scientific perspective to bear on weather-forecasting. So it is understandable that a typical microcosm-macrocosm engraving relating the signs of the zodiac to the different parts of the human body was strategically placed on the title page and that all sorts of "rules" for weather-forecasting, like the significance of the day of the week on which the new year fell, were outlined. That this was regarded as entirely in keeping with the new science is nowhere more clearly evident than in his son's new edition of the work. For here the old Ptolemaic system that Leonard had relied on was replaced by Thomas with the new heliocentric system thereby bearing out the claim that almanac makers were among the first in England to convert to Copernicanism. So yet again we have with the Diggeses, the intermingling—to use modern designations—of scientific knowledge and knowledge based on other "nonrational" sources of belief.

The influence of magical thinking on studies of anthropological variation—astrological ethnology as it has been called—can be traced to ancient times when it was believed that the four elements were connected with theories of location because in different places different combinations of the elements were to be found. In this way the determining influence of the physical environment could be linked to the influence of the stars. Such conceptions were to be found in the thinking of thirteenth-century figures like Albert the Great and Roger Bacon (Glacken). In Albert's case it was the connection between the seven *klimata* and elemental combinations that was of great significance, while for Bacon—for whom accurate knowledge of places was crucial to discerning divine meanings in the world—different planets exercised influence over particular regions. For the Renaissance era this tradition of astrological ethnology is perhaps best exemplified in the writings of Jean Bodin, who was equally at home with Hippocrates's medicine, Plato's laws, Aristotle's politics, and Ptolemy's geography. To him national character—including such traits as perfidy, treachery, drunkenness, insanity—was to be explained in terms of the government of the stars. Each region, he believed, was ruled by different signs of the Zodiac and these, together with the different combinations of humors, produced varying physical and mental characteristics.

While magical modes of thinking were progressively to decline in the wake of the Scientific Revolution of the seventeenth century—resulting as much as anything else from Protestant critics in search of a biblicist religion—it would be mistaken to conclude that they entirely disappeared from Western purview. Indeed various brands of nature mysticism have persisted in certain strands of the environmental movement, and in recent years a postmodernist rejection of the rationalism of what is often called the "Enlightenment project" has encouraged a resurgence of interest in premodern ways of knowing as a means of reversing the "disenchantment of nature" that modern science effected.

David N. Livingstone

Bibliography

Cosgrove, Denis. "Environmental Thought and Action: Pre-Modern and Post-Modern." *Transactions of the Institute of British Geographers* N.S. 15 (1990): pp. 344–358.

———. "The Geometry of Landscape: Practice and Speculative Arts in Sixteenth-Century Venetian Land Territories." In *The Iconography of Landscape: Essays on the Symbolic Representation, Design and Use of Past Environments,* edited by Denis Cosgrove and Stephen Daniels, pp. 254–276. Cambridge: Cambridge University Press, 1988.

Debus, Allen G. *Man and Nature in the Renaissance.* Cambridge: Cambridge University Press, 1978.

Dobbs, B.J.T. *The Foundations of Newton's Alchemy, or "The Hunting of the Greene Lyon."* Cambridge: Cambridge University Press, 1975.

Garin, Eugenio. *Astrology in the Renaissance. The Zodiac of Life.* London: Routledge and Kegan Paul, 1983.

Glacken, Clarence J. *Traces on the Rhodian Shore: Nature and Culture in Western Thought from Ancient Times to the End of the Eighteenth Century.* Berkeley: University of California Press, 1967.

Henry, John. "Magic and Science in the Sixteenth and Seventeenth Centuries." In *Companion to the History of Modern Science,* edited by R.C. Olby, G.N. Cantor, J.R.R. Christie, and M.J.S. Hodge, pp. 583–596. London: Routledge, 1990.

Livingstone, David N. *The Geographical Tradition: Episodes in the History of a Contested Enterprise.* Oxford: Blackwell, 1992.

———. "Science, Magic and Religion: A Contextual Reassessment of Geography in the Sixteenth and Seventeenth Centuries." *History of Science* 26 (1988): pp. 269–294.

Thomas, Keith. *Religion and the Decline of Magic: Studies in Popular Beliefs in Sixteenth- and Seventeenth-Century England.* London: Weidenfeld and Nicolson, 1971.

Vickers, Brian, ed. *Occult and Scientific Mentalities in the Renaissance.* Cambridge: Cambridge University Press, 1984.

Webster, Charles. *From Paracelsus to Newton: Magic and the Making of Modern Science.* Cambridge: Cambridge University Press, 1982.

Yates, Frances A. "The Hermetic Tradition in Renaissance Science." In *Art, Science, and History in the Renaissance,* edited by Charles S. Singleton, pp. 255–274. Baltimore, Md.: Johns Hopkins University Press, 1967.

See also Agricultural Meteorology; Atmosphere, Discovery and Exploration of; Climate, Ancient Ideas; Cosmology and the Earth; Elizabethan Geography; Foucault's *Order of Things;* Geography and Natural Theology; Historiography, Eighteenth-Century England; Meteorological Ideas in Europe; Meteorological Ideas in Folklore and Mythology; Meteorological Ideas in the Pre-modern Orient; Meteorology, Medical; Occult Philosophy and the Earth in the Renaissance; Tides, before Newton

Geography: The Word

One of the oldest words referring to knowledge of the Earth.

"Geography" was adapted by Renaissance scholars from the Hellenistic "earth *(γεω)* writing *(γραφια)*" reputedly coined by Eratosthenes (ca. 275–194 B.C.E.). Some scholars adhered to the authoritative logic of Claudius Ptolemy (ca. 90–168 C.E.) who argued (1.1.1) that geography is properly the study of the whole world, the study of a particular region *(χορος)* being chorography. More intuitively, geography is the description of the world, its constituent regions, and their inhabitants, at all scales. Before 1800, that description was both textual and graphic in form. Disciplinary specialization progressively restricted geography to writing; map-making became cartography, first used in 1839 for the "study of maps" (Harley and Woodward, vol. 1, p. 12).

Matthew H. Edney

Bibliography
Harley, J.B., and David Woodward, eds. *The History of Cartography.* Chicago: University of Chicago Press, 1987– . 6 vols. in 8 books.
Ptolemy. *The Geography of Claudius Ptolemy.* Translated by Edward L. Stevenson. New York: New York Public Library, 1932. Reprint. New York: Dover, 1991.

See also Cartography; Geography; Geology: The Word; Geomorphology: The Word; Geophysics: The Word: Geothermics: The Word

Geological Astronomy

The integration of geological investigation in a larger astronomical perspective.

The Aristotelian distinction between the sublunar world and the heavens beyond, each made of different elements and ruled by different physical laws, little encouraged the forging of intellectual links between geology and astronomy. Not until the Scientific Revolution of the sixteenth and seventeenth centuries did the universe become one in the collective imagination of Homo sapiens. And not until the twentieth century was there much interaction between geological and astronomical hypotheses.

A potentially productive attempt to link geology and astronomy occurred when the geologist Thomas Chrowder Chamberlin (1843–1928) at the University of Chicago and the director of the Mount Wilson Observatory, George Ellery Hale (1868–1938), attempted in 1915 to draw from Chamberlin's planetesimal hypothesis regarding the origin of the solar system ideas that might provide focus for a research program on spiral nebulae.

As Chamberlin had noted, a cold and arid climate for the Earth in the past, as indicated by glaciation and salt deposits, was incompatible with the exceedingly extensive, dense, warm, and moist atmosphere postulated for earlier times by the nebular hypothesis of Simon de Laplace (1749–1827), in which the solar system was formed by separation and condensation of parts of a whirling cloud of hot gas. Furthermore, if a molten Earth had condensed from a gaseous mass, the temperature of the Earth's atmosphere probably would have been so great that water vapor would have evaporated and been lost into space. Alternatively, if water vapor had not been evaporated and lost into space, it would have dissociated into hydrogen and oxygen, and the hydrogen would have escaped quickly into space. Thus Laplace's hypothesis of a molten Earth seemed untenable to Chamberlin.

Astronomical tests further weakened faith in the theory and served to forestall acceptance of a modified form of the Laplacian hypothesis in which meteoroids slowly aggregated. A large portion of the solar system's momentum resides in the outer regions, but the mass is heavily concentrated near the center, an unlikely occurrence within Laplace's nebular hypothesis. The unsymmetrical distribution of matter and momentum suggested to Chamberlin that the solar system had been formed by a collision between a small nebula with large momentum and the periphery of a large nebula with very little momentum. Spiral nebulae might represent such collisions.

Chamberlin worked at the Mount Wilson Observatory in the summer of 1915, and from his planetesimal hypothesis came a suggestion to study motions of concentrations of material in spiral nebulae. The astronomer Adriaan van Maanen (1884–1946) purportedly detected motions of small condensations in the spiral nebula M 101, motions which— if real—indicated that the nebula was not as distant as generally supposed. (Were M 101 even one-fifth as large as the estimated size of our own galaxy and were M 101 rotating with the period claimed by van Maanen, the outer edge of the nebula would have had to be traveling faster than the speed of light. Thus the purported rotation contradicted belief in spiral nebulae as extragalactic systems. Now we know that van Maanen's measurements were spurious.)

Even before van Maanen began comparing photographs, Hale circulated among astronomers at Mount Wilson Chamberlin's paper prepared during the summer of 1915 on the nebular problem. The astronomers, however, were narrowly focused on particular observational problems and evinced little interest in more abstract theory. In retrospect, the task of drawing detailed quantitative observational predictions out of the planetesimal theory was beyond the mathematical and computational capabilities of the age, and without specific observational suggestions, there was little for observational astronomers to sink their teeth into.

Also, as the historian of science Stephen Brush (b. 1935) has written, Chamberlin was trying to develop an "interfield" theory, a theory generated within one scientific field (geology) but requiring for its testing observations from another field (astronomy). In ranging over many diverse fields, interfield theories inevitably perform less well in each individual field than do special theories limited to a single field. And since scientists are more often specialists than generalists, they more often judge a theory primarily by its usefulness in a very narrow context.

Chamberlin did initiate an interdisciplinary research team at the University of Chicago, and, had it continued beyond his death in 1928, a new field of planetary science encompassing geology, astronomy, physics, chemistry, and mathematics might have been established decades before the discipline finally came into its own. As early as 1902, the Carnegie Institution of Washington advisory committee on geophysics, of which Chamberlin was a member, had defined its field as "founded on pure physics and chemistry; its data are supplied chiefly by geology; and the ramifications of its superstructure extended into astronomy and astrophysics."

Chamberlin's planetesimal theory also may have had some influence on observations at the Lowell Observatory, particularly in the aftermath of a bitter quarrel following the 1908 publication of *Mars as the Abode of Life* by Percival Lowell (1855–1916). Adopting Laplace's hypothesis, Lowell precipitated a quarrel with adherents of Chamberlin's theory. Eliot Blackwelder (1880–1969), professor of geology at the University of Wisconsin (where Chamberlin had been president before moving to Chicago), stated that Lowell's book was being foisted upon a trusting public as a popular exposition of science when it was fantasy. The misbranding of intellectual products was

as immoral as the misbranding of manufactured products; censure could "hardly be too severe upon a man who so unscrupulously deceives the educated public merely in order to gain a certain notoriety and a brief, but undeserved, credence for his pet theories." Rebuttals and replies flew back and forth. Perhaps both the most colorful and the least dignified emanated from Forest Ray Moulton (1872–1952), Chamberlin's colleague in astronomy at Chicago. He described Lowell as "that mysterious "watcher of the stars" whose scientific theories, like Poe's vision of the raven "have taken shape at midnight." It was in the context of Lowell's interest in the evolution of planetary systems that he had directed Vesto M. Slipher (1875–1969) to study spiral nebulae, and the unseemly exchange of personal remarks may well have provided additional stimulus. Late in 1912, Slipher succeeded in measuring both the rotation and the radial velocity of the Andromeda nebula. The latter remarkable discovery eventually led to the realization that the universe is expanding.

Another interesting link—or conflict—between geology and astronomy arose in the 1930s, when the accepted geological age of the Earth proved embarrassingly greater than the age of the universe newly inferred from the relativistic, expanding, and homogeneous model of the universe created by Edwin Hubble (1889–1953). Strongly moved by the spirit of relativity theory, Hubble refused to accept falsification of his model of an expanding universe by contradictory observations. Rather than bow to the dictate of geological time (and also to some contrary observations from the field of astronomy), Hubble instead clung to philosophical values and to a theory in conflict with observation and prediction. (Eventually, when the distance scale was recalibrated in the 1950s, astronomers derived an age for the universe greater than the age of the Earth.)

Were there a single indispensable characteristic unfailingly distinguishing scientific theories from the nonscientific, many would follow the philosopher of science Sir Karl Popper (b. 1902) in positing falsifiability as the sine qua non of scientificness. Historians of science, however, including Stephen Brush, have recognized that in some instances direct experimental tests of hypotheses have been accorded less weight than the conformity of the hypotheses with general theoretical superstructures. The conflict between geological time and the age of the universe inferred by Hubble is one such instance.

Linkages between geology and astronomy have multiplied during the later half of the twentieth century, to the benefit of each of the particular sciences and to the advantage of science as a whole. Correspondingly, the history of geological astronomy (or of astronomical geology) is now a fertile field ripe for exploration.

Norriss S. Hetherington

Bibliography

Brush, Stephen G. "The Age of the Earth in the Twentieth Century." *Earth Sciences History* 8 (1989): pp. 170–182.

———. "A Geologist among Astronomers: The Rise and Fall of the Chamberlin-Moulton Cosmogony." *Journal for the History of Astronomy* 9 (1978): pp. 1–41, 77–104.

———. "Should the History of Science Be Rated X?" *Science* 183 (1974): pp. 1164–1172.

Hetherington, Norriss S. "Converting an Hypothesis into a Research Program: T.C. Chamberlin, His Planetesimal Hypothesis, and Its Effect on Research at the Mount Wilson Observatory." In *The Earth, the Heavens and the Carnegie Institution of Washington,* edited by Gregory A. Good, pp. 113–123. American Geophysical Union: History of Geophysics Series, vol. 5. Washington, D.C.: American Geophysical Union, 1994.

———. "Geological Time versus Astronomical Time: Are Scientific Theories Falsifiable?" *Earth Sciences History* 8 (1989): pp. 167–69.

Kushner, David. "Sir George Darwin and a British School of Geophysics." *Osiris* 8 (1993): pp. 196–223.

Mitton, Daniel J. "Astrogeology in the 19th Century." *Geotimes* 14, no. 6 (1969): p. 22.

See also Age of the Earth, since 1800; Chemistry, Terrestrial and Cosmical; Geophysics; Heat, Internal, Twentieth Century; Nebular Hypothesis; Planetary Science; Popper's Ideas on Falsifiability

Geological Education

First formal instruction in geology in the eighteenth century. Scientists and educators know that geology has been taught throughout the world over many years. Many studies regarding geology education have appeared in the literature, however these works have emphasized particular time periods, students, and places. If geological education is to advance by not only training geologists but also by informing the public, then a more detailed exploration of the history of geological education seems to be needed.

A review of teaching texts, reference books, abstracts, and articles suggests that research involving geological education falls into several distinct categories. First, many articles discuss the development of geological education at American undergraduate institutions between 1749 and the present. Examples include Robert M. Norris on early teaching at Berkeley and Stanford, James X. Corgan on Tennessee Colleges in the mid-nineteenth century, Margaret Rossiter on geology in nineteenth-century women's education, Brian J. Skinner and Barbara L. Narendra on Yale, Carol Faul on geology at the early University of Pennsylvania, Markes E. Johnson on reforms in geological education at Rensselaer, and Daniel J. Jones on teaching geology at the universities of Oklahoma and Chicago.

The second type of historical study involves the broad topic of earth-science education reform. These studies usually do not emphasize one institution, but strive to consider a broader geographic region. Examples include articles by Eileen Marie Starr, Larry A. Irwin, and John R. Carpenter. These have focused on curricular developments in the United States since World War II.

Although these studies do not cover all of the information available regarding geological education, they appear representative of this aspect of the history of the geosciences. Clearly many issues in geological education must be evaluated in greater detail. First, the overall development of geological education at the college and precollege level throughout the world must be investigated. Special attention must be paid to education before roughly 1900. Although reform movements within the United States have been discussed, more needs to be described with regard to reform in other countries.

Other issues should also be explored. For example, how have geology texts changed through time and how do texts compare from country to country? Some have discussed the development of texts, but additional research regarding geology texts is needed. Likewise, what specific changes in geology teaching techniques have occurred over the years? When did hands-on labs begin at the college and precollege level? When, where, and how were field trips introduced into the geology curriculum? William R. Ogden and Robert H. Roy have provided some insight into this issue, but more historical research is needed.

Another issue that might help document the development of geology education could be an investigation of the interplay of academia, industry, and the geology curriculum. In different regions of the world, how has geology education been affected by these factors? When and why were specific topics of study added, expanded, and deleted from a geology curriculum? Finally, although much has been written about the research contributions of Abraham Gottlob Werner, William Buckland, Adam Sedgwick, and others, extended investigation of the teaching techniques and choices of curriculum are almost completely lacking. One exception is Rachel Laudan's *From Mineralogy to Geology: The Foundations of a Science, 1650–1830* (1987), which examines geological education in late-eighteenth-century France and Germany (pp. 51–55). How did each of these individuals approach the teaching of geology, and how did their courses affect classes elsewhere? Historical research on these topics would enrich the history of the geosciences generally.

William J. Boone

Bibliography

Carpenter, John R. "An Overview of Geoscience Education Reform in the United States." *Journal of Geological Education* 41 (1993): pp. 304–311.

Corgan, James X. "Geology in Tennessee Colleges 1826–1850." *Journal of Geological Education* 29 (1981): pp. 160–168.

Faul, Carol. "A History of Geology at the University of Pennsylvania: Benjamin Franklin and the Rest." *Geological Society of America Centennial Special* 1 (1985): pp. 376–389.

Irwin, Larry A. "A Brief Historical Account and Introduction to the Earth Science Curriculum Project." *High School Journal* 53 (January 1970): pp. 241–249.

Johnson, Markes E. "Geology and Early American Reforms in Education: The Rensselaer and New Harmony Schools." *Geological Society of America Abstracts* 12 (1980): p. 456.

Jones, Daniel J. "Early Geologic Education at the Universities of Oklahoma and Chicago: Comparisons and Contrasts." *Geological Society of America Abstracts* 12 (1980): p. 456.

Norris, Robert M. "Early Geologic Education in California: Berkeley and Stanford Show the Way." *Journal of Geological Education* 29 (1981): pp. 169–175.

Ogden, William R., and Robert H. Roy. "Secondary School Earth Science Teaching, 1918–1972: Objectives as Stated in Periodical Literature." *Journal of Geological Education* 26 (1978): pp. 96–101.

Rossiter, Margaret W. "Geology in Nineteenth-Century Women's Education in the United States." *Journal of Geological Education* 29 (1981): pp. 228–232.

Skinner, Brian J., and Barbara L. Narendra. "Rummaging through the Attic: Or, A Brief History of the Geological Sciences at Yale." *Geological Society of America Centennial Special* 1 (1985): pp. 355–376.

Starr, Eileen Marie. "The History of the Development of Earth-Science Programs in Higher-Education." *Journal of Geological Education* 39 (1991): pp. 48–51.

See also Geology; Geophysics in Universities; Mining Academies

Geological Maps

A relatively recent cartographic method to visually illustrate the location, succession, and configuration of rock units in the Earth's crust (Rudwick, p. 159).

Prior to the late 1700s, the words "geology" and "geologist" rarely if ever appear in the literature. By implication, the term "geological map" suffered the same fate, appearing in map titles only starting in the early 1800s. Titles of maps prior to that used words such as "mineralogical," "petrographic," "geognostic," or simply "map."

On pre-1800s maps, the primary emphasis was to show, using symbols or letters, the location of minerals, fossils, mines, springs, coal, and other occurrences of isolated natural phenomena. There was little, if any, concern for rock sequences or their stratigraphic succession as we know it today. Furthermore, these maps were produced by individuals with their own personal ideas about geology and cartography. Even generalized, acceptable guidelines for producing such maps did not exist. Thus, prior to the early 1800s, geological maps were in their embryonic stages, as Arthur H. Robinson has argued (chap. 4). But just as maps produced in the 1700s were improvements over their predecessors, maps of the 1800s brought forth the modern geological map.

During the 1800s, geological cartography changed dramatically for several reasons. First, the value of fossils was recognized for their age significance and thus, their value for stratigraphic correlation. Second, the subject of geology became an academic discipline, producing many geologists and quantities of information. Third, printing methods greatly improved over the outdated symbols and hand coloring. Fourth, accurate topographic base maps became available. Fifth, standard stratigraphic names, structural symbols, cross-sections, and stratigraphic columns were accepted.

Major contributions to geological maps in the 1900s included vast areas mapped and correlated worldwide, the use of isotopes to date rocks and establish stratigraphic ages, satellite imagery and aerial photography to examine large and remote areas, geophysics to explore the subsurface, oil and gas-well logs for detailed subsurface data, and a better understanding of the Earth's evolution and plate tectonics.

The oldest geological map known to exist is referred to as the Turin papyrus and is dated ca. 1150 B.C.E. The papyrus, measuring 41 centimeters by 2.82 meters (16 by 111 inches), is colored to show sedimentary rocks, igneous/metamorphic rocks, and also an ancient gold mining area and a stone quarry in eastern Egypt. The sedimentary rocks are shown as black hills, and the igneous/metamorphic rocks are shown as pink hills. Even the main wadis (dry river beds) have colored spots to illustrate the colored alluvial gravels they contain. This three-thousand-year-old geological map was made during the reign of Rameses IV (1151–1145 B.C.E.) and is now located in the Egyptian Museum in Turin, Italy. The map is in fragments, but its reconstruction depicts the area of Wadi Hammamat, about 500 kilometers (310 miles) south of Cairo (Harrell and Brown).

In 1539, Olaus Magnus (1490–1557) produced a map from wood blocks measuring 170 x 125 centimeters (66.3 by 48.8 inches) that shows the location of mineral deposits in Scandinavia. The map, entitled "Carta Marina . . . ," uses symbols to illustrate copper (shaded triangle), gold (star), iron (circle), and silver (shaded rectangle). A reduced, copper-plate edition, at a scale of 1:6,500,000, was made in 1572 (Ehrenberg, p. 9).

Georgius Agricola (1494–1555) wrote *De Re Metallica* (published in 1556), which included numerous woodblock prints of mining methods and ore veins. These latter prints are sketches of the land (not maps) showing how ore veins cut across hills, valleys, and other ore veins, and also the veins' directions and inclinations. In 1664, Abbé Coulon (fl. 1660s) produced a small geological map of France that was included in the book *Les Rivieres de France* (Ireland, p. 1231).

The history of geological maps must include Martin Lister (1638–1712), who never made such a map, but proposed ideas that led to later contributions. Lister wrote a paper in 1684 with a title that begins, "An Ingenious Proposal for a New Sort of Map of Countrys." On the first page he suggests "that a Soil or Mineral Map . . . were devised," and further notes, "The Soil might either be coloured, by variety of Lines, or Etchings; but the great care must be, very exactly to note upon the Map, where such and such Soils are bounded." Clearly, he is proposing a geological map with colored formations and exact contacts.

Modern geological maps include stratigraphic sequences, dip of bedding, faults, and unconformities. One of the earliest to recognize these was John Strachey (1671–1743), who drew a cross-section through coal mines in Somersetshire, England, in 1719. An examination of his section shows seven coal veins in their proper succession dipping 17° to the southeast, with a fault in the middle. The entire stratigraphic sequence is overlain by horizontal limestone, marl, and "yellowish spungey earth," indicating an unconformity. He also noted that one shale stratum could always be identified by the "Cockle Shells & Fern Branches" it contained.

Other geological maps followed in the 1700s and soon accounted for more maps than had been produced since the Egyptian papyrus, nearly three thousand years earlier. In 1726, Luigi Ferdinando Marsigli (1658–1730) showed mining and mineral locations in the Danube River basin on his "Mappa Metallographica." Christopher Packe (1686–1749) produced a map in 1743 of Canterbury illustrating "stone-hills" and "clay-hills." In 1755, Lewis Evans (1700–1756) produced "A General Map of the Middle British Colonies, in America" showing deposits of petroleum, clay, coal, freestone [sandstone], salt, and the glaciated part of northern Ohio. This map was reprinted with and without credit at least twenty-six times. The 1762 map by Georg Christian Füchsel (1722–1773) illustrated the Triassic strata of Thuringen, Germany, using numbers and letters described in the accompanying text (Ehrenberg, p. 12). The first hand-colored map is usually credited to Friedrich Gottlieb Gläser (17?–?) for his 1775 map, "Karte der Grafschaft Henneberg in Thuringen" ("Map of the Henneberg Dukedom"), published in Leipzig (Ireland, p. 1232).

In 1778, the map by Thomas Hutchin (1730–1789) of the Middle Atlantic States included "the Ohio River and all the Rivers which Fall into it." He showed locations of petroleum, coal, clay, and freestone, while noting in the text locations of salt springs, iron ore, and lead deposits. During the same year, Johann Friedrich Wilhelm Toussaint von Charpentier (1728–1805) published a map, "Petrographische Karte Des Churfürstenthums Sachsen . . . ," ("Petrographic Map of the Principality of Saxony"), in Germany, using eight colored tints to show granite, gneiss, schist, limestone, gypsum, sandstone, river sand, clay, and loam. Charpentier used a color-coded legend, but arranged the color boxes arbitrarily. Abraham Gottlob Werner (1749–1817) wrote that colors on geognostic maps should match those of the rocks with the bottom of each unit intensely colored. He also stressed the use of arrows to show the direction of dip and their length to reflect the angle of dip (Taylor, pp. 20–23).

Perhaps the most important geological maps of the 1700s were those published by Jean-Etiénne Guettard (1715–1786) in association with Philippi Buache (1700–1773), Antoine-Laurent Lavoisier (1743–1794), and Antoine Grimoald Monnet (1734–1817) (Taylor, pp. 18–20). The first, published in 1746, is a mineralogical map of France and England and illustrates three bands of rocks surrounding Paris (the sandy band, marly band, and schistose band). The bands were truncated at the English Channel, but Guettard carried them across to southern England, based primarily on information from the literature (Ehrenberg, pp. 11–12).

The second geological map by Guettard, "Carte Minéralogique . . . ," drawn by Buache, was of North America and showed the same three large belts of rocks: *Bande Sabloneuse* (sand) of the continental shelf along the East Coast, *Bande Marneuse* (marl) along the Gulf and Atlantic coastal plain, and finally the *Bande Schisteuse ou Métallique* (schist) covering the entire Mississippi Valley. There were thirty-nine symbols used on this first geological map of North America to show locations of rocks, minerals, springs, and fossils between the Atlantic and Rocky Mountains. The map was dated 1752, when it was presented before the Academie Royale des Sciences, although it was published only in 1756 (figure 1).

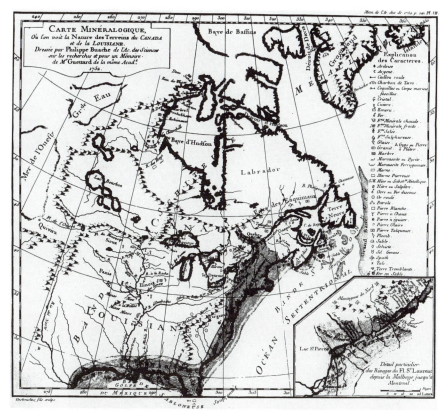

Figure 1. Jean-Etiénne Guettard's map entitled Carte Minéralogique Ou l'on voit la Nature des Terreins du Canada et de la Louisiane. *This first geological map of North America (reduced from the original scale of 1:19,300,000) shows three large bands of rocks:* Bande Sabloneuse, Bande Marneuse, *and* Bande Schisteuse ou Métallique. *The map is dated 1752, when it was presented before the Academie Royale des Sciences, although it was published only in 1756. Photograph courtesy of the University of Illinois Library at Champaign-Urbana.*

The last maps produced by Guettard, in collaboration with Lavoisier and Monnet, are in the *Atlas of France,* but only 31 of the 214 quadrangles were published. These maps, dated between 1766 and 1780, showed quarries, mines, and minerals by symbols. One innovation by Lavoisier was the addition of type sections in the margins of the maps; more precisely, they were composite sections. Monnet also put sections in the map margins, but these represented rock sections he had actually observed (Rudwick, p. 166).

The 1800s ushered in the modern geological map with stratigraphic order, structural symbols, cross sections, columns, and color. The map by William Smith (1769–1839) entitled "A Delineation of the Strata of England and Wales, with Part of Scotland" was published in 1815, with manuscript copies dated 1801. The colors used were extremely close to the actual colors of the various rocks and were also shaded with the darkest tones at the stratigraphic base of each unit (á la Werner) (Ehrenberg, p. 14). Smith's stratigraphic succession, but not age, was based on fossils found during his construction of canals and observations in collieries. Concerning fossils, Smith wrote in 1796 of the "wonderful order and regularity with which Nature has disposed of these singular productions and assigned to each Class its particular Stratum."

In 1809, William Maclure (1763–1840) published "A Map of the United States of America," with four later editions in 1811 and 1817. This copperplate-engraved map, with watercolors applied by hand, was the first geological map printed in America (Ehrenberg, pp. 20–21).

The geological map of the Paris Basin was published in 1811 by Georges Cuvier (1769–1832) and Alexandre Brongniart (1770–1847), showing the Tertiary stratigraphic succession and correlation based on fossils. They also established the convention of vertical color-keyed boxes, but with inverted spatial order. Other maps followed, such as the 1826 map entitled "Geognostische Karte von Deutschland" ("Geognostic Map of Germany") by Leopold Von Buch (1774–1852); the Geological Survey of Great Britain's inch-to-the-mile map series started in 1839 by Sir Henry Thomas de la Beche (1796–1855); the 1845 "Geological Map of the United States, Canada . . ." by Charles Lyell (1797–1875); and in the same year, the map of Russia by Roderick Impey Murchison (1792–1871) (Ireland, p. 1239).

The production of geological maps exploded by the mid-1800s with the successful use of chromolithography, which removed the necessity of hand coloring (Woodward, chap. 4). Two early examples are the 1843 "Carte géognostique das Plateau Tertiaire Parisien" by Félix Victor Raulin (1815–1905), which used four primary colors to produce eleven different tints, and the 1843 geological map "Essai d'une Carte Géologique du Globe Terrestre" at 1:50,000,000 scale by Ami Boué (1794–1881). In 1883, a method combining colors with patterns of dots and lines was developed by the August Hoen Company in the United States.

Another aspect that improved geological maps was the depiction of relief. Maps in the 1700s used a combination of shading and hachures, but hachures suggested relatively flat land with flat terraces. Contour lines first appeared in 1584 to indicate water depth (isobathic lines) (Robinson, p. 210), but their use was limited on land and hachures were used more extensively. Contour lines required accurate topographic measurements, and were initiated in Europe only in the 1830s and 1840s. European map-makers finally adopted contours in 1913, although the geological map of Belgium (1878–1894) used them.

Other important maps of the 1800s include an early map of Peru (1827); the map of the Andes (1835–1838) by Alcide Charles Victor Dessalines D'Orbigney (1802–1857); maps of various parts of Africa (1843, 1852, 1871); maps of the United States (1855 and 1884); a map of India (1855); several maps of Australia (1872–1875); the Western surveys of the United States (1870s-1880s); the first map of Japan (1899); and numerous, more detailed maps of selected areas (Marcou and Marcou, pp. 22–32; Ireland, p. 1270).

The 1900s expanded and improved upon maps of the late 1800s with more area being mapped, stratigraphic names correlated with adjacent regions, and improved base maps at uniform scales. Topographic base maps were normally produced in the field with a transit, but in the 1930s, aerial photography replaced this older method. Map scales by the U.S. Geological Survey went from 1:125,000 to 1:62,500 to 1:24,000 by the mid-1900s, affording greater detail. By the 1970s, satellite imagery and side-looking airborne radar (SLAR) provided synoptic views of the entire world. Improved base maps and various aerial images coupled with geophysics, drill holes, and computer techniques now provided the field geologist with new tools (figure 2). Many areas were mapped in detail for the first time and compilations of states, countries, and continents were

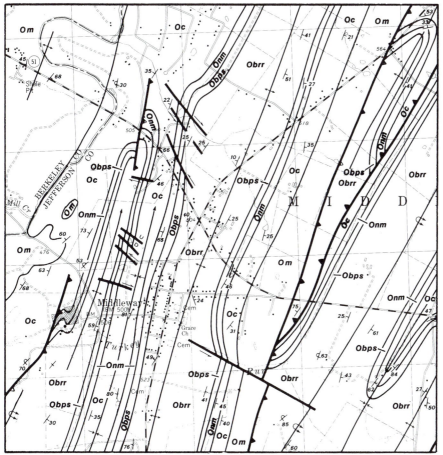

Figure 2. Part of a detailed geological map from eastern West Virginia at a scale of 1:24,000. Note the use of structural symbols (strike and dip, fold axes, faults) and formation contacts. All of the formations are Ordovician: Om = Martinsburg Formation, Oc = Chambersburg Limestone, Onm = New Market Limestone, Obps = Pinesburg Station Dolomite, and Obrr = Rockdale Run Formation. From the original color map by Dean, Lessing, and Kulander, 1990. With permission of the West Virginia Geological Survey.

published. These geologic overviews, along with ideas of plate tectonics, provided geologists with a new understanding of Earth.

Significant geological maps of the 1900s include the "Geologic Atlas of the United States" by the U.S. Geological Survey (1884–1945), a map of North America (1912), a map of Brazil (1919), a map of Russia (1922), a map of South Africa (1925), a map of Australia (1931), a map of the United States (1974), and a map of the world (1932–1939) (Ireland, p. 1270). In addition to these small-scale maps, thousands of detailed, large-scale maps have now been published worldwide.

Although many published articles discuss various aspects of the history and significance of geological maps, there are many areas where further research could be undertaken. A valuable aid to historians and geologists would be a computer compilation of geological maps that could be sorted by title, date, author, scale, source, or any combination, with a description, or discussion, of each map. Another topic with scant information is the development of structural symbols. Historical mapping techniques might be better un-

derstood by examining old field notes and correspondence. The influence of mapping ideas between individuals, countries, and continents also needs research. Very little has been written of historical geological maps from Africa, Asia, and South America. Also, the influence of aerial photography and topographic base maps would be an interesting contribution. Finally, the deteriorating maps and literature of geology must be preserved and archived for future research.

Peter Lessing

Bibliography

Ehrenberg, Ralph E. *The Earth Revealed—Aspects of Geologic Mapping.* Washington, D.C.: Library of Congress, 1989.

Harrell, James A., and V. Max Brown. "The World's Oldest Surviving Geological Map: The 1150 B.C. Turin Papyrus from Egypt." *Journal of Geology* 100 (1992): pp. 3–18.

Ireland, H. Andrew. "History of the Development of Geologic Maps." *Geological Society of America Bulletin* 54 (1943): pp. 1227–1280.

Marcou, Jules, and John B. Marcou. *Mapoteca Geologica Americana—A Catalogue of Geological Maps of America (North and South) 1752–1881 in Geographic and Chronologic Order.* Washington, D.C.: U.S. Geological Survey Bulletin 7, 1884.

Robinson, Arthur H. *Early Thematic Mapping in the History of Cartography.* Chicago: University of Chicago Press, 1982.

Rudwick, Martin J.S. "The Emergence of a Visual Language for Geological Science 1760–1840." *History of Science* 14 (1976): pp. 149–195.

Taylor, Kenneth L. "Early Geoscience Mapping, 1750–1830." *Proceedings of the Geoscience Information Society* 15 (1985): pp. 15–49.

Woodward, David, ed. *Five Centuries of Map Printing.* Chicago: University of Chicago Press, 1975.

See also Cartography; Geological Periodization; Geological Surveys; Geological Time; Geology; Humboldtian Science; Isolines; Mappaemundi; Mineralogy; Minerals and Crystals, Fifteenth to Eighteenth Centuries; Mining and Knowledge of the Earth; Paleontology; Stratigraphy

Geological Periodization

The historical process of naming and describing the periods of the Earth's history, including the timescale.

Every student of geology is expected to memorize the Geological Time Scale (see figure 1). Where did this extraordinary scale come from? In its present form it is less than a hundred years old, but it is a scale with its roots well back in the eighteenth century. The development of the scale (the recognition of geological eras, periods, and epochs) is closely linked with ideas about the age of the Earth and geological time. Eras, periods, and epochs define slices of time, the rocks formed during periods being referred to as systems, those deposited during an epoch forming a series.

The idea of a chronological sequence among the rocks of the Earth's crust originated independently in different countries. In regions where mineral deposits, and especially coal seams, had been mined, it was familiar knowledge from as early as the seventeenth century that a certain definite order could be recognized in the rock layers.

Important workers during the eighteenth century were Giovanni Arduino (1713–1795) in Italy, Johann Gottlob Lehmann (1719–1767) in Germany, and Peter Simon Pallas (1741–1811) in Russia. Other major contributors were Jean-Etienne Guettard (1715–1786), Antoine-Grimoald Magnate (1734–1817), Antoine Laurent Lavoisier (1743–1794), and Abbé J.L. Giraud-Soulavie (1753–1813) in France; Alberto Fortis (1741–1804) and others in Italy; and John Strachey (1671–1743) and John Michell (1724–1793) in England

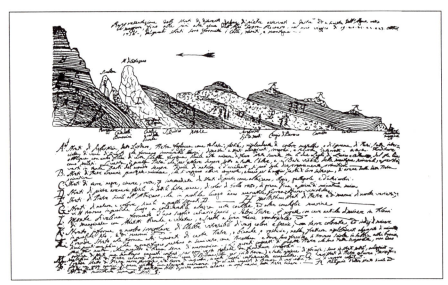

Figure 1. Giovanni Arduino drew this astonishing geological sketch of a section in the Valley del Agno, 35 kilometers (57 miles) northeast of his home town, Verona, Italy, in four days in 1758. Fourteen units are recognized over 26 kilometers (43 miles). The section is both stratigraphically and structurally accurate, thicknesses being indicated for the units M to Q. Intrusive bodies are recorded within the lowest unit A (crystalline Palaeozoic schists), at the bottom left, and several unconformities are implied (between H and I and L and M). Reproduced from Stegagno, G., Il Veronese Giovanni Arduino e il su contributo al progresso della scienza geologica. Verona, 1929.

(figure 2). This period is discussed in detail in François Ellenberger's *Histoire de la Geologie* (1988 and 1994), Gabriel Gohau's *A History of Geology* (English translation, 1991), and in Ezio Vaccari's *Giovanni Arduino (1714–1795)* (1993). By the end of the century there was a basic knowledge of the geology of Europe, and a stratigraphical succession had evolved and was systematized by Abraham Gottlob Werner (1747–1817). Werner distinguished four principal rock "formations" (in French, *terrain*), meaning a group of beds of the same or different nature, but formed in the same epoch: Primitive *(Ur Gebirge),* Transitional *(Übergangs Gebirge),* Secondary *(Flötz Gebirge),* and Tertiary and Volcanic *(Aufgeschwemmte Gebirge).* Alexander M. Ospovat (pp. 164–165), and Robert Jameson (chap. 4) explain and discuss in some detail Werner's concepts, and their influence, and Albritton (chap. 10) also covers this period of development.

The framework of the modern geological timescale was established between 1790 and 1840 (Zittel, chap. 6). During these decades there was enormous progress in the observation of geological phenomena and of their recording on maps, sections, and in reports. There was wide dissemination of information through publications of societies, governments, and wealthy individuals. Probably more important was the opportunity to travel (particularly after the Napoleonic wars), which many geologists used to advantage, and following personal contacts there was continuing correspondence between a wide range of personalities. An example was the Continental journey undertaken by William Buckland (1784–1856) in 1816, when he met Werner and Goethe and worked with many younger field geologists.

Nicolaas Rupke argues that the most formative period of stratigraphy was between 1810 and 1830, when the idea of a universal

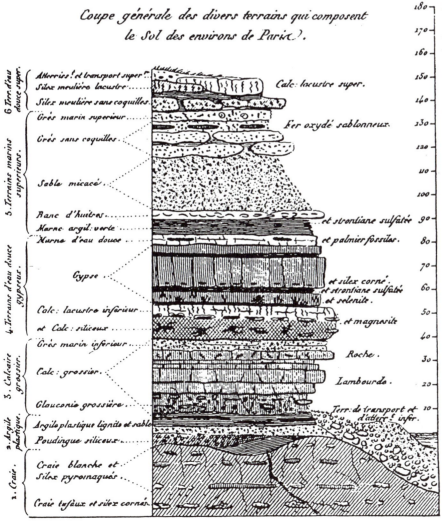

Figure 2. Baron Georges Cuvier published this stratigraphic section with Alexandre Brogniart of the rocks in the Paris Basin in 1822. Cuvier believed that the rapid changes in rock type and fossils were caused by catastrophic events. While the observations were correct, the catastrophic theory was generally not accepted by geologists. Reproduced from Branagan, D.F., et al. Beneath the Scenery. *Sydney: Science Press, 1970.*

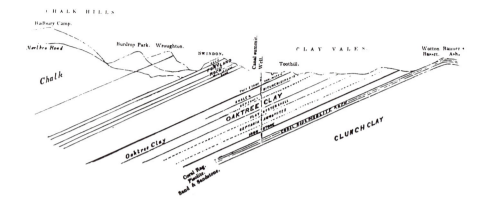

Figure 3. William Smith used the topography in his mapping, noting the characteristic landforms of various stratigraphic units. Section A (above) in Wiltshire, England, and of purely local extent, contrasts the Clay vales and the Chalk hills. The section below runs across Britain from Snowdon, Wales to London, and, insofar as possible, is three-dimensional, with an indication of the vertical exaggeration. The lower figure was drawn in 1817 and reproduced in the Philosophical Magazine *in 1833. Reproduced from Sheppard, T., "William Smith: His Maps and Memoirs."* Proceedings of the Yorkshire Geological Society *19 (1917): pp. 75–253; and Cox, Leslie Reginald, "New Light on William Smith and His Work."* Proceedings of the Yorkshire Geological Society *25 (1942): pp. 1–99.*

timescale was still a matter of controversy. Buckland was a key figure in the acceptance of such a scale, which he built up in four editions between 1814 and 1818, with an increasing emphasis on Secondary and Tertiary successions. Other geologists throughout Europe followed suit with stratigraphical scales during the 1820s, although Alexander von Humboldt (1769–1859) warned geologists to avoid national vanity and keep to accepted names. However, there had been a shift from Wernerian stratigraphy, with its emphasis on Primary rocks and their composition, to the historical geology of Cuvier, based on the fossiliferous rocks and their paleontology (Rupke, chap.10).

Georges Cuvier (1769–1832) with Alexandre Brongniart (1777–1847) established new standards and methods in stratigraphic geology. Cuvier thought that changes in the fossils found in rock successions indicate sudden revolutions when deposition was halted and living forms destroyed, to be replaced later by new forms, newly created (figure 3) (Laudan, chap. 7). This "catastrophic theory" exerted a great influence in geology for many years.

An important influence during these decades—despite some criticisms of it by Rachel Laudan (pp. 165–168) and Anthony Hallam (chap. 3)—was the work of William Smith (1769–1839), his method of stratigraphical succession based on fossils (as particular items and without specific zoological identification), and his excellent geological maps. Smith's ideas, maps, and sections (figure 3), rather than his scanty writings, justify his important place in the history of geology.

In 1815 Smith wrote that his accurate surveys and study of the strata prove that there is great regularity in their position and thickness, and that each stratum has distinctive properties and contains specific fossils. Smith arranged the rocks in their true order from his Killas (present Cambrian and Silurian) of Wales up to the Tertiary rocks of the London Basin. Hugh Torrens (pp. 108–117) discusses how Smith's ideas and the use of fossils in stratigraphy were transmitted from Europe to America between 1800 and 1840.

In 1822 Cuvier was still using Werner's terms Primary, Secondary, and Tertiary, but they were now three divisions of geological time, with no reference to the origin of the rock materials on which Werner had based much of his classification. Similarly William Maclure in the United States used Wernerian terms because they were "generally understood," and he wished to avoid a proliferation of names, but he did not accept Werner's theory of origin of the rocks (Jameson, pp. 251–259). In 1822 the local names used by Smith and others for units of the Secondary rocks in England began to be modified into the period names used today. In their book *The Geology of England and Wales,* William D. Conybeare (1787–1857) and William Phillips (1775–1828) used the word "Carboniferous" for the popularly called "Coal Measures," including also the underlying Carboniferous limestone and Old Red Sandstone, suggesting that the Carboniferous fell somewhere between Werner's Flötz and Transitional Classes.

The year 1822 also saw the publication of Omalius d'Halloy's geological map covering a large part of Western Continental Europe based on his ten years of fieldwork, largely on foot (Berry, pp. 69–72). He divided the "Secondary terrains" into five parts. Of the names he suggested, only Cretaceous continues to be used, for "what has already been called the chalk" (Latin *creta* = "chalk"). The term was rapidly used in North America by Lardner Vanuxem (1792–1848).

Alexander von Humboldt, in 1795, used the term "Jura limestone" for a rock unit occurring in the Jura mountains, regarding it as a distinct formation, but it included only part of the present Jurassic (Berry, pp. 74–75). D'Halloy had shown the extent of the Jurassic rocks in the Paris Basin in 1813, calling them "Old horizontal limestone," which he showed lying unconformably over Palaeozoic slates. However it was not until 1829 that Ami Boué fixed its position in the stratigraphic succession and Alexandre Brongniart used the term *Terrain Jurassique,* which was quickly accepted.

About 1830 Adam Sedgwick (1785–1873) began mapping deformed rocks in Wales. His friend Roderick Murchison (1792–1871) also became involved, looking at the slightly younger rocks in the same region. Over the next four years they carried out remarkable fieldwork in quite difficult country.

In the same year Charles Lyell discussed the subdivisions of the Tertiary into epochs in his *Principles of Geology,* basing the divisions on a comparison of their respective fossils. All formations since the coming of humans he called "Recent." The older tertiary strata he

divided into four, the oldest containing an extremely small number of fossils identifiable with living species, with the progressively younger strata each containing more and more identifiable living species. On this basis he named the Newer and Older Pliocene, Miocene, and Eocene epochs.

Field activity continued at a rapid rate in Europe and around the world at this time. In 1834 Friedrich A. von Alberti (1795–1878) studied the three series of Bunter (at the base), Muschelkalk, and Keuper in Germany. He worked around Wurtemberg, examining the rocks for their economic mineral content. After learning of the work on similar rocks in the Vosges Mountains by Élie de Beaumont and others, he published his monograph grouping the three rock units as the Trias[sic] (that is, three layers) formation. The name was reinforced by Friedrich A. Quensted (1809–1889) in 1843, although there were differences of opinion with Alberti's interpretation and their followers continued to differ for years (Zittel, pp. 461–462; Woodward, p. 114).

A year later Roderick Murchison, who worked at a furious pace, published the first results of his work on the Silurian System. He wrote, "There was required a comprehensive term [for] the whole group and distinguished from the old red sandstone above, and the slaty rocks below. . . . I suggest, that as the great mass of rocks . . . traverses the kingdom of our ancestors the Silures, the term 'Silurian System' should be adopted" (Wilmarth, p. 80; Secord, p. 98).

In August of the same year Sedgwick divided the old Transition (greywacke or slate) series of northern England and Wales into three groups: Lower Cumbrian, chiefly slates containing no fossils; Middle Cumbrian, composed of slates, conglomerates, and porphyries, containing fossils; and Upper Cumbrian, containing fossiliferous limestone that "approaches the lower beds of Mr. Murchison's Silurian System." This last phrase was to prove the germ of a long-lasting feud (Secord, pp. 107–109).

Further mapping showed that the Silurian system as defined by Murchison overlapped Sedgwick's Cambrian system, and argument on these divisions persisted for many years, and the two great contributors to stratigraphy ceased to work together and even to communicate. However, unlike controversies such as the Devonian argument, the quarrel had little effect on other geologists. James Secord's *Controversy in Victorian Geology: The Cambrian-Silurian Dispute* tells this story.

The first attempt to group together periods and epochs came in 1838 when Sedgwick suggested the name "Palaeozoic" (ancient life) era for the previously named periods (Silurian and part of the Cambrian System). The lower, apparently unfossiliferous portion of the Cambrian he called "Protozoic" (Secord, pp. 137–141). John Phillips (1800–1874) extended the term "Palaeozoic" in 1840 to include the Devonian and the Protozoic. He also mentioned the similar terms "Mesozoic" (middle life) and "Kainozoic" (recent life) as useful and the following year pressed this idea of three major eras more strongly. William Barton Rogers and Henry Darwin Rogers adopted the term "Palaeozoic" for rocks in the United States in 1844, earning the ire of James Hall, who preferred using "New York System" (Rabbitt, vol. 1: p. 66).

Lyell continued to work in detail on the young successions in 1839, giving the name Pleistocene to rocks he had earlier (1833) called Recent, noting they contained some extinct forms. Desnoyers in 1829, separated these rocks as a group, the Quaternary, as post-Tertiary, but Henri Reboul in 1833 used the term "Quaternary" in its presently accepted sense as a period. The much older name Diluvium continued to be used in Germany into the twentieth century. Terms such as Anthropozoic, Anthropogene, and Holocene were hopefully proposed by some authors. Only the last term caught on, being now used in some modern classifications for the Recent rocks, younger than Pleistocene.

In 1837 William Lonsdale (1794–1871) recognized that fossils from Devon are younger than those in Silurian rocks and older than those found in Carboniferous rocks. This was a spur to naming the Devonian Period by Murchison and Sedgwick in 1839. The definition originated in work begun some years earlier mapping Transition greywacke and limestone rocks, Old Red Sandstone, and the sorting out of rocks that were complexly folded and faulted and containing a variety of fossils. These were more difficult to map than the relatively undeformed Secondary strata. Sedgwick and Murchison in cooperation, and working in opposition to Henry De la Beche (1796–1855) but with a large cast of contributors (as is excitingly told in Martin Rudwick's book *The Great Devonian Controversy*), sorted out much of the stratigraphy in southwestern England. Sedgwick and Murchison wrote that "as Devonshire affords the best type of the fossils of this intermediate system [between the Carboniferous and the Silurian], the authors propose to substitute the term Devonian for old red sandstone, and they

hope that the organic remains, discovered in that county, will enable continental geologists to detect . . . a system of strata hitherto supposed to be almost peculiar to the British Isles" (Wilmarth, p. 79). And so it proved. In fact the best sequence of the Devonian was found in Belgium and the Rhineland, and while Murchison and Sedgwick worked there, Ferdinand Roemer (b. 1818) and André-Hubert Dumont (1809–1857) were among those who carried out detailed mapping on the continent. Sedgwick and Murchison were aware that American geologists had been studying rocks, in the Lake Erie region, of similar age to those they named Devonian, and, in fact, hurried publication of their results to gain priority for the Devonian system, which might otherwise have ended up as the Erian (Speakman, p. 76).

Murchison's annual journeys into Continental Europe took him to Russia in May 1840. He was joined by Philippe É. de Verneuil (b. 1805). Entertained by Humboldt in Berlin, Murchison wrote to Sedgwick: "Our classification [Cambrian, Silurian, and Devonian] is already accepted by the Prussian geologists. . . . The Devonian is . . . greeted . . . a good name." As well as studying the Devonian and older Palaeozoic rocks, Murchison and Verneuil examined a succession ("a vast series of marls, schists, limestones, sandstones and conglomerates") found above the Carboniferous rocks west of the Ural Mountains. From this work the Permian system was named in 1841 by Murchison.

Thus, much of the geological timescale had come into use by the early 1840s, and it began to be carried by explorers, official geologists, and traveling gentlemen to many parts of the world. However it would be many years before the necessary fieldwork, fossil collecting, and analysis would establish its universal validity. Detailed work on the Tertiary saw the term "Oligocene" suggested by Heinrich Beyrich (1815–1896) in 1854 to include the rocks regarded by Lyell as Upper Eocene and by himself earlier as Lower Miocene. Otherwise the scale served well in Europe. Across the oceans it was not so simple. Coal measures in the antipodes did not seem to be quite Carboniferous, and so it proved many years later (most were Permian). North American geologists did not find the term "Carboniferous" ideal, and many years after its original naming a subdivision of Pennsylvanian (coal-bearing succession) separated by a significant time break from the underlying Mississippian became the established terminology in that region. Alexander Winchell (b. 1824) proposed "Mississippian" in 1869, and H.S. Williams modified this in 1891, also suggesting the term "Pennsylvanian."

The Cambrian/Silurian controversy remained unresolved until 1879, when Charles Lapworth (1842–1920) pointed out that amid all the confusion one fact stood out— that the strata contain three distinct faunas, the oldest being in well-accepted Cambrian rocks, while the youngest fauna occur in clearly defined Silurian beds. The second fauna occurs in the rocks of the intermediate or so-called Upper Cambrian or Lower Silurian system. Lapworth wrote that these intermediate rocks "lie within the territory of the Ordovices: a tribe as undaunted in its resistance to the Romans as the Silures. . . . Here [is] the . . . appropriate title for the central system of the Lower Palaeozoic. It should be called the Ordovician System, after the name of this old British tribe" (Wilmarth, pp. 83–84; Zittel, p. 444).

The rocks below the quite fossiliferous Cambrian rocks took a long time to sort out, and much of the story belongs to the New World. Nurtured on the rocks of Wales, William Logan (1798–1875) spent many years after 1842 trying to unravel the complex geology of eastern Canada, and adjacent states of the United States, but there were many disagreements between various workers. Logan and T. Sterry Hunt (1826–1892) in 1855 used the terms "Huronian" and "Laurentian" systems, although they believed the former was equivalent to Sedgwick's Cambrian. Later workers (a committee made up of American and Canadian workers in the Lake Superior region in 1905) placed the Huronian in the pre-Cambrian, using the term "Pre-Cambrian" as the major heading.

J.W. Foster and J.D. Whitney introduced the term "Azoic" in 1850 for unfossiliferous rocks in the Lake Superior region that appeared to underlie rocks apparently containing the lowest forms of animal life (Rabbitt, vol. 1, p. 85). Azoic became widely used, for instance in Central Europe by Joseph Barrande in 1852 (Zittel, p. 446) and was accepted by James D. Dana in 1855 (Rabbitt, vol. 1, p. 119). But Dana suggested the alternative term "Archaean" in 1872 when he described rocks in the Northeastern United States which he believed were "equivalents of the oldest known Azoic rocks of Canada . . . [but] because . . . the era was not . . . destitute of life, I propose to use . . . the general term Archaean from the Greek, pertaining to the beginning." This term became accepted for the oldest known rocks, and sev-

enteen years later (1879) S.F. Emmons wrote, "The Huronian, Keweenawian, and Grand Canyon Series, and whatever other clastic formations occur between the Cambrian and the Archean, should be included in one grand group of equivalent rank with the Archean, Paleozoic etc., I . . . suggest the name Proterozoic for this new group, signifying that its life was earlier than that of the other groups, without committing ourselves as yet to the statement that it was the first to appear on earth." C.R. Van Hise in 1892 supported Proterozoic and noted the U.S. Geological Survey's preferred general scheme for the lower part of the geological column: Paleozoic (consisting of Carboniferous, Devonian, Silurian, and Cambrian), Proterozoic (Algonkian), and Archean (Zittel, pp. 439–440).

However Archibald Geikie (1835–1924) in Scotland was not happy about such proposals, and in 1893 he felt that to prove any crystalline schists were "Archaean" they had to be found overlain by the oldest fossiliferous rocks. If such evidence was not available, the use of a precise term to denote a particular geological era was undesirable. Geikie thought it "less objectional to adopt some vague general term which nevertheless expresses the only homotaxial relation [that is, containing the same fossils] about which there can be no doubt. For this purpose the designation 'Pre-Cambrian,' already in use, seems suitable." Nevertheless Geikie had earlier (1862 and 1876) used the term "Laurentian" for some of the Scottish gneisses. This episode is discussed in J.G.C. Anderson's 1979 article and in David Oldroyd's *The Highlands Controversy* (1990). As late as 1925 the U.S. Geological Survey used the term "Proterozoic" as synonymous with Pre-Cambrian, but today Precambrian (without a hyphen) includes Proterozoic and Archean.

With the establishment of the International Geological Congress movement in the 1870s, there was an attempt to systematize the geological timescale, and by 1886 most terms were agreed upon, although some European geologists wanted to have similar endings for systems, replacing Cretaceous, Carboniferous, Devonian, and Silurian by Cretacic, Carbonic, Devonic, and Siluric (Rabbitt, vol. 2, p. 132), an idea that never eventuated.

Thus the story is a complex one. In this attempt to establish an order of formation of rock layers, at times there has been a desire to subdivide, at others to group layers together. The story began locally, but expanded to comprehend a theory of universality, the expectation that the same succession would occur worldwide. Only when study of the problem moved back to the local level and detailed maps and sections were compiled could a solution be envisaged. Exchange of information and travel during the early nineteenth century saw the story unravel, first through work on the gently inclined, relatively undisturbed Secondary strata of England and France. The older strata caused more problems because of their structural complexity, deformation, and frequent absence of fossils. The younger Diluvium, in many parts of Europe the result of the Pleistocene Ice Age, was also a puzzling complication that did not begin to unravel until the mid-nineteenth century.

By 1900 the geological scale of eras, periods, and epochs as we know it was essentially defined, and generally accepted worldwide, although, surprisingly, the absolute ages of the strata were not yet established. This was not possible until radioactivity had been discovered and geologists began to look forward to knowing, with some accuracy, the age of the Earth (Kummel, chap. 1). Did this mean the end of the geological timescale? Not a bit of it. Students still have to learn it. Its growth may be extraordinary, but it is much better than it might have been. Terms such as Psychozoic, Progonic, and Anthracolithic fortunately never gained popularity!

Of the terms presently used we can note the following sequence of growth, determined from evidence in various localities.

Tertiary Period, named by Arduino (Italy, 1760)

Jurassic Period, suggested by Humboldt (Italy, 1799), Boué (France, 1829)

Carboniferous Period, Conybeare and Phillips (England, 1822)

Cretaceous Period, Omalius d'Halloy (Belgium, 1822)

Quaternary, Desnoyers (France, 1829)

Recent Epoch, Lyell (France, 1833)

Pliocene Epoch, Lyell (France, 1833)

Miocene Epoch, Lyell (France, 1833)

Eocene Epoch, Lyell (France, 1833)

Triassic Period, Alberti (Germany, 1834)

Silurian Period, Murchison (England and Wales, 1835)

Cambrian Period, Sedgwick (England and Wales, 1835)

Palaeozoic Era, Sedgwick (England, 1838)

Pleistocene Epoch, Lyell (England, 1839)

Devonian Period, Sedgwick and Murchison (England, 1839)

Cainozoic Era, Phillips (England, 1840 and 1841)

Mesozoic Era, Phillips (England, 1840 and 1841)

Permian Period, Murchison (Russia, 1841)

Oligocene Epoch, Beyrich (Germany, 1854)

Mississippian (originally an Epoch), A. Winchell (United States, 1869)

Archaean Period, Dana (United States, 1872)

Ordovician Period, Lapworth (England, 1879)

Proterozoic Era, S.F. Emmons (United States, 1888)

Pre-Cambrian, A. Geikie (Scotland, 1889)

Pennsylvanian (Epoch), H.S. Williams (United States, 1891)

Tertiary remains as a tribute to the eighteenth-century pioneers, such as Arduino, and Quaternary is an added tribute to these pioneers by following the same method of classification. We have a series of names based on locality of key regions: these are Jurassic, Devonian, Permian, Mississippian, and Pennsylvanian. Silurian, Cambrian, and Ordovician are also essentially locality names. Carboniferous and Cretaceous are based on dominant composition. There are a series of Tertiary epochs using variations of fossil content and Greek terms to indicate the dawn of recent, major recent, and most recent eras based on Early Life (Palaeozoic), Middle Life (Mesozoic), and Recent Life (Cainozoic). The unfortunate introduction of Cenozoic for Cainozoic makes nonsense of the original derivation, for Cenos means empty! Triassic remains the odd one out. It is merely the threefold grouping of a set of well-defined rock types.

As examples of scientists coming to consensus in the face of ambiguous data, there are few cases to rival the development of the names of the geological periods. The processes of controversy and building consensus have been examined thoroughly in a few cases, notably by Martin Rudwick, James Secord, and David Oldroyd. Similar instances in this complex story merit similar treatment by historians. Such studies would serve also to reinforce the idea of the universality of geology and that its growth as a science was the product of work all over the world, by geologists from widely differing backgrounds, forming an interactive network and not merely a hierarchy.

The spate of publications in various languages in the past ten years or so on the history of the earth sciences, and particularly related to the development of stratigraphy, indicates a vigorous scholarship has developed on matters that had previously been widely interpreted in a simplistic manner and taught to generations of geologists as proclaimed gospel. While this is particularly important for an understanding of the fabric of geology, there have been some excesses in degrading the work of formerly important founding figures, such as William Smith and Charles Lyell. It must not be forgotten that they remain significant contributors to the development of the science. Perhaps the most important change in interpretation and understanding of the history is that although we know there have been some key players, the growth of the subject during the eighteenth and early nineteenth centuries depended on a network of contributors, many of whose work for various reasons, has, in the past, been neglected.

David F. Branagan

Bibliography

Albritton, Claude C. *The Abyss of Time: Changing Conceptions of the Earth's Antiquity after the Sixteenth Century.* Los Angeles: Jeremy P. Tarcher, 1986.

Anderson, J.G.C. "The Concept of Precambrian Geology and the Recognition of Precambrian Rocks in Scotland and Ireland." In *History of Concepts in Precambrian Geology,* edited by W.O. Kupsch and W.A.S. Sarjeant. *Geological Association of Canada Special Paper* 19 (1979): pp. 1–11.

Berry, William B.N. *Growth of a Prehistoric Time Scale, Based on Organic Evolution.* San Francisco: W.H. Freeman and Company, 1968.

Ellenberger, François. *Histoire de la Geologie.* 2 vols. Paris: Technique et Documentation (Lavoisier), 1988, 1994.

Gohau, Gabriel. *Les Sciences de la Terre aux XVII et XVIIIᵉ siecles. Naissance de la geologie.* Paris: Albin Michel, 1990. *A History of Geology.* Revised and translated by Albert V. Carozzi and Marguerite Carozzi. New Brunswick and London: Rutgers Press, 1991.

Hallam, Anthony. *Great Geological Controversies.* Oxford and New York: Oxford University Press, 1989.

Jameson, Robert. *The Wernerian Theory of the Neptunian Origin of Rocks.* Edited by George W. White. Contributions to the History of Geology. New York: Hafner Press, 1976.

Kummel, Bernhard. *History of the Earth: An Introduction to Historical Geology.* San Francisco: W.H. Freeman and Company, 1961.

Laudan, Rachel. *From Mineralogy to Geology: The Foundations of a Science, 1650–1830.* Chicago: University of Chicago Press, 1985.

Lyell, Charles. *Principles of Geology.* New introduction by Martin J.S. Rudwick. Chicago: University of Chicago Press, 1990.

Oldroyd, David. *The Highlands Controversy: Constructing Geological Knowledge through Fieldwork in Nineteenth Century Britain.* Chicago: University of Chicago Press, 1990.

Ospovat, Alexander M. "Werner's Concept of the Basement Complex." In *History of Concepts in Precambrian Geology,* edited by W.O. Kupsch and W.A.S. Sarjeant, *Geological Association of Canada Special Paper* 19 (1979): pp. 161–170.

Rabbitt, Mary C. *Minerals, Lands, and Geology for the Common Defence and General Welfare: United States Geological Survey.* Vol. 1, before 1879. Vol. 2, 1879–1904. Washington, D.C.: United States Government Printing Office, 1979, 1980.

Rudwick, Martin J.S. *The Great Devonian Controversy.* Chicago: University of Chicago Press, 1985.

Rupke, Nicolaas A. *The Great Chain of History: William Buckland and the English School of Geology 1814–1849.* Oxford: Clarendon Press, 1983.

Secord, James A. *Controversy in Victorian Geology: The Cambrian-Silurian Dispute.* Princeton: Princeton University Press, 1986.

Speakman, Colin. *Adam Sedgwick: Geologist and Dalesman 1785–1873.* Broadoak, U.K.: Broadoak Press, 1982.

Torrens, Hugh. "The Transmission of Ideas in the Use of Fossils in Stratigraphic Analysis from England to America, 1800–1840." *Earth Sciences History* 9, no. 2 (1990): pp. 108–117.

Vaccari, Ezio. *Giovanni Arduino (1714–1795).* Firenze: Leo S. Olschki, 1993.

Wilmarth, M. Grace. *The Geological Time Classification of the United States Geological Survey Compared with Other Classifications, Accompanied by the Original Definitions of Era, Period, and*

Epoch Terms. U.S. Geological Survey Bulletin 769. Washington, D.C.: U.S. Government Printing Office, 1925.

Woodward, Horace B. *History of Geology.* London: Watts and Co, 1911.

Zittel, Karl Alfred von. *History of Geology and Palaeontology.* Translated by Maria M. Ogilvie-Gordon. London: Walter Scott, 1901. Reprint. Weinheim, Germany: J. Cramer, 1962.

See also Actualism, Uniformitarianism, Catastrophism; Age of the Earth; Cycle of Erosion; Deluge; Dendrochronology; Diluvialism; Earth in Decay; Evolution and the Geosciences; Geological Time; Geology; Paleomagnetism; Paleontology; Plutonists, Neptunists, Vulcanists; Stratigraphy; Taconic Controversy

Geological Societies

Formed as geology became a specialized science.

Developments in the geological sciences are linked to the work of various scientific societies. The early scientific societies generally began with broad agendas, but some eventually became specialized, corresponding to the increased specialization of the scientific community.

Four years after the Royal Society of London was founded, the French Academy of Sciences held its first meeting in 1666. Philippe Buache became *adjoint geographe* of the academy in 1730 and held that position until his death three years later. This was the only academy position that was specifically associated with an earth science until a 1785 reorganization led to the formation of a class for natural history and mineralogy. The French Revolution abolished the academy in 1793 (Faul and Faul).

Another scientific society that would become instrumental in the development of the earth sciences was formed in Edinburgh, Scotland, around 1739. The Philosophical Society had been organized by Colin Maclaurin. Maclaurin's protégé, James Hutton, joined the Philosophical Society in 1767. Hutton's work in geology largely influenced the direction of modern geology. In his *Abstract of a Dissertation,* Hutton proposed that the Earth changed over a long period of time because of natural processes. The society was superseded by the Royal Society of Edinburgh, where Hutton became an officer. The first volume of the *Society's Transactions* was published around 1788 and contained Hutton's *Abstract* (Dean).

Several general scientific societies sprang up in the mid to late 1700s and served the earth sciences through the interests of their members. One example is the American Philosophical Society, founded in Philadelphia in 1743. The society merged with the American Society for Promoting Useful Knowledge in 1769. The merged organization was served by one of its presidents, Thomas Jefferson. Jefferson was involved in many scientific pursuits, one of which was his involvement in paleontology. He was responsible for naming the fossilized ground sloth, *Megalonyx,* and presented a paper to the society on this topic in 1797 (Faul and Faul; Schneer, p. 97).

Around 1800 scientific societies became notably specialized in geological topics. In 1799, the British Mineralogical Society was founded predominantly by mineral collectors. One of its influential members, the mineralogist and geologist William Babington, served as president from 1822 to 1824 (Faul and Faul). Another specialized society, the American Mineralogical Society, formed in 1799 to investigate minerals and fossils and to explore their natural and chemical histories in the United States (Merrill, pp. 19–21).

Shortly after, in 1807, the first learned society dedicated specifically to geology was founded (Rudwick, p. 325). The Geological Society of London sought to maintain a geological library and collection, to discuss and disseminate observations, and to standardize nomenclature. The membership rose to two hundred in 1811. The Geological Society of London's *Transactions* first appeared in 1811, followed three years later by its second volume. Among the work published in the *Transactions* were reports and papers by John Maculloch. Maculloch's "Sketch of the Mineralogy of Skye" was published in 1816, while he was president of the society (Faul and Faul, pp. 116–123).

Differences in geological thought of the eighteenth and nineteenth centuries centered around theories of geological formation proposed by Abraham Gottlob Werner and James Hutton, whose interests were supported by different scientific societies. One of Werner's followers, Robert Jameson, founded the Wernerian Natural History society in Edinburgh in 1808. Jameson became the first president of the society and retained that position for forty-six years. Werner was the society's first honorary member. The society's *Memoirs* were published from 1811 to 1839. Where the Wernerians found support in the Wernerian Natural History Society, many supporters of the competing school of thought, proposed by Hutton, were found in the Royal Society of Edinburgh (Dean).

Other scientific societies formed that were directly or peripherally interested in geological developments, including the American Geological Society, founded in New Haven in 1819. The society did not publish, dissolving in 1828. Four years later, the Geological Society of Pennsylvania was established. The society was composed of both scientific and business-oriented individuals interested in promoting a geological survey. After an act was passed in 1836 authorizing such a survey, the group disbanded (Faul and Faul, pp. 161–165).

In 1831, the British Association for the Advancement of Science (BAAS) was formed. Evidence of the association's continued interest in geology existed in the publication of a considerable series of earthquake reports by Robert Mallet from 1850 to 1858. The association also established a seismological committee whose secretary was the seismologist John Milne. Milne began producing the association's seismological *General Reports* in 1881 (Hall).

The Edinburgh Geological Society, founded in 1834, largely represented the Huttonian position. The Association of American Geologists and Naturalists, formed in Philadelphia in 1840, later became the American Association for the Advancement of Science (AAAS) in 1848 (Dean, p. 229; Faul and Faul, p. 162). Descending from the AAAS was the Geological Society of America, formed in 1888 (Fairchild, p. 61).

International exchange of research and development in geology followed some years later. In 1878, the first International Geological Congress was held in connection with the Paris Exposition. Organized by the Geological Society of France, the congress attracted 325 geologists. The congress served as a forum for presentations of papers and as an exhibition site for rocks, fossils, maps, and other geologic materials (Thurston, pp. 16–17).

The course of several centuries showed the gradual change from predominantly general scientific societies to the rise of the more specialized geological societies. Numerous geological societies have since formed around the world, some devoted to specific interests within geology.

The influence geological societies had on the progress of geology is questionable. For example, Laudan argues that institutional historians erroneously credit the development of nineteenth-century geology to the formation of the Geological Society of London. Rather she maintains that for a number of years the society contributed to the "stagnation" and "deterioration" of geology (Laudan, p. 527).

Some geological societies have been studied reasonably well, while there are many other major and provincial geological societies that have yet to be investigated in any way by science historians. For a history of geological societies see one-time secretary of the society Herman LeRoy Fairchild's *The Geological Society of America: 1888–1930* and M.J.S. Rudwick's "The Foundation for the Geological Society of London: Its Scheme for Co-Operative Research and Its Struggle for Independence." For other more specialized societies see W. Campbell Smith's article "The Mineralogical Society 1876–1976" and Earl Ingerson's "The Geochemical Society." For discussions of geological societies outside North America and England, see Karl Andrée's and Raymond Hocart's articles listed in the bibliography.

Valerie N. Morphew

Bibliography

André, Karl. "Aus der Geschichte der Deutschen Geologische Gesellschaft." *Deutsche Geologische Gesellschaft Zeitschrift* 100 (1950): pp. 1–24.

Dean, Dennis R. *James Hutton and the History of Geology.* Ithaca, N.Y.: Cornell University Press, 1992.

Fairchild, Herman LeRoy. *The Geological Society of America: 1888–1930.* New York: Geological Society of America, 1932.

Faul, Henry, and Carol Faul. *It Began with a Stone: A History of Geology from the Stone Age to the Age of Plate Tectonics.* New York: John Wiley and Sons, 1983.

Geikie, Sir Andrew. *The Founders of Geology.* 2d ed. New York: Dover Publications, Inc., 1962.

Hall, D.H. *History of the Earth Sciences during the Scientific and Industrial Revolutions with Special Emphasis on the Physical Geosciences.* Amsterdam: Elsevier Scientific Publishing Company, 1976.

Hocart, Raymond. "La Société Française de Mineralogie de 1928 à 1953," *Bulletin de la Société Française de Mineralogie* 77, nos. 1–3 (1954): pp. 13–22.

Ingerson, Earl. "The Geochemical Society." *Geotimes* 6 (1962): pp. 8–14.

Laudan, Rachel. "Ideas and Organizations in Geology: A Case Study in Institutional History." *ISIS* 68 (1977): pp. 527–538.

Merrill, George P. *The First One Hundred Years of American Geology.* New York: Hafner Publishing Company, 1964.

Rudwick, M.J.S. "The Foundation for the Geological Society of London: Its Scheme for Co-operative Research and Its Struggle for Independence." *British Journal for the History of Science* 1 (1963): pp. 325–355.

Schneer, Cecil J., ed. *Two Hundred Years of Geology in America: Proceedings of the New Hampshire Bicentennial Conference on the History of Geology.* Hanover, N.H.: University Press of New England, 1979.

Smith, W. Campbell. "The Mineralogical Society, 1876–1976." *Mineralogical Magazine* 40 (1976): pp. 430–439.

Thurston, William. "The First International Geological Congress." *Geotimes* 13 (1968): pp. 16–17.

See also Geographical Societies; Geological Surveys; Geology; Geophysical Societies and International Organizations; International Organizations in Oceanography; Jesuits and the Earth; Masons and the Earth; Meteorological Societies; Meteorological Observing Systems, Early History

Geological Surveys

Government agencies sponsoring geological mapping.

Most of the literature by historians about geological surveys focuses on institutions sponsored by regional or national governments for the mapping of geological structures and identifying of geological resources within their boundaries. Earlier texts chronicle geological surveys and offer celebratory rather than analytical biographies. More contemporary pieces probe into the social and intellectual contexts in which geological surveys were undertaken. By studying the institutions under which surveys were organized and the discipline of geology itself, historians have gained a deeper understanding of the roles of geological surveys in geoscience.

The British Geological Survey grew out of the interests of both the Geological Society of London and the Royal Society of London. Among the early histories of British geological surveys are John Flett's *First Hundred Years of the Geological Survey of Great Britain* (1937) and Sir Edward Bailey's *Geological Survey of Great Britain* (1952). While Flett and Bailey are primarily chronological, more recent works, such as Harold Wilson's

Down to Earth: 150 Years of the British Geological Survey (1985), offer a more comprehensive account. All of these texts, however, provide a useful sketch of the major events and individuals associated with geological surveys in Great Britain.

Appointed in 1835, Henry Thomas De la Beche (1796–1855) became the first director of the British Geological Survey. De la Beche gained his early experience on the Ordnance Survey and belonged to both the Geological Society and the Royal Society. His publications include *Manual of Geology* (1831) and *Theoretical Researches in Geology* (1834).

Working for the first four years as the only member of the British Geological Survey, De la Beche was also responsible for the Museum of Economic Geology and the Mining Record Office of the survey. De la Beche played a key role in founding the Royal School of Mines, which remained a division of the survey until 1872. It later became known as the Imperial College of Science. Having simultaneously created a geological bureaucracy and a research institution, De la Beche is considered one of the most influential institution builders in nineteenth century geology.

In "The Geological Survey of Great Britain as a Research School, 1839–1855," James A. Secord analyzes De la Beche's role in the organization of the British Geological Survey as well as his intellectual perspectives on geology. Secord argues that while the establishment of the survey was certainly important to the professionalization of science in Britain, the theoretical issues associated with the survey and De la Beche are often overlooked. Interested in ancient environments, De la Beche focused the theoretical work of the survey around that concern. One example of this approach was De la Beche's "demand for extremely detailed studies of the stratigraphy of individual localities" (Secord, p. 244).

De la Beche's successor also made substantial contributions to the survey. Sir Roderick Murchison (1792–1871), appointed second director in 1855, was known for his abilities with stratigraphy. A member of the Geological Society and the Royal Society, too, Murchison wrote *The Silurian System* (1839), *The Geology of Russia in Europe and the Ural Mountains* (1845), and *Siluria* (1854) before being appointed to the directorship.

Bailey's *Geological Survey of Great Britain* stresses the focus during Murchison's directorship on the Scottish Highlands, rivers, glaciers, and coal deposits. More recent scholarship emphasizes Murchison's role in assisting the expansion of the British Empire during the nineteenth century. Robert A. Stafford, in "Geological Surveys, Mineral Discoveries, and British Expansion, 1835–71," discusses how geologists under Murchison traveled the globe with the Survey and the Royal School of Mines. They surveyed in Canada, Australia, India, South Africa, Tasmania, Trinidad, and Jamaica.

Little research has been done on the history of geological surveys in many areas of the former British empire; however, Canada is an exception. Two texts that present a comprehensive history of survey work in Canada are Morris Zaslow's *Reading the Rocks: The Story of the Geological Survey of Canada, 1842–1972* (1975) and Don W. Thomson's *Men and Meridians: The History of Surveying and Mapping in Canada* (1969–1975). While Thomson's three volume work is a compilation of all types of surveys, including geological surveys, Zaslow focuses on the geological. A third work, Suzanne Zeller's *Inventing Canada: Early Victorian Science and the Idea of a Transcontinental Nation* (1987), places the Geological Survey of Canada in the context of the construction of Canada (chaps. 3, 4).

As a result of the efforts of the Natural History Society of Montreal and the Literary and Historical Society of Quebec, the Canadian provincial government appointed William Edmond Logan (1798–1875) the first director of the Geological Survey of Canada in 1842. The Canadian-born Logan, the son of wealthy Scottish merchants, went to school in Scotland and worked for Forest Copper Works in South Wales. In that position he produced a geological map of the Welsh District that was later recognized by De la Beche. Logan was also a member of the Geological Society of London, and his most notable work, *Geology of Canada,* was published in 1863.

The lack of topographical maps of Canada concerned Logan and others into the twentieth century. All subsequent directors of the Canadian Geological Survey worked at some point in their careers on mapping western Canada. After the founding of a Topographical Division in 1908, the Canadian Geological Survey began to examine and emulate the success of the United States Geological Survey in mapping the American southwest.

Much of the historical literature about geological surveying in America during the nineteenth century concerns exploration in the West. Beginning in the 1950s, historians have addressed specific geological surveys and leaders of geological expeditions. Among the more prominent texts are Richard Bartlett's *Great Surveys of the American West* (1962), William Goetzmann's *Exploration and Empire: The Explorer and the Scientist in the Winning of the American West* (1966), and Wallace Stegner's *Beyond the Hundredth Meridian: John Wesley Powell and the Second Opening of the West* (1954).

Great Surveys of the American West recounts four prominent surveys conducted in the 1870s. Bartlett focuses on the work of Ferdinand Vandeveer Hayden (1829–1887), Clarence King (1842–1901), John Wesley Powell (1834–1902), and George Montague Wheeler (1842–1905). Working simultaneously but independently, all four commanded federally funded western geological surveys. During this era, no formal policy existed for such programs to be sponsored or organized by the federal government. By 1874, Powell proposed a consolidation of the four surveys, under the directorship of the federal government, in order to eliminate waste. Powell's vision was realized in 1878 when Congress passed legislation initiating the organization of the U.S. Geological Survey. Powell served as the agency's second director after Clarence King.

John Wesley Powell, a memorable character who attracted much attention during his lifetime, has been the subject of several biographies, including William Culp Darrah's *Powell of the Colorado* (1951), Paul Meadows's *John Wesley Powell: Frontiersman of Science* (1952), and John Terrell's *The Man who Rediscovered America: A Biography of John Wesley Powell* (1969). Other works place more emphasis on Powell's survey work. Among the most notable is Stegner's *Beyond the Hundredth Meridian.*

Stegner analyzes Powell's application of science to his exploration of the Colorado River and his role in developing the Western states. Powell received financial assistance from Illinois Normal University until 1872 and from the federal government afterwards. Powell, who was not university educated, published two reports on his work in the West: *Report on the Exploration of the Colorado River of the West and Its Tributaries* (1875) and *Report on the Geology of the Eastern Portion of the Uinta Mountains* (1876).

Stegner describes Powell's 1875 report as somewhat sensational. Powell had his "eye partly on the scientific" and on Congress's appropriations committees. The report was so lavishly illustrated and such an exciting adventure story that popular magazines continually offered to publish it in a more accessible venue. Articles from the report were actually published in such mainstream magazines as *Harper's Magazine* and *Scribner's* (Stegner, p. 148).

Powell's report on the Uinta Mountains contained more scientific analysis and less adventure. Stegner declares that out of this work emerged the modern science of physical geology. The ideas about topography and erosion that Powell developed about the Plateau Province earned him respect from the scientific community, and eventually, a primary role in the development of the Western states.

Powell worked for the U.S. Geological Survey until his resignation in 1894. During that time, Powell "established models for the later Forest Service, National Park Service, Soil Conservation Service, and other government agencies, mainly under Interior and Agriculture, which have been notable for the disinterested effectiveness of their work" (Stegner, p. 345).

Unlike earlier works that promote the romance of the Western survey expedition, Goetzmann's *Exploration and Empire* exhibits a more sophisticated approach. Instead of analyzing exploration as a "sequence of discoveries," Goetzmann addresses the impact that explorations in the American West made on that region, the nation, and science. Goetzmann concludes that while surveys of the West took many forms during the nineteenth century, the federal government maintained a continuous presence and influence over the surveys that shaped the finished products offered by the surveyors (Goetzmann, p. xi).

Some of the most recent works on the history of geological surveys go far toward bridging the gap between the romantic chronicle and thoughtful analysis. Among these are *Toward a History of Geology* (1969) and *Two Hundred Years of Geology in America* (1979), both edited by C.J. Schneer, which offer a more comprehensive review of the history of geological surveys in America. Mary Rabbitt's *Minerals, Lands, and Geology for the Common Defence and General Welfare* (1979) also provides a more extensive account.

While most historical works concern geological surveying in England, Canada, and the United States, there is a growing body of literature that addresses other regions. Among the works on Australian geological surveys is *History and the Role of Government in Australia* (1976), edited by R.K. Johns. Within this work is a piece by P.W. Crohn entitled "His-

tory of the Northern Territory Geological Survey." Thomas Darragh's "The Geological Survey of Victoria under Alfred Selwyn, 1852–1868" (1987) examines Selwyn's leadership at the Australian Survey.

Geological survey work in Europe has received little attention from scholars. William Topley's *The National Geological Surveys of Europe* (1885) is one of the earliest chronicles of European surveys. Martin Guntau's "The History of the Origins of the Prussian Geological Survey in Berlin" (1988) focuses on institutional development. Survey work in Czechoslovakia is addressed by Jan Urban in "On the History of Geological Mapping in Czechoslovakia" (1980).

Scholars have also given little attention to Africa and South America. Among the works on Africa are Anne Godlewska's *The Napoleonic Survey of Egypt* (1988) and Maxine Taylor's "Scientific Expeditions during the July Monarchy: The French in Abyssinia" (1990). Milton Vargas's "Louis Agassiz and the Story of Geological Surface Formations in Brazil" (1991) presents one of the few studies on South American surveys; the article focuses on Agassiz's 1865 Brazilian expedition and his interest in glaciation.

Another area that has received little attention is Asia and the South Pacific islands. "Imperial Geological Survey of Japan: Its History, Organization, and Work" (1924), written by Kinosuke Inouye, is the only history of Japanese survey work. While there is virtually no historical literature on China, two works accessible to Western scholars address survey work in India. A.K. Ghosh's "Geological Survey of India (1851–1951)" (1951) and *Centenary of the Geological Survey of India, 1851–1951: A Short History of the First Hundred Years* (1951), produced by the Geological Survey of India, are quite similar in their content. Michel Durand-Delga's "L'affaire Deprat: L'honneur retrouvé d'un geologue" (1991) illustrates a recent interest in Indochina. New Zealand is the only South Pacific island that has received historical attention. However, P. Burton's *The New Zealand Geological Survey, 1865–1965* (1965) is more a guide to New Zealand surveys than a historical analysis.

Two areas of recent interest to scholars are Greenland and the Arctic. One of the works on Greenland, Curt Teicher's "A Geological Expedition to East Greenland, 1931–1932" (1991), analyzes a particular expedition; Peter Dawes's "Lauge Koch: Pioneer Geo-explorer of Greenland's Far North" (1991) is more concerned with the individual explorer. Geir Hestmark studies the intellectual work of Scandinavian geologists in his article "Fridtjof Nansen and the Geology of the Arctic" (1991).

Historians have primarily addressed geological survey work in Great Britain, Canada, and the United States, and thus there is only a small body of literature on other areas. A great amount of the Earth's surface, representing many political and cultural contexts for geology, needs scholarly attention. Although many of the comprehensive works on geological surveys include the twentieth century, most of the individual case studies examine the nineteenth century almost exclusively, a situation that encourages further scholarship in this field. Moreover, it is time that chronologies and celebrations be supplanted uniformly by careful analyses, of the sort represented by Suzanne Zeller's and Anne Godlewska's books.

Anne-Marie Turnage

Bibliography

Darragh, Thomas A. "The Geological Survey of Victoria under Alfred Selwyn, 1852–1868." *Historical Records of Australian Science* 7 (1987): pp. 1–25.

Dawes, Peter Robert. "Lauge Koch: Pioneer Geo-explorer of Greenland's Far North." *Earth Sciences History* 10 (1991): pp. 130–153.

Durand-Delga, Michel. "L'affaire Deprat: L'honneur retrouve d'un geologue." *Recherche* 22 (1991): pp. 1342–1346.

Ghosh, A.K. "Geological Survey of India (1851–1951)." *Science as Culture* 16 (1951): pp. 307–313.

Goetzmann, William H. *Exploration and Empire: The Explorer and the Scientist in the Winning of the American West.* New York: Knopf, 1966.

Guntau, Martin. "The History of the Origins of the Prussian Geological Survey in Berlin (1873)." *History and Technology* 5 (1988): pp. 51–58.

Hestmark, Geir. "Fridtjof Nansen and the Geology of the Arctic." *Earth Sciences History* 10 (1991): pp. 168–212.

Inouye, Kinosuke. "Imperial Geological Survey of Japan: Its History, Organization, and Work." *Journal of Geography* 36 (1924): pp. 11–22.

Secord, James A. "The Geological Survey of Great Britain as a Research School, 1839–1855." *History of Science* 24 (1986): pp. 223–275.

Stafford, Robert A. "Geological Surveys, Mineral Discoveries, and British Expansion, 1835–71." *Journal of Imperial and Commonwealth History* 3 (1984): pp. 5–32.

Stegner, Wallace. *Beyond the Hundredth Meridian: John Wesley Powell and the Second Opening of the West.* Boston: Houghton Mifflin, 1954.

Taylor, Maxine F. "Scientific Expeditions during the July Monarchy: The French in Abyssinia." In *Proceedings of the 13th and 14th Meetings of the French Colonial Historical Society,* edited by Phillip P. Boucher, pp. 103–118. Lanham, Md.: University Press of America, 1990.

Teichert, Curt. "A Geological Expedition to East Greenland, 1931–1932." *Earth Sciences History* 10 (1991): pp. 259–273.

Urban, Jan. "On the History of Geological Mapping in Czechoslovakia." *Annals of Science* 37 (1980): pp. 413–432.

Vargas, Milton. "Louis Agassiz and the Story of Geological Surface Formations in Brazil." *Quipu* 8 (1991): pp. 379–388.

Geological Surveys, U.S. State

Government bureaus charged with researching and mapping the geology of a political unit.

Every state in the United States has sponsored a geological survey; some states, several surveys. The Association of American State Geologists recently offered this definition of state surveys: "While they are diverse in size, in name, and in detailed functions, each has the basic responsibility to delineate the geologic resources and conditions as they impact upon the economic and environmental well-being of the respective state" (Socolow, preface). The definition is historically accurate. State surveys began in the 1820s as unique and temporary organizations. Within a century the survey became a permanent agency of most states, a research department in public service. During the interim, surveys figured prominently in the professionalization of geology and in the institutionalization of science in government, and they contributed to geological literature and knowledge.

Initially states established geological surveys—sometimes broadly identified as natural history or natural resource surveys—as temporary organizations with specific, legislatively defined tasks. North Carolina set the precedent by establishing the first state survey in 1823,

BASALTIC COLUMNS, LAKE SUPERIOR.

Figure 1. Geological surveys of the region south of Lake Superior were originally undertaken by scientists under contract to the U.S. Treasury Department. These scientists-explorers reported sometimes romantically, sometimes descriptively, of such formations as basaltic columns. Reproduced from Owen, David Dale, Report of a Geological Survey of Wisconsin, Iowa, and Minnesota; and incidentally of a Portion of Nebraska Territory. Made under Instructions from the United States Treasury Department, *p. 384.* Philadelphia: Lippincott, Gambo, 1852.

and South Carolina authorized the second in 1824. Both were short-lived. In 1830 Massachusetts approved the third state survey; then a movement for state surveys spread across the country, reaching some new states almost as soon as they achieved statehood. Tennessee established a survey in 1831, Maryland in 1833, and Connecticut, New Jersey, and Virginia in 1835. Five states—Georgia, Maine, New York, Ohio, and Pennsylvania—established surveys in 1836. Twenty states had sponsored geological surveys by 1850, and almost forty states by 1900 (figure 1). Oklahoma established a territorial survey in 1900 and provided for a state geological survey in the state's constitution of 1907. Similarly, Alaska and Hawaii began surveys under territorial governments and, upon becoming states, transformed the surveys into state agencies.

Surveys undertook geological reconnaissance, topographical mapping, agricultural investigations, and studies of natural history and natural resources. They employed chemists, paleontologists, mineralogists, zoologists, and botanists, as well as geologists. While nineteenth-century surveys were the most numerous and most visible scientific agency within state government, twentieth-century surveys became one of several scientific organizations performing routine work for their respective states (figure 2).

The literature on state surveys varies in breadth and depth. The widest coverage appears in *The State Geological Surveys, a History,* published by the Association of American State Geologists. This collection of articles examines geological surveys state by state from the 1820s to the 1980s, but the individual articles are brief (from one to twenty-two pages in length) and the quality uneven. Each entry provides the dates of one state's surveys and the names and terms of the survey directors. Some entries have excellent bibliographies, though most list no sources. The book has no introductory or concluding remarks about surveys in general or the context of American science and society, and no index. Moreover, the volume lacks detail available in earlier state-by-state compilations, which cover very little of the twentieth century.

Originally published in 1924, *The First One Hundred Years of American Geology,* by George P. Merrill, is still a basic reference for nineteenth-century surveys; no comparable review of twentieth-century surveys exists. A curator of geology at the Smithsonian Institution, Merrill had previously compiled detailed administrative histories of the geological surveys of thirty-four states. In *The First One Hundred Years,* he argued that the period from

GENERALIZED SKETCH OF THE CHARACTERISTIC TOPOGRAPHY OF THE KETTLE MORAINE.

Figure 2. Not surprisingly, glacial features such as these Kettle Moraines featured prominently in the reports of the Wisconsin state survey. From Chamberlin, T.C., Geology of Wisconsin. Survey of 1873–1879, vol. 1, p. 277. 4 vols. Madison: Commissioners of Public Printing, 1877–1883.

1830 to 1880 was an "era of state surveys," followed by an "era of national surveys." According to Merrill, the 1830s was a feverish decade for public surveys, but the next decade was a quiet interlude amid financial depression. In contrast, the 1850s was an "era of publication, not merely of state survey reports, but of books and general treatises" (p. 293). Despite the turmoil and interruptions caused by the Civil War, new leadership emerged in the 1860s in state surveys and geology in general (p. 392). In the 1870s individual states continued or started surveys while the federal government became increasingly active in science. With the authorization of the United States Geological Survey in 1879, Merrill closed his era of state surveys.

The classic text on federal science in the United States is A. Hunter Dupree's *Science in the Federal Government*, which traces geology's "metamorphosis from a series of ad hoc military expeditions to a permanent civilian agency" (p. 214), from the Lewis and Clark Expedition to the U.S. Geological Survey (chaps. 2, 5, 10). Since Dupree's book appeared in 1957, historians have written monographs on the different federal surveys, including early Army explorations, the several territorial surveys of the 1860s and 1870s, and the national Geological Survey, as well as biographies of nineteenth-century federal geologists such as Clarence King, John Wesley Powell, and Ferdinand V. Hayden. The federal surveys and the federally employed geologists provide both context and content for the history of state geological surveys.

Multiple case studies appear in Anne Millbrooke's dissertation on *State Geological Surveys of the Nineteenth Century*. Her four cases—South Carolina, Pennsylvania, Illinois, and California—represent different periods of time, different geographic regions, and different organizational formats. She examines the surveys during Merrill's "era of state surveys" and what happened to the state organizations as national surveys entered the geological landscape. New York, California, and other states are also subjects of doctoral dissertations on the history of individual state surveys. Begun as a doctoral dissertation, Robert G. Hays's book on *State Science in Illinois* is a case study that encompasses both the nineteenth and twentieth centuries. Within the context of Illinois state history and from the perspective of political science, Hays chronicles that state's geological, natural history, and water surveys from their inceptions in the mid-nineteenth century to 1978. Many state surveys have published historical monographs, usually on the occasion of an anniversary; these include Georgia, Illinois, Kansas, Minnesota, Oklahoma, Vermont, and Wisconsin. Geologist Rex C. Buchanan, for example, prepared the centennial publication of the Kansas Geological Survey, *To Bring Together, Correlate, and Preserve*.

Autobiographies and biographies exist for numerous employees and directors of state surveys. Nathaniel Southgate Shaler, Kentucky state geologist in the 1870s, and Olaf P. Jenkins, a geologist with the California survey from the 1920s to the 1950s, are among the state-employed geologists who wrote personal accounts. James Dwight Dana, James Hall, Edmund Ruffin, Shaler, and Josiah Dwight Whitney are nineteenth-century subjects of biographies. David N. Livingstone's biography of Shaler, for example, illustrates recent efforts to place state geologists (and surveys) in, as his subtitle says, "the culture of American science"—both the social and intellectual context of American science. Shaler exemplifies the emergence of geology as a profession. A graduate of the Lawrence Scientific School and a student of Louis Agassiz's, he spent most of his career at Harvard University. He worked part time as director of the reactivated Kentucky

Geological Survey for seven years, and later he worked for the U.S. Geological Survey. He advocated college reform and the academic training of geologists. He became president of the Geological Society of America, a professional organization founded by geologists mostly associated with state surveys. Intellectually, Shaler accepted evolution of a neo-Lamarckian variety as well as an evolutionary theology, what his biographer called his "vestiges of natural theology." Other state geologists joined professional debates about mountain-building, the geosyncline concept, glacial theory, the Taconic question, extinctions, and, more recently, plate tectonics.

The politics of public patronage created and sustained, and sometimes suspended and closed, geological surveys. During the nineteenth century, Millbrooke argues, public perceptions of the utility of geology extended beyond economic benefits to stimulating curiosity, enriching intellectual life, testing European theories in the American setting, entertaining amateur scientists, teaching moral lessons, reforming society, and aiding state or national progress. Depending upon geography and other local factors, the economic promise varied. In South Carolina agriculture dominated the economy and the geological surveys. The development of transportation systems and coal-related businesses in Pennsylvania generated public support of geology there. Illinois tried to promote transportation and agriculture through geology. California sought to develop mineral resources, encourage agriculture, and locate water resources for use in mining and agriculture. In a later example, an oil boom helped transform the Kansas survey into a permanent agency (Buchanan, pp. 2, 55–58), and, in a final example, Hawaii sought to manage water resources, particularly for agricultural irrigation (Manabu Tagomori in Socolow, p. 86).

Public utility made geology a form of internal improvement during the Antebellum period. Internal improvements encompassed public works within the boundaries of individual states, such as canals and roads. Geological surveys began in the favorable climate created by the internal-improvements movement and at a time when private and federal patrons failed to support geological surveys of any state. While interpretations of the U.S. Constitution limited federal activity within state jurisdiction, state legislatures debated the role of science in government—and established surveys within their respective boundaries. Most of the early state surveys were small, temporary institutions. States like Kan-

sas and Pennsylvania founded additional surveys to complete the work and update the data of earlier efforts. But as the federal government increased its scientific programs, the state survey evolved into a bureaucratic, administrative agency that continuously compiled data about geologic resources. Established in 1880, the California State Mining Bureau became a model of the survey as a permanent state agency. Millbrooke identifies three related developments that allowed state surveys to evolve into permanent agencies: (1) the emergence of the university, (2) the rise of federal science, and (3) the movement for conservation. In tracing the evolution of the state scientific surveys in Illinois, Hays also observes these influences, there epitomized by the formation of a state Board of Natural Resources and Conservation in 1917. The U.S. Geological Survey represented a growth of the federal bureaucracy of civilian science. Federal and state surveys divided labor. The federal survey assumed some tasks more scientific or more expensive in nature, including paleontological research and topographic mapping, and this permitted the state surveys to focus upon economically useful activities specified by their respective state legislatures.

The history of state geological surveys provides opportunities for research. Most existing work pertains to the institutional history of a survey or surveys and to the role of surveys in the professionalization of American science, mostly in the nineteenth century. Additional general and case studies could add insight to these and other themes. The twentieth-century surveys remain only lightly examined. Research is needed on the instruments, field methods, and laboratory techniques of the various surveys through time. Other subjects open for study include the influence of politics, the nature of state employment, state participation in professional debates, the relationship between state and federal geologists and institutions, geological ideas as developed and applied in the state surveys, individual and collective contributions of state surveys to geological knowledge, the career paths of geologists, the multidisciplinary agendas of certain surveys, state bureaucracies as institutional settings for science, geology and the public, government patronage, and biography. The general chronology is available, as are various bibliographies, archival files of the surveys, manuscript collections, and other resources, including a growing body of secondary literature.

Anne Millbrooke

Bibliography

Buchanan, Rex C. *"To Bring Together, Correlate, and Preserve"—A History of the Kansas Geological Survey, 1864–1989*. Bulletin 227. Lawrence: Kansas Geological Survey, 1989.

Dupree, A. Hunter. *Science in the Federal Government: A History of Policies and Activities* [1957]. Baltimore, Md.: John Hopkins University Press, 1986.

Hays, Robert G. *State Science in Illinois, the Scientific Surveys, 1850–1978*. Carbondale: Southern Illinois University Press, 1980.

Livingstone, David N. *Nathaniel Southgate Shaler and the Culture of American Science*. Tuscaloosa: University of Alabama Press, 1987.

Merrill, George P. *The First One Hundred Years of American Geology* [1924]. New York: Hafner Publishing Company, 1969.

Millbrooke, Anne Marie. *State Geological Surveys of the Nineteenth Century*. Ann Arbor, Mich.: University Microfilms, 1981.

Socolow, Arthur A., ed. *The State Geological Surveys, a History*. Grand Forks, N.D.: Association of American State Geologists, 1988.

See also Conservation of Natural Resources; Evolution and the Geosciences; Geological Societies; Geological Surveys; Geology; Geosyncline; Mineralogy; Paleontology; Petroleum Geology to 1920; Taconic Controversy

Geological Time

A fundamental concept now seen as basic to the development of modern geology, evolutionary biology, and cosmology.

At present the Earth is believed to be somewhat less than five billion years old and the cosmos as a whole perhaps between two and four times older. But these figures are of very recent date and are certain to be further refined—or even superseded entirely—as new methodologies continue to be developed. It is commonly held that extensive views of time are modern and scientific. In actuality, however, the most extensive estimates ever made for the duration of the Earth and its universe were those of the ancient world.

In Vedic and later Indian religious traditions, for example, the world is eternal, but its history is divided into lesser and greater ages of predictable duration, effects, and recurrence. Thus, as yugas become mahayugas and they, kalpas and manvantaras (one such cycle being equivalent to more than sixty trillion years), the universe is periodically born, destroyed, and reborn as part of an infinite pattern in which even the gods are not eternal, but material existence is. For both Hindus and Buddhists, time is limitless, and we are endlessly returned within it until our personal Nirvana is attained.

Although only the Pythagoreans similarly affirmed metempsychosis, we know that cyclical conceptions of the Earth's history were also popular among the Greeks. Anaximander, perhaps the earliest pre-Socratic philosopher to hold such views, was followed by Empedocles and the Pythagoreans, who then—utilizing Chaldean antecedents—formulated the influential doctrine of the cyclical Great Year, which was popularized by the Babylonian scribe Berossus (third century B.C.E.) and spread throughout the Hellenistic world. According to this doctrine, the universe, though eternal, undergoes cyclical destructions from either fire or flood at variously specified long but regular intervals.

Between the first century B.C.E. and the third century C.E., however, more apocalyptic beliefs were common, often deriving from the Zoroastrian tenet that a single mahayana cycle of four yugas lasting a total of twelve thousand years represents the entire history of the Earth. Roman, Jewish, and Christian chronologers then shortened this much abridged allotment still further, as biblical scholars in particular came to believe that God intended to destroy the Earth after an existence of six thousand years.

If so, it was a matter of no small importance to determine from a close analysis of Scripture just when the Creation had occurred. Utilizing the remarkably complete Old Testament records of the generations of mankind (those otherwise tedious begats), several Christian scholars of the third to fifth centuries C.E. independently affirmed a Creation date of about 5500 B.C.E. The inescapable outcome of this research was to suppose that the six thousandth year was indeed imminent. Though St. Augustine in *The City of God* (413–426) affirmed the Earth's duration to be six thousand years, he denied that it was soon to end. Some later writers then either added a seventh period of one thousand years to the Earth's history or accepted durations of longer than one thousand years for each of the figurative "days" composing the biblical scheme.

Since it was through his unmistakable structuring of time that God revealed himself to mankind, any suggestion of essentially amorphous duration stabbed dangerously close to the heart of medieval theology. Augustine (again in *The City of God*) therefore attacked pagan eternalism vigorously, and most of his significant successors did the same. Despite this nearly universal theological support for a short-lived Earth, however, the eternalist tradition (with Aristotle at its head) was by no means defeated. Arab scholars having no special stake in biblical chronology began to study the Greek philosopher's works, first in tenth-century Baghdad and then two centuries later on at Cordoba. Once translated into Latin, the commentaries of Avicenna and Averroes seriously challenged previous medieval thought.

Aristotle and his Arab commentators were vigorously attacked for their eternalist beliefs well into the seventeenth century, as increasing acceptance of their heretical position spread from its stronghold in Padua through France and into England. As the Reformation, beginning in 1517, kept narrowly defined theological issues before an increasingly literate public (printing having been introduced to Europe), eternalism was regularly equated with atheism. The turmoil of the times, moreover, convinced many that the long-predicted end of the world was indeed near.

Virtually all of the commentaries written upon Genesis in Europe between 1525 and 1633 affirm that time began with God's creation of the world, and many of them specifically oppose Aristotle's opinion to the contrary. Though it was possible to argue that biblical "days" were only figurative (Creation being instantaneous), almost everyone regarded them as literal. Once beyond the Creation week, times derived from Patriarchal genealogy, but there were two distinct textual traditions by now, and in the matter of chronology one version of the Bible contradicted the other. This difficulty was of major significance to the Renaissance because Genesis was their sole authority for human history prior to the Flood—a period that lasted for 1,656 years according to the Hebrew text and for 2,342 years according to the Greek (Septuagint). In attempting to resolve these differences, and to discredit Aristotle, commentators increasingly called upon the book of God's works, which is to say the natural history of their time.

Although earlier reluctance to accept the Bible literally had derived at first from textual considerations, or from alternative traditions or the state of humanity, beginning with the latter seventeenth century it became increasingly usual to challenge the adequacy of Genesis on geological grounds. Two related and especially pertinent controversies concerned the identity of fossils and the nature of the Flood. Depending on one's theological position, it was possible to date fossils (not yet definitely established as the remains of once-living creatures) from the Creation, from the Flood, or from various other and perhaps continuing times. Chronological questions were therefore central to major aspects of the later seventeenth-century geological theorizing by such major figures as Descartes, Hooke, Ray, Lhwyd, Burnet, Woodward, and Whiston. For all of these, biblical chronology had largely failed. If some new proof in its favor were not forthcoming, they assumed, then the history of both humanity and the Earth would have to be rewritten.

However distressing to more orthodox denominations, this presumed inadequacy of the Bible accorded perfectly with deism, the aggressive Enlightenment theology that looked to nature rather than Scripture for its truths. As a group, deists tended to deny that either of the Testaments had been divinely inspired and turned instead to evidence from nature, some of which they used against the Bible. Although deism was primarily British in origin, flourishing especially between 1690 and 1740 (later in Scotland), there were also deists in France, many of them in the early eighteenth century.

Stressing the inadequacy of biblical time, these French writers increasingly recognized that geological processes had been of immense duration. In a paper of 1720, for example, René de Reamur agreed with earlier British speculators that the fossil record attests to a duration long preceding the Flood. Less adventurous thinkers circulated their skeptical opinions clandestinely, often with false imprints and pseudonymous authorship. Thus, in his *Lettres persanes* ("Cologne" [for Amsterdam]) the next year, Montesquieu recalled La Peyrere and other philosophers who distinguished two creations, that of things and that of men. Such thinkers felt unable to believe that matter and life are only six thousand years old, or that God postponed his creative work for an eternity. Benoit de Maillet's posthumous *Telliamed* (1748) allowed human existence four hundred thousand years, and extended the Earth's age indefinitely. Diderot, in *Lettrè sur les avuegles* (1749, "London" [for Paris]) and Buffon, in *Histoire naturelle* (1749, Paris) proposed similarly unbiblical time schemes, though Buffon was chastised by clerical authorities as a result. By 1751, if Rousseau's *Les confessions* (1782–1789) can be trusted, François Mussard and Nicolas Boullanger were also among those fascinated with this still-forbidden question of the Earth's age, as many of Baron D'Holbach's coterie would be. Never one to hide his innermost thoughts, Rousseau himself affirmed in 1755 that the development of man's mind to its present level must have required thousands of ages. In 1769 Diderot required "hundreds of millions of years," and Jean Terrasson felt free to interpret the biblical six days of creation as six years, six centuries, six thousand years, or even six million years. Though all of these thinkers were influenced by geological evidence, however, they seldom relied on it exclusively, and none hazarded anything like a specific chronology.

A number of earlier theorists, including Avicenna, Da Vinci, Steno, and Hooke, had envisioned chronologies derived from geological phenomena, but their ideas were never actually developed. During the eighteenth century, however, as time became increasingly important to natural science, physical evidence for the age of the Earth gradually supplanted all other kinds in credibility. There was little agreement as to which phenomena were really chronological and how they might be read, but we can usefully divide their various attempts into several overlapping categories.

Although most arguments derived from stratification concerned fossils, Leonardo Da Vinci foresaw (without subsequent influence) that sedimentation might be a seasonal or annual activity. In 1668 Robert Hooke thought it possible to derive a chronology from fossils, including their development and vicissitudes; John Ray, John Wallis, and Carl Linnaeus made similar, more limited, suggestions. Meanwhile, John Strachey had begun to propose stratigraphic sequences in 1719 and 1725. But it was only later on in France that such writers as Del la Croix Rouelle, and especially Jean Louis Giraud-Soulavie in 1779 clearly associated fossils with strata. Despite such anticipations, few would reliably correlate stratification, fossils, and chronology before the nineteenth century.

Some progress had been made toward morphological chronology, the recognition that sequences of geological change can be deduced from landforms. Although Nicolaus Steno's *De solido* (1669) proposed a six-stage chronology for Tuscany, its author continued to believe the Earth no more than six thousand

years old. The late seventeenth-century British Deluge geologists Burnet, Woodward, and Whiston all affirmed before-and-after global change, the primeval Earth for them having been totally disrupted by the Flood. It had been general throughout the seventeenth century to argue down the Aristotelians by emphasizing erosion (that is, the Earth could never have lasted from eternity), but no one is known to have actually tried to date a landform on that basis, probably because all landforms were assumed to be coeval, dating either from the Creation or the Flood.

During the mid-eighteenth century, however, it was commonly assumed that landforms (and the rocks composing them) had been created at different times. Granites, for example, were primeval; sediments, derivative; and a third class of volcanic and loosely consolidated rocks, adventitious since then. Thus, Johann Lehmann in 1756 distinguished three kinds of mountains—and a sequence of rock types—created before, during, and after the Deluge, respectively. Giovanni Arduino in 1760 and George Fuchsel in 1762 and 1773 then generalized this tripartite progression so that it no longer depended on the Flood and could not therefore be dated by any means then known, a position that coincided nicely with the concurrent retreat of biblical chronology. Eventually, Abraham Gottlob Werner announced in 1787 a unique, nonrepetitive petrological sequence of worldwide applicability, based on successive deposits from a retreating universal ocean. His many students and other followers endeavored for years to support this strictly local scheme through competent fieldwork on several continents. Yet it soon became apparent that geological formations were both locally diverse and frequently recurring. Lacking a theory of universal applicability and reliable ideas about sequence, Wernerians could at best establish only relative chronology. No theory based solely upon rock types offered reliable proofs of the Earth's immense age, which Werner and most of his followers extended beyond scriptural limits but continued to abbreviate.

A third category of evidence, growth phenomena, was especially useful to the eighteenth century, which devised several attempts to gauge geological time from steady, measurable increases (like Da Vinci's varving). Edward Lhwyd, for example, regarded the slow accumulation of boulders strewn about in two valleys of northern Wales as evidence that the Earth was many thousands of years older than commonly believed. Similarly, Edmond Halley proposed in 1715 to determine the world's age by extrapolating from the sea's allegedly regular increase in salinity. Several mid-century geologists, including Maillet, Buffon, and Linnaeus, believed that the ocean's waters were steadily diminishing. If so, then an objective (but not necessarily absolute) chronology becomes possible, based on the expansion of the continents. Alternatively, J.T. Needham, an associate of Buffon's, attempted to calculate the age of the Earth from sedimentation rates—and found the result so staggering that he could not accept it. Though all these theories embody unprovable assumptions about geological change (its uniformitarian character especially), such attempts toward a purely geological chronology are deeply significant indications of how the science was abandoning the authority of books and turning to the Earth itself.

The last category of evidence is decay phenomena, the opposite of growth. One important specialization of this approach was Buffon's attempt to establish an absolute chronology for the Earth by measuring the decline of its residual heat. More generally, however, arguments from decay dealt primarily with erosion, regarding which there were three major positions. A common one during the first half of the eighteenth century was simply to deny or to minimize the reality of day-to-day erosion. Another common, but older, tradition emphasized the rapidity of decay: our planet's vulnerability to erosion proved that its history was brief, thereby refuting Aristotle and affirming Genesis. A third school emphasized decay but saw the need for some sort of regenerative principle if the Earth were to endure for even its allotted span. Perhaps the most conspicuous advocate of this last position prior to James Hutton (1726–1797) was the frequently anonymous Baron de Holbach who (along with Montesquieu and others) argued for sequential, destructive revolutions in the geological realm but—unlike Hutton—specified that these permutations of eternal matter are entirely devoid of either design or purpose.

James Hutton agreed with Holbach and others in regarding the surface of the Earth as a geological theater in which the seemingly rival forces of destruction and creation are constantly at work. Unlike Holbach, however, Hutton was a deist rather than an atheist. Where Holbach had seen the natural world as a chaos of random chance, Hutton saw sure evidence of divine contrivance and benevolent intention. Having no doubt that the Earth had been created by God as a home for mankind, Hutton maintained the seemingly paradoxical belief that the destruction of soil through erosion actually helped to maintain the Earth's fertility, which was constantly being renewed by the creation of fresh soil from eroding rock.

Because the destruction and creation of rock was far too slow to be readily observed by short-lived humans (who nevertheless could comprehend it rationally), Hutton required immense amounts of time if his theory were to be valid. Though, in response to a chief critic, he specified that the Earth had a beginning, his operative belief was that its duration was virtually limitless. As he wrote in his famous theory (1788, 1795), "Time, which measures every thing in our idea, and is often deficient to our schemes, is to nature endless and as nothing." He is the first major geological theorist who takes for granted a duration of geological time resembling our own. His theory is therefore among the first to dispense with a Creation whose relics have persisted to this day (Hutton believed nothing to be "original"). Unlike Werner and his predecessors, Hutton did not believe that the various types of rocks had been created sequentially; thus, granites and basalts for him were not the products of particular episodes in the Earth's history but were being created constantly. Because Hutton paid little attention to fossils, however, he did not accept the idea that species could become extinct or that life on Earth was ever significantly different from what it is now. Furthermore, he had no quarrel with the biblical chronologers who limited the duration of mankind to six thousand years. But he believed the biblical days of creation to be figurative only and in practice disregarded them altogether, unlike preceding theorists (including Buffon) who had attempted to accommodate them somehow.

By the beginning of the nineteenth century, the prevalent geological theories in Europe were Werner's and (somewhat later on) Hutton's, neither of which paid the slightest attention to biblical chronology, except regarding the history of mankind. Neither Werner nor Hutton ever endorsed the still-popular concept of a universal flood subsequent to the creation of mankind, though biblicists did. Werner's theory involved a sequence of rock types (and fossils) that sharply distinguished eras in the Earth's supposed past from one another. Hutton's theory, on the other hand, was largely ahistorical, being almost always concerned with processes rather than events. Neither theory was capable of estimating durations reliably, but together they destroyed for a time much of whatever remaining credibility biblical chronology still had.

Because geology had become such a popular science during the nineteenth century, one pursued at all levels of sophistication, generalizations as to its contents must necessarily admit of many exceptions. Throughout most of the centuries, however, concepts of geological time derived primarily from paleontological evidence. Stimulated by Werner, and often in opposition to him, field-workers throughout the world attempted to establish stratigraphical sequences for their particular areas and remained in hopes of deriving a succession that would be valid everywhere. The first great stratigraphers (despite significant eighteenth-century anticipations) were Alexander Brongniart in France and William Smith in England, whose work around 1815 is especially relevant. Yet neither of these endorsed extended geological time, and both affirmed some version of the biblical Deluge, which Werner and Hutton had abandoned.

Together with Brongniart, the brilliant comparative anatomist Georges Cuvier at the same time popularized a strongly catastrophic view of geological change in which abrupt dislocations of strata and extinctions within the history of life—concepts that Cuvier was foremost in establishing—took place rapidly, as if modeled on earthquakes rather than erosion. But even erosion (for Hutton, immensely slow) was for Cuvier an extremely short-lived phenomenon and therefore one that must have been caused by geological forces different in kind and power from what we now observe. This outlook dominated European and American geological thought during the 1820s, when it was widely assumed that a certain very considerable body of evidence (later to be explained as glacial) attested to the most recent of a series of geographically extensive debacles or floods, popularly the flood of Noah.

Writing in opposition to Cuvier, Constant Prevost in France and Charles Lyell in England denied the uniqueness of the geological past, asserted the adequacy of present-day forces—if given enough time—and argued that it was fundamentally unscientific to discard known causes in favor of unknown ones. Having been led to a position later described as uniformitarian, which Hutton had also affirmed, Lyell demonstrated the explanatory power of known causes in a famous book, *Principles of Geology* (1830–1833), "being an attempt to explain the former changes of the Earth's surface, by reference to causes now in operation." The attempt was remarkably successful, as Lyell's book achieved twelve editions (to 1875), and a considerable degree of influence.

Lyell's influence was nowhere more important than in the mind of Charles Darwin, whose *Origin of Species* (1859) required vast amounts of geological time in order for its slow process of evolution by natural selection to work. Opponents of Darwin therefore attacked his sometimes too literal adherence to Lyell and disputed with him the length of geological time. A particularly effective challenge to both Lyell and Darwin was vigorously advanced during the latter nineteenth century by the physicist William Thomson, Lord Kelvin (1824–1907), who argued mistakenly that the Sun is consuming itself too rapidly to allow for the vast eons that uniformitarians required.

Though Kelvin's arguments seemed irrefutable for a time, the discovery of radioactivity around 1900 proved that solar activity included fission as well as combustion and was far longer lived than Kelvin had imagined. Equally influential was the discovery that radioactive decay within terrestrial rocks provides a reliable means of dating them, one isotope changing into another at a fixed rate and therefore (by the percentage of each) establishing when the less stable, decaying isotope had come into existence. Enjoying the advantage of an agreed-upon methodology, twentieth-century geophysicists have been able to date a wide variety of rocks, establishing not only the beginnings and endings of geological periods with relative accuracy but even approaching the age of the Earth itself. The oldest rocks yet found on Earth are gneisses from Greenland dated around 3.7 billion years. The assumed origin of the Earth 4.6 billion years ago is based on datings from lunar rocks and meteorites.

Because geological time is such a fundamental concept, it is often mentioned in books dealing with the history of geology, including the standard surveys by Zittel, Geikie, and Adams. Davies and Dean provide further examples. Preceding all these is Lyell, whose *Principles of Geology* (all editions) begins with a self-serving but nonetheless impressive critique of earlier beliefs. Lyell's own point of view is not entirely modern. Many textbooks of geology also remark on developing ideas about geological time; their historical assertions are often poorly informed and should be used with caution.

The best book to read first, superseded in part but by no means obsolete, is Haber's *The Age of the World: Moses to Darwin* (1959), parts of which appeared the same year in *Forerunners of Darwin, 1745–1859* (Baltimore, Md.: Johns Hopkins University Press, 1959), edited by Bently Glass, Owsei Tomkin, and William L. Straus, Jr. Haber was the first modern scholar to reestablish direct connections between the anti-Aristotelian Christian fathers and later scientific debates. Whereas late-nineteenth-century historians like John W. Draper and Andrew White ridiculed Archbishop Ussher's laboriously derived Creation date of 4004 B.C.E. and mistakenly characterized him as ignorant, Haber more reasonably described the efforts of Christian chronologers as scholarly investigations based on assumptions now thought to be false. But it was the fossil record, rather than the biblical one, that proved to be decisive. Haber sketched classical, medieval, and early modern opinions concerning fossils briefly. The first major advance was to realize that fossils are the remains of once-living creatures; the second was to realize that not all fossils are relics of the biblical Deluge (Noah's flood). Necessarily, then, discussion of geological time had to follow. Haber reviewed the chronological assertions of selected eighteenth-century geological theorists, including Maillet, Buffon, Werner, and Hutton. His final episodes considered "The Lyellian Revolution" and "Darwinian Time." Almost every chapter of Haber's book has since been redone in more detail by later scholars, who point out that Darwin's was by no means the last word and that fossils provide only one argument among others regarding the duration of geological time.

As his title indicates, Albritton's *The Abyss of Time* (1980) did not attempt to recount classical or medieval contributions, but he went beyond Haber in treating of twentieth-century topics. In a series of well-written, pleasantly anecdotal chapters, Albritton dealt in turn with Steno, Hooke, Burnet, Maillet, Buffon, Hutton, Smith, Werner, Lyell, Darwin, Kelvin, and Holmes. Arthur Holmes's *The Age of the Earth* (1913 and later editions) reviewed all the various methods then current in modern geochronology, together with their diverse results, and effectively demonstrated the superiority of radiometric dating. From 1927 to 1960 Holmes proposed successive versions of a geological time scale calibrated in years. His work has been continued since then by others, with newly found rocks on Earth and the Moon to aid them. Albritton's

book originated as a series of popular lectures and its analyses are intended to be easily comprehensible. He emphasized biographical details, so most of the illustrations are portraits.

Among more specialized works now available, R.C. Dales, *Medieval Discussions of the Eternity of the World* (1990), and J.B.M. Wissink, ed., *The Eternity of the World in the Thought of Thomas Aquinas and His Contemporaries* (1990), illuminate medieval controversy. Paolo Rossi, *The Dark Abyss of Time* (1984), covers seventeenth- and eighteenth-century figures (from Hooke to Vico) whose growing awareness of the world's immense antiquity challenged biblical chronology. Dennis R. Dean, *James Hutton and the History of Geology* (1992), summarizes opinions from 1785 to 1905. William B.N. Berry, *Growth of a Prehistoric Time Scale Based on Organic Evolution* (1968), is most valuable for chapters six to nine, in which the origins of our familiar geological periods (Tertiary, Quaternary, Carboniferous, Cretaceous, Jurassic, Triassic, Silurian, Cambrian, Devonian, Permian, Ordovician, and subdivisions of the Cenozoic or Cainozoic) are explained. Highly specialized studies on the Cambrian/Silurian and Devonian debates, by James Secord (1986) and Martin Rudwick (1985), have since appeared. Joe D. Burchfield, *Lord Kelvin and the Age of the Earth* (1975), is comprehensively researched, including not only Kelvin but also Geikie, Croll, Sollas, and Holmes, among others. The Albritton Memorial Issue (1989) of *Earth Sciences History* is devoted to geological time. Finally, G. Brent Dalrymple, *The Age of the Earth* (1991), explains modern methods for determining the age of the Earth and why the various earlier methods did not work. These more specialized treatments usually presuppose a working knowledge of the general topic (such as one gains from Haber and Albritton), are more challenging to read, and are often superior in scholarship.

Dennis R. Dean

Bibliography

Albritton, Claude C., Jr. *The Abyss of Time: Changing Conceptions of the Earth's Antiquity after the Sixteenth Century.* San Francisco: Freeman, Cooper, 1980.

Dean, Dennis R. "The Age of the Earth Controversy: Beginnings to Hutton." *Annals of Science* 38 (1981): pp. 435–456.

Haber, Francis C. *The Age of the World: Moses to Darwin.* Baltimore, Md.: Johns Hopkins University Press, 1959.

Herries Davies, Gordon L. *The Earth in Decay: A History of British Geomorphology, 1578–1878.* London: Macdonald, 1969.

Holmes, Arthur. *The Age of the Earth.* New York: Harper, 1913, 1927, 1937.

———. "A Revised Geological Time-Scale." *Transactions of the Geological Society of Edinburgh* 17 (1960): pp. 183–216.

See also Actualism, Uniformitarianism, Catastrophism; Age of the Earth, before 1800; Age of the Earth, since 1800; Cosmology and the Earth; Dendrochronology; Deluge; Earth in Decay; Fossilization; Geological Periodization; Geology; Geomorphology; Radioactivity in the Earth; Stratigraphy; Taconic Controversy

Geology: Disciplinary History

A science that provides a classic case for discussion of discipline formation and of the meaning of scientific disciplines.

According to most historians of the sciences of the Earth, it is not legitimate to speak about geology as a definite science until at least the end of the eighteenth century. The consideration of the period between 1760 and 1840 (called by the traditional historiography the heroic period of geology) as a fundamental phase in the development of modern geology is also widely accepted (Guntau, "Emergence of Geology," p. 284; Laudan, "History of Geology," p. 314). Studies about the first appearance and development of the use of the word "geology" show clearly that this definition came to be used by scientists for indicating a scientific discipline from the last decades of the eighteenth century and especially from the 1780s onward.

The historiographical legacy coming from the classic late-nineteenth-century histories of geology such as Karl Zittel's *Geschichte der Geologie und Paläontologie* (1899: *History of Geology and Paleontology,* English edition, 1901) and Archibald Geikie's *Founders of Geology* (1897; 2d enlarged edition, 1905), followed also by Frank Adams's *Birth and Development of the Geological Sciences* (1938) and by other authors, seems to demonstrate that the eighteenth century was definitively crucial for a disciplinary history of geology.

However, the long process that determined the establishment of geology as a scientific discipline was gradual because, as Kenneth L. Taylor writes (p. 78), "Ideas emerge slowly, in stages. This is likely to be true especially for the idea of a discipline, which encompasses

purposes, methods and procedural rules. There may occur, in the evolution of a disciplinary concept, substitutions of symbolic terms in parallel with shifts in the idea." The first roots of this evolution may be traced in the second half of the seventeenth century, and the evidence of this now is better documented in Gabriel Gohau's *Les Sciences de la Terre aux XVIIe et XVIIIe siècles* (1990) and François Ellenberger's *Histoire de la geologie* (2d vol., 1994). It is significant that, also in other prominent works of the history of earth sciences, the period examined starts from the 1650s or the 1660s and ends between 1810 and the 1840s (Porter, *The Making of Geology;* Laudan, *From Mineralogy to Geology;* Herries Davies and Orme). The choice of such chronological limits follows a historiographical consciousness, which rejects the so-called "whig" interpretation in the history of the geosciences and is founded instead on the accurate study of the primary sources within their cultural, social, and economical contexts.

During the late seventeenth century the trend to elaborate "theories of the Earth" was evident, including well-known theoretical systems by Thomas Burnet (1635–1715), John Woodward (1665–1728), William Whiston (1667–1752), and Gottfried Wilhelm Leibniz (1646–1716). These theories were published between 1680 and 1695, but René Descartes (1596–1650) had already given an account of the Earth's formation in his *Principia Philosophiae* (Amsterdam, 1644). Another two important factors that marked the development of studies of the Earth in this century were the strong influence of ideas about Noah's Flood on the "theories of the Earth" and the debate about the origin of fossils. The latter determined the birth of paleontology.

However, a turning point for the establishment of a research methodology in the sciences of the Earth was certainly represented by what Gordon Herries Davies called in 1984 the "Stenonian Revolution." In fact the Danish scholar Niels Stensen (Nicholas Steno, 1638–1686) in his *De Solido intra Solidum Naturaliter Contento Dissertationis Prodromus* (Forerunner to a dissertation on a solid naturally enclosed within a solid, Florence, 1669) introduced a new interpretation of strata as the records of the Earth's history: "It was Steno who first clearly explained strata as sequential deposits: implicit in his work is that principle which was later to be known as the law of superimposition; and it was Steno who first explained and illustrated that most significant structural feature known to stratigraphy, the unconformity. . . . It was this Stenonian revolution, with its novel interpretation of rocks as historical documents, which made fully possible the historical reaction that for the next three hundred years was to dominate events in the interface of terrestrial object and human observer" (Herries Davies and Orme, p. 17).

The eighteenth-century scholars who were involved in studying the Earth's surface gradually adopted this methodological view, which necessarily was based on data collected in the field. Consequently, by 1800 a great quantity of information of an empirical nature was accumulated and an immense body of geological literature was published, as both Rhoda Rappaport and Victor Eyles stated in the historical literature of the 1960s: the latter has strongly put forward the thesis that in spite of the fact that the sciences of the Earth were "undeveloped" and "unorganized" during most of the eighteenth century, the earth sciences were nevertheless "the subject of widespread interest, and often of close study throughout the century, both because of their intrinsic interest and because of their economic interest" (Eyles, p. 160).

This was confirmed during the late eighteenth century, by the existence of an eclectic European community of "oryctologists" or "lithologists" (earth scientists), formed of naturalists, scientists involved in chemical or medical studies, but also of scholars with a technical background coming particularly from mining. They were often in contact with each other through personal correspondence. They were not necessarily linked to universities, but they could find an institutional base in the scientific societies usually sponsored by governments, such as the Academies of Sciences in Paris, Berlin, Bologna, and St. Petersburg.

The birth of this "identity" was also supported by an increase in field-researches on different phenomena and geological features within several different regional contexts. In fact most of these eighteenth-century researches could be related to each other because they investigated the same problems in different geographical areas. Consequently the scholars contacted each other or at least were often very well informed about the available literature and works in progress on the subjects of their interest—that is, many aspects of the physical environment.

Concerning these only a short outline of names and topics can be given here. Extinct volcanoes and igneous rocks were studied by Jean Etiénne Guettard (1715–1786) and Nicolas Desmarest (1725–1815) from France, and also by Italians such as Alberto Fortis (1741–1803), and Britons like John Strange (1732–1799) between the 1750s and the 1770s. The origin of springs was actively debated in the early eighteenth century and a decisive contribution was given by Antonio Vallisneri (1661–1730) in 1715. The strata and their lithological components were extensively investigated, particularly by English scholars such as John Strachey (1671–1743) and John Michell (1724–1793), by the Italian Giovanni Arduino (1714–1795), the Frenchman Jean-Louis Giraud-Soulavie (1752–1813), and by the Germans Johann Gottlob Lehmann (1719–1767) and Georg Christian Füchsel (1722–1773), but above all by William Smith (1769–1839), who published the results of his studies early in the nineteenth century. The mountains and their different rocktypes were classified in different units by Anton Lazzaro Moro (1687–1764), Giovanni Targioni Tozzetti (1712–1783), Lehmann, Arduino, Füchsel, Peter Simon Pallas (1741–1811), and Abraham Gottlob Werner (1749–1817). Theories about earthquakes were elaborated for example by John Michell and Rudolf Erich Raspe (1737–1794). Georges Louis Leclerc, Comte de Buffon (1707–1788) suggested a chronology for the history of the Earth in his *Époques de la nature* (1778). After the "theories of the Earth" published in 1748 and 1749 by Benoit de Maillet (1656–1738) and by Buffon himself, some new general theories based more on field evidences were elaborated by British scientists at the end of the century, first of all by James Hutton (1726–1797), who published the final version of his *Theory of the Earth* in 1795, but also for example by John Whitehurst (1713–1788) in 1778. Also several detailed researches on geomorphological aspects, on the figure of the Earth, on terrestrial magnetism, on minerals, crystals, and other subjects began to be produced regularly.

This does not mean that all the branches of the modern geological sciences were mostly established during this period of time, because, as Victor Eyles stated, "During the eighteenth century, very little subdivision of geology into subsidiary sciences took place, and such subdivisions as were used were imprecise" (Eyles, p. 161).

Nevertheless, the growing community of future geologists was gradually acquiring the characters of an autonomous scientific discipline. One characteristic was the increase and the specialization of collections exclusively devoted to lithological and mineralogical specimens. In the heterogeneous world of eighteenth-century scientific travelers, mineralogical and geological travels began to have their own specific place. The result was a significant production of published works containing accounts of these travels, which described and also compared the geological features of the different areas visited by the same traveler. Travel soon became an indispensable instrument of knowledge for a geologist who had previously explored only his own geographical region. It also represented the best way for meeting other scientists involved in similar researches within other cultural, political, economical, and social contexts.

Although this period is commonly accepted as important for the birth of the scientific discipline of geology, there have been different historical evaluations of the characteristic of these crucial years. According to Martin Guntau, who concentrates his work more on the eighteenth century, the important events of the process of formation of geology as a science were accompanied by specific social changes. On one hand, there were the conditions in the mining industries of several European countries, which required geological knowledge in order to ensure high production. On the other hand was the new attitude toward nature and science determined by the Enlightenment: this new vision was essentially freed from religious tutelage and inspired with deep intellectual optimism. Because of these changes, what we call today geological activities—such as description, measuring, and classification of geological-mineralogical facts, corresponding experimental and theoretical work, prospecting for deposits and geological mapping—came to form a stable and developing combination (Guntau, "The Emergence of Geology"; *Die Genesis der Geologie*).

Others historians have concentrated their attention on the possible links between the rising science of geology and mining, as for example during the time of the Industrial Revolution in Britain. Concerning this topic Roy Porter argues that any immediate relationship between industrialization and the making of geology was rather problematic (Porter, "The Industrial Revolution"). Nevertheless Porter himself has also emphasized that, in general, mining and quarrying greatly stimulated the development of the Earth sciences, showing the superposition of strata

down perpendicular shafts, the dip and the faults along horizontal galleries underground, and a consistent order among bedded rocks (especially in coal mines), which suggested to the scientists the conditions of their formation during sedimentation. This was true for scholars with a technical mining background and who were based in Continental Europe, such as Giovanni Arduino in Italy, who developed his litho-stratigraphical system thanks to knowledge obtained during his work as supervisor of mines. With regard to Porter's doubts, Rachel Laudan has recently stated that "a detailed examination of the evidence suggests that the Industrial Revolution and the development of English geology were largely independent. Most English geologists were gentlemen amateurs who neither contributed know-how to the industrializing north nor relied on new data from, say, the opening-up of new industrial mineral resources," while by contrast, on the Continent, "The development of industry, particularly mining and porcelain industries, went hand in hand with the development of geology from the mid-eighteenth century on" (Laudan, "History of Geology," p. 324).

Guntau again states that during the eighteenth century, the religiously oriented conception of the Earth came into ever-increasing contradiction with developing geological knowledge (Guntau, "Physikotheologie," p. 104). It is true, he writes, that "physicotheologists" essentially contributed to the progress achieved in geological knowledge; yet in the Age of Enlightenment the concepts of the Earth began to move away from religious motivation. The new bourgeois ideal of science, which was based on reason and which praised usefulness of knowledge as its ultimate goal, greatly stimulated geological knowledge. Essential changes in geological thinking manifested themselves among others in the understanding of the historical character of the Earth's past, the overcoming of biblical ideas about the Earth's age, and the interpretation of the nature of fossils. This argument, concludes Guntau, was an important prerequisite for the development of geology as a natural science in the end of the eighteenth century.

Other historical perspectives, such as Anthony Hallam's *Great Geological Controversies* (1983), pay particular attention to the role of the scientific controversies that took place from the eighteenth to the twentieth century. Around 1800 the controversies on the origin of rocks such as basalt and granite led not only to mineralogical or lithological problems but also to more general views on the role of the main geological agents: fire and water.

The simultaneous appearance of two contrary theories in the 1780s, Neptunism and Plutonism, which were respectively connected to the studies by Abraham Gottlob Werner and James Hutton, determined a decisive qualitative change in the formation of geology as a scientific discipline. Guntau has considered this change in *Die Genesis der Geologie als Wissenschaft* (*The Genesis of Geology as a Science*, pp. 61–106) as the development of the systemic character of geology—that is to say, the transition stage from empirical understanding of geological phenomena to theoretical interpretations of the nature of geology. The Neptunists supposed that all the rocks of the Earth's surface had been deposited from and consolidated in a formerly universal ocean (this was like a cosmogony, which seemed to many historians more linked to Genesis than to field work); on the other hand, the Plutonists thought that the rocks had been eroded from older land surfaces, deposited in the ocean and there consolidated by heat. "According to the Wernerians, the present land surface was revealed when the waters that had deposited the rocks gradually receded; but according to the Huttonians, the present land surface was revealed when the rocks consolidated under the ocean were elevated" (Laudan, "History of Geology," p. 315).

Within this controversy Laudan has highlighted the decisive European impact of the "Wernerian school" in her *From Mineralogy to Geology* (1987). This school was more powerful than the "Huttonian" from 1790 to the late 1820s, because of the authority of Werner as distinguished professor in the Mining Academy of Freiberg, which attracted students from all over the world. Mott Greene's *Geology in the Nineteenth Century* (1982), his history of geotectonics theories, has also attempted to correct the overemphasis given in the classic histories of geology to the importance of James Hutton and other British geologists, who had been preceded by decades on the European continent by the work of Desmarest, Guettard, Lehmann, Pallas, Werner, but also Torbern Bergman (1735–1784) and Horace Bénédict de Saussure (1740–1799).

Unfortunately, the lack of knowledge of the development of eighteenth-century terrestrial sciences in several national and regional contexts, especially non-European, is still an open historical question and represents the main problem for the acquisition of a fully satisfactory synthesis about the process of institutionalization of geology. Martin Guntau has tried, in his *Die Genesis der Geologie als Wissenschaft* (1984, pp. 37–57), to summarize and to compare the eighteenth-century development of geological studies in Great Britain, Russia, France, Germany, and Spain.

The French situation in the eighteenth and nineteenth centuries has been analyzed in detail by various valid contributions, above all by François Ellenberger, Gabriel Gohau, Kennard Bork, and Kenneth Taylor. The latter has analyzed the beginnings of a French geological identity, (considered to be strongly associated with empiricism, secularism, and practical utility) through the significant figures of De Saussure, Déodat de Dolomieu (1750–1801), Barthélémy Faujas de Saint Fond (1741–1819), and Jean-Claude Delamétherie (1743–1817). In Germany the attention of historians has long been concentrated on Werner and his early-nineteenth-century pupils at Freiberg Academy. These included Alexander von Humboldt (1769–1859) and Leopold von Buch (1774–1853), who subsequently moved from a Neptunistic concept of the Earth to a view influenced more by the Vulcanistic theory. However other countries, such as Italy, still need an accurate general historical account of the development of the earth sciences in the period.

In Great Britain, the investigation of the history of geology has probably received the most attention, especially in relation to the early nineteenth century. After the classic books like Charles Gillispie's *Genesis and Geology* (1959), Gordon Davies's *The Earth in Decay* (1969) on British geomorphology, and Roy Porter's *Making of Geology* (1977) in Britain from the 1660s to the years after 1810, other studies like Nicolaas Rupke's *Great Chain of History: William Buckland and the English School of Geology, 1814–1849* (1983), Martin Rudwick's *Great Devonian Controversy* (1985), James Secord's *Controversy in Victorian Geology: The Cambrian-Silurian Debate* (1986), David Oldroyd's *Highlands Controversy* (1990), and Dennis Dean's *James Hutton and the History of Geology* (1992) have enriched the historical knowledge of an important context. It now appears clear that during about thirty years before 1820 an immense work of research was realized, entirely based in the British area: strata and their fauna were studied, geological sections and maps were drawn, a coherent nomenclature was established, and the history of the Earth was reconstructed with the use of its rocks. A community of geologists was well constituted and operating after 1820 in the United Kingdom, and it had already an institutional support, its first textbooks and chairs of teaching.

Certainly during these years the central figure in European geology was Charles Lyell (1797–1875). The above-mentioned studies, however, have also enlarged the historical view of other prominent geologists of the British Isles, such as John Playfair (1748–1819), Richard Kirwan (1733–1812), Robert Jameson (1774–1854), William Buckland (1784–1846), Roderick Impey Murchison (1792–1871), and Adam Sedgwick (1785–1873).

The uniformitarian theory advocated by Lyell in his famed *Principles of Geology* (1830–1833) clashed with the catastrophist idea explained by the French scientist Georges Cuvier (1769–1832) in his *Discours sur les révolutions de la surface du globe* (*Discourse on Revolutions of the Globe's Surface*, 1812). Lyell demonstrated the validity of Hutton's thesis that slowly acting natural processes, such as those operating today, are entirely adequate to explain all geological phenomena. According to the uniformitarian theory, the geological agents of the past were the same as those of the present, both in their type and intensity. The catastrophist hypothesis, which was supported in the later nineteenth century also by William Buckland, Leopold von Buch, and Léonce Élie de Beaumont (1798–1874), instead postulated large periodic catastrophic events (such as violent volcanic eruptions) to explain modifications of the Earth's crust.

As in the case of Hutton, the importance of Lyell for the establishment of geology as a modern scientific discipline has been widely emphasized, especially in the early historiography of geology, which often considered the making of modern geology mainly a British accomplishment. Rachel Laudan ("Redefinitions of a Discipline," pp. 81–84, 87–91, 94–95, 99–100) argues that Lyell's historical introduction to the *Principles of Geology* (which influenced most subsequent English-speaking historiography) was intended to promote a revolution in geology by showing how previous methodology had prevented geology from becoming a respected science. Laudan's lower estimation of William Smith's role and her claim in *From Mineralogy to Geology* (pp. 164–168, 221) that the position of Élie de Beaumont could have been even more influential than that of Lyell attracted some critics. But certainly the development of geology, in particular stratigraphy, was also significant in early-

nineteenth-century France, for example with the researches by Georges Cuvier and Alexandre Brogniart (1770–1847).

François Ellenberger in his *Histoire de la geologie* (1994) has suggested the concept of *"révolution scientifique créatrice"* for indicating the big change, in the years from 1800 to 1825, that determined the establishment of modern geology both as an organized discipline and as a methodology recognized by a large scientific community (pp. 294–295). Geology also became fashionable and popular among a wide audience, especially in England and France. The three main concepts, entirely new, that characterized this "revolution," according to Ellenberger, were: the immensity of the past times and of the age of the Earth; the radical modifications of the living world in the time, shown by the succession of fossil fauna and flora; and the transformation of the rocks (pp. 295–317).

Until the mid-nineteenth century, some fundamental stages of the disciplinary history of geology took place: the institutionalizing of teaching, the publication of the first textbooks, and the establishment of geological national surveys and societies or institutions.

According to the majority of historians, the first chair of geology was established in France in the new *Muséum d'Histoire Naturelle* of Paris, which replaced the *Jardin de Roi* in 1793: in the same year Barthélémy Faujas de Saint Fond was appointed as the first professor of geology in the *Muséum* (Guntau, "The Emergence of Geology," p. 286; Gohau, *Histoire de la geologie,* pp. 7, 236).

In the European universities the teaching of mineralogy (usually associated with chemistry) had instead been introduced since the mid-eighteenth century in countries with a strong mineralogical tradition, such as at Uppsala University in Sweden. Already in the Mining Academies that had been established in the late eighteenth century, some teaching courses were very nearly courses of geology, such as the course of *Gebirgslehre* (rock theory) given by Werner in the Mining Academy of Freiberg from 1778 to 1817, which was called Geognosy from 1786.

In those institutions the predominant subject was mineralogy, which also included the study of rocks and the Earth's surface. It was complementary to the teaching of mining techniques. However geology became an established discipline in the mining academies before it did in the universities. Apart from the courses of Geognosy given by Werner, in Mexico City the local mining academy established a new chair of geology in 1794, while in the *École des Mines* of Paris, Élie de Beaumont held the first chair of geology, set up in 1835.

The teaching of geology within European universities had long been included in the vast eighteenth-century disciplinary area of Natural History (for example, in the Italian universities), but it was also connected to the first chairs of chemistry. In France, the chemistry courses given between 1742 and 1768 by Guillaume-François Rouelle (1703–1770) in the *Jardin de Roi* in Paris involved mineralogy but also geological subjects. Several of Rouelle's pupils were later engaged in geological researches. Among the earliest formal lectures on geological subjects were those given in the Scottish universities, such as Edinburgh and Aberdeen, from the mid-eighteenth century, while university chairs or lectureships in geology were established in the nineteenth century (Eyles, pp. 178–180). In the English universities less attention was paid to geology and mineralogy in the eighteenth century. Cambridge, in spite of the existence of a Woodwardian chair since 1728 (which, according to Victor Eyles, was never used for delivering any formal lectures on geology), started a lectureship in geology around 1818, while Oxford started one in 1819 (Eyles, pp. 180–181; Guntau, "Geologische Institutionen," p. 235).

Departments of geology and mineralogy with respective chairs and teaching programs began to be established especially from the 1840s all over Europe and in North America and particularly in the English-speaking world. In Germany the first chair of mineralogy and geology was set up in Berlin in 1810, and it was followed by similar chairs in Bonn and Heidelberg (1818), in Tübingen (1837), in Leipzig (1842), in Munich (1843) and so on until the end of the 1870s (Guntau, "Geologische Institutionen," p. 235). Other countries created their first chairs of geology within the universities belatedly: in Italy they were established mostly after the 1860s, also because of political reasons connected to the unification of the country in those years; in France Constant Prévost (1787–1856) in 1831 held the first chair of geology independent from mineralogy within the faculty of Mathematical and Physical Sciences in Paris (Gohau, *Histoire de la géologie,* p. 8).

Contemporary to the beginnings of academic teaching of geology was the publication of the first generation of geological textbooks, which, as Roy Porter has stated, "presuppose

that working first principles are adequately established, and point to a popular audience seeking instructions" (Porter, *The Making of Geology,* p. 210). Among the first textbooks were Robert Jameson's *Treatise of Geognosy* (Edinburgh, 1808) and Jean-André de Luc's *Traité élémentaire de Géologie* (Paris, 1809). They also included popular classics such as Robert Bakewell's *Introduction to Geology* (London, 1813) and Parker Cleaveland's *Elementary Treatise on Mineralogy and Geology* (Boston, 1816), but also the lesser-known *Elementos de Orictognosia* by Andrés Manuel del Río (Mexico City, 1795–1805), the *Introduzione alla Geologia* by Scipione Breislak (Milan, 1811), William Phillips's *Outline of Mineralogy and Geology* (London, 1815), Jean François d'Aubuisson de Voisins's *Traité de géognosie* (Paris and Strasbourg, 1819), Ebenezer Emmons's *Manual of Mineralogy and Geology* (Albany, 1823), and others.

From 1830 (particularly during the decade up to 1840), the didactic works increased rapidly everywhere: some significant textbooks until midcentury were Henry Thomas de la Beche's *Geological Manual* (London, 1831), Karl Caesar von Leonhard's *Lehrbuch der Geognosie und Geologie* (Stuttgart, 1835), Lyell's *Elements of Geology* (London, 1838), Jean-Jacques Huot's *Nouveau cours élémentaire de geologie* (Paris, 1837–1839), J.J. d'Omalius d'Halloy's *Élements de géologie* (Paris, 1839, 3d ed.), François Sulpice Beudant's *Géologie* (Paris, 1841), Karl Vogt's *Lehrbuch der Geologie* (Braunschweig, 1846–1847), Alcide d'Orbigny's *Cours élémentaire de paléontologie et de géologie stratigraphiques* (Paris, 1849–1852), and Karl Friedrich Naumann's *Lehrbuch der Geognosie* (Leipzig, 1850–1854).

In this period a significant change in geological cartography and illustrations took place: "If we survey a broad range of late eighteenth century books and journals on topics relevant to the future science of 'geology'"—wrote Martin Rudwick in 1976— "one of their most striking features (with of course a few exceptions) is the scarcity and poor quality of their illustrations. A similar survey of material published in the 1830s shows a remarkable change: the texts are now complemented by a wide range of maps, sections, landscapes and diagrams of other kind. During the period in which 'geology' emerged as a self-conscious new discipline with clearly defined intellectual goals and well established institutional forms, there was thus a comparable emergence of what I shall call a 'visual language' for the science, which is reflected not only in a broadening range of kinds of illustration, but also in a great increase in their sheer quantity" (Rudwick, p. 150).

The recognition that geology could provide benefits for industrialization and national prosperity encouraged many governments to promote and finance geological surveys for compiling inventories of local geological and mineral resources. The establishment of these new institutions obviously improved the quality and the diffusion of geological cartography, particularly from the 1830s. The earliest geological survey was planned in France in 1822 within the *Corps Royal des Mines* and the fieldwork for mapping the whole country started in 1825. A short time later several national geological surveys began to be established in Europe and in North America. In the United States, most of the state surveys were founded quite early, between the 1830s and the 1850s: the earliest were in Massachusetts (1831), Tennessee (1831), and Maryland (1833). The Geological Survey of England and Wales was established in 1835 under Henry Thomas de la Beche (1796–1855) and was followed by similar institutions in Canada (1842), Ireland (1845), and India (1851). In Europe geological surveys appeared in Austria-Hungary and Spain (1849), later in Sweden and Norway (1858), Switzerland (1859), France (around 1868), Portugal (1869), Prussia (1873), Italy (1873), Belgium (1878), and Russia (1882). The national geological survey of the United States was eventually founded in 1879, although the national government had sponsored geological surveying since the 1830s (Guntau, "Geologische Institutionen," pp. 238–240).

Up to the early nineteenth century there had been no society or scientific academy devoted exclusively to geological topics. The scientific academies and societies, established in Europe, especially during the eighteenth century, show different levels of interest for geological researches, according to their cultural-scientific "policy," the preparation of their members, and the geological features of the area where they operated. But it is important to notice that the proceedings of these institutions, such as the *Philosophical Transactions* of the Royal Society of London, the *Transactions* of the Royal Society of Edinburgh, or the *Memoires* of the French Academy of Sciences, included several studies on geological subjects and contributed to the diffusion of these new researches.

In the British Isles, where the interest in geology had rapidly increased after 1780, the need for an institution devoted to accumulating geological data collected in the field was stronger than elsewhere, particularly in surveying and mapping the strata. The first geological society was established in London in 1807 and its first president was George Bellas Greenough (1778–1855); the society published the *Transactions* of the Geological Society of London from 1811 to 1856. After 1845 it was largely superseded by the *Quarterly Journal*. The *Transactions* have long been regarded as the first periodical publication in geology, but Martin Guntau ("The Emergence of Geology," p. 286; *Die Genesis der Geologie*, p. 109) has also quoted the earlier *Taschenbuch für die gesamte Mineralogie* (published in Frankfurt-am-Main since 1807). Nevertheless we still know very little about the growth of the geological-mineralogical journals in other national contexts. Consequently a rigid judgment of priority or significance of geological textbooks and journals is rather problematic.

Between 1800 and 1860 many geological societies were founded in the British Isles, for example in Cornwall (1814), Dublin (1831), Edinburgh (1834), Manchester (1848), London (Geologists' Association, 1858), and Glasgow (1858). The *Société Géologique de France* was founded in 1830, while the *Deutsche Geologische Gesellschaft* in Germany and a similar institution in Hungary were established in 1848. Among the numerous European and non-European societies founded after the mid-nineteenth century may be mentioned those in Ireland (1864), Sweden (1871), Italy (1881), Switzerland (1882), and the United States (1888) (Guntau, "Geologische Institutionen," p. 234).

In the second half of the nineteenth century the discipline of geology was definitively established in several contexts: the geologist is a figure completely settled in the academic research and teaching system, but the role is also totally recognized within the international scientific community, and geologists also increased the links with technology and the economy for the exploitation of the natural resources via applied geology.

Very significant developments took place particularly in the thirty years between 1885 and 1915: we must remember the tectonic theory by Eduard Suess (1831–1914) published in his *Das Antlitz der Erde (The face of the earth,* 1883), Lord Kelvin's calculation of the age of the Earth (1899), the "continental drift" of Alfred Wegener (1880–1930), first announced in 1912, up to the most recent "revolution" of plate tectonic theory, which has dominated geology since the mid-1960s (Laudan, "Redefinitions of a Discipline," pp. 84–87, 95–100). Meanwhile the science of geology developed a gradual specialization in different branches within the universities and the institutes of research. The International Union of Geological Sciences was founded in 1878, and the first International Geological Congress was held the same year in Paris with participants from twenty-three countries. The congresses continued to be organized every three or four years in different countries (Guntau, "Geologische Institutionen," pp. 234–235).

In 1979 Kenneth Taylor suggested that "the science of geology as it came to be conceived in the train of the term's invention was not a direct, lineal descendant of a more primitive eighteenth century version of the same thing. Instead, the late eighteenth century developments that set the stage for the emergence of geology as a new discipline included a reordering or reorganization of the sciences, making room in a new way for a distinct science of the Earth" (Taylor, p. 83). This distinct science was that established mainly in the first two decades of the nineteenth century. It is interesting to report that François Ellenberger has noticed that today's geologists feel themselves in a strange world when facing eighteenth-century geological literature, but suddenly feel at home with the writings from the 1830s. There they recognize the characters of their own present discipline: specific nomenclatures and methodologies.

Ellenberger, Guntau, and other historians agree in stating that the rise of geology as a scientific discipline did not occur on the basis of a single event or of the theories of a few prominent scientific figures, but depended on a series of conditions, a combination of factors. These included social and economical situations (for example the professionalization of the geologist, and the role of the Industrial Revolution), qualitative changes (accumulation of geological knowledge, and a new relationship with religion), and institutionalization (establishment of geological societies and surveys, and publication of textbooks).

Rachel Laudan pointed out in her 1990 article "The History of Geology" (p. 314) the need to update the "received view" of the history of geology with the acquisition of more information about what she called the social history of geology, the methodology of geology, and the relation between geology and religion. Because history of geology is one of the youngest histories of science, the aim toward a disciplinary history of geology still needs more investigations based on the primary sources, but not only about strictly scientific questions. These investigations must also ask new questions about the nature of geological controversies, about the social setting of geology, about its relationships with other sciences, about the importance of theories, experiments, and fieldwork, and about the development and the institutionalization of the discipline within national contexts, especially in the nineteenth century.

Ezio Vaccari

Bibliography

Ellenberger, François. *Histoire de la géologie. Tome 2. La grande éclosion et ses prémices 1660–1810.* Paris: Technique et Documetation (Lavoisier), 1994.

Eyles, Victor A. "The Extent of Geological Knowledge in the Eighteenth Century, and the Methods by which It was Diffused." In *Toward a History of Geology,* edited by Cecil J. Schneer, pp. 159–183. Cambridge, Mass. and London: M.I.T. Press, 1969.

Gohau, Gabriel. *Histoire de la géologie.* Paris: Éditions de la Découverte, 1987. *A History of Geology,* revised and translated by Albert V. Carozzi and Marguerite Carozzi. New Brunswick and London: Rutgers University Press, 1990.

———. *Les Sciences de la Terre aux XVIIe et XVIIIe siècles. Naissance da la géologie.* Paris: Albin Michel, 1990.

Guntau, Martin. *Die Genesis der Geologie als Wissenschaft.* Berlin: Akademie Verlag, 1984.

———. "The Emergence of Geology as a Scientific Discipline." *History of Science* 16 (1978): pp. 280–290.

———. "Geologische Institutionen und Staatliche initiativen in der Geschichte." In *Geosciences/Geowissenschaften,* III.Teil. *Proceedings of the Symposium of the XVIIIth International Congress of History of Science,* edited by M. Büttner and E. Kohler, pp. 229–239. Bochum: Universitätsverlag, 1991.

Guntau, Martin. "Pysikotheologie und Aufklärung in ihren Beziehungen zur geologischen Erkenntnis im 18. Jahrhundert." *Zeitschrift für Geologischen Wissenschaften* (Berlin) 8 (1980): pp. 87–106.

Herries Davies, Gordon L., and Anthony R. Orme. *Two Centuries of Earth Science 1650–1850*. Papers presented at a Clark Library Seminar, November 3, 1984. Los Angeles: William Andrews Clark Memorial Library, 1989.

Laudan, Rachel. *From Mineralogy to Geology: The Foundations of a Science 1680–1830*. Chicago: University of Chicago Press, 1987.

———. "The History of Geology, 1780–1840." In *Companion to the History of Science*, edited by M.C.R. Olby, G.N. Cantor, and M.J.S. Hodge, pp. 314–325. London, Routledge, 1990.

———. "Redefinitions of a Discipline: Histories of Geology and Geological History." In *Function and Uses of Disciplinary Histories*, edited by Loren Graham, Wolf Lepenies, and Peter Weingart, pp. 79–104. Dordrecht, Boston, and Lancaster: D. Reidel Publishing Company, 1983.

Porter, Roy. "The Industrial Revolution and the Rise of the Science of Geology." In *Changing Perspectives in the History of Science*, edited by M. Teich and R. Young, pp. 320–343. London: Heinemann, 1973.

———. *The Making of Geology. Earth Science in Britain 1660–1815*. Cambridge: Cambridge University Press, 1977.

Rappaport, Rhoda. "Problems and Sources in the History of Geology, 1749–1810." *History of Science* 3 (1964): pp. 60–77.

Rudwick, Martin J.S. "The Emergence of Visual Language for Geological Science 1760–1840." *History of Science* 14 (1976): pp. 149–195.

Taylor, Kenneth L. "Geology in 1776: Some Notes on the Character of an Incipient Science." In *Two Hundred Years of American Geology*, edited by Cecil E. Schneer, pp. 75–90. Hanover, N.H.: University Press of New England, 1979.

See also Actualism, Uniformitarianism, and Catastrophism; Age of the Earth, before 1800; Age of the Earth, since 1800; Cartography; Continental Drift and Plate Tectonics; Deluge; Diluvialism; Disciplinary History; Earthquakes, Theories; Economic Geology; Geological Societies; Geological Surveys; Geology; Geomorphology; Mineralogy; Mining Academies; Mining and Knowledge of the Earth; Paleontology; Plutonists, Neptunists, Vulcanists; Presentism; Sacred Theory of the Earth; Stratigraphy; Volcanoes, Theories before 1800

Geology in the Laboratory ca. 1800

An important and neglected aspect of early geology.

Until recently, students of the history of geology might have concluded that in the eighteenth century when geology was emerging as a science it advanced exclusively by an interplay of field evidence and theory. Eminent geologists espoused theories such as Plutonism or Neptunism, and went to the field to observe and find instances that might support their positions, such as a baked clay next to a rock intrusion, igneous veins crosscutting sedimentary rock, or marine fossils under a volcanic layer. However, neither major theory could produce definitive instances, and both were hampered by the assumption that all rocks must be formed by one agency only—either heat, or precipitation from water suspension or solution. The laboratory provided another kind of evidence. While its function was more to disprove some instances of rock origin than to resolve the claims of overarching theories, it contributed to a lack of resolution between those theories.

The historiography of geology has generally not dealt extensively with evidence from laboratory experiment. An interesting trend can be seen in this history. In the period of about 1890 to 1910, experimentation was rather fully discussed, especially that of Lazzaro Spallanzani, Horace Bénedict de Saussure, and Sir James Hall, among others. In the mid-twentieth century, the place of the laboratory was a minor theme, essentially equated with the work of Sir James Hall, who was said to have provided proof of the Huttonian thesis. Later, Rhoda Rappaport in a 1964 article and Mott Greene in *Geology in the Nineteenth Century* (1982) both noted the lack of work on experimental geology. This has been addressed lately in Rachel Laudan's *From Mineralogy to Geology* (1987), Sally Newcomb's 1990 article on British experimentalists, and Bernhard Fritscher's *Vulkanismusstreit und Geochemie* (1991). But a large eighteenth-century literature remains to be investigated.

Experimentation on earth materials began early. In the late seventeenth century Nicholas Lemery mixed powdered sulfur and iron filings, buried the damp mixture, and later watched as the surrounding earth swelled and gave off sulfurous fumes. This reaction was invoked as a mechanism for volcanism for more than a century. In the early and mid-eighteenth century there were others such as René-Antoine Ferchault de Réaumur and Johann Heinrich Pott who experimented with fusion of minerals and earths and their mixtures, and whose discoveries entered the fund of eighteenth-century knowledge. They were not testing geological theory, but rather were attempting to reproduce the process for making Chinese porcelain. However, Pott pointed out in his *Lithogéognosie* (1753) that thorough investigation of the properties of natural substances by true experiments could lead to discovery of both connections between and the proper distribution of various natural products in nature. In Johann Friedrich Henckel's *Pyritologia,* originally published in 1725, and translated into English in 1757, he wrote that discussing the laboratory took more than a few pages, and that while this enterprise led to a good knowledge of nature, there was a good bit of trouble associated with the making of proper experiments, despite the pleasure to be gotten from it. Jean Darcet continued this work with better furnaces and control, and added fusing of a natural rock that we now identify as basalt, as reported in his *Mémoire sur l'Action d'un Feu Egal* (1766).

Laboratory equipment was increasingly available during the course of the eighteenth century. Iron, glasshouse, and the more dependable porcelain furnaces were used, as well as small laboratory furnaces that were essential for analysis "in the dry way" or by fusion (Eklund). Later, methods were devised that subjected samples to increased temperatures while under pressure. Josiah Wedgwood's pyrometer pieces introduced in the 1780s, while not accurate, allowed the first measurement of high temperatures. Work at high temperatures or with strong reagents was encouraged by availability of containers made of Réaumur's porcelain or of platinum. During the latter part of the eighteenth century the blowpipe, which had a long history in technology, was used for mineral analysis (Oldroyd). About the same time, methods of wet chemical analysis became productive and were applied both to mineral and other natural waters, and to minerals and rocks. Both wet and dry analyses were used in support of geological theories (Laudan, chap. 3; Fritscher, chap. 8).

Experimentation specifically designed to answer questions about rock origin began at this fertile period toward 1800, and benefited from the insights gained about elemental substances and gases by chemists. Experiments to learn about fusion, solution, and crystallization characteristics of minerals and rocks often were done by investigators as well known in chemistry as in geology. Much of this was done to explore and clarify theories of rock origin.

The origin of basalt was a primary preoccupation around 1800, but granite and limestone/marble were also of considerable interest because their behavior could corroborate either Plutonism or Neptunism (Newcomb; Fritscher). Beginning with Jean Darcet in 1766 and others, basalt was readily fused and generally yielded a glassy solid upon cooling. There were efforts to make an association between the amount of heat required and the heat possibly available to account for volcanism. Despite the clear association of crystalline basalt with extinct volcanoes, its ready fusion and lack of a crystalline texture upon cooling implied it could not have solidified from fusion. While Sir James Hall's investigations of slowly cooled basalt to reproduce partially crystalline textures, reported to the Royal Society of Edinburgh in his "Experiments on Whinstone and Lava" (1805), seemed to favor an igneous origin, Richard Kirwan in 1794 and others had contended that the texture was the result of volatiles being driven off. This was supported by analyses showing the presence of volatiles in basalts. In 1805 Robert Kennedy examined both some basalts and some "crystallites," the somewhat crystalline results of slow cooling of fused basalts produced by Hall, and found the definite presence of saline substances. Another theory tested in the laboratory was that of the role of sulfur or another combustible in both the fluidity of lava and the origin of volcanism, and the effect this would have on the resultant solidified rock. Lazzaro Spallanzani and Déodat de Gratet de Dolomieu were among those who investigated this problem (von Zittel, p. 98).

Whole rock analysis was done by processes surprisingly similar to wet rock analysis of the twentieth century. An important connection is that silica was identified, both in rocks and in mineral waters. Examples of this are Joseph Black's "Analysis of Hot Spring Water from Iceland" (1794) and Robert Kennedy's 1805 article. Rock deposition from water solution was a mechanism that could be more readily demonstrated in the laboratory than could a source for the enormous heat required to fuse entire formations of rock.

The origin of granite also could not be easily explained as the result of cooling from fusion. De Saussure and others attempted to fuse granite and saw that the quartz was unaffected, as he reported in *Voyages dans les Alpes* (1779). Hall reported in "Observations on the Formation of Granite" in 1794 that he was unable to demonstrate recrystallization of granite after attempted fusion. In granite, well developed crystals of feldspar surrounded by less well-developed crystals of quartz were difficult to explain, when it was known that feldspar has a much lower fusion temperature.

Limestone/marble could not readily be explained as products of consolidation by heat, when the process of producing lime from limestone had been used since antiquity. Attempts to actually fuse limestone were failures. Hall's claims to have fused powdered limestone to a marble texture under pressure without loss of carbon dioxide were impressive in his 1812 "Account of a Series of Experiments, Shewing the Effect of Compression in Modifying the Action of Heat." However, there were arguments that natural processes could not mimic the pressures projected for consolidation under a mass of sea water.

Despite the similarity of some of those processes used in the laboratory and the kinds of conclusions drawn from them to ongoing methods of gaining knowledge about earth materials, the function of the investigations was very much consonant with, indeed inseparable from, the eighteenth-century frame of reference. The two possibilities in the pressing problem of rock origin dictated investigation by modes of fire ("dry" analysis) and water ("wet" analysis). This built on the history of mineral identification and classification in the eighteenth century (Laudan, chap. 3).

In early geology, the laboratory was a window on the natural world. Many sources, particularly those in German, French, Italian, and Swedish, remain to be investigated.

Sally Newcomb

Bibliography
Eklund, Jon. *The Incompleat Chymist.* Smithsonian Studies in History and Technology, no. 33. Washington, D.C.: Smithsonian Institution Press, 1975.
Fritscher, Berhhard. *Vulkanismusstreit und Geochemie.* Stuttgart: Franz Steiner Verlag, 1991.
Greene, Mott T. *Geology in the Nineteenth Century.* Chicago: University of Chicago Press, 1982.
Laudan, Rachel. *From Mineralogy to Geology.* Chicago: University of Chicago Press, 1987.
Newcomb, Sally. "Contributions of British Experimentalists to the Discipline of Geology: 1780–1820." *Proceedings of the American Philosophical Society* 134, no. 2 (1990): pp. 161–225.
Oldroyd, David R. "Edward Daniel Clarke, 1769–1822, and his Role in the History of the Blowpipe." *Annals of Science* 29 (1972): pp. 213–235.
Rappaport, Rhoda. "Problems and Sources in the History of Geology." *History of Science* 3 (1964): pp. 60–77.
Zittel, Karl Alfred von. *History of Geology and Paleontology.* London: Walter Scott, 1901.

See also Chemical Revolution; Matter, Properties at High Pressure and Temperature; Petrology; Plutonists, Neptunists, Vulcanists

Geology: The Word

First appeared as *Geologia* in certain Latin book titles in seventeenth-century Europe.

The English word "geology" was not used until 1735, when Benjamin Martin used it to mean the study of the Earth, as opposed to astronomy, the study of the heavens. Geology had a similarly broad meaning ("the knowledge of the state and nature of the Earth") in Samuel Johnson's great English dictionary of 1755. After related developments in France, the terms "geology," "geological," and "geologist" all appeared in English during the 1780s. The first writers to use them consistently, in the 1790s, were James Hutton's most outspoken opponents, Jean André Deluc and Richard Kirwan. Hutton himself did not use these terms regularly before 1794. But John Playfair treated all three as normal English in his famous *Illustrations of the Huttonian Theory* in 1802. The Geological Society of London was founded in 1807, by which time the name of the science was thoroughly established, although its exact subjects and methods were still hotly debated.

Dennis R. Dean

Bibliography
Dean, Dennis R. "The Word 'Geology.'" *Annals of Science* 36 (1979): pp. 35–43.

See also Disciplinary History; Geochemistry: The Word and Disciplinary History; Geography: The Word; Geology: Disciplinary History; Geomorphology: The Word; Geophysics: The Word; Geothermics: The Word

Geomagnetism in Nineteenth-Century Italy

An example of the importance of placing science in cultural context.

In the nineteenth century the Italian scientific community, almost entirely concentrated in the universities, was extremely small and distributed on a wide arch of disciplines; the proportion of university chairs in science to those in other fields was very low. In 1894, as Roberto Maiocchi writes in his book *Non solo Fermi (Not Only Fermi,* p. 11), there were 15 chairs of experimental and mathematical physics and 47 of mathematics, while there were 87 in the humanities, 166 juridical and administrative subjects, and 195 in medicine. Research supported by industry or private organizations was practically unknown.

From a methodological and cultural viewpoint, furthermore, the scientific community was strongly divided between scientists in physics, chemistry, astronomy, astrophysics, meteorology, and geomagnetism on the one side. On the other side there were mathematicians. The former, in the main, strongly criticized—rhetorically appealing to Galileo—the use of mathematics in natural sciences. Mathematics was sometimes seen as an obstacle to the knowledge of nature, which, instead, could be reached only through experimentation and induction, without any use of hypothetical models.

Mathematicians, in contrast, conducted very abstract researches on traditional problems. Mathematical-physicists, moreover, were not a bridge between the two communities: they saw in physics a source of strictly mathematical studies. For them it was unimaginable that mathematics could be constitutive of physics.

Some historians of science, who have studied this period in Italy (for example Gerald Holton in his book *Immaginazione scientifica [The Scientific Imagination]),* agree that from Alessandro Volta, around 1800, until Enrico Fermi, in the 1930s, Italian physics lacked creativity. Other historians, such as Barbara Reeves in her article "Tradizioni," have strongly underlined as a significant episode in nineteenth-century Italian physics the so-called "School of Pisa," which with Carlo Matteucci (1811–1868), Ottaviano Mossotti (1791–1863), Riccardo Felici (1819–1902), and Enrico Betti (1823–1892) kept step with the most innovative international scientific environment and established a research tradition.

There was another tradition in Italy of research in terrestrial and cosmic physics, an area including meteorology, geomagnetism, and astrophysics. In the middle of the century, in fact, these disciplines, as they were deemed as having nothing to do with astronomy, moved away from astronomical observatories, which were dedicated to classical astronomy. The "cosmic" side of this new tradition can be connected, in many documented ways, to the development of Italian physics in the 1930s, but that is another story.

Besides methodological and cultural problems, there were also political problems: Italy was divided into states characterized since 1800 by great political instability subsequent to the quakes created in Europe by the French Revolution of 1789. Industrial development was, moreover, strongly inhomogeneous and concentrated essentially in northern Italy, which in the late eighteenth century had taken advantage of enlightened policies of Austrian government.

The necessary conditions for the development of physics were lacking, and thus meteorology, geomagnetism, and astrophysics, which seemed to be realizable without mathematics, flourished instead. They seemed to fit better the scientific culture of Italian scientists. These scientists faced research problems essentially experimentally, very often in a deep religious context, in order to show the regularity of natural phenomena on a cosmic scale and the interconnection of different phenomena. They sought the unity of the cosmos, the fruit of a single act of a divine creation. In that context it isn't surprising that the *Kosmos* (1845–1858) of Alexander von Humboldt (1769–1859), or the *Physique du Globe* (1861) of Lambert Quetelet (1796–1874), provided scientific research models that strongly influenced Italian scientists. Visits of the two famous scientists to Italy reinforced this effect.

Concerning geomagnetism specifically, the publication of Gauss's works on this topic in the 1830s represented for Italy, as it did other nations, a revolutionary event in the field. The other significant occurrence for the study and practice of geomagnetism in Italy was the political unification of the country, starting in the 1860s. As a result we can distinguish three periods in the study of geomagnetism in Italy during the nineteenth century, with well-distinguished characteristics.

In the first period, from 1800 until the publication of the "Intensitas" of Gauss in 1833, the study of geomagnetism was carried out essentially in the astronomical observatories as an ancillary activity. Measurements of magnetic declination and its diurnal variations, in some cases also of inclination, but not of intensity, were carried out as discussed by Ciro Chistoni in 1890. The involvement of astronomers was not accidental: they already used related instruments and had the necessary skill to determine the geographic meridian, to measure small angles with reliable precision, and, finally, they had watches for a precise measurement of time (see Cawood). Besides astronomers, geodesists also measured geomagnetic elements. Magnetic declination measurements were made from 1806 to 1823 by the Istituto Geografico Militare di Milano (Geographic Military Institute of Milan) during the topographic survey of Northern Italy and the hydrographic survey of the Adriatic Sea.

In summary, in this first period, measurements of the declination and of its variation were carried out by astronomers and by geodesists, as they considered them useful for their main activity. These measurements were made with various instruments and methods, but none of them were of any theoretical interest. These measurements usually were not even published. Even if some researcher introduced innovative methods in the study of geomagnetism, these innovations did not enter into a cumulative scientific research tradition because they lacked the context that could give them value and continuity.

The second period runs from the 1833 publication of the "Intensitas" of Gauss until the early 1860s, when the political unification of Italy started. It is the period of the diffusion of instrumentation and of the methods of measurements proposed by Gauss, even if "non-Gaussian" instrumentation and methods continued to be used. Moreover, more institutions carried out geomagnetic observations and, in some astronomical observatories, qualified researchers were specifically oriented to geomagnetism, according to Gauss's approach.

Of the two main memoirs by Gauss on geomagnetism—the "Intensitas" and the "Allgemeine Theorie des Erdmagnetismus" in 1839—the former was extremely important in Italy, whereas the latter was practically without consequence. This is further evidence of the low interest of natural scientists in a mathematical approach to science and of mathematicians in pursuing researches in new fields—as the application of the potential theory to real physical situations.

The "Intensitas" was translated into Ital-ian by Paolo Frisiani Sr., second astronomer of the astronomical Brera Observatory in Milan, with the title "Misura assoluta" ("Absolute Measurement"), and with the addition, written by Frisiani in "Annotazioni," of several comments explaining the mathematical contents. Frisiani, a theoretician, published between 1860 and 1874 four memoirs discussing the results of his researches on the Earth's magnetism. Karl Kreil, first-assistant astronomer of the astronomical observatory in Milan, furthermore described, in his 1837 article "Descrizione Apparati," the instruments and the methods of measurements of Gauss. The translation of the "Intensitas" and the work of Kreil were published in 1837 in the "Supplemento alle Effemeridi Astronomiche di Milano per il 1838" (pp. 133–197).

Among the Italian institutions, only the astronomical observatory of Brera in Milan participated in the international scientific collaboration proposed by Gauss and known as *Magnetischer Verein* ("magnetic union"). The Milanese institution was the most southern point of the European network. The participation of Brera in Gauss's program was a consequence of the visit, in autumn 1834, of two pupils of Gauss's—Wolfgang Sartorius Waltershausen (1809–1876) and Johann Listing (1808–1882)—who had undertaken a journey in Italy and elsewhere to set up magnetic observations, with instrumentation and methods corresponding to Gauss's in Göttingen.

Kreil, later on destined to become the first director of the Zentralanstalt für Meteorologie und Erdmagnetismus (Central Office for Meteorological and Earth Magnetism) in Vienna in 1851, with the aid of other collaborators, was charged with magnetic observations. The measurements in Milan were both spatial and temporal studies of the laws of the local magnetic field; Kreil and his fellow workers, furthermore, periodically carried out the "term" measurements provided for by the *Magnetischer Verein*. They initially used two unifilar magnetometers, similar to those of Sartorius and Listing, the first magnetometer for declination and absolute intensity measurements and the other to detect the variations; both instruments had been built by the technician at the observatory. In 1836 a magnetometer built by Moritz Meyerstein, Gauss's technician, was purchased from Karl Littrow, director of the Vienna astronomical observatory. Meyerstein's magnetometer was used in Milan until 1922, and it is still there on permanent exhibition.

In 1839 a bifilar Gaussian magnetometer was purchased to measure the variations of the horizontal intensity. For the measurements of the inclination, an inclinometer by Jean-Etienne Lenoir was used. In Milan, furthermore, Kreil measured the variation of the inclination with an oscillatory inclinometer similar to that used by the two pupils of Gauss, built by the technician of the Milanese Observatory. In this period only Kreil in Milan and Adolph Kupffer in St. Petersburg directly measured the inclination variations. From the collected data Kreil deduced a periodic variation law of Earth's magnetic field and, in particular, he found a correlation between variation of the Earth's magnetic field and the position of the Moon, as he and Pietro Della Vedova wrote in the "Osservazioni" (p. 187). The Milanese observers, who corresponded with the most important European scholars about problems connected with geomagnetism, also published twice-daily declination measurements for land surveyors in a newspaper in Milan. In 1840 the Brera Observatory associated with the "Magnetic Crusade" organized by the British Association for the Advancement of Science and, in 1843, also with the program established by Johann Lamont, director of the Munich Observatory. Data from the international collaborations were sent to Gauss, to the Royal Society of London, and to Lamont. Gauss and Lamont published them: the first in the "Resultate aus den Beobachtungen des Magnetischen Vereins" (Results from the Observations of the Magnetic Union), the second in the "Annalen für Meteorologie, Erdmagnetismus und Verwandte Gegenstände" (Annals for Meteorology, Geomagnetism, and Applied Conditions).

When in 1845 the Royal Society of London convened all the participants in the Magnetic Crusade in Cambridge to decide whether to continue the work, it was decided that individual observers were free to continue simultaneous observations at specified times of the year. This decision was very well accepted by the Milanese Observatory, because some collaborators had abandoned the activity, but, above all, because there was a widespread conviction in astronomical observatories that magnetic observations were too onerous for astronomers and too far afield.

In a report sent to the Austrian government in 1846, Francesco Carlini (1783–1862), director of the Brera Observatory, underlined the importance of processing geomagnetic data already collected rather than collecting more, a course suggested at the Cambridge meeting. Declination observations in Milan continued and represent one of the richest collections of magnetic declination in the nineteenth century.

In this period we see, moreover, the flourishing of new meteorological observatories, which very often carried out geomagnetic observations too. In 1861, about fifty meteorological observatories were operating; many of them were managed by members of religious orders. Their independent disciplinary status was often acknowledged, even inside astronomical observatories.

The third period started in the 1860s, when the political union of Italy was realized. One of the problems that the new government had to face was the reorganization of universities and of institutions that conducted scientific research. Directors of astronomical and meteorological observatories proposed a diminution in the number of astronomical observatories and the construction and reorganization of fewer observatories in suitable areas (Tacchini). It was suggested, furthermore, that the meteorological and geomagnetic activities of the astronomical observatories should cease completely and be transferred to new meteorological observatories to be distributed over all Italian territory. A new central meteorological establishment was proposed to coordinate these activities.

It was widely held that for geomagnetism the observations to be made should be divided into two well-distinguished branches. The first was the magnetic survey of Italy. The second branch addressed the periodic variations and perturbations of magnetism and their relations to cosmical and meteorological phenomena.

It was underlined that, although there were many common points between meteorology and geomagnetism, the research methods were fully different, as different as the maturity of the disciplines. The Earth's magnetism, according to professional astronomers, was subject to regular laws and the study of its mathematical phase had already begun. Meteorology was, instead, a science still in its infancy. For this reason it was considered useful to split the central institution into two sections, meteorological and geomagnetic, under a single direction.

Although meteorology was thought to be less mature than geomagnetism, the problems of meteorology were felt to be more important. It was widely thought that observations carried out in connection with other European countries would allow forecasting of weather conditions.

But a meteorological and geomagnetic central observatory was realized only about two decades later. In this period, Italian scientists were backward compared with those in other European countries as concerns meteorology and geomagnetism. By 1860 France and England already had a regular meteorological service, and the Kew observatory was already famous for its contributions to geomagnetism.

In the 1860s and 1870s two figures emerged: the Jesuit Father Angelo Secchi (1818–1878) and the Barnabite Father Francesco Denza (1834–1894). They contributed fundamentally from observational, organizational, and theoretical viewpoints to meteorology and geomagnetism. Secchi, famous for the first classification of stars according to their spectra, founded a geomagnetic observatory in 1859 at the Collegio Romano in Rome. The instruments and the measurements were the most advanced for that period. The only modern technique missing was photographic registration. It is worth emphasizing that Secchi began his meteorological, geomagnetic, and astrophysical activity as an organic (or holistic) research program regarding the construction of the Heavens and Earth, starting from observations. He explicitly referred to William Herschel's approach.

Secchi's aim was to study various phenomena, such as meteorological, geomagnetic, and astronomical, in order to establish correlations. His theoretical background is exposed in his book *L'unità delle forze fisiche* (The unity of physical forces, 1864), whose aim was to give a unitarian description of different natural phenomena as manifestations of the same forces. This approach was not new; among others, Humboldt claimed, in the introduction to his *Kosmos,* that "if we look at the study of physical phenomena in reference to . . . the general progress of the human mind, we will find its most beautiful results in disclosing those mutual relations, which tie together different natural forces." But, whereas Humboldt looked at the natural world as a living body moved by internal forces, Secchi, instead, had in mind a more mechanistic explanation of natural forces and passive molecular movements. It had been the divine creator who had communicated the force, from outside, to inert matter. As Secchi wrote, "the energy [of the movement comes] . . . from the initial push of the First Mover" (p. 499).

The solar eclipse in 1870 was the occasion for Denza to venture into the field of Earth magnetism. He became the first direc-tor of the Specola Vaticana (Vatican Astronomical Observatory) in 1893, but was then famous for his work in meteorology. The Italian government, in fact, financed two scientific missions in Sicily, where geomagnetism could be observed under best conditions: Secchi was responsible for the first mission and asked Denza to undertake the meteorological and geomagnetic observations. In the other mission Demetrio Emilio Diamilla Müller (1826–1908) and Luciano Serra (1842–1925) undertook the geomagnetic observations.

Diamilla Müller, an eclectic and notorious freelancer, in 1870 had already organized a campaign of intense single-day observations, on August 30, 1870, executed every ten minutes in order to verify whether the diurnal variation of the Earth's magnetism is connected with the Sun. Thirty Italian observatories, scattered over all the territories, took part in his plan, in addition to some foreign observatories. Almost all of these observatories participated later that year in Müller's observations during the solar eclipse.

Father Denza, who in 1859 had founded a meteorological observatory in Moncalieri, near Turin, eagerly became acquainted with Secchi's geomagnetic instrumentation. Coming back home from Sicily, he asked Secchi for the instruments and began a systematic magnetic survey of the Italian territory, to draw its first magnetic map (Denza).

The need for maps was strongly felt, mainly by the navy, for the calibration of its compasses. The survey, then, proceeded with instruments specifically purchased for the purpose. Such instruments are still kept at the College Alberoni in Piacenza. But Denza did not completely analyze the data, which have never been published. A partial processing of the data was made by Dionigi Boddaert (1874–1951) and it is kept in the archives of the College of Moncalieri, still in manuscript form.

Finally, a central organization to coordinate and stimulate the collection and analysis of geomagnetic data was created in 1872, Istituto Idrografico della Marina (Hydrographic Institute of the Navy) in Genoa, which concentrated all the different services of the navy and had the specific task of magnetic research concerning the Italian seas. In 1876, the Ufficio Centrale di Meteorologia (Meteorological Central Office) was constituted by the Italian government and it started its activities in Secchi's meteorological and geomagnetic observatory in 1879 (Palazzo). Pietro Tacchini, an astrophysicist, was appointed first director of the office. Tacchini was also the founder of the Società degli Spettroscopisti Italiani (Italian Spectroscopists' Society), the first society of this kind in the world.

The Meteorological Office had a physical section; the task of this section was to undertake the observations necessary for the drawing of geomagnetic maps as quickly as possible. In 1887 the section of geodynamics for the study of earthquakes was created. The office began to publish observations and articles in the *Annali* in 1879.

The magnetic survey of the territory began in 1881. The maps of equal declination and equal inclination were presented at the first Italian geographic congress held in Genoa in 1892; the map of equal intensity was shown to the geographic congress of Naples of 1904.

For the survey of Italy the office had purchased an Elliot magnetometer and an inclinometer, both manufactured by Dover, but soon thereafter Ciro Chistoni modified the magnetometer. He engineered a new instrument and Ernst Schneider of Vienna built a new magnetometer for the office that was first used in 1883–1884. The method used by Chistoni was that of Gauss, modified by Lamont. The magnetic survey of Italy was the main task of the physical section of the office, but Chistoni and Luigi Palazzo also researched methods and instruments. Both specialized in geomagnetism, having studied at geomagnetic observatories around Europe.

The office was an institution set up to forecast the weather and, in geomagnetism, to draw maps. Other institutions continued to make observations, in coordination with and financed by the office; others, above all, in the case of university scientific faculties, carried out researches that, at the beginning of our century, made possible the creation of a new discipline—geophysics—with an independent scientific status.

In conclusion we can say that Italian participation in the *Magnetischer Verein* in the early nineteenth century and the constitution, in the later half, contributed to the founding of a Meteorological Central Office, within which there was a physical section whose task was to draw magnetic maps of Italian territory. These were important episodes that characterized Italian geomagnetic studies. Above all magnetic mapping of the territory was a very complicated task. In his article "Scientific Sovereignty" (p. 11), Gregory A. Good has enumerated the difficulties that arose for developing a magnetic survey of a territory: the uncommon level of expertise required,

high costs, knowledge of magnetic principles far beyond those required for topographical surveying, and so on. In Italy the problem was even more difficult to solve, because of the fragility of the new political and economic structures in that period. What then made possible such a development?

We have seen that studies on geomagnetism were carried out inside astronomical observatories, which in Italy had a rather good tradition of scientific research, centered essentially on classical astronomy. New techniques such as spectroscopy, photometry, and photography were introduced in the observatories very late and with some suspicion, because they were considered a matter for physics rather than astronomy. So inside the astronomical community a new group of scientists arose, formed by individuals trained in astronomy, but in fact closer to astrophysics, geomagnetism, and meteorology. Secchi, Tacchini, and others were in this new breed, whose prestige was high enough to control new institutions specifically oriented to carry out researches in their field of interest.

Classical astronomers helped the birth of these new institutions because they considered this process a sort of parthenogenesis which, from one side, allowed them to improve their main astronomical activity and, from the other side, to control the new institutions.

Maria Basso Ricci
Pasquale Tucci

Bibliography

Cawood, John. "Terrestrial Magnetism and the Development of International Collaboration in the Early Nineteenth Century." *Annals of Science* 34 (1977): pp. 551–587.

Chapman, Sydney, and Julius Bartels. *Geomagnetism.* 2 vols. Oxford: Clarendon, 1940.

Chistoni, Ciro. "Contributo allo studio del magnetismo terrestre in Italia e lungo le coste dell'Adriatico. (Riassunto di determinazioni degli elementi del magnetismo terrestre fatte prima del 1880)." *Annali dell'Ufficio Centrale Meteorologico e Geodinamico Italiano* 9, no. 1 (1890): pp. 183–352.

Denza, Francesco. *Determinazione dei valori assoluti degli Elementi Magnetici in Italia.* Torino: Tipografia S. Giuseppe, Collegio Artigianelli, 1988.

Frisiani, Paolo. "Annotazioni." *Primo Supplemento alle Effemeridi Astrono-*

miche di Milano per l'anno 1838 (1837): pp. 58–112.

Gauss, Carl Friedrich. "Misura Assoluta della Forza Magnetica Terrestre." *Primo supplemento alle Effemeridi Astronomiche di Milano per l'anno 1838* (1837): pp. 1–57.

Good, Gregory A. "Scientific Sovereignty: Canada, the Carnegie Institution and the Earth's Magnetism in the North." *Scientia Canadensis* 38 (1990): pp. 3–37.

Holton, Gerald. *The Scientific Imagination: Case Studies.* Cambridge: Cambridge University Press, 1978.

Humboldt, Alexander von. *Kosmos: Entwurf einer physischen Weltbeschreibung.* Stuttgart: Cotta, 1847.

Kreil, Karl. "Descrizione degli apparati magnetici e dei metodi con cui si eseguiscono le osservazioni." *Primo supplemento alle Effemeridi Astronomiche di Milano per l'anno 1838* (1837): pp. 133–197.

Kreil, Karl, and Pietro Della Vedova. "Osservazioni sull'intensità e sulla direzione della Forza magnetica istituite negli anni 1836, 1837, 1838 all'I.R. Osservatorio di Milano." *Secondo supplemento alle Effemeridi Astronomiche di Milano per l'anno 1839* (1839).

Maiocchi, Roberto. *Non solo Fermi.* Florence: Le Lettere, 1991.

Palazzo, Luigi. "'Meteorologia e Geodinamica' a cura dell'Accademia dei Lincei." In *Cinquanta Anni di Storia Italiana (1860–1910),* vol. 2, pp. 1–51. Rome: Reale Accademia dei Lincei, 1911.

Quetelet, L. *Sur la Physique du Globe.* Brussels: Hayes, 1861.

Reeves, Barbara J. "Le tradizioni di ricerca fisica in Italia nel tardo diciannovesimo secolo." In *La scienza accademica nell'Italia post-unitaria,* edited by Ancarini, vol. 5, pp. 53–95. Milan: Franco Angeli, 1989.

Secchi, Angelo. *L'unità delle forze fisiche. Saggio di filosofia naturale.* Rome: Tipografia Forense, 1864.

Tacchini, Pietro. "Sulle Attuali Condizioni degli Osservatori Astronomici in Italia." Reprinted in *Memorie Degli Spettroscopisti Italiani* 4 (1875): pp. 1–20.

Geomagnetism, Theories before 1800

Explanations of the magnetism of the Earth.

Although ancient Chinese and Western Medieval thinkers and navigators developed coherent theories and techniques, modern understanding of the Earth as a magnet began in 1600. Many subsequent developments in physical theory led to complex dead ends.

If we take geomagnetism to mean the Earth's magnetic field, and its probable production through a self-exciting electromagnetic dynamo action of its conducting outer core, then it has no history before the twentieth century. That, however, would be a naive and absurd restriction, especially because recent understandings build on centuries of knowledge of geomagnetic phenomena, such as the attractive and directional properties of naturally occurring loadstone, and, since the Middle Ages, the behavior of compass needles. But to widen the history to include this cumulative empirical base also leads to an absurdity. Before the publication in 1600 of *De Magnete,* by the English royal physician William Gilbert (1544–1603), most writers believed in cosmological or heavenly causes of magnetic phenomena, which merely happened to have terrestrial representations. Thus the word "geomagnetism" must be used cautiously if violence is not to be done to earlier views. Put crudely, the early history of "geomagnetism" is that of an expanding corpus of easily obtained though poorly understood data, which were interpreted through widely differing theories, and which cannot be arranged in a sequence evolving toward modern geomagnetism. When we turn to the first recorded details, we are immediately plunged into historiographical difficulties.

There is no doubt that between 500 B.C.E. and 1200 C.E. knowledge of geomagnetic phenomena was much more developed in China than in Europe. First records of the attractive power of loadstones occur in both East and West around 500 B.C.E. But, while little development took place in Europe, the sophisticated Chinese work is now well known through Joseph Needham's monumental work (Needham, pp. 1–59). He concludes that "south-pointing" spoons of loadstone were in use by the first century C.E. By 1100 the magnetization of iron, the polarity of loadstones, the use of compasses, and even the declination of magnetic from geographical north were established, a century before they became known, probably via trade routes, to Western scholars.

But is Needham right to treat this as early geomagnetism? Little theory was offered, the

Chinese being in general more content with description and use. Furthermore, Chinese concerns were primarily geomantic—"compasses" were first used as divining spoons, and for orienting buildings according to the local flow of spiritual forces. Nevertheless, in this radically different cultural context, Chinese, much more than medieval Western, writers explained magnetism as an *Earthly* (admittedly Taoist) force. Thus, from the perspective of the history of modern, Western science, there is a tension between the technical and empirical legacy of Chinese work, and its conceptual strangeness. Historians like Needham preserve the strangeness in order to foreground the specifically Chinese nature of the achievement. But at the same time they filter it unhelpfully through categories like "physics" and "geomagnetism" because they wish to integrate it with a progressivist history of science.

The center of innovation shifted from China, first to Islamic and then to medieval Christian investigators, whom Smith has recently analyzed. Until the late sixteenth century, strong sociocultural divisions existed between philosophy (the preserve of a leisured, learned elite, and directed at a contemplative understanding of God's creation), and "art" (applied, technical, and practical manipulations of nature). A very important consequence was an effective divorce between theories of magnetic action and increasing knowledge among navigators of geomagnetic phenomena, especially of the compass.

Influential philosophers from the mid-thirteenth century to the mid-sixteenth century rarely experimented, and empirical claims depended upon navigators' measurements. Philosophers developed theories of the cause of the magnet's attractive and directional properties, which were of two kinds, but neither treated them as general properties of the Earth. One tradition, based like much else in late medieval thought on concepts of Aristotle (384–322 B.C.E.), was developed by Thomas Aquinas (1226–1274), treating magnetism as a specific form or occult quality of magnetite—more obscure and interesting than the specific yellow, malleable form of gold, but of the same ontological order. This led to theories of huge magnetic islands or rocks, situated near the geographical poles, toward which magnets and compasses were drawn. A second tradition developed Renaissance neo-Platonist theories of a network of correspondences and forces between the celestial and terrestrial worlds. The Pole Star was an oft-cited cause, the more plausible because,

like the compass, it declined slightly from true north. In 1269 Petrus Peregrinus (fl. ca. 1269) had hoped to produce a terrestrial replica of the heavens' diurnal and spherical perpetual motion about its axis by experimenting with spherical loadstones (Gilbert, pp. 1–15). Writers before Smith wrongly singled out Peregrinus as a magnetic experimenter ahead of his time, although it is true that Gilbert acknowledged an influence. Neither Peregrinus nor any other learned writer had a concept of geomagnetism.

As David Waters (pp. 152–247) has shown, within the largely separate realm of Renaissance navigation, seagoing practitioners were skeptical about cosmological speculations concerning magnetism. They concentrated on reliable rules of art for direction-finding at sea using the mariner's compass. Thus, while directionality data gathered rapidly, manuals often dismissed the cause of magnetism as a mystery beyond philosophers. Two questions predominated. First, how could a needle receive magnetism "properly"? The answer was to employ a trusted supplier of needles and stones. It was while improving the design of his instruments that the leading Elizabethan compass-maker Robert Norman (fl. ca. 1580) found in 1581 that magnetic inclination was not an artifact of poorly balanced needles (figure 1). The second was how to interpret the declination of the compass from true north. By 1600, after a century of colonial exploration, experts generally agreed that much if not all of the declination, and discrepancies between observations, were attributable to bad practice, but that real declination exists—and that it never changes. Some argued that patterns of declination data pointed to "prime meridians" of zero declination, and possibly a regular pattern of direction toward two magnetic poles, mountains, or islands, which might hold the solution to the pressing problem of finding the longitude at sea. Those such as the English, who sailed in high latitudes with wilder patterns of declination, were skeptical of such "solutions." In 1599 the Dutchman Simon Stevin (1548–1620) likewise argued that the only useful correlations were those of local declination values with local geography.

It is only if one views scientific progress in very empirical and technical terms, as Waters tends to do, that we can regard navigators as proto-geomagneticians. Nevertheless, the birth of geomagnetism with *De Magnete* in 1600 came about from an unprecedented and unorthodox fusion of practical and natural philosophical approaches. Gilbert collaborated

Figure 1. The title page of Robert Norman's 1581 Newe Attractive . . . , *a critical work in early research on magnetism of the Earth.*

THE

newe Attractiue,

Containyng a ſhort diſcourſe *of the* Magnes oʒ Lodeſtone *, and* amongeſt other his bertues, of a newe diſcouered ſecret and ſubtill pʒopertie, concernyng the Declinyng of the Meedle, touched therewith bnder the plaine of the Hoʒizon. Mow firſt founde out by *Robert Norman* Hydrographer.

❧ Herebnto are annered certaine neceſſarie rules foʒ the art of Mauigation, by the ſame *R. N.*

❧ *Imprinted at London by Ihon Kyng-ſton, for Richard Ballard.*

1581.

closely with London's maritime community, especially its leading instructor, Edward Wright (1561–1615), who wrote parts of *De Magnete* and probably influenced its matter-of-fact style. The Marxist historian Edgar Zilsel has thereby argued for a link, although a positivistic one, between the emergence of capitalism and of modern geomagnetic science.

Although a historiography of heroic discoverers is almost always wrong, this collabo-ration is one of the few reasons to deny Gil-bert the title of founder of (geo-)magnetic sci-ence. The longer title of *De Magnete*, "A New Philosophy of the Magnet, Magnetic Bodies and the Great Magnet the Earth," makes the geomagnetic conclusion of Gilbert's treatise clear. Not only was its conclusion novel, but also its method to establish it. The work be-gins with a dismissive book rejecting previous "fables" on the magnet, and a section arguing

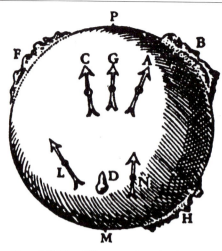

Figure 2. William Gilbert argued in 1600 that the magnetic needle is attracted by large landmasses. From Gilbert's De Magnete.

that magnetism had, uniquely, an immaterial cause. The bulk is devoted to experimental proof by analogy of terrestrial magnetism. Gilbert adapts Peregrinus's spherical loadstone, which he calls a *terrella,* or little Earth, and applies to it miniature compass needles, called *versoria.* He records the orientation of these *versoria* as they are moved over the surfaces of *terrellae.*

Gilbert painstakingly showed that his *versoria* exhibited the phenomena of direction, Norman's inclination, and declination. Using a *terrella* deformed to imitate the irregularities of continents and oceans, he argued from the patterns of declination exhibited on his artificial Earth that geomagnetic declination is caused by the greater (or lesser) net attraction exerted by landmasses (or oceans) (figure 2). He assumed that only major geological changes would alter the declination. For Gilbert (and Wright) this provided not merely further proof of geomagnetism, but also an endorsement of Stevin's local position-finding method, and a disproof of universal ones.

Gilbert's creation of a "magnetical philosophy" was, by seventeenth-century standards, a rapid success that shaped subsequent work, particularly because it united technical and philosophical concerns. Historians (including Zilsel) used to see in this proof of Gilbert's modernity, especially in his experimental method, and dismissed his "speculative" concluding argument that the Earth, driven by an immaterial magnetic soul, performs Copernican rotations. Recent work (Pumfrey, pp. 48–50) has shown how contemporaries like Galileo Galilei (1564–1642)

were impressed by his Copernican cosmology.

Navigators and governments were more impressed by the prospect, raised by magnetic philosophy if not by *De Magnete,* of geomagnetic solutions to the longitude, and other navigational problems. French workers like Guillaume de Nautonnier (fl. ca. 1600) agreed with Gilbert that the Earth is a large spherical magnet but, by reintroducing separate magnetic poles and insisting that magnetic meridians are regular, rekindled hopes for a complete magnetic navigation that government prizes sustained for thirty years. The discovery by Henry Gellibrand (1597–1636), in 1634, that declination is not time-invariant, resulted from the endorsement that Gilbert's paradigm gave to the English tradition of careful measurement in pursuit of an empirical solution. Yet Gellibrand's work led immediately to the first hypothesis, made in 1639 by the navigator Henry Bond (ca. 1600–1678), that there are separate, rotating magnetic poles that create regular patterns of declination. Such work was clearly more driven by practical and empirical than by theoretical concerns. The famous 1692 hypothesis by Edmond Halley (1656–1742) that the Earth consists of an inner sphere and outer shell, each with a north and south pole and rotating at different speeds, can be read in part as the culmination of this tradition. But Halley's voyages to measure geomagnetic data, and *The Longitude and Latitude Found by the Inclinatory or Dipping Needle* (London, 1721) by William Whiston (1667–1752) mark the decline of sustained utilitarian investigations into geomagnetism.

Returning to philosophers' reactions, a series of works by Jesuits culminated in *Magnes* (Rome, 1641) of Athanasius Kircher (1602?–1680). These works addressed magnetic navigation, because the utilitarianism of the Jesuit teaching was part of its appeal, but their main purpose was to render geomagnetic science orthodox, especially by refuting Copernicanism. With the exception of Jean Daujat, historians ignored these neoconservative "losers" until very recently. Yet Kircher's compendia and his geomagnetic theory had great influence. The latter incorporated Gellibrand's secular variation, elaborating a theory of randomly shifting subterranean "fibres" of magnetic minerals. Importantly, Kircher's explanation also lent no support to Copernicanism.

Even the more "progressive" developers of magnetic philosophy could not accept Gilbert's proposition of a magnetic Earth soul, and they explored the mechanistic theory of René Descartes (1596–1650). For Cartesian

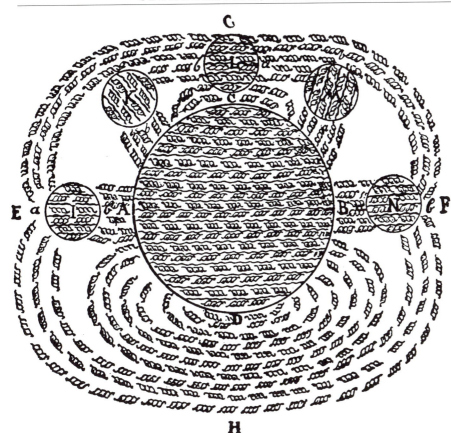

Figure 3. Descartes's representation of Earth's magnetism, from his Principia philosophiae (Amsterdam, 1644). Source: Adam, Charles, and Paul Tannery, eds. Oeuvres de Descartes. *12 vols. with supplement. Vol. 8 (1905), p. 290. Paris: Léopold Cerf, 1897–1913.*

mechanists the Earth, like small magnets, emits streams of screw-shaped corpuscles, whose strongest flow is between the geographical poles. Direction and attraction are the consequence of the particles boring into receptive channels, which are the defining property of magnetic bodies such as compass needles (figure 3).

As mechanists elaborated corpuscular hypotheses, most successfully in the field of pneumatics, the geosphere became filled with particulate streams, including magnetic effluvia, whose behavior was in principle altered by an extraordinary variety of factors, especially meteorological ones. As a result, philosophical interest in geomagnetism had also subsided by the turn of the century. Indeed the collapse of a distinctive magnetic research program is counter-evidence to the common historiographical tendency to see mechanical philosophy as a thoroughly "progressive research program."

It is true that Newton's early-eighteenth-century reinstatement of magnetism as a fundamental, and genuinely attractive principle, like gravity but also like electricity and "fermentation," revived British interest. But it did so without a geomagnetic focus, and concentrated, as in electricity, upon the experimental elucidation of the active powers in matter. In the same period Continental investigators developed post-Cartesian fluid mechanical explanations. Indeed Leonhard Euler (1707–1783) and all the co-winners of the 1746 Paris Academy of Sciences prize on "the explanation of the magnet and iron, the pointing of the magnetised needle towards the north, its declination and inclination" invoked the flow and pressure of magnetic fluids.

Roderick Home, the chief historian of this topic, has rightly claimed that there was little division, conceptual or national, between Newtonian "attractionnaires" and "impulsionnaires" (Aepinus, pp. 151–164). Indeed the two approaches fused into the later-eighteenth-century notion of a subtle yet active magnetic fluid. All these theories were plausible but led, especially when applied to the Earth, to mathematical analysis of impossible complexity. Franz Aepinus (1724–1802) attempted a more instrumental approach, analyzing magnetic "fields" of force, which he extended to geomagnetism. He was able to provide the mathematics for magnetic couples, to distinguish between magnetic attraction and direction, and to make telling criticisms of Halley's four-pole hypothesis. But faced with the irregularity of isogonic, and isoclinic charts, he too was defeated by the complexity of the calculations. Similarly mathematical approaches also led Johann Tobias Mayer (1723–1762) to criticize Halley. Mayer, the subject of Forbes's study, made the important supposition of treating the Earth as an indefinitely small central dipole, whose axis is inclined, irregularly, to the axis of rotation. These later developments have been well reviewed by Gregory Good.

The history of early modern geomagnetism gives a challenging perspective on the historiography of science because, despite the praise heaped upon the pivotal *De Magnete* for its elegant discovery, simple experiments, and practical utility, subsequent work refused to confirm simple dipole models. By 1800 the incompatibility of Laplacian micro-explanations, and mathematical analyses of forces, both with each other and with increasingly detailed geomagnetic data, had brought a decline in clarity, progress, and interest. Geomagnetism required what Good calls a "nineteenth century re-awakening."

Stephen Pumfrey

Bibliography

Aepinus, Franz U.T. *Essay on the Theory of Electricity and Magnetism.* Introductory monograph by R.W. Home. Translated by P.J. Connor. Princeton: Princeton University Press, 1979.

Daujat, Jean. *Origines Et Formation de la Théorie des Phénomènes Electriques et Magnétiques.* 3 vols. Paris: PUF, 1945.

Forbes, Eric G. *Tobias Mayer (1723–62): Pioneer of Enlightened Science in Germany,* pp. 206–218. Göttingen: Vandenhoeck und Ruprecht, 1980.

Gilbert, William. *De Magnete.* Translated by P. Fleury Mottelay. New York: Dover Publications, 1958.

Good, Gregory A. "Follow the Needle: Seeking the Magnetic Poles." *Earth Sciences History* 10 (1991): pp. 154–167.

Needham, Joseph. *The Shorter Science and Civilisation in China: An Abridgement of Joseph Needham's Original Text.* Vol. 3. Cambridge: Cambridge University Press, 1986.

Pumfrey, Stephen. "Magnetical Philosophy and Astronomy, 1600–1650." In *Planetary Astronomy from the Renaissance to the Rise of Astrophysics. Part A: Tycho Brahe to Newton.* Edited by René Taton and Curtis Wilson, pp. 45–53.

Cambridge: Cambridge University Press, 1989.

Smith, Julian A. "Precursors to Peregrinus—the Early History of Magnetism and the Mariner's Compass in Europe." *Journal of Medieval History* 18 (1992): pp. 21–74.

Waters, David W. *The Art of Navigation in England.* 3 vols. London: Hollis and Carter, 1958.

Zilsel, Edgar. "The Origins of William Gilbert's Scientific Method." *Journal of the History of Ideas* 2 (1941): pp. 1–32.

See also Cosmology and the Earth; Exploration, Age of; Geography, Elizabethan; Geomagnetism; Gravity, Newton, and the Eighteenth Century; Historiography, Eighteenth-Century England; Instruments, Geomagnetic; Occult Philosophy and the Earth in the Renaissance

Geomagnetism, Theories between 1800 and 1900

A period of rejection of long-held ideas, rapid extension of observation, testing and rejection of new physical theories, and the development of new mathematical approaches to geomagnetism.

The status of nineteenth-century geomagnetic theory was presented by the English natural philosopher John Herschel (1792–1871) in 1840, on the eve of what was called the Magnetic Crusade. He wrote that although in experimental sciences situations can be manipulated to get directly at efficient causes, in observational sciences such as astronomy and the study of Earth's magnetism, theories provide coherence to records otherwise disjointed. In such sciences, he wrote, "the theory *is* the science" (Herschel, p. 66). Herschel saw geomagnetic theories as temporary structures, scaffolds: "tentative, transient, and empirical conceptions" (p. 67). Terrestrial magnetism in the nineteenth century was no mere inductive science, but its theories were also not solidly established. Not surprisingly, then, ideas about the causes of the Earth's magnetism did indeed come and go.

The main theories of the Earth's magnetism in 1800 came from two well-established traditions: theories of magnetic fluids and theories based on multiple magnetic poles. The first arose in the successful use of imponderable fluids by eighteenth-century investigators of subjects such as electricity, heat, and light. The second was most famously associated with the name of Edmond Halley (1656–1742), although other proponents both preceded and followed him. During the nineteenth century, both of these views came into doubt as new approaches arose. Some of the most important emergent approaches included theories based on discoveries in electrodynamics and electromagnetism by André-Marie Ampère (1775–1836), Michael Faraday (1791–1867), and others, and a new mathematical approach introduced by Carl Friedrich Gauss (1777–1855) in 1839. Gauss's approach, while initially presented as separable from physical theory, ultimately allowed scientists to explore new explanations of the Earth's magnetism. Finally, the comprehensive treatment of electromagnetic fields by James Clerk Maxwell (1831–1879) provided a basis for new investigations as the twentieth century dawned.

By 1800, magnetism generally and for the first time "occupied its own space on the map of natural philosophy" (Fara, p. 83). Although not the result of great discoveries but rather of complex social developments, this situation rested on certain ideas about magnetism. Gowin Knight (1713–1772) was a foremost proponent of magnetic fluid theory (see Fara, pp. 44–60). Knight in 1748 (pp. 66–77) maintained that the curved lines of iron filings near a magnet indicate the paths of magnetic fluids (Fara, p. 150). His was a fluid of corpuscles, separated by a repulsive force, and present within iron. Meanwhile, Leonhard Euler (1707–1783) and Charles-François Du Fay (1698–1739)—among others—based their work on circulating subtle matter, somewhat like that proposed by René Descartes (1596–1650). Various magnetic fluids or ethers were actively explored and advocated for on either side of 1800 by Tiberius Cavallo, Thomas Young, John Robison, and John Dalton (Fara, pp. 247–257).

Franz Aepinus (1724–1802) developed an alternative, detailed, mathematical theory in 1759 that assumed a different sort of magnetic fluid (Home, chap. 4). His was a noncirculating magnetic fluid, its particles attracted to iron, but mutually repelled. Critically, it was the sums of these unexplained forces acting at-a-distance that really mattered. His magnetic theory posited two magnetic states, positive and negative, depending on whether a body had more or less of its "natural" amount of magnetic fluid (Home and Conner, pp. 166–167). Aepinus's physical theory was semiquantitative but macroscopic. He also argued that the Earth has "quite a large" magnetic core, by which he meant a conventional magnet, but which he

refused to explain mechanistically, saying rather that it is due somehow to "the immediate action of the creator" (quoted in Home, p. 183). The alignment of the compass needle was often explained as being due to the flow of a magnetic fluid through its length; Aepinus explained it instead in terms of the joint action of two opposite poles on the needle (Home, pp. 182–186). He was mostly interested in magnetic laws and action generally, however, and considered secular (and perhaps other) variations of the Earth's magnetism to be beyond mathematical analysis, perhaps because of the "generation and destruction of magnetic ores."

A second major variety of magnetic fluid theory supposed that every iron particle (and perhaps that of other materials) contains equal amounts of boreal and austral magnetic fluids. Particles of the one fluid were held to attract those of the other, but to repel those of the same kind. Generally, these fluids were considered inseparable from iron, restricted to motion over only very small distances.

Charles Augustin Coulomb (1736–1806) represents the height of magnetic theory in 1800. Heir to these theories of magnetic fluids, he did not shed them entirely, but he radically transformed their possible meaning. The best historical discussion of his work on magnetism is in C. Stewart Gillmor's biography (chap. 6). Coulomb criticized the notion of circulating ethers, the one-fluid theory of Aepinus, and the various two-fluid theories. None of these accounted adequately, in his view, for some very simple experimental results. Between 1777 and 1799, Coulomb developed a theory in which two magnetic fluids were restricted to movement within individual molecules, whose forces acted at a distance (as had those of Aepinus's one-fluid theory) and were subject to calculation (Gillmor, pp. 210–221). These two characteristics differentiated it from previous theories. His theory was further developed in the nineteenth century by, among others, Jean-Baptiste Biot (1774–1862) and Siméon Denis Poisson (1781–1840) (Gillmor, p. 218). Poisson's theory of magnetism, presented to the *Académie Royale des Sciences* in 1826 was perhaps the highest development of magnetic fluid theory. Herschel and Gauss, among others, knew and used it.

However, some early-nineteenth-century natural philosophers began to doubt fluid models and entertain alternatives. In this, they perhaps unknowingly followed the lead of eighteenth-century writers such as Pieter van Musschenbroeck (1692–1761), who considered that magnetic fluid existed only in certain people's heads (Home, pp. 161–162). Tobias Mayer (the elder, 1723–1762) maintained in 1760 that the fluid theory obstructed progress in magnetic investigation. He called it a "useless and inept" hypothesis, and advocated an approach based only on experiment and calculation (Forbes, pp. 65–67). David Brewster (1781–1868) echoed this view in 1857, stating that circulating fluids such as those of Euler's or Daniel Bernoulli (1700–1782) were "useless speculations" (p. 4)—although he ignored the fact that they were widely applauded in their time. Neither the objections of van Musschenbroeck and Mayer nor the discoveries in the 1820s and 1830s regarding the magnetic effects of electric currents entirely ended discussion of magnetic fluids, but they did shift the focus to the flow of electricity and its induced magnetic effects.

John Canton (1718–1772) originated an explanation of diurnal variation that was still taken seriously in the mid-nineteenth century. (The daily periodic change of magnetic declination was discovered by George Graham in 1722.) Canton supposed that the Sun's heat acting on the parts of the Earth east of the dawn demarcation line somehow weakens their magnetism, thus allowing a compass needle to swing toward the west before dawn. Then in the afternoon, he stated, as the Sun warms more of the planet west of the observer, the magnetism in that region would be weakened, and the needle would swing eastward (Brewster, p. 6). This was based on the laboratory experience that heat weakens magnets, but Canton provided no clear explanation of how this might work on a terrestrial scale.

The 1820 discovery by Hans Christian Oersted (1777–1851) that electric currents produce magnetic effects is well known, but its immediate effect on theories of terrestrial magnetism is not. Historian John Cawood sketches (pp. 578–581) how François Arago (1786–1853) brought news of the discovery to Paris, where he, Alexander von Humboldt (1769–1859), and others were already active in terrestrial magnetic research. Ampère's two-fluid theory of electromagnetism was in part a result of this, and he and Humboldt both speculated on how these discoveries could explain geomagnetism.

The possibility that the relations between electricity, magnetism, and heat would help explain geomagnetism was strengthened by other discoveries of the 1820s and 1830s. Thomas Johann Seebeck (1770–1831) dis-

covered thermoelectricity in 1821. Humboldt and Edward Sabine (1788–1883) were especially impressed by the similarities between the globe's isothermal lines and the lines of equal magnetic intensity. Faraday's discovery in 1831 that magnetism can produce electric currents reinforced ideas about the unity of natural phenomena. Peter Barlow explained geomagnetism as a whole in terms of electric currents flowing in the Earth's crust. In 1839, Gauss suggested that discussions based on magnetic fluids or on electromagnetism could produce the same appearances (p. 49). John Herschel in 1840 attributed periodic variations such as diurnal variation to electrical currents in either the atmosphere or in the Earth's crust, induced by temperature variations (Herschel, p. 95). The relationships between studying magnetism in the global context and in that of the laboratory in the early nineteenth century are problematic, and require much closer historical interpretation.

The history of the understanding of the Earth's magnetic poles is a complex topic (see Good, "Follow the Needle"). Two meanings, sometimes confused, were discussed in the nineteenth century. In the first, a freely suspended magnetic needle pointed vertically downward at Earth's magnetic poles. Other ways to say this were that declination needles converged on this place, or that the horizontal intensity vanished there, although this depended on the theory held. The second meaning considered the magnetic poles to be regions of maximum magnetic intensity, there being such a region in Canada and another in Siberia.

The foremost proponent of the theory in the nineteenth century that Earth has two magnetic axes (or four poles) was Christopher Hansteen (1784–1875). He presented this theory in *Untersuchungen über den Magnetismus der Erde* (Investigations concerning the magnetism of the Earth, 1819). This theory was influential, despite the rejection of Halley's version of it by many eighteenth-century investigators. Hansteen could not accept a single-axis, two-pole theory partly because the magnetic equator (the path along which the magnetic inclination or dip is zero) is not a great circle. Hansteen carefully distinguished between "points of force" and "points of convergence," the former being to him the real magnetic poles and the latter a superficial appearance (Good, "Follow the Needle," p. 161). About 1830 Hansteen and others journeyed across Siberia in search of a region of maximum magnetic intensity, and James C.

Ross (1800–1862) sought the pole of vertical dip in northern Canada, clearly illustrating the practical consequences of different ideas.

The four-pole theory guided not only expeditions but also analysis in the 1820s and 1830s. The main distinction between Halley's and Hansteen's theories was that whereas Halley lacked a law of magnetic attraction, Hansteen used quantitative laws and could calculate from his theory the declination and other magnetic variables that should be observed at various locations on Earth (Hansteen, chaps. 5, 6). His calculations were made possible by Henry Cavendish (1731–1810) and Coulomb (Cawood, pp. 553–557). Hansteen did not entirely forswear speculation about the ultimate cause of magnetism, but he carried his application of quantitative law to geomagnetism much further than his predecessors had.

Despite widespread use of and admiration for Hansteen's theory, there were doubts. Biot, who had researched geomagnetism on the ground and in balloons, proposed a detailed mathematical theory based on a single magnetic dipole near the Earth's center (Good, "Follow the Needle," p. 161; Cawood, pp. 563–564). More important, by the 1830s the geomagnetic data were interpreted by some as incompatible with any theory based on one or two dipoles. Barlow concluded in 1833 that every point on Earth has its own poles and own secular magnetic variation. Others agreed, including Herschel and Gauss (Good, "Follow the Needle," pp. 162–163).

The ultimate source of geomagnetic phenomena was much debated in the nineteenth century. Hansteen and Brewster were firmly convinced that the real causes lie beyond the Earth: the Sun and Moon. Gauss, like Halley and Mayer, was equally convinced that most geomagnetic phenomena have their origin within the Earth. To Hansteen, the Sun and Moon seemed likely to produce changes in Earth's magnetism, just as they produce the tides. He also speculated that the rotation of his two magnetic axes was due to the precession of the equinoxes (Hansteen, pp. 102–105). Brewster admitted the presence of magnetic metals in the Earth's crust, but he thought they were the source of local disturbance, not of the main magnetic phenomena. If the primary source of this magnetism were in the crust or deep in the Earth's interior, he wrote, the intensity measured on the ocean, on mountains, or in balloons should be much less than it is. Brewster posited instead that the atmosphere contains metallic vapors, especially iron. This envelope of atmospheric iron, magnetized by induction from an external cause, would, he said, produce the same appearances as a dipole deep in the Earth, but it would also be affected by temperature differences from the Sun's heat and by electrical discharges. Thus Brewster explained diurnal and magnetic storm variations, lightning, and even auroral noise. The source of all these induced effects, Brewster had no doubt, is the Sun, although he said it was for future research to decide whether they are due to solar heat, light, direct magnetic action, or to some unknown rays (Brewster, pp. 63–68).

Two figures overshadow all others in the history of nineteenth-century work in geomagnetism: Alexander von Humboldt and Carl Friedrich Gauss. The former proposed no theory of great importance, but he conducted several important investigations, including that of sudden disturbances of magnetic compasses, called magnetic storms. He also inspired generations of researchers to undertake arduous geomagnetic observational programs. At Humboldt's instigation, a network of magnetic observatories was established first in Europe in the 1830s, and then worldwide in the 1840s (Biermann, passim; Cawood, pp. 583–587). Gauss, working with Wilhelm Weber (1804–1891), achieved breakthroughs in both instrumentation and in geomagnetic theory. In many ways, geomagnetic research followed out the patterns set by Humboldt and Gauss until well into the twentieth century.

Humboldt simultaneously speculated boldly on the causes of geomagnetic phenomena and illustrated the painstaking empiricism required to critically assess the value of such ideas. Largely because of his example, much nineteenth-century geomagnetic research aimed at intricate, quantitative description. This is not to be disparaged. Humboldt's long passage on terrestrial magnetism in the *Cosmos* (vol. 5, pp. 50–156) provides an exhaustive chronology of what researchers learned up to mid-century about the morphology of magnetic variations, magnetic distribution, and magnetic storms. An even longer story could be told about descriptive research done after the *Cosmos* appeared. It should be noted that although Humboldt explicitly limited the *Cosmos* to "positive knowledge," he also told the reader that he did indeed entertain and value physical hypotheses.

Gauss's accomplishments are well summarized in G.D. Garland's 1979 article and in Christa Jungnickel and Russell McCormmach's *Intellectual Mastery of Nature* (vol. 1, pp. 63–

77). Gauss, like Humboldt, provided some of the stimulus for the establishment of magnetic observatories. He made this possible partly through the design of new magnetic instruments intended for specific variables, and partly through the rigorous mathematical analysis of those instruments and of the measurements taken with them. More important, in 1832 he established a method (called the absolute method) by which the intensity of magnetism can be measured in terms of mass, length, and time (Garland, pp. 7–10). Up to this time, magnetic intensity was a relative measurement, based on the oscillation of a magnetic needle suspended by a fiber. Gauss's new method made it possible to conduct comparable magnetic intensity measurements around the globe and over long periods of time.

Gauss's longest-lasting effect on geomagnetic research was his development of spherical harmonic analysis, a mathematical representation of Earth's magnetism. Although Gauss thought of his theory as calculating the varying density of magnetic fluid, he did not think this physical hypothesis was necessary to his theory (Gauss, p. 47). More important, Gauss also did not assume that the Earth has two or four poles, nor did he use any other physical supposition. Rather, he assumed magnetism to be generally distributed within the Earth and on its surface. He assumed moreover that the magnetic force at any given point is due to the summation of forces from all other points. That is, he denied any efficacy to particular magnetic poles. Indeed, he denied that the chord between the two poles of vertical dip should even be termed the Earth's magnetic axis (p. 45). His method made it possible for the first time to locate the relative contributions of various causes to geomagnetic phenomena (Garland, pp. 14–22; Good, "Study of Geomagnetism," pp. 220–221).

Another critical development in mid-century was James Clerk Maxwell's synthesis of electromagnetism, embodied in "Maxwell's equations," which made it possible to treat Faraday's ideas about electric and magnetic fields quantitatively. His *Treatise on Electricity and Magnetism* (1873) epitomized his theory. While it is well known that these equations unified the studies of electricity, magnetism, and light, and that they are part of the story of technologies such as radio, their connection to the study of geomagnetism has yet to be told. Jungnickel and McCormmach offer a suggestive review of reaction to Maxwell (vol. 2, pp. 227–245). Maxwell's theory provided another set of mathematical tools, but also a new physical basis that replaced both fluids and action-at-a-distance forces. From the 1880s onwards, geomagnetic theorists wrote invariably of Earth's magnetic field, not of its magnetic forces nor of its magnetic elements.

This was in itself a revolution. A generation of magneticians raised on mathematical physics was coming of age. Arthur Schuster (1851–1934) had worked with Hermann Helmholtz (1821–1894) in Berlin and with Maxwell in Cambridge. Louis Agricola Bauer (1865–1932) did doctoral studies with Max Planck (1858–1947) and Wilhelm von Bezold (1837–1907). Geomagnetic research grew explosively in the 1890s. Existing venues for publication no longer sufficed, leading to the founding of the journal *Terrestrial Magnetism* in 1896. International organization expanded; national magnetic surveys and permanent observatories multiplied. These institutional developments arose partly in practical concerns, but the increasing theoretical capability of researchers was also a factor.

A better representation of the Earth's magnetic field than was possible in Gauss's time was needed to answer several physical questions. First was the question of the location of the cause of the main field, and of various disturbance fields. Gauss had concluded from his analysis that the main field is caused internally (Garland, pp. 18–20). In 1889, Schuster demonstrated that the diurnal variation is very likely caused by external events, but not entirely. His development of Gauss's spherical harmonics showed how the approach could be used to investigate both electrical currents in the upper atmosphere and the electrical conductivity of the Earth's crust (Good, "Study of Geomagnetism," pp. 223–225). Likewise, with adequate observations to work from, Gauss's theory could reveal whether there is an electrical current flowing vertically through the Earth's surface, as well as whether magnetic monopoles exist. Gauss had noted both of these implications (Garland, pp. 21–22) but did not follow up on them. These questions motivated research by Bauer, among others (Good, "Study of Geomagnetism," pp. 220–221).

The massive accumulation of magnetic data since 1839 allowed Georg von Neumayer (1826–1909), H. Fritsche, and others to enlarge on Gauss's calculations. Whereas Gauss had had to restrict his calculations to a spherical Earth, Adolf Schmidt (1860–1944) had adequate data to consider a spheroidal Earth (Chapman and Bartels, chaps. 17, 18).

Whereas Gauss included only the terms of the harmonic expansion relating to causes within the Earth, both John Couch Adams (1819–1892) and Schmidt could include terms relating to external causes, too. Moreover the precision of the representation was carried much further in the 1880s and 1890s than Gauss could have done. Gauss had included terms to the fourth order of the expansion (that is, 24 constants), Schmidt to the sixth order, while Adams included 120 constants for causes internal and 120 for causes external to Earth.

Because of the greater precision of these later analyses of the Earth's magnetism, it became possible to test certain assumptions of Gauss's theory. Not only had Gauss assumed the permanent part of geomagnetism to be due to internal causes, he had also assumed these causes to be referable to a potential. With his more precise calculations Schmidt concluded that another factor was possible: perhaps as much as 1/40th of the total magnetic intensity could be due to an electric current passing vertically from the Earth into the atmosphere (Schmidt, passim; Nippoldt, pp. 98–99). Not an easy question to test, this led to several years of active research, as related in 1900 by Alfred Nippoldt (1874–1936) (pp. 99–101).

Just as extensions of Gauss's theory allowed a closer analysis of the Earth's permanent magnetic field, investigators also analyzed anew the variations of the Earth's magnetism (Good, "Study of Geomagnetism," pp. 221–225; Nippoldt, pp. 106–109). Schuster examined spherical harmonic terms related to external causes and demonstrated their connection to diurnal variation; he speculated on the existence of electrical currents in the upper atmosphere. Bauer stressed in 1895 that the first term of the Gaussian harmonic corresponds to a uniform magnetization of the Earth, a basic physical interpretation. He also calculated a "residual field," which he related to the diurnal variation field (Nippoldt, pp. 102–104). Meanwhile, V. Carlheim-Gyllenskiöld (1859–1934), Schuster, Arthur Korn (1870–1945), William Sutherland (1859–1911), and others attempted to apply Maxwell's theory and the work of Heinrich Hertz (1857–1894) on electromagnetic induction to various physical models and hypotheses (Nippoldt, pp. 104–106).

Arthur Schuster is a crucial geomagnetic theorist. His numerous articles examined and rejected many proposed theories of geomagnetism, usually because of shortcomings in their mathematics or physics. Among his articles is the neglected "Critical Examination of the Possible Causes of Terrestrial Magnetism." Published in 1912, it reflects well the state of geomagnetic theory at the turn of the century. In it, Schuster specifically omits theories of the periodic variation and disturbances to concentrate on the origin of the main field. His discussion reflects activity both of theorists and of field and experimental workers intent on testing the various theories. It certainly does not reflect a moribund or unimaginative research community. Indeed, the lively investigations undertaken by this community set the stage for the better-known 1919 memoir of Joseph Larmor (1857–1942) on the magnetism of rotating bodies.

Schuster considered and evaluated each of the available theories of the main geomagnetic field. It was a safe starting point, he wrote, to assume that "the near approach between the geographical and the magnetic poles is intimately connected with the ultimate cause of terrestrial magnetism" (pp. 121–122). He judged that geomagnetic writers had prematurely ruled out an explanation based on permanent, normal magnetization of some portion of Earth. Indeed, his laboratory was investigating the effects of pressure on magnetization. He felt that too much hope was placed on explanations based on electric currents circulating within the Earth, either as the result of some other energy source or "as a survival of an old state of things"—that is, of an originally much stronger electric current (pp. 123–124). Factors Schuster could not have taken into account later disqualified his objections to this theory. He also argued against the theory that the magnetism of the Earth's core is induced by external causes. A group of theories worth much closer scrutiny related rotation of bodies to the generation of magnetism (pp. 125–130). Magnetism could be produced if molecules were magnetic or if they carried an electrical charge. He also considered an intricate relationship between gravity, electrons, and the positive charges in atoms (pp. 133–135). Schuster ultimately, however, drew no firm theoretical conclusion, resting content to have pointed out possibilities, as well as both experimental and theoretical difficulties with each approach. In this, he symbolized geomagnetic theory at the turn of the twentieth century.

The nineteenth century is sometimes considered bereft of serious theories of the origin of geomagnetism and its variations, as rather a time for gathering of data and for clearing away of fanciful ideas. While there is an element of truth to these views, scientists nevertheless proposed and explored numerous geomagnetic theories. That none of these theories provided a complete physical and mathematical explanation of geomagnetism is beside the point. No matter how incorrect, incomplete, or incomprehensible they may now seem, these theories motivated some of the most ambitious large-scale geoscientific research and were entertained by some of the best known scientists of the time. No history of this terrestrial science could be complete without an examination of these theories. They must stand ultimately in juxtaposition to the histories of observing programs and of the cultural and institutional changes that made this science possible.

A starting point for the history of nineteenth-century geomagnetic research is still Chapman's and Bartels's *Geomagnetism* (1940). However, one must be careful not to take this book as a comprehensive reflection of sources, researchers, or issues explored before about 1880. Many earlier investigations and views did not fit the post-Gaussian, post-Maxwellian perspective of the authors. For earlier periods, it's important to consult not only the secondary sources noted above, but also a wide range of primary sources. To transcend positivist historiography and truly read magnetic researchers such as Hansteen in their own context, not ours, is not an easy task. It is especially important that historians examine geomagnetic research in relation to instrument-making, the mathematical practitioner community, astronomy, meteorology, and, finally, theoretical physics (Good, "Geomagnetics and Scientific Institutions").

Gregory A. Good

Bibliography

Biermann, K.-R. "Alexander von Humboldts und Carl Friedrich Gauss organisatorisches Wirken auf geomagnetischen Gebiet." *Forschungen und Fortschritte* 32 (1958): pp. 1–8.

Brewster, David. "Magnetism." In *Encyclopaedia Britannica,* vol. 14, pp. 1–92. Boston: Little, Brown, 1857.

Cawood, John. "Terrestrial Magnetism and the Development of International Cooperation in the Early Nineteenth Century." *Annals of Science* 34 (1977): pp. 551–587.

Chapman, Sydney, and Julius Bartels. *Geomagnetism.* 2 vols. Oxford: Oxford University Press, 1940.

Fara, Patricia. "Magnetic England in the Eighteenth Century." Ph.D. diss., University of London, 1993.

Forbes, Eric G. *The Unpublished Writings of Tobias Mayer. Vol. III. The Theory of the Magnet and Its Application to Terrestrial Magnetism.* Göttingen: Vandenhoeck and Ruprecht, 1972.

Garland, G.D. "The Contributions of Carl Friedrich Gauss to Geomagnetism." *Historia Mathematica* 6 (1979): pp. 5–29.

Gauss, C.F. "Allgemeine Theorie des Erdmagnetismus." In *Resultate aus den Beobachtungen des magnetischen Vereins im Jahre 1838,* edited by Carl Friedrich Gauss and Wilhelm Weber, pp. 1–57. Leipzig: Weidmannsche Buchhandlung, 1839.

Gillmor, C. Stewart. *Coulomb and the Evolution of Physics and Engineering in Eighteenth-Century France.* Princeton: Princeton University Press, 1971.

Good, Gregory A. "Follow the Needle: Seeking the Magnetic Poles." *Earth Sciences History* 10 (1991): pp. 154–167.

———. "Geomagnetics and Scientific Institutions in 19th-Century America." *EOS: Transactions of the American Geophysical Union* 66 (July 2, 1985): pp. 521–526.

———. "The Study of Geomagnetism in the Late 19th Century." *EOS: Transactions of the American Geophysical Union* 69 (April 19, 1988): pp. 218–228.

Hansteen, Christopher. *Untersuchungen über den Magnetismus der Erde.* Christiania (Oslo): Lehmann and Gröndahl, 1819.

Herschel, John F.W. "Terrestrial Magnetism." In *Essays from the Edinburgh and Quarterly Review,* pp. 63–141. London: Longmans, 1857. Originally published in the *Quarterly Review* in 1840.

Home, R.W., and P.J. Conner. *Aepinus's Essay on the Theory of Electricity and Magnetism.* Introductory monograph and notes by R.W. Home. Translation by P.J. Conner. Princeton: Princeton University Press, 1979.

Humboldt, Alexander von. *Cosmos: A Sketch of a Physical Description of the Universe* [1845]. Translated by E.C. Otté and W.S. Dallas. 5 vols. New York: Harper, 1867, 1868.

Jungnickel, Christa, and Russell McCormmach. *Intellectual Mastery of Nature: Theoretical Physics from Ohm to Einstein.* 2 vols. Chicago and London: University of Chicago Press, 1986.

Nippoldt, Alfred. "The Present Status of the Theory of the Earth's Magnetism." *Terrestrial Magnetism and Atmospheric Electricity* 5 (1900): pp. 97–110.

Schmidt, Adolf. "Der magnetische Zustand der Erde zur Epoche, 1885." *Archiv der deutsche Seewarte* (Hamburg) 21, no. 2 (1898).

See also Auroras, before the International Geophysical Year; Geomagnetism; Geophysics; Humboldtian Science; Instruments, Geomagnetic; Isolines; Magnetic Storms or Disturbances; Solar-Terrestrial Relations; Solar Wind

Geomagnetism, Theories since 1900

Concerning production of the main magnetic field of the Earth, its secular and diurnal variation, and induced fields.

A definitive history of geomagnetism is yet to be written, but brief accounts have appeared in various publications. The story up to 1940 has been summarized (Chapman and Bartels, pp. 898–936). Perhaps the most complete account is by David R. Barraclough (pp. 584–592). Brief accounts have also been given by Stuart Malin (in Jacobs, *Geomagnetism,* vol. 1, pp. 1–50), and others (Multhauf and Good, pp. 1–46; Good, pp. 524–526; and Parkinson, pp. 347–355).

The explanation of the Earth's magnetic field has been one of the major problems in earth science for many years. The explanation given by William Gilbert (1544–1603) in 1600 of permanent magnetization within the Earth had to be abandoned when it was realized that the temperature within most of the Earth is higher than the Curie point of magnetic materials. The hope that the Curie point increases with pressure was investigated experimentally in 1931 by Leason Heberling Adams and J. Wilbur Green and theoretically by J.C. Slater (presented at the 1932 meeting of the New England Section of the American Physical Society) and found to be groundless. The position in 1939 can be summarized by this statement (Chapman and Bartels, p. 701): "It cannot be said that at present any satisfactory explanation of the Earth's main field is available."

It is useful to summarize the observed phenomena for which any satisfactory theory of the main field must allow. To a first approximation the field is that of a centered dipole almost parallel to the axis of rotation. Changes amounting to a large fraction of the field have occurred in the geologically short time span of a few centuries. These changes are known as secular variation. A prominent feature is the tendency for the field to drift westward at a rate of several degrees per century. These facts have been known for a long time. Since 1943 more evidence has come from the magnetization of rocks. Over tens of thousands of years the magnitude of the field has varied by a factor of three or four. In spite of this rapid variation, the field has behaved much as it does today for the last three billion years. During that time there have been many sudden (that is, taking less than ten thousand years) reversals of the field in which the direction everywhere changed by 180°. The close relationship between the magnetic and rotational axes appears to have persisted throughout.

In 1948 Horace Welcome Babcock measured the magnitude of the magnetic fields of the Sun and some stars. The result suggested a relation between angular momentum and magnetic moment, as pointed out by Patrick M.S. Blackett in 1947. A plethora of papers appeared offering various relations between the angular momentum and magnetic moment, some claiming the authority of unified field theory. Attempts to settle the question by determining the vertical gradient of the field, however, gave contradictory results. Finally, on the basis of laboratory experiments, Blackett himself abandoned the idea in 1952.

When Blackett's idea was abandoned, attention was confined to various ways in which electric currents could continue in the interior of the Earth. The possibility that the magnetic field is caused by the rotation with the Earth of a system of electrostatic charges was discussed by several authors. The idea goes back to William Sutherland who suggested in 1903 that an anisotropic distribution of polar molecules within the Earth would furnish sufficient charge density. Various authors have suggested ways of accounting for the necessary distribution of charge.

Most twentieth-century ideas of the mechanism of generation of the Earth's magnetic field originated with a brief publication by Joseph Larmor in 1919. One of his suggestions was that the magnetic field of the Sun might be generated by convective motion driving a dynamo that might generate electric currents sufficient to support the observed field. Of his several suggestions, this was the one he favored.

The Earth's field is approximately, but not exactly, axisymmetric. Thomas George Cowling, a mathematician who collaborated with Chapman, investigated the feasibility of Larmor's idea. In 1934 he showed on physical grounds that an axisymmetric field could not be produced by a hydromagnetic dynamo. This was the first of a number of "antidynamo" theorems. Summaries can be found in the literature (Jacobs, *The Earth's Core*, pp. 129–130; *Geomagnetism*, vol. 2, p. 206). The restriction to axisymmetric fields in Cowling's theorem was not appreciated and, for many years, it inhibited the development of the idea of a dynamo. Cowling himself later stated (Cowling, p. 9) "Too much emphasis was put on my theorem."

Walter M. Elsasser, a product of the famous Göttingen school of physicists, came to California in 1936 as a result of the Third Reich's purges, and abandoned nuclear physics for geophysics. The modern era in main field theory may be said to have begun with a series of papers by Elsasser, starting in 1939. These papers showed that a self-excited magneto-hydro-dynamic dynamo is possible in a simply connected medium, such as the Earth's core, provided the symmetries expressed in the antidynamo theorems are avoided. But Elsasser gave no numerically calculated results. Those first came in 1954.

Edward (Teddy) Crisp Bullard (1907–1980) was a product of the Cavendish Laboratory when Lord Rutherford was in charge. He became one of the most important innovators in the revolution in geology known as plate tectonics. Perhaps his most important work was in marine geophysics. His interest in geomagnetism grew out of his work on degaussing ships during World War II. He was one of the few prominent geophysicists of his generation able to use the novel electronic computers. He and H. Gellman in 1954 calculated the action of an alpha-omega type dynamo. The omega effect is the conversion of a poloidal field to a toroidal one by the differential rotation of the conducting medium. The alpha effect, first discovered by Eugene N. Parker and developed by S.I. Braginski, is the contrary conversion of a toroidal field into a poloidal one by the vertical convection of the medium together with twisting from the Coriolis force. A self-sustaining dynamo will occur if the resulting poloidal field sufficiently augments the original poloidal field, as occurs in the homopolar generator. References are in Jacobs (*Geomagnetism*, vol. 2, p. 246).

To illustrate the idea of a homopolar generator, Bullard in 1955 considered a modification of the disk dynamo invented by Michael Faraday: a rotating disk electrically connected to a concentric coaxial coil. A very interesting extension of this was produced by Tsuneji Rikitake in 1958. He considered two coupled disk dynamos in which the coil of one was attached to the disk of the other. The interesting feature of this arrangement is that it can show the kind of reversals observed in the geomagnetic field.

A concept central to the work of Bullard and Gellman, and many others, is the idea of "frozen flux lines." A system of currents once set up in the core (assuming reasonable conductivity) will persist for tens of thousands of years. This implies a slow migration of flux lines through the conductor. If the conductor moves appreciably in a sufficiently short time, the magnetic field must move with it, as if the field were "frozen" into the moving conductor. This concept, which is also of great importance in magnetospheric physics, originated with Hannes Alfven. In 1950 he suggested what has come to be known as the "twisted kink" theory. It differs only in details from the alpha-omega dynamo and is of historical interest as an early application of the idea of frozen flux, a concept that is often called Alfven's theorem. Despite the widespread use of this theorem in the physics of the core, Gerry Bloxham and David Gubbins presented evidence, in 1985, that diffusion of flux through the core might be an important feature in the generation of secular variation.

Difficulties with the alpha-omega dynamo as presented by Bullard and Gellman were pointed out by R.D. Gibson and Paul Harry Roberts (pp. 108–120), and others. The difficulty is that each spherical harmonic considered generates higher-order harmonics because of the asymmetry necessary to avoid the antidynamo restrictions. These higher-order terms form a divergent series. George Backus in 1958 overcame this divergence by the rather unnatural step of requiring that the flow stop periodically while the higher-order terms decay. At about the same time Arvid Herzenberg devised a dynamo consisting of two rotating spheres with their axes of rotation at right angles. A working model of this dynamo was constructed in 1963 by Frank J. Lowes and I. Wilkinson. Although rather unlikely in nature, these models did show that a self-excited dynamo is a possibility and that the objections to the Bullard-Gellman dynamo are not fundamental.

E. Harry Vestine, a Canadian physicist

working at the Department of Terrestrial Magnetism in Washington, proposed in 1954 that poloidal currents could possibly be generated by temperature differences at the core-mantle boundary. In the presence of a poloidal magnetic field they would produce toroidal Hall currents in the lower mantle that might in turn augment the original poloidal field, thus resulting in a self-sustaining dynamo. The mechanism depends on the Hall coefficient and conductivity of the lower mantle, neither of which are well determined. An interesting feature of this mechanism is that no toroidal magnetic field is required, so that the energy required is less than for dynamos of the alpha-omega type.

In 1895 John Hopkinson estimated the decay time of currents in the Earth to be thousands of millions of years, and on this basis, hypothesized that the magnetic field is a remnant of a field generated early in the Earth's life. A more realistic estimate of the conductivity of the core led Elsasser to realize in 1947 that the decay time is small compared with the age of the Earth, and that a permanent source of energy was required. The source of this energy is still controversial. Elsasser originally (1939) considered that thermo-electric power derived from temperature differences in different parts of the core-mantle boundary would supply the required energy. David R. Inglis and Edward Teller also supported the idea of thermo-electric power. Bullard in 1940 favored thermal energy, produced by cooling of the core or by radioactivity. The inefficiency of this process became clear with the application of thermodynamics by Bachus, Gubbins, and David Loper between 1975 and 1979.

In 1971 Gary H. Higgins and George C. Kennedy estimated the melting point of iron at the pressures of the outer core. Their conclusion was that the thermal gradient through the core would be less than the adiabatic gradient. This means that the liquid core would be stably stratified and purely thermal convection could not occur. However, as pointed out by Don L. Anderson, the estimate of the temperature gradient depends on the melting point discontinuity at the inner core boundary, which in turn depends on the influence of impurities in the liquid iron. In 1971 these were thought to be mainly sulfur.

An interesting mechanism was envisaged by Willem V.R. Malkus in 1963. The torque imposed on the Earth by the Sun and Moon, because of its ellipticity, causes a precession of the axis of rotation about the normal to the ecliptic with a period of twenty-six thousand years. The torque imposed on the core, with its smaller ellipticity, is less, so it tends to precess at a slower rate. Nevertheless it is forced to precess with the rest of the Earth. Therefore the mantle imposes a torque on the core, which tends to cause fluid flow in the core. There is some controversy as to whether this flow is adequate to power the dynamo, as M.G. Rochester and his co-workers pointed out in 1975.

The most popular theory in the late twentieth century concerning the source of power has involved freezing of the material of the liquid outer core onto the solid inner core. The outer core is thought to be composed of liquid iron, but its density is too low for pure iron at the prevailing pressure. There is a light component, which has been variously considered to be silicon, sulphur, or oxygen. As the core loses heat, pure iron freezes onto the inner core, leaving liquid rich in the light component. This material is less dense than the surrounding material and therefore convects upward, forming a flow with a vertical component. This mechanism was first suggested by Braginskiy in 1964 and was developed by Gubbins and Loper about 1977. If this mechanism were valid, there should be a compositional difference between the outer and inner core. T.G. Masters found evidence to support this difference, based on Earth oscillations (Gubbins and Masters, pp. 24–25).

Henry T. Hall and Rama Murthy in 1971 realized that the residual liquid left at the inner core boundary would be buoyant. They seem to have been unaware of Braginskiy's suggestion, and considered that "although the fluid motions of the outer core are dominated by thermal convection due to the presence of ^{40}K, low density, sulfur rich material rejected from the inner core may play an important role in the convective motion of the outer core" (Cox and Cain, p. 592).

All theories of the origin of the Earth's main field in the twentieth century depend upon the physical properties of the core, as derived from seismic data and Earth oscillations. Although these have proven more reliable than any other data, several details have not been clarified, and these can have an influence on the validity of some theories of the source of the main field (Gubbins and Masters, pp. 1–50).

Interest in the structure of the core-mantle boundary was initiated by the discovery by Raymond Hide and Malin in 1971 that there is a correlation between the global gravitational and magnetic fields. This suggested some topography on the boundary, but negative seismic evidence precluded the existence of topography of greater than 2 kilometers. Seismic waves reflected from the core-mantle boundary indicated a lateral variation in reflectivity. In the 1980s the idea of "crypto-continents" was expressed by some authors. These would be patches of mantle, at its base, of continental size, that are hotter and better electrical conductors than the rest of the mantle. They have been considered to be the cause of areas of low secular variation. Gubbins considered in 1979 that the present decrease in the axial dipole field (5 percent per century) is due to the increase in intensity and southward movement of a patch of reversed flux at the core-mantle boundary, at present south of Africa. He considered reversals to occur when the intensity of the reverse flux regions increases enough to exceed the effect of the normal flux regions.

Another fruitful field of research has been that of turbulent dynamos. The general theory was outlined in 1950 by George Keith Batchelor. The idea of "mean field electrodynamics," in which a steady and possibly axisymmetric flow and field are perturbed by small-scale fluctuations, was initiated by M. Steenbeck and F. Kraus in 1969. The closely similar theory of magnetohydrodynamic waves in the Earth's core was treated at length by Braginskiy and summarized in his 1967 paper.

The early workers in the subject, such as Elsasser and Bullard, tried to deal with all aspects of the problem of the origin of the main field. After 1980 the tendency was to deal separately with three aspects: (1) the source of energy; (2) the kinematic dynamo, in which a flow of conducting fluid is assumed, and the resulting field calculated; and (3) the dynamical problem, in which a flow pattern is determined from the imposed forces, including the Lorentz force, which depends on the magnitude of the magnetic field. The dynamical problem is the most difficult and the one upon which least headway has been made to date. So many variables are involved, several of which are poorly determined, that most treatments omit some variables, often without justification. Perhaps the most important advances in this field were made by Friedrich H. Busse and reported in a series of papers from 1975 to 1978. He found that the liquid would flow in a series of rolls with axes parallel to the axis of rotation (thus accounting for the proximity of the geomagnetic and rotational axes) and showed that these can produce a magnetic field.

The magnetohydrodynamic mechanism for the main geomagnetic field, as outlined above, accounted for most of its observed features, such as its almost axisymmetric form and approximation to a dipole. It allowed for, but did not predict, secular variation and reversals. Several other mechanisms were suggested but none accounted as well for the observed properties of the field.

Bibliography for the origin of the main field can be found in several reviews, such as Gubbins and Masters (pp. 48–50), Jacobs (*Geomagnetism,* vol. 2, pp. 177, 246, 303), and in the appropriate volumes of *Physics Abstracts*. An important conference on the core-mantle interface took place in March 1972 and was reported by Allan Cox and Joseph Cain (pp. 591–623). The report has a useful bibliography as well as abstracts of the papers presented.

Diurnal variation is another topic in geomagnetism about which theories have developed since 1900. Like many advances in geomagnetism, the discovery of diurnal variation resulted from an improvement in instrumentation. In 1722 George Graham constructed a compass that could be read more precisely than any before. While observing with this he noticed that the north-seeking end of the compass needle declines more to the east during the mornings and more to the west during the afternoons. This phenomenon, which involves the whole field, has been called "diurnal variation." In 1759 J. Canton found a seasonal effect in diurnal variations, strongly suggesting a solar control. In 1850 K. Kriel, in Prague, found a small but distinct variation with a period of half a lunar day (that is, 12 hours 25 minutes). Attempts to explain the phenomenon appeared occasionally during the nineteenth century, such as Faraday's suggestion involving the paramagnetism of oxygen. In the 1882 edition of *Encyclopedia Britannica,* Balfour Stewart put forward his dynamo theory of diurnal variation. Work since then has been devoted to justifying and filling in details of this theory.

Soon after Stewart's suggestion, Arthur Schuster showed, using Gauss's harmonic analysis technique, that the major part of the diurnal variation originates outside the Earth. This was implicit in Stewart's theory, in spite of the fact that the atmosphere was then considered to be an insulator; indeed little was known about the electrical properties of gases. Several similar analyses in terms of spherical harmonics have been done since (Chapman and Bartels, pp. 684–698; Parkinson, pp. 263–264).

For several decades the science of geomagnetism was dominated by the figure of Sydney Chapman (1888–1970). After studying engineering at Manchester (where Schuster was professor of physics), he read mathematics at Cambridge. He held positions at Manchester, Cambridge, Greenwich Observatory, and Imperial College before becoming professor of natural philosophy at Oxford in 1946. Here his important work on the theory of plasmas, the ionosphere, and magnetic storms was started. Before having to retire from Oxford, he resigned and spent the last seventeen years of his life shuttling seasonally between Fairbanks, Alaska, and Boulder, Colorado, spending the winters in Alaska: "You can't see the aurora in the summer." He was one of the leading organizers of the International Geophysical Year (1957–1958). He was a prolific writer. Cowling, in the Royal Society obituary, listed 406 papers and seven books of which Chapman was author or co-author. One of his early contributions (1913) was to devise a notation for the various types of diurnal variations, which is still in use. Thus the variation with a period of one solar day and derived from quiet days is designated Sq, for the lunar variation, L, for solar variations derived from disturbed days, SD, and so on.

The effect of solar heating, as suggested by Stewart, is hard to quantify, but the lunar effect must be entirely due to gravitational tides and therefore subject to calculation. The semidiurnal lunar tides were well known and, in a series of papers starting in 1913, Chapman analyzed in detail the lunar variations that should result from the known lunar tides. Two significant results appeared. The phase of the upper atmosphere winds was opposite to that required, and an integrated conductivity of 2.5×10^4 siemens was required in the upper atmosphere. This unlikely conductivity led Ross Gunn, in 1928, to look back to a variation of the paramagnetic theory of Faraday. He considered the paramagnetic effect of gyrating ions in the ionosphere as a mechanism for the diurnal variation. Gunn appeared to overestimate the number of ions. Geoffrey Ingram Taylor's work on atmospheric oscillations showed that, with a realistic model, a nodal surface develops in the middle atmosphere, so that the flow of air is in opposite directions above and below this surface, thus explaining the phase contrast found by Chapman. In 1927 G.H. Pedersen pointed out that electrons could travel across the magnetic field only by virtue of collisions. Meanwhile radio exploration of the ionosphere, initiated by Gregory Breit and Merle Tuve in the United States and Edward Victor Appleton in Britain, revealed an electron density that gave an integrated conductivity of only 5 siemens.

In 1937 Chaim Leib Pekeris investigated the dynamics of tidal flow and concluded that the quantity that remains constant with height is the kinetic energy density, not the velocity, as had been assumed by earlier workers. The resulting higher velocity in the ionosphere required a conductivity of only 25 to 50 siemens. The theory was finally cleared up by William George Baker and David Forbes Martyn in 1953, when they recalculated the ionospheric conductivity taking into account the effect of electrostatic charges that confine the current flow to the ionosphere, and make it act like a thin conducting shell.

David Forbes Martyn (1906–1970) was one of the most prominent physicists in Australia in the mid-twentieth century. After obtaining a B.S. in his home town of Glasgow, and a Ph.D. from London University, he migrated to Australia in 1929. He was soon involved in researching the behavior of charged particles in electromagnetic fields, and the propagation of radio waves in the ionosphere. He held a number of positions in government instrumentalities in the early days of radio sounding of the ionosphere. Finally he was head of the Upper Atmosphere Laboratory at Camden, near Sydney.

The same calculations of Baker and Martyn explained a phenomenon noticed after recording at the Huancayo Observatory, Peru, started in 1922. The observatory is situated very close to the magnetic equator, where the inclination is zero. At all low latitude stations the diurnal variation rises during the morning to a northward maximum at noon. At Huancayo the noon maximum was found to be two or three times as great as at other low-latitude sites. By 1947 the same phenomenon had been found at other sites sufficiently close to the magnetic equator. This indicated a narrow stream of electrical current running eastward close to the magnetic equator. In 1951 Chapman named this the "equatorial electrojet." The explanation offered by Baker and Martyn involved the electric field caused by electrostatic charges on the upper and lower surfaces of the thin conductor formed by the lower ionosphere, which has the effect of increasing the conductivity in an east-west direction.

The height at which the electrojet and other dynamo currents flow cannot be determined from surface measurements of the diurnal variation field. Stewart considered that the upper troposphere might be their location. When the height distribution of electron density was determined by radio probing of the ionosphere, the region of maximum conductivity appeared to be the E region, at a height of between 100 and 150 kilometers (60 and 90 miles). This site for the dynamo current was confirmed by rocket-borne magnetometers. However in 1975 Malin expressed some doubts about this, based on the relation between L and the height of the E-layer.

Since the paper by Baker and Martyn, a number of papers on diurnal variation have appeared, several being improved analyses using the greater number of observatories available during and after the International Geophysical Year. On the theoretical side, Hiroshi Maeda in 1953 discussed coordinates that fit the behavior of the diurnal variations better than either geographic or geomagnetic coordinates. He also commented on the difficulty of defining Sq at high latitudes in a paper in 1973 entitled "What is Sq?" In 1969 V.M. Mishin and his colleagues in Irkutsk pointed out the effect of field-aligned currents that effectively link the Northern and Southern hemispheres. A considerable amount of work has been done on specifying details of the equatorial electrojet; this was summarized by R.G. Rastogi (Jacobs, *Geomagnetism*, vol. 3, pp. 461–526).

Since the advent of space probes there has been some interest in the interaction between the magnetosphere and the ionosphere. However the atmospheric dynamo as originally suggested by Stewart and quantitatively developed by Baker and Martyn appears to be the main source of the diurnal variation, with the possible exception of some high latitude phenomena, discussed elsewhere in this volume. Reference to the early work on diurnal variation will be found in Chapman and Bartels (pp. 964–968), and later work in Parkinson (pp. 398–424). The most recent summary is by Wallace Campbell (Jacobs, *Geomagnetism*, vol. 3, pp. 455–460).

One of the by-products of Schuster's 1889 analysis of the diurnal variation was the realization that varying external fields can induce appreciable fields of internal origin. Because the vertical components of the external and internal fields are of opposite phase, the resultant vertical field is much less than expected from a purely external field.

Chapman and Bartels summarized the situation in 1939. They presented detailed calculations of the induced currents flowing in the "uniform core model"—that is, a model consisting of a uniform concentric sphere whose radius and conductivity were chosen to fit the data derived from solar and lunar diurnal variations (pp. 711–749). They also quoted the work of Chapman and Albert Price on the main phase of magnetic storms, which did not agree with the model derived from diurnal variation. Mention was also made of a landmark paper by B.N. Lahiri and Price in 1939 in which they treated the conductivity as a continuously increasing function of depth, with a conducting shell near the surface, which they tentatively identified as the effect of the oceans. Earth currents were discussed (pp. 417–448), and some attempt was made to explain them in terms of induction by the varying magnetic field, but there was no suggestion that by combining geomagnetic and telluric results some information about earth resistivities could be obtained.

After 1950 the subject developed along two lines. One was the determination of the distribution of global conductivity, treating the Earth as having spherical symmetry. The second was the determination of conductivity structure locally, including the detection of lateral gradients in conductivity.

The work of Chapman, Price, and their collaborators had put the theory of overall global conductivity on a firm basis by 1939. The principal advance since then has been to probe to greater depths by using variations with periods longer than one day, and the development of inversion theories. The most prominent work in the former field was that by Roger J. Banks published in 1969 and 1972.

The second, and more extensively studied, branch of the subject has dealt generally with local conditions, although it has been used to probe to considerable depths. The idea of combining earth (or "telluric") currents with geomagnetic variations originated with Andrei Nikolaivich Tikhonov in 1950, and it was more fully developed in 1953 by Louis Cagniard, who coined the name "magneto-tellurics." The potential difference between two probes in the ground is compared with simultaneous magnetic variations of the same frequency. High frequency ratios are controlled by conditions at shallow depth while low frequencies probe to greater depths. Thus a great range of frequencies is required, which taxes the instrumentation. Much of the early work was done by Thomas Madden and his students at the Massachusetts Institute of Technology during the decade starting in 1967.

After Cagniard's paper in 1953, James Wait criticized some of the assumptions implicit in the magneto-telluric technique. There followed an interesting exchange of letters published in *Geophysics,* volume nineteen. The principal contention was the uniformity of the primary field. Wait quoted observations at high latitudes and claimed that a more exact formula, containing higher orders of the reciprocal propagation constant, should have been used. The primary field can be expressed as the sum of a number of waves, but whether these are physical waves or merely mathematical concepts, was left in doubt. Cagniard eventually agreed with Wait, but it was not at all clear that he was convinced of the reality of waves traveling at imaginary angles. Workers in the 1970s and 1980s tended to follow Cagniard's approach.

One of the most prominent names in the development of magneto-tellurics is that of Albert Price. Essentially a mathematician, he was professor of applied mathematics at Exeter University for many years. Apart from his early work with Chapman and Lahiri, he investigated the assumptions inherent in Cagniard's work in 1962. He initiated the theory of induction in thin layers in papers published in 1949 and 1950, later applied to the oceans. In collaboration with Walter Jones he initiated the method of calculating the response of "two-dimensional" models in 1970, in which the conductivity depends not on depth alone but also on one horizontal dimension. This was later extended by Jones in 1974 and by John Weaver in 1976, and has been used as a standard part of the process of forward modeling.

After 1970 a considerable effort was devoted to devising inversion methods for magneto-telluric data. An inversion method is an algorithm for which the input is a sequence of observed data (usually the ratio of electric to magnetic fields) and the output is a distribution of electrical conductivity. The earlier interpretation methods ("forward modeling") consisted of modeling a distribution of conductivity, calculating a corresponding parameter, and comparing this with the observed value of the same parameter. Almost all inversion methods are fundamentally based on the work of Gel'fand and Levitan, published in 1955. An inversion method applicable to geophysics generally was enunciated by Backus and Gilbert in 1967, and it was adapted to

magneto-telluric data by Robert Parker in 1970. Peter Weidelt, in 1972, devised a slightly different method and suggested a number of criteria to ensure that the data are consistent with a model in which the conductivity depends on depth only. Later algorithms, such as that of Gaston Fischer and B.V. LeQuang, published in 1981, try to define a family of models all of which are consistent with the data.

The difficulty of calculating the response to three-dimensional bodies is severe, especially if they are of irregular shape. Therefore scale modeling, such as that performed by Harry Dosso and his co-workers in Canada since the early 1960s has been of great help. The calculation of induced currents in a number of conductors of particular shapes has been summarized by Rikitake (pp. 126–220).

Julius Bartels, as early as 1939, observed that even closely spaced observatories often record rather different time variations, especially in the vertical component. This was recognized as being the result of lateral inhomogeneities in underground conductivity. During the 1950s study of these conductivity anomalies was pursued by two schools: the German school of Horst Wiese, Ulrich Schmucker, and others, and the Japanese school with Rikitake as principal investigator. In 1959 Parkinson drew attention to the effect of the oceans on magnetic variations at coastal sites.

According to theory, a uniform horizontal inducing field over a conductivity distribution depending on depth only (as was assumed by Cagniard) produces no vertical component. Thus the ratio of vertical to horizontal fields is a measure of the lateral gradient of conductivity. This technique was developed by James Everett and R.D. Hyndman in 1967 and later used by many investigators such as Ian Gough and his co-workers in North America in 1982, Edward Lilley in Australia in 1972, and Rokityansky, Van'yan and others in Eastern Europe during the 1970s and 1980s.

Much work has gone into solving the problem of electromagnetic induction in the oceans. The first attempt was made by Bullard and Robert Parker in 1970. Since then a series of papers by Rod Hewson-Brown, Peter C. Kendall, and their collaborators, (1973–1983), Bruce Hobbs and Graham Dawes (1979), and others have appeared. The oceans are of such irregular shape that generally some simplifications must be made.

The conductivity distribution of the ocean floors is a parameter of considerable geological interest. The challenge of operating magneto-telluric equipment on the ocean floor was taken up by Charles Cox and Jean Filloux at Scripps Institute of Oceanography from 1971. Details are given by Filloux (Jacobs, *Geomagnetism*, vol. 1, pp. 143–248).

The results of induction field surveys give much more significant information if the conductivity results can be interpreted in terms of rock type and physical properties. The early work on the conductivity of minerals, such as that of R.D. Harvey in 1928, concentrated on economic minerals such as oxides and sulfides. Apart from deposits of such minerals, the commonest control on the conductivity of near surface rocks are porosity and the salinity of the interstitial water. This was first studied by K. Sundberg in 1932 and John J. Jakosky and R.D. Hopper in 1937, and, expressed by the empirical law that bears his name, by G.E. Archie in 1942. The linear conductivity anomalies often located by measurements of the time varying magnetic field, have usually been ascribed to zones of higher than average porosity. A feature that may be important is the presence of graphite, which can change the conductivity greatly even in minute amounts.

The principal hope in deep geomagnetic probing is that a knowledge of conductivity will give information on temperature. Work on the temperature dependence of the conductivity of mantle material was done by Takesi Nagata in 1937, and was continued by H.P. Coster in 1948, by Harry Hughes in Cambridge, and by K. Noritomi in Japan in the mid-1950s. The relation is complicated because temperature is only one of the variables controlling conductivity. Oxygen fugacity, impurities, crystal form and chemical composition can all have important effects. Comprehensive bibliographies are given by E.I. Parkhomenko (pp. 243–262, 297–308).

Science, like other activities, can often be seen more clearly from a distance. In the mid-1990s we can see some of the major breakthroughs of the 1960s, but only in the future will we be able to see clearly the relative importance of later work. The situation is complicated by the greater number of scientists working during the latter half of the twentieth century. When a Faraday or a Maxwell stood alone in the field, producing monumental publications at rare intervals, the target for historians was clearer than in the latter half of the twentieth century, when great numbers of scientists are busy writing papers about their narrow specialties. When Sir

Arthur Schuster discovered the induced field he remarked, "This we might have expected" (p. 469). Editors a century later would be loath to waste space on such remarks. Autobiographical articles, such as that of T.G. Cowling (pp. 1–18) are all too rare.

The few authoritative accounts of the history of geomagnetism usually specialize on the early periods. Several articles by Crichton Mitchell and H.D. Harradon are examples. Barraclough (p. 584) states, "For the present century no attempt has been made to be at all comprehensive and the choice of topics is, no doubt, influenced by my own interests."

Perhaps it is not too much to hope that the articles in this volume may guide others to a more detailed investigation of the history of geomagnetism during the twentieth century.

W. Dudley Parkinson

Bibliography

Barraclough, David R. "Geomagnetism: Historical Introduction." In *The Encyclopedia of Solid Earth Geophysics,* edited by David E. James, pp. 584–592. New York: Van Nostrand Reinholt, 1989.

Chapman, Sydney, and Julius Bartels. *Geomagnetism.* Oxford: Oxford University Press, 1940.

Cowling, T.G. "Astronomer by Accident." *Annual Review of Astronomy and Astrophysics* 23 (1985): pp. 1–18.

Cox, Allan, and Joseph C. Cain. "International Conference on the Core-Mantle Interface." *EOS* 53 (1972): pp. 591–597.

Crichton Mitchell, A. "Chapters in the History of Terrestrial Magnetism." *Terrestrial Magnetism and Atmospheric Electricity* 37 (1932): pp. 105–146; 42 (1937): pp. 241–280; 44 (1939): pp. 77–80.

Gibson, R.D., and Paul Harry Roberts. "Some Comments on the Theory of Homogeneous Dynamos." In *Magnetism and the Cosmos,* edited by W.R. Hindmarsh, F.J. Lowes, P.H. Roberts, and S.K. Runcorn, pp. 108–120. Edinburgh: Oliver and Boyd, 1965.

Good, Gregory A. "Geomagnetism and Scientific Institutions in the 19th Century." *EOS* 66 (1985): pp. 521, 524–526.

Gubbins, D., and T.G. Masters. "Driving Mechanism for the Earth's Dynamo."

Advances in Geophysics 21 (1979): pp. 1–50.

Harradon, H.D. "Some Early Contributions to the History of Geomagnetism." *Terrestrial Magnetism and Atmospheric Electricity* 37 (1932): pp. 105–146; 42 (1937): pp. 185–198.

Jacobs, J.A. *The Earth's Core.* London: Academic Press, 1975.

———, ed. *Geomagnetism.* London: Academic Press, vols. 1, 2, 1987, vol. 3, 1989.

Multhauf, Robert P., and Gregory Good. *A Brief History of Geomagnetism.* Washington, D.C.: Smithsonian Institution Press, 1987.

Parkhomenko, E.I. *Electrical Properties of Rocks.* New York: Plenum, 1967.

Parkinson, W.D. *Introduction to Geomagnetism.* Edinburgh: Scottish Academic Press, 1983.

Rikitake, Tsuneji. *Electromagnetism and the Earth's Interior.* Amsterdam: Elsevier, 1966.

Schuster, Arthur. "The Diurnal Variation of Terrestrial Magnetism." *Philosophical Transactions of the Royal Society of London* A180 (1889): pp. 467–512.

See also Auroras, before the International Geophysical Year; Auroras, since the International Geophysical Year; Geomagnetism; Geophysics; Humboldtian Science; Instruments, Geomagnetic; Isolines; Magnetic Storms or Disturbances; Solar-Terrestrial Relations; Solar Wind

Geomorphology: Disciplinary History

Study of the surface of the Earth.

The history of geomorphology is better written as a history of ideas rather than of a discipline. An outline history may be found in Keith Tinkler's 1985 *Short History of Geomorphology,* which shows that an interest in the Earth's surface has always been central to human use of that surface; thus it is not difficult to trace in philosophical writings from the early Greeks to the present a concern with how the surface works. Insofar as Western science shares a common culture through a shared intellectual language it may be said that Greek and Roman knowledge has been well known in the Western world since whenever it first became available, and it may be said too that a comparable body of material was probably known in China dating at least as far back as the early Greek writings.

However, although an understanding of commonplace erosional events—such as the collapse of cliffs, soil erosion, the meandering of rivers, and the building of beaches—has long been with us, placing these into an overall system of change required the development of a comprehensive theory of the Earth. Broadly it may be said that since the Renaissance, as "geological" theories of the globe have waxed and waned, as described in François Ellenberger's books *L'aube de la géologie moderne: Henri Gautier (1660–1737)* (1975) and *Histoire de la géologie* (1988), so has the sophistication of attempts to understand that surface, a point also well made for British literature for the three centuries before 1878 in Gordon L. Herries Davies's *The Earth in Decay* (1969). For these reasons, the history of geomorphology is more profitably studied as a history of ideas than as the history of an academic and isolated discipline.

However, there is inevitable divergence in knowledge with the rise of nations and languages, and although there may well be parallels between the state and type of knowledge known in English in, say the seventeenth century, and that known in other European languages, it is too early yet to say how common, or how different, these varied perceptions of the world have been. A preliminary view of the diversity, if not the unity, however, may be glimpsed in Keith Tinkler's 1989 volume *History of Geomorphology: From Hutton to Hack.*

The seventeenth century saw the gradual emergence of something resembling modern science, headed by the Royal Society of London, and subsequently by equivalent scientific societies elsewhere in Europe, and many of them in mutual communication about matters scientific. It would be incorrect to say that the bulk of their scientific interests lay in the area of earth science, but, by 1700 much English "earth science" was being written in the light of Newtonian science or its European competitors, although it is far from saying that it used that knowledge in a way scientists would regard as rigorous today. The numerous theories of the Earth then written in Britain sought to find a rational and complete explanation of global development that was harmonized with both contemporary science and theological scholarship. To this end the principle of universal gravitation, operating via mechanisms such as passing comets and tilting terrestrial axes, was used to engender floods, earthquakes, eruptions, and in their wake mountains, lakes, valleys, and marine fossils. Such authors included John Woodward (1665–1728), William Whiston (1667–

1752), James Burnett (1635–1715), and Robert Hooke (1635–1703). The fledgling scientific method of public discourse and experimentation was not yet adapted to deal with phenomena that could not be brought to the laboratory as entities. As Dennis Dean has revealed in his 1981 paper on the age of the Earth controversy, a catastrophic cast to earth histories also seemed to be demanded by theological insistence on an age of the Earth measured in a few millennia.

Although by virtue of abundant reprints of popular theories the eighteenth century is often seen as one of increasingly wild theoretical speculation about the terraqueous globe, there is now an increasing realization that there were also abroad the seeds of a different approach based on careful, and eventually extensive, field description and specimen sampling. Essays by François Ellenberger, "Les Méconnus: Eighteenth Century French Pioneers of Geomorphology," and Keith Tinkler, "Worlds Apart: Eighteenth Century Writings on Rivers, Lakes and the Terraqueous Globe," in Tinkler's *History of Geomorphology: From Hutton to Hack* (pp. 11–36 and 37–71, respectively) document some of these examples for France, Britain, and India. The work of Pálsson (1762–1840) on glacial processes in Iceland, Giovanni Targioni-Tozzeti (1712–1784) on rivers and landscape in Italy, Georges Louis Leclercs, Comte de Buffon (1707–1788), Nicholas-Antoine Boulanger (1722–1759), and Nicholas Demarest (1725–1815) on landscape in France, Lewis Evans (1700–1756) on the Appalachian landscape, and François Pouchot (1712–1769) on Niagara Falls, and doubtless many others elsewhere, all show that a new type of field science was being bred, but one less likely to erupt into public prominence by reason of its more carefully observed and argued character. Its philosophy was an unconscious adaption of a universalist view of the world, that like things—stones falling in Europe and America—must be interpreted in similar ways. Applied to interpreted sequences of sediments this led, via the current principles of universalism, to the assumption that the world should possess an identical sedimentological and erosional history in all its parts. This gave rise to what we may call a universalist phase in geological reasoning, an argument made in Tinkler's "Worlds Apart."

The eighteenth century was noteworthy too for loosening the theological shackles placed upon temporal reasoning about the age of the Earth. All geological processes are slow upon a human timescale, and this was even-

tually becoming clear from the gathering mass of local descriptions and interpretations. Although most readers sought an appeasement with scriptural authority on the age of the Earth, the extreme theology of the Deists—those who recognized a God without the benefit of a revealed religion—enabled geological reasoners to see this world as an abode designed for man (the design hypothesis) without being constrained to a specific timescale. The work of James Hutton (1726–1797) in his 1795 book *A Theory of the Earth,* and explicated by John Playfair (1747–1819) in his 1802 *Illustrations of the Huttonian Theory of the Earth,* typified this approach, although many of Hutton's ideas had been known, in bits and pieces, for centuries. Although Hutton and Playfair enunciated an episodic cycling of rock, their accounts are most successful, according to Frank Cunningham's 1977 *Revolution in Landscape Science,* or perhaps we should say have been most enduring, where they deal with surficial processes.

By 1800 the gathering Industrial Revolution began to foster specialist scientific societies and to provide and require increasing information on the Earth's interior in addition to its surface. The science of geology was named and, in retrospect, a century-long enterprise to establish the geological column was begun. An interest in the surface was left far behind, although a number of controversies sputtered along through the century. The primary one, which has long been of interest, was the debate over the origin of valleys. Entirely catastrophic views (rents from earthquakes, or carving by flood waters were the favored mechanisms) eventually gave way to gradualist views in light of the accounts by Charles Lyell (1797–1875) and Roderick Impey Murchison (1792–1871) in the 1820s of the repeated phases of valley cutting and lava filling in the *Massif Centrale* in France. The evidence had been known and explained in the French literature for nearly a century (Ellenberger in Tinkler, *Hutton to Hack,* p. 24). But perhaps the reason for the late acceptance of the very clear evidence was that its reasoned explanation had to be as a clearly public rebuttal to the assault forces of the catastrophists within a formal geological setting. Eighteenth-century geological arguments were essentially conducted as guerrilla warfare; by the nineteenth century formal wars were fought and lost.

Shortly after this gradualist and partial resolution of the fluvial origin of valleys—partial because problems still remained over the issue of lake basins (very common throughout Europe)—several smoldering accounts of glacial action beyond its present limits began to surface. Once more, these accounts had authentic eighteenth-century roots, both of evidence and interpretation, but again it seemed as though there had to be a public confrontation to raise the stakes. Louis Agassiz (1807–1873) proved an adept publicist in the early 1840s, but the glacial theory then in vogue was primarily depositional, and it was not until the 1860s that evidence from North America and Europe was drawn together by Andrew Ramsay (1814–1891) to provide an integrated depositional and erosional view of landscapes capable of explaining excavated rock basins as the overdeepened beds of glaciers. With this resolution quickly endorsed by James Geikie (1839–1915) in *The Great Ice Age* (1874, 1877, and 1894), the explanation of fluvial landscapes both within glaciated terrains and beyond them became unproblematic. Further convincing evidence for the efficacy of gradualist erosion was provided in *Exploration of the Colorado River of the West* (1875) by John Wesley Powell (1834–1902), with his geological and physiographic account of his descent of the Colorado River through the Grand Canyon (see figure).

In consequence of these discoveries, the nineteenth century tacitly endorsed Lyell's much published philosophy of uniformitarianism. Although not all parties agreed with the details of his scheme as it applied to particular parts of the geological column, or the philosophical implications of unlimited time, there were few convincing alternatives. Gratuitous catastrophism was expunged, and although large-scale natural disasters such as volcanic eruptions, earthquakes, floods, and tidal waves were accepted as agents of change, there was as yet no systematic study of the magnitude of events in relation to timescales. The emergence of evolution by natural selection after 1859 likewise made enormous demands on the length of geological time and fitted well with uniformitarian philosophy of gradual, slow change.

The stage was therefore set for a renewed vision for surface processes, and this was provided by William Morris Davis (1850–1934), whose biography appears in Richard Chorley, Robert Beckinsale, and Anthony Dunn, *History of the Study of Scenery,* vol. 2 (1973). The cycle was adapted to new notions of mountain-building taking place in short bursts followed by sustained continental stability. The cycle laid out the normal course of erosional processes and associated forms through geo-logical time, and it treated aberrations as either special cases, with forms adapted to particularly dominant processes, as with wind in deserts, or as "climatic accidents," as in the case of glaciation. The word "geomorphology" came into being at the end of the nineteenth century and was quickly adopted.

The geographical cycle is claimed to have held sway throughout the first half of the twentieth century, to be displaced in part by new directions—an emphasis on process rather than form—placed upon earth scientists through experiences in World War II. Another reason for its displacement was that the tectonic underpinnings of the theory were completely replaced by 1950, according to Chorley's 1963 paper "The Diastrophic Basis to Twentieth-Century Geomorphological Thought." However, it is well to point out that there was much sound process work in progress through the 1920s and 1930s, as testified by the work of Douglas W. Johnson (*Shoreline Processes and Shoreline Development,* 1919), F. Hjulstrom (*Studies of the Morphological Activity of Rivers Illustrated by the River Fyris,* 1935), Ralph A. Bagnold (*Physics of Blown Sand and Desert Dunes,* 1941), and Frank E. Horton ("Erosional Development of Streams and Their Drainage Basins: Hydrophysical Approach to Quantitative Morphology," *Geological Society of America Bulletin,* 1946, but based on papers already published in the 1930s). This early process work may have lost or lacked momentum during the Depression years, but certainly it emerged with completely new directions after World War II.

After World War II the work of the U.S. Geological Survey (USGS) on flood problems and attempts by North American academics to redirect landscape analysis along statistical lines caused a radical shift. This shift matured through the next two decades toward a dominating interest in surface processes, at least in English-speaking areas. This also led to the relative neglect of forms. The 1964 textbook by Luna B. Leopold, M. Gordon Wolman, and John P. Miller, *Fluvial Processes in Geomorphology,* was radically different from early geomorphology texts and reflected the tone set by the new research at the USGS. Although there have not yet been any thorough studies of the matter, it would seem as though French and German work was more balanced in its approach to form and process (and remains so). In both countries there was a considerable interest in climatic geomorphology, which traced a genealogy back to European contemporaries of William Morris Davis.

This section of the Grand Canyon shows one of John Wesley Powell's boats at the bottom, with first granite, then dikes and volcanic beds (marked a *and* a*), then nonconforming beds, and on up to the lip of the canyon. Powell wrote: "Three times has this great region been left high and dry by the ever shifting sea; three times have the rocks been fractured and faulted; three times have floods of lava been poured up through the crevices, and three times have the clouds gathered over the rocks, and carved out valleys with their storms." Reproduced from John Wesley Powell,* Exploration of the Colorado River of the West and Its Tributaries. Explored in 1869, 1870, 1871, and 1872, under the Direction of the Secretary of the Smithsonian Institution. *Figure 79, p. 113. Washington, D.C.: Government Printing Office, 1875.*

This line of thinking is well summarized in J. Büdel's 1982 *Climatic Geomorphology.* Former Eastern-bloc countries, and especially Poland, developed geomorphology along practical lines with an emphasis on national- and regional-scale geomorphological mapping, and interpretations of the surface for land use and land planning purposes. This development is reviewed for Poland by Leszek Starkel in "Different Aspects of Polish Geo-morphology: Palæogeographic, Dynamic and Applied" in Tinkler (*Hutton to Hack,* pp. 257–282). As Suzuki explains, Japan has developed a very active school of geomorphology, in part because of the intensely practical needs for surface understanding in a country with alpine terrain on a plate margin subject to volcanism, tectonism, and tsunamis.

If geomorphology achieved a name only at the end of the nineteenth century, and an international standing at the end of the twentieth century, can it be said to stand on its own as a discipline, as is implied in Robert Beckinsale's 1972 essay on the I.G.U. and physical geography? Complicating the placement of the subject as an academic discipline has been its uncertain alliances with sister disciplines, primarily geology and geography. In the United Kingdom, for example, geomorphology in the twentieth century has been almost entirely the prerogative of geography departments. Outside the English-speaking world the situation of the discipline is even less clear. Without the unity of a common language, or language group, disciplinary development and specialty interests have often been dominated by the requirements of national governments. This was long the case in the former communist-bloc countries, particularly and dominantly the USSR and Poland. In smaller countries, with few academic departments of either geology or geography (or both together), the dominating effects of particular individual scientists or cliques have been a primary control on the disciplinary flavor in the country. The numerous and uneven entries in H.J. Walker's 1989 *History of Geomorphology*, and in H.J. Walker's and W.E. Grabau's updated *Evolution of Geomorphology: A Nation-by-Nation Summary of Development* (1993), reveal these trends quite markedly. Although the latter volume is derived from and built upon the earlier one, many countries' entries changed between the volumes. For example, the entries on France are entertainingly and instructively different. A comparison demonstrates the way particular cliques have been thought to dominate twentieth-century lines of enquiry and actual field practice in France. Similar arguments have been made for the entire English-speaking world at an earlier point in time for the instance of William Morris Davis (1850–1934) and his alleged effect on the twentieth-century development of American, and even world, geomorphology. This is clearly revealed by the way the volumes are structured and the titles are phrased for the *History of Geomorphology* (1964, 1973, 1991, in progress) by Robert Beckinsale, Richard Chorley, and Anthony Dunn. Small countries, too, often focus necessarily on landforms within their territories, and thus they may appear very unbalanced in their treatment of surface forms, compared, say, to a standard textbook.

The question of what properly constitutes geomorphology has been complicated further by the needs of the geophysical community. Geophysics has used the constraints provided by an accurate knowledge of the deformation of the Earth's surface during postglacial isostatic rebound, in developing rheological models of the Earth's interior. Increasingly too, the decipherment of surface change has required the use of more elaborate dating mechanisms, and thus alliances have been forged with the methodology of Quaternary scientists. Thus it may be said that while there are fifty academic journals that advertise some interest in geomorphology (World List of Scientific Serials) there are about thirty that contain the name geomorphology in their title. Of these, about a third are refereed academic journals.

Other indices of the health of the incipient discipline exist: an *Encyclopaedia of Geomorphology* edited by R.W. Fairbridge in 1968 was issued, and a new edition is being planned. The abstracting service *Geomorphological Abstracts* began in 1960 and has since developed into a large-scale geoscience abstracting journal. The first volume of an ongoing series on the *History of Geomorphology* was issued in 1964 (and subsequently in 1973 and 1991, with one more promised). Other significant contributions on the history of the discipline, in English, have appeared in 1969 (Herries Davies), 1977 (Cunningham), 1985 (Tinkler), 1989 (Tinkler), 1989 (Walker), and 1993 (Walker and Grabau). Very recently, as an aftermath of the Third International Association of Geomorphologists (IAG) meeting in Hamilton, Ontario, Canada, a worldwide electronic mail list of geomorphologists was instituted in 1993 and is maintained by Jeffery Lee at Texas Tech University in Lubbock, Texas. This disseminates information and maintains communications among over three hundred worldwide members.

National Societies for Geomorphology have thrived in some countries (United Kingdom), whereas elsewhere (Canada, United States) the subject's needs are met by specialty groups meeting within other societies such as the Association of American Geographers and the Geological Society of America. In Canada, meetings are initially scheduled to be with the Canadian Quaternary Association. The United Kingdom has had an extremely active British Geomorphological Research Group (BGRG) since 1961, a group which, although initially independent, is now affiliated with the Institute of British Geographers and with the Geological Society of London. The group has issued a successful series of *Technical Bulletins*, has held regular independent conferences, and started the journal *Earth Surface Processes* in

1976. It added *and Landforms* to the title in 1981.

The initiative of individuals in the BGRG led to the first big independent International Conference in Geomorphology (now the IAG), held in Manchester in September 1985. Conferences have been held at four-year intervals—in Frankfurt in 1989 and in Hamilton, Ontario, Canada in 1993. The next one is scheduled for Bologna in 1997. Regional meetings are also held. The fledgling international organization has now been recognized by the International Union of Scientific Societies, but the price of initial independence has been to avoid temporal competition with the IGU (International Geographical Union) and the IGC (International Geological Congress). The problems of disciplinary affiliation mentioned earlier have caused initial difficulties in setting up properly representative National Committees for Geomorphology (required for affiliation to the International Society) in some countries—for example in the United States and Canada, although these difficulties have now been overcome.

Keith J. Tinkler

Bibliography

Beckinsale, Robert P. "The I.G.U. and the Development of Physical Geography with Special Reference to Geomorphology." In *Geography through a Century of International Congresses,* edited by Ph. Pinchemel et al. Paris: UNESCO, 1972.

———. "The International Influence of William Morris Davis." *Geographical Review* 66 (1976): pp. 448–466.

Beckinsale, Robert P., and R.J. Chorley. *History of the Study of Scenery, or the Development of Geomorphology. Volume 3, Contemporaries of W.M. Davis to 1930.* London: Methuen, 1991.

Büdel, J. *Climatic Geomorphology.* Princeton: Princeton University Press, 1982.

Chorley, Richard J. "The Diastrophic Basis to Twentieth-Century Geomorphological Thought." *Geological Society of America, Bulletin* 74 (1963): pp. 953–970.

Chorley, Richard J., Anthony J. Dunn, and Robert P. Beckinsale. *History of the Study of Scenery, or the Development of Geomorphology.* 2 vols., London: Methuen, 1964, 1973.

Cunningham, Frank. *The Revolution in Earth Science.* Vancouver: Tantalus Research Ltd., 1977.

Czechówna, L. *Historia geomorfologii w polsce w latach 1840–1939 na tle rozwoju geomorfologii swiatowej.* Poznan: Praca Wydana Z Zasilku Polskiej Academii Nauk, 1969.

Dean, Dennis R. "The Age of the Earth Controversy: Beginnings to Hutton." *Annals of Science* 38 (1981): pp. 435–456.

Ellenberger, François E. *A l'aube de la géologie moderne: Henri Gautier 1660–1737. Histoire et Nature* 7, 9, 10 (1975).

———. *Histoire de la géologie.* Tome 1. Paris: Lavoisier, 1988.

Herries Davies, Gordon L. *The Earth in Decay: A History of British Geomorphology to 1878.* London: MacDonald, 1969.

Scott, H.I. *The Development of Landform Studies in Australia.* Artama, NSW, Australia: Bellbird Publishing House, 1977.

Suzuki, T. "Recent Trend of Geomorphology in Japan." *Transactions of the Japanese Geomorphological Union* 10-A (1989).

Tinkler, Keith J. *A Short History of Geomorphology.* London: Croom Helm, 1985.

———, ed. *History of Geomorphology: From Hutton to Hack.* London: Unwin/Hyman, 1989.

Walker, H.J. "History of Geomorphology." *Transactions of the Japanese Geomorphological Union* 10-B (1989).

Walker, H.J., and W.E Grabau. *The Evolution of Geomorphology: A Nation-by-Nation Summary.* New York: John Wiley and Sons, 1993.

See also Age of the Earth, before 1800; Age of the Earth, since 1800; Cycle of Erosion; Deluge; Diluvialism; Geography; Geological Time; Geology; Geomorphology: The Word; Pedology; Sacred Theory of the Earth; Soil Science; Volcanoes, Theories before 1800

Geomorphology: The Word

Currently construed as concerned with the shape of the Earth's surface and with the processes responsible for changing it through time (Tinkler, chap. 1).

The global aspects of Earth *(geo),* shape *(morph),* and science *(logos)* implied in the word itself are not usually included in its study. The study of Earth's shape taken at the global scale is the province of geophysics, or more precisely, geodesy, in which subject it was already securely lodged by the time the word "geomorphology" came into general use after about 1890. Nevertheless, there are interactions between the concerns of geophysics and geomorphology at global, continental, and regional scales wherever the surface is deformed by the varying loads placed upon it by water, ice, and sediment and their corollaries, the melting of ice, the erosion of sediment from the continents, and the changing sea levels of the last two million years. Examples of works that exemplify the interplay between geomorphology and physics at various scales are *Lake Bonneville* (1890) by Grove Karl Gilbert (1843–1918), *The Evolution of Earth Structure with a Theory of Geomorphic Changes* (1903) by Thomas Mellard Reade (1832–1909), *Morphology of the Earth* (1962) by Lester Charles King (birth date unknown), and *Post-Glacial Uplift of Arctic Canada* (1970) by John T. Andrew (b. 1937).

The word "geomorphology" probably was used first in the German language in *Lehrbuch der Geognosie* (1858) of Carl Friedrich Naumann (1797–1873) (Roglic, p. 1), but it first appeared in English in two papers by W.J. McGee (1853–1912) in 1888, who attributed it first to John Wesley Powell (1834–1902) but later claimed it for himself and credited Powell with the term "geomorphic geology" in an 1893 work. McGee spoke of the subject in 1888 as novel, and as constituting the New Geology:

Such genetic study of topographic forms (which has been denominated geomorphology) is specially applicable in the investigation of the Cenozoic phenomena of the eastern United States and has been successfully employed in the region herein described; and, probably for the first time, important practical conclusions involving the consideration of hypogeal structure and orogenic movement have been based on the interpretation of topography and on inferences from the present behaviour of the streams by which the topography has been determined. (McGee, Geology of the Head of Chesapeake Bay, p. 547)

General use of the word in English, French, and German probably followed its use by both McGee and Powell at the International Geological Congress of 1891. The word quickly attracted general use and it was used in book titles, or their prefaces, without special explanation, by 1900—for example, *Earth Sculpture* by James Beikie (1898), *Scientific Study of Scenery* (1900) by John Edward Marr (1857–1933), and *Evolution of Earth Structure* by T.M. Reade (1903). Several variants were proposed with the intent of stressing descriptive and tectonic applications respectively: geomorphography and geomorphogeny. The 1905 essay on "Complications of the Geographical Cycle" by William Morris Davis (1850–1934) mentioned the latter, but he seems never to have adopted even geomorphology. Occasional but not pervasive use has been made of these terms; for example, Andrew Cowper Lawson (1861–1952) used "geomorphogeny" in 1894. Arthur N. Strahler in 1992 (p. 68) proposed the term "geomorphysics" to emphasize the application of physical principles to geomorphic processes. Another recent variant, anthropo-geomorphology, has been used by E. Fels (1965) to reflect human shaping of the landscape.

Keith J. Tinkler

Bibliography

Fels, E. "Nochmals: Anthropogene Geomorphologie." *Petermanns Geographische Mitteilungen* 109 (1965): pp. 9–15.

Lawson, A.C. "The Geomorphogeny of the Coast of Northern California." *Bulletin of the Department of Geology, University of California* 1 (1894): pp. 241–247.

McGee, William John. *The Geology of the Head of Chesapeake Bay.* Washington, D.C.: Government Printing Office, 1888.

Roglic, J. "Historical Review of Morphologic Concepts." In *Karst: Important Karst Regions of the Northern Hemisphere,* edited by M. Herak and V.T. Springfield. Amsterdam: Elsevier, 1972.

Strahler, Arthur N. "Quantitative/Dynamic Geomorphology at Columbia 1945–60: A Retrospective." *Progress in Physical Geography* 16 (1992): pp. 65–84.

Tinkler, K.J. *A Short History of Geomorphology.* London: Croom Helm, 1985.

See also Disciplinary History; Geochemistry: The Word and Disciplinary History; Geography: The Word; Geology: The Word; Geomorphology; Geophysics: The Word; Geothermics: The Word

Geophysical Societies and International Organizations

An important institutional context for geophysics.

Societies have usually been voluntary or honorific groups of individuals interested in the physical sciences of the Earth. Scientific societies such as the Royal Society of London or the French Academy of Sciences had accepted members with geophysical interests since their founding in the 1660s. Beginning in the nineteenth century, specialist societies in fields related to the geosciences were established, including societies for geology, meteorology, and mineralogy. The most famous is the Geological Society of London, founded in 1807, but scores of others appeared around Europe, the Americas, and the world in the nineteenth century. Although such societies included members interested in the physical investigations of the Earth, this was not the main purpose of these societies. Societies dedicated to geophysical topics emerged alongside an independent discipline of geophysics, a complex process that began in the early nineteenth century (Schröder, "Emil Wiechert"). National and international organizations for geophysical topics first appeared late in the nineteenth century.

The first collections of individuals to come together around geophysical topics were generally interested in promoting a particular research project. The Mannheimer Meteorologische Gesellschaft (Palatine Meteorological Society) is a well known research network of the late eighteenth century (see Colacino). In the 1830s, Carl Friedrich Gauss and Wilhelm Weber founded the Göttinger Magnetischer Verein (Magnetic Union) to initiate cooperative research on the Earth's magnetism (Jungnickel and McCormmach, vol. 1, pp. 63–77). Franz Neumann also encouraged geophysical research at the University of Königberg, through his physics seminar—another sort of social grouping, but not a society (see Olesko).

Industrialization also provided an impetus to the development of geophysics. The opening of navigation and of economic markets outside of Europe in the late nineteenth century and then later of aviation raised new geophysical problems to prominence. The investigation of tides, ocean currents, storms, and magnetism at sea required new methods unavailable in traditional disciplines such as physics, geography, and astronomy. New theories and practical methods were needed. The monetary profit attainable helped geophysics to become an independent branch of science.

One part of geophysics, seismology, developed in the decades around 1900 in Japan, Italy, Russia, Great Britain, Germany, and elsewhere. Like other parts of geophysics, seismology required coordinated effort in many countries. In 1898 Emil Wiechert started a broad seismological program, based at the University of Göttingen. Its observatories in Samoa and China cooperated with American and other investigators. The Königliche Gesellschaft der Wissenschaften (Royal Society of Science) in Göttingen, it should be noted, sponsored this collaboration.

However, it was still true that all geophysical organizations were focused on particular research areas. International organizations rather than local societies became the rule for the geosciences, perhaps because the phenomena required worldwide coordinated research. An early effort at international cooperation in geodesy in the 1860s ultimately produced a Permanent Commission, which sponsored seventeen general conferences between 1864 and 1912. The first International Meteorological Congress, which met in Vienna in 1873 (Schröder and Wiederkehr, pp. 80–86), and the first International Polar Year in 1882–1883 pointed the way. International meetings in many geosciences proliferated in the 1890s. Meteorologists, geodesists, and investigators of terrestrial magnetism and seismology met repeatedly. An international Permanent Commission on Terrestrial Magnetism and Atmospheric Electricity was established in 1896, as part of the International Meteorological Organization. V. Rebeur-Paschwith published a proposal for an international network of seismological observatories in 1895, and the International Congress of Geographers formalized such plans. The First International Conference on Seismology was held in Strasbourg in 1901, convened by Georg Gerland, which resulted in the establishment of the International Seismological Association.

A further consequence of international organizing was the development of national organizations for geophysics. National organizations for meteorology, geodesy, geomagnetism, and so on, were founded in most European countries, the United States, Japan, and elsewhere (Schröder-Gudehus, pp. 911–915). Meteorology and astronomy having been established at some universities early in the nineteenth century, the first geophysics professorships and courses appeared around 1900. Wiechert, a theoretical physicist trained in Königsberg, became the first director of the Geophysical Institute at the University of Göttingen in 1898. Louis Bauer, with a Berlin Ph.D. in theoretical physics, became instructor in geophysics at the University of Chicago in 1896.

Despite all this active organizing of individual geophysical sciences, however, there was no significant effort to unite them under one association for geophysics until after World War I. The old international associations and permanent commissions, which had depended strongly on German leadership, were dissolved. Under the general guidance of the new International Research Council, the umbrella organization International Union for Geodesy and Geophysics (IUGG) was established in 1918–1919. Various "sections" (later again called associations) were established for the various geophysical sciences: terrestrial magnetism and atmospheric electricity (now geomagnetism and aeronomy), oceanography, geodesy, and so on). In each of the member countries, national groups were established, such as the American Geophysical Union in 1919 (Fleming, pp. 5–9). The Deutsche Geophysikalische Gesellschaft (German Geophysical Society) was founded in 1922, although it was separate from the IUGG until 1939. Others were founded in Italy, France, Austria, and around the world.

No extended historical investigation has yet been published on the development of the early geophysical societies, commissions, congresses, and so forth. The relations of the different subfields of geophysics and of their supporting organizational activities have been discussed mostly in isolation from each other, and usually as parts of celebrations. A historical analysis of the establishment of, say, geomagnetic or seismological associations would contribute importantly to understanding the consolidation of geophysics. An analysis that related several subfields to each other and to other sciences could open many new questions. An analysis that placed these organizations in political, social, and economic context would be especially welcome.

Wilfried Schröder

Bibliography

Colacino, M., and M.R. Valensise. "The Role of the Cimento Accademy and the Meteorologica Societat Palatina." In *Geophysics,* edited by W. Schröder and M. Colacino, pp. 9–29. Bremen: Science Ed., 1994.

Fleming, J.A. "Origin and Development of the American Geophysical Union." *Transactions of the American Geophysical Union* 35, no. 1 (1954): pp. 5–46.

Jungnickel, Christa, and Russell McCormmach. *The Intellectual Mastery of Nature: Theoretical Physics from Ohm to Einstein.* 2 vols. Chicago and London: University of Chicago Press, 1986.

Olesko, Kathryn M. *Physics as a Calling: Discipline and Practice in the Königsberg Seminar for Physics.* Ithaca, N.Y.: Cornell University Press, 1991.

Rothe, J.P. "Fifty Years of History of the International Association of Seismology, 1901–1951." *Bulletin of the Seismological Society of America* 71 (1993): pp. 905–923.

Schröder, Wilfried. *Disziplingeschichte als Wissenschaftliche Selbstreflexion der historischen Wissenschaftsforschung.* Frankfurt: Lang, 1982.

———. "Emil Wiechert und seine Bedeutung für die Entwicklung der Geophysik." *Archive for the History of the Exact Sciences* 27 (1982): pp. 369–389.

Schröder, Wilfried, and K.H. Wiederkehr. "Georg von Neumayer (1826–1909) und die Fortschritte in der Meteorologie und Geomagnetik." In *Exploring the Earth: Progress in Geophysics since the 17th Century,* pp. 76–100. Bremen-Roennebeck: International Association of Geomagnetism and Aeronomy, 1992.

Schröder-Gudehus, Brigitte. "Nationalism and Internationalism." In *Companion to the History of Modern Science,* edited by R.C. Olby, G.N. Cantor, J.R.R. Christie, and M.J.S. Hodge, pp. 909–919. London and New York: Routledge, 1990.

See also Disciplinary History; Geographical Societies; Geological Societies; Geophysics; International Geophysical Year; International Organizations in Oceanography; International Polar Years; Meteorological Societies; Planetary Science; Space Science

Geophysics in Australia

A case study of the development of one geoscience in a regional context.

Geophysical observations in the Australian region began as early as the seventeenth century and the subject has largely paralleled developments in other parts of the world, with a few important exceptional cases. In 1642 the Dutch explorer Abel Tasman (1602–1659) made magnetic measurements during a voyage in which he discovered Tasmania and New Zealand, and the early British and French explorers made magnetic and pendulum gravity observations in the late eighteenth and early nineteenth centuries. In 1840, a complete magnetic observatory was set up by the British navy at Hobart in Tasmania, as part of a network of observatories to study global magnetism, and to check the model of the geomagnetic field proposed by Carl Friedrich Gauss (1777–1855), as discussed in Savours's and McConnell's "History of the Rossbank Observatory, Tasmania" and by Home in "Humboldtian Science Revisited." The Hobart observatory was closed in 1854, but the German Georg Neumayer (1826–1909) carried out pioneering magnetic observations in Melbourne and Victoria from 1858 to 1864 (Home, "Humboldtian Science," passim). The Melbourne-Toolangi magnetic observatories in Victoria have since produced one of the longest sets of magnetic data available. In 1919 the Carnegie Institution of Washington set up the Watheroo Magnetic Observatory in Western Australia (Home, "To Watheroo and Back").

The early gravity observations were important in studies of the shape of the Earth, and the magnetic data for navigation, because in the nineteenth century ships were sailing regularly in the southern waters from Europe to Australia and elsewhere.

By the mid-nineteenth century, scientific societies and journals had been established in Sydney, Melbourne, Hobart, and Adelaide, and universities were founded in Sydney and Melbourne. This, plus the gold rushes and economic boom of the 1850s, accelerated technical progress in the colonies. (Federation of the colonies did not occur until 1901.)

Seismology began in 1900 with the installation of Milne seismographs at some state astronomical observatories. A seismic network was set up in the Snowy Mountains of New South Wales in 1957, and networks were later operating in several states. Over one hundred seismological stations have been opened by the Bureau of Mineral Resources, Geology, and Geophysics (BMR, now the Australian Geological Survey Organisation), plus others in Antarctica. The pattern of moderate seismicity recorded is related to the position of Australia away from plate boundaries. However, seismicity in Australia has increased in the late twentieth century with, for example, magnitude 6.9 and 6.2 earthquakes wrecking small towns in Western Australia in 1968 and 1979, and a series of shocks up to magnitude 6.8 near Tennant Creek in the Northern Territory. The Newcastle earthquake of December 1989 was the first known to cause deaths (thirteen).

Keith Bullen (1906–1976), from New Zealand, but who worked for most of his ca-

reer in Australia, was well known for the J.B. travel-time tables, done in collaboration with Harold Jeffreys (1891–1989). His models of the Earth as discussed in his two books on seismology and the Earth's density are notable.

British nuclear blasts in South Australia in the 1950s were recorded by field parties from the Australian National University and the BMR, making the first accurate determinations of Australian crustal velocities and thickness. Australian stations proved valuable in recording American nuclear explosions in the Pacific in the 1960s to improve travel-timetables, and indicated faster velocities beneath shield areas, as in Western Australia (see Doyle, "Geophysics in Australia").

In 1965, a seismic array was set up at Tennant Creek in the Northern Territory by British authorities, to detect underground nuclear tests worldwide. In the 1970s a national Seismological Monitoring Centre was established at the BMR in Canberra and began exchanging seismic data regarding nuclear explosions with other organizations overseas.

An Australian continental reflection profiling program was started in the 1980s with long reflection and refraction traversing by the BMR. Offshore seismic data from around the coasts has been obtained by commercial surveys, overseas research institutes, and the BMR. These data have elucidated the formation of the continental margins by plate rifting and drift.

Submarine gravity measurements were made off the Western Australian coast and some inland by Felix Vening Meinesz (1887–1966) as early as 1935, revealing the first evidence of deep sediments in the Perth Basin. Australia was the first continent to be covered by reasonably accurate gravity surveys, station density being one per 50 square miles (130 square kilometers). This was largely through a program carried out by the BMR, using helicopters in remoter areas (see Dooley, p. 113). Absolute gravity determinations by pendulum observations have been made since the 1950s at sites around the continent by BMR personnel and U.S. and Russian parties (Dooley and Barlow).

Geophysics was not taught in an Australian university until 1950, when Sydney University appointed the first lecturer. In 1951, John C. Jaeger (1907–1979) was appointed to the chair in geophysics at the Australian National University (ANU) in Canberra and developed a department in geophysics with a worldwide reputation, now the Research School of Earth Sciences. Jaeger was a well-known applied mathematician and later became known for his work on heat-flow and rock mechanics (for example, see Jaeger and Cook). With his students he was the first to publish a statement on the different heat flow between a Precambrian shield (the Western Shield) and a younger province (southeastern Australia) (Jaeger and Thyer, p. 458). The School of Earth Sciences at the ANU concentrated its research program (no undergraduate teaching) almost entirely in general geophysics and geochemistry rather than exploration geophysics, and has included paleomagnetism, rock mechanics, heat flow, seismology, geochronology, crust-mantle conductivity, rheology, and fluid dynamics.

An important success at the ANU was the work of Edward Irving (b. 1927) in paleomagnetism, which he began in Australia in 1955. His work provided some of the first convincing evidence for continental drift by showing the likely large-scale northward movement of Australia. Irving also wrote an early volume on paleomagnetism in 1964.

The ANU geochronology laboratory has become well known for its dating, by William Compston (b. 1931) and associates, of lunar samples and of 4.3-billion-year-old zircons from Western Australia, and also for developing an important new ion microprobe mass spectrometer in the late 1970s.

Other well-known researchers at the ANU since the 1960s have been Alfred (Ted) Ringwood (1930–1993) and David Green (b. 1936) in geochemistry, the former also known for work on the origin of the Earth and Moon; Stuart Ross Taylor on lunar studies and geochemistry; Mervyn S. Paterson on rock mechanics; Frank Stacey on rock magnetism; Michael McElhinny on paleomagnetism; and Kurt Lambeck on Earth's rotation, gravity, geodesy, and sea level variations (see Doyle, "Geophysics in Australia").

Exploration geophysics in Australia has been marked by the importance of government involvement, as in the Imperial Geophysical Experimental Survey (1928–1930), the Aerial, Geological and Geophysical Survey of Northern Australia (1935–1940), the Bureau of Mineral Resources, Geology and Geophysics (since 1946), and the Mineral Physics Division (now Exploration Geoscience Division) of the Council for Scientific and Industrial Research Organisation or CSIRO (since 1970), plus that in various state geological surveys. The former survey (I.G.E.S.) resulted in one of the first books on exploration geophysics: *The Principles and Practice of Geophysical Prospecting* (1931),

by Broughton Edge and Thomas Laby (1880–1946).

Since about 1949 there have been a succession of mineral discoveries in Australia that have opened up new land and led to increased settlement, just as the gold rushes did in the 1850s. The Western Mining Corporation (WMC) contracted the first aeromagnetic survey in the country in 1947, near Southern Cross in Western Australia. Induced polarization and magnetic surveys were used along the Kalgoorlie-Wiluna mineral belt in the early 1960s, contributing to the discovery of the nickel deposit at Kambalda in 1966 by WMC. The company also discovered the huge copper-uranium-gold deposit under 300 meters of barren sediments at Olympic Dam (Roxby Downs) in South Australia in 1975, partly from magnetic and gravity data that indicated the likely presence of source rocks.

The BMR's regional magnetic maps, originally published with gold and iron ore in mind, were a basic tool for the nickel explorers of the 1960s. This use of the magnetic maps was repeated in the gold boom of the late 1980s, again particularly in Western Australia. Detailed low-level aeromagnetic mapping by contract companies became popular in the 1980s, particularly for gold exploration but also in diamond exploration and has led to much-improved geological mapping.

As Thyer (p. 251) pointed out, many mining companies were slow to introduce geophysics into their exploration programs, and government encouragement and example were necessary, particularly up to the 1960s. Also important have been the participation and expertise of geophysical contracting companies and the early importation and use of new instruments and techniques developed in North America and Europe. Examples are induced polarization, the common depth point, digital techniques, and data processing in seismic reflection surveys.

Geophysics has not been as dominant in metals exploration in Australia as it has been in Canada, for example. This was because of the deep weathering often encountered and so the sometimes disappointing results from frequency electromagnetic (EM) and induced polarization (IP) methods developed in Europe and North America (see Doyle, "Geophysics in Australia"). However, geophysics has become more important, as targets are now deeper and geological mapping less diagnostic. The development of detailed aeromagnetic surveys and pulsed EM instruments has boosted geophysical exploration in Australia, the latter because of the ability often to separate out overburden anomalies.

The Mineral Physics Division of the CSIRO had a significant success in the 1970s with its improved transient EM instrument, the SIROTEM. This was the first geophysical instrument designed for the Australian environment of deep weathering. As well, the Scintrex Company developed the magnetic induced polarization (MIP) technique in the 1980s specifically for such conditions, as in the Western Australian Yilgarn Shield.

In 1970 the Australian Society of Exploration Geophysicists was formed and its *Bulletin* first published (renamed *Exploration Geophysics* from volume 15 in 1984). The society has held national biennial meetings since the 1970s.

At least until the 1950s, most geological thinking in Australia has concentrated on hard-rock exploration, a factor influenced by the gold rushes of the nineteenth century and later mineral discoveries. Geologists from Australia and overseas were pessimistic about the possibilities for oil on the continent, regarded as too old, stable, and with few oil seeps. However, mapping by State Geological Surveys and the BMR revealed the great extent of the sedimentary basins that cover more than half the continent. Australia also has the world's largest exclusive offshore economic zone. As in Canada, extra finance and expertise for the exploring companies had to come from overseas, usually from North America and Britain.

Before 1946, the use of geophysics for hydrocarbon exploration was very limited, although an extensive gravity and magnetic reconnaissance of southern Queensland was made by Shell between 1939 and 1943, followed by further work after the war. The BMR undertook gravity and magnetic work near Roma, in south-east Queensland, in 1947–1948 (see Dooley).

In 1961 an aeromagnetic survey was carried out for Haematite Exploration Party Ltd. (Broken Hill Proprietary Ltd.), over the Bass Strait region between Victoria and Tasmania. A seismic reflection survey by Western Geophysical then covered 9,600 kilometers in 1962–1963 (a two boat operation). Large amounts of gas and oil were found in the Gippsland Basin in 1965–1967, using techniques such as air guns, common depth point surveying, and digital recording and processing. It is noteworthy that the delay in introducing such new techniques from overseas was often only one or two years. The Gipps-

land Basin has since provided up to 90 percent of Australia's oil and much of its gas output.

The Woodside and Mid-Eastern Oil companies began exploration of the Northwest Shelf off Western Australia in 1963–1964, by contracting reconnaissance aeromagnetic profiles, revealing basement ridges and troughs. In 1964–1965, the Burmah Oil Company (Australia) and Shell Development (Australia) and partners joined Woodside's search, organizing reconnaissance seismic surveys by the Western Geophysical Company. In 1968, the BMR contracted marine surveys on the North-West Shelf, combining gravity, magnetic, and seismic sparker six-channel measurements. Logistics and survey control were difficult for exploration companies, as much of the program was 300 to 500 kilometers from the coast, and there was a lack of suitable ports. An exploration team could be closer to Timor in Indonesia than to Australia, and 3,200 kilometers from headquarters in Perth.

Until 1968, the quality of seismic data was fair to poor, but it improved with the rapid evolution of marine seismic methods. In 1971–1972 major gas field discoveries were made at North Rankin (160 kilometers offshore, on the North-West Shelf) and at Goodwyn and Angel wells. Export of liquefied natural gas began to Japan in the 1980s. Remoteness also retarded exploration in the Eromanga and Cooper Basins in Queensland and South Australia, the nearest city being Adelaide, 800 kilometers to the south, and the environment semidesert or worse. The early gravity and magnetic work by Shell between 1939 and 1943 has been described by Sprigg as an epic of exploration geophysics.

The development of geophysics in Australia in both academic and exploration geophysics has been discussed by Jaeger and Thyer (pp. 450–461), Day (pp. 33–60), and Doyle ("A Short History"; "Geophysics in Australia"), exploration geophysics by Thyer (pp. 244–251), and exploration for oil and gas by Dooley (pp. 109–118) and Doyle and Howard (pp. 286–291). Further historical work is desirable, particularly on exploration geophysics in recent years—for example, the development and impact of modern detailed aeromagnetic surveys, as in gold exploration in Western Australia.

H.A. Doyle

Bibliography
Bullen, Keith E. *The Earth's Density.*
    London: Chapman and Hall, 1975.

———. *An Introduction to the Theory of Seismology.* Cambridge: Cambridge University Press, 1947.

Day, Allen A. "The Development of Geophysics in Australia." *Journal and Proceedings, Royal Society of New South Wales* 100 (1966): pp. 33–60.

Dooley, James C. "An Overview of Geophysical Exploration for Oil and Gas in Australia." In *Petroleum in Australia—The First Century,* pp. 109–118. Sydney: Australian Petroleum Exploration Association Ltd., 1988.

Dooley, James C., and Brian C. Barlow. "Gravimetry in Australia: 1819–1976." *BMR Journal of Geology and Geophysics* 1 (1976): pp. 261–276.

Doyle, Hugh A. "Geophysics in Australia." *Earth Sciences History* 6 (1987): pp. 178–204.

———. "A Short History of Australian Geophysics." *Exploration Geophysics* 20 (1989): pp. 491–496.

Doyle, Hugh A., and Ken W. Howard. "History of Seismic Exploration in Australia." In *Petroleum in Australia— The First Century,* pp. 286–291. Sydney: Australian Petroleum Exploration Association, 1988.

Edge, A.B. Broughton, and Thomas H. Laby. *The Principles and Practice of Geophysical Prospecting.* Cambridge: Cambridge University Press, 1931.

Home, Roderick W. "Humboldtian Science Revisited: An Australian Case Study." *History of Science* 33 (1995): pp. 1–22.

———. "To Watheroo and Back: The DTM in Australia, 1911–1947." In *The Earth, the Heavens and the Carnegie Institution of Washington,* edited by Gregory A. Good, pp. 149–160. American Geophysical Union, *History of Geophysics Series,* vol. 5. Washington, D.C.: American Geophysical Union, 1994.

Irving, Edward. *Palaeomagnetism and Its Application to Geological and Geophysical Problems.* New York: John Wiley, 1964.

Jaeger, John C., and Neville G.W. Cook. *Fundamentals of Rock Mechanics.* London: Methuen, 1969.

Jaeger, John C., and Robert F. Thyer. "Report on Progress in Geophysics, Geophysics in Australia." *Geophysical Journal Royal Astronomical Society* 3 (1960): pp. 450–461.

Lambeck, Kurt. *The Earth's Variable Rotation: Geophysical Causes and Consequences.* Cambridge: Cambridge University Press, 1980.

———. *Geophysical Geodesy: The Slow Deformation of the Earth.* Oxford: Oxford University Press, 1988.

McElhinny, Michael W. *Palaeomagnetism and Plate Tectonics.* Cambridge: Cambridge University Press, 1973.

Paterson, Mervyn S. *Experimental Rock Deformation: The Brittle Field.* New York: Springer-Verlag, 1978.

Ringwood, Alfred E. *Origin of the Earth and Moon.* New York: Springer-Verlag, 1979.

Savours, Ann, and Anita McConnell. "The History of the Rossbank Observatory, Tasmania." *Annals of Science* 39 (1982): pp. 527–564.

Stacey, Frank D. *Physics of the Earth.* New York: John Wiley, 1969.

Stacey, Frank D., and Subir K. Banerjee. *The Physical Principles of Rock Magnetism.* Amsterdam: Elsevier, 1973.

Thyer, Robert F. "Georoots—Early Geophysical Exploration in Australia." *Bulletin of the Australian Society of Exploration Geophysicists* 10 (1979): pp. 244–251.

See also Disciplinary History; Geophysical Societies and International Organizations; Geophysics; Geophysics in Universities; Paleontology in Australia

Geophysics: Disciplinary History

An umbrella discipline including many aspects of the investigation of the Earth's physical properties.

Until geophysics emerged, many main branches of this discipline were part of physics or its predecessors—for example, terrestrial magnetism, the size of the Earth, gravity, density, and the temperature of the Earth. They were understood as, for example, physics of the Earth, physical geology, terrestrial physics, *théorie de la terre,* and *physique de la monde.* All terms were used as synonyms of geophysics. Elements now composing the discipline of geophysics were treated in astronomy, meteorology, geography, geology, and physics.

Physicists and (to a lesser extent) astronomers developed those elements of geophysics to which their mathematical-physical methods could be applied. These elements were part of the physical sciences. Another part was rooted in the empirical geosciences of that time, such as geography and geognosy, from which geology emerged.

Geography was the discipline that promoted geophysics to such an extent that a separate scientific discipline was finally born. The roots go back to the eighteenth century when Johann Lulofs (1711–1768) published his introduction to the mathematical and physical knowledge of the globe in 1743. He treated the Earth as a unique body, as a whole including its shape, size, movement within the cosmos, and also its surface. At that time, an anthropocentric geography was emphasized. However, worldwide expeditions in combination with scientific experiments and measurements, such as those by Alexander von Humboldt (1769–1859) and many other scientists, evoked a revision in geography. In 1800, Johann Ernst Ehregott Fabri (1755–1825) was one of the first to propose a new system of geography, which he subdivided into physical, mathematical, and political branches. This followed the line of argument of the Nuremberg "cosmographers" of the mid-eighteenth century (Forbes, pp. 417–421). These efforts provided an outline for including geography as part of the natural sciences.

Further efforts to measure physical properties at the Earth's surface contributed to the development of a new discipline that might necessarily be separated from pure physics. From the viewpoint of physics, the Earth is only a special object with general physical phenomena and properties. Therefore, many physicists did not have a general interest in the physics of the Earth. On the other hand, geographers sought for a scientific basis of their discipline and decorated some branches of geography with attributes resembling a natural science.

The combination of the search by geographers for foundations of their discipline in natural sciences and the more marginal interest of physicists in the physics of the Earth prepared the way for geophysics as an independent discipline. This science was based on physical laws and methods and was applied to the whole Earth.

The first steps were certainly taken in geography by proposing a scientific frame in which geography itself could not fit. The state of development lasted more than half a century, during which geophysical researches were done in many countries by, for example, William Hopkins (1793–1866) and Edward Sabine (1788–1883) in Britain, Dominique François Jean Arago (1786–1853) in France, Alexander von Humboldt (1769–1859) and

Carl Friedrich Gauss (1777–1855) in Germany, Christopher Hansteen (1784–1873) in Norway, Adolph Theodor von Kupffer (1799–1865) in Russia, and Alexander Dallas Bache (1806–1867) in the United States. This separate development in geography and in physics was finished in 1884 and 1885 when Sigmund Günther (1848–1923) tied together knowledge of the physics of the Earth and of physical geography in his *Lehrbuch der Geophysik und der physikalischen Geographie* (Textbook of Geophysics and Physical Geography).

A straight route to this climax cannot be seen; that is, the development of geophysics was complex (Kertz, pp. 50–51; Kushner, pp. 213–219; Schröder, pp. 165–168). Certainly most of the geophysical elements were treated within physics, and physicists used the expression "physics of the Earth." They also wrote books about this special physics, the first of which was written in 1815 by Georg Friedrich Parrot (1767–1852).

In the 1830s, the *Comptes Rendues de l'Académie des Sciences* in Paris began issuing reports on *physique du globe,* and in the 1850s a journal on proceedings of physics was first issued by the Physical Society in Berlin containing also a separate column on *Physik der Erde.* Mathematics and astronomy also contributed to the development of geophysics by providing foundations (such as potential theory and spherical harmonic analysis) without which geophysics is unthinkable.

As explained, the main impulse for geophysics came from the earth sciences such as geography. The word "geophysics" itself was coined by the geographer Julius Fröbel (1805–1893) in 1834 (Buntebarth, p. 101). Over four decades passed during which the term "geophysics" was only sporadically used. Carl Friedrich Naumann (1797–1873), a geognosist and mineralogist, defined and used "geophysics" as that part of geognosy that treats the Earth on a whole. After 1850 the word "geophysics" seemed to be forgotten in the literature. Baron Ferdinand Paul Wilhelm von Richthofen (1833–1905) initiated the discussion of geophysics again with his geographical book on China in 1877, because he used geophysics as a separate auxiliary science in his scientific geography comprising the physics of the solid Earth, omitting climatology and meteorology (von Richthofen, vol. 1, pp. 730–732).

The revival finally was begun by the editor of the *Geographisches Jahrbuch,* Hans Karl Hermann Wagner (1840–1929), in Königsberg. His introductory essay as editor was an article on the recent state of the methodology of geography in 1878. He was the first person to pick up von Richthofen's task of a new scientific geography. Within a few years, Wagner acquired several scientists on the editorial board of the *Geographisches Jahrbuch* who became well-known geophysicists, such as Georg Gerland (1833–1919), who founded the first geophysical journal in 1887, Sigmund Günther, who wrote the first monograph on geophysics, and Karl Zöppritz (1838–1885), who was responsible for the geophysics column in the *Geographisches Jahrbuch* from 1881 until 1885. This geophysical part was always placed at the first pages of the journal and demonstrated the great interest of the editor in this discipline.

Wagner promoted geophysics with such vigor that this discipline could no longer be ignored in Germany. No wonder that in 1898 the first university chair was founded in Göttingen, the town where Wagner was geographer. He was also involved in the continuous support of the newly emergent discipline in Germany. Wagner wanted more global activities, in order to demonstrate that the entire Earth is the object of geophysics.

At that time, international relations began to take shape with meetings of geophysicists following the First International Polar Year in 1882–1883. The International Seismological Association was founded in 1899 and the first International Conference on Seismology was held in Strasbourg in 1901. The foundation of the International Union of Geodesy and Geophysics in 1919 was certainly the most important step for the international cooperation in geophysical research. Several national associations for geophysicists were also founded at the beginning of the twentieth century, and they contributed much to the development of the discipline with the issuing of journals devoted exclusively to geophysicists (such as the "Geophysical Supplement" in the *Monthly Notices of the Royal Astronomical Society London* in 1922 and the *Zeitschrift für Geophysik* in 1924–1925).

In order to measure physical properties not only in fixed stations but also elsewhere on the Earth's surface, portable instruments were constructed for measuring magnetic and gravitational effects as well as other physical properties, such as elastic wave velocities in connection with earthquakes. These portable instruments allowed scientists to distinguish materials deep within the Earth with different physical properties, from which a new branch in geophysics emerged: applied geophysics.

This time marked the end of the first of three main periods of activity during which the Earth as a whole body was the object of investigations. From the 1920s, the second period of activity was dominated by the applied branch, the goals of which were to explore and exploit the resources of the Earth. This branch was most prosperous during the first half of the twentieth century in prospecting for ores and oil. The development of seismic exploration techniques was especially important, because this method was able to distinguish geological structures. A further development arose with the use of computers in the 1950s. This method, which can analyze a huge amount of data, is still being furthered by rapidly growing computer technology. The focus of the applied branch differs from that of nineteenth-century geophysical research. In this case, the entire Earth is not the object of research but rather details of the crust or even of only its uppermost part are stressed.

Another transformation occurred in the late twentieth century that was influenced by neither scientific nor economic but by political or social reasons. The search for economically less valuable substances (such as water in an arid climate) initiated a new thinking in the application of geophysical methods. This development seems to lead toward a new climax in the near future. The pollution of air, soil, and water in the highly developed industrial countries requires different foundations in applied geophysics than those of fifty years ago. In geophysical research centers, petrophysical topics are now emphasized.

Since the 1980s great efforts have been made to investigate and limit the extent of pollution and the destruction of nature, in order to preserve the Earth. Recent manmade problems have introduced a new quality into geophysics that was unknown hitherto and in which human life is involved. This development departs from pure natural science.

In general geophysics, increasing knowledge of the entire Earth remains the unchanged goal. Success in seismology at the beginning of the twentieth century made available the principal structure of the Earth's interior—that is, its subdivision into core, mantle, and crust. Emerging space techniques since the 1960s have accentuated research of the higher atmosphere, and thus the physics of the upper atmosphere has become a substantial branch in geophysics. The Moon has also been brought into geophysical investigations. The Earth's magnetism and gravity have been investigated with great success by the use of satellites.

Geophysics owed a new research area to the continental drift theory of Alfred Wegener (1880–1930), to the later formulated sea-floor spreading, and finally to plate tectonics. From these topics, geodynamics, which was already defined by C.F. Naumann in his *Lehrbuch der Geognosie* in 1849 (vol. 1, pp. 9–10), developed as a branch between geophysics and geology. It is in part speculative and does not, strictly speaking, fit into the original geophysics, although physical laws are used.

Much geophysical research is based on measurements around the Earth either at the surface or from satellites. This work requires much financial support, so that a relation exists between nongeophysical interests and the development of special branches in geophysics. This relation has been poorly investigated. During the twentieth century, applied geophysics resulted from the search for ores and oil, and political decisions supported the rapid development of space techniques, which yielded much knowledge about the Earth's magnetic field and gravity. Geophysics presents many different facets, all inviting extended historical investigation.

Günter Buntebarth

Bibliography
Buntebarth, Günter. "Zur Entwicklung des Begriffes Geophysik." *Abhandlungen der Braunschweigischen Wissenschaftlichen Gesellschaft* 32 (1981): pp. 95–109.
Fabri, Johann Ernst. *Abriss der natürlichen Erdkunde insonderheit Geistik in ausführlicher Darstellung für Akademien und Gymnasien.* Nuremberg: Bieling, 1800.
Forbes, Eric G. "Mathematical Cosmography." In *The Ferment of Knowledge: Studies in the Historiography of Eighteenth-Century Science,* edited by G.S. Rousseau and Roy Porter, pp. 417–448. Cambridge: Cambridge University Press, 1980.
Günther, Sigmund. *Lehrbuch der Geophysik und der physikalischen Geographie.* 2 vols. Stuttgart: F. Enke, 1884, 1885.
Kertz, Walter. "Die Entwicklung der Geophysik zur eigenständigen Wissenschaft." *Mitteilungen der Gauss-Gesellschaft e.V. Göttingen* 16 (1979): pp. 41–54.
Kushner, David. "Sir George Darwin and the British School of Geophysics." *Osiris* 8 (1993): pp. 196–224.
Lulofs, Johann. *Introductio ad cognitionem atque usum utriusque globus, institutionibus domesticis accommodatus.* Leyden, 1743.
Parrot, Georg Friedrich von. *Grundriss der theoretischen Physik, Theil 3: Grundriss der Physik der Erde und Geologie.* Riga und Leipzig: Meinshausen, 1815.
Richthofen, Freiherr Ferdinand von. *China, Ergebnisse eigener Reisen und darauf gegründeter Studien.* Berlin: Reimer, 1877.
Schröder, Wilfried. "Emil Wiechert and the Foundation of Geophysics." *Acta Geodaetica, Geophysica et Montanista Hungariae* (Budapest, Akadémiai Kiadó) 23 (1988): pp. 165–185.
Wagner, Hans Karl Hermann. "Der gegenwärtige Standpunkt der Methodik der Erdkunde." *Geographisches Jahrbuch* 7 (1878): pp. 550–636.

See also Disciplinary History; Geography; Geology; Geophysical Societies and International Organizations; Geophysics in Australia; Geophysics in Universities; Geophysics: The Word; International Polar Years; International Geophysical Year; International Organizations in Oceanography; Oceanography, Physical; Planetary Science; Space Science

Geophysics in Universities

One of several institutional settings for geophysics.

Modern geophysics was first incorporated into universities in the nineteenth century. Its subsequent growth occurred in several stages. Early studies of geomagnetism were conducted by prominent academic astronomers and physicists, among them François Arago, Carl Friedrich Gauss, Alexander von Humboldt, and Joseph Henry. Not until the 1890s, however, did universities begin appointing individual faculty in geophysics. Emil Wiechert established one of the first formal academic institutes of geophysics at Göttingen University in 1901, but individual university appointments in geophysics—including Louis A. Bauer's at Chicago (1896) and Harry F. Reid's at Johns Hopkins University (also 1896)—were more common when academic geophysics was represented at all. Not until the 1920s and 1930s did undergraduate and graduate programs in meteorology, solid-earth geophysics, and oceanography emerge at a scattering of universities in Europe and North America. Sustained growth in academic geophysics occurred only after World War II. The nascent space age, the discovery of sea-floor spreading in the early 1960s, and military interest in geophysical results accelerated the expansion of new undergraduate and graduate programs and the creation of additional university-based institutes of geophysics.

Geophysics was not a core discipline like such older sciences such as astronomy and chemistry, and thus it entered the university through diverse interdisciplinary channels that varied considerably from one national context to another. Academic geophysics in Germany largely resulted from interest by physicists in geomagnetic phenomena and the physical structure of the Earth. In Great Britain, the Tripos examination encouraged scientists to address problems in geodesy and global structure from a highly analytical, Newtonian perspective; George Darwin and Harold Jeffreys, both at Cambridge, became internationally recognized exemplars of this tradition. By contrast, geophysical research at the McGill and Toronto universities in Canada, although developed within their departments of physics, began in response to demands for improved methods of geophysical prospecting. Frequent regional earthquakes helped stimulate seismological work by Beno Gutenberg at Caltech and Percy Byerly at Berkeley, while access to the Woods Hole Marine Biology Laboratory inspired meteorological and oceanographic studies at the Massachusetts Institute of Technology. Patronage from benefactors outside traditional departmental structures also played a significant role in nurturing academic geophysics. Grants from the operating boards of the Rockefeller Foundation instituted new programs in academic geophysics in the United States and Europe at a half-dozen universities in the early 1930s, including Percy Bridgman's high-pressure studies at Harvard. Bridgman's work in turn became the nucleus of Harvard's interdisciplinary Committee on Experimental Geology and Geophysics, begun in 1931 and the first of its kind at a major American university.

Before World War II few universities offered instruction or conducted research in more than one of the component fields of geophysics. German universities were exceptions to this general rule. Berlin offered graduate training in solid-earth geophysics, meteorology, and oceanography, while Hamburg, Frankfurt, Göttingen, Leipzig, Jena, Prague, and Vien-

na—all then in greater Germany—fielded world-class investigations in varied areas of geophysics through the 1930s. Scientists exposed to German traditions of geophysics, among them Vilhelm Bjerknes, Harald Sverdrup, and Carl-Gustav Rossby, came to influence the growth of academic geophysics in Scandinavia and the United States. Physical scientists fleeing from National Socialism, including Walter Elsasser, similarly strengthened programs of academic geophysics in the United States.

Of all the branches of geophysics, the most well developed within the university setting was seismology. Because of its relevance to studies of earthquakes, seismology became incorporated into numerous university programs worldwide. The British-trained John Milne became professor of geology and mining at the Imperial College of Engineering in Tokyo in 1875, where he concentrated on earthquake seismology through the early twentieth century. Wiechert similarly emphasized seismological research at his Göttingen-based institute by the late nineteenth century, and in the United States Frederick L. Oldenbach, S.J., established a seismological station at St. Ignatius College in Cleveland, Ohio, in 1900. Nine years later Oldenbach invited researchers at other Jesuit colleges in the United States and Canada to participate in seismological research. This effort ultimately led to the creation of a Department of Geophysics at St. Louis University in 1925 under the direction of James B. Macelwane. Seismic observatories were situated at a number of universities by the 1920s, but whether and how their presence stimulated geophysical research or instruction at these host facilities remains unclear.

Other fields of geophysics gained university toeholds more slowly and sporadically. The rapid expansion of the petroleum industry in North America and Europe inspired the creation of academic training and research in applied (or exploration) geophysics, typically in departments of geology. A distinct department of geophysics was created at the Colorado School of Mines in 1927. Instruction in applied geophysics was also offered at the American universities of Texas, Rice, and Stanford, and at Delft University in Holland. Academic meteorology was likewise aided by the rapid growth of aviation in the early twentieth century, and by increased recognition of the importance of meteorological knowledge for agriculture, commerce, and warfare. Rossby began teaching meteorology at MIT in

1928, Caltech launched a short-lived department of meteorology in 1933, and New York University established a department of meteorology and oceanography in 1937. Emergency war-related undergraduate and graduate instruction in meteorology began at Chicago and UCLA in the early 1940s, resulting in the training of thousands of students. Other initiatives in academic geophysics had more idiosyncratic origins. At Princeton, Richard Field, fascinated by undersea geology, trained graduate students in oceanography, while Scripps Institution of Oceanography, closely tied to UCLA, likewise became an academic center for this field. Desire for improved survey techniques ultimately allowed Felix Vening Meinesz to teach geodesy and gravimetry at Utrecht University after 1927. Mathematical geophysics was taught at Moscow State University by Otto Iu. Shmidt, the polar explorer and national hero who founded the Moscow-based Institute of Theoretical Geophysics in 1934.

In nations with less developed scientific traditions—indeed, in most nations other than the United States—geophysics emerged within departments of physics or applied mathematics rather than within departments of geology. Frequently academic geophysics rose in connection with neighboring governmental facilities of geophysics: in Finland, for example, Helsinki University collaborated closely with the Central Meteorological Institute, enabling Oscar V. Johansson to receive an appointment in climatology in 1909. In the colony states, including those in Indonesia, southern Africa, and South America, European and British models of academic geophysics predominated. Emil Bose, trained in Germany, established a physics institute at the National University of La Plata in Argentina in the early twentieth century, specializing in atmospheric physics. Networks linking seats of empire with autonomous local universities facilitated the recruitment of instructors and reinforced particular methodological approaches. When the newly created Australian National University established a chair in geophysics in 1951, close connections to England aided the recruitment of the Cambridge physicist John C. Jaeger, whose initial research program in solid-earth geophysics resembled that of E.C. Bullard at Cambridge.

The benchmark for rapid growth of academic geophysics was World War II. In the United States, dramatic increases in federal and military funding for geophysics expanded the range of fields investigated and taught. This funding permitted universities to establish distinct departments or institutes of geophysics such as Columbia's Lamont-Doherty Observatory, established by Maurice Ewing in 1948. Federal appropriations also funded institutes of geophysics at the universities of California (1944), Alaska (1946), Ohio State (polar studies, 1960), and Hawaii (1961). Training and research in geophysics expanded rapidly within departments of geology at Caltech, Berkeley, Wisconsin, MIT, and Princeton; leading academic geophysicists of the postwar generation included Louis Slichter, Roger Revelle, and (in Canada) J. Tuzo Wilson. Already by 1950, eight departments of geophysics and nine departments of meteorology granted advanced degrees, while twelve universities offered at least some instruction in oceanography. (Comparable growth occurred in the Soviet Union, yet it characteristically occurred within institutes of the Soviet Academy of Sciences, rather than at universities.) Worldwide, centers of academic geophysics tended toward ever more comprehensive investigations of phenomena. In Great Britain, S. Keith Runcorn and colleagues led new geomagnetic studies within the Department of Geodesy and Geophysics at Cambridge and at Newcastle-upon-Tyne, while P.M.S. Blackett initiated research on paleomagnetism and general magnetic theory at Manchester University. Well represented fields included solar-terrestrial relations, the upper atmosphere, and ionospheric research. New ionospheric studies were launched at Wuhan University in China by C.T. Kwei, paralleling expanded university-based programs in upper atmospheric and ionospheric physics at Harvard, Chicago, Colorado, Michigan, Iowa, Utrecht, Hamburg, and Manchester. The development of the International Geophysical Year, or IGY (1957–1958), the advent of space exploration, and the fervor over continental drift and plate tectonics in the 1960s galvanized the creation of new academic departments of geophysics and space sciences in North America and Europe. Oceanography grew especially rapidly. By the early 1970s graduate studies in oceanography were launched at Oregon State University, Texas A&M University, and several others, supplementing established programs at Scripps and at Woods Hole; the appointment of geophysicists as chairs of American departments of geology was no longer uncommon.

Some accounts of academic geophysics written by scientists have stressed the triumph of physical and quantitative methods over what they judge to be the backward discipline of geology. Traditional field geologists have often been portrayed as conservative proponents of qualitative, unproductive studies and jealous guardians of the preserve of academic geology. Geophysics, by contrast, has been seen as symbolic of the precision and power of modern physical approaches. The perceived triumph of the IGY and the development of plate-tectonics theory have been contrasted with the difficulties geologists faced in producing explanatory frameworks for mountain-building and other large-scale terrestrial phenomena. Academic centers of oceanography, meteorology, and ionospheric studies have been viewed as natural, unproblematic outgrowths of the burgeoning expansion of research universities in the postwar period. With few exceptions, these accounts have devoted limited attention to geophysical research programs within academic departments of physics or astronomy.

More recently, studies of academic research programs in physics, astronomy, and geology have resulted in new perspectives about the significance of geophysical studies within these disciplines during the nineteenth and twentieth centuries. Historians now stress that seismology and terrestrial magnetism were important components of university research in Europe, Canada, and the United States by the late nineteenth century. Scholars have also gained new appreciation of the vigor of meteorology and ionospheric studies at academic centers before and especially after World War II. This perspective has emerged in part from focused attention to these subjects, but it has also come from new investigations of military patronage of university science after World War II. Such studies have stressed the importance that government planners and military scientists placed on diverse areas of geophysics, including upper atmospheric physics (to aid communications and the design of ballistic missiles), oceanography (to facilitate submarine warfare), and seismology (to improve methods of detecting subterranean atomic bomb tests). For these scholars, the growth of academic geophysics illuminates military influence on the intellectual and institutional growth of science after 1945. Nonetheless, few historical studies have examined academic research programs in space science, climatic studies, seismology, hydrology, or volcanology; fewer still have addressed such issues as methodology, instrumentation, or the emergence of research schools of geophysics within the university community.

The Center for History of Physics of the American Institute of Physics has surveyed leading geophysicists, identified archival holdings in the discipline's component fields, and studied collaborative research in geophysics, particularly within the United States, Canada, and Western Europe. The Department of Space History of the National Air and Space Museum of the Smithsonian Institution, the Center for History of Physics, and Texas A&M University all hold collections of oral history interviews with geophysicists; oral history interviews and other materials from the AIP Center's study of Multi-Institutional Collaborations in Space Science and Geophysics, which primarily addresses research undertaken after 1970, should become available to historians beginning in 1994. Very little is known about academic geophysics in any national context, the evolution of research programs or research schools, the interaction of academic geophysics with colleagues in external institutions, or the teaching of geophysics on the undergraduate or graduate level. How the IGY affected the growth of academic geophysics, and how applied geophysics created opportunities for this discipline at universities, remain singularly unexplored topics.

Ronald E. Doel

Bibliography
Bartels, Julius. *Studienführer: Geophysik.* Berlin: Carl Winter, Universitätsverlag, 1944.
Bates, Charles C., Thomas F. Gaskell, and Robert B. Rice. *Geophysics in the Affairs of Man: A Personalized History of Exploration Geophysics and Its Allied Sciences of Seismology and Oceanography.* Oxford: Pergamon, 1982.
Cannon, Susan F. *Science in Culture.* New York: Dawson and Science History Publications, 1978.
Davis, Neil. *The College Hill Chronicles: How the University of Alaska Came of Age.* Fairbanks: University of Alaska Foundation, 1993.
DeVorkin, David H. *Science with a Vengeance: The Military Origins of Space Science.* New York: Springer-Verlag, 1993.
Doyle, H.A. "Geophysics in Australia." *Earth Sciences History* 6, no. 2 (1987): pp. 178–204.
Fleming, James Rodger. *Meteorology in America, 1800–1870.* Baltimore, Md.: Johns Hopkins University Press, 1990.
Friedman, Robert Marc. *Appropriating the Weather: Vilhelm Bjerknes and the Construction of a Modern Meteorology.*

Ithaca, N.Y.: Cornell University Press, 1989.

Good, Gregory A. "The Rockefeller Foundation, the Leipzig Geophysical Institute, and National Socialism in the 1930s." *Historical Studies in the Physical and Biological Sciences* 21, no. 2 (1990): pp. 299–316.

Goodstein, Judith. *Millikan's School: A History of the California Institute of Technology.* New York: Norton, 1991.

Hufbauer, Karl. *Exploring the Sun: Solar Science since Galileo.* Baltimore, Md.: Johns Hopkins University Press, 1991.

Kelly, Sherwin F. "A Perspective of Geophysics." *Transactions of the American Institute of Mining and Metallurgical Engineers* 138 (1940): pp. 23–33.

Menard, Henry William. *This Ocean of Truth: A Personal History of Global Tectonics.* Princeton: Princeton University Press, 1986.

Mukerji, Chandra. *A Fragile Power: Scientists and the State.* Princeton: Princeton University Press, 1989.

Olesko, Kathyrn M. *Physics as a Calling: Discipline and Practice in the Königsberg Seminar for Physics.* Ithaca, N.Y.: Cornell University Press, 1991.

Pyenson, Lewis. *Cultural Imperialism and Exact Sciences: German Expansion Overseas, 1900–1930.* New York: Peter Lang, 1985.

———. *Empire of Reason: Exact Sciences in Indonesia.* Leiden: E.J. Brill, 1989.

Shrock, Robert Rakes. *Geology at M.I.T., 1865–1965: A History of the First Hundred Years of Geology at Massachusetts Institute of Technology.* Vol. 1: *The Faculty and Supporting Staff.* 1977. Vol. 2: *Departmental Operations and Products.* Cambridge: MIT Press, 1981.

Shuleikin, V.V. "Development of Soviet Geophysics." Akademia Nauk S.S.S.R. Izvestia. *Seria geograficheskaia i geofizicheskaia* 12 no. 4. Translation in Box 167, Joint Research Development Board files, National Archives, Washington, D.C., 1948.

Veldkamp, J. *History of Geophysical Research in the Netherlands and Its Former Overseas Territories.* New York: North-Holland Publishing Company, 1984.

Wood, Robert Muir. *The Dark Side of the Earth: The Battle for the Earth Sciences, 1800–1980.* London: Allen and Unwin, 1985.

See also Disciplinary History; Geophysics in Australia; Planetary Science; Space Science

Geophysics: The Word

The physics of the Earth.

Geophysics was formed as a separate discipline during the second half of the nineteenth century. However, several synonyms were used earlier: physics of the Earth, physical geology, terrestrial physics, *théorie de la terre,* and *physique de la monde.* The German term *Physik der Erde* was used in 1800 by L.W. Gilbert (p. 304). The first monograph on *Physik der Erde* was written by the physicist Georg Friedrich Parrot (1767–1852) in 1815. Physicists used this term throughout the last century.

In the 1830s geographers began to think about a new system in geographical science, in order not to restrict it as a descriptive science, but to bring geography to the level of a natural science, which sought knowledge of physical causes and laws. Julius Fröbel (1805–1893) was the first who criticized mere descriptive geography in 1832 and proposed a new system in 1834, including a branch in geography that he demanded be a natural science. He proposed several terms, among them the word "geophysics" *(Geophysik)* (Fröbel, p. 27). This word did not begin to replace "physics of the Earth" or similar terms until 1848, when it appeared as an encyclopedia article in volume twelve of Meyer's *Conversationslexikon* (Kertz, p. 43). The term was used again in 1849 by Carl Friedrich Naumann (1797–1873) in his *Lehrbuch der Geognosie* (vol. 1, 9–10), but the word did not then come into general use. Another few decades passed during which the term was used only sporadically.

Since 1881 (Zöppritz, p. 1) geophysics was regularly used in the *Geographisches Jahrbuch,* which was edited by Hans Karl Hermann Wagner (1840–1929). Afterwards the word "geophysics" became common. In 1884–1885 the first textbook on geophysics was written by Sigmund Günther (1848–1923). In the English and French literature this term was adopted widely after 1900.

Günter Buntebarth

Bibliography

Bowler, Peter J. *The Norton History of the Environmental Sciences.* New York and London: W.W. Norton, 1993. First published as *The Fontana History of the Environmental Sciences,* London: Fontana Press, 1992. The pagination is the same.

Buntebarth, Günter. "Zur Entwicklung des Begriffes Geophysik." *Abhandlungen der Braunschweigischen Wissenschaftlichen Gesellschaft* 32 (1981): pp. 95–109.

Fröbel, Julius. "Entwurf eines Systems der geographischen Wissenschaften I." *Mittheilungen aus dem Gebiete der Teoretischen Erdkunde* (Zürich: Füssli) 1 (1834): pp. 1–35.

Gilbert, L.W. "Physikalische Merkwürdig-keiten, aus der Beschreibung von De La Perouse's Entdeckungsreise: ausgezogen vom Herausgeber." *Annalen der Physik* 6 (1800): p. 304.

Kertz, Walter. "Die Entwicklung der Geophysik zur eigenständigen Wissenschaft." *Mitteilungen der Gauss-Gesellschaft e.V. Göttingen* 16 (1979): pp. 41–54.

Zöppritz, Karl. "Der gegenwärtige Standpunkt der Geophysik." *Geographisches Jahrbuch* (Gotha: Perthes) 8 (1880): pp. 1–76.

See also Disciplinary History; Geochemistry: The Word and Disciplinary History; Geography: The Word; Geology: The Word; Geomorphology: The Word; Geothermics: The Word

Geopolitics

The study of the connections between geography and state power, particularly as expressed in international politics.

Geopolitical thought usually focuses on the role of geographical factors in conflict between states. Characteristic themes of geopolitical writing have included the importance of control of the seas and strategic landmasses, global dimensions of international competition, the spatial expansion of state power, the struggle to obtain "natural" borders, and the organic character of states.

Geopolitics had its roots in the Western nations in the closing years of the nineteenth century, developing in response to intensified global political and economic struggle. The term "geopolitics" itself originated outside the geosciences in the work of the Swedish political scientist and journalist Rudolf Kjellén, who coined the word in 1899 and who in 1916 gave geopolitics its first extended elucidation in his book *Staten som Livsform* (The State as an Organism).

Geopolitical analysis of the relationship between politics and geography has been characterized traditionally by the use of regional and global frameworks. This is especially clear in the works of the major geopolitical thinkers of the pre–World War I period, including Alfred Thayer Mahan in the United States, Sir Halford MacKinder in Great Britain, and Friedrich Ratzel in Germany. Mahan's portrayal of control of maritime routes as the key to world political power, expounded at length in 1890 in *The Influence of Sea Power upon History,* had a tremendous impact in England and on the European continent (Parker, pp. 15–16). MacKinder argued in 1904 that world history was dominated by cyclical power struggles between continental and seafaring peoples, and that control of the Eurasian landmass ("the pivot of the world's politics" or, as he later called it, "the heartland") gave its possessor an almost impregnable position of political power (MacKinder, pp. 421–444). Ratzel was extremely influential on the Continent and, through his follower Ellen Semple, in the United States. His *Politische Geographie* (Political Geography) in 1897 introduced a powerful Darwinist current into geopolitical thought, portraying states as biological organisms in constant competition for favorable living space, or *Lebensraum,* a term Ratzel introduced in 1901 that later had a profound influence on German geopolitical theories (Bakker, pp. 170–171; Korinman, chaps. 1, 2).

The period between the world wars was the classical era of geopolitical thought in Europe and Japan. English geopoliticians including MacKinder, James Fairgrieve, and Vaughan Cornish devoted most of their writings to delineating the geographical sources of Western world power, finding them in climate and agriculture, advantageous access to maritime lanes, easily obtained energy in coal deposits, and other factors. English geopolitical writing of the period, like that in other lands, displayed an intense concern with contemporary politics, particularly in the geographical analysis of the growth of British world power and its search for geographically founded policies that would preserve Britain's position.

On the Continent, geopolitical ideas were most popular in Germany and, to a lesser degree, in France. German geopolitics gained wide popular currency between the wars, as Karl Haushofer, Otto Maull, Erich Obst, and a host of other German geographers expanded upon the legacy left by Ratzel. The influence of Darwin on geopolitical thought was most evident in Germany, where the organic model of state development was taken most literally, and where violent struggle between states was widely accepted as a "natural" part of state relations. Here, too, Ratzel's efforts went furthest to construct a nomothetic "science" (that is, a science based on universal laws) of geopolitics. His "Law of Expanding Spaces," whereby states "naturally" attempt to occupy sparsely settled land on their borders, is a good example. A geo-determinist view that accorded geography decisive formative influence on national political structures and relations between states gained wide adherence. As in England, the relationship of geopolitical thought to contemporary politics was instrumental in shaping the concerns and rhetoric of geopolitical writers. The geopoliticians viewed themselves as practitioners of an applied science, whose end was the reassertion of German primacy in central Europe. After the Nazi seizure of power in 1933, geopolitics was elevated to the status of a state science, geopolitical writing and research were supported by the state, and geopolitical concepts such as *Lebensraum* became a common part of the German political discourse. There has been considerable debate about the role of geopolitics in National Socialist ideology, but it is clear that Adolf Hitler was familiar with the terms and theories of geopolitics and that rhetoric taken from geopolitics was commonly used by the Nazis (Bakker, p. 178; Brunn and Mingst, p. 61).

In France, Paul Vidal de la Blache had been something of a lone geopolitical voice before World War I, but many Frenchmen turned to the field in the wake of the devastating conflict. Their concerns mirrored those of geopoliticians in other nations. Albert Demangeon, for example, concluded from his study of the British empire that European world hegemony was on the decline before the rising powers of America and Japan. Demangeon and other French geopoliticians, including Lucien Febvre, were much less deterministic than the Germans and even than the English, and certainly a bit more optimistic. They focused on the interplay between culture and geography as much as on that between geography and politics, and while conceding that European culture was decadent they tended to view human cultural interaction with geography generally as giving evidence of a triumph of human will and spirit.

Not surprisingly, the one non-Western state to develop a strong geopolitical tradition was Japan. This was the nation most closely engaged with the emerging Western world political system and one in which, as elsewhere, geopolitical theories of a militaristic and Darwinist cast flourished in the era between the world wars (Takeuchi, pp. 188–203). Built upon a mixture of traditional Japanese imperial geographic theories, with a significant admixture of German ideas introduced by German-trained Japanese geographers, Japanese geopolitics in the interwar era was concerned primarily with justifying Japan's political expansion.

World War II had the paradoxical effect of discrediting and spurring geopolitical thought simultaneously. The association of geopolitics with the Nazis temporarily destroyed the legitimacy of the field in Europe and Japan. In America, wild stories of a geopolitical master plan that supposedly guided Hitler's conquests and entirely unfounded stories, repeated in Anglo-American histories into the late 1980s, of the existence of a Nazi institute for geopolitics in which thousands of geographers allegedly concocted Hitler's strategies, spurred a widespread American interest in geopolitics for the first time (Parker, pp. 57, 102–109). Although Isaiah Bowman had written on geopolitical themes before the war, the first few years of American participation in the conflict produced an unprecedented outpouring of new geopolitical works, authored by Bowman, Derwent Whittlesey, Robert Strausz-Hupé, Hans Weigert, Nicholas Spykman, and others.

Geopolitics has always been extremely sensitive in reflecting the changing face of international politics, and the field evolved significantly in the postwar world in response to the political transformations caused by the war. The term "geopolitics" itself, for example, was so thoroughly tarred with the Nazi brush that it practically disappeared from use until the mid-1970s. A comprehensive survey of developments in French and German geography from 1969, for example, shows no mention of the term and little evidence of interest in any form of political geography (Dickinson, chaps. 14, 21). Geopolitical themes and theories, however, continued under other names to occupy geographers like Spykman, Saul Cohen, and others. Technological advances also contributed to the transformation of geopolitics in the postwar world. The advent of advanced aviation technology, for example, lent a new geopolitical significance to polar regions, which were now included in analyses of global power relations.

The development of nuclear weapons with intercontinental range also stimulated the heterogeneity of geopolitical thought. Some geopolitical theorists, focusing on the apparently bipolar world of the Cold War, continued to find concepts like "Heartland" and "Rimland" productive in analyzing the global political struggle. Beginning in the mid-1960s, however, some geopolitical thinkers began to argue that these terms had lost much of their earlier significance, thanks to technological change, decolonization, and other factors, and that the structure of power distribution among states was now multipolar rather than bipolar. The relative decline of European world power, and the rise of regional powers to fill the vacuums created by decolonization, stimulated a growing interest in the use of smaller-scale regional analytical frameworks in geopolitical writing, a phenomenon illustrated in Saul Cohen's influential *Geography and Politics in a World Divided*.

After its brief golden age in the interwar period, geopolitics passed through a postwar dark age and, beginning in the late 1970s, experienced an unmistakable renaissance. In that period, geopolitics returned to book and journal titles throughout the West, but it was in many ways a quite different geopolitics from that practiced earlier. The term was always an ambiguous umbrella expression for a variety of issues involving politics, culture, and geography, but the revived geopolitics displayed a range of interests considerably broader than the classical, prewar variety. It was concerned as much with symbiosis and integration between states, especially at regional levels, for example, as with the conflict around which earlier geopolitical studies had centered. Many of the new geopolitical works were written from a peace-studies perspective, and employed systems analysis, game theory, quantitative methods, and other relatively new analytical tools to address the geopolitics of issues such as deterrence, the distribution and production of world energy supplies, arms control, hunger, and production and distribution of food resources.

This geopolitical concern with new and previously unexplored aspects of conflict and competition between states was also reflected in a move away from concentration on the bipolar, East-West concerns that grew out of Cold War geopolitics, and the rise of studies devoted to the geopolitics of global North-South relations in their economic, cultural, and political manifestations. Many of these studies, such as J.R. Short's *Introduction to Political Geography*, expanded upon ideas formulated in Immanuel Wallerstein's influential and controversial works on the development of the capitalist world system, replacing what

they viewed as outmoded heartland theories with models of center versus periphery, in which the northern regions of the globe as the "center" exert enormous economic and political influence in less-developed "peripheral" regions.

Historical evaluations of geopolitics have varied greatly over the course of time. During and after World War II, scholars in Germany, the Netherlands, and America all argued that geopolitics as developed before the war had been too narrowly focused on war and struggle, misled by the use of organic models, and too easily misused for propagandistic rather than scientific purposes (Ante, pp. 1–12; Bakker, pp. 1–17; Weigert, chap. 1). They did not, however, dispute the validity of the fundamental geopolitical preoccupation with the role of geography in relations between states, calling instead for the further investigation of these ties divorced from politicized and reputedly pseudo-scientific geopolitical theories. Others, like the French writer Paul Claval, later lamented the tendency of geopolitical theorists to focus on overly simplistic models that failed to take account of the multiplicity of variables affecting relations between states (Claval, pp. 63–64). The heartland/rimland model, its supposedly more sophisticated successor, the center-periphery model, and the old organic model of state growth were all subjected to this criticism.

Other lasting controversies in considerations of geopolitics have centered on both fundamental questions of geopolitical theory as well as on the uses of the field. Many critics have asked in what ways, if any, does geopolitics differ from political geography (Brunn and Mingst, pp. 41–51)? The question of the exact degree to which geography determines political processes and choices, as opposed to merely setting the physical bounds within which political actors make choices, has always demanded the attention of geopolitical thinkers. Early trends toward a relatively crude determinism, evident especially in German geopolitics, gave way in later decades to a possibilist framework, in which "objective, geographic reality" merely provides the setting, albeit a highly influential one, in which political action occurs (O'Sullivan, pp. 9–16). The disciplinary identity of geopolitics has proven over time to be a persistently thorny issue and the source of considerable debate. Practitioners of geopolitical analysis have traditionally integrated elements of political geography with political science, history, and at times other fields, including anthropology. Geopoliticians practicing within the field of geography (arguably the largest contingent of geopolitical theorists) generally argue for the existence of the field as a distinct discipline, while those trained in political science and other fields tend to disagree (Brunn and Mingst, pp. 62–63).

These controversies and historiographical debates about the precise nature of the geopolitical endeavor may be seen in large part as the long-term working out of the questions created by the Nazi exploitation of geopolitical ideas, and the willing participation of many of Germany's most distinguished geographers in that process (Rössler, chap. 1). They should not, however, obscure those aspects of geopolitical theory that have, amid all its heterogeneity, defined it and in the eyes of its exponents given it lasting value. These unifying themes have been identified as the need to address the issue of conflict between states, the utilization of binary models to analyze political-geographic structures, and a persistent hegemonic model, in which an inner or central geographic area exerts direct or indirect control over an outer or peripheral territory (Parker, pp. 178–179). All these traits characterize accurately some of the major geopolitical studies of recent years (O'Sullivan, pp. 1–5).

The political uses and abuses to which geopolitical ideas have been put suggest some of the elements that would compose a future geopolitical research agenda. The very ambiguity of the term facilitated its misuse in the past, and those who utilize a geopolitical approach, both geographers and social scientists who incorporate a spatial perspective in their work, will profit from an integrative and interdisciplinary effort at defining the term and its methods with some degree of specificity. The cloud of vague associations still hovering about geopolitics, which is sometimes used arbitrarily to refer to a method of analysis, a style of foreign policy, or the effect of geography on politics all in the same work, is necessarily detrimental to analytical rigor. An important aspect of this definitional task would be addressed by more research devoted to the history of geopolitics, locating the field in its broader (nongeographical) social, historical, political, and cultural settings. Recent investigations of the relationship between understandings of geography and nationalism represent a step in this direction (Anderson, pp. 18–39). A better understanding of the term's history, and the characteristic role it has played in both the scholarly and the public political discourses, would refine and sharpen it for contemporary use by separating the valuable MacKinderesque geopolitical grain from the pseudo-scientific geopolitical chaff of the Nazi period.

A more diversified geopolitical approach to the definition, interpretation, and investigation of state power would also yield valuable results. In the postcolonial and post–Cold War era, geopolitical theory faces the task of developing new models of the extension of state power as old models of hegemony are rendered obsolete by political change. A good start here exists in the move toward the application of geopolitics to a wider range of issues and the interest in regional and north-south questions. Entire vistas for research lie open in the application of spatial geopolitical analysis to questions of cultural development and interaction on a global or regional scale: How does geography help define culture (particularly political culture), and what is its role in contributing to or hindering the spread of certain cultures? This will, however, require a softening or even elimination of the traditional identification of geopolitics with the analysis of conflict between states. This is not to suggest that the geopolitical analysis of foreign policies and the role of geography in defining the state ought not continue, but rather that geopolitics realize its potential. It thus remains to be seen what sort of identity for "geopolitics" will finally emerge from the era of rapid technological change and international confrontation that marked its birth.

David T. Murphy

Bibliography

Anderson, J. "Nationalist Ideology and Territory." In *Nationalism, Self-Determination and Political Geography,* edited by R.J. Johnston, D.B. Knight, and E. Kofman, pp. 18–39. London: Croom Helm, 1988.

Ante, Ulrich. *Zur Grundlegung des Gegenstandsbereiches der politischen Geographie: Über das "Politische" in der Geographie.* Stuttgart: Steiner Verlag, 1985.

Bakker, Geert. *Duitse Geopolitiek, 1919–1945: een imperialistische ideologie.* Utrecht: Van Gorcum and Co., 1967.

Brunn, S.D., and K.A. Mingst. "Geopolitics." In *Progress in Political Geography,* edited by Michael Pacione, pp. 41–76. London, Sydney, and Dover, N.H.:

Croom Helm, 1985.

Claval, Paul. "Centre/Periphery and Space: Models of Political Geography." In *Centre and Periphery: Spatial Variation in Politics,* edited by J. Gottmann, pp. 63–72. London: Sage, 1980.

Cohen, Saul Bernard, *Geography and Politics in a Divided World.* New York: Random House, 1963.

Dickinson, Robert E. *The Makers of Modern Geography.* London: Routledge and Kegan Paul, 1969.

Enggass, P.M. *Geopolitics: A Bibliography of Applied Political Geography.* Monticello, Ill.: Vance Bibliographies, 1984.

Hepple, Leslie W. "The Revival of Geopolitics." *Political Geography Quarterly* 5 (October 1986): pp. 21–36.

Korinman, Michel. *Quand l'Allemagne pensait le monde: Grandeur et décadence d'une géopolitique.* Paris: Fayard, 1990.

MacKinder, Halford J. "The Geographical Pivot of History." *Geographic Journal* 23 (1904): pp. 421–437.

O'Sullivan, Patrick. *Geopolitics.* London and Sydney: Croom Helm, 1986.

Parker, Geoffrey. *Western Geopolitical Thought in the Twentieth Century.* New York: St. Martin's Press, 1985.

Rössler, Mechtild. *"Wissenschaft und Lebensraum." Geographische Ostforschung im Nationalsozialismus.* Berlin and Hamburg: Hamburger Beiträge zur Wissenschaftsgeschichte, 1990.

Takeuchi, Keiichi. "The Japanese Imperial Tradition, Western Imperialism and Modern Japanese Geography." In *Geography and Empire,* edited by Anne Godlewska and Neil Smith. Oxford, and Cambridge, Mass.: Blackwell, 1994.

Weigert, Hans. *Generals and Geographers: The Twilight of Geopolitics.* New York: Oxford, University Press, 1942.

See also Colonialism and Imperialism; Geographical Societies; Geography; Geography and Imperialism

Geosyncline

A term descriptive of stratigraphic structure, also associated with a nineteenth-century theory of mountain-building.

"Fixism" had as a basic tenet the idea that movement of the Earth's crust is restricted mainly to the vertical: the rising or subsidence of the crust. The limited, local, lateral movement that occurred during these episodes was thought caused by the contraction of a cooling earth. It was in this fixist, cooling/contracting, uniformitarian world of Newtonian science in the nineteenth century that the theory of geosynclines emerged.

The new theory accounted, among other things, for the growth of mountains, and for that reason it was especially welcomed by European geologists. It occupies a special place in history also, because it was the first "American" geological theory to gain worldwide acceptance and because it has been influential in the development of a whole-Earth geology to the present day. First put forward by James Hall in his presidential address to the American Association for the Advancement of Science at Montreal in 1857, it sparked immediate interest and debate in the geological community both in America and overseas.

James Hall (1811–1898) graduated from Rensselaer Polytechnic Institute in 1832 and in 1836 was appointed to the newly formed Geological Survey of New York. Hall was put in charge of the Fourth District, which covered the northern Appalachian Mountains, an area ideally suited to his work as a paleontologist because it is the least disturbed part of the state, and, therefore, an area where the stratigraphy is more clearly defined. Hall put forward the revolutionary idea that most of the mountains on Earth had been uplifted from more depressed regions where they had originated. He believed there had been a great open sea in the center of the American continent and thought that currents flowing parallel to the coast from the northeast had led in the Paleozoic to the accumulation of an immense body of shallow-water sediments, under the weight of which the seafloor subsided. The sediments consolidated and folding occurred along these "synclinal axes." However, he did not attempt to relate folding to the later uplift of the sediment as a mountain chain. James Dwight Dana (1813–1895) soon refined and extended Hall's work.

Dana studied under Benjamin Silliman (1779–1864) at Yale College, where Werner's system of stratigraphy was still being taught in 1830. He was an assistant to Silliman in 1836, and, when twenty-four years old, brought out his widely used *System of Mineralogy.* For four years, until 1842, he traveled widely throughout the world as geologist and mineralogist with the Wilkes Exploring Expedition, after which many publications followed. Then in 1850, he was appointed professor of natural history at Yale College. For the rest of his life, he was plagued by bouts of ill health; yet, beginning in 1866, he was able to make a lasting contribution to geosynclinal theory (see Dana). The celebrated American geologist Joseph Le Conte (1823–1901) well summed up Dana's contribution to geological science by describing him as being the first to study geology from "the standpoint of evolution of the earth through all time."

Dana agreed with Hall that the Appalachians had originated from a mass of shallow-water sediments that had subsided as the sediment had accumulated. Jean Aubouin has noted in his *Geosynclines* (p. 9) that Dana, like Hall, believed subsidence closely related to accumulation—one foot accumulation for one foot subsidence—but did not agree that subsidence was solely due to the weight of the sediment. Dana believed that the Earth's contraction played a part in this process. It was he who gave the name "geosynclinal" to the areas Hall had called "synclinal" axes. Aubouin (p. 10) mentioned that this term was later changed to "geosyncline." Dana also introduced the idea that there were areas of progressive uplift, geanticlinal zones, that were balanced by the sinking of the neighboring geosynclinal areas and thus linked the sediments in a synclinal zone to their possible source from the uplifted areas. Dana did not favor the idea that sinking was the cause of folding. Nor did he agree with Le Conte, who said in 1872 that folding caused the uplift of a mountain range. He believed that lateral pressure in the crust of the cooling Earth—the drying apple analogy—was the cause of mountain-building. One far-reaching aspect of Dana's work was his introduction of the concept of a geosynclinal cycle: deposition, folding, and uplift to form a mountain chain. This concept was still being debated more than a century later by the American geologist Peter J. Coney, who saw the geosynclinal cycle as one phase in a larger process. Another aspect of Dana's work that had long-term consequences was his notion that continents grow by accretion as mountain chains are formed toward the ocean in successive cycles.

By the end of the nineteenth century, opinions in Europe and America had diverged markedly. The French geologist Émile Haug (1861–1927) argued in 1900 that geosynclines were areas where a great thickness of sediments had been deposited, but he believed that the rate of sedimentation could vary and the life of the cycle would be speeded up when the "trough" filled more rapidly. His concept of a "trough" marked the most radical departure from the theory as proposed by the Americans. Hall and Dana always conceived of the synclinal zone as a basin marginal to the continent and filled with shallow-water sediment, but Europeans, led by Haug, envisioned the geosyncline as a trough between two continental areas filled with deep-water sediments.

Aubouin (p. 17) notes that "as the geological inventory of the planet grows, the differences in detail from one geosyncline to another are multiplied." It was these differences that led to energetic attempts by geologists in the early part of the twentieth century to classify geosynclines. As workers such as Charles Schuchert (1858–1942), Leopold Kober (1883–1970), and J. Hans Stille (1876–1966) moved into the field, neologisms to describe the differences in geosynclines proliferated. This culminated in the 1950s with the complicated nomenclature devised by Marshall Kay (1904–1975), which for American geologists became definitive.

By the start of the 1970s, the climate of geological thought had radically changed: there were few fixist geologists remaining, and contractionists were reconsidering their position. Plate tectonics became the new global theory. During this "revolution," the geosynclinal theory (or more specifically the geotectonic cycle, which had become an integral part of the theory) came under examination. According to the American geologist Peter Coney, the geotectonic cycle consisted of a geosynclinal phase when sediments accumulated; a tectogenic phase, or period of deformation and plutonism; and the orogenic phase of uplift, collapse, volcanism, and incorporation into the continental block. In 1970, Coney (p. 739) reached the conclusion that this cycle is "obsolete as a model of mountain system evolution." Robert H. Dott (b. 1929) had questioned the validity of this concept as early as 1964 and in 1974 (p. 3) he pointed out that the "tectonic cycle implied that all orogens [mountain systems] developed in just the same manner." Coney noted that workers in the 1960s reached the conclusion that in some cases "drifting continents" produced mountains and the tectonics of geosynclinal development should be kept "separate from subsequent tectonic events": he argued (p. 742) not for the abandonment of the geosynclinal concept, but for a new model and terminology, and suggested (p. 739) that "the concept of multiple origins for mountain systems" is preferable. He said (p. 745) that to claim "geosynclinal prisms lead to mountain systems is a little like saying automobile fenders lead to accidents."

Almost simultaneously with the rise of plate tectonics, a number of West-Coast American geologists, William P. Irwin (b. 1919), David L. Jones (b. 1930), and Charles A. Ross (b. 1933), from the U.S. Geological Survey, and James W.H. Monger (b. 1937) from the Canadian Geological Survey proposed the allochthonous (exotic) terrane concept, a corollary of plate tectonics. An account of this new development by Adrian Sharpe in 1991 demonstrated that there were many other geologists, particularly from the West Coast, who also contributed to the idea that some portions of the continents were not genetically related to the ancient cratons, but had originated elsewhere and then accreted to the cratons. It seemed that Alaska, for example, is the final repository for many fragments of the Earth's crust that have traveled even thousands of miles. David G. Howell (b. 1944) of the U.S. Geological Survey has said that it has been termed the "garbage dump" of the Pacific Ocean (Sharpe).

All this was happening when Coney proposed the abandonment of the geotectonic cycle. The geosynclinal concept had lost precise meaning and the term "geosyncline" itself was interpreted and used in a variety of ways. With the advent of plate tectonics, the theory of geosynclines seemed to sink under the weight of anomalies and inconsistencies. Terranes seemed, at first glance, to deal a death blow to the theory. However, the terrane concept may be considered a reworking of the classical geosynclinal concept. Despite the dramatic change in thinking that has seen the overthrow of fixism in favor of a mobile Earth, the basic geology of geosynclines, as envisioned by Hall and Dana, is still valid: continents are still depositing huge amounts of sediment into the oceans. The ultimate destination and fate of these compacted sediments may be subject to debate, but the basic concept of the geosyncline as the repository of sediments is yet unaltered.

Philosophical models of scientific change have been proposed in Thomas Kuhn's *Structure of Scientific Revolutions* (1962, 1970), Imre Lakatos's "Falsification and the Methodology of Scientific Research Programmes" (1970, 1987), and Larry Laudan's *Progress and Its Problems* (1978). The "revolutionary" model proposed by Kuhn has been particularly influential and seems to reflect the changes that took place in the 1970s when fixist beliefs were overthrown by mobilism. However, the Kuhnian concept of a sudden change of paradigm or "gestalt" switch in the outlook of the geological community poorly describes the rise and especially the presumed fall of the geosynclinal concept. In one sense proposed by Kuhn, that a paradigm consists of "the entire constellation of beliefs, values, techniques, and so on shared by members of a given community," geosyncline theory was a part of a developing paradigm that included fixism, contractionism, and uniformitarianism. In another sense suggested by Kuhn, the theory of geosynclines was one element in the "constellation." In both senses, as revolutionary as the notion of geosynclines may have been, its acceptance during the nineteenth century did not involve a massive and sudden switch in the overall paradigm. Neither did the plate-tectonics revolution, which cast out fixism, entail the scrapping of the geosyncline concept, although it came under scrutiny and underwent modification.

Lakatos, whose concept of a research program resembles in some degree a Kuhnian paradigm, maintains that a research program has a "hard core" that remains unchanged. His model fits many aspects of the geosynclinal story, but the hard core of the research program did change over time. Moreover, although Lakatos allows the possibility of one or more competing programs, "geosynclines" was not in competition with any other theory—the theory was a unique concept that developed alongside and within the "constellation" of beliefs that included fixism (later mobilism), uniformitarianism, and contractionism.

Larry Laudan's notion of a research tradition seems to describe well many of the changes in geological theory that occurred during the nineteenth and twentieth centuries. An advantage of his model is that he allows for the pursuit of one or more research traditions. Viewed from a Laudanian perspective, the theory of geosynclines could be seen as either a tradition in its own right or as one of a number of theories within a tradition that underwent drastic alteration over the best part of two hundred years: fixism to mobilism, contractionism to steady state. Whether a tradition in its own right, or part of a larger methodological and philosophical commitment, "geosynclines" have been remarkably durable.

There have been several detailed histories of aspects of the geosyncline. Jean Aubouin, for example, has dealt with the theory mainly from the viewpoint of Alpine geology. However, much remains to be studied. There have been many geoscientists whose contributions to the topic lie beyond the scope of this essay. Dott has suggested that an examination of the concept as applied by the Europeans, such as Haug, would be a fertile area of investigation, as would a study of changing conceptions of the Tasman orogenic belt of eastern Australia. Also inviting are the debate about the developing theory of isostasy and the push by geophysicists for greater input into the geosciences as the geosynclinal theory was applied in the twentieth century.

Adrian P. Sharpe

Bibliography

Aubouin, Jean. *Geosynclines.* Amsterdam: Elsevier, 1965.

Coney, Peter J. "The Geotectonic Cycle and the New Global Tectonics." *Geological Society of America Bulletin* 81 (1970): pp. 739–748.

Dana, James Dwight. "On Some Results of the Earth's Contraction from Cooling, including a Discussion of the Origin of Mountains, and the Nature of the Earth's Interior." *American Journal of Science,* series 3, vol. 5 (1873): pp. 423–443; vol. 6, pp. 6–14, 104–115, 161–172.

Dott, Robert H., Jr. "Tectonics and Sedimentation a Century Later." *Earth Science Reviews* 14 (1978): pp. 1–34.

Dott, Robert H., Jr., and Robert H. Shaver, eds. *Modern and Ancient Geosynclival Sedimentation.* Tulsa, Okla: Society of Economic Paleontologists and Mineralogists, 1974. (Special Publication No. 19).

Greene, Mott T. *Geology in the Nineteenth Century.* Ithaca, N.Y.: Cornell University Press, 1982.

Lakatos, Imre. "Falsification and the Methodology of Scientific Research Programmes." In *Criticism and the Growth of Knowledge,* edited by Imre Lakatos and Alan Musgrave, pp. 91–196. New York: Cambridge University Press, 1970, 1987.

Sharpe, Adrian. "A Controversy in Science: The Debate about Allochthonous Terranes on the West Coast of North America." M.A. thesis, University of Melbourne, 1991.

See also Actualism, Uniformitarianism, and Catastrophism; Continental Drift and Plate Tectonics; Geology; Isostasy; Lakatos's Idea of Scientific Research Programs; Ocean Currents; Paleontology; Paleontology in Australia; Sedimentary Geology; Stratigraphy

Geothermics: The Word

Heat of the Earth.

Synonyms of "geothermics" were used since about 1800 in several languages, written in separate words. In 1829 with the use of numerous data, Adolph Theodor von Kupffer (1799–1865) elaborated that the mean annual temperatures do not generally coincide between the air and the soil near the surface of the Earth. It had been common practice to call the lines of equal air temperature isotherms (Humboldt, p. 102). Therefore, Kupffer had to distinguish the lines of equal soil temperature, which he represented as isogeotherms *(Isogeothermen)* (Kupffer, Tab. 11). With that, the vocabulary of geothermics was born, even though it was not generally applied.

In 1849, Carl Friedrich Naumann (1797–1873) wrote a chapter (vol. 1 pp. 41–76) on the temperature of the Earth's interior, and used the word "geothermics" *(Geothermik)* (Naumann, p. 41). Naumann also coined the specific term of "geothermal depth-step" *(geothermische Tiefenstufe),* meaning the depth interval in which the temperature in the subsurface increases by 1°. This term came into general use and it is still favored above "temperature gradient" by many geologists.

The word "geothermics" was rarely used until the twentieth century, with the development of applied geophysics. At that time, the word "geothermy" *(Geothermie)* was also introduced in the German literature, with "geothermics" used for the applied branch and "geothermy" for the general heat of the Earth.

In the English and French literature heat of the Earth or similar expressions have often been favored above geothermics until the last decades of the twentieth century.

Günter Buntebarth

Bibliography

Humboldt, Alexander v. "Sur les lignes isothermes." *Annales de Chimie et de Physique* 5 (1817): p. 102.

Kupffer, Adolph Theodor v. "Über die mittlere Temperatur der Luft und des Bodens auf einigen Punkten des östlichen Rußlands." *Annalen der Physik und Chemie* 91 (1829): pp. 159–192.

Naumann, Carl Friedrich. *Lehrbuch der Geognosie.* Leipzig: W. Engelmann, 1849.

See also Geological Maps; Heat, Internal, Eighteenth and Nineteenth Centuries; Heat, Internal, Twentieth Century; Humboldtian Science; Isolines

Geysers

The eruption of a mixture of steam and water from the ground into the atmosphere.

The Geysir at Haukadal, 48 kilometers (30 miles) east of Reykjavik, Iceland, was first mentioned in 1294, and the name "geysir" was applied in 1647 from *geysa* (to rush forth) or *gjósa* (to gush). The theory specifically designed to account for the activity of The Geysir dates from 1846, based on the idea that a narrow column of water would, when rapidly heated at the bottom, form a continuously boiling spring. Slower heating from below, and a wider column would permit cooling at the surface. The temperature gradually increases because of the entry of hot steam until boiling temperatures are obtained at 12–15 meters (39–49 feet), causing eruption. Recent studies of water chemistry indicate that all thermal water is of meteoric origin—that is, from atmospheric precipitation. No history of the investigation of geysers has been written.

D. Philip Commander

Bibliography
Barth, T.F.W. *Volcanic Geology, Hot Springs and Geysers of Iceland.* Washington, D.C.: Carnegie Institution, 1950.

See also Artesian Water; Dowsing; Drilling; Drilling, Scientific; Geothermics; Heat, Internal, Eighteenth and Nineteenth Centuries; Heat, Internal, Twentieth Century; Hydrologic Cycle; Mineral Waters; Ocean Chemistry; Precipitation, Theories of; Water Quality; Water Wells in Antiquity

Gravimetry

The measurement of the Earth's gravity.

Since prehistoric times, humans have generally been aware of the property of weight. They applied the term "gravity" to this property and to the tendency of downward motion on Earth. Aristotle (384–322 B.C.E.) hypothesized that the downward speed of a falling object is proportional to its weight. Astonishingly, this view was accepted, and left unexamined, for almost two thousand years until the sixteenth century, when Galileo Galilei (1564–1642), in a series of experiments conducted during 1589–1591, showed that bodies of different weight fall with the same speed if the effect of air resistance is re-

moved. His findings, combined with the contemporary work of Dutch mathematician Simon Stevin (1548–1620), began to redefine gravity for the first time in a modern sense. In 1686, Isaac Newton (1643–1727) published his *Principia Mathematica.* In it, Newton discussed his law of gravitation, which he claimed he had formulated in 1666. He said he could not publish it then because of the difficulty of proceeding from mass particles to extended bodies such as Earth. This difficulty was overcome when he showed that bodies having spherically symmetrical distribution of mass can be treated as if their mass is concentrated at their centers. In his treatise, Newton showed that gravity, usually denoted by g, is a special case of gravitation. A force varying with the inverse square power of the distance from the Sun had already been proposed by such notables as Robert Hooke (1635–1703), and by Newton's contemporaries such as Edmond Halley (1656–1742) and Christopher Wren (1632–1723), but that had been applied only to circular motion. Even prior to Hooke, René Descartes (1596–1650) had proposed a nonquantitative, mechanical theory of gravitation based on inward pressure of vortices on planets. The credit for discovering and scientifically stating the universal law of gravitation, however, goes entirely to Newton, who put gravity on its modern scientific footing.

Once gravity was defined (frequently described as a force, but in fact it is the acceleration caused by the gravitational and centrifugal forces), the next natural step in the process of historical evolution was to attempt to measure it. The subject that deals with the measurement of gravity at or near the surface of the Earth came to be known as gravimetry. More recent, space-age definitions of gravimetry tend to extend it to include the measurement of the gravity fields of the planets and other celestial bodies. However, this aspect will not be a part of this historical review.

The unit of measurement traditionally used in gravimetry is the milligal (mgal), which is derived from the unit gal, named after Galileo. One mgal is 10 gal. One gal is 1 cms^{-2}—that is, an acceleration of 1 centimeter per second per second. In the International System of Units, the unit of gravity is ms^{-2}. The average value of g is 9.80 ms^{-2}. Since one of the major interests in gravimetry is the measurement of much smaller gravity variations from this average value, smaller units such as μms^{-2} = 10^{-6} ms^{-2} and nms^{-2} = 10^{-9} ms^{-2} are used in practice.

Interestingly, the first major development in gravimetry—the invention of a pendulum that would be used later to measure gravity, owes its origin to the marine navigational needs of keeping accurate time and finding accurate longitudes for overseas trade and commerce. This is a powerful reminder how economic needs drive science. The possible connection between clock rates and gravity was recognized early and pointed out by, among others, Francis Bacon in 1620. The first working pendulum clock was designed in 1657 by Christiaan Huygens (1629–1695) and built by Salomon Coster. During the period 1666–1669, Huygens formulated the period of a pendulum in terms of its length and gravitational acceleration. He published his results in 1673 in *Horologium Oscillatorium*. These results established the pendulum, in principle, as a gravity-measuring device, although it was not used for this purpose until several years later. The concept of the periodic simple harmonic motion of a pendulum was known to the tenth century Arab astronomer Ibn-i-Yunus. Galileo is said to have rediscovered it in 1583 as he observed and timed the oscillations of a swinging lamp in a cathedral in Pisa, Italy.

A few years after the introduction of the clock pendulum in 1657, it was observed that a given pendulum will beat more slowly at lower latitudes than at higher latitudes. Of course, we know now that it is because gravitational acceleration increases from equator to poles. But this was not known then. Jean Richer, who led an expedition from Paris to Cayenne in 1672–1673 primarily for astronomical observations, confirmed that his pendulum lost $2^{1}/_{2}$ minutes per day in Cayenne. A few years later, in 1677–1678, Edmond Halley discovered that his pendulum clock lost time at the island of St. Helena. These observations were later explained by Newton as due to the variation of gravity from equator to pole. This latitude dependence of gravity was later confirmed by French expeditions to Peru in 1735–1744 and to Lapland in 1736–1737. These findings made it possible to use the pendulum as an apparatus to compare gravity at different latitudes. However, the pendulums used so far were not very precise. Their precision did not improve enough to become useful tools of gravimetry until around 1800. Later on, the latitude dependence of gravity also led to the latitude correction—a very important development in gravimetry.

In the meantime, Robert Hooke conducted a series of experiments between 1662 and 1666 to check if gravity varies with height. The initial suggestion for such a variation had been made by Francis Bacon in 1620. Hooke's results were inconclusive. It was not until 1749 that Pierre Bouguer discovered the vertical variation of gravity while interpreting the pendulum observations made in the mountainous areas of the Andes during his 1735–1744 expedition to Peru. This led him to develop a method of reducing gravity observations to sea level. This height correction was another important development in gravimetry. Later on, Hooke's law of elasticity—formulated in 1678—formed the basis of modern gravimeters.

During the late eighteenth century, progress related to gravimetry was occurring on another front as well. There were several attempts to determine the universal gravitational constant G (in Newton's law of gravity) by determining the attraction of large features such as mountains. The best of these determinations was by Nevil Maskelyne in 1774. He determined G by measuring the deflection of the vertical due to the attraction of a mountain. But these methods are much inferior to the laboratory method in which the gravitational attraction between known masses is measured. The laboratory method was first used by the English scientist Henry Cavendish, in 1798, who used a torsion balance built by John Michell to determine the first reliable value of G. Cavendish's determination of G turned Newton's law of gravitation from a proportionality statement into a quantitatively exact one. This was the most important advance in gravitation since Newton. Since measurements of the acceleration of gravity are equivalent to finding the product of G and mass of the Earth, finding G was then frequently referred to as "weighing the Earth."

The Cavendish experiment has since been repeated, with progressively improved apparatus, by Ferdinand Reich in 1838, Francis Bailey in 1842, Philipp von Jolly in 1881, Wilsing in 1889, John Henry Poynting in 1891, Charles Vernon Boys in 1895, Karl Ferdinand Braun in 1896, Rudolf von Eötvös in 1896, F. Richarz in 1898, George Kimball Burgess in 1901, Paul R. Heyl in 1930, J. Zahradnicek in 1932, and Heyl and Peter Chrzanowski in 1942. Of these, the value established by Paul R. Heyl of the then U.S. National Bureau of Standards in 1930 is the most accepted. This value is 6.670×10^{-11} ± 0.005 m³/(kg s²). A new effort involving an angular acceleration method of measuring gravitational interaction was devised in 1960 by J.W. Beans. This method has the promise of much higher accuracies. Such high accuracies will be needed indeed to detect a possible slow secular temporal dependence of G, as suggested by a number of investigators since the early twentieth century. P.A.M. Dirac was the first to make such a proposal in 1937. Since then, P. Jordan and D.W. Sciama and, in 1961, C. Brans and R.H. Dicke have proposed cosmological theories applying this principle. Brans and Dicke suggest a change of 2 x 10^{-11} per year. T.C. Van Flandern predicts a change of 1 x 10^{-10} per year. I.I. Shapiro, based on radar ranging experiments, suggests an upper limit of 4 x 10^{-10}. However, J.C. Barrow, based on cosmological arguments, argues an upper limit of 1.5 x 10^{-12}. If G does change, it will have profound implications on phenomena ranging from the evolution of the universe to the evolution of the Earth.

Going back to the development of instrumentation for gravimetry, J.C. Borda and J.D. Cassini De Thury, using a wire pendulum and determining its oscillation time by the coincidence method suggested by Rudjer Boškovic (1711–1787), achieved a gravity measurement accuracy of 10^{-5}g in 1792. The wire pendulum was improved further by F.W. Bessel (1784–1846). In 1818, Henry Kater, a British geodesist, constructed a reversible pendulum and used it to measure the absolute value of gravity at a site in London. The development of invariable pendulums made it possible to measure gravity difference with respect to a site, rather than the absolute value of g. This led to increased gravimetric activity. By 1862, the reversible pendulum built by J. Repsold for Bessel was being used by several countries, including the U.S. Coast and Geodetic Survey (USCGS) to measure gravity differences. In 1878, Charles S. Pierce built his invariable pendulum, which replaced the Repsold model at USCGS. In 1887, R.V. Sterneck constructed a pendulum, also known as "$1/2$ second pendulum" or "four-pendulum apparatus," which was used widely for relative gravity measurements. Most of the relative gravity measurements were tied to the Potsdam datum. The absolute value of g at Potsdam, Germany, was determined, using a reversible pendulum, by F. Kühnen and Ph. Furtwängler during 1898–1904 at the behest of F.R. Helmert (1843–1917). It was discovered later that this value of g was too high and required a correction of about 14 milligals. Between 1901 and 1909, O. Hecker obtained

about 250 gravity observations at sea using a hypsometer and a mercury barometer. This was a milestone in gravimetry. The major impediment to measuring gravity at sea aboard a moving ship or submarine was the Eötvös effect—the influence of the east-west component of the velocity of a body on the observed gravity value, first pointed out by R. von Eötvös (1848–1919). Its computation required a highly precise knowledge of the ship's east-west velocity component—something that did not become really possible until satellite position fixes were introduced in the late twentieth century. By 1912, there were about twenty-five hundred gravity values available. Some of these data had been used by Helmert in 1901 to formulate a normal gravity formula based on the Potsdam datum.

In 1930, International Association of Geodesy (IAG), an arm of the International Union of Geodesy and Geophysics (IUGG), adopted the International Gravity Formula (based on the International Reference Ellipsoid it had adopted earlier) in order to ensure standardization and consistency in the emerging global gravimetric database. The use of this formula was recommended for the reduction of all gravity observations.

Further developments in pendulum instrumentation, and a better understanding of their error sources and their corrections, increased their accuracy and made them less laborious to use. The development of a two-pendulum apparatus and of the Gulf pendulum, based on the principle of the minimum pendulum and developed by Gulf Research and Development Company, made pendulum measurements less laborious. The Gulf pendulum was even used for gravimetric prospecting. The oil companies also successfully tried the Askania torsion balance, first developed in principle by Eötvös in 1896, to map geophysical prospects between 1920 and 1940. These developments improved the measurement accuracy to about ±10–20 μms^{-2}(10^{-6}g) and reduced the observation time to 1 to 6 hours per station, down from about one day per station. But in spite of these improvements, the pendulum and torsion balance observations were still costly, cumbersome, and time-consuming. The torsion balance had the additional disadvantage that it could be used only in flat areas for identifying single geophysical prospects. As a result, there had been periodic attempts to develop alternative gravity-measuring instrumentation that would be more convenient, quick, and preferably more accurate. The gravimetric use of pendulums on land peaked during 1880–1920. Their use in submarines lasted between 1920 and 1960. The use of the torsion balance also came to an end by 1940. In fact, during the second quarter of the twentieth century, the gravimetric equipment of choice for relative gravity measurements was already gravimeters, and the use of pendulums had been reduced to measure and monitor the absolute value of g for a few selected base stations. These base stations needed to be used to calibrate gravimeters and tie in their observations.

The basic principle of gravimeters had essentially been stated by Robert Hooke in the seventeenth century in his law of elasticity. John Herschel suggested in 1833 the use of a spring balance to measure gravity. Even in the eighteenth century, Boškovic had conceived the idea of a kind of gravimeter to measure gravity "even in the oceans." By the second quarter of the twentieth century, gravimeters, in their early stages of development, were becoming an equipment of choice for relative gravity measurements. Their early development is ascribed to Adolf Schmidt in 1914 and G. Ising in 1918, but there was a surge of design development and construction in the 1930s. Gravimeters were of three types initially: dynamic, gas-pressure, and static. Most dynamic gravimeters used the Holweck-Lejay inverted pendulum developed by F. Holweck and P. Lejay in 1930. Lejay successfully used the Holweck-Lejay gravimeter around the globe for geodetic purposes. This type did not become popular in geophysical prospecting. The gas pressure gravimeter was developed by H. Haalck in 1931, who followed up on O. Hecker's experiments conducted in 1903. This type did not find much use either, partly because it was awkward to transport. Static gravimeters claimed most development effort and were most accepted. In 1930, O.H. Truman developed the lever-spring balance, which was used in oil prospecting by Humble Oil Company. In 1932, Harlety described a linear measurement system that resulted in the development of the Gulf gravimeter built by A. Hoyt in 1938 and the Nørgaard gravimeter. The former was extensively used for oil prospecting by Gulf Oil Company. In 1934, Alfred Schleusener, of the firm Seismos GmbH, built a gravimeter based on the design of St. von Thyssen that found fairly widespread use. In 1934, L.J.B. LaCoste introduced the idea of a long-period vertical seismometer. This, along with the concept of a zero-length spring, was used later

on to develop the highly precise LaCoste-Romberg gravimeters, popularly known as G meters. The North American gravimeter is also based on the same principle.

These devices found widespread use. This design was improved further when Sam P. Worden used a quartz spring to build the Worden gravimeter, which became the most popular in geophysical prospecting. It was also used, along with the Gulf pendulum, to establish a worldwide, gravimetric, base-station network for geodetic purposes by George P. Woollard and his group in the mid-twentieth century. The Askania gravimeter, developed by A. Graf, was also used widely. The gravimeters provided convenience, speed, cost-effectiveness and improved accuracy. The average observation time was reduced from 1 to 6 hours to about 10 minutes per station. At the same time, the measurement accuracy improved from ± 10–20 $\mu ms^{-2}(10^{-6}g)$ to ± 2–5 μms^{-2} (slightly less than $10^{-7}g$) for gravimeters in field use. Modern gravimeters now yield accuracies of slightly better than $10^{-7}g$ for field use and $10^{-8}g$ for stationary use. By 1940, gravimeters had replaced pendulums and torsion balances for all geophysical prospecting work and for much of the gravimetric baseline work for geodetic purposes. Gravimeters gave such a boost to gravity measurement efforts worldwide that by 1940 the number of gravity observations had risen to ten thousand. In 1945, IAG set up a permanent section of gravimetry to coordinate and promote gravimetric observations and their geodetic and geophysical uses. In 1951, an International Gravity Commission was set up to ensure international cooperation and consistency in gravity observations and their reduction. By the early 1960s, there were over a quarter of a million gravity values available between the Heiskanen group at Ohio State University, the Woollard group at the University of Hawaii, and some other smaller allied groups.

Although by about the mid-twentieth century considerable gravimetric data had accumulated, it was not uniformly distributed and did not have the type of dense coverage needed for many geodetic applications. Consequently, major studies were conducted on how to interpolate and extrapolate such data. There was also considerable debate on whether the free air-gravity anomalies or isostatic gravity anomalies were best suited for such purposes.

The gravimetric surveys at sea also got a boost. The Gulf underwater gravimeter developed by T.B. Pepper was used for gravity measurements for the shallow shelf areas starting in 1940. Meanwhile, in 1921 F.A. Vening Meinesz developed a two-pendulum apparatus that was expanded to a three-pendulum Sterneck-type apparatus for use in submarines. Between 1923 and 1960, the United States, the Soviet Union, and several other countries of Europe conducted marine cruises to gather gravity data at more than five thousand stations. In 1957, sea gravimeters were developed for use aboard ships. These replaced the submarine pendulum apparatus. In the 1960s, borehole gravimeters were developed for use at drilling sites.

In the 1970s, the reversible pendulum apparatus to perform absolute gravity measurements was replaced largely by the equipment using the free-fall method based on the work of A. Guillet in 1938, C.H. Volet in 1946, J.E. Faller in 1963, A. Sakuma in 1963, and Alan H. Cook in 1965. The basic principle of this method is the same as used by George Atwood (1746–1807). However, these determinations use the highly sensitive interferometric method of simultaneous measurement of distance and time. The accuracy of these determinations is reported to be ± 0.1 $\mu ms^{-2}(10^{-8}g)$.

The improvements in instrumentation, the geodetic requirements of a consistent global gravity database, the U.S. Department of Defense's (DoD's) precision weapon-launching and national defense requirements, the emerging awareness on the international level that gravimetric data are critical in the understanding of global geodynamics, and increased geophysical prospecting activity led to the establishment of the International Gravity Standardization Network 1971 (IGSN71). This gravity network is gradually being extended and improved with new gravity observations and better determinations of the existing base stations. In the early stages of IGSN71's development, a major contribution was made by, among others, George P. Woollard and his group, located first at the University of Wisconsin and later at the University of Hawaii, and by W.A. Heiskanen and his group at the Ohio State University. Additionally, DoD played the role of a major catalyst for extending gravimetric coverage and supported a number of groups both within its organizations and outside to carry out gravity surveys. At present, the DoD's Defense Mapping Agency (DMA) has the most comprehensive data-base, with over twenty-five million gravity values. But parts of DMA's data-base are either classified or proprietary and not available for nonrestricted use. In addition, the International Gravimetric Bureau in France has over five million gravity values. The National Geophysical Data Center of the National Oceanic and Atmospheric Administration (NOAA) has about fourteen million gravity values. While these databases will be regarded prodigious by any standards, the gravity values are not well distributed over the globe. Instead, they are clustered in selected areas that may have been of geophysical or strategic interest. This leaves vast areas of the globe, including large areas of the ocean, for which no or very little gravity data are available for a variety of reasons. Thus, if one had to depend entirely on the traditional surface gravity measurements for the definition of the Earth's gravity field, one would not be in a very enviable position.

The knowledge of the global gravity field made an unprecedented leap with the advent of the artificial Earth satellite era in 1957. Soon it became apparent that analysis of the satellite orbits and their perturbations yields the long-wavelength components of the Earth's gravity field to an accuracy not even imaginable with surface gravity data analysis. Many such analyses have been conducted by a number of groups over the past three decades. Since the satellite orbital analysis techniques yield the constant coefficients in the spherical harmonic expansion of the Earth's gravity field, the resultant gravity field solutions are called the spherical harmonic models of the Earth's gravity field. As it happens, the satellite orbital analyses provide information on the long wavelengths of the gravity field, while the gravimetric data contains information on the short wavelengths. As a result, the satellite orbital perturbation data and the gravimetric data are used in what are called combination solutions. The more recent combination solutions also utilize space-platform data types such as satellite altimetry data, satellite-to-satellite tracking data, and satellite-laser tracking data. As the basic data for these models have accumulated in size and diversified in type, these solutions have required long-term commitment of enormous computer, manpower, and financial resources that cannot be provided by individuals or small groups. Thus, the computational efforts, mainly concentrated in United States, have gradually converged at the National Aeronautics and Space Administration's (NASA's) Goddard Space Flight Center, DoD's Naval Surface Weapons Center, and, in the earlier stages, the Smithsonian Astrophysical Observatory, Cambridge, Massachusetts. The improvement of gravity field models is still an ongoing process, and NASA's Goddard Center is the most active agency in this regard.

The more recent satellite technique of satellite altimetry has provided detailed knowledge of the instantaneous sea surface, which, with the knowledge of certain oceanographic factors, can be converted to the geoidal surface. These geoidal undulations can be converted to gravity anomalies but with some loss of resolution. Considerable altimetry data were acquired in the 1970s and 1980s on several satellite missions, such as GEOS-3 and SEASAT. The improved altimeters designed for the most recent TOPEX/Poseidon and ERS-1 satellite missions are providing sea-level height measurements to an accuracy of 2–3 centimeters with a half-wavelength of a few kilometers.

Frequently, the study of temporal variations of gravity is included in gravimetry. There is no solid evidence of any secular changes in gravity. But time-dependent changes occur because of ocean tides, solid earth tides, earthquakes, volcanism, isostatic adjustment, and so forth.

Apart from their geodetic uses, the gravity anomalies have been used extensively for detecting and modeling tectonic features of geophysical interest. The geophysical applications range from their uses in oil and mineral prospecting to the study of global geodynamical phenomena such as plate tectonics, the Earth's internal structure ranging from the upper mantle to the core-mantle interface, and earthquakes. The long-wavelength components have been interpreted by some as originating from bumps at the core-mantle boundary that are thought to play a role in the electromagnetic coupling of the core and mantle.

Many individuals and institutions have made significant contributions to the development of this subject. There is, surprisingly, no detailed history of the study of gravity. Especially to be desired is a history that places this science in the contexts of other sciences and of their social and institutional settings. Clearly, for example, the roles of private mineral prospecting firms and of the military require careful scrutiny. Basic information is available in various articles in the *Dictionary of Scientific Biography*, the McGraw-Hill *Encyclopedia of Science and Technology*, and in other encyclopedias. Ultimately, however, this history must rest on both published and unpublished primary materials.

M.A. Khan

Bibliography

Heiskanen, W.A., and F.A. Vening Meinesz. *The Earth and Its Gravity Field.* New York: McGraw-Hill Book Co. Inc., 1958.

Khan, M.A. "Some Geophysical and Geodetic Contributions of Satellite-Determined Gravity Results." *Geophysical Surveys* 2 (1976): pp. 469–496.

Torge, Wolfgang. *Gravimetry.* New York: Walter de Gruyter, 1989.

See also Earth, Figure of in the Satellite Era; Earth, Models of before 1600; Earth, Size of; Geodesy; Gravity before Newton; Gravity since 1800; Gravity, Newton, and the Eighteenth Century; Instruments, Gravity; Isostasy; Continental Drift and Plate Tectonics; Plate Tectonics and Space-Based Platforms; Scientific Rocketry to Sputnik; Tides, Earth

Gravity before Newton
Heaviness and lightness.

Heaviness and lightness were explained by early philosophers in terms of the four elements: earth, air, fire, and water. Earth and water were heavy, and all things made of them tended to fall down. More specifically, heavy things moved by nature toward the center of the *Kosmos,* which was assumed to be at the center of the Earth. Air and fire, on the other hand, were light and moved by nature away from the center toward the outer limits of the *Kosmos.* If a heavy object moved in a direction other than down, that motion was unnatural and was due to external force. Or, if a light object did not move upward, it was being forcefully kept out of its natural place.

In those terms, gravity could be given by Aristotle (384–322 B.C.E.) as a reason for the spherical shape of the Earth. If every heavy thing moved down, each would strike and move other things that also moved downwards. If they were free to move naturally, all would continue toward the same center until there was no more space for motion, and each would provide resistance to the motion of others. This would result in a huge bulk that looked like a ball, because any other shape would allow space for further motion of things to get closer to the center. Thus, the Earth is a sphere because of gravity.

This notion of gravity was quite satisfactory for many purposes, but it was not the only idea about elemental substances or about weight. Thales for example had proposed only one element (water), whereas Anaximander had proposed another (air), as basic for all things. Fire was favored by Greek and Roman alchemists, who experimented with its strange and often unexpected effects on every sort of material.

In the fourteenth century, however, a new question of gravity arose in a different context. Earth was a sphere, and *mappae-mundi* showed inhabitants on both north and south sides of the equator. But only the continents of Asia, Africa, and Europe were actually known, and they lay in one-quarter of the orb surrounded by water. Why were they above water? Could it be that the element *terra* (earth) and the element *aqua* (water) each form a separate natural sphere because of gravity? Jean Buridan (1295–1358 C.E.) and several scholars after him proposed to describe two spheres of earth and water interacting. They argued that the center of the water must move when there is a great flood or a storm at sea changing the shape of the gathered waters; and the center of the element earth must move when large bodies of land shift, as result of an avalanche or earthquake or volcanic eruption. But where then is the center of the *Kosmos* toward which each heavy object moves because of gravity? (See Vogel).

The ancient concept of gravity was being severely tested against other cosmological ideas during the fourteenth to sixteenth centuries. It was probably the tension of ideas about spheres of *terra* and *aqua* that Nicolaus Copernicus (1473–1543) had in mind when he said in the preface to *De revolutionibus* (1543) that his new astronomy would once more harmonize the elements (Vogel).

Another aspect of gravity was that heavy things moved in some cases by attraction rather than by nature or by force. What caused some metals to attract each other? The work of William Gilbert (1540–1603) on magnetism stimulated many people to experiment with heavy objects. It also encouraged Johannes Kepler (1571–1630) to speak about the attraction of the Sun toward the planet Mars, as greater when near and less when far away (*Astronomia nova,* 1609; *Harmonices mundi,* 1619). This made no sense to Galileo (1564–1642), who had no taste for spiritual forces, and in fact Kepler's "third law" could only describe those motions in geometry but not account for such an attractive force. But it was the formula that Isaac Newton (1642–1727) used to justify his new theory of gravity, though not to prove it (see Goodman and Russell).

Wesley M. Stevens

Bibliography

Goodman, D. and C.A. Russell, eds. *The Rise of Scientific Europe, 1500–1800.* Sevenoaks, U.K.: Hodder and Stoughton, 1991.

Lindberg, David. *The Beginnings of Western Science.* Chicago: University of Chicago Press, 1992.

Vogel, Klaus. A. "Das Problem der relativen Lage von Erd- und Wassersphäre im Mittelalter und die kosmographische Revolution." *Mitteilungen der Öster-reichische Gesellschaft für Wissenschafts-geschichte* 13 (1993): pp. 103–143.

See also Cosmology and the Earth; Earth, Models of before 1600; Earth, Size of; Geodesy; Gravimetry; Gravity since 1800; Gravity, Newton, and the Eighteenth Century; Instruments, Gravity; Isostasy

Gravity, Newton, and the Eighteenth Century

An active and varied period in research of phenomena associated with Earth's gravity.

In 1687 the theory of universal gravitation was presented by Isaac Newton in his *Philosophiae Naturalis Principia Mathematica* (Mathematical Principles of Natural Philosophy). The scientific problems Newton had claimed to solve in the *Principia* provided scientists with more than a century of testing activity.

Many consequences of universal gravitation had a direct relation to terrestrial issues. For eighteenth-century scientists, problems concerning the Earth's shape, the Moon's orbit, and the effect of the Moon on ocean tides were of great importance. As the eighteenth century progressed and these issues were explored, an increasing number of scientists became convinced of the truth of Newton's theory.

Gaining acceptance was not so straightforward. Developments in mathematics, according to John L. Greenberg's articles, and improvements in instrumentation and observational techniques, argues Mary Terrall, played important roles in the acceptance of Newton's theory on the European continent. Fierce debate over the intelligibility of gravity as an attractive force played a role as well. Newton's theory also faced the challenge of replacing an already widely accepted Cartesian cosmology.

Objections to Newton's idea of gravitational attraction were metaphysical in nature. Gravitational attraction, if considered as action-at-a-distance through a vacuum or without some intervening medium, was thought "impossible to conceive" (Buchdahl, p. 82). This interpretation of Newtonian attraction was not endorsed by Newton, but he was still charged with introducing scholastic occult qualities into causal explanations. Some of the charges stemmed from misinterpreting Newton's assertions about the status of gravity as a cause (Hall, p. 238). For Newton, gravitational attraction was an explanatory principle whose own cause needed to be explained.

By the eighteenth century the mechanical approach of René Descartes (1596–1650) had a strong hold on natural philosophers. Within Cartesian mechanics natural phenomena were produced by impulse mechanisms. For Descartes, force and motion were imparted to objects only by contact with other objects or by impulse through an intervening medium. Descartes equated extension with matter and matter with space. In the Cartesian universe there was no empty space—no void. Space did not exist without matter. So, action-at-a-distance without an intervening medium violated Cartesian concepts of space as well as force. Newtonian and Cartesian science were incompatible on metaphysical grounds.

The incompatibility of the Newtonian and Cartesian systems was not the only factor influencing the reception of Newton's *Principia*. John Greenberg ("Mathematical Physics," pp. 59–60) argues that Parisian mathematics in the early eighteenth century lagged behind in developments of the calculus. Not until the 1720s did Parisian mathematicians catch up to the work of Jacob (1654–1705) and Johann I. Bernoulli (1667–1748) in Basel. According to Greenberg ("Mathematical Physics," p. 66) the economic stress of war, as well as an atmosphere of intolerance and the censorship of ideas from abroad, contributed to an unproductive intellectual environment in France. Scientific greats such as Christiaan Huygens (1629–1695) and Joseph-Nicolas Delisle left the intellectual community of Paris disenchanted (p. 62; "Degrees," p. 152).

It was not until the late 1720s, through the use of Leibnizian calculus taught him by Johann Bernoulli, that Pierre Louis Moreau de Maupertuis (1698–1759) made Newton's *Principia* accessible in France. (For the relationship between Maupertuis and Bernoulli, see Brown, pp. 167–206.) Maupertuis thought Newton's mathematics was impenetrable. Only when Newton's problems were worked by us-

ing Leibnizian calculus did Newtonian attraction gain acceptance in France (Terrall, p. 222). Determining the Earth's shape was one application that gained much attention during the eighteenth century.

Maupertuis's first work relevant to geodesy was published in the *Philosophical Transactions* of the Royal Society of London in 1732 and is reckoned as beginning the revival of geodesy in Paris (Hall, p. 235). In "Two Problems concerning the Figures of Rotating Fluids," Maupertuis argued Newton's case about the Earth's shape being the result of gravitational and centrifugal forces acting on the planet (Hankins, p. 37). Printed the same year but in Paris, and so having influence in France, was Maupertuis's "Discours sur les differentes figures des astres." In this paper Maupertuis "treated universal gravitation as inscrutable-but no more so than Cartesian mechanism" (Greenberg, "Mathematical Physics," p. 71; Aiton, p. 203). Maupertuis asserted that attraction is not a metaphysical impossibility to be excluded *a priori*. These assertions made him enemies in France (Aiton, p. 201). What ensued was a long dispute over the shape of the Earth. This dispute took place in but was not confined to the Royal Academy of Sciences at Paris. Not only theoretical considerations but also traditional methods of measuring and calculating the Earth's shape were disputed (see Terrall).

Spearheading the debate against Maupertuis was Jacques Cassini (1677–1756). In 1718 Cassini had published the results of geodetic measurements begun under the direction of his father, Jean-Dominique Cassini (1625–1712). These measurements were produced originally as part of an ambitious project to accurately map the kingdom of France. The elder Cassini began the project in 1683 to determine the length of a degree of latitude. He wanted to extend measurements made over an arc of only 1°21' by Jean Picard (1620–1682) from 1668 to 1670. Cassini measured an arc of 8°30'. The new measurements were needed not only for the mapping project, but also to settle the growing debate over the shape of the Earth.

Jean Richer (1630–1696) had observed in 1672 that a pendulum oscillating with a frequency of 1 second was shorter in the island of Cayenne than in Paris, a result that Newton reported in his *Principia*. These experiments measured the variations of effective gravity at different latitudes on the Earth's surface and provided Newton with evidence that the Earth is an oblate spheroid (Greenberg, "Degrees," p. 152). The Cassinis' measurements suggested the length of 1° of latitude measured on the Earth's surface increased as the latitudinal measurements went North. The results published by Jacques Cassini in 1718 provided evidence for concluding that the Earth is elongated at the poles, or a prolate spheroid. This conclusion directly conflicted with Newtonian predictions based on Richer's pendulum experiments. Cassini's calculations of an elongated Earth were accepted at the Academy of Sciences at Paris for nearly fifteen years.

Contrary to historical accounts that portray the period between 1718 (Cassini's published results) and Maupertuis's "Discours" of 1732 as having had little impact on geodesy in France, it appears more investigation is warranted. Individuals such as Joseph-Nicolas Delisle (1688–1768) in 1720, Giovanni Poleni (1683–1761) in 1724, and British scientist John T. Desaguliers (1683–1744) in 1725 called into question the accuracy of Cassini's measurements. For instance Desaguliers in his "Dissertation concerning the Figure of the Earth" (1725) responded to a 1720 Paris Academy mémoire of Jean-Baptiste Dortous de Mairan (1678–1771) in which de Mairan defended Cassini's geodetic measurements. Desaguliers criticized de Mairan's reasoning in the *Philosophical Transactions* in 1725 by showing that the oblong spheroidal Earth of Cassini "cannot be consistent with the experiments on pendulums" (p. 69). Desaguliers also criticized de Mairan by showing that the margin of error resulting from instrumentation in Cassini's measurements was much greater than the increments the measurements were designed to measure. Although there is some disagreement among historians, such as Terrall, Greenberg, and Hall, concerning the impact of Desaguliers's 1725 "Dissertation," it appears there was critical discussion of these issues prior to Maupertuis's "Discours" in 1732.

Cassini's calculation of the Earth's shape was supported by his geodetic observations and ultimately rested on their accuracy. Some historians suggest that the debate over the Earth's shape was over the relative superiority of theoretical reasoning and observational data, as if Cassini was the only one armed with observations. Generally, the only observations historians acknowledge that Newton had in support of the flattened Earth are Richer's pendulum experiments. On the contrary, Newton also had the pendulum results of Edmond Halley at the island of St. Helena and at London around 1677 and at the Royal Observatory of Paris in 1682, among others.

Newton cited these in the *Principia* (pp. 430–433). But he possessed other evidence as well, which has been ignored. Proposition XVIII Theorem XVI of the *Principia* (p. 424) asserts that the Earth is higher at the equator than at the poles because if not the oceans "would subside about the poles and rising towards the equator, would lay all things there under water." It is interesting to note that Desaguliers used this same fact in disputing the assertions of de Mairan.

The most important evidence Newton possessed for concluding that the Earth is flattened at the poles was, ironically, supplied by Jean-Dominique Cassini himself. Under Proposition XIX, Problem III, Newton asserted (p. 428) that "Cassini observed in the year 1691, that the diameter of Jupiter reaching from east to west is greater by about a fifteenth part than the other diameter." This observation made by Cassini should have at least raised some questions in the minds of philosophers like the Cassinis or de Mairan in considering the Earth's shape.

In the early 1730s Cassini's geodetic measurements were called into question by a contingent of Paris Academy mathematicians. Though Jacques Cassini defended his measurements, his use of only local measurements to determine the Earth's shape appeared inadequate. Criticizing the accuracy of Cassini's data was an assault on his reputation as an observer and cast doubt on the value of the French mapping project. This also made suspect the reliability of the astronomical instruments and techniques used by French astronomers (for accuracy of the measurements of Picard, the Cassinis, and Maupertuis, see *Geographical Journal*, 1941, pp. 291–293).

Drawing attention to the problem of determining the Earth's shape through the use of mathematics was not enough to settle the dispute. What was needed was a new set of observations from points on the Earth's surface that would reveal the greatest disparity in the length of a degree of latitude. What resulted was the Lapland and Peru expeditions. The Lapland Expedition headed for the Arctic Circle in 1736, under the direction of Maupertuis and Alexis Clairaut (1713–1765). With the two mathematicians went astronomer Pierre LeMonnier (1715–1799), astronomer Anders Celsius (1701–1744), and clockmaker Charles-Louis Camus (1699–1768). The Lapland team returned to Paris in 1737. Their observations and calculations took them fifteen months to complete. The equatorial expedition faced almost insurmountable difficulties. Hindered by internal conflicts, it did not return to Paris for over ten years (see Terrall).

When the Lapland results were reported to the Paris Academy in August 1737, Cassini raised objections to their findings at once. His main criticisms were procedural, having to do with the use of the Graham Sector, a device unfamiliar to Cassini that was used to observe the zenith star. Grappling over the reliability of the Lapland team's observations continued for over two years. Consensus on a flattened Earth was finally managed, even in absence of the Peru expedition results, with a new set of measurements of the Paris meridian taken by César François Cassini de Thury (1714–1784), son of Jacques Cassini. Cassini de Thury, having used new French instruments, announced no disparity with the results of Maupertuis. The dispute over the shape of the Earth was finally resolved and Newton's theory vindicated. Universal gravitation had taken a giant step in gaining acceptance on the European continent.

Newton's theory of universal gravitation had many crucial tests to pass before it would be accepted by the most critical skeptics. Predicting the motion of the Earth's satellite was an issue that occupied the most acute mathematicians. It was considered "the greatest controversy," and Newton claimed that it made his head ache to account for the movement of the lunar apogee, which advances 40° per year (Wilson, p. 140). This problem was the "application of Newtonian theory to the problem of perturbation" and constituted a "crucial test for the acceptance of universal gravitation: indeed it was this problem and its various ramifications that was the primary concern of eighteenth century celestial mechanics" (Chandler, p. 37).

Mathematicians such as Alexis Clairaut, Leonhard Euler (1707–1783), and Jean le Rond d'Alembert (1717–1783) attempted solutions of the lunar apogee. To calculate the motion of the Earth's satellite required solving the "three body problem." This problem Newton described in Proposition 66 of Book I of the *Principia*. The Moon is strongly attracted by the Earth and the Sun. The competition for finding the solution to this "three-body problem" was fierce (Hankins, p. 39).

Clairaut, Euler, and d'Alembert had failed. They agreed that it was Newton's law of gravitation that was in error. Clairaut declared publicly at the Academy of Sciences at Paris

"that Newton's law would not account for the observed motions of the moon" (Hankins, p. 39). His memoir "Du Système du monde, dans les principes de la gravitation universelle" ("On the System of the World using the Principle of Universal Gravitation") was read to the academy in November 1747. In 1749 Clairaut reversed himself and declared that Newton's theory was "perfectly in accord with the observations" (Wilson, p. 140). Newton's theory did account for the 40° movement of the apogee. Clairaut did not reveal his method, only his results at that time. Euler, desperate for the solution, persuaded the Russian Academy of Sciences to sponsor an essay contest for the best paper on the movement of the lunar apogee. This motivated Clairaut to reveal his method. His prize-winning "Theories de la lune" was published in St. Petersburg in 1752 (Chandler, p. 369).

Euler, named one of the commissioners for the Petersburg prize of 1751, had a copy of Clairaut's essay by March 1751 (Wilson, p. 142). In that year Euler wrote Clairaut, elated that he was "altogether clear concerning the motion of the lunar apogee" (Wilson, p. 142). It was in complete agreement with Newton's theory. The introduction to Euler's "Theoria Motus Lunae" ("Theory of Lunar Motion") published in 1752 states that "consideration of the apogee offers the safest means of deciding on the sufficiency of the Newtonian theory . . . surely no stronger argument by which the truth of this theory might be demonstrated can be desired" (Wilson, pp. 143–144). With this evidence, the truth of Newton's theory gained added support.

Another terrestrial consequence of Newton's theory of universal gravitation that drew great interest was his theory of tides. This theory also used the three-body problem. The Earth's oceans were not only attracted to the Earth but were also attracted by the gravitational forces of the Moon and Sun. Newton's quantitative work on the inequalities of tides is based on the assumption that the ocean "assumes a position of equilibrium under the attractive forces of the sun and moon" (Aiton, "Tides," p. 206). Newton's tidal theory was based only on the vertical components of the attractive forces of Sun and Moon and could not account for all the tidal phenomena. Euler's important contribution to the tidal theory was his accounting for the horizontal component of the attractive forces acting on ocean tides. Daniel Bernoulli's 1752 essay, "Traité sur le flux et reflux de la mer" took into account the properties of the ellipse and the variations in the distance of the Moon from the Earth for computing a table of tides (Aiton, "Tides," pp. 215–220). These tables were the first to have a theoretical basis. In 1774 Pierre Simon de Laplace (1749–1827) undertook the first dynamical theory of the motion of fluids, which was elaborated in his *Mécanique Celeste* (Aiton, "Tides," p. 223).

Newton's theory of universal gravitation by the end of the eighteenth century was held in such high esteem because it accounted for very diverse phenomena. Predicting and accounting for the Earth's shape and the motions of the Moon and tides were just a few applications that drew attention in the eighteenth century. These issues place Newton's work, as well as that of the Cassinis, Desaguliers, Cavendish, and others, in a neglected terrestrial context.

Andy Pintus

Bibliography
Aiton, E.J. "The Contributions of Newton, Bernoulli, and Euler to the Theory of the Tides." *Annals of Science* 11 (1955): pp. 206–223.
———. *The Vortex Theory of Planetary Motions.* New York: American Elsevier Publishing Company, Inc., 1972.
Brown, Harcourt. *Science and the Human Comedy.* Toronto and Buffalo, N.Y.: University of Toronto Press, 1976.
Buchdahl, Gerd. "Gravity and Intelligibility." In *The Methodological Heritage of Newton,* edited by Robert E. Butts and John W. Davis. Toronto: University of Toronto Press, 1970.
Chandler, Philip. "Clairaut's Critique of Newtonian Attraction: Some Insights into His Philosophy of Science." *Annals of Science* 32 (1975): pp. 369–378.
Desaguliers, John T. "Dissertation concerning the Figure of the Earth." *Philosophical Transactions* (1725): pp. 62–69.
Greenberg, John L. "Degrees of Longitude and the Earth's Shape: The Diffusion of a Scientific Idea in Paris in the 1730's." *Annals of Science* 41 (1984): pp. 151–158.
———. "Mathematical Physics in Eighteenth-Century France." *ISIS* 77 (1986): pp. 59–78.
———. *The Problem of the Earth's Shape from Newton to Clairaut: The Rise of Mathematical Science in 18th Century Paris and the Fall of "Normal" Science.*
Cambridge: Cambridge University Press, 1994.
Hall, A. Rupert. "Newton in France: A New View." *History of Science.* 13 (1975): pp. 233–250.
Hankins, Thomas L. *Science and the Enlightenment.* Cambridge: Cambridge University Press, 1985.
Maupertuis, Pierre L.M. de. "Two Problems concerning the Figures Assumed by Revolving Fluids; with Conjectures concerning Stars Which Sometimes Appear and Disappear; and on Saturn's Ring." *Philosophical Transactions* (1732): pp. 519–528.
Newton, Isaac. *Mathematical Principles of Natural Philosophy.* Translated by Andrew Motte, 1729; revised, Florian Cajori. Berkeley: University of California Press, 1946.
Terrall, Mary. "Representing the Earth's Shape, the Polemics Surrounding Maupertuis's Expedition to Lapland." *ISIS* 83 (1992): pp. 218–237.
Wilson, C.A. "From Kepler's Laws, So Called to Universal Gravitation: Empirical Factors." *Archive for the History of Exact Sciences* 6 (1970): pp. 89–170.

See also Earth, Figure of in the Satellite Era; Earth, Models of before 1600; Earth, Size of; Geodesy; Gravimetry; Gravity before Newton; Gravity since 1800; Instruments, Gravity

Gravity since 1800

Studied in this period not only in connection with the figure of the Earth, but also in its relations to mineral prospecting and questions of isostasy and plate tectonics.

The measurement and interpretation of the gravity field of the Earth was, by 1800, in a position of theoretical maturity but observational infancy. The basic physics of the gravitational field was generally accepted as being that developed by Newton and further developed by his successors, such as A.C. Clairaut (1713–1785); this acceptance was further cemented throughout the nineteenth century by the triumphs of Newtonian celestial mechanics. Those studying the Earth's gravity thus had the advantage of a theoretical framework that was lacking, for example, in the parallel case of terrestrial magnetism. However, the actual making of observations was far more difficult. The largest change in gravitational acceleration, g, (from the equator to the poles) is only about 0.5 percent of its total value; the variations caused by anomalies of density are at most 0.03 percent, and usually much less. (By comparison, determining the direction of the magnetic field to 1° needs only 2 percent accuracy). Until the 1930s, the only way to measure gravity was by timing the swings of a pendulum, a difficult and cumbersome procedure. An important aspect of the development of gravity studies was thus the gradual accumulation of data; much of what could be done was determined by what data happened to be available, often for reasons quite beyond the control of those who wanted to use them.

Gravity in the Earth, as in the heavens, was initially the province of astronomers, but was naturally carried into the field of geodesy as it emerged during the nineteenth century. The initial goal of these investigations, as for many in the eighteenth century, was the determination of the shape, or figure, of the Earth. That it was an ellipsoid flattened at the poles was established, but the degree of flattening (in modern terms the ellipticity) remained to be found. The usual technique for finding the flattening was to compare the lengths of arcs of parallel, determined by geodetic surveying, with the difference in latitude, found astronomically. For a sphere the ratio of arc length to latitude difference would give the radius of the Earth; for an ellipsoid the apparent radius would change with the average latitude of the arc, and so give the flattening. Conversely, an accurate value for the flattening was needed if the most accurate results were to be obtained in large-scale surveys. It was known, and had been quantified by Clairaut, that the change in gravity with latitude depends on the flattening; measurements of this change thus offered an independent check of the results from surveying.

While a few gravity measurements had been made in connection with the French geodetic expeditions of the eighteenth century, the first global investigations came after the invention of the reversible and invariable pendulum by Henry Kater (1777–1835) in 1818. Gravity measurements were included in a number of expeditions in the 1820s (Grant, pp. 150–157), and in several surveys in India after 1860; but by 1880 the total number of measurements for the world was just under one hundred, enough to determine the flattening of the Earth but hardly to do more.

During this period important information on the gravity field had also come from extensions of the geodetic surveys described above. Finding the latitude of a place depended on measuring the positions of stars relative to the local vertical (the direction of gravity), and it was well appreciated that the results could be affected by any deflection of this vertical away from the direction it would have on a uniform ellipsoid. Such local deflections would be largest near large elevations: the first such juxtaposition of a precise survey and high mountains occurred in 1847, when the geodetic surveys of India approached the Himalayas. In 1855 J.H. Pratt (1800–1871) calculated the deflection of the vertical given what was known of the mountain topography, and found that the value expected was much greater than that observed. An explanation of this discrepancy was provided by George Biddle Airy (1801–1893), who argued that given the fluid nature of most of the Earth, such a result would be expected, since the mountain masses could be supported only by a greater thickness of light material beneath, as in a floating log. In 1859 Pratt (who for other reasons was skeptical of the Earth's fluidity) argued that an alternate explanation was that, down to some depth, the overall density depended on the elevation, with high mountains being underlain by less dense material (Kushner, pp. 95–117).

The interpretation of these results in more general geological terms came with the concept of isostasy, first described at length by Clarence E. Dutton (1841–1912) in 1889. This idea generalized the notion that the density distribution within the Earth was such that many of its features were close to hydrostatic equilibrium. Dutton appreciated that additional gravity measurements could test isostasy, thus adding a new motivation for measuring gravity to the old one of determining the flattening. This spawned several new measurement programs, both of the direct measurement of gravity and of larger-scale analyses of deflections of the vertical; one of the most notable of the latter was by J.F. Hayford (1868–1925). These results seemed to most geodesists to support the idea of isostasy, with elevations extending even over small areas being balanced by density changes. Many geologists were skeptical of this, and the debate over the extent of isostasy continued throughout much of the first part of the twentieth century (Greene, pp. 267–270; Heiskanen and Vening Meinesz, chap. 7).

This debate was complicated by the increasing number of gravity observations throughout the Earth. Improvements in pendulums reduced the time needed for a single measurement from several weeks to a single day; as important, F.A. Vening Meinesz (1887–1966) showed, starting in 1923, how to extend gravity measurements to the ocean areas, previously devoid of any precise coverage at all. These gravity measurements were generally interpreted to show that most of the ocean is underlain by dense material, as expected from isostasy, but they also showed large departures from isostasy along the ocean trenches, and other anomalies that were not easy to explain (Oreskes; Menard, chap. 10).

In the 1920s gravity measurements also became important for determining very local density changes, such as might be caused by ore deposits. The detection of such small changes was first made possible by the torsion balance developed by Roland von Eötvös (1848–1919) around 1900. Its use underwent an explosive growth after 1920, thanks largely to the oil industry: gravity measurements were for a time the best way to detect salt domes, which were known to be a primary area of oil accumulation. Though soon replaced by seismic methods as the preferred method of finding the details of structure, gravity measurements remained an important method of reconnaissance in exploring for petroleum and was widely used in other kinds of geophysical exploration as well. The large economic incentives in this field led to considerable development in gravity measurement, culminating in the development of workable gravimeters, and also in very extensive surveys, far beyond what was possible for geodesy. Much of the resulting data were not usable for other studies, either because they were kept secret for commercial purposes or because they were given relative only to some base station and not tied to a larger framework; but in many cases summaries of the data were made available and could be used to supplement the still sparse pendulum data.

The increasing number of gravity measurements allowed a refinement of the older method of determining the flattening; the interpretation of these data drew on mathematical advances in the subject of potential fields during the nineteenth century. By a theorem developed by George Gabriel Stokes (1819–1903) in 1849, if the variation of gravity were known all over the Earth (strictly speaking on the geoid, the surface of mean sea level), the shape of this surface could be determined: not just the flattening, but all the

variations. It is testimony to the gap between theory and data that the first global application of this theorem, by R.A. Hirvonen, came eighty-five years later, in 1934. This technique of computing the Earth's shape from measurements of surface gravity was pursued by a number of investigators, most especially the group led by W.A. Heiskanen (1894–1971), first at the Isostatic Institute in Finland and later at Ohio State University. It was greatly accelerated in the period after World War II, when George P. Woollard (1908–1979) was able to tie together many local gravity systems to form a unified global framework. Another development of the postwar period was the commercial availability of gravimeters to groups not engaged in geophysical prospecting, who could thus extend gravity measurements to areas not of commercial interest. Much of this work was the extension to previously unexplored areas of measurements, and methods of understanding them, that had been used elsewhere: in this sense, much of the gravity work after roughly 1950 was the use of a standard "black box."

It had been known since the eighteenth century that the variation in the gravitational field caused by the flattening would cause a perturbation in the motion of any satellite, and the motion of the Moon had been used to provide another estimate of this quantity. Such perturbations are larger for a closer satellite; even approximate observations of the orbits of the first few artificial satellites in 1957 and 1958 were enough to provide a more accurate measure of the effect of the flattening on the Earth's gravitational field than had the previous 150 years of measurements. The initial result of the satellite data was to revise the values both of the actual flattening and of the flattening expected for a body in hydrostatic equilibrium (Lambeck, "Earth's Shape"). These had appeared to agree closely; the satellite data revealed, not without controversy, that they did not, a result taken by many at the time to demonstrate the long-term strength of the Earth and the impossibility of convection and continental drift (Menard, chap. 18). The acceptance of plate tectonics a few years later made the interpretation of these anomalies in terms of convection the only acceptable interpretation, which it remains. Indeed, the main trend of global gravity studies since the mid-1960s has been the use of satellite data (often combined with surface gravity data) to map long-wavelength variations in the gravitational field, and to interpret these as being caused by density anomalies related to convection. This has been supplemented, since 1980, by satellite radar measurements that provide a detailed picture of the gravity field over the oceans, to some extent now better known than that over many continents (Lambeck, *Geophysical Geodesy*).

Though the study of gravity as a force would now be regarded as a part of physics, it was originally considered the province of astronomers and geodesists. It is notable that all the early experiments to determine what is now referred to as the gravitational constant, G, were always cast in terms of finding the mean density of the Earth. Some of the earliest ones (Grant, pp. 158–160) used pendulums or deflections of the vertical, but these were superseded by laboratory measurements. A resurgence of geophysical measurements to study the physics of gravity occurred when it was realized that such measurements offered one way of testing the applicability of Newton's theory of gravity over distances intermediate between those of the laboratory and the Solar System. Though such measurements had been proposed by F. Stacey in 1978, the main impetus for them came from the proposal of a "Fifth Force" by E. Fischbach and others in 1986, based on high-energy physics results and a reanalysis of experiments by Eötvös. The possibility of detecting a departure from the inverse-square law led to several experiments in measuring the vertical gradient of gravity in regions of known density (up towers, down a hole in the Greenland icecap, and in the ocean) to look for any anomalies. Some initial results indeed showed systematic anomalies, but it was eventually concluded that these could all be explained by variations in local density; to within the errors in the measurement, there appears to be no departure from Newton's law (Franklin).

There is certainly room for additional historical studies of how gravity data impinged on thinking about the Earth. Most notably, there is the question of how differently geologists, geodesists, and geophysicists viewed the data and the interpretation of it. The career of isostasy in the twentieth century is a good example: it was agreed by all concerned that it was an important idea, but the extent to which it really occurred, and the larger implications, were very much debated; gravity data provided much of the fuel for this debate. This leads to the related question of why these data were gathered at all, and the way in which they were transformed from quantities of at most academic interest to something first of commercial and later of military importance (MacKenzie), so that the largest collection of gravity data in the world is held by the U.S. Defense Department.

Duncan Carr Agnew

Bibliography

Franklin, Allan. *The Rise and Fall of the "Fifth Force": Discovery, Pursuit, and Justification in Modern Physics.* New York: American Institute of Physics, 1993.

Grant, Robert. *History of Physical Astronomy, from the Earliest Ages to the Middle of the 19th Century.* London: R. Baldwin, 1852.

Greene, Mott T. *Geology in the Nineteenth Century: Changing Views of a Changing World.* Ithaca, N.Y.: Cornell University Press, 1982.

Heiskanen, W.A., and F.A. Vening Meinesz. *The Earth and Its Gravity Field.* New York: McGraw-Hill, 1958.

Kushner, David S. "The Emergence of Geophysics in Nineteenth Century Britain." Ph.D. diss., Princeton University, 1990.

Lambeck, K. "The Earth's Shape and Gravity Field, a Report of Progress from 1958 to 1982." *Geophysical Journal of the Royal Astronomical Society* 74 (1983): pp. 25–54.

———. *Geophysical Geodesy: The Slow Deformations of the Earth.* Oxford: Clarendon Press, 1988.

MacKenzie, Donald A. *Inventing Accuracy: An Historical Sociology of Nuclear Missile Guidance.* Cambridge: MIT Press, 1990.

Menard, H.W. *The Ocean of Truth: A Personal History of Global Tectonics.* Princeton: Princeton University Press, 1986.

Oreskes, Naomi. "Weighing the Earth from a Submarine: The Gravity Measuring Cruise of the U.S.S. S-21." In *The Earth, the Heavens, and the Carnegie Institution of Washington,* edited by Gregory A. Good, pp. 53–68. Washington, D.C.: American Geophysical Union, 1994.

See also Continental Drift and Plate Tectonics; Earth, Figure of in the Satellite Era; Earth, Size of; Geodesy; Gravimetry; Gravity before Newton; Gravity, Newton, and the Eighteenth Century; Instruments, Gravity; Isostasy; Plate Tectonics and Space-Based Platforms; Scientific Rocketry to Sputnik; Tides, Earth

Greenhouse Effect

The natural absorption and reemission of infrared radiation by gases such as water vapor, carbon dioxide, and methane regulates the Earth's surface temperature.

As early as 1681 Edme Mariotte wrote that although the Sun's light and heat easily pass through glass and other transparent materials, heat from other sources (*chaleur de feu*) does not. In 1818 Jean-Baptist-Joseph Fourier wrote on the heating of enclosed spaces, specifically greenhouses. In 1824, citing work by Horace Bénédict de Saussure and others, Fourier compared the transparency of the atmosphere to *chaleur lumineuse* and its inability to transmit *chaleur obscure* to the effect of a sheet of glass covering a vase.

Beginning in 1859 John Tyndall conducted experiments on the radiative properties of gases and later suggested that changes in the amount of aqueous vapor, carbonic acid, or hydrocarbons in the atmosphere could cause dramatic changes in the climate. In 1899 Thomas C. Chamberlin proposed that changes in the CO_2 content of the atmosphere were the cause of ice ages and interglacial warming. Svante Arrhenius (beginning in 1896) calculated the warming that would result from increased levels of CO_2 and suggested that human activities, such as burning large amounts of coal, could alter the heat balance of the atmosphere.

In the twentieth century G.S. Callendar in 1938 and Charles Keeling in 1957 measured the rising levels of CO_2 in the atmosphere. Syukuro Manabe and Richard T. Wetherald in 1967 first used computers to model the effect of doubling the CO_2 concentration. The debate over global warming—the threat of rapid climatic change caused by human activities—became a public issue in 1988 following Hansen's testimony to the U.S. Congress.

There is no general history of the greenhouse effect, but a good bibliographic source, particularly for developments after 1970, is by M.D. Handel and J.S. Risbey. Elisabeth Crawford also provides a close analysis of one particularly important researcher (chap. 10).

James Rodger Fleming

Bibliography

Crawford, Elisabeth. *Arrhenius: From Ionic Theory to the Greenhouse Effect.* Canton, Mass.: Science History Publications/USA, 1996.

Handel, M.D., and J.S. Risbey. "An Annotated Bibliography on the Greenhouse Effect and Climate Change." *Climatic Change* 21, no. 2 (June 1, 1992): pp. 97–255.

See also Atmosphere; Climate Change before 1940; Climate Change, since 1940; Climates, Pleistocene and Recent; Environmental History; Ice Ages; International Geophysical Year; Ocean-Atmosphere Interactions; Solar Constant